MASTERING
Real Estate Principles

Gerald R. Cortesi

Real Estate
Education Company®
A Kaplan Professional Company

This publication is designed to provide accurate and authoritative information in regard to the subject matter covered. It is sold with the understanding that the publisher is not engaged in rendering legal, accounting or other professional service. If legal advice or other expert assistance is required, the services of a competent professional person should be sought.

Vice President: Carol L. Luitjens
Executive Editor: Diana Faulhaber
Senior Development Editor: Nikki Loosemore
Managing Editor: Ronald J. Liszkowski
Art Manager: Lucy Jenkins
Interior Designer: Norman Baugher
Cover Design: DePinto Studios

Published by Real Estate Education Company®,
a division of Dearborn Financial Publishing, Inc.®
155 North Wacker Drive
Chicago, IL 60606-1719
(312) 836-4400
http://www.dearborn.com

Printed in the United States of America.

99 00 01 10 9 8 7 6 5 4 3 2 1

Library of Congress Cataloging-in-Publication Data

Cortesi, Gerald R.
    Mastering real estate principles / Gerald R. Cortesi. — 2nd ed.
        p.   cm.
    Includes index.
    ISBN 0-7931-2990-7
    1. Real estate business—United States—Problems, exercises, etc.
  2. Real estate business—Law and legislation—United States.
  3. Real property—United States   I. Title.
HD255.C65 1999   98-39821
333.33'076—dc21   CIP

CONTENTS

Unit III   Real Estate Ownership

ABOUT THE AUTHOR

Gerald R. Cortesi is the coauthor of *Modern Residential Financing Methods,* published by Real Estate Education Company®, and serves as the principal content advisor for their *Success Master*™ software series. In addition to being an adjunct faculty member in the business school at Oakton and Triton Colleges, Cortesi is a computer audit specialist in the financial services industry. He holds an Illinois broker's license and is a member of the Real Estate Educators Association, the Association of Illinois Real Estate Educators and the Information Systems Audit and Control Association. Cortesi holds both BA and MBA degrees from Loyola University in Chicago.

EDITORIAL REVIEW BOARD

The author and publisher wish to acknowledge assistance of the following reviewers, whose comments and suggestions have had a profound impact on the development of this book:

- Darryl Bradshaw, Mykut Real Estate School
- Patricia Crilley, Pat Crilley Schools
- Charles Gaba, 4 Star Real Estate School
- Helen L. Grant, Moseley-Flint Schools of Real Estate, Inc.
- John Hamilton, Polley Associates
- LaVern Kohl, Action School of Real Estate, Inc.
- Rick Larson, Prosource Educational Services
- John D. Mayfield, Jr., The Southeast Real Estate Prep School
- Wade R. Ragas, University of New Orleans
- Dan Sarrett, Real Estate Education Company
- Marie S. Spodek, DREI, Professional Real Estate Services
- Paul W. Turner, University of Memphis
- Paul F. Wilkinson, CRS, Long & Foster Institute of Real Estate
- Judy Wolk, Charleston Trident Association of REALTORS® School

PREFACE

When the first edition of *Mastering Real Estate Principles* was published three short years ago, there was uncertainty as to how readers would react to a book that used a significantly different approach and format to present information. The favorable response to the book has exceeded our expectations and has been most gratifying. We believe *Mastering Real Estate Principles* provides an effective tool for learning real estate concepts. While feedback from users of the book has been positive, we will continue to enhance and update the book to maintain its value to all who use it.

In this edition you will find that the section on real estate organizations has been replaced by a section on real estate Internet sites. The evolution of computer technology provides new opportunities to access real estate information. We have included Internet sites for many real estate organizations, government agencies and other entities to provide the reader with useful real estate information.

Material in this edition has also been updated to reflect changes in the tax laws and agency law, including designated agency and transaction brokerage.

Gerald R. Cortesi
December 1998

INTRODUCTION

IMPORTANT!

Please Read the Introduction Before Using the Book!

This introduction is the most important part of the book; it should be read to understand the design, organization and formatting techniques incorporated into the book. The introduction also includes suggested instructions on how best to use *Mastering Real Estate Principles*.

WELCOME

Congratulations for your interest in the fascinating world of real estate. Hopefully this book will start you on a new adventure and perhaps fun and profit in real estate. The concept, design and format of this book are intended to provide an effective learning tool for the reader.

OBJECTIVE

The primary purpose of this book is to provide a practical learning tool to be used in real estate licensing courses. The content includes all of the topics necessary to prepare for the real estate licensing exam; however, unlike traditional real estate textbooks, the format is designed to "instruct" rather than "present" information. While the book focuses on the real estate topics necessary to become a licensed real estate professional, it can also be used by those seeking information on real estate basics for their personal knowledge.

FORMAT

The format of this book is not quite like most other texts. The narrative is combined with examples, exercises and solutions. Using this format, a topic is explained and illustrated, and the reader is asked to immediately practice applying the information and is given the answers with explanations to provide feedback. This is repeated for each section in the chapter so that the book becomes interactive and the reader feels as though the topics are being taught.

The book uses a variety of format techniques to provide helpful "signposts" to guide you through the material. These techniques also provide the emphasis an instructor would use in a classroom environment. Techniques used include

Hints: Provide tips to help explain or remember terms and concepts.

Tips: Highlight common mistakes made by students.

Notes: Add additional information that will enhance an understanding of the topics.

Examples: More than 300 examples have been included to illustrate each concept taught in the book. Both positive and negative examples are used. These illustrate "what it is" and "what it is not," to present an overall understanding of the concept and how it is applied.

Boldface lettering: Mastering real estate terminology is critical to understanding real estate principles. All key real estate terms are printed in boldface lettering to highlight them.

Italics: Italics are used to provide *emphasis* in the print. Italics are also used when listing subparts of a topic.

ORGANIZATION

Text Organization

The overall structure of the book includes the components listed below.

____ UNIT

____ CHAPTER

____ SECTION

The book is divided into two parts. The first part is the core of the book and comprises 26 chapters that contain the basic information for all of the topics. This part also includes Unit Diagnostic Tests, which are used to practice applying the real estate concepts presented in the chapters and measure your comprehension of the material. The second part of the book is the **Study Tool Kit,** which is intended to provide you with tools that can be used as a quick reference and for review. These include two Comprehensive Tests and answers with explanations for both the Diagnostic and Comprehensive tests.

Units

There are eight units in the book. Each unit contains several chapters that group similar topics (e.g., Real Estate Law, Real Estate Brokerage) together. A Diagnostic Test follows each unit and includes questions on the topics in the unit.

Chapters

Each chapter in the book addresses a specific topic. Each chapter begins with a short description of the topic and why it is important to the reader, the learning objectives of the chapter and key terms. The content of each chapter is divided into sections.

Sections

Each section in a chapter presents a specific part of the chapter topic. Section exercises provide practice and reinforce real estate concepts. Solutions are given at the end of the chapter so that you can evaluate progress in understanding the section content.

STUDY TOOL KIT

The kit has helpful tools for reviewing and studying the material in the book. Use these tools as you progress through the chapter sections or when preparing for state licensing exams. When the *Study Tool Kit icon* appears in the margin, it indicates that additional information related to the subject is in the Study Tool Kit.

The contents of the Study Tool Kit are described below.

- Progress Chart—Allows you to track completion of topics and assignments.
- List of Real Estate Abbreviations.
- Real Estate Internet Sites.
- Summary of Laws Affecting Real Estate—A brief description of each law.
- Real Estate Math Review—Various real estate math problems with examples and solutions.
- Comprehensive Practice Examinations—Two examinations include all of the topics used in the book. Answer keys are also provided.

Hint: The book includes an extensive glossary of real estate terms. Terminology of real estate is very important to understanding the concepts and is one of the obstacles students new to real estate have difficulty with. Refer to the glossary frequently as you read and study the material so that you become familiar with the language of real estate.

HOW TO USE THIS BOOK

The content, presentation of topics and format of the book have been carefully developed to provide the reader with a learning tool for mastering the principles of real estate. To derive the greatest benefit from this book, please read this section carefully. Listed below are the suggested approach and hints on using the book.

1. Start with Unit I. This introductory unit includes chapters that cover basic terms and principles of real estate. Many of these terms and concepts appear in later chapters, so it is recommended that these be completed first. After covering the chapters in Unit I, other units can be used in any order; however, we do recommend doing them in the order they appear.
2. Do the chapters in each unit in the order in which they appear. The chapter topics are arranged progressively, so that each chapter builds on the one that precedes it.

3. Complete the review exercises for each section in the chapter, and review your answers before starting the next section. Chapter sections cover specific subtopics and should be understood before proceeding to the next section.
4. Track your progress by checking off the Learning Objectives and Key Terms included at the beginning of each chapter.
5. After completing the chapters in a unit, complete the Unit Diagnostic Test. These tests will provide you with important feedback on your progress in understanding and applying real estate principles.
6. After completing all of the units, try taking the comprehensive test.

Remember

The Study Tool Kit is available for your use and assistance while you cover the topics in the book. Become familiar with the information included in the Tool Kit, and it will become a valuable assistant.

I. Complete Each Chapter in a Unit

1. Read chapter introduction and learning objectives

2. Complete each chapter section

- Read section material
- Complete section exercise
- Review answers in answer key at the end of the chapter
- Review section if necessary
- Check off completed learning objectives and key terms
- Repeat for each section

II. Complete Unit Diagnostic Test

1. Answer questions in test

2. Review answers in answer key

- Note weak content areas
- Review chapter material if necessary
- Repeat unit test as necessary to establish knowledge and proficiency

III. Complete Comprehensive Test

1. Answer questions in test

2. Review answers in answer key

- Note weak content areas
- Review chapter material if necessary

U N I T

1

INTRODUCTION
TO REAL ESTATE

CHAPTER 1
INTRODUCTION TO REAL ESTATE

Real estate is a huge business and plays an important part in the country's economy. This chapter presents an introduction to real estate and the real estate business. *Section 1* introduces services provided by the real estate industry and classes of real estate. *Section 2* describes the physical and economic characteristics of real estate. *Section 3* describes the real estate market and factors that affect the supply and demand for real estate. Remember to use the Study Tool Kit at the end of the book to reference key information and to update your progress checklist.

Tip: If you have not done so, please read "How to Use This Book" in the Introduction to the Text. The format of this book is different from most texts, and by following the suggested approach, you will derive greater benefits from your efforts.

Learning Objectives

Track your progress as you work through the chapter by checking each learning objective when you complete it.

____ List and describe the various services provided by the real estate business.

____ List the five classes of real estate and give examples of each.

____ List three physical characteristics of real estate.

____ List four economic characteristics of real estate.

____ Describe the effects on real estate values due to changes in supply and demand.

____ List factors affecting supply.

____ List factors affecting demand.

Key Terms and Phrases

Track your progress as you work through the chapter by checking each term when you understand its meaning.

____ Agricultural real estate

____ Appraisal

____ Brokerage

____ Commercial real estate

____ Demographics

____ Fixity

____ Immobility

____ Indestructibility

____ Industrial real estate

____ Market segmentation

____ Modification

____ National Association of REALTORS® (NAR)

____	Nonhomogeneity	____	Situs
____	REALTOR®	____	Special purpose real estate
____	Residential real estate	____	Vacancy levels
____	Scarcity		

SECTION 1

REAL ESTATE SERVICES AND CLASSES OF REAL ESTATE

SERVICES PROVIDED BY THE REAL ESTATE INDUSTRY

Most people think that real estate is only selling houses. While selling residential property is a major sector of real estate activity, many other services are provided by the real estate profession.

Brokerage

Real estate **brokerage** is bringing together parties (the buyer and the seller or landlord and tenant) in a real estate transaction. The broker (or sales associates working for the broker) usually acts as an agent on behalf of the party or parties in negotiating the sale, purchase or rental of the property. This is the most visible activity performed by real estate professionals, and most people who hold real estate sales or broker licenses are engaged in this type of service.

Appraisal

Appraisal is the process of estimating the market value of real estate. Appraisals are needed for many types of real estate activities, including lending, tax assessments and insurance adjusting. Some appraisers are employed by lenders and government agencies; others work as independent appraisers. Appraisers now need to be licensed or certified to perform appraisals for federally related property transactions. Professional designations, such as Member of the Appraisal Institute (MAI), are offered by the major appraisal organizations.

Counseling

Real estate counselors provide advice to individuals and firms regarding the purchase and use of real estate investments. Counselors need an extensive knowledge of real estate, tax laws and investing.

Education

Real estate education includes instruction for both real estate practitioners and the general public. Instruction may take the form of courses or seminars and can be held at universities, community colleges, private schools and business organizations.

Financing

Most real estate transactions require financing. Some real estate brokers are also mortgage brokers and may assist in finding real estate financing for buyers.

Property Development

Real estate development involves dividing larger parcels of land (called subdividing) and the construction of improvements such as roads and utilities. Buildings constructed by developers can range from single-family homes to large shopping centers or office complexes.

Property Management

Many investors in larger income-producing properties such as large apartment buildings and shopping centers may not have the time, interest or expertise to take care of the daily operation of these buildings. They hire property managers to run the property for them and maximize the income flow while maintaining the property value. Property managers are typically responsible for finding tenants, collecting rents and ensuring that the property is maintained. Some real estate firms specialize in property management, and larger firms may have separate property management departments.

PROFESSIONAL ORGANIZATION

The National Association of REALTORS®

The **National Association of REALTORS®** (NAR) is the largest and best-known trade association in the real estate industry. Founded in 1908, it has worked to promote high standards of professionalism in the real estate industry and has more than 700,000 members.

The term REALTOR® is a registered trademark of the NAR and may be used only by its members. Most real estate professionals belong to the NAR, its affiliates or councils. The NAR performs many important functions, three of which are discussed here. First, it sponsors several affiliated institutions and societies that offer educational and training programs in specialized areas of real estate such as property management and appraisal. Many of these training programs lead to professional designations. Second, it takes positions on legislation affecting real estate and provides testimony to Congress and to government and regulatory agencies on important real estate issues. Third, it has established a code of ethics designed to protect the public and serve as a behavior model for real estate professionals.

CLASSES OF REAL ESTATE

Real estate can be divided into five classifications, based on the use of the property. Because it is difficult to become an expert on all types of real estate, brokers tend to specialize in one or two types of property.

1. **Residential real estate** is used for housing. This includes single-family residences, condos, cooperatives, apartments, duplexes and triplexes, town homes and mobile homes. It also includes dwellings used for vacation homes and retirement housing.
2. **Commercial real estate** is used for business and includes retail stores and shopping malls, office buildings, theaters and parking lots.
3. **Industrial real estate** includes factories, warehouses and research and development facilities.
4. **Agricultural real estate** includes farms, orchards, timberland, ranches and hatcheries.

5. All other types of property that do not fit the previous classes are **special purpose real estate.** This includes: churches, government land and schools.

 Note: While it is possible for a real estate company to be involved with all classes of property and provide all of the real estate services, this is impractical and is seldom done. Companies and licensed individuals usually specialize in the type of service they provide, as well as the class of property they handle. For example, a company may specialize in brokerage services for residential property or a property manager may manage only commercial property.

BEFORE READING THE NEXT SECTION, COMPLETE THE SECTION 1 REVIEW EXERCISES AND COMPARE YOUR ANSWERS WITH THE SOLUTIONS AT THE END OF THE CHAPTER.

SECTION 1
REVIEW EXERCISES

1. Name the *service* provided by the real estate profession that best fits each description.
   a. _____ Providing instruction to both the general public and real estate professionals
   b. _____ Operating a property for the owner
   c. _____ Bringing buyers and sellers together
   d. _____ Assisting buyers in securing a loan
   e. _____ Estimating the value of real estate
   f. _____ Dividing larger tracts of land and building homes
   g. _____ Providing advice on such topics as real estate investments

2. Name the *class* of real property that best fits each description.
   a. _____ Store
   b. _____ Condominium
   c. _____ Farm
   d. _____ Church
   e. _____ Warehouse

Are the following statements true (T) or false (F)?

3. ____ The term REALTOR® includes anyone who is licensed in real estate.

4. ____ Brokers tend to specialize in one or two types of real estate.

Supply the term that best matches each of the following descriptions.

5. _____ A registered trademark of the NAR that can only be used by its members

6. _____ Property used for housing

7. _____ The service of bringing buyers and sellers together

8. _____ Property used for businesses such as stores and office buildings

9. _____ A large professional organization for the real estate industry

10. _____ Determining the market value of real estate

REAL ESTATE CHARACTERISTICS

Real estate has *physical* and *economic* characteristics that make it distinct from other commodities. These characteristics affect the value of real estate and the real estate market. Physical characteristics describe the physical attributes of the land. Economic characteristics affect the value of real estate. This section discusses the physical and economic characteristics of real estate and some of the resulting consequences of the characteristics. Some of the consequences pertain to real estate topics discussed in later chapters.

PHYSICAL CHARACTERISTICS OF REAL ESTATE

Three physical characteristics of real estate are immobility, indestructibility and nonhomogeneity.

Immobility

An important *and unique* characteristic of real estate is **immobility**. Even though a property's minerals, topsoil and other substances can be moved, the *geographical location* of the property always remains the same.

Hint: To illustrate the significance of this characteristic, think of another commodity, such as automobiles. If there is a sudden demand for autos in a particular area of the city, dealers can send autos from other areas of the city or from other cities or states. If there is a sudden demand for houses in a particular area, brokers can't ship in houses from anywhere else. Conversely, if demand for housing drops in a certain area, brokers can't ship them to other areas where demand is high.

Because the location for real estate is fixed, the following consequences occur:

- The *location* of real estate is an important factor in determining its value.
- Real estate markets are *local*, and real estate professionals need to be familiar with the market in their area.
- Land is easily regulated and taxed by local governments.
- The value of real estate is heavily influenced, either favorably or unfavorably, by changes in the surrounding area.
- An exact description of the property's location, including definite reference points, is required when title to property is transferred.

Indestructibility

The characteristic of **indestructibility** is also referred to as *durability*. Land cannot be destroyed or worn out. Its appearance may be altered but it continues to exist. Also, improvements to land, such as buildings, usually have a long life. Because land is indestructible the following effects occur:

- Real estate investments are relatively stable and long term.
- Land cannot be depreciated because it does not wear out.
- Land is not insured by property insurance because it cannot be destroyed.

Nonhomogeneity

Nonhomogeneity means that no parcels of real estate are exactly alike. Differences between parcels of real estate include the type of buildings located on the property, the size and shape of the property, the type of minerals or soil on the property and so on. Even if two parcels of real estate look exactly alike, they always will be different because of their unique locations. Another way of expressing this characteristic is *uniqueness* or *heterogeneity*.

- Because of this lack of standardization, real estate professionals must work very hard to match a property to a buyer's needs.
- Because each property is different, it takes buyers longer to select and purchase real estate.
- Another consequence of nonhomogeneity is in contract remedies. If a seller breaches a real estate sales contract with the buyer, the courts may not allow the seller to substitute money or another parcel of land. Another term to describe the concept that real estate is nonsubstitutable is *nonfungible*.

ECONOMIC CHARACTERISTICS OF REAL ESTATE

Four economic characteristics of real estate are scarcity, modifications, fixity and area preference.

Scarcity

Scarcity means that the supply of real estate is limited. There is no shortage of land for use; however, there frequently is not enough in certain popular areas to meet demand. A term used by economists to describe a commodity with a *fixed supply,* such as real estate, is *inelastic.*

A consequence of this characteristic is that a strong demand in an area will increase property values. The owner of property in a highly desirable area will have an almost monopolistic advantage.

Modification

The economic characteristic of **modification** (also called *improvements*) states that changes in a parcel of land affect its value. The effect may be either *favorable* or *unfavorable.*

EXAMPLE: An apartment building owner has the grounds around the building landscaped. This change (modification) to the property probably will increase its value.

Fixity

Fixity means that investments in real estate are long term (also called *permanence of investments*). This is primarily due to the physical characteristics of *immobility* and *indestructibility.* Because land is immobile, investment in property becomes fixed; it cannot be moved if the market becomes more favorable elsewhere. Also, because real estate transactions are complex and involve large amounts of money, they are not made as frequently as other transactions and require more time to consummate. A consequence of this characteristic is that real estate investment decisions should be viewed as *long-term* investment decisions.

Area Preference

Area preference (also called **situs**) refers to people's preference for certain areas. For instance, many people would probably prefer houses near good schools. Area preference is considered the most important economic characteristic of real estate.

Consequences of this characteristic are

- Prospective purchasers of property will attach great importance to the surrounding area when making their decision and determining the amount they are willing to pay.

EXAMPLE: Families with young children often desire housing near good schools.

- The preference for certain areas that meet their needs will affect the amount they are willing to pay and therefore the value of the property.

EXAMPLE: A family looking for a house finds an area that has good schools, a low crime rate and other favorable factors. They will be agreeable to making a higher offer to the seller of a house in this area.

BEFORE READING THE NEXT SECTION, COMPLETE THE SECTION 2 REVIEW EXERCISES AND COMPARE YOUR ANSWERS WITH THE SOLUTIONS AT THE END OF THE CHAPTER.

SECTION 2
REVIEW EXERCISES

1. List the physical characteristic of land that best fits each description.
    a. _____ Land is not standardized.
    b. _____ Location of land cannot be changed.
    c. _____ Land is durable and does not wear out.

2. List the economic characteristic of land that best fits each description.
    a. _____ Investments in land are long term.
    b. _____ Changes in land will affect its value.
    c. _____ Buyers prefer some locations over others.
    d. _____ The supply of land is fixed.

Are the following statements true (T) or false (F)?

3. ____ Land's indestructibility makes it easily regulated by local government.

4. ____ Scarcity means that we do not have enough land to satisfy demand.

5. ____ The characteristic of *modification* means that the changes will always increase a property's value.

List the term that best matches each of the following descriptions.

6. _____ The physical characteristic of real estate that land cannot be destroyed.

7. _____ The economic characteristic of real estate that changes in land may affect its value as well as the value of surrounding properties.

8. _____ The physical characteristic of real estate that land cannot be moved.

9. _____ The economic characteristic of real estate that refers to the limited supply of land.

10. _____ The physical characteristic of real estate that no two parcels of real estate are alike.

11. _____ Investments in real estate are for the long term.

12. _____ Refers to people's preference for some areas over others.

THE REAL ESTATE MARKET

Real estate can be bought and sold like other types of commodities. The real estate market is the mechanism whereby real estate is bought and sold, prices can fluctuate up or down, and the supply and demand for the product are always changing. To be effective in real estate, it is important to understand the characteristics of the real estate market and the forces that affect the supply and demand for real estate.

CHARACTERISTICS OF THE REAL ESTATE MARKET

Supply/Demand and Price

In the real estate market, supply and demand interact to affect property prices. As in any market, supply and demand are continually adjusting, and this causes changes in the price of property.

- Prices *increase* when demand increases or supply decreases.
- Prices *decrease* when demand decreases or supply increases.
- If supply and demand *increase together,* prices remain stable.
- If supply and demand *decrease together,* prices remain stable.

HINT: Price changes usually go the same way as demand changes. Price changes usually go the opposite way to supply changes.

Figure 1.1 illustrates the relationship between supply and demand.

Local Market

One of the physical characteristics of real estate is *immobility.* Because property cannot be moved around to satisfy demand in different areas, the real estate market is very *local* in character. Markets may differ among cities, or even in different sections of the same city. Because of this, each local market must be considered separately.

Market Segmentation

In addition to being localized, the real estate market may be *segmented,* that is, several different markets may operate in the same area. **Market segmentation** may occur in several different ways, including the type of property and the price range for property.

EXAMPLE: The market for residential property in a city may be different from the market for office buildings.

FIGURE 1.1
*Relationship Between
Supply, Demand and Price*

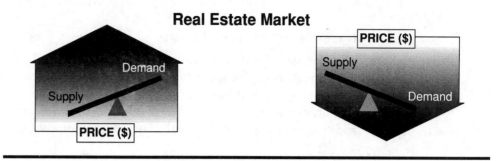

Real Estate Market

EXAMPLE: The market for houses priced from $100,000 to $200,000 may be different from the market for houses priced above $200,000.

Market Adjustments

As the forces of supply and demand change, the speed at which prices respond is determined by the *standardization* and *mobility* of the product. Because real estate is *non-mobile* and *nonstandard*, the price of real estate is slow to adjust. Also, the construction of improvements to real estate takes longer to complete, slowing increases in supply.

Note: While the supply of real estate may be slow to adjust, the demand for real estate may change quickly. For instance, if mortgage rates were to drop suddenly, more people could afford a home, and the demand for real estate might increase quickly as home buyers rushed to buy homes and lock in the lower rates.

FACTORS AFFECTING THE SUPPLY OF REAL ESTATE

The Supply of Labor and Construction Materials

It takes significant amounts of labor and materials to construct a house. Many skilled laborers, such as carpenters, masons, plumbers, etc., are required for the construction. The availability of skilled labor and materials will affect the supply of housing that can be built.

EXAMPLE: A shortage of lumber will delay construction of homes.

Government Controls

The federal government and its many agencies affect the supply of real estate through regulatory controls. These controls can affect the amount of money available for real estate loans, which are critical for building new structures.

EXAMPLE: Changes to the income tax code can affect the desirability of investing in real estate, thus reducing the availability of investment funds to build new commercial buildings.

Local government controls real estate through zoning and building ordinances. These also influence the supply of housing.

EXAMPLE: A suburb changes its zoning rules to require larger lot sizes for houses. In this case fewer houses can be built.

EXAMPLE: A town designates an enterprise zone with low real estate taxes to attract commercial developers. This will increase the supply of commercial buildings.

Government Financial Policy

The large size of real estate transactions requires the availability of mortgage money at a reasonable cost. The supply and cost of financing therefore are important factors in determining the quantity and timing of new additions to real estate supply. These are significantly affected by government economic and financial policy. Construction of additional housing (supply of real estate) diminishes when the cost of financing is high.

EXAMPLE: The government could increase spending programs such as aid to low income housing. This may increase the supply of housing.

EXAMPLE: Increased government spending could raise interest rates because the government needs to borrow money. This in turn decreases the affordability of loans and the ability of people to purchase housing.

FACTORS AFFECTING THE DEMAND FOR REAL ESTATE

While the factors that affect the demand for real estate are the same as those that affect the demand for most other commodities, real estate markets are generally local (because of the characteristic of immobility). Because of this, local demand factors will influence the market.

Population

It should be obvious that if the population increases so will the demand for housing. More important than the number of people, however, is the **demographics** of the population. The term *demographics* refers to the characteristics of the population: age distribution, family size and population movements. Demographics affect not only the total demand for real estate but also the type of housing demanded.

EXAMPLE: As children of the baby boomer generation reached adulthood, the demand for apartments increased. As they grew older and had families of their own, the demand for single-family housing increased.

EXAMPLE: The movement of people to the western and southern states created a greater demand for housing in those areas.

Employment and Wage Levels

Employment and wage levels directly affect people's ability to pay for real estate. This is especially important for a durable commodity such as real estate because people have the option of deferring the purchase to a later time if they are fearful of losing their jobs.

EXAMPLE: People may decide to rent and put off purchasing a house until their income rises or they are more certain of employment.

Vacancy Levels

A vacancy rate is the percentage of all units that are not occupied. **Vacancy levels** indicate the need and demand for property in an area, and there may be several rates based on the type of property.

EXAMPLE: A town may have a vacancy rate of 5 percent for apartment units, 20 percent for retail space and 20 percent for office space.

EXAMPLE: If the vacancy rate for apartment units has recently fallen from 6 percent to 3 percent, there is increasing demand in this section of the market.

COMPLETE THE SECTION 3 REVIEW EXERCISES AND COMPARE YOUR ANSWERS WITH THE SOLUTIONS AT THE END OF THE CHAPTER.

SECTION 3
REVIEW EXERCISES

1. Name the factor affecting the supply or demand for real estate that best fits each description.

   a. _____ A measure for the number of units that are not occupied

   b. _____ The availability of carpenters and other workers

   c. _____ The number of people in an area

   d. _____ Zoning laws regulating the type of real estate construction

   e. _____ The number of people without jobs

   f. _____ Setting interest rates for the country's money supply

   Are the following statements true (T) or false (F)?

2. ____ The real estate market is relatively quick to adjust to the forces of supply and demand.

3. ____ Most real estate professionals do not try to advise clients regarding property outside the area in which they are actively engaged.

4. ____ If the demand for real estate decreases and the supply increases, prices will increase.

5. ____ If the supply of real estate decreases and the demand increases, prices will increase.

   Supply the term that best matches each of the following descriptions.

6. _____ Divides real estate markets into submarkets

7. _____ Details the characteristics of the population

8. _____ The percentage of building units that are not occupied

SOLUTIONS
FOR SECTION REVIEW EXERCISES

SECTION 1

1. a. Education   b. Property management   c. Brokerage   d. Financing
   e. Appraisal   f. Property development   g. Counseling

2. a. Commercial   b. Residential   c. Agriculture   d. Special purpose
   e. Industrial

3. FALSE Only members of the National Association of REALTORS® may use the term REALTORS®

4. TRUE

5. REALTOR®

6. Residential real estate

7. Brokerage

8. Commercial real estate

9. National Association of REALTORS® or NAR

10. Appraisal

SECTION 2

1. a. Nonhomogeneity   b. Immobility   c. Indestructibility

2. a. Fixity   b. Modifications   c. Situs   d. Scarcity

3. FALSE Land's *immobility,* not its indestructibility, makes it easily regulated by local government.

4. FALSE Scarcity means that the supply of real estate is fixed.

5. FALSE The characteristic of modification means that changes may either increase or decrease the property's value.

6. Indestructibility

7. Modification

8. Immobility

9. Scarcity

10. Nonhomogeneity

11. Fixity

12. Situs

SECTION 3

1. a. Vacancy rate   b. Supply of labor   c. Population   d. Government controls
   e. Employment levels   f. Government financial policy

2. FALSE The real estate market is relatively slow to adjust to the forces of supply and demand.

3. TRUE

4. FALSE Prices will decrease because there will be an oversupply of real estate.

5. TRUE

6. Market segmentation

7. Demographics

8. Vacancy levels

CHAPTER 2

REAL ESTATE CONCEPTS

In Chapter 2 you learn some of the basic real estate terms and legal concepts. Real estate licensees must be aware of basic concepts of real estate law; however, only lawyers are authorized to practice law. Licensees should advise their clients to seek legal counsel. They should not attempt to provide legal advice. *Section 1* covers basic real estate terms. *Section 2* covers the concept of real and personal property. Remember to use the Study Tool Kit to reference key information and to update your progress checklist.

Learning Objectives

Track your progress as you work through the chapter by checking each learning objective when you complete it.

____ List what is included in the terms *land, real property* and *real estate*.

____ Explain the concept of a bundle of rights.

____ Explain the differences between real and personal property.

____ Explain the differences between a fixture and a trade fixture.

____ List and describe the tests for a fixture.

Key Terms and Phrases

Track your progress as you work through the chapter by checking each term when you understand its meaning.

____ Accession	____ Land
____ Air rights	____ Personal Property
____ Allodial system	____ Property
____ Attachment	____ Raw land
____ Common law	____ Real estate
____ Emblements	____ Real property
____ Fixture	____ Severance
____ Fruits of industry	____ Subsurface rights
____ Fruits of nature	____ Tangible property
____ Improvement	____ Trade fixture
____ Intangible property	

BASIC CONCEPTS AND BACKGROUND OF REAL ESTATE LAW

HISTORICAL BACKGROUND

Allodial System

For hundreds of years land in Europe was held by royalty under the feudal system. Real estate in the United States follows the **allodial system,** a legal system that recognizes full property ownership rights of individuals. Individual ownership includes the rights of possession, control, enjoyment and disposition.

Common Law

Common law is a body of law recognized by the courts based on custom and usage. While federal, state and local legislatures enact *statutes,* which affect real estate, statutes cannot cover every situation, and common law provides remedies for these situations.

BASIC LEGAL CONCEPTS

Property

Property *rights* are the rights someone has in something and are often defined as a "bundle of legal rights." A symbol of property rights is a bundle of sticks. Each stick represents a different right. An owner may choose to sell or give away one of the rights and retain the rest. These rights include the following:

- *Possession*   The right to occupy the property
- *Enjoyment*   The right to possess the property without interference
- *Disposition*   The right to sell or give the property to someone else
- *Control*   The right to use the property the way the owner wishes within the limits of the law
- *Exclusion*   The right to keep other people from using the property

Ownership of property is not unlimited. A property owner's rights are restricted by certain powers of the government. The seller also may retain some rights through deed restrictions. These concepts will be discussed in later chapters.

Figure 2.1 illustrates the concept of a bundle of rights.

FIGURE 2.1
The Bundle of Legal Rights

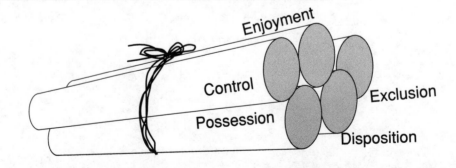

Land

The term **land** refers not only to the surface of the earth but also to the area below it to the center of the earth, above it to infinity and to all *natural* things permanently attached. Thus, the land includes such things as the minerals below the surface, planted vegetation and the space above the surface. An owner's rights to use the surface, the subsurface and the air above the land are called *surface rights, subsurface rights* and *air rights.* Subsurface and air rights will be explained later in the section.

Real Estate

Real estate includes all of the components in the definition of land plus *artificial* things (placed by humans) permanently attached. Thus, the definition of real estate also includes, for example, buildings, garages and fences.

Real Property

The term **real property** includes everything in the definition of real estate and also the legal interests, rights and privileges associated with the ownership of real estate. These include the bundle of rights discussed earlier.

Note: While there are slight differences in meaning among the terms real estate, real property and realty, they are almost always used interchangeably.

Improvements

Any type of land development is considered an **improvement** to the property. Improvements include buildings, streets, fences and sewers. Land that is *unimproved* is called **raw land.**

Air Rights

Property ownership includes rights to the space above the surface of the earth. These are called **air rights.** The rights to use, control or occupy the space above the land can be very valuable, especially in the business sections of large cities where land is scarce. Large commercial buildings have been built over railroad tracks in space gained by purchasing the air rights.

Subsurface Rights

Property ownership includes rights to the ground below the surface of the earth. These are called **subsurface rights** and include ownership of all minerals in the ground (called *mineral rights*). An owner may transfer ownership of the surface rights but retain the subsurface rights.

EXAMPLE: An oil company sells a large section of real estate to a developer but retains the mineral rights. The developer can construct and sell buildings on the property while the oil company continues to own the oil.

Figure 2.2 illustrates the components included in the terms used in this section.

FIGURE 2.2
*Land, Real Estate
and Real Property*

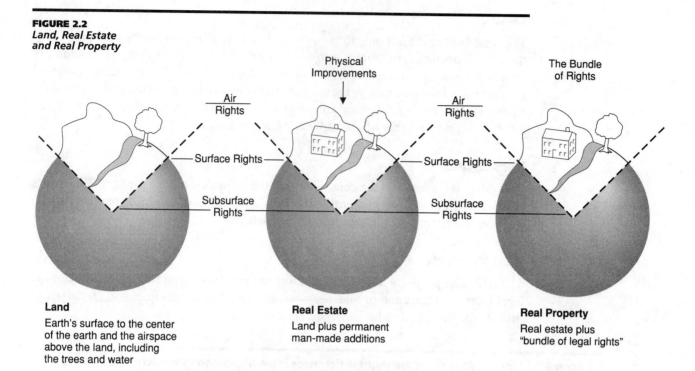

Land
Earth's surface to the center
of the earth and the airspace
above the land, including
the trees and water

Real Estate
Land plus permanent
man-made additions

Real Property
Real estate plus
"bundle of legal rights"

**BEFORE READING THE NEXT SECTION, COMPLETE THE SECTION 1
REVIEW EXERCISES AND COMPARE YOUR
ANSWERS WITH THE SOLUTIONS AT THE END OF THE CHAPTER.**

SECTION 1
REVIEW EXERCISES

1. List the components included in each of the following terms:
   a. Land _____
   b. Real estate _____
   c. Real property_____

Are the following statements true (T) or false (F)?

2. _____ It is possible for one person to own the air rights and another person to own the remaining rights to the same parcel of land.

3. _____ Trees and shrubs found naturally growing on the property would be considered improvements.

4. _____ Land that is unimproved also might be called raw land.

Supply the term that best matches each of the following descriptions.

5. _____ Laws recognized by the courts based on custom and usage

6. _____ Rights a property owner has in anything below the surface

7. _____ Additions to the property that are created artificially rather than by nature

8. _____ Rights a property owner has in anything above the surface

9. _____ A legal system that recognizes private ownership of land

SECTION 2

REAL AND PERSONAL PROPERTY

REAL VERSUS PERSONAL PROPERTY

Property may be classified as either real property or personal property, and distinguishing between the two is important for several reasons. In a real estate transaction all property that is real goes to the purchaser while all personal property stays with the seller (unless provisions in the contract specify differently). Another reason is that taxes are levied differently on real and personal property. Also, a deed is used to transfer title to real estate, whereas a bill of sale is used to transfer title to personal property.

Real Property

Real property and real estate are terms that may be used interchangeably. As we saw in Section 1, *real property* includes the land, the air above it to infinity, the ground below to the center of the earth and anything permanently attached by nature or humans, as well as the legal rights associated with ownership.

Note: In most states mobile homes on permanent foundations are regarded as real property.

Personal Property

Personal property (also called *chattel property* or *personalty*) includes any property that is not real property. Its principal characteristic is that it is *movable,* whereas real property is immobile.

Tangible and Intangible Property

Personal property can also be classified as either *tangible* or *intangible.* **Tangible property** includes physical things that can be seen and touched. Because **intangible property** cannot be seen or touched, it is represented by some type of document, such as a stock certificate.

EXAMPLE: A car, a book and money are all tangible personal property.

EXAMPLE: A trademark is intangible property.

Changing Property's Status

Property may be changed from real to personal or from personal to real. Real property may be changed to personal property by **severance.** Personal property may be changed to real property by **attachment.**

EXAMPLE: A tree is cut down for lumber. Real property (the tree) has now become personal property (the lumber) by severance.

EXAMPLE: Lumber is used to build a house. Personal property (the lumber) has now become real property (the house) by attachment.

Note: The distinction between real and personal property is not always obvious. Conflicts often arise between buyers and sellers over whether an item "goes with the house." Items such as appliances, bookcases and carpeting often are at issue.

Plants and Crops

Naturally growing plants and trees that do not require cultivation are classified as real property and are called *fructus naturales,* **fruits of nature.** Cultivated annual crops are considered personal property. These are called **emblements** or *fructus industriales,* **fruits of industry.**

EXAMPLE: Shrubs and native trees growing on the property are fruits of nature and belong with the real estate.

EXAMPLE: Tenant farmers may be allowed to harvest the crops (fruits of industry) they have grown if a landowner terminates the lease.

FIXTURE VERSUS TRADE FIXTURE

Fixtures

A **fixture** is an object that *once was personal property* but has been attached to the land or a building so that it *now is real property.* Fixtures are real property.

EXAMPLE: Built-in kitchen cabinets and bathtubs are examples of fixtures.

Trade Fixtures

A **trade fixture** is an article attached by the tenant to the building for use in conducting a trade or business. Trade fixtures are also called *chattel fixtures.* Trade fixtures remain the *personal property* of the tenant. Trade fixtures can be removed by the tenant when the property is no longer rented, but the tenant is responsible for any damage to the property from their removal. If trade fixtures are not removed, they become the property of the landlord through what is called **accession.**

EXAMPLE: Bowling alleys, neon signs, display counters, store shelves, bars and restaurant equipment are all examples of trade fixtures.

See Figure 2.3 for a summary of the differences between fixtures and trade fixtures.

FIGURE 2.3
Characteristics of Fixtures and Trade Fixtures

Fixtures	Trade Fixtures
Real Property	Personal Property
Become part of the building	Can be removed
Are owned by the landowner	Are owned by the tenant
Are included in the real estate sales contract	Change owners by separate agreement

TESTS OF A FIXTURE

To determine whether property is real or personal (i.e., whether it is a fixture), courts generally apply four tests.

1. Intention of the Parties

If there is no agreement between the parties (i.e., the owner and tenant or the buyer and seller), the *courts* must determine the *intention* of the parties.

EXAMPLE: A seller places a sign that says "Not Included" on the drapes whenever a salesperson shows the property to prospective buyers.

2. Method of Attachment

Is the method of attachment of a permanent nature or can it be removed without causing significant damage to the property? If removing the object would cause permanent damage to the real estate, it will be considered a fixture.

EXAMPLE: Tacked-down wall-to-wall carpeting may damage the floor if removed and will be considered a fixture.

3. Agreement of the Parties

The existence of an agreement between the parties identifying whether the item is a fixture or personal property.

EXAMPLE: The buyer lists several items in the sales contract and their inclusion is agreed to by the seller. These items then will be regarded as personal property, not fixtures.

4. Adaptation of the Item

If the item is adapted or custom built to fit the property, it will be considered a fixture.

EXAMPLE: Storm windows that are custom made are fixtures.

If the results of the tests are inconclusive, the law will look at the *relationship of the parties*. The law generally favors the following relationships:

- The buyer over the seller
- The tenant over the landlord
- The lender over the borrower

 Note: To avoid conflicts and misunderstandings between buyer and seller, the listing and sales contracts should clearly specify which items are considered part of the real property in the transaction and any personal property that is to be included.

**COMPLETE THE SECTION 2 REVIEW
EXERCISE AND COMPARE YOUR ANSWERS WITH THE
SOLUTIONS AT THE END OF THE CHAPTER.**

REVIEW EXERCISES

1. List the test for a fixture that corresponds to each description.

   a. _____ The item is securely bolted to the wall.

   b. _____ The listing agreement between the broker and seller lists the item.

   c. _____ The item was constructed that so that it would fit into the wall space next to the fireplace.

   d. _____ The item is specifically listed in the lease agreement.

Are the following statements true (T) or false (F)?

2. ____ Another name for personal property is chattel property.

3. ____ The primary characteristic of personal property is mobility.

4. ____ A trade fixture is considered real property.

5. ____ Objects can be converted from personal property to real property, but not from real property to personal property.

6. Determine if the following items are likely to be real or personal property.

   a. _____ Refrigerator

   b. _____ Furnace

   c. _____ Fence

   d. _____ Garage

   e. _____ Bowling alleys

   f. _____ Planted shrubs

   g. _____ Window air conditioner

Supply the term that best matches each of the following descriptions.

7. _____ An item that was once personal property but has been attached to the real estate and has become real property

8. _____ Annual crops on the property that are cultivated by the owner

9. _____ The process of changing real property to personal property

10. _____ A type of fixture that remains personal property and can be removed by the tenant

11. _____ The process of changing personal property to real property

SOLUTIONS
FOR SECTION REVIEW EXERCISES

SECTION 1

1. a. Land — Earth's surface, below to the center, above to infinity, natural things attached.

    b. Real estate — Earth's surface, below to the center, above to infinity, natural and artificial things attached.

    c. Real property — Earth's surface, below to the center, above to infinity, natural and artificial things attached, and the rights of ownership in the land.

2. TRUE

3. FALSE Improvements are *artificial* enhancements to the land, such as buildings and fences.

4. TRUE

5. Common law

6. Subsurface rights

7. Improvements

8. Air rights

9. Allodial system

SECTION 2

1. a. Method of attachment to the real estate   b. Intention of the parties   c. Adaptation of the article to the real estate   d. Written agreement of the parties

2. TRUE

3. TRUE

4. FALSE Trade fixtures remain the personal property of the tenant.

5. FALSE Objects can be converted from real property to personal property through severance.

6. a. Personal property   b. Real property   c. Real property
    d. Real property   e. Personal property (these are trade fixtures)
    f. Real property   g. Personal property

7. Fixture

8. Emblements *or* fruits of industry

9. Severance

10. Trade fixture

11. Attachment

THIS IS THE LAST CHAPTER IN THE UNIT. TAKE THE UNIT I DIAGNOSTIC TEST.

INSTRUCTIONS FOR USING THE UNIT DIAGNOSTIC TESTS

There is a Diagnostic Test covering each of the units in this book. Answers with explanations and solutions to any math questions are in the Study Tool Kit. To gain the most benefit from the test, read the instructions below.

The purpose of the diagnostic test is to provide valuable practice and feedback that will enable readers to evaluate comprehension of the material and practice answering tests. A diagnostic worksheet is provided for recording and analyzing the results of each test, both in total and by chapter. This analysis identifies areas in which readers are proficient and those in which they are weak.

- Answer sheets for the tests are perforated so that they can be removed from the book, making them easier to use.
- The test for each unit consists of 50 questions (30 in the Unit I and VIII tests) that cover all of the topics in the unit.
- After completing a test, refer to the diagnostic worksheet. Compare your answers with the answer key and write a "C" in the box provided for each question answered correctly.
- Total the number correct for each chapter and enter it in the test summary.
- Compare your score with the score breakdown for (1) the test as a whole (listed below the chapter totals) and (2) by chapter (listed in the test summary at the right of each chapter).
- This will provide you with an indication of your learning comprehension, both overall and by specific topic. It is recommended that you review the material in the text for each question that was answered incorrectly.
- You may want to photocopy the blank answer sheet and diagnostic page in this book for future use with new tests that you create. It is recommended that any new test be created using the questions that you answered incorrectly.

UNIT
DIAGNOSTIC
TEST

1. The physical characteristic of real property that no two parcels of land are exactly alike is called

   a. immobility.
   b. nonhomogeneity.
   c. situs.
   d. indestructibility.

2. Bowling alleys, store shelves and restaurant equipment are examples of which of the following:

   a. Real property
   b. Real estate
   c. Trade fixtures
   d. General fixtures

3. Intent of the parties, method of annexation, adaptation to real estate and agreement between the parties are the legal tests for determining whether an item is

   a. a trade fixture or personal property.
   b. real property or real estate.
   c. a fixture or personal property.
   d. an improvement.

4. A shopping mall is an example of what type of real estate?

   a. Industrial
   b. Commercial
   c. Residential
   d. Special purpose

5. Laws developed through the years by the courts based on custom and usage are referred to as

   a. the allodial system.
   b. common law.
   c. statute law.
   d. emblements.

6. The economic characteristic of scarcity refers to which of the following?

   a. No two parcels of land are exactly alike.
   b. There may not be enough land in certain areas to satisfy demand.
   c. People prefer certain areas.
   d. The real estate industry has run out of land to continue sufficient development.

7. Included in the term *real property* is

   a. anything permanently affixed to the land.
   b. the air rights to the property.
   c. mineral rights to the property.
   d. All of the above

8. The economic characteristic of situs refers to which of the following?

   a. No two parcels of land are exactly alike.
   b. There may not be enough land in certain areas to satisfy demand.
   c. People prefer certain areas.
   d. Land cannot be destroyed.

9. A warehouse is an example of what type of real estate?

   a. Residential
   b. Special purpose
   c. Industrial
   d. Commercial

10. A system of laws that recognizes private ownership of land is referred to as

   a. the allodial system.
   b. common law.
   c. statute law.
   d. feudal law.

11. Of the following items, which is considered personal property?

    a. A store's display counters
    b. A garage
    c. An installed dishwasher
    d. Growing bushes

12. In general, when the supply of real estate increases

    a. prices tend to increase.
    b. prices tend to decrease.
    c. demand tends to increase.
    d. demand is unchanged.

13. Which of the following describes the act by which real property can be converted to personal property?

    a. Severance
    b. Accession
    c. Conversion
    d. Separation

14. A buyer and seller of a home are debating whether a certain item is real or personal property. The buyer believes it is real property and should be conveyed with the house; the seller believes it is personal property and may be conveyed separately with a bill of sale. In determining whether the item is real or personal property, a court would consider all of the following *except*

    a. adaptation of the item to the real estate.
    b. the method of attachment.
    c. permanence of the installation.
    d. the length of time the item has been attached to the property.

15. In the real estate market there are several factors that affect the supply and demand for real estate. Which of the following would affect the demand for real estate?

    a. Number of real estate brokers in the area
    b. Number of full-time real estate salespeople in the area
    c. Wage levels and employment opportunities
    d. Price of new homes being built in the area

16. The term REALTOR® can be used only by:

    a. licensed brokers.
    b. full-time licensed salespersons or brokers.
    c. all licensed salespersons and brokers.
    d. licensees who are members of the National Association of REALTORS®.

17. Harold owns a building in a commercial area. Tom rents space in the building and operates a bookstore. In Tom's bookstore, there are large tables fastened to the walls, where customers are encouraged to sit and read. Shelves create aisles from the front of the store to the back. The shelves are bolted to both the ceiling and the floor. Which of the following best characterizes the contents of Tom's bookstore?

    a. The shelves and tables are trade fixtures and will be sold with the building.
    b. The shelves and tables are trade fixtures and may be removed before Tom's lease expires.
    c. Because Tom is a tenant, the shelves and tables are fixtures and may not be removed except with Harold's permission.
    d. Because the shelves and tables are attached to the building, they are treated the same as other fixtures.

18. An office building is an example of what type of real estate?

    a. Residential
    b. Special purpose
    c. Industrial
    d. Commercial

19. A mobile home on a permanent foundation most likely would be considered

    a. chattel property.
    b. a trade fixture.
    c. real property.
    d. personal property.

20. The economic characteristic of fixity refers to which of the following statements?

    a. Investments in real estate are usually for the long term.
    b. Land cannot be destroyed.
    c. Land cannot be removed.
    d. No two parcels of land are exactly alike.

21. James is building a new enclosed front porch on his home. A truckload of lumber has been left on James's driveway for use in building the porch. At this point, the lumber is considered what kind of property?

    a. A fixture because it will be permanently affixed to existing real property
    b. Personal property
    c. Real property
    d. A trade fixture

22. Property management, appraisal, financing and development are all examples of

 a. factors affecting demand for real estate.
 b. services provided by the real estate industry.
 c. non-real estate professions.
 d. government regulation of the real estate industry.

23. Which of the following is considered to be personal property?

 a. Trees growing on the property
 b. Trade fixtures installed on the property
 c. A garage
 d. A driveway

24. Which economic characteristic of real estate refers to the concept that changes in a parcel of land affect its value either favorably or unfavorably?

 a. Fixity
 b. Scarcity
 c. Nonhomogeneity
 d. Modifications

25. A tenant occupies a rental unit in an apartment building and installs new wooden kitchen cabinets. At the end of the lease the tenant wishes to remove the cabinets. Which of the following is true regarding removal of the cabinets?

 a. The cabinets can be removed by the tenant.
 b. The cabinets can be removed, but the tenant owes compensation to the property owner.
 c. The cabinets must stay, but the tenant is entitled to compensation.
 d. The cabinets must stay.

26. A church is an example of what type of real estate?

 a. Residential
 b. Special purpose
 c. Industrial
 d. Commercial

27. A restaurant owner occupying a leased space in a commercial building installs a large neon sign in the window. The sign would probably be considered:

 a. an emblement
 b. a trade fixture
 c. real property
 d. a fixture

28. What physical characteristic makes real estate easy for local governments to tax and causes it to be heavily influenced by changes in the surrounding areas?

 a. Indestructibility
 b. Nonhomogeneity
 c. Immobility
 d. Situs

29. Which of the following is included in the definition of real estate but not the definition of land?

 a. The air rights
 b. The property's surface
 c. Below the property to the center of the Earth.
 d. Fixtures on the property

30. Which economic characteristic of real estate refers to the concept that the supply of land is limited and therefore strong demand in certain areas will increase property values?

 a. Fixity
 b. Scarcity
 c. Nonhomogeneity
 d. Modifications

U N I T I
DIAGNOSTIC TEST
ANSWER SHEET

This sheet is perforated for easy pullout. Write your answers on this sheet as you complete the exercises. Refer to the diagnostic worksheet after completing the test to evaluate your strong and weak content areas. Review material in the appropriate chapter and sections.

1. _____

2. _____

3. _____

4. _____

5. _____

6. _____

7. _____

8. _____

9. _____

10. _____

11. _____

12. _____

13. _____

14. _____

15. _____

16. _____

17. _____

18. _____

19. _____

20. _____

21. _____

22. _____

23. _____

24. _____

25. _____

26. _____

27. _____

28. _____

29. _____

30. _____

REAL ESTATE
LAW

CHAPTER 3

GOVERNMENT POWERS

Real estate is subject to certain restrictions by the government. *Section 1* covers the government's police powers, which are used to protect the public health and safety. Police powers include zoning laws and building codes. *Section 2* covers other government powers. These include taxation, eminent domain and escheat. *Section 3* covers environmental considerations including federal environmental laws written to protect the environment. The government powers discussed in this chapter are summarized in Figure 3.1. Remember to use the Study Tool Kit to reference key information and to update your progress checklist.

Learning Objectives

Track your progress as you work through the chapter by checking each learning objective when you complete it.

____ List and describe the four government powers.

____ Explain the differences between zoning variance, nonconforming use and zoning amendment.

____ Explain the difference between zoning laws and building codes.

____ List and describe the three requirements for eminent domain.

Key Terms and Phrases

Track your progress as you work through the chapter by checking each term when you understand its meaning.

____ Amendment	____ Home rule powers
____ Building codes	____ Inverse condemnation
____ Building permit	____ Nonconforming use
____ Certificate of occupancy	____ Planned Unit Development
____ Condemnation	____ Police powers
____ Downzoning	____ Taxation
____ Eminent domain	____ Variance
____ Enabling legislation	____ Zoning
____ Escheat	

FIGURE 3.1
Government Powers

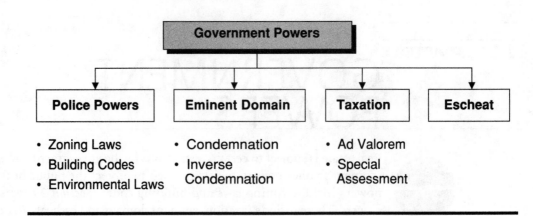

POLICE POWERS

PURPOSE OF POLICE POWERS

Under the government's **police powers** the state has the power to pass legislation to protect the public health and safety as well as to promote the general welfare. Local governments get their authority through **enabling legislation** passed by the state. In some states this power is created through **home rule powers** provided in the state's constitution.

EXAMPLE: Through the government's police powers it may enforce zoning laws, building codes, rent controls and environmental laws.

Under the police powers the government may have buildings that are unsafe or unfit for occupancy ordered vacated and destroyed through the process of condemnation. In this case no compensation is given to the property owner. The government can also assess fines or remove property that is in violation of zoning laws.

However, the exercise of the government's police powers must be *reasonable* and applied *equitably* to everyone. If government regulation is too arbitrary or restrictive it may violate the safeguards of due process and equal protection included in the U.S. Constitution. Regulations found to be in violation will be considered void.

ZONING

Zoning regulates and controls the use of land. Common areas controlled by zoning laws include types of structures permitted, building heights, setbacks and density. Zoning laws are enforceable under the government's police powers. Zoning rules are set by local governments, such as the county or city. There are no federal zoning laws. Zoning powers are given to local governments by state enabling acts. Each county, city and town then passes zoning ordinances that regulate property within its jurisdiction.

Zoning Classifications

Land is divided into designated areas or *zones*, which are then identified by a coding system that defines how the land may be used. Typical zoning classifications include R for residential, C for commercial, I for industrial and A for agriculture. There are usually subcategories within each classification, and some tracts of land may be allowed *mixed uses*.

A **Planned Unit Development,** or PUD, is an example of mixed use zoning. PUDs are developments of several acres that set aside areas for residences, commercial property, public areas such as schools or parks, and even industrial property.

EXAMPLE: Subcategories of residential zoning in Anytown USA include R1, single-family houses; R2, residential buildings of two to four units; R3, residential buildings of five to eight units; R4, residential highrises.

EXAMPLE: Zoning laws in Anytown USA include the *mixed land use* category of RO, which allows a building to include both apartments and office units.

Note: There is no uniformity throughout the country for zoning classifications. One city may use "I" to designate industrial property, and another may use "I" for institutional property such as schools.

Zoning laws dictate additional rules besides defining how the land can be used. These include minimum square footage requirements for buildings on the property; *setback* requirements, which state how far from the lot lines a building must be located; and the maximum height permitted for any buildings on the property.

EXAMPLE: Zoning laws in Anytown USA state that all buildings bordering the town lake must not exceed one story, to protect the sunlight and flow of air to neighboring properties.

Nonconforming Use

If a property's use existed prior to the current zoning rules, it generally will be allowed to continue as a **nonconforming use.** In this situation the use is *permitted*, and the zoning will not retroactively stop the preexisting use.

Although nonconforming uses are allowed to exist, they are usually subject to various requirements that are intended to gradually bring the property into conformance with the zoning laws. These may include such requirements as the following:

- Establishment of a reasonable period of time by which the nonconforming use must be phased out.
- If the nonconforming use structure is *destroyed*, it cannot be replaced with another nonconforming use structure.
- If the nonconforming use is *abandoned*, the owner can continue to use the property only for purposes that conform to the zoning code.
- If title to the property is *transferred*, the nonconforming use may have to cease.
- The owner may make necessary repairs to the structure but may *not expand* the nonconforming use.

Downzoning

Downzoning occurs when zoning is changed from higher-density uses to lower-density uses. *Density* zoning regulates the number of units the buildings on the property can include or the number of buildings that may be built on a tract of land. Downzoning often is used to prevent the overloading of public services and infrastructure in an area.

EXAMPLE: A residential area is downzoned from multiunit buildings to single family use.

EXAMPLE: An area is downzoned from multistory office buildings to one-story office buildings.

EXAMPLE: A zoning ordinance increases the minimum size of a lot on which a house may be built from 10,000 to 20,000 square feet. This cuts in half the number of houses that can be built.

Amendment

A zoning law can be changed by an **amendment.** The amendment can be requested by either property owners or the local government. Requests for amendments are usually heard by the zoning board. The board will consider the request at a public hearing and allow any citizens groups or neighbors to offer input. The board then makes its recommendation to the local government, which will make the final decision.

Zoning Appeals

A property owner who wants to do something to the property that is not permitted by the zoning law can appeal to the zoning appeals board. The appeals board hears zoning complaints on specific properties and may grant *variances* to the zoning law.

Variance

Property owners who are successful with their complaints to the zoning appeals board are granted a variance. A **variance** is an *exception* to the zoning law. Variances often are granted if strict enforcement of the zoning law would result in undue hardship to the property owner.

EXAMPLE: The zoning law requires driveways to be at least ten feet from the lot line. A property owner wishes to build a driveway for a new garage that will be only nine feet from the lot line. Because the garage may be useless without the driveway, the appeals board may grant a variance.

Hint: The terms amendment and variance appear similar but have different meanings. An amendment changes the zoning law, whereas a variance allows an exception to the zoning law but does not change it.

Some uses of property may be inconsistent with zoning but desirable for public convenience. To accommodate these situations, zoning codes allow special permissions called *conditional use permits* or *special-use permits* to be given.

EXAMPLE: A church located in a residential neighborhood may be given a conditional use permit.

If an owner's request for a variance has been denied and the owner has exhausted the zoning appeal process, the owner may turn to the courts. The owner may sue and have the property *rezoned* if it is proved that the zoning law was arbitrary or unlawfully enacted or enforced.

BUILDING CODES

 Note: Individuals purchasing property and real estate professionals need to be aware of local zoning laws because they have a significant impact on a property's value. Expensive changes may be required to bring a property into compliance with local zoning laws.

Under the government's police powers, **building codes** are enacted to protect the public health and safety from inferior construction practices. Through building codes, state and local governments set minimum standards for construction methods and materials. This includes requirements for fire safety standards; carpentry, plumbing and electrical work; heating equipment; and sewerage facilities. Building codes are usually enforced by building inspectors and fire and health officials.

Building Permits

Building inspectors issue **building permits** for construction of new buildings or altering existing structures. Compliance with all zoning laws is checked before the permit is issued. This ensures zoning laws are enforced. An owner who builds without a permit may be required to dismantle the structure.

Certificate of Occupancy

Before a new building may be occupied, a **certificate of occupancy** must be issued. The building is inspected, and if it complies with the building codes a certificate is issued. The building cannot be legally occupied without the occupancy certificate.

BEFORE READING THE NEXT SECTION, COMPLETE THE SECTION 1 REVIEW EXERCISES AND COMPARE YOUR ANSWERS WITH THE SOLUTIONS AT THE END OF THE CHAPTER.

SECTION 1
REVIEW EXERCISES

1. Name at least two examples of police powers.

    a. _____

    b. _____

Are the following statements true (T) or false (F)?

2. ____ Building codes regulate the purposes for which buildings may be used.

3. ____ Amendments, unlike variances, require a change to the zoning laws.

4. ____ Zoning laws are not set by the federal government.

5. How does a town obtain its power to control land through zoning laws?

    _____

6. Under what circumstances might a nonconforming use be brought back into conformance with zoning laws?

    a. _____

    b. _____

c. _____

d. _____

Supply the term that best matches each of the following descriptions.

7. _____ The government power to create laws to protect the public health and safety and promote the general welfare

8. _____ Local laws that regulate the control and use of land

9. _____ Use in existence prior to the zoning law that is allowed to continue

10. _____ Changing an area from higher-density use to lower-density use

11. _____ Permission for a property owner to use the land in a way not allowed under the zoning law

12. _____ Enacted to protect the public health and safety from inferior construction practices

13. _____ Permission granted by a local government to build a specific structure

14. _____ A document issued by a local government permitting a new building to be occupied that is issued only if the building is in compliance with building codes

---

SECTION 2
OTHER GOVERNMENT POWERS

In addition to police powers, governments have other powers that affect real estate. These are taxation, eminent domain and escheat.

TAXATION

Taxation is a charge on real estate to meet the financial needs of government. Real estate is easily taxed because it is immobile and ownership is in the public records.

Real estate taxation will be discussed in more detail in Chapter 5.

EMINENT DOMAIN

Under the power of **eminent domain** the government or its agencies may take title to privately held land for public use without the owner's consent. When exercising eminent domain, the government must pay fair compensation to the property owner. This power may be delegated by the government to other entities such as schools and utilities. The actual taking of title to the property is acquired through the process of **condemnation**.

Condemnation

There are three requirements for condemnation:

1. The proposed use must be declared by the court to be for the *public good*.

2. The property owner is entitled to *fair compensation* from the government. The owner may refuse the amount offered by the government and may have the court determine fair compensation. When only part of the property is taken by the government, resulting in a decrease in property value, the owner is entitled to compensation for the loss of value.

3. The rights of the property owner must be protected by *due process of law.*

Inverse Condemnation

Property owners can force **inverse condemnation** of their property if government action has forced a loss of value or inability to use the property.

EXAMPLE: The city builds a new airport runway that ends near a homeowner's property, significantly diminishing its suitability as residential property. The homeowner may force the city to condemn and purchase the home.

ESCHEAT

If a person dies and leaves no will or heirs, title to the property will revert to the state or county where the property is located through the government power of **escheat.** Chapter 10, Transferring Title, discusses escheat in more detail.

Hint: To help you remember the government powers think of the name PETE (P = Police powers, E = Eminent domain, T = Taxes, E = Escheat).

BEFORE READING THE NEXT SECTION, COMPLETE THE SECTION 2 REVIEW EXERCISES AND COMPARE YOUR ANSWERS WITH THE SOLUTIONS AT THE END OF THE CHAPTER.

SECTION 2
REVIEW EXERCISES

1. Name the requirement for condemnation that best fits each description.
   a. _____ Protecting the rights of the property owner
   b. _____ What use will be made of the property
   c. _____ What the property owner will receive

2. Name the government power that best fits each description.
   a. _____ Forcing the government to take property
   b. _____ Rasing money to meet the financial needs of government
   c. _____ Passing title of property to the state if no heir can be found
   d. _____ Acquiring title to property by the state to allow a highway to be built

Are the following statements true (T) or false (F)?

3. ____ If a property owner dies leaving no heirs, title to the property may pass to the government through its powers of eminent domain.

4. ____ Real estate is easily taxed because it is immobile and ownership is in the public records.

Supply the term that matches each of the following descriptions.

5. _____ The government power of taking private land for the public good

6. _____ The government power whereby property reverts to the state or county if the owner dies without a will and leaves no heirs

7. _____ The government power that is used to raise money for funding local government

8. _____ Action initiated by property owners to force the government to buy their property

9. _____ The legal process used by the government to carry out its power of eminent domain

---

SECTION 3

ENVIRONMENTAL CONSIDERATIONS AFFECTING REAL ESTATE

Several federal and state laws have been passed to protect the environment and address the problems caused by hazardous substances. These laws often affect the usability and value of real estate. Environmental laws are usually enforced by government regulatory agencies, but some laws allow individuals to bring law suits for pollution violations.

REGULATORY AGENCIES AND ENVIRONMENTAL LAWS

The U.S. Environmental Protection Agency (EPA)—EPA was established as an independent agency in 1970. It is responsible for administering and enforcing several comprehensive environmental protection laws.

The National Environmental Policy Act (NEPA), 1969—NEPA promotes efforts to reduce damage to the environment. It requires the filing of an Environmental Impact Statement with EPA to ensure proposed land projects do not adversely affect the environment.

The Clean Air Act (CAA), 1967—The CAA (as amended in 1990) requires the EPA to establish and enforce air quality standards to protect human health, safety and the environment. In 1993 the EPA issued regulations that affect property owners and businesses that own or repair a wide range of appliances (such as air-conditioners and refrigerators) that use refrigerants.

The Clean Water Act (CWA), 1972—The purpose of CWA is to restore and maintain the quality of the country's waters. The CWA regulates the discharge of pollutants into U.S. waters. A permit must be obtained for effluent discharges. The permit specifies limitations on the discharges so that the water quality does not drop below certain levels. Another important section of the CWA establishes federal authority for protection of the nation's wetlands. The *Army Corps of Engineers* and the EPA have concurrent jurisdictional authority over the dredging and filling of waters (including wetlands) in the country.

The Resources Conservation and Recovery Act, 1976—This act defined hazardous materials and regulated their transportation, storage, use, treatment, disposal and cleanup. A 1984 amendment to the act established a program for regulation of underground storage tanks (USTs), for the installation and maintenance of tanks, monitoring for leaks and recordkeeping requirements. It also requires the property owner to have sufficient financial resources to cover damages resulting from leaking tanks.

The Comprehensive Environmental Response, Compensation and Liability Act (CERCLA), 1980—This act was passed to correct the environmental problems caused by abandoned hazardous waste sites. Sites containing hazardous substances are identified, action is taken to ensure the sites are cleaned up, and reimbursement for cleanup expenses is sought from the parties responsible for creating the problem. CERCLA established a Superfund of several billion dollars to clean up hazardous waste dumps and spills; money is recouped in cost recovery actions from the parties responsible. Buyers and lenders should be concerned about the financial burden of complying with federal cleanup requirements, which affect both the property that is the source of the contamination as well as any adjacent contaminated property.

The Superfund Amendments and Reauthorization Act (SARA), 1986—This act defines stringent clean-up standards for sites containing hazardous substances and expands liability for the clean-up costs. Parties that may be held responsible under this act include current owners and operators of the property, previous owners and operators, and persons who arranged for hazardous substance disposal at the site. The amendments also created the concept of *innocent landowner immunity*. This established certain conditions under which a landowner, who was completely innocent of all wrongdoing, may not be held liable.

The Coastal Zone Management Act (CZMA), 1972—Under CZMA the government implemented a coastal management scheme that places stringent controls on activities that adversely impact the coastal environment, including coastal wetlands.

The Lead Based Paint Hazard and Reduction Act requires that individuals receive certain information before renting, buying or renovating pre-1978 housing. Many houses and apartments built before 1978 have lead-based paint. Lead from paint, chips and dust can pose serious health hazards if not taken care of properly. Under the rules

- Landlords must disclose known information on lead-based paint hazards before leases take effect. Leases will include a federal form about lead-based paint.
- Sellers must disclose known information on lead-based hazards before selling a house. Sales contracts must include a federal form about lead-based paint in the building. Buyers will have up to ten days to check for lead hazards.
- Renovators must provide property owners with the EPA pamphlet, "Protect Your Family from Lead in Your Home," before starting work.

COMPLETE THE SECTION 3 REVIEW EXERCISES AND COMPARE YOUR ANSWERS WITH THE SOLUTIONS AT THE END OF THE CHAPTER.

SECTION 3
REVIEW EXERCISES

Are the following statements true (T) or false (F)?

1. ____ Under the Superfund Amendments and Reauthorization Act (SARA) an owner of property containing hazardous substances cannot escape liability under any circumstances.

2. ____ Federal lead disclosure rules pertain to property constructed before 1978.

3. ____ The Clean Water Act prohibits the discharge of any effluent into the nation's waters.

4. ____ Environmental acts often affect the value of real estate.

Name the act that best fits the following descriptions.

5. _____ Established federal authority for protection of the nation's wetlands

6. _____ Established a Superfund to clean up hazardous waste dumps and spills

7. _____ Intended to ensure proposed land projects do not adversely affect the environment

8. _____ Defined stringent cleanup standards for hazardous waste sites and extended liability for the cleanup

9. _____ Regulates underground storage tanks

SOLUTIONS

FOR SECTION REVIEW EXERCISES

SECTION 1

1. Zoning laws and building ordinances are the two primary police powers. Other examples are rent controls and environmental laws.
2. FALSE Zoning laws regulate a property's use.
3. TRUE
4. TRUE
5. Local governments obtain the power to regulate property through zoning laws from state enabling acts.
6. a. Following a reasonable time period for phasing out the nonconforming use.
   b. The structure is destroyed.   c. The nonconforming use is abandoned.
   d. Title to the property is transferred.
7. Police power
8. Zoning laws
9. Nonconforming use
10. Downzoning
11. Variance
12. Building codes
13. Building permit
14. Certificate of occupancy

SECTION 2

1. a. Due process of law   b. For the public good   c. Fair compensation
2. a. Eminent domain (inverse condemnation)   b. Taxation   c. Escheat
   d. Eminent domain (condemnation)
3. FALSE The government may obtain title to property through its powers of escheat.
4. TRUE
5. Eminent domain
6. Escheat
7. Taxation
8. Inverse condemnation
9. Condemnation

SECTION 3

1. FALSE SARA created the concept of innocent landowner in which the owner may not be liable under certain conditions.
2. TRUE
3. FALSE The act regulates the amount of effluent discharge through permits so that water quality levels may be maintained.
4. TRUE
5. The Clean Water Act
6. The Comprehensive Environmental Response, Compensation and Liability Act
7. National Environmental Policy Act
8. The Superfund Amendments and Reauthorization Act
9. The Resources, Conservation and Recovery Act

CHAPTER 4
ENCUMBRANCES

In this chapter you will learn about liabilities on the property called *encumbrances*. There are several types of encumbrances, including easements, liens and deed restrictions. This chapter discusses easements and deed restrictions, while liens are presented in Chapter 5. *Section 1* covers general information on encumbrances and easements. *Section 2* covers common types of easements. Remember to use the Study Tool Kit to reference key information and to update your progress checklist.

Learning Objectives

Track your progress as you work through the chapter by checking each learning objective when you complete it.

____ List and describe the two ways easements can be classified.

____ Explain the difference between appurtenant easements and easements in gross.

____ List and describe six common ways easements are created.

____ List and describe five common ways easements are terminated.

____ Explain the difference between an easement, an encroachment and a license.

____ List the common types of easements and their distinguishing characteristics.

____ Explain the difference between the dominant and servient tenements.

Key Terms and Phrases

Track your progress as you work through the chapter by checking each term when you understand its meaning.

____ Appurtenant easement

____ Commercial easements in gross

____ Deed restrictions

____ Dominant tenement

____ Easement

____ Easement by necessity

____ Easement by prescription

____ Easement in gross

____ Encroachment

____ Encumbrance

____ Landlocked

____ License

____ Negative easement

____ Party wall

____ Positive easement

____ Prescriptive easement

____ Run with the land

____ Servient tenement

____ Tacking

GENERAL NOTES ON ENCUMBRANCES AND EASEMENTS

ENCUMBRANCES

An **encumbrance** is a charge, claim or liability on real estate. An encumbrance may reduce a property's value or place restrictions on how it can be used; however, it does not necessarily *prevent* title to the property from transferring to someone else.

There are two types of encumbrances (see Figure 4.1):

1. Encumbrances that affect only *title,* such as liens and deed restrictions
2. Encumbrances that affect both the *title and physical condition* of the property, such as easements and encroachments

EASEMENTS

An **easement** is the *right* to use someone's land. The right may be to use the land's surface or the air space above it. Easements are called *nonpossessory* interests in real estate because they give the easement holder the right to *use* the property but not to *possess* it.

Classifying Easements

Easements can be classified in *two* ways:

1. Easements that are *appurtenant* or *in gross*
2. Easements that are *positive* or *negative*

Appurtenant easements belong to the land and transfer with the title. *Easements in gross* are held by individuals and end on the death of either the party giving the easement or the easement holder. Easements appurtenant and in gross are discussed in detail in Section 2 of the chapter.

Positive easements *allow* a person to use another's property for some stated purpose.

EXAMPLE: Able and Baker own separate lots that are next to each other. Able has an easement to cross Baker's land to reach a public road.

Negative easements *prevent* an owner from using the property in some manner.

EXAMPLE: A property owner is prevented from erecting a tall building that would restrict the view of the owner of the negative easement.

Creation of Easements

Easements can be created in the following ways:

- By *written agreement*—A written agreement between the easement parties. This is the most commonly used way to create easements. The agreement names the parties and describes the property over which the easement will run (the *servient tenement*) and, if it is

FIGURE 4.1
Common Types of Encumbrances

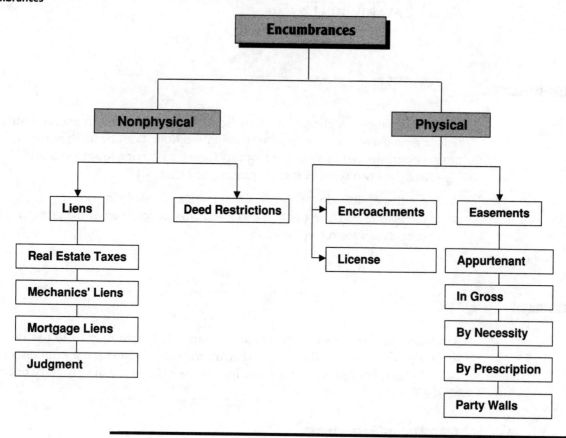

an appurtenant easement, the *dominant tenement.* The agreement also describes the use that is allowed. It is signed by the parties.

- By *express grant* in a deed—The deed, which includes the easement, is given by the owner of the property over which the easement will run.

EXAMPLE: A developer has set aside an area for a park and includes in the deed to each lot owner in the development an easement right to enter the park.

- By *express reservation* in a deed—The party giving the title (grantor) reserves an easement right over the property.

EXAMPLE: A father sells his summer cottage on the lake to his son and reserves in the deed an easement right for himself to enter the property in the future to fish.

- By *condemnation*—Through the government's power of eminent domain (discussed in Chapter 3), the easement can be acquired for a public purpose. The owner must be compensated for any loss of value to the property.
- By *prescription*—Using another's land in compliance with certain requirements defined by state law will create an easement by prescription.
- By *necessity*—This type of easement is created by law to allow owners access to their land. (Easements by *prescription* and *necessity* are discussed in detail in Section 2 of this chapter).

Termination of Easements

Easements can be terminated in the following ways:

- *Expiration*—If the easement was created for a specified period of time, the easement automatically ends when the time period expires.
- *End of purpose*—If the purpose for the easement no longer exists.

EXAMPLE: An easement by necessity ends if the property now includes land that provides access.

- *Merger*—If the owner of the dominant or servient property becomes the owner of *both* properties, the easement terminates by merger.
- *Agreement*—The owner of the easement can always agree to terminate the easement right. The agreement should be in writing and recorded in the public records to give notice that the easement right no longer exists.
- *Abandonment*—If the easement is not used over a period of time, it may be ended by abandonment. The length of time required before the easement is considered abandoned will vary among states and from case to case.

EXAMPLE: A manufacturing company owns an easement over neighboring properties so that trailer trucks can pick up goods from the plant. If the company removes its processing plant, the easement is extinguished.

LICENSE

A **license** is a privilege to use the land of another for a specific purpose. A license is a personal privilege granted only to the person to whom it is given; therefore, it cannot be assigned to someone else. The license ends if it is revoked by the licensor, on the death of either party, on sale of the land, by expiration or by abandonment.

EXAMPLE: A property owner gives someone a license to hunt or fish on his or her property.

 Hint: Both a license and an easement allow someone to use the land. However, they are different because a license can be terminated at any time by the party granting the license.

ENCROACHMENTS

Encroachments are *unauthorized physical intrusions* of a building or other form of real property onto an adjoining property.

EXAMPLE: A fence extends beyond the boundary line of an owner's property onto his neighbor's property.

Encroachments can usually be discovered either by a visual inspection of the property or by a *spot survey*. A spot survey (also called an Improvement Location Certificate or ILC in some areas) shows the location of property improvements and the lot lines. The owner of the property being encroached on can take court action either to force the removal of the encroachment or to recover damages.

Figure 4.2 illustrates an example of encroachments.

FIGURE 4.2
Encroachments

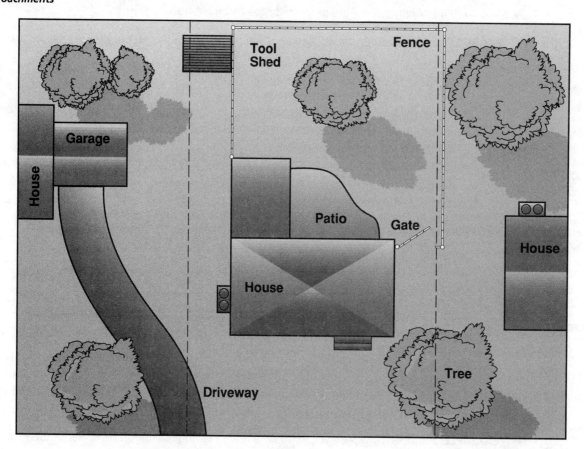

 Hint: An encroachment of long-standing use may result in an easement right by prescription or adverse possession. Section 2 discusses easements by prescription.

DEED RESTRICTIONS

Deed restrictions are conditions or limitations placed in a deed by the owner when property is transferred to another party. While deed restrictions are created by individual parties and affect a particular property, *restrictive covenants* are conditions placed in the deeds by developers and usually affect an entire subdivision. These restrictions affect how the land can be used. If deed restrictions or covenants place unreasonable or unlawful restraints on an owner's use of the land, they will be unenforceable. If there is a conflict between a deed restriction and zoning rules, whichever is the more restrictive will usually prevail.

(Deed restrictions also are discussed in Chapter 10, Transferring Title.)

EXAMPLE: A seller gives the buyer a deed to a parcel of land but includes a restriction in the deed keeping the rights to minerals on the land.

EXAMPLE: To protect scenic views, a builder places a restrictive covenant in the deeds limiting trees to 15 feet tall.

EXAMPLE: A restrictive covenant in the deeds for a subdivision prohibits owners from selling their property to a particular ethnic group. This covenant is unenforceable because it violates fair housing laws.

EXAMPLE: A property is zoned for multifamily buildings, but the deed restrictions limit use to single-family buildings. The deed restrictions will prevail.

BEFORE READING THE NEXT SECTION, COMPLETE THE SECTION 1 REVIEW EXERCISES AND COMPARE YOUR ANSWERS WITH THE SOLUTIONS AT THE END OF THE CHAPTER.

SECTION 1
REVIEW EXERCISES

1. List two ways easements can be classified.

   a. _____ or _____

   b. _____ or _____

2. List six ways easements can be created.

   a. _____

   b. _____

   c. _____

   d. _____

   e. _____

   f. _____

3. List five ways easements can be terminated.

   a. _____

   b. _____

   c. _____

   d. _____

   e. _____

Are the following statements true (T) or false (F)?

4. ____ Encumbrances usually prevent title to the property from passing.

5. ____ Expressed reservation in a deed is the most commonly used way to create an easement.

6. ____ Because both a license and an easement allow a person to enter another's property, they are essentially the same thing.

7. ____ Encroachments can usually be discovered by a survey rather than by looking in the public records.

8. Determine whether each of the following is an example of a license, an encroachment, a positive easement or a negative easement.

   a. _____ A property owner can prevent her neighbor from building a second story that would block the sun to her garden.

   b. _____ A parking lot allows you to park your car for a fee.

   c. _____ The eaves of a house hang over the property line of the adjoining property.

      d. _____ You are given the right to enter your neighbor's property to launch your boat.

Supply the term that best matches each of the following descriptions.

9. _____ Illegal physical intrusion on another's land by an improvement

10. _____ A charge, claim or liability on the property

11. _____ A personal privilege to enter another's land for a specific purpose

12. _____ The right to use another's land

13. _____ A clause in the deed that limits the owner's use of the property

---

SECTION 2

TYPES OF EASEMENTS

APPURTENANT EASEMENTS

Appurtenant easements allow the owner of a parcel of land to use the land next to it. For this easement to exist there must be *two* conditions:

1. There must be at least *two* parcels of land located *next* to each other.
2. The parcels must be owned by *different parties*.

When an easement appurtenant situation exists, the parcels of land involved are called dominant and servient tenements.

Dominant tenement—The parcel of land that benefits from the easement is called the dominant tenement.

Servient tenement—The parcel of land over which the easement runs is called the servient tenement.

Figure 4.3 illustrates an example of dominant and servient tenements.

EXAMPLE: A and B own properties next to each other, but only B's property has access to a lake. B may grant A an easement to cross B's property to reach the lake. In this situation B is the servient tenement and A is the dominant tenement.

 Hint: Remember that the dominant tenement uses or dominates the other property. The servient tenement serves the other property.

Appurtenant easements are said to **"run with the land."** This means that if the dominant property is conveyed to another party, the easement right transfers with it. The obligations also transfer with the servient tenement if the servient property is conveyed. The easement right of the dominant property will transfer with the property forever unless there is a specific limitation on the time of the easement or it is released by the owner.

FIGURE 4.3
Appurtenant Easement

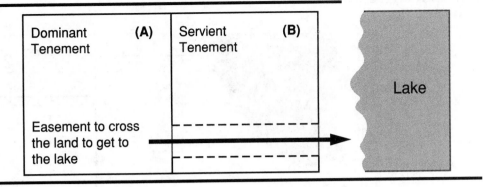

Easement by Necessity

Owners of land have the right to enter (right of *ingress*) and leave (the right of *egress*) their property. An easement is created by court order to prevent landowners from becoming **landlocked,** making the property useless. An **easement by necessity** therefore is created by law over the adjoining property. This situation often arises when an owner sells part of his land that has no access to a public way except over the seller's remaining land.

Party Wall Easements

Sometimes the wall of a building straddles the boundary line of two separate properties. This is called a **party wall.** In this situation each property owner owns that portion of the party wall on his or her property and has a *party wall easement* in the other portion of the wall. Expenses to either build or maintain the wall are usually shared. To create the easement rights, a party wall agreement must be used.

EASEMENT IN GROSS

An **easement in gross** is the *personal right* to use another's land. Such easements are given to individuals or corporations. Easements in gross cannot be assigned to someone else, and they terminate on the death of the easement owner. Unlike appurtenant easements, an easement in gross has a servient tenement but no dominant tenement.

Commercial Easements in Gross

Most easements in gross are given to commercial entities such as utility companies to maintain the pipelines, telephone lines or power lines necessary to provide utilities and other services. These are called **commercial easements in gross** and usually may be assigned or conveyed by the easement holder.

EXAMPLE: The local telephone company has been given a commercial easement over the rear ten feet of each residential lot in a city. The company may enter residential lots to install and repair its telephone equipment and may sell its rights to a cable company to lay TV cable on the easement.

FIGURE 4.4
Common Easements

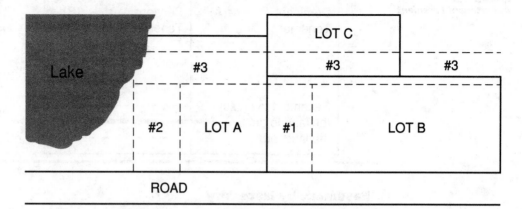

1. C has an easement by necessity across B's land.
2. The public has an easement right over A's land to the lake.
3. A utility easement in gross crosses the land of A, B and C.

EASEMENT BY PRESCRIPTION (PRESCRIPTIVE EASEMENT)

An **easement by prescription** (also called a **prescriptive easement**) is acquired when a claimant uses another's land for a period of time as defined by state law. Requirements for acquiring an easement by prescription vary; however, they usually include the following:

- An uninterrupted *use* of the property (usually from 5 to 21 years).
- The use must be *continuous* (see the description of tacking below).
- The use must be *adverse, without* the owner's consent.
- The use must be *visible, open and notorious,* so that the owner can easily learn of it.

EXAMPLE: A driveway at the edge of property A extends partly on to property B. If used by the owner of A for the prescribed period of time, the use may result in a permanent easement right by prescription.

Successive periods of use by different parties, called **tacking,** may be combined to meet the requirement of continuous use. This will allow a party not using the property for the entire period to establish an easement by prescription. Tacking will be allowed only if the parties are successors in interest.

EXAMPLE: A mother uses the property and now the son continues the use. The time both used the property may be "tacked" together to meet the time requirement.

 Note: To legally establish an easement by prescription, a "quiet title" lawsuit is often used.

Figure 4.4 illustrates several types of common easements.

**COMPLETE THE SECTION 2 REVIEW EXERCISES AND COMPARE YOUR
ANSWERS WITH THE SOLUTIONS AT THE END OF THE CHAPTER.**

REVIEW EXERCISES

1. Determine which of the requirements for an easement by prescription best fits each description.

    a. _____ The use of the property is uninterrupted.

    b. _____ The use can be readily seen by the owner.

    c. _____ The property is used without the owner's consent.

Are the following statements true (T) or false (F)?

2. ____ One of the requirements for an appurtenant easement is that at least two parcels of real estate be in close proximity to each other.

3. ____ Easements in gross are said to "run with the land."

4. ____ Easements by necessity are created to prevent an owner from becoming landlocked.

5. ____ Easements by necessity and party wall easements are both examples of easements appurtenant.

6. ____ The parcel of land that is subject to an easement appurtenant is considered the dominant tenement.

Supply the term that best matches each of the following descriptions.

7. _____ Easements belonging to properties that are adjacent to one another

8. _____ An easement right given to a person to enter someone's land for a specific purpose

9. _____ An easement right granted by court order when there is no access to a person's land

10. _____ Acquiring an easement right by using the property without the owner's consent

11. _____ The right given to utility companies to go onto the land to maintain their equipment

12. _____ A tract of land that benefits from an easement appurtenant right

13. _____ A tract of land over which an appurtenant easement right runs

14. _____ An easement right acquired by the use of another's property for the period prescribed by law

15. _____ Easement rights that are passed on to the successive owners of the property

16. _____ Combining successive periods of property use

SOLUTIONS
FOR SECTION REVIEW EXERCISES

SECTION 1

1. a. Easements appurtenant or easements in gross   b. Positive easements or negative easements
2. a. By written agreement   b. By expressed grant in a deed   c. By expressed reservation in a deed   d. By condemnation   e. By prescription   f. By necessity
3. a. By expiration   b. By end of purpose   c. By merger   d. By agreement   e. By abandonment
4. FALSE An encumbrance may reduce a property's value or place restrictions on how it can be used, but it usually does not *prevent* title to the property from transferring to someone else.
5. FALSE The most commonly used way to create an easement is by a written agreement between the parties.
6. FALSE A license is a privilege that can be terminated by the party granting the license, whereas an easement is a right to use the land.
7. TRUE
8. a. Negative easement   b. License   c. Encroachment   d. Positive easement
9. Encroachment
10. Encumbrance
11. License
12. Easement
13. Deed restriction

SECTION 2

1. a. Continuous   b. Open and notorious   c. Adverse
2. FALSE One requirement for an appurtenant easement is that at least two parcels of real estate be *next* to each other.
3. FALSE Easements *appurtenant* are said to "run with the land."
4. TRUE
5. TRUE
6. FALSE The parcel of land that is subject to an easement appurtenant is considered the *servient* tenement.
7. Appurtenant easement
8. Easement in gross
9. Easement by necessity
10. Easement by prescription
11. Commercial easement in gross
12. Dominant tenement
13. Servient tenement
14. Easements by prescription
15. Run with the land
16. Tacking

SEE ▼ STUDY TOOL KIT

CHAPTER 5
ENCUMBRANCES: LIENS

The last chapter introduced the concept of encumbrances and discussed the encumbrances of easements and deed restrictions. This chapter focuses on other types of encumbrances, called *liens*. Several of the most common types of liens are explained. *Section 1* covers how liens are classified and prioritized. *Section 2* covers real estate tax liens. *Section 3* covers other types of liens. Remember to use the Study Tool Kit to reference key information and to update your progress checklist.

Learning Objectives

Track your progress as you work through the chapter by checking each learning objective when you complete it.

____ Explain the differences between: specific and general liens, voluntary and involuntary liens, statutory and equitable liens.

____ List and explain three ways liens can be created.

____ Explain how liens are prioritized.

____ Explain the difference between ad valorem and special assessment tax liens.

____ List the types of properties exempted from real estate tax liens.

____ List the steps for computing a real estate tax bill.

____ Describe the tax sale process.

____ Describe the special assessment process.

____ Classify the various types of liens included in the chapter.

Key Terms and Phrases

Track your progress as you work through the chapter by checking each term when you understand its meaning.

____ Ad valorem   ____ Judgment

____ Assessment   ____ Lien

____ Equalizer   ____ Lienee

____ Equitable liens   ____ Lienor

____ Equitable redemption rights ____ Lis Pendens

____ General lien   ____ Mechanic's lien

____ Involuntary lien   ____ Mills

____	Mortgage lien	____	Tax rate
____	Special assessment	____	Tax sale
____	Specific lien	____	Vendee lien
____	Statutory liens	____	Vendor lien
____	Statutory redemption rights	____	Voluntary lien
____	Subordination agreement	____	Writ of attachment

SECTION 1
GENERAL NOTES ON LIENS

DESCRIPTION OF LIENS

A **lien** is a claim or charge against the property to provide security for a debt or obligation. The lien allows the creditor to have the property sold to satisfy the debt in case of default. To enforce a lien, the creditor must take legal action and obtain a court order to have the property sold.

Liens against real estate may reduce the value of the property; however, the owner can still convey title to another party. Because the liens remain as a liability for whomever owns the property, they are usually settled before the closing as a condition of the sale.

The party holding the lien is called the **lienor.** The party who has property encumbered by the lien is called the **lienee.**

CLASSIFYING LIENS

Liens can be classified by how they affect property (specific or general) or how they are created (voluntary or involuntary).

Specific versus General

A **general lien** is a claim against *all* of a person's property, both real and personal.

EXAMPLE: Inheritance tax, judgments and IRS liens.

A **specific lien** is a claim against a specific property. The property affected may be either real or personal.

EXAMPLE: Specific liens secured by real estate include mortgage, mechanic's lien and real estate taxes.

EXAMPLE: An auto loan is a specific lien secured by personal property.

Voluntary versus Involuntary

Voluntary liens are made with the owner's consent.

EXAMPLE: An owner obtains a loan to purchase real estate. The owner signs mortgage documents that create a lien on the property.

Involuntary liens are created by law and do not require the owner's consent.

EXAMPLE: Local governments are granted real estate tax liens on property in their jurisdictions to enforce the collection of taxes.

Involuntary liens can be further classified as either statutory or equitable. Involuntary **statutory liens** are created by state laws. Involuntary **equitable liens** are created by the court either when *fairness* requires that a lien right exist or when the conduct of the parties *implies* that a lien exists.

CREATION OF LIENS

As seen in the discussion above, liens can be created in three ways:

1. Contractual—by agreement of the parties.
2. Statutory—by law.
3. Equitable—by the courts to ensure fairness and justice.

Figure 5.1 summarizes how liens are classified.

PRIORITY OF LIENS

When there are two or more liens on a property, the *priority* of the liens determines the order in which the liens will be satisfied if the property must be sold to satisfy one or more of the liens. Outstanding real estate taxes and special assessments take *priority over all other liens*. The priority of the remaining liens is usually established by the *date and time they were recorded* in the public records. Liens are recorded in the county where the property is located.

Tip: An exception to the rule of liens taking priority as of the date they are recorded is the mechanic's lien. Rules for mechanics' liens vary by state and may take effect when the work is ordered or started. These are discussed later in the chapter.

A holder of a lien may want to make it subordinate to another lien. To change priority of the liens, a written **subordination agreement** can be made between the lienholders.

EXAMPLE: The holder of a mortgage on a tract of land may subordinate it to a construction mortgage for a building on the land because it will enhance the value of the property.

BEFORE READING THE NEXT SECTION, COMPLETE THE SECTION 1 REVIEW EXERCISES AND COMPARE YOUR ANSWERS WITH THE SOLUTIONS AT THE END OF THE CHAPTER.

FIGURE 5.1
Classifying Common Liens

Types of Liens	General	Specific	Voluntary	Involuntary
Real Estate—Ad Valorem		X		X
Real Estate—Special Assessment		X	X	X
Mortgage		X	X	
Deed of Trust		X	X	
Judgment	X			X
Mechanic's		X		X
Debts of a Decedent	X			X
Vendor		X		X
Vendee		X		X
Municipal Utilities		X		X
Bail Bond		X	X	
Income Tax	X			X

Note that special assessments can be either voluntary or involuntary, depending on the circumstances.

SECTION 1

REVIEW EXERCISES

1. List two ways liens can be classified.

   a. _____ or _____

   b. _____ or _____

Are the following statements true (T) or false (F)?

2. ____ The party who holds the lien right is called the lienor.

3. ____ Specific liens can be used to affect all of the property of the debtor.

4. ____ Voluntary liens are created by law (statute).

5. ____ Mechanics' liens take priority over all other liens.

6. List three ways liens can be created.

   a. _____

   b. _____

   c. _____

7. If a property has a mortgage lien, a mechanic's lien and a real estate tax lien attached to it, which lien would be paid first if the property were foreclosed?

   _____

Supply the term that best matches each of following descriptions.

8. _____ A charge against property for a debt or obligation of the property owner

9. _____ A lien that applies to all of a person's property

10. _____ Created by law either by statute or by the courts

11. _____ A lien that applies to a specific property

12. _____ A written agreement between lienholders to change priority of their liens

13. _____ Created without the property owner's consent

SECTION 2

REAL ESTATE TAX LIENS

One of the government powers discussed in Chapter 3 was the power to tax real estate. The physical characteristic of immobility facilitates the assessment and collection of taxes by the government, and their priority over other liens provides assurance that they will be collected. Real estate tax liens are specific, involuntary liens created by statute. There are two types of real estate taxes; *ad valorem* and *special assessments*. This section of the chapter discusses both types.

GENERAL (AD VALOREM) REAL ESTATE TAX

The general or **ad valorem** real estate tax raises money for the operation of various local government agencies. It is called *ad valorem* because the tax is based on the *assessed value* of the property being taxed.

Not all property is subject to real estate taxes. The following types of property are exempt from real estate taxes under most state laws:

- Property owned by local, state and federal governments
- Municipal property such as parks and schools
- Most property owned by religious and charitable organizations
- Hospitals
- Educational institutions

In addition to certain types of properties that are exempt from real estate taxes various programs to reduce real estate taxes are available in many states. These include

- tax reductions to attract businesses to an area;
- reduction in a home's assessed value for homeowners to offset inflation, for making improvements or for senior citizens; and
- tax reductions for agricultural land.

Ad Valorem Property Tax Process

While the specifics for levying and collecting real estate taxes may vary among states, the general process includes three steps:

1. Local governments prepare their budgets to determine how much money they will need.
2. An **assessment** of value is made for all the taxable property in the taxing district.
3. The **tax rate** is determined and used to calculate the tax bill for each property.

Budget and Appropriation. *Budget*—A budget is prepared for the coming *fiscal year.* (Note that a fiscal year may not be the same as the calendar year. A school district's fiscal year may run from July 1 through June 30.) Once the budget is prepared, sources of revenue other than real estate taxes are identified and subtracted from the expenditure total. The amount remaining must be raised from real estate taxes.

Appropriation—Appropriate action is taken to *authorize* the expenditures in the budget. This usually involves adopting an ordinance or passing a law in the taxing district.

Assessment. A value for individual parcels of real estate is calculated (or assessed) by the county or township appraisers (or assessors) where the property is located. *Assessed values* are based on a percentage of the *fair market value,* which is determined by reviewing the sales price of similar homes. In determining the assessed amount the land is usually appraised separately from buildings and other improvements.

EXAMPLE: A property's land is valued at $20,000, the improvements at $100,000, and it is to be assessed at 40 percent. The amount of the assessed value is ($20,000 + $100,000) × .4 = $48,000.

The frequency of the assessment is usually determined by state law. Property owners have the right to challenge (or appeal) the assessed amount if they believe errors were made. The process usually includes filing a protest and appearing before an assessment appeals board. A property owner who still is not satisfied with the board's decision can pursue the case in court.

Some states use an **equalizer** that raises or lowers the assessed value to achieve uniformity and correct inequalities in statewide assessments. The assessed value is multiplied by the equalizer, resulting in an equalized value. The tax rate then is applied to determine the amount of tax.

Hint: The equalizer is actually a percentage that is converted to a decimal. Thus, an equalizer of 1.5 means the property's equalized assessed value is 150 percent of the current assessed value.

A property's assessed value will be raised if the equalizer is more than 100 percent (i.e., 1.0) or lowered if the equalizer is less than 100 percent. The first example shows an assessed value that is raised by the multiplier, while the second example lowers the assessed value.

EXAMPLE: A property is assessed for tax purposes at $80,000, and the equalizer is 1.2. The equalized assessed value of the property would be $96,000 ($80,000 × 1.2).

EXAMPLE: A property is assessed for tax purposes at $80,000, and the equalizer is .8. The equalized assessed value of the property would be $64,000 ($80,000 × .8).

The steps to calculate a tax bill are summarized in Figure 5.2.

The Tax Rate and Tax Bill. The following process for determining the real estate tax rate is performed for *each government entity* entitled to tax real estate.

First, a tax levy is passed by a vote of the taxing district's governing body to impose the tax on property owners. The maximum tax rate that can be levied is often limited by law or local referendum.

The tax rate is then calculated by dividing the total assessed value of all the properties in each taxing district by the total amount of money needed for the budgets.

FIGURE 5.2 *Computing a Real Estate Tax Bill*	Step 1	$	Market value of property
		×	Assessment rate
	Step 2	$	Assessed value
		×	Equalizer (if necessary)
	Step 3	$	Equalized assessed value
		×	Tax rate
		$	Tax bill

EXAMPLE: Budget $ 30,000,000
            Other revenue   – 5,000,000
            Property tax needed $ 25,000,000

            Total assessed value $500,000,000
            Tax rate: $25,000,000 ÷ $500,000,000 = .05

The tax rate can be expressed several ways. Three of the most common methods are listed here. The rate in each method is equal; it is simply expressed differently.

1. As a *percentage* (i.e., 5% or .05)
2. In **mills** (a mill is ¹⁄₁₀₀₀ of a dollar or $.001)
3. In *dollars per hundred* of assessed value

EXAMPLE: The real estate tax on a property with an assessed value of $1,000 would be $50, using all three ways of expressing the tax rate.

1. $50 = $1,000 × .05 (i.e., 5%)
2. $50 = $1,000 × 50 mills (.001 × 50 = .05)
3. $50 = $1,000 ÷ $100 × $5

The steps to calculate a tax rate are summarized in Figure 5.3.

After the assessed value, equalizer and tax rate are calculated on each property, the owner receives the tax bill. Usually the tax for all of the taxing bodies is included in one bill. However, in some areas separate bills are prepared. The schedule for making tax payments is set by local law, and if taxes are not paid by the due date, interest on the amount owed may be added as a penalty. In some jurisdictions if the tax is paid early the property owner receives a discount. When the property is sold, the amount of real estate taxes owed must be computed, requiring an understanding of the local tax rules. Following are some of the ways taxes may be paid:

• The number of installments may be semiannual, quarterly or monthly.
• Taxes may be paid in advance.

EXAMPLE: 1999 taxes are paid at the start of 1999.

• Taxes may be paid through the current year.

EXAMPLE: 1999 taxes are paid throughout 1999.

• Taxes may be paid partially or fully after the current year.

EXAMPLE: Part of 1999 taxes paid in 1999 and the rest in 2000.

               or

1999 taxes are paid in 2000.

Hint: The math review in the Study Tool Kit includes examples of real estate tax calculations.

FIGURE 5.3
Computing a
Real Estate Tax Rate

Step 1	$		Revenue needed
	–		Revenue from other sources
Step 2	$		Revenue from taxes
	÷		Assessed value of properties
		%	Tax rate

ENFORCEMENT OF TAX LIENS

Only *"valid"* real estate taxes may be enforced. To be valid the tax must be

- properly levied;
- for a legal purpose; and
- applied equitably to all properties.

Note: If the tax is paid on the wrong property, it is usually's the owner's responsibility to try to recover the taxes paid. While trying to correct the problem, the owner will probably also have to pay the outstanding tax on the property.

Tax Sale

If the real estate taxes on a property have not been paid for the length of time specified in the law, the government can exercise its lien right and have the property sold at a **tax sale** to satisfy the outstanding taxes plus any interest and penalties. The procedures for tax sales vary among states; however, the general process is basically the same.

1. A court renders a *judgment* and orders the sale of the property.
2. *Notice* of the sale must be published according to rules set in the law.
3. At the tax sale the property is sold to recover the amount of the taxes, interest and penalties owed.
4. The winner at the sale usually receives a *tax certificate* after paying the delinquent tax and may ultimately apply for a *tax deed*.

Note: A mortgage foreclosure does not clear tax liens on the property.

Redemption Rights

The owner of the tax delinquent property is usually given certain rights to redeem the property. Redemption rights vary from state to state but in general can be classified into two types.

1. Equitable right of redemption: **Equitable redemption rights** allow the owner to redeem property any time *before the tax sale* by paying back taxes, penalties and court costs.
2. Statutory right of redemption: **Statutory redemption rights** are created by state laws and can be exercised *after the tax sale*. In most cases the owner may redeem the property if the following expenses are paid: interest to the winner at the tax sale, back taxes and penalties.

SPECIAL ASSESSMENTS

A **special assessment** is a tax levied on specific parcels of real estate to pay for local improvements. The property owners are required to pay for the public improvements because their real estate will benefit. The tax is usually apportioned among the property owners according to the benefit each will receive.

EXAMPLE: Sidewalk improvements, repaving of streets, new curbs, installation of streetlights.

Special assessments are always *specific*, but can be either *voluntary* or *involuntary*. If a government agency initiates the improvements, the lien is involuntary. If the homeowners initiate a request to the government for the improvements, it is voluntary.

Assessment Process

A *proposal for an improvement* can be made by either a group of property owners or the local government. The proposal is taken to the local authority in charge of levying assessments. A public notice is issued and a hearing is held for the proposed improvement.

If the hearings result in a decision to proceed, a local *ordinance is passed*, describing the nature of the improvement.

The *cost of the improvement is allocated over the properties* that will benefit from the improvement. Each parcel of real estate is not necessarily assessed the same amount. Common methods of spreading the cost are on a *fractional* basis or *cost-per-foot* basis.

EXAMPLE: Fractional basis. Ten houses on a block share the cost of a repaved street equally.

EXAMPLE: Cost-per-foot basis. Ten houses on a block are assessed different amounts, depending on the width of each lot.

Petition and approval is also called "confirming the assessment role." The local court either approves or rejects the assessment proposal. If approved, the assessment now becomes a lien on the property.

When the improvement is completed, a *special assessment warrant* is issued. This gives the local collector the right to issue special assessment bills.

Special assessment liens are usually payable in equal installments over five to ten years. Interest may be charged on the tax, and the owner has the right of prepayment to stop the interest from accruing.

BEFORE READING THE NEXT SECTION, COMPLETE THE SECTION 2 REVIEW EXERCISES AND COMPARE YOUR ANSWERS WITH THE SOLUTIONS AT THE END OF THE CHAPTER.

SECTION 2
REVIEW EXERCISES

1. List the two types of real estate tax liens.

   a. _____

   b. _____

2. List three examples of property that probably would be exempt from real estate tax liens.

a. _____

b. _____

c. _____

Are the following statements true (T) or false (F)?

3. ____ In most states the winner at a tax sale receives a tax deed to the property.

4. ____ Property owners can redeem their property after the tax sale by exercising their statutory redemption rights.

5. ____ A mill is equal to $.01.

6. List three ways the real estate tax rate can be expressed.

a. _____

b. _____

c. _____

7. A property's market value is $200,000, it is assessed for tax purposes at 25 percent of market value, there is an equalizer of 1.5 and the tax rate is $5 per hundred. Using this information, compute the following:

a. _____ Assessed value

b. _____ Equalized assessed value

c. _____ Tax bill

8. Name the step that corresponds to each of the following procedures in the special assessment process.

a. _____ Allocating the cost over the properties to be improved

b. _____ Proposing the improvement

c. _____ Enforcing collection of the tax

d. _____ Confirming the assessment role

e. _____ Passed after the hearing

f. _____ The right to issue special assessment bills

Supply the term that best matches each of the following descriptions.

9. _____ Special real estate tax for improvements that benefit the property

10. _____ The borrower's right to redeem the property after the foreclosure sale

11. _____ A real estate tax based on the value of the property

12. _____ A value put on real estate as a basis to calculate the amount of tax

13. _____ The borrower's right to redeem the property prior to a foreclosure sale

14. _____ Used to adjust property assessments so that they are equitable throughout a state

15. _____ An amount equal to one tenth of a cent

SECTION 3

LIENS OTHER THAN REAL ESTATE TAXES

MORTGAGE LIEN

When a lender makes a loan using real estate as security, the property owner signs a mortgage document that creates a lien against the property. When the loan is repaid, the lien ends. If the loan is not paid, the lender may foreclose and sell the property. A **mortgage lien** is a *specific, voluntary* lien. Mortgages are discussed in Chapter 20, Loan Instruments.

 Note: Lenders will usually insist on a first lien, meaning their liens have priority over any other liens against the property (except real estate tax liens).

MECHANICS' LIENS

A *mechanic,* in real estate terminology, is someone who provides *materials* (lumber companies, building materials suppliers) or *services* (carpenters, plumbers, etc.) for the real estate. The law protects them through a **mechanic's lien,** which is used if the property owner does not pay for the work or materials provided. A mechanic's lien is granted by statute and is a *specific and involuntary* lien. The rules for mechanics' liens vary by state. General characteristics of mechanics' liens are listed below.

- Both general contractors and subcontractors are entitled to mechanics' liens, and payment to the *general* contractor may *not* relieve the owner from the *subcontractor* claims.
- The priority of the lien is dependent on when the lien "attaches" to the real estate. This varies by state. It could be the date the contract was signed, the work was started, the work was completed, the notice of the lien was filed or some other date.
- Mechanics'-lien holders must enforce their liens within a time period set by state law, otherwise their lien rights will expire.
- A person claiming a mechanic's lien must file a notice in the public records within the time period set by state law. However, a purchaser of property must be cautious because mechanics' liens may be *unrecorded* but still enforceable.
- To protect title to their property, owners may obtain waivers of mechanics' liens from both the general and subcontractor, as well as suppliers of materials.

EXAMPLE: A state requires the lien notice to be recorded within three months after the work is completed but attaches (is effective) *as of the date the work was started.* A purchaser might not find the notice in the public records between the time the work was ordered and completed.

JUDGMENT LIEN

A **judgment** is a decree issued by the court at the conclusion of a lawsuit. When a judgment is recorded, it creates a lien on both the real and personal property of the defendant in the same state. Judgments that involve a definite sum of money are called *money judgments.* Judgments are *general, involuntary* liens.

After a judgment has been issued, the court will, if requested, issue a *writ of execution* instructing the sheriff to seize and sell the debtor's property. When the property is sold to satisfy the debt, the debtor should get a *satisfaction of judgment,* which should be recorded to clear the judgment lien. The judgment lien's priority is set by state law and may be based on the date when the judgment was passed by the court, the judgment was filed or the writ of execution was written. Statutory limitations set the time period judgments are effective. This is generally seven to ten years unless renewed.

To prevent an owner from transferring title to real estate while a court suit is being decided, a plaintiff may obtain a **writ of attachment** from the court. The court then will retain custody of the property until the suit is over. This assures the plaintiff that there will be property to place the judgment against.

LIENS AGAINST A DECEASED PERSON'S ESTATE

Liens may be placed against a deceased person's estate by creditors and by the state and the federal governments for estate and inheritance taxes. These liens are cleared in probate proceedings and are superior to any rights of the estate's heirs. Liens against the estate are classified as *general, involuntary* liens.

VENDOR'S AND VENDEE'S LIENS

A *vendor* is a seller. This lien represents the seller's (vendor's) claim if the full purchase price is not received. A **vendor's lien** is classified as a *specific, involuntary* lien.

EXAMPLE: The seller of the property provides a loan to the buyer as part of the purchase. The seller obtains a lien on the property for the loan. The lien can be enforced by selling the property and paying the seller if the buyer does not pay the loan as agreed.

A *vendee* is a buyer. This lien is the buyer's (vendee's) claim if the seller (vendor) fails to deliver title to property that is purchased. A **vendee's lien** is classified as a *specific, involuntary* lien.

EXAMPLE: The buyer of a property gives the seller a deposit. The seller then defaults and refuses to go through with the transaction. The buyer has a lien against the property for the amount of the deposit.

INCOME TAX LIEN

The Internal Revenue Service and state revenue departments may place liens on property for taxes owed by a taxpayer. A federal tax lien is effective for ten years, whereas the time period for other tax liens varies based on the type of tax. The priority of federal and state income tax liens is based on the date of recording. Income tax liens are classified as *general, involuntary* liens.

MUNICIPAL UTILITIES LIEN

A local municipality may place a lien on property to satisfy unpaid utility bills. A municipal utility lien is classified as a *specific, involuntary* lien.

EXAMPLE: A lien may be placed on a residence for unpaid water bills.

LIS PENDENS (PENDING LITIGATION)

A **lis pendens** is a notice in the public records of a pending lawsuit involving the real estate. This acts as a public warning to anyone interested in the property. A purchaser acquiring land under lis pendens takes it subject to the possible future judgment against the property.

COMPLETE THE SECTION 3 REVIEW EXERCISES AND COMPARE YOUR ANSWERS WITH THE SOLUTIONS AT THE END OF THE CHAPTER.

SECTION 3
REVIEW EXERCISES

1. Classify the following liens as either voluntary or involuntary.
   a. Mortgage _____
   b. Judgment _____
   c. Real estate tax _____
   d. Mechanic's lien _____
   e. Vendor's lien _____

2. Classify the following liens as either specific or general.
   a. Mortgage _____
   b. Judgment _____
   c. Real estate tax _____
   d. Mechanic's lien _____
   e. Vendor's lien _____

Are the following statements true (T) or false (F)?

3. ____ A mechanic's lien does not apply in a situation where the owner has paid the general contractor for the work but the general contractor has not paid the subcontractors and suppliers.

4. ____ To clear a judgment lien, the debtor should obtain a satisfaction of judgment.

5. ____ Liens against a deceased person's estate are superior to the rights of the estate's heirs.

6. What type of lien would be filed against the real estate in each of the following situations?
   a. _____ The seller fails to deliver title to the buyer as promised.
   b. _____ The owner does not pay for services and materials used to replace the roof.
   c. _____ A plaintiff wins a $100,000 lawsuit against the property owner.

d. _____ The owner obtains a loan using the real estate as security.

e. _____ The owner decides not to pay taxes on income from the property.

Supply the term that best matches each of the following descriptions.

7. _____ Decree issued by the court at the conclusion of a lawsuit

8. _____ Notice in the public records of a pending lawsuit

9. _____ A lien that protects the suppliers of goods and services to the real estate

10. _____ A lien that protects the seller

11. _____ A lien that protects the buyer

SOLUTIONS
FOR SECTION REVIEW EXERCISES

SECTION 1

1. a. general or specific   b. voluntary or involuntary
2. TRUE
3. FALSE Specific liens attach only to a single property, whereas general liens affect all of the property of the debtor.
4. FALSE Involuntary liens are created by law (statute).
5. FALSE Real estate tax liens take priority over all other liens.
6. a. By agreement of the parties (contractual)   b. By law
   c. By the court (equitable)
7. Real estate tax liens take priority over the other liens.
8. Lien
9. General lien
10. Involuntary lien
11. Specific lien
12. Subordination agreement
13. Involuntary lien

SECTION 2

1. a. Ad valorem   b. Special assessment
2. Examples of property that would probably be exempt from real estate tax liens include property owned by the government, parks, schools, religious and charitable organizations, hospitals.
3. FALSE In most states the winner at a tax sale receives a certificate. Winners may ultimately obtain a tax deed to the property after the redemption period.
4. TRUE
5. FALSE A mill is equal to $.001.
6. a. As a percentage   b. In mills   c. In dollars per hundred of assessed value
7. a. $50,000 = $200,000 \times .25$ b. $75,000 = $50,000 \times 1.5$
   c. $3,750 = $75,000 \div $100 \times 5
8. a. Assessment role spread   b. Improvement recommended   c. Tax lien
   d. Petition and approval   e. Ordinance is passed   f. Special assessment warrant
9. Special assessment
10. Statutory redemption rights
11. Ad valorem tax
12. Assessment
13. Equitable redemption rights
14. Equalizer
15. Mill

SECTION 3

1. a. Voluntary   b. Involuntary   c. Involuntary   d. Involuntary
   e. Involuntary
2. a. Specific   b. General   c. Specific   d. Specific   e. Specific

3. FALSE Subcontractors and suppliers of material have mechanics' liens even though the general contractor has been paid.

4. TRUE

5. TRUE

6. a. Vendee's lien   b. Mechanic's lien   c. Judgment lien
   d. Mortgage lien   e. IRS tax lien

7. Judgment

8. Lis pendens

9. Mechanic's lien

10. Vendor lien

11. Vendee lien

CHAPTER 6

LEGAL DESCRIPTIONS

In this chapter you will learn what legal descriptions are and how they are used in the real estate industry. The chapter explains three methods for legally describing real estate. Section 1 covers the metes-and-bounds method. Section 2 covers the rectangular survey system. Section 3 covers the plat of survey method and datum, which is used for measuring elevations. Remember to use the Study Tool Kit to reference key information and to update your progress checklist.

Learning Objectives

Track your progress as you work through the chapter by checking each learning objective when you complete it.

____ Explain the process of creating a legal description using the metes-and-bounds method.

____ Explain the role of the POB, monuments and directions in metes-and-bounds descriptions.

____ Explain the process of creating a legal description using the rectangular survey method.

____ Describe the various lines that are used in the rectangular survey method.

____ Divide sections and determine the number of acres.

____ Explain the process of creating a legal description using the plat of survey method.

____ Describe how benchmarks and datum are used in measuring elevations.

____ Describe various units of measurement.

Key Terms and Phrases

Track your progress as you work through the chapter by checking each term when you understand its meaning.

____ Air lots	____ Monuments
____ Base lines	____ Plat of survey method
____ Benchmark	____ Point of beginning (POB)
____ Boundary lines	____ Principal meridians
____ Correction line	____ Range lines
____ Datum	____ Ranges
____ Fractional sections	____ Rectangular survey system
____ Government lots	____ Sections
____ Guide meridian	____ Spot survey
____ Legal description	____ Township lines
____ Metes and bounds	____ Townships

METES-AND-BOUNDS METHOD

PURPOSE OF LEGAL DESCRIPTIONS

If someone asked you to identify a parcel of real estate, you might use its street address, "123 Easy Street"; describe it as, for example, "the second house from the corner of Easy and Main Street"; or use a common name, for example, "the Double D Ranch" or "The White House." While we use these *informal* methods to describe real estate in everyday life, they are not precise or accurate enough for legal purposes. A property's boundaries cannot be determined by these methods, and the property address or name may change over the years, adding more uncertainty.

A **legal description** is an exact way of describing the location of real estate that will be accepted by a court. Courts will not accept a street address as a legal description because it is not specific enough to describe the property. The legal description of a property is used in many documents including deeds, mortgages, liens, trust deeds and sales contracts.

Note: The informal method may be used for situations where the exact description of the property is not necessary. A street address is sufficient in an apartment lease. However, if the apartment building were being purchased, a legal description would be needed.

Common methods used to describe real estate are *metes and bounds, rectangular survey system* and *plat of survey method* (also called *lot and block* or *recorded plat method*). These methods can be used independently or can be combined in describing a property.

METES-AND-BOUNDS DESCRIPTION

Metes and bounds is the oldest method of developing legal descriptions and is used in approximately 20 states. Metes refers to *distance* (measured in feet) and bounds refers to *direction*.

A metes-and-bounds description starts at a definite point called the **point of beginning (POB)**. From the POB the circumference of the property is described until the description ends back at the POB. A metes-and-bounds description includes (1) a POB, (2) distances and (3) directions.

Monuments

Monuments are fixed objects used in the metes-and-bounds description to establish boundaries. They may be either natural (e.g., an oak tree or large boulder) or artificial- (e.g., made of stone or concrete, or a steel rod or stake driven into the ground). The POB in the metes-and-bounds description is usually a monument. Monuments are placed at the end of measurements such as at the corners of the property. Figure 6.1 contains a metes-and-bounds description and illustrates the parcel of land it describes.

FIGURE 6.1
A Metes-and-Bounds Description

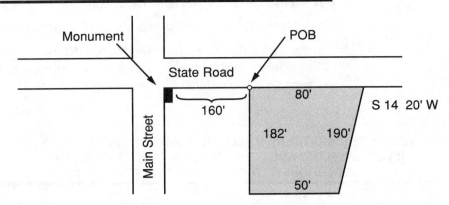

Starting at a monument located at the SE point of the intersection of State Road and Main Street, proceed 160 feet directly East along State Road to the Point of Beginning (POB); then 80 ft. farther directly East along State Road; then S 14° 20′ W for 190 ft.; then West 50 ft.; then 182 ft. directly North to the POB.

Boundary Lines

Boundary lines define the boundaries of the property and are drawn from monuments. Boundary lines are referenced by distance and direction from the monuments, and at each corner of the property the boundary lines are marked with a monument.

Directions

Compass bearings (adjusted to true north rather than magnetic north) are used to describe the *direction* of the property's boundary lines and include degrees (°), minutes (′) and seconds (″). Figure 6.2 illustrates the use of compass bearings for directions. The following measurements are used as part of the description.

Circle	=	360° (degrees)
Each degree	=	60′ (minutes)
Each minute	=	60″ (seconds)

EXAMPLE: N 44° 31′ 56″ E = North 44 degrees, 31 minutes, 56 seconds East.

FIGURE 6.2
Directions Used in a Metes-and-Bounds Description

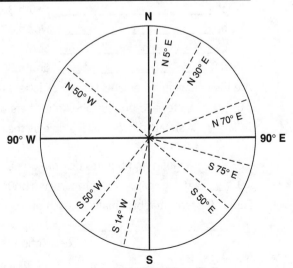

Compass directions such as those above are used to determine the direction between corners of the property. Directions are read clockwise.

Problems with Metes and Bounds

There are two major problems with descriptions using the metes-and-bounds method.

1. They are usually very long, complicated and difficult to understand.
2. Monuments used in the description can be destroyed or deteriorate over time, making them difficult to identify.

BEFORE READING THE NEXT SECTION, COMPLETE THE SECTION 1 REVIEW EXERCISES AND COMPARE YOUR ANSWERS WITH THE SOLUTIONS AT THE END OF THE CHAPTER.

SECTION 1
REVIEW EXERCISES

1. List the three common methods of describing real estate.

   a. _____

   b. _____

   c. _____

2. Compass bearings used to describe the boundary lines include

   a. _____

   b. _____

   c. _____

3. List the components of a metes-and-bounds description.

   a. _____

   b. _____

   c. _____

4. List the problems with using monuments in legal descriptions.

   a. _____

   b. _____

5. Write the compass bearings for the following descriptions.

   a. _____ South 36°, 28 minutes, 36 seconds East

   b. _____ North 4°, 11 minutes, 18 seconds East

   c. _____ South 15°, 0 minutes, 0 seconds West

   d. _____ South 80°, 0 minutes, 0 seconds East

Are the following statements true (T) or false (F)?

6. ____ Metes-and-bounds descriptions are usually brief and easy to understand.

7. ____ A street address is acceptable by the courts as a legal description for the sale of real estate.

8. ____ A metes-and-bounds description begins and ends at a point of beginning.

9. ____ At each corner of a property the boundary lines are often marked with a monument.

Supply the term that best matches each of the following descriptions.

10. _____ Fixed objects used to establish boundaries in a legal description

11. _____ The starting and ending point in a legal description

12. _____ An exact way of describing the location of real estate

13. _____ A method of describing real estate that uses distance and direction

14. _____ Lines referenced from monuments

SECTION 2

RECTANGULAR SURVEY SYSTEM

The **rectangular survey system**, also called the *government survey system* and *geodetic survey system*, was established by Congress in 1785 to create a faster, simpler and more accurate method of identifying land. This system describes the location of property by using two sets of intersecting lines, which form a grid. Four types of lines are used: (1) principal meridians, (2) base lines, (3) range lines and (4) township lines. This system is used in 30 states.

Hint: To better understand the concept of using the rectangular survey, think of a checkerboard. It has intersecting lines that form a grid of squares.

PRINCIPAL MERIDIANS AND BASE LINES

The first set of intersecting lines are called **principal meridians** (PMs), which run north and south, and **base lines,** which run east and west.

There are 36 principal meridians. Each is named or numbered and has an intersecting base line. The meridian used to describe a parcel of land may *not* be the *nearest one* because the meridians are not located at equal distances from each other. Each parcel of land is measured from only *one of the meridians.* Figure 6.3 shows the location of principal meridians and base lines in the United States.

RANGE LINES

Range lines run north and south and are *parallel* to the PMs. The range lines are six miles apart.

The columns of land formed by these range lines are called **ranges.** In writing a legal description ranges are numbered east or west of the PM.

EXAMPLE: Range 3 East of the 3rd PM or Range 4 West of the 3rd PM.

TOWNSHIP LINES

Township lines run east and west and are parallel to the base lines. The range lines are *six miles apart.*

FIGURE 6.3
Public Land Survey Systems of the United States

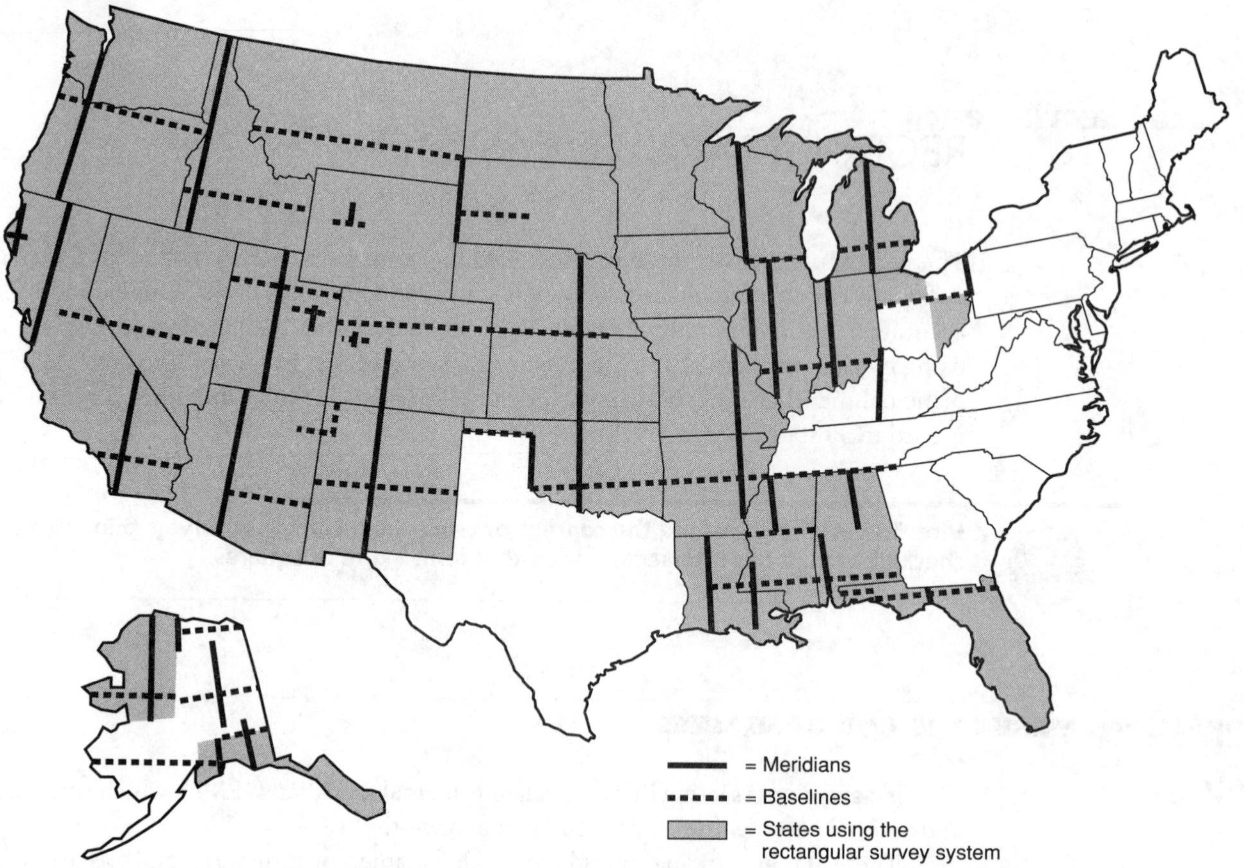

--- = Meridians

••••• = Baselines

■ = States using the rectangular survey system

The square strips of land formed by the township and range lines are called townships or tiers. In writing a legal description townships are numbered north and south of the base line.

EXAMPLE: Township 2 North (T2N) or Township 3 South (T3S).

Because the lines that make up a township (range and township lines) are all six miles apart, townships are 6 miles square and have an area of 36 square miles, or 23,040 acres. Figure 6.4 illustrates ranges and townships and how they are incorporated into a legal description.

SECTIONS

Each township can be further divided into **sections**.

- There are 36 sections in a township.
- Each section contains 1 square mile or 640 acres.
- Sections are numbered 1 through 36, starting with 1 in the northeast (top right hand) corner and continuing west (left) along the top row to the northwest (left) corner; the second row is numbered west (left) to east (right); and the remaining four rows continue the pattern. See Figure 6.5 for an example of the numbering.

FIGURE 6.4
*Townships in
the Rectangular
Survey System*

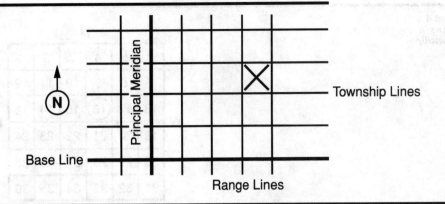

- Section 16 is set aside for school use. This section was chosen for schools because of its central location in the township. The sale or rental proceeds from this land were available for school use.

Sections can be further divided into *halves* and *quarters,* referred to as *aliquot parts.* To calculate the size of a tract of land from the legal description, start with the fact that each section has 640 acres and divide by the denominator in the description.

EXAMPLE: To calculate the number of acres in the following description: the W½, NE¼, SE¼. Divide 640 ÷ 2 = 320 ÷ 4 = 80 ÷ 4 = 20 acres.

Portions of a section can be combined in a description, or a parcel of land may overlap two sections. To calculate the area of tract of land, both portions are calculated and added together.

EXAMPLE: To calculate the number of acres in the following description: W½, NW¼; E½, NW¼.

Step 1: Divide 640 ÷ 2 = 320 ÷ 4 = 80 acres.
Step 2: Divide 640 ÷ 2 = 320 ÷ 4 = 80 acres.
Step 3: Add 80 + 80 = 160 acres.

Tip: Notice that the semicolon in the description means "and"; therefore, two parts must be calculated.

Figure 6.6 illustrates how a section can be divided and the areas calculated.

LEGAL DESCRIPTION

A legal description using the rectangular survey system is written using the following format:

1. The part (or parts) of the section
2. The section number
3. The township row
4. The range column
5. The name or number of the principal meridian

EXAMPLE: The NW¼ of the S½ of Section 2, Township 3 North, Range 4 East, of the 3rd Principal Meridian.

FIGURE 6.5
Sections in a Township

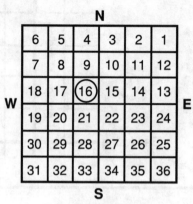

16 = School Section

This can be also written as NW¼, S½, Section 2, T3N, R4E, 3rd PM.

CORRECTION LINES

Correction lines and guide meridians are used to compensate for the curvature of the earth. Because the world is round, the range lines (which run north and south) converge and would eventually meet at the North Pole.

Every fourth township line is called a **correction line** (sometimes called a *standard parallel line*), and every fourth range line is called a **guide meridian**. Guide meridians run *true north* and the intersecting correction line is *shorter* than a township line.

FRACTIONAL SECTIONS AND GOVERNMENT LOTS

Because of the crude instruments used to survey in the past and errors in earlier work by surveyors, few townships are actually 36 miles square. Established rules provide for adjustments to be made in the north and west boundaries of a township in sections 1–7, 18, 19, 30 and 31. Sections that are either under- or oversized are called **fractional sections**.

Areas smaller than full quarter sections are designated as **government lots** and are numbered and placed in the fractional sections.

TIP: The term government lots does not mean the property is owned by the government.

FIGURE 6.6
Section

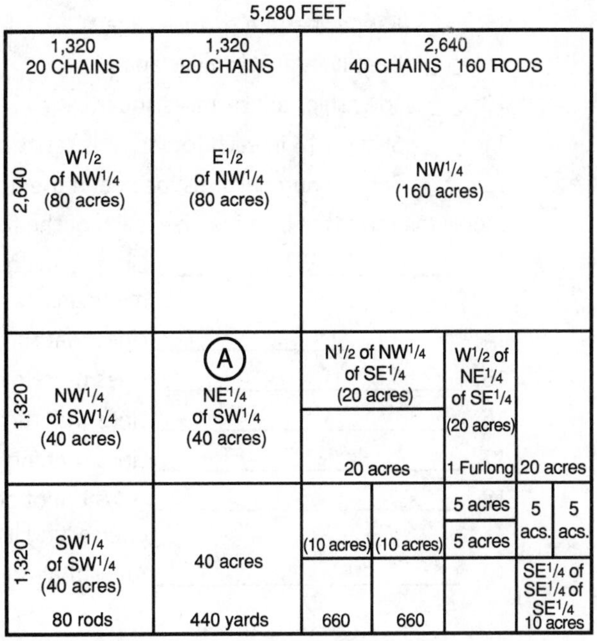

		5,280 FEET		
1,320 20 CHAINS	1,320 20 CHAINS	2,640 40 CHAINS 160 RODS		

BEFORE READING THE NEXT SECTION, COMPLETE THE SECTION 2
REVIEW EXERCISES AND COMPARE YOUR ANSWERS WITH THE
SOLUTIONS AT THE END OF THE CHAPTER.

SECTION 2
REVIEW EXERCISES

1. List types of lines used in the rectangular survey system.

   a. _____

   b. _____

   c. _____

   d. _____

2. Enter the value for each of the following measures.

   a. _____ Number of square miles in a township

   b. _____ Number of sections in a township

   c. _____ Number of acres in a township

   d. _____ Distance between township lines

   e. _____ Distance between range lines

3. Calculate the number of acres for the following descriptions.

   a. _____ S½, NW¼, SE¼

   b. _____ NW¼, S½

   c. _____ N½, SE¼ and the S½, NW¼

   d. _____ NW¼, S½ and the N½, SE¼

Are the following statements true (T) or false (F)?

4. ____ Principal meridians run east and west.

5. ____ Base lines run north and south.

6. ____ The principal meridian nearest to a parcel of land is always used in its description.

7. ____ Ranges are numbered north and south of the base line.

8. ____ Range lines are six miles apart.

9. ____ Base lines are six miles apart.

10. ____ Townships are six miles square.

11. ____ Section 14 in each township is set aside for school purposes.

12. ____ Section number six is located in the northwest corner of a township.

Supply the term that best matches each of the following descriptions.

13. _____ Lines running east and west that intersect principal meridians

14. _____ Lines that run parallel to base lines

15. _____ Lines used to compensate for the curvature of the earth

16. _____ Lines that run parallel to principal meridians.

17. _____ Lines running north and south that intersect base lines

18. _____ A system of describing real estate by using sets of intersecting lines

19. _____ Areas that are not full quarter sections

SECTION 3
PLAT OF SURVEY METHOD AND MEASURING ELEVATIONS

PLAT OF SURVEY METHOD

The third method of describing real estate is the **plat of survey method,** also called the *recorded plat method* and *lot-block-tract method.* The system is used in urban areas when land is subdivided into numbered lots, blocks and tracts, and a recorded survey called a *plat map* is referenced.

This method is used to some degree in all states and is always used in conjunction with a metes-and-bounds or rectangular survey description.

A surveyor's plat map is recorded with the county and placed in a *plat book* or *map book.* The survey plat divides the land into lots, blocks and tracts. The survey plat also shows public streets, the lot sizes and utility easements. Once properly recorded, the plat becomes part of the legal description.

EXAMPLE: Lot 12, Hill Valley Estates 3, located in the northwest quarter of Section 6, Township 4 North, Range 3 East of the 3rd Principal Meridian in Baker County, Illinois.

Figure 6.7 illustrates a subdivision plat map.

Preparation of a survey is required for most real estate transactions. A *survey sketch* is used to determine the location and dimensions of a parcel of land. When a survey shows the location and size of buildings on the property, it is called a **spot survey.**

Some states have *plat acts.* These laws specify the smallest parcel of land that can be subdivided and sold.

FIGURE 6.7
Subdivision Plat Map

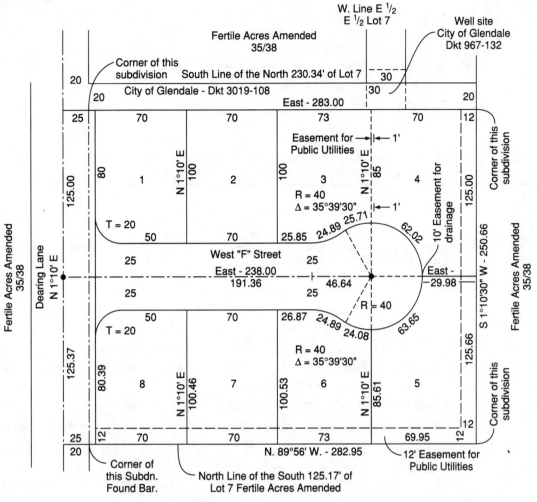

MEASURING ELEVATIONS

A **datum** is a level surface from which elevations are measured. Every large city has a datum, but surveyors use the United States Coast and Geodetic Survey (USGS) datum, which is the mean sea level in New York harbor.

Benchmarks are usually bronze markers, placed by the United States Coast & Geodetic Survey, that indicate the elevation above sea level. Benchmarks are used as reference points by surveyors to locate a parcel of land and to measure elevations. Multistory condominiums use elevations in their descriptions.

AIR LOTS

A property owner may divide the space above the property's surface into **air lots.** The descriptions of condominiums located in multistoried buildings are usually described using air lots.

KEY MEASUREMENTS TO REMEMBER

- Township = 6 miles square or 36 square miles
- Section = 1 square mile or 640 acres
- Mile = 5,280 feet or 1,760 yards or 320 rods
- Acre = 43,560 square feet or 160 square rods
- Rod = 16½ feet or 5½ yards
- Chain = 66 feet or 4 rods

COMPLETE THE SECTION 3 REVIEW EXERCISES AND COMPARE YOUR ANSWERS WITH THE SOLUTIONS AT THE END OF THE CHAPTER.

SECTION 3
REVIEW EXERCISES

Are the following statements true (T) or false (F)?

1. ____ A property owner may divide the space above the property into sections called datums.

2. ____ Survey plats include public streets, lot sizes and easements.

3. ____ The plat of survey method is used in conjunction with metes-and-bounds and rectangular survey descriptions.

Supply the term that best matches each of the following descriptions.

4. _____ A survey that shows the location of buildings on the property

5. _____ Markers placed to indicate the elevation above sea level

6. _____ A system that uses a recorded survey to show land divided into lots and blocks

7. _____ A level surface from which elevations are measured

THIS IS THE LAST CHAPTER IN THE UNIT. TAKE THE UNIT II DIAGNOSTIC TEST.

SOLUTIONS

FOR SECTION REVIEW EXERCISES

SECTION 1

1. a. Metes and bounds   b. Rectangular survey   c. Plat of survey
2. a. degrees   b. minutes   c. seconds
3. a. Point of beginning   b. Distance   c. Direction
4. a. Can be destroyed or deteriorate   b. Difficult to locate
5. a. S 36° 28′ 36″ E   b. N 4° 11′ 18″ E   c. S 15° 0′ 0″ W   d. S 80° 0′ 0″ E
6. FALSE Metes-and-bounds descriptions are very long and difficult to understand.
7. FALSE A street address is not precise enough and therefore is not acceptable by the courts.
8. TRUE
9. TRUE
10. Monuments
11. Point of beginning
12. Legal description
13. Metes and bounds
14. Boundary lines

SECTION 2

1. a. Principal meridians   b. Base lines   c. Range lines   d. Township lines
2. a. 36 square miles   b. 36 sections   c. 23,040 acres   d. 6 miles   e. 6 miles
3. a. 20 acres   b. 80 acres   c. 160 acres   d. 160 acres
4. FALSE Principal meridians run north and south.
5. FALSE Base lines run east and west.
6. FALSE Land is not always measured from the nearest principal meridian.
7. FALSE Ranges are numbered east and west of base lines.
8. TRUE
9. FALSE While range and township lines are six miles apart, base lines are fewer and more widely distributed.
10. TRUE
11. FALSE Section 16 in each township was set aside for school purposes.
12. TRUE
13. Base lines
14. Township lines
15. Correction lines
16. Range lines
17. Principal meridians
18. Rectangular Survey System
19. Government lots

SECTION 3

1. FALSE A property owner may divide the space above the property into air lots.
2. TRUE
3. TRUE

4. Spot survey
5. Benchmarks
6. Plat of survey method
7. Datum

UNIT II
DIAGNOSTIC TEST

1. 1. Which of the following most likely would be controlled through buiilding codes?

   a. Size of a building
   b. Height of a building
   c. Type of materials to be used in the building
   d. Number of buildings in a given area

2. Sarah and Andrew own adjacent lots. Sarah's lot has an appurtenant easement that allows her to run a sewer line across Andrew's property. If Sarah sells the lot to someone else, the easement

   a. reverts to Andrew.
   b. remains with Sarah.
   c. transfers to the new owner.
   d. is abandoned.

3. The market value for a house is $90,000 and the assessment ratio is 20 percent. What is the amount of the real estate tax if the tax rate is $5 per $100 of assessed value?

   a. $75
   b. $ 900
   c. $1,800
   d. $9,000

4. What type of legal description is being used if it reads, "A tract of land beginning at the corner of State and Main St. and proceeding south 36 degrees 30 minutes for 200 feet, then due east 100 feet, then due south 100 feet to the big oak tree, then due west for 100 feet to the place of beginning" ?

   a. Metes and bounds
   b. Rectangular survey
   c. Government survey
   d. Subdivision plat

5. A town enacts a new zoning code. Under the new code, commercial buildings are not permitted within 1,000 feet of the town park. A commercial building is permitted to continue its former use, even though it is built next to the park. This building is an example of a(n)

   a. nonconforming use.
   b. special use.
   c. zoning variance.
   d. entitlement.

6. The type of easement that results from a landowner's rights of ingress and egress to and from his or her land is an

   a. easement by prescription.
   b. easement by necessity.
   c. easement in gross.
   d. adverse easement.

7. How many square miles are contained in a township?

   a. 6 square miles
   b. 24 square miles
   c. 36 square miles
   d. 64 square miles

8. What type of liens are real estate ad valorem and special assessments taxes?

   a. Specific and involuntary
   b. General and voluntary
   c. Specific and voluntary
   d. General and involuntary

9. A right created by law that provides security to anyone who performs labor or furnishes materials for the improvement of real estate is a(n)

   a. judgment.
   b. easement.
   c. mechanic's lien.
   d. general lien.

10. The property of a person who dies without a will and without heirs may be taken by the government through its powers of

    a. descent.
    b. eminent domain.
    c. zoning.
    d. escheat.

11. In the rectangular survey method the line running east and west that is used to describe land as north or south of it is called a

    a. base line.
    b. range line.
    c. boundary line.
    d. principal meridian.

12. If a driveway extends over a property line by one foot, it is called a(n)

    a. encroachment.
    b. easement by necessity.
    c. easement in gross.
    d. license.

13. The real estate tax rate for a property with a tax assessment of $22,000 and an annual tax of $800 is

    a. 2.6 percent.
    b. 3.6 percent.
    c. 3.75 percent.
    d. 4.25 percent.

14. Land in the northwest corner of a township is located in section number

    a. 1.
    b. 6.
    c. 30.
    d. 36.

15. Mary is losing title to her real estate through condemnation. Mary's real estate is involved in the process

    a. through adverse possession.
    b. by mortgage default.
    c. by eminent domain.
    d. by enforcement of a mechanic's lien.

16. The type of easement created by continuous use of real property for a period of years without the consent of the property owner is called

    a. necessity.
    b. prescription.
    c. eminent domain.
    d. reservation.

17. Real estate taxes are considered ad valorem because they

    a. are based on the zoning of the property.
    b. are based on income produced by the property.
    c. affect each property equally.
    d. are based on the property's value.

18. Which section in each township is designated for school purposes?

    a. Section 1
    b. Section 16
    c. Section 25
    d. Section 36

19. Zoning powers are conferred on municipal governments in which of the following ways?

    a. By eminent domain
    b. Through planned unit developments
    c. By state enabling acts
    d. Through escheat

20. The type of easement usually given to a utility company so it can service equipment is an

    a. easement by prescription.
    b. easement by necessity.
    c. easement in gross.
    d. adverse easement.

21. What is the annual real estate tax bill if the assessed value of a property is $20,000, the tax rate is $5.25 per $100 of assessed value, and the equalization factor is 1.45?

    a. $290
    b. $1,050
    c. $1,523
    d. $10,050

22. A governmental body has the right to take the land of an individual for the public good through

    a. eminent domain.
    b. adverse possession.
    c. descent.
    d. escheat.

23. The concept of "tacking on" is used with an easement

    a. appurtenant.
    b. in gross.
    c. by necessity.
    d. by prescription.

24. Tom has the legal right to pass over the land owned by his neighbor. Tom has a(n)

    a. estate in land.
    b. police power.
    c. easement.
    d. encroachment.

25. A government body has the right to regulate real estate for the protection of the public through

    a. eminent domain.
    b. police power.
    c. descent.
    d. escheat.

26. What is the amount of real estate taxes on a property worth $150,000 if the assessment ratio is 20 percent and the tax rate is $5 per $100 of assessed value?

    a. $1,500
    b. $2,500
    c. $3,000
    d. $30,000

27. How many acres are contained in the N½ of the SE¼ of the SW¼ of a section?

    a. 20
    b. 40
    c. 160
    d. 640

28. Kate has recently installed a fence on her property. The fence extends one foot onto the property of a neighbor. Kate's fence is a(n)

    a. easement by prescription.
    b. easement by necessity.
    c. encroachment.
    d. lien.

29. All of the following regarding a property with a preexisting nonconforming use are true *except* that

    a. it may end when the property is sold.
    b. if abandoned the property's future use must conform.
    c. it may not be expanded.
    d. it was created by a zoning variance.

30. The courts may grant a landowner who is landlocked an easement:

    a. by prescription.
    b. by necessity.
    c. in gross.
    d. by variance.

31. In the legal description, "the northwest ¼ of the southwest ¼ of Section 6, Township 4 North, Range 3 East" is defective because there is no reference to

    a. a principal meridian.
    b. boundary lines.
    c. lot numbers.
    d. a record of survey.

32. A property has several liens and is being sold to satisfy the lien holders. Which of the following liens on the property has the highest priority?

    a. A mechanic's lien
    b. A real estate tax lien
    c. The first lien recorded
    d. The first lien agreed to by the property owner

33. If suffering a severe hardship through compliance with a zoning ordinance, a property owner should apply for a(n)

    a. nonconforming use.
    b. variance.
    c. exemption.
    d. There is no recourse.

34. A lien for a mortgage is what type of lien?

    a. Specific and involuntary
    b. General and voluntary
    c. Specific and voluntary
    d. General and involuntary

35. A section contains

    a. 36 acres.
    b. 6 square miles.
    c. 36 square miles.
    d. 640 acres.

36. An example of mixed use zoning is a(n)

    a. condominiums.
    b. planned unit developments.
    c. shopping malls.
    d. apartment buildings.

37. Bob and Sam own adjacent lots. Sam grants Bob an appurtenant easement to cross Sam's property to reach the lake. In this situation Sam

    a. has an easement right.
    b. may rescind Bob's easement at any time.
    c. owns the dominant tenement.
    d. owns the servient tenement.

38. Anne is considering the purchase of an empty lot on which she intends to build a store. To determine whether she can put the property to this type of use, she should examine the

    a. building code.
    b. list of permitted nonconforming uses.
    c. housing code.
    d. zoning ordinance.

39. In the rectangular survey method the horizontal rows measured every six miles from base lines are called

    a. townships.
    b. ranges.
    c. sections.
    d. principal meridians.

40. A mechanic's lien is what type of lien?

    a. Specific and involuntary
    b. General and voluntary
    c. Specific and voluntary
    d. General and involuntary

41. The right of a defaulted taxpayer to recover his or her property before the sale for unpaid real estate taxes is the

    a. equitable right of redemption.
    b. equitable right of appeal.
    c. statutory right of assessment.
    d. right of escheat.

42. In the rectangular survey method the vertical rows measured from principal meridians are called

    a. townships.
    b. ranges.
    c. sections.
    d. base lines.

43. Which of the following would be classified as a general lien?

    a. Mechanic's lien
    b. Bail bond lien
    c. Real estate tax lien
    d. Judgment lien

44. A young couple are having a new house built. Before they can move into their newly built home

    a. the lender must approve the house.
    b. the local government must issue an occupancy permit.
    c. mechanics liens must be waived.
    d. an appraisal must be made.

45. Which of the following liens usually is given the highest priority?

    a. Mortgage dated last year
    b. Mechanic's lien for work started before the mortgage was made
    c. Real estate taxes due
    d. Judgment entered after the mortgage lien was made

46. A building occupies a space that is 520′ × 520′ on property that measures 1,040′ × 1,040′. What percentage of the property does the building occupy?

    a. 20 percent
    b. 25 percent
    c. 50 percent
    d. 80 percent

47. If the government wishes to exercise its right of eminent domain through the process of condemnation, it must meet all of the following requirements *except*

   a. pay fair compensation.
   b. obtain the consent of the owner.
   c. prove a public good.
   d. follow the proper legal procedure.

48. A judgment lien most likely will be filed against the real estate if:

   a. the owner does not pay the real estate taxes on the property.
   b. the owner does not pay a carpenter who made repairs.
   c. the owner obtains a loan using the property as collateral.
   d. a plaintiff wins a $10,000 lawsuit against the owner.

49. In describing real estate, the method that uses feet, degrees and natural and artificial markers as monuments is

   a. rectangular survey.
   b. metes and bounds.
   c. government survey.
   d. lot and block.

50. Which of the following properties would be exempt from real estate taxes under most state laws?

   a. Someone's house
   b. A privately owned day care center
   c. A park
   d. An industrial complex

U N I T II
DIAGNOSTIC TEST
ANSWER SHEET

This sheet is perforated for easy pullout. Write your answers on this sheet as you complete the exercises. Refer to the diagnostic worksheet after completing the test to evaluate your strong and weak content areas. Review material in the appropriate chapter and sections.

1. _____
2. _____
3. _____
4. _____
5. _____
6. _____
7. _____
8. _____
9. _____
10. _____
11. _____
12. _____
13. _____
14. _____
15. _____
16. _____
17. _____

18. _____
19. _____
20. _____
21. _____
22. _____
23. _____
24. _____
25. _____
26. _____
27. _____
28. _____
29. _____
30. _____
31. _____
32. _____
33. _____
34. _____

35. _____
36. _____
37. _____
38. _____
39. _____
40. _____
41. _____
42. _____
43. _____
44. _____
45. _____
46. _____
47. _____
48. _____
49. _____
50. _____

REAL ESTATE
OWNERSHIP

CHAPTER 7

FREEHOLD INTERESTS IN REAL ESTATE

This chapter describes the types of ownership interest (called an *estate*) one can have in real estate. *Section 1* covers fee simple and defeasible freehold estates. *Section 2* covers life estates. *Section 3* covers water rights. Remember to use the Study Tool Kit to reference key information and to update your progress checklist.

Learning Objectives

Track your progress as you work through the chapter by checking each learning objective when you complete it.

____ Describe the concepts of estates in land and the allodial system.

____ Describe the characteristics of freehold estates.

____ Describe the difference between fee simple absolute and defeasible fee estates.

____ List and describe the two types of defeasible fee estates.

____ Describe the difference between ordinary and pur autre vie life estates.

____ Describe the difference between conventional and statutory life estates.

____ List and describe the three legal life estates.

____ Describe the difference between a remainder and a reversion interest.

____ Describe the difference between littoral and riparian rights.

____ List and describe the terms used to describe the impact of nature on land.

Key Terms and Phrases

Track your progress as you work through the chapter by checking each term when you understand its meaning.

____ Accretion

____ Allodial system

____ Alluvion

____ Avulsion

____ Conventional life estate

____ Curtesy

____ Dower

____ Erosion

____ Fee simple absolute

____ Fee simple defeasible

____ Fee simple subject to condition precedent

____ Fee simple subject to condition subsequent

____ Freehold estate

____ Homestead

____ Leasehold estate

____ Legal life estate

____ Life tenant

____ Littoral rights

____	Ordinary life estate	____	Remainder interest
____	Prior appropriation	____	Reversion interest
____	Pur autre vie	____	Riparian rights
____	Reliction	____	Waste

FEE SIMPLE AND DEFEASIBLE FREEHOLD ESTATES

ESTATES IN LAND

An *estate* refers to the *degree, quantity, nature* and *extent* of interest (ownership rights) a person can have in real estate. Estates can be divided into two general groups: (1) **freehold estates,** which are of indefinite length, and (2) **leasehold estates** (less than freehold), which are for a fixed term. Leasehold estates are covered in Chapter 8. Figure 7.1 lists the different types of freehold and leasehold estates in land.

Allodial versus Feudal Ownership

Under the *feudal system* the king or government owned the land, and individuals were merely tenants. Under the **allodial system,** the system used in the United States, individuals can hold absolute ownership rights in land. This is called *allodial* or *private ownership.*

Inheritable versus Noninheritable Freehold Estates

Inheritable freehold estates can be left to heirs. Inheritable freehold estates include *fee simple absolute* and *fee simple defeasible* estates.

A *noninheritable freehold* estate cannot be left to heirs and terminates on the death of the person on whose life it is based. Noninheritable freehold estates include *conventional life estates* and *legal life estates.*

Fee Simple Absolute

Fee simple absolute estates are also called *fee simple estates.* This is the *highest form of ownership* interest recognized by law. It is *complete ownership.* This estate exists for an *unlimited time.* It may be inherited, given away or sold by the owner. However, it is still subject to government powers including police powers, eminent domain, escheat and taxation. (Government powers are covered in Chapter 3.)

Fee Simple Defeasible

A **fee simple defeasible** estate is subject to a *condition* to determine when it will begin or when it will end. It is also referred to as *determinable fee, conditional fee* or *qualified fee.*

Hint: To help you remember them, think of defeasible fees as being "defeated" by some condition.

FIGURE 7.1
Estates in Real Estate

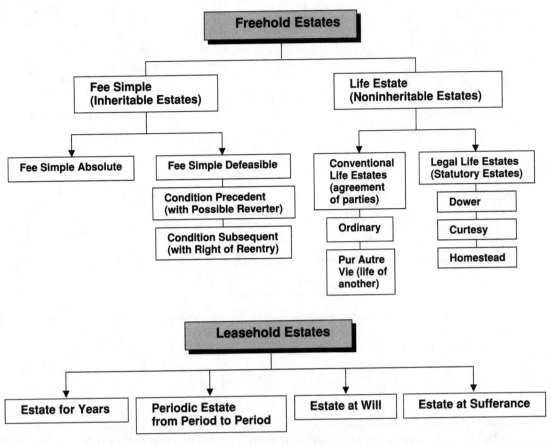

When a fee simple defeasible estate ends, title will pass by one of *three* possibilities:

1. To the *original grantor* (reversion interest).
2. To the original grantor's *heirs* (reversion interest).
3. To a specified *third party* (remainder interest).

Figure 7.2 illustrates reversion and remainder interests.

Two Types of Fee Simple Defeasible. *Fee Simple Subject to Condition Subsequent*—If the estate includes a prohibited use of the property, it is called a **fee simple subject to condition subsequent.** This is sometimes called a *must not do* or a *but if* estate.

EXAMPLE: A grantor gives a church group 10 acres of land; however, they "*must not*" allow any gambling activities on the property, otherwise the estate is terminated.

Note that the condition continues to exist even if the church group conveys the property to someone else. The grantor has the *right of reentry,* that is, the right to "take back" the estate if the condition is not met.

Fee Simple Subject to Condition Precedent—If the estate remains in effect as long as a specified condition is satisfied, it is called a **fee simple subject to condition precedent.** This is sometimes called an *as long as* estate. The grantor (or the grantor's heirs) retain right of *reversion* interest should the condition no longer be met.

FIGURE 7.2
Reversion and Remainder

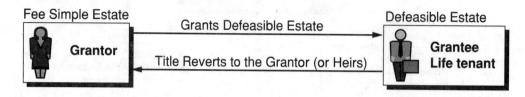

Reversion

Fee Simple Estate		Defeasible Estate
Grantor	Grants Defeasible Estate →	**Grantee** **Life tenant**
	← Title Reverts to the Grantor (or Heirs)	

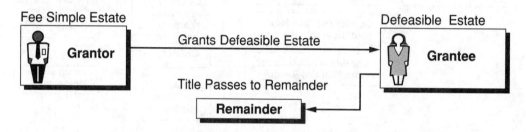

Remainder

Fee Simple Estate		Defeasible Estate
Grantor	Grants Defeasible Estate →	**Grantee**
	Title Passes to Remainder	
	Remainder ←	

EXAMPLE: Land is deeded to an environmental group with the condition that the estate will continue "as long as" a bird sanctuary is operated on the property. When the condition is no longer met, the property reverts back to the grantor.

Tip: Notice that the condition precedent estate ends automatically when the condition is not met and that the reversion interest is automatic. In the condition subsequent estate it is not automatic. The right of reentry means that grantors (or their heirs) must take action by physically reentering the property or going to court to terminate the estate.

**BEFORE READING THE NEXT SECTION, COMPLETE THE SECTION 1
REVIEW EXERCISES AND COMPARE YOUR ANSWERS WITH THE
SOLUTIONS AT THE END OF THE CHAPTER.**

SECTION 1
REVIEW EXERCISES

1. Determine whether each of the following estates is inheritable or noninheritable.

   a. _____ Fee absolute

   b. _____ Conventional life estates

   c. _____ Fee simple defeasible

   d. _____ Legal life estates

2. Name the three possibilities by which title passes when an estate ends.

   a. _____ To the original grantor

   b. _____ To the grantor's heirs

   c. _____ To a specified third party

Are the following statements true (T) or false (F)?

3. ____ A defeasible estate that includes a condition prohibiting the use of alcohol on the property is a fee simple subject to condition subsequent.

4. ____ Fee simple estates represent complete ownership and supersede government powers.

5. ____ The right of reentry is associated with a fee simple subject to condition precedent estate.

6. ____ The extent of ownership rights a person may have in real estate is referred to as an *estate*.

7. ____ A defeasible estate that is granted as long as the property is used in a certain manner is a fee simple subject to condition precedent.

8. ____ In a fee simple subject to condition precedent estate, a reversion interest is retained by the grantor.

Supply the term that best matches each of the following descriptions.

9. _____ Recognizes that individuals can hold ownership rights in land

10. _____ Highest form of ownership recognized by law

11. _____ A fee subject to a condition

12. _____ A defeasible fee that prohibits certain uses of the property

13. _____ A defeasible fee that takes effect when a certain condition is met

SECTION 2

LIFE ESTATES

Life estates are freehold estates based on someone's *life*. The party who *owns the life estate* is called the **life tenant**. Remember that the rights of the life tenant are *not inheritable*, that is, they cannot be passed on to heirs. There are two types of life estates:

1. **Conventional life estates** are created by the actions of a grantor by means of a deed, will or trust.
2. **Legal life estates** are created by statute (law). (These are also known as *statutory estates.*)

CONVENTIONAL LIFE ESTATES

There are two kinds of conventional life estates, (1) ordinary and (2) pur autre vie, or *for the life of another.*

If the estate is based on the *life tenant's life*, it is an **ordinary life estate**. This type of life estate is limited in time to the life of the owner. When the owner dies, the estate is terminated.

EXAMPLE: A gives to B an ordinary life estate. B is the life tenant "owner" of the property, and the life estate will continue as long as B is alive.

If the estate is based on the life of a person *other than the life tenant*, it is called a **pur autre vie** life estate. Pur autre vie means *for another's life.*

FIGURE 7.3
Life Estates

Ordinary Life Estate, Based on Life Tenant's Life

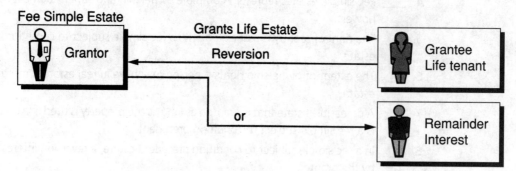

Pur Autre Vie Life Estate, Based on Another's Life

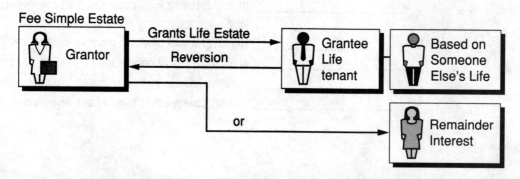

EXAMPLE: A gives a life estate to B for as long as C is alive. Here B is the life tenant "owner" of the property, and the life estate will continue as long as C is alive.

Figure 7.3 illustrates ordinary and pur autre vie life estates.

Life Tenant

The life tenant has a true ownership interest; may enjoy all the income and profits from the property; and may lease, sell or mortgage his or her life estate. However, a life tenant may not perform acts that would injure the property. This is called "committing" waste. Waste could result from the unauthorized use or neglect of the property.

EXAMPLE: Failure of the life tenant to make repairs or pay the property taxes could be considered committing waste.

Future Property Interests

Because the life estate will not continue indefinitely, a future ownership is established after the death of the life estate owner. When the life estate is terminated, there will be either a *remainder* or *reversionary* interest in the property.

Under a **remainder interest,** ownership will pass to a third party named in the deed. Thus, a remainder person has a *nonpossessory, future interest* in the property.

EXAMPLE: A grants to B a life estate and designates C to have a remainder interest. When B dies the ownership of the property goes to C.

If there is no remainder interest, the property "reverts" back to the original owner. This is called a **reversion interest**. If the original owner has died, it will revert back to the *heirs*.

EXAMPLE: A grants to B a life estate and designates a reversion interest. When B dies, the ownership of the property reverts back to A (or to A's heirs if A is dead).

Note: If a pur autre vie life tenant (life estate based on a third party's life) dies, the life tenant's heirs may inherit the life estate until the third party dies.

LEGAL LIFE ESTATES

The conventional life estates previously discussed were all created by the action of the grantor. Legal life estates, however, are created automatically by *law*. They are sometimes called *statutory life estates*. The laws creating legal life estates vary among states, and not all states recognize the three legal life estates described in this section.

1. The legal life estate of **curtesy** pertains to the *husband's life estate* in real estate of his deceased's *wife's property.*
2. The legal life estate of **dower** pertains to the *wife's life estate* in real estate of her deceased's *husband's property.*

Other characteristics of dower and curtesy:

- Dower and curtesy rights cannot be assigned or transferred to someone else.

EXAMPLE: If the husband sells the property without his wife's consent, the wife can demand return of her dower interest when the husband dies.

- Legal life estates can be released if both spouses sign a deed of conveyance.
- The portion of the real estate included in curtesy and dower varies by state law but is usually one-half or one-third.
3. Under the legal life estate of **homestead,** a portion of the value of a homeowner's principal residence (the homestead) is protected from certain judgments for debts.

Rules governing property that qualifies for homestead protection and the amount protected from creditors vary among states. State laws usually exempt real estate taxes and mortgages from the homestead rules. The signatures of both spouses are needed on contracts and mortgages to release homestead rights.

BEFORE READING THE NEXT SECTION, COMPLETE THE SECTION 2 REVIEW EXERCISES AND COMPARE YOUR ANSWERS WITH THE SOLUTIONS AT THE END OF THE CHAPTER.

SECTION 2
REVIEW EXERCISES

1. In each of the situations state whether there is a remainder or a reversion interest.

a. _____ A grantor gives a life estate to a grantee. The grantee dies and the property passes to the grantor

b. _____ A grantor gives a life estate to a grantee. The grantee dies and the property passes to the grantor's heirs.

c. _____ A grantor gives a life estate to a grantee. The grantee dies and the property passes to a third party.

Are the following statements true (T) or false (F)?

2. ____ Most life estates are inheritable by the life tenant's heirs.

3. ____ Another name for legal life estate is statutory life estate.

4. ____ A life tenant may collect income from the property and lease, sell or mortgage the life estate.

Supply the term that best matches each of the following descriptions.

5. _____ Life estates created by law

6. _____ Wife's life estate in the husband's property

7. _____ The party who holds a life estate

8. _____ The act of injuring the property

9. _____ A conventional life estate based on the life tenant's life

10. _____ Ownership passes to a third party when an estate ends

11. _____ Protection of the principal residence from some judgments

12. _____ Life estates created by the action of the parties

13. _____ A conventional life estate based on another's life

14. _____ Ownership passes back to the original owner when an estate ends

15. _____ Husband's life estate in the wife's property

_____ **SECTION 3**

WATER RIGHTS

Owners of property that borders water or landowners who use water may have certain rights.

RIPARIAN RIGHTS

Riparian rights pertain to land bordering flowing water, such as streams or rivers. The extent of ownership depends on whether the water bordering the land is navigable.

- If the water is *nonnavigable,* ownership generally extends to the center of the water.
- If the water is *navigable,* ownership extends to the high-water mark at the water's edge. In this situation the government owns the water and the submerged land, and the public has an easement right to travel on the water.

Figure 7.4 illustrates riparian ownership rights.

FIGURE 7.4
Riparian Rights

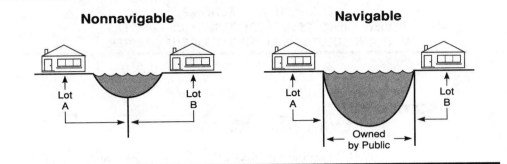

LITTORAL RIGHTS

Littoral rights refer to the rights of an owner of property along a large body of water that is not flowing, such as the ocean, a sea or a lake. Ownership of the land usually extends to the high-water mark

Hint: Both riparian and littoral rights are appurtenant, meaning they are "attached" to the land. Therefore, the rights belong to whoever owns the land and are not retained by former owners.

PRIOR APPROPRIATION

Prior appropriation rights apply in Western states where water is scarce. Ownership and use of the water are controlled by the state. To obtain the right to appropriate (divert) water, the landowner applies for a permit with the proper state office.

ACCRETION AND EROSION

Various terms are used to describe the impact of nature on real estate. These include the following:

- **Accretion,** the gradual addition of land by the forces of nature.
- **Alluvion,** new deposits of land as a result of accretion. *Alluvion* deposits are common at the mouth of large rivers such as the Mississippi. The landowner is entitled to all additions.
- **Erosion,** the gradual loss of land through the natural forces of nature such as water, wind or ice. The owner may lose land through the natural process of erosion.
- **Avulsion,** the sudden removal of land by forces of nature.

EXAMPLE: A hurricane washes away a beach area.

- **Reliction** is the gradual subsiding of water leaving additional land. The new land usually belongs to the owner of the area that was covered with water.

**COMPLETE THE SECTION 3
REVIEW EXERCISES AND COMPARE YOUR ANSWERS
WITH THE SOLUTIONS AT THE END OF THE CHAPTER.**

SECTION 3
REVIEW EXERCISES

1. Select the term that best describes each situation.

   a. _____ An owner's beachfront is reduced by half through water currents.

   b. _____ Additional beach area is acquired by the owner through the action of water currents.

   c. _____ Most of a ranch's grazing land is lost when a flash flood from a nearby river flows through the area.

   d. _____ Over several years winds result in a farm owner's soil base being depleted.

Are the following statements true (T) or false (F)?

2. ____ Ownership rights in land that borders a large body of water generally extend to the low-water mark.

3. ____ Ownership rights in land that borders navigable water generally extend to the center of the water.

4. ____ Riparian water rights are appurtenant, that is, attached, to the land.

5. ____ To use water in states where prior appropriation rights are recognized, a land-owner applies to the state for a permit.

Supply the term that best matches each of the following descriptions.

6. _____ New deposits of land through natural forces

7. _____ Rights associated with land bordering large bodies of water such as a lake or the ocean

8. _____ The right to divert water

9. _____ Gradual loss of land through natural forces

10. _____ Rights associated with land bordering water such as a stream or river

11. _____ Gradual addition of land

12. _____ The sudden loss of land through natural forces

SOLUTIONS
FOR SECTION REVIEW EXERCISES

SECTION 1

1. a. Inheritable   b. Noninheritable   c. Inheritable   d. Noninheritable
2. a. Reversion   b. Reversion   c. Remainder
3. TRUE
4. FALSE Fee simple estates are subject to government powers.
5. FALSE The right of reentry is associated with a fee simple subject to condition subsequent estate.
6. TRUE
7. TRUE
8. TRUE
9. Allodial system
10. Fee simple (or fee simple absolute)
11. Fee simple defeasible
12. Fee simple subject to condition subsequent
13. Fee simple subject to condition precedent

SECTION 2

1. a. Reversion   b. Reversion   c. Remainder
2. FALSE Life estates are *not* inheritable.
3. TRUE
4. TRUE
5. Legal life estates
6. Dower
7. Life tenant
8. Waste
9. Ordinary life estate
10. Remainder interest
11. Homestead
12. Conventional life estates
13. Pur autre vie life estate
14. Reversion interest
15. Curtesy

SECTION 3

1. a. Erosion   b. Alluvion   c. Avulsion   d. Erosion
2. FALSE Ownership rights generally extend to the high-water mark.
3. FALSE Ownership rights extend to the water's edge.
4. TRUE

5. TRUE

6. Alluvion

7. Littoral rights

8. Prior appropriation

9. Erosion

10. Riparian rights

11. Accretion

12. Avulsion

CHAPTER 8
LEASEHOLD ESTATES IN REAL ESTATE

Chapter 7 covered freehold estates. This chapter covers another type of estate, called a *leasehold* estate. *Section 1* covers the different types of leasehold estates. *Section 2* covers several types of lease agreements. *Section 3* covers lease characteristics, including lease requirements, how leases are terminated and remedies available to the landlord and tenant if the lease is breached. Remember to use the Study Tool Kit to reference key information and to update your progress checklist.

Learning Objectives

Track your progress as you work through the chapter by checking each learning objective when you complete it.

____ Describe the characteristics of the four common types of leasehold estates.

____ Describe the characteristics of the lease agreements included in the chapter and the situations for which they are best suited.

____ Calculate the rent amount for a percentage lease.

____ List and describe the requirements for a valid lease.

____ List and describe several of the provisions included in a lease agreement.

____ Explain the difference between an assignment and sublease.

____ List and describe various ways leases can be terminated.

____ List and describe landlords' and tenants' remedies for breach of a lease.

Key Terms and Phrases

Track your progress as you work through the chapter by checking each term when you understand its meaning.

____ Actual eviction	____ Lease-purchase
____ Assignment	____ Lease with option to buy
____ Constructive eviction	____ Lessee
____ Estate for years	____ Lessor
____ Graduated lease	____ Net lease
____ Gross lease	____ Oil and gas lease
____ Ground lease	____ Percentage lease
____ Holdover tenancy	____ Periodic estate
____ Index lease	____ Recapture clause
____ Lease agreement	____ Reversion right
____ Lease option	____ Right of first refusal

____	Sale and leaseback	____	Tenancy at sufferance
____	Sublease	____	Tenancy at will
____	Suit for possession	____	Variable lease

SECTION 1

TYPES OF LEASEHOLD ESTATES

A leasehold estate includes fewer ownership rights than does a freehold estate and is of limited duration. Leasehold estates are created by a **lease agreement.** The lease agreement is both (1) a contract and (2) a transferring of an ownership interest (the right of possession) in return for payment of rent and other obligations. The landlord keeps a **reversion right** to retake possession. The owner of the property (the landlord) is called the **lessor** and the tenant the **lessee.** The *statue of frauds* requires that a lease for a period longer than one year must be in writing to be enforceable. An oral lease for one year or less may be enforceable. (The statute of frauds will be discussed in more detail in Chapter 14, Real Estate Contracts.)

Figure 8.1 illustrates the types of leasehold estates.

Hint: Remember there is an "o" in lessor and owner and an "e" in lessee and tenant. Lessor = owner or landlord. Lessee = tenant or renter.

ESTATE FOR YEARS

The most common type of leasehold estate is an **estate for years.** This type of estate continues for a *definite period of time.* The lessee must vacate the premises at the end of the lease and *no notice is required to terminate* this type of estate.

While it is called an *estate for years,* the length of the leasehold estate can be for *any fixed period of time* (e.g., a month, six months, a year). It is probably more accurate to refer to is as an *estate for a stated period.*

Sale of the property or death of either the tenant or the landlord *does not terminate* the leasehold. If the tenant dies, the leasehold estate goes to the tenant's heirs. The lease may be terminated prior to the expiration date by consent of the parties.

Note: State laws set the maximum term for leasehold interests.

PERIODIC ESTATE

Periodic estates, also called *estates from period to period,* do not have an expiration date; therefore, they continue for an indefinite period of time. The rent is paid at definite intervals and each time it is paid the lease is automatically renewed for a like period. Because it continues indefinitely, notice must be given to end a periodic estate.

FIGURE 8.1
Types of
Leashold Estates

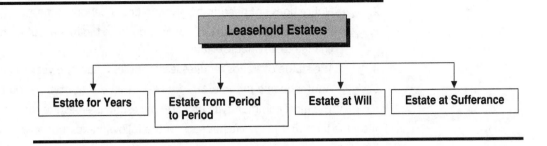

EXAMPLE: A landlord and tenant agree to the rental of an apartment by the month without specifying the number of months the lease will run. The lease will continue until one of the parties gives proper notice to terminate.

The length of notice that must be given to terminate a periodic estate varies from state to state but in general is

- for week-to-week tenancy, one week's notice.
- for month-to-month tenancy, one month's notice.
- for year-to-year tenancy, from three to six months.

TENANCY (ESTATE) AT WILL

Under a **tenancy at will,** the tenant may possess the property with the consent of the landlord. The term is for an *indefinite* period of time and can be terminated by either party if sufficient notice is given. The tenancy also will be terminated if the property is sold or on the *death or insanity* of either landlord or tenant.

EXAMPLE: At the end of a lease, the landlord tells the tenants that her parents will be moving into the apartment in the next few months. The landlord gives the tenants the option to continue renting until her parents are ready to move in. If the tenants agree, a tenancy at will is created.

TENANCY (ESTATE) AT SUFFERANCE

In a **tenancy at sufferance (holdover tenancy)** the tenant wrongfully remains in possession of the property after the right to possess has expired. The tenant differs from a trespasser only in that original entry on the property was legal. If the landlord accepts rent, then the tenancy changes to a periodic tenancy.

**BEFORE READING THE NEXT SECTION, COMPLETE THE SECTION 1
REVIEW EXERCISES AND COMPARE YOUR ANSWERS WITH THE
SOLUTIONS AT THE END OF THE CHAPTER.**

SECTION 1
REVIEW EXERCISES

Are the following statements true (T) or false (F)?

1. ____ A tenancy at will ends if the property is sold.

2. ____ Notice does not need to be given to end a periodic estate.

3. ____ If a landlord accepts a rent payment during a tenancy at sufferance, the tenancy may change to a periodic estate.

4. ____ The statue of frauds requires leases for less than one year to be in writing.

5. ____ Another name for an *estate for years* is an *estate from period to period*.

6. ____ The most common type of leasehold estate is an estate for years.

Supply the term that best matches each of the following descriptions.

7. _____ An estate that continues for an indefinite period of time

8. _____ A tenant wrongfully stays on the property

9. _____ Another term for the tenant

10. _____ An estate that continues for a definite period of time

11. _____ A contract that transfers the right of possession

12. _____ A tenancy with the consent of the landlord that can be terminated at any time

13. _____ A landlord

14. _____ The right of the landlord to retake possession of the premises

---

SECTION 2
TYPES OF LEASES

This section discusses some common types of lease agreements. These are illustrated in Figure 8.2.

GROSS LEASE

The most common type of lease is the **gross lease** (also called a *straight lease* or a *flat lease*). Under this lease the tenant pays a *set amount of rent* each month, whereas the landlord pays all of the building's expenses. This type of lease most often is used for *residential* units.

NET LEASE

Under a **net lease** the tenant pays a set amount of rent plus some or all of the building expenses. Expenses paid by the tenant include operating expenses, taxes and insurance. This type of lease is most often used in *commercial* or *industrial* property.

This type of lease can be a net, a net-net (*double-net*) or a net-net-net (*triple-net*) lease. The number of nets refers to the number of expenses paid by the tenant. The more nets, the more expenses paid by the tenant.

Tip: Expenses paid by the tenant do not include the building's debt expense (i.e., mortgage payments for any loans on the property).

PERCENTAGE LEASE

Percentage leases are used almost exclusively for *commercial* property. The rent is determined by a percentage of the *gross income* of the tenant. A percentage lease may also be either a *gross* or a *net* lease, depending on whether the tenant must also pay the building's expenses.

A percentage lease agreement usually provides for a fixed minimum amount of rent *plus* a percentage of gross income over a base amount.

EXAMPLE: A lease agreement calls for $10,000 annual rent and 2 percent of gross sales in excess of $500,000 per year. If yearly sales are $600,000, what is the rent?

$10,000 annual rent + $2,000 ($600,000 – $500,000 = $100,000, × .02) = $12,000 rent.

Percentage leases may include a **recapture clause.** This clause allows the lessor to reclaim the property if a minimum sales amount is not met.

VARIABLE LEASES

A **variable lease** agreement allows for future changes in the amount of rent. There are several ways this could be arranged, including *graduated leases* and *index leases.*

A **graduated lease** arrangement allows for rent changes at *predetermined future dates.*

EXAMPLE: A three-year lease agreement provides for rent of $800 a month in the first year, $1,000 a month in the second year and $1,200 a month in the third year.

Property in which the rent would fluctuate based on the time of year might use a graduated lease.

EXAMPLE: A resort owner may charge a rent of $300 a week during the off-peak season and $700 a week during the peak season.

In an **index lease** the rent change is *based on a common index,* such as the consumer price index (CPI). An escalator clause in the lease ties the rent increase to the index. The escalator clause may include other factors in determining the rent increase, such as an increase in property taxes or utility expenses.

GROUND LEASE

A **ground lease** is a long-term lease (usually for a period of 50 or more years). The tenant leases the land and often agrees to erect a building as part of the lease agreement. The tenant also pays the building's expenses, thus making the lease a net lease. Ground leases

FIGURE 8.2
Types of Lease
Agreements

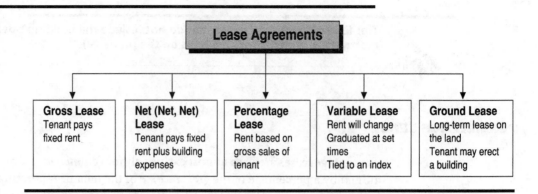

are most often used by *business* to lease undeveloped *industrial* or *commercial* property. The lease is not terminated if the building is destroyed.

EXAMPLE: ABC Company leases a ten-acre plot of land from the owner to build and operate its corporate headquarters.

OIL AND GAS LEASES

In an **oil and gas lease,** the landowner receives rent from a company for allowing drilling on the property. If no gas or oil is found, a flat rent is charged. If gas or oil is found, the landlord receives a royalty.

LEASE-PURCHASE

In a **lease-purchase** arrangement, a tenant leases the property for a period of time with the *intention of purchasing the property* at a later date. The delayed purchase may be for tax or financing purposes.

EXAMPLE: ABC company agrees to lease a property for six months and then purchase. The company believes that by waiting it will be able to secure financing at a lower rate.

SALE-LEASEBACK

Under a **sale and leaseback** arrangement, an owner (usually a business) sells the property where the business is located to an investor and then leases the property back. The *seller* (who is now the *lessee*) benefits because it frees up capital from the sale, and the rent now can be deducted as a business expense. The *buyer* (who is now the *lessor*) benefits because it has a stable tenant and a favorable return on its investment. A long-term net lease is usually used in this situation.

BEFORE READING THE NEXT SECTION, COMPLETE THE SECTION 2
REVIEW EXERCISES AND COMPARE YOUR ANSWERS WITH THE
SOLUTIONS AT THE END OF THE CHAPTER.

SECTION 2

REVIEW EXERCISES

1. List the benefits to the parties in a sale and leaseback arrangement.

   The seller/lessee   a. _____

   b. _____

   The buyer/lessor   a. _____

   b. _____

Are the following statements true (T) or false (F)?

2. ____ Net leases are commonly used with industrial property.

3. ____ Gross leases are most often used with commercial property.

4. ____ Expenses paid by the tenant under a net lease include the mortgage payment.

5. ____ A percentage lease also may be either a gross or a net lease.

Supply the term that best matches each of the following descriptions.

6. _____ An arrangement in which a tenant leases a property with the intention of purchasing it

7. _____ A lease arrangement in which part of the rent amount is determined by the gross income the tenant receives

8. _____ A long-term lease under which the tenant usually agrees to construct a building

9. _____ The owner sells the property to an investor and then leases the property

10. _____ A lease arrangement in which changes to the rent are made at set future dates

11. _____ A lease arrangement in which changes to the rent are based on a common index

12. _____ A lease arrangement in which the tenant pays a fixed amount of rent and the owner pays the expenses on the building

13. _____ Allows the lessor to reclaim the property if a minimum sales amount is not met

14. _____ A lease arrangement in which the tenant pays a fixed amount of rent and some or all of the expenses on the building

SECTION 3

LEASE CHARACTERISTICS

REQUIREMENTS FOR A VALID LEASE

A valid lease includes the basic elements needed for all contracts and some additional elements unique to lease agreements. (Basic contract requirements are covered in more detail in Chapter 14, Real Estate Contracts.)

Basic Contract Requirements

- *Capacity to contract*—The parties must be legally competent.
- *Offer and acceptance*—There must be mutual agreement by the parties on all the terms of the lease.
- *Legal objectives*—The lease terms must be legal.

EXAMPLE: A lease that included provisions to discriminate would be illegal.

- *Consideration*—Rent is usually given by the tenant, and the owner gives up the right of possession.

Basic Lease Elements

- *Description of premises*—A description of the property to be rented.
- *Term*—The length of the lease.
- *Names and signatures*—The names of the parties and their signatures.
- *Use*—Description of the specific use of the premises allowed the tenant. If use will be limited, limitations should be clearly stated.
- *Security deposit*—Amount held by landlord to be applied against repairs necessary at the end of the lease. There is no obligation for the tenant to pay a security deposit unless the lease provides for it.
- *Habitability*—Landlord warrants that the property is safe and meets specific state requirements for habitability.
- *Quiet enjoyment*—Tenant is entitled to use the property without interference from the landlord or other tenants. This is usually implied by law even if it is not in the lease.
- *Reentry clause*—Gives the landlord the right to enter the premises to make repairs or show it for rent. Notice to the tenant in advance is usually required.
- *Rent*—The amount of rent (or formula for calculating the rent). An escalator clause may provide for rent increases.
- *Maintenance*—Provisions detailing who is responsible for various repairs. Tenant is required to return the premises in same condition, less ordinary wear and tear. The landlord must make the repairs necessary to keep the building habitable.
- *Improvements*—Neither party is *obligated* to make improvements. The tenant will usually be allowed only to make improvements with permission of the owner. Improvements become *fixtures* and are the property of the landlord. Any *trade fixtures* (fixtures used in a trade or business) should be identified because they may be removed by the tenant.
- *Options*—Conditions for the right to renew the lease or purchase the property. This may include a **right of first refusal,** allowing the tenant the opportunity to buy the property before the owner can accept an offer from a third party.
- *Holdover*—A clause providing for a rent penalty if the tenant does not give up possession at the end of the lease.
- *Exculpatory clause*—The tenant agrees not to hold the landlord liable for any loss or injury incurred on the property. This also is called a *hold harmless* clause. Such clauses were once common but are now unenforceable for residential property in many states.
- *Assignment and sublease*—Establishes rights given to the tenant to assign or sublease the premises. Usually requires owner's approval.

DESTRUCTION OF PREMISES

If the building is partly or completely destroyed the following generally will apply:

- If leasing *part* of the building, the tenant usually is not required to continue paying rent.

- If leasing *all* of the building (or in the case of a ground lease), the tenant usually is required to continue paying rent.

TRANSFER OF LEASEHOLD INTERESTS

Assignment—Transfer of All Leasehold Interests

In an **assignment** the lessee (or the lessor) transfers all the remaining terms of the lease. The assignee is *primarily obligated* under the lease, but the original lessee may be *secondarily obligated.*

Sublease—Transfer of a Portion of the Leasehold Interest

In a **sublease** agreement, the original lessee becomes a sublessor and takes on a new tenant (sublessee). The subtenant makes payments to the original lessee. There is no obligation between the party subleasing and the landlord, and the *original lessee* is still *primarily obligated* to pay rent to the landlord. Subleasing can be prohibited in the lease agreement.

OPTIONS

A **lease option** (also called a *renewal option*) is a provision in the lease that grants the lessee the right to renew the lease if notice is given before a specified date.

A **lease with option to buy** allows the tenant to purchase the property during a specified time period. The tenant is usually given credit toward the purchase price for part of the rent paid if the option is executed.

 Tip: Note that in a lease with option to buy the tenant is not required to purchase. In a lease-purchase agreement (covered in Section 2 of this chapter) the tenant is usually required to purchase after the rental period.

BREACH OF LEASE

If either party to the lease agreement does not live up to the terms of the agreement, a breach has occurred.

Landlord's Remedies

- *Actual Eviction*—The landlord can regain possession (**actual eviction**) by filing a **suit for possession.** The landlord must give notice to the tenant before filing the suit. If the tenant does not leave, the courts may forcibly remove the tenant and his or her possessions.
- *Suit for rent*—May sue to recover past-due rent.
- *Suit for damages*—May sue for any damages incurred because of the tenant's breach of the lease terms.

Tenant's Remedies

- *Suit for damages*—May sue for any damages incurred because the landlord breached the terms of the lease.
- *Constructive eviction*—**Constructive eviction** may occur if the premises become uninhabitable, forcing the tenant to leave. If this occurs, the tenant may not be liable for any future rent.

EXAMPLE: The property does not have heat, the plumbing does not work or the building is structurally unsafe.

TERMINATION OF LEASES

Leases may be terminated in a number of ways. The more common methods are listed below.

- *Expiration of term*—Expiration of the lease or by giving proper notice to terminate the lease at the end of the renewal period.
- *Surrender and acceptance*—Mutual agreement of the parties to cancel the remaining portion of the lease. This is not the same as abandonment by the tenant. If the tenant abandons the property without permission of the landlord, the tenant remains liable for the rent.
- *Bankruptcy*—The tenant's bankruptcy generally terminates the lease.
- *Destruction of premises*—This will generally terminate the lease.
- *Eminent domain*—Loss of the property through eminent domain terminates the lease.
- *Breach*—If either the lessor or the lessee breaches the provisions of the lease, it may be terminated.
- *Eviction*—If the owner successfully evicts the tenant, the lease is terminated. In many states constructive eviction also will terminate the lease.
- *Merger*—If the lessee becomes the owner of the leased property, the leasehold interest terminates.

Note: In most cases if the owner dies or the property is sold, the leases remain in effect.

UNIFORM RESIDENTIAL LANDLORD AND TENANT ACT

This model law was created by the National Conference of Commissioners on Uniform State Laws. It is intended to *clarify* and *standardize* state landlord-tenant law and protect both tenants and landlords. Variations of this act have been included in many state laws. The act addresses the following issues:

- Landlord's right of reentry to the premises
- Landlord's obligation to perform maintenance and ensure habitability
- Guidelines for handling security deposits
- Protection from landlord's retaliation for tenant complaints
- Prohibition of exculpatory clauses (which allows the landlord to escape all liability)
- Prohibition of judgment clauses by which tenants waive their rights or legal remedies

**COMPLETE THE SECTION 3 REVIEW EXERCISES AND COMPARE YOUR ANSWERS
WITH THE SOLUTIONS AT THE END OF THE CHAPTER.**

REVIEW EXERCISES

1. Supply the lease element that best matches each of the following descriptions.

   a. _____ An amount held by the landlord to be applied against unpaid rent or repairs

   b. _____ The right to renew the lease or purchase the property

   c. _____ Prevents interference from the landlord and other tenants

   d. _____ Warrants the property is safe

   e. _____ A hold-harmless clause excluding the landlord from liability for injuries incurred on the property

   f. _____ A rent penalty if the tenant does not give up possession at the end of the lease

   g. _____ Landlord's right to enter the premises to make repairs

2. Supply the reason to terminate a lease that best matches each of the following descriptions.

   a. _____ A fire consumes the property.

   b. _____ The lease renewal period passes and no notice to renew is given.

   c. _____ The landlord has the tenant removed from the premises.

   d. _____ The lessee becomes the owner of the leased property.

   e. _____ The parties mutually agree to end the lease.

Are the following statements true (T) or false (F)?

3. ____ The tenant is entitled to use the property without interference from the landlord and other tenants, even if there is no clause in the lease stating this.

4. ____ Exculpatory clauses are difficult for landlords to enforce.

5. ____ Under an assignment all liability is transferred to the assignee.

6. ____ In a lease with option to buy the tenant is not required to purchase.

7. ____ A landlord's remedies include suit for rent, suit for damages and constructive eviction.

8. ____ If the property is sold, the leases are terminated.

Supply the term that best matches each of the following descriptions.

9. _____ Transfer of the remaining terms of the lease by the tenant

10. _____ Gives the lessee the right to renew the lease

11. _____ Allows the tenant to buy the property during a specified time period

12. _____ The original lessee becomes a lessor with a new subtenant

13. _____ Landlord's remedy to remove the tenant

14. _____ The tenant is forced to leave owing to the condition of the building

SOLUTIONS
FOR SECTION REVIEW EXERCISES

SECTION 1

1. TRUE
2. FALSE Because periodic estates continue for an indefinite period of time, notice must be given to end the estate.
3. TRUE
4. FALSE The statute of frauds requires leases for *more* than one year to be in writing.
5. FALSE A periodic estate is also called an estate from period to period.
6. TRUE
7. Periodic Estate
8. Tenancy at sufferance
9. Lessee
10. Estate for years
11. Lease agreement
12. Tenancy at will
13. Lessor
14. Reversion right

SECTION 2

1. The seller/lessee (a) frees up cash from the sale, which can be used for other purposes; (b) can deduct rent as a business expense.
   The buyer/lessor (a) has a stable tenant; (b) receives a favorable return on the investment.
2. TRUE
3. FALSE Gross leases are most often used with residential property.
4. FALSE Expenses paid by the tenant under a net lease include operating expenses, taxes and insurance, but not the debt expense.
5. TRUE
6. Lease purchase
7. Percentage lease
8. Ground lease
9. Sale and leaseback
10. A graduated lease
11. An index lease
12. A gross lease
13. Recapture clause
14. Net lease

SECTION 3

1. a. Security deposit b. Options c. Quiet enjoyment d. Habitability
   e. Exculpatory clause f. Holdover g. Reentry clause
2. a. Destruction of premises b. Expiration c. Eviction d. Merger
   e. Surrender and acceptance
3. TRUE
4. TRUE

5. FALSE These clauses are unenforceable for residential property in many states.

6. TRUE

7. FALSE A landlord's remedies include actual eviction. Constructive eviction is one of the tenant's remedies.

8. FALSE Usually if the property is sold, the leases remain in effect.

9. Assignment

10. Lease option

11. Lease with option to buy

12. Sublease

13. Actual eviction

14. Constructive eviction

CHAPTER 9

FORMS OF OWNERSHIP

This chapter covers the various forms of ownership, or how title to real estate can be held. The method used to hold title is important because it determines who must sign documents when the property is sold. Legal and economic considerations are also associated with some forms of ownership. *Section 1* describes sole ownership and several ways title may be held by more than one person (co-ownership). *Section 2* describes methods commonly used in business to hold title to property. *Section 3* describes other forms of ownership. Figure 9.1 illustrates the various ways title can be held that will be discussed in the chapter. Remember to use the Study Tool Kit to reference key information and to update your progress checklist.

Learning Objectives

Track your progress as you work through the chapter by checking each learning objective when you complete it.

____ Explain the differences between joint tenancy and tenants in common.

____ List and describe the four unities for forming a joint tenancy.

____ Explain how co-ownership can be terminated.

____ Describe the characteristics of severalty, tenancy by entirety and community property.

____ Explain the differences between general and limited partnerships.

____ List and describe the forms of ownership available to businesses.

____ List and describe the parties to a trust.

____ List and describe the different types of trusts.

____ List and describe the advantages of using the land trust form of ownership for real estate.

____ Explain the differences and similarities between the cooperative and condominium forms of ownership.

Key Terms and Phrases

Track your progress as you work through the chapter by checking each term when you understand its meaning.

____ Beneficiary   ____ Corporation

____ Community property   ____ Declaration

____ Condominium   ____ General partnership

____ Condominium bylaws   ____ Joint tenancy

____ Condominium owners' association   ____ Joint venture

____ Cooperatives   ____ Land trust

____	Limited liability Company (LLC)	____	Syndication
____	Limited partnership	____	Tenancy by the entirety
____	Living trust	____	Tenants in common
____	Partnership	____	Testamentary trust
____	Real estate investment trust (REIT)	____	Time-sharing
____	Right of partition	____	Trust
____	Right of survivorship	____	Trustee
____	S corporation	____	Trustor
____	Severalty		

SECTION 1

SEVERALTY AND CO-OWNERSHIP

OWNERSHIP IN SEVERALTY

Ownership in **severalty** is the same as *sole owner*. While it may seem that severalty should mean "several" owners, in law it means *separate* or *severed*. This is the simplest form of ownership and the easiest title to transfer because only one party is needed to sign the deed.

Note: Even though the property is held in severalty, the spouse may still need to sign the sales contract to release curtesy, dower and homestead rights.

JOINT TENANCY

Characteristics of Joint Tenancy

Joint tenancy is ownership by two or more people with **right of survivorship**. Right of survivorship means that when one co-owner dies, his or her share goes to the surviving co-owner(s). Right of survivorship also *supersedes* passing of title by *will* and *dower and curtesy* rights. (Dower and curtesy are covered in Chapter 7.)

EXAMPLE: A husband forms a joint tenancy in property with someone other than his wife and then dies. The wife has no dower or inheritance rights in the property.

Hint: Right of survivorship does NOT mean that the ownership share passes to the deceased tenant's heirs. It passes to the surviving joint tenants.

Joint tenancy must be *expressly created*. That is, the deed must clearly show joint tenancy. If there is no indication of what type of co-ownership is being created, the courts assume tenancy in common rather than joint tenancy.

FIGURE 9.1
Forms of Ownership

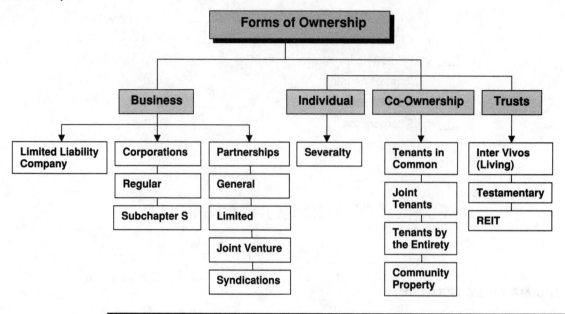

EXAMPLE: If A and B wish to take title as joint tenants, the language used might be "A and B as joint tenants with right of survivorship."

New joint tenants cannot be added later. Joint tenants may sell or convey their interest in a property, but the new owner becomes a *tenant in common* because there is no unity of title. Of course, all of the owners could decide to form a new joint tenancy together. This is illustrated in Figure 9.2.

EXAMPLE: A, B and C are joint tenants. C sells her interest to X. X is now a tenant in common with A and B, who are joint tenants.

All joint tenants have **right of partition.** If one of the parties wants to end the tenancy, he or she can go to court and force it to be dissolved and the assets distributed to the various tenants.

Unities for Joint Tenancy

A basic concept of joint tenancy is *unity of ownership*. To create a joint tenancy, *four unities are required.*

1. *Unity of time*—Ownership is acquired by all tenants at the *same time.*
2. *Unity of title*—All tenants' ownership is created by the *same instrument.*

EXAMPLE: A, B and C are named as joint tenants in the same deed.

3. *Unity of interest*—All tenants *own equal percentages* in the property and have the same type of ownership estate. (Estates in real estate are covered in Chapters 7 and 8.)

EXAMPLE: A, B and C are named as joint tenants, all owning a fee simple, one-third interest in the property.

4. *Unity of possession*—All tenants have *equal rights to access and possession* in the property.

FIGURE 9.2
Interest in Joint Tenancy

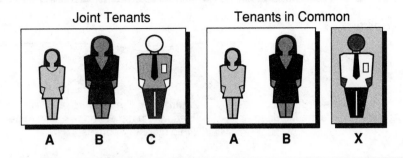

Joint Tenants — A B C   Tenants in Common — A B X

Hint: To help remember the four unities, think of TTIP. With this "tip" you may remember Time, Title, Interest and Possession.

TENANTS IN COMMON

Tenants in common hold an undivided interest in a property. An *undivided interest* is a share of the *entire* property, rather than ownership of a *particular part* of the property. Interest is held by each owner in severalty. None of the owners can exclude the others. All tenants in common have what is called *unity of possession:* They all have an equal right to occupy the property.

There is *no right of survivorship.* If one of the tenants dies, that tenant's interest in the tenancy goes to his or her heirs.

Tenants in common may hold *different percentages* of ownership in the property. The deed must specify the percentage of each tenant's share in the property; otherwise the courts assume each owns an equal share.

Each tenant in common can sell or mortgage his or her interest without the consent of the others. This does not destroy the tenancy; the new owner will become a tenant in common. Just as in joint tenancy, tenants in common have a *right of partition* to end the tenancy.

EXAMPLE: A, B and C are tenants in common. C sells his interest to X. X is now a tenant in common with A and B.

If the deed does not specify the form of ownership under which the parties are taking title, the law assumes it is tenancy in common.

TERMINATION OF CO-OWNERSHIP

Whether it is a tenancy in common or a joint tenancy, there are several ways to end the co-ownership.

- The parties may voluntarily agree to end the co-ownership.
- One or more tenants may file a *suit of partition,* asking the court to end the tenancy and divide the property.
- By operation of law.

FIGURE 9.3
Community Property

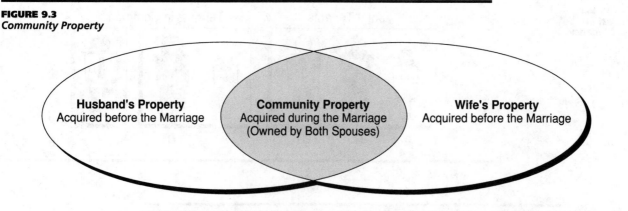

Husband's Property	Community Property	Wife's Property
Acquired before the Marriage	Acquired during the Marriage (Owned by Both Spouses)	Acquired before the Marriage

EXAMPLE: Bankruptcy or foreclosure may end the tenancy.

- Joint tenancy is destroyed if one of the unities is destroyed.

EXAMPLE: A, B and C are joint tenants, and C sells to D. A and B are still joint tenants, but they are tenants in common with D (unities of time and title are destroyed).

TENANCY BY THE ENTIRETY

Tenancy by the entirety is a special form of joint tenancy that exists only between *husband and wife.* Title to the property is placed in the marital unit, with each spouse owning an undivided interest in the property. Like joint tenancy, there is *right of survivorship.* This tenancy has five unities: time, title, interest, possession and *person. Unity of person* refers to the husband and wife's being considered one person.

During the owners' lives, title can be conveyed only by a deed *signed by both parties.* One party cannot sell his or her interest without the other, and there usually is no right of partition. Also, a creditor's lien cannot be levied against the property unless both parties are debtors of the creditor. Tenancy by entirety may be terminated by death of either spouse, divorce or mutual agreement of the parties. Tenancy by entirety is not recognized in all states.

COMMUNITY PROPERTY

The concept of **community property** is that property acquired by the joint efforts of husband and wife should be shared equally. In community property states two types of property rights are recognized: (1) property that is *separately owned* by either spouse and (2) community property, owned by *both spouses.* This is illustrated in Figure 9.3. Only a few states recognize community property.

The general rules for determining whether property is separate or community property are

- property owned *prior* to the marriage remains the *separate property* of the owning spouse;
- property acquired *during* the marriage is *community property,* and each spouse owns one half;
- property acquired by *gift or inheritance* is always *separate property,* even if acquired during the marriage.

If one spouse dies, the surviving spouse automatically owns *one-half* of the *community property. Separate property* is distributed according to the deceased's will. Therefore, there is *no right of survivorship.* Community property states do not recognize curtesy and dower rights. To convey or encumber community property requires the consent of *both parties.* To convey separate property, the consent of only the owning spouse is required.

**BEFORE READING THE NEXT SECTION, COMPLETE THE SECTION 1
REVIEW EXERCISES AND COMPARE YOUR ANSWERS WITH THE
SOLUTIONS AT THE END OF THE CHAPTER.**

SECTION 1
REVIEW EXERCISES

1. Name the form of ownership that best fits each description.
   a. _____ Applies only between husband and wife.
   b. _____ Owners may hold different percentages of ownership.
   c. _____ A spouse may own property either separately or with the other spouse.
   d. _____ Includes the right of survivorship.

2. Name the type of unity that best fits each description.
   a. _____ All tenants own equal percentage of the property.
   b. _____ All tenants acquired ownership at the same time.
   c. _____ All tenants were listed on the same deed.
   d. _____ All tenants have the right to occupy the property.

Are the following statements true (T) or false (F)?

3. ____ Right of survivorship means that the property passes to the deceased tenant's heirs.

4. ____ All tenants in both a joint tenancy and a tenancy in common have the right of partition.

5. ____ The simplest form of ownership is severalty.

6. ____ Tenants in common must be expressly stated.

7. ____ A tenant in common can sell his or her ownership to someone else and not end the tenancy.

8. ____ A tenancy by the entirety will be ended by the death of either spouse or by divorce.

9. ____ In community property states, property acquired during the marriage belongs to both spouses.

Supply the term that best matches each of the following descriptions.

10. _____ Tenants hold an undivided interest with no right of survivorship.

11. _____ A joint tenancy between husband and wife.

12. _____ Property held before the marriage remains the individual's property, whereas property acquired after the marriage is owned by both spouses.

13. _____ The simplest form of ownership.

14. _____ The tenants have the right to ask the courts to force a dissolution of the tenancy.

15. _____ A form of ownership that includes four unities.

16. _____ When a joint tenant dies, his or her share goes to the remaining joint tenants.

FORMS COMMONLY USED BY BUSINESS

Common forms of ownership used in business are illustrated in Figure 9.1.

PARTNERSHIPS

A **partnership** is an agreement of two or more people to conduct a business. Under the *Uniform Partnership Act,* a model act adopted by most states, title to real estate can be held in either the partners' names or the partnership's name. If property is held in the partnership's name it is called *tenancy in partnership.* Forms of partnership may include general partnerships, limited partnerships, joint ventures and syndications.

General Partnerships

The partners in a **general partnership** have a right to participate in the management of the partnership. However, a disadvantage is that the general partners have unlimited liability for all of the partnership debts.

EXAMPLE: A, B and C are general partners. A and B each contribute $100,000 to the partnership, and C contributes $500,000. If the partnership incurs debts totaling $1 million, the creditors will take all of the assets of the partnership and can then pursue the personal assets of all partners or any one partner for the remaining $300,000.

Note: In an attempt to avoid liability general partners may place personal assets in a trust.

Limited Partnerships

A **limited partnership** includes at least one general partner and one or more limited partners. The limited partners do not run the business and have limited liability. Limited partners are liable only to the extent of their investments.

CORPORATIONS

A **corporation** is an artificial person created by a *charter* in the state where it files. The corporation is run by its *board of directors* and exists forever or until it is dissolved. A corporation can hold title to real estate and, because it is regarded as a person, the property actually may be *held in severalty.*

Shareholders invest in the corporation by purchasing *stock.* The stock held by the shareholders is personal property. Shareholders' *liability is limited* to the amount of their investments.

There are several *advantages* to the corporation ownership form. These include

- *continuity of life*. Because a corporation is a person created by law, the death of its officers does not end the corporation.
- *limited liability*. If the corporation loses money, the stockholders can lose only the amount of their investment (i.e., the amount they paid for the stock).
- *ease of transferring ownership*. Because title to the real estate is held by the corporation, stockholders only have to sell their shares of stock to liquidate their investment.

There also are some *disadvantages* with title to real estate being held in the form of a corporation. These include

- *double taxation*. Because the corporation is a person, it must file an income tax return and pay tax on its profits. It then distributes the profits in the form of *dividends* to the shareholders. The shareholders declare the dividends as income on their personal income tax returns, thus paying income tax a second time on the corporation's income.
- *inability to pass along losses*. If a corporation suffers a loss, it cannot pass the loss to the shareholders. Thus, the shareholders cannot use the corporation's losses on their income tax returns to offset (i.e., shelter) income from other sources.

Note: Because a corporation can exist forever, it cannot hold title as a joint tenant with right of survivorship.

S CORPORATION

An **S corporation** (formally called a *subchapter S corporation*) combines the features of a general corporation and a partnership. Stockholders in an S corporation enjoy the *limited liability* feature of limited partnerships and general corporations but *avoid* the *double taxation* of profits of a general corporation.

Note: While an S corporation has some advantages, there are limitations that prevent all companies from being S corporations (e.g., there must be 75 or fewer shareholders).

LIMITED LIABILITY COMPANIES

A new form of ownership for businesses is a **limited liability company (LLC)**. An LLC includes the attractive features of corporations and limited partnerships. Under an LLC owners are called *members* and, like corporations, have *limited liability*. Unlike corporations, LLCs do not require all of the cumbersome administrative procedures, such as shareholders' meetings and publishing minutes. They also *avoid the double taxation* of regular corporations because they are taxed like a partnership. An advantage of LLCs over S corporations is that there are no restrictions on who can be in them. LLCs are best suited for a small, closely held business and are recognized in most states.

SYNDICATIONS

Syndications are formed by two or more people to operate a real estate investment. The syndication may take *any ownership form* but usually is a limited partnership. The syndicator is the general managing partner and the investors are limited partners.

 Note: Most syndicate investments are treated like securities and must comply with the rules of the Securities and Exchange Commission.

JOINT VENTURE

A **joint venture** is usually created for a single project. It is usually intended to last a limited time, and when the project is finished, the joint venture is dissolved. Joint ventures may take any ownership form.

BEFORE READING THE NEXT SECTION, COMPLETE THE SECTION 2 REVIEW EXERCISES AND COMPARE YOUR ANSWERS WITH THE SOLUTIONS AT THE END OF THE CHAPTER.

SECTION 2
REVIEW EXERCISES

1. Name the form of ownership that best fits each description.

   a. _____ Investors hold shares.

   b. _____ Partners have unlimited liability.

   c. _____ Owners are called members and have limited liability.

   d. _____ Most partners may not manage the business.

   e. _____ Includes a managing partner, many investors and usually takes the form of a limited partnership.

Are the following statements true (T) or false (F)?

2. ____ Under the Uniform Partnership Act, title to real estate can be held by partnerships.

3. ____ Limited partnerships include both limited and general partners.

4. ____ Corporations have limited life.

5. ____ If a corporation suffers a loss, it cannot pass the loss on to its shareholders.

6. ____ A joint venture is usually intended for a limited time.

Supply the term that best matches each of the following descriptions.

7. _____ Artificial person created by a charter

8. _____ Includes partners liable only up to the amount of their investment

9. _____ Business ownership with attractive features of limited liability, reduced administrative overhead and single taxation; owners called "members"

10. _____ Form of ownership created for a single project

11. _____ Agreement by two or more people to conduct a business

12. _____ Special form of corporation that combines the advantages of limited liability and single taxation

13. _____ All partners can manage the business and have unlimited liability

OTHER FORMS OF OWNERSHIP

TRUSTS

Any assets, including real estate, may be held in a **trust.** Trusts are created by a legal instrument such as a *trust agreement, will, trust deed* or *deed in trust.* There are three parties to a trust: **trustor, trustee** and **beneficiary.**

Trustor—the party who transfers the property into the trust.

Trustee—the party who holds legal title to the assets of the trust and manages the trust assets. The trustee is a *fiduciary* and has a special legal, confidential relationship to the beneficiary. The trustee's powers are defined in the document that establishes the trust.

Beneficiary—the party who benefits from the trust. This includes possession of the property and any income generated.

Note: An owner of property can create a trust and be both the trustor and the beneficiary.

SOME TYPES OF TRUSTS

Living Trusts

A living trust is one created by the owner of the property during their lifetime. These are also called *inter vivos trusts.* There are two types:

1. *Irrevocable trust*—These cannot be changed once they are created.
2. *Revocable trust*—The owner can be both trustor and beneficiary and retain the control and benefits of the property.

The goals of the living trust are to

- avoid the *cost* and *delay* associated with probate;
- provide for the *automatic transfer* of property when the owner dies; and
- provide for *management* of the property if the owner becomes mentally or physically incapacitated. This is done by naming an alternate (successor) trustee to take over.

Testamentary Trust

A testamentary trust is created by *will* after the property owner's death.

Land Trusts

Land trusts are recognized in several states. Real estate is the only asset of a **land trust**, and legal title to the property is held by the trustee. Real property is transferred into the trust by a *deed in trust*. The trustee who creates the trust may retain the beneficial interest in the real estate.

The trust is for a definite term, usually 20 years, but the time period can be extended. Also, the trustee may resign at any time and convey title to the beneficiary. The property is deeded out of trust using a *trustee's deed*.

Note: Because the beneficial interest created by a trust is personal property, land trusts convert the ownership benefits of real property to personal property. This beneficial interest can be pledged as collateral for a loan without a mortgage being placed in the public records.

Among the reasons to form a land trust are that it

- *provides privacy.* The trustee's name and not the beneficiary's are disclosed in the public records. However the beneficiary's identity may have to be revealed under certain circumstances, such as an IRS lien, a court order, building code violations and an arson investigation.
- *simplifies transferring ownership benefits.* Only requires an assignment by the trust's beneficiary, making a deed unnecessary.
- *avoids transfer tax.* Because beneficial interests in property in a trust are personal property, transfer taxes may be avoided in some states.
- *protects from encumbrances.* The beneficiary's interest is personal property. Most liens attaching to the beneficiary may not attach to the property in the land trust.
- *limits personal liability.* General partners may place personal assets in trust to avoid unlimited liability of partnership.
- *avoids questions of marital rights.* The beneficial interest is usually not subject to marital property rights of curtesy and dower.

Real Estate Investment Trust

The **real estate investment trust (REIT)** form of business organization was created by Congress. The purpose of REITs is to encourage small investors to pool their money and participate in larger real estate projects. Investors transfer title to real estate to a trustee, who agrees to manage the property for the benefit and profit of the investors (the beneficiaries). The investors receive certificates of ownership as evidence of their investments. These certificates are similar to shares of stock and can be freely traded to anyone else. The income from the trust is distributed to the certificate owners. If the REIT meets certain IRS conditions, it can qualify for tax-exempt status; therefore, profits (when received by the beneficiaries) are *taxed only once*.

CONDOMINIUMS

All states have passed *condominium acts* (also called *horizontal property acts, strata titles acts* or similar names) that recognize the formation of condominium ownership. In **condominium** ownership all occupants in a multiunit building own separate property (the unit they live in) and a specified share of the common areas. Common areas include the roof, hallways, parking lot, sidewalks, pool, yard, etc. Condominium ownership is usually used in residential buildings, but also can be used as commercial property and office buildings.

Condominium ownership has the following characteristics:

- Taxes are assessed against each unit and unit owners receive their own tax bills.
- Unit owners secure their own financing.
- Surveys and legal descriptions can be made on individual units.
- Each occupant is responsible for maintaining his or her unit.
- Each unit owner pays a monthly maintenance fee (also called *association dues*). Non-payment of the fee may create a lien against the owner's unit.
- A *reserve fund* is established for unusual costs (e.g., a new roof). If the fund is not adequate, the owners will be charged a *special assessment.*
- Title is conveyed by a *unit deed,* which conveys title to both the unit and the common elements.

The Declaration

The **declaration** is also known as the *master deed, declaration of conditions, covenants and restrictions* or *enabling declaration.* This document legally establishes the condominium. The declaration is filed with the county and usually includes a legal description and *recorded plat* of each unit. This is a three-dimensional description of the unit and common areas. The declaration also

- establishes the *condominium owners' association* board.
- gives the owners' association board power to assess and collect money to maintain the condominium.
- describes the individual units and common elements.
- provides for the possible use of professional property management and for insuring the property.
- establishes covenants and restrictions governing the property.
- establishes the percentage of the common elements owned. This is important because it may affect (a) the number of votes an owner has on matters brought before the association and (b) the amount the owner will be assessed for maintenance and real estate taxes.

Condominium Owners' Association

Articles of association create the **condominium owners' association**, which controls and maintains the common elements. It also enforces the condominium bylaws.

Bylaws

Through the **condominium bylaws,** the *board of directors* of a condominium owners' association regulates and administers the condominium. Items covered by the condominium's bylaws could

- define the power, authority and duties of officers and directors.
- establish the rights and duties of condominium owners.
- define the use and maintenance of the common areas.
- establish an operating budget.
- collect monthly maintenance charges and enforce a lien for unpaid amounts.
- provide for professional property management.
- establish rules for use of recreational facilities.
- provide for hazard and liability insurance.

CC&Rs

Covenants, conditions and restrictions (CC&R) are regulations filed by the condominium developer that must be followed by anyone purchasing a unit. These include restrictions to preserve the overall appearance of the building.

EXAMPLE: A condo's CC&Rs include rules prohibiting the installation of TV dishes and storing personal property on the balconies.

Right of First Refusal

If condominium owners wish to sell their units, the condominium's bylaws may give the association the *right of first refusal.* This right allows the association to purchase a unit at the fair market value before it is offered for sale to the general public. The bylaws require that unit owners notify the association of their intention to sell. Right of first refusal *cannot* be used to illegally discriminate in the sale of the unit.

COOPERATIVES

Cooperatives were an early method for tenants to gain control of the building they lived in. The tenants formed a nonprofit corporation that purchased the building. The *shares* of stock the tenants held in the corporation gave them a long-term lease right (called a *proprietary lease*) to occupy a unit in the building. A cooperative is created by filing *Articles of Incorporation.* The cooperative is governed by a board of directors elected by the tenants.

The corporation actually holds title to the real estate. Thus, tenants are said to hold *personal property* (the shares), even though they enjoy all the rights of owners of real estate. The corporation usually retains a *right of first refusal,* which requires that shareholders first offer their stock to the corporation before selling it to someone else. Taxes, maintenance expenses and mortgage liens are placed against the corporation, and tenants (shareholders) pay an assessment to cover the costs.

TIME-SHARING

Time-sharing allows an individual to own or lease a specified time interval in a property. Time-share is usually used for resort property, and the time-share owner has the right to occupy the unit for a specific time period (usually one week) each year. There are two legal formats:

1. *Time-share estate*—A *fee simple interest* in the unit is purchased. The purchaser owns the unit for the same time period each year in perpetuity.
2. *Time-share use*—The *contractual right to use* the property for the same time period each year for a certain number of years. After that period, any rights held by the owner end.

The time intervals are usually priced according to the season, and financing is usually available from the developer or a lender. In addition to the price of the time-share, there also usually are maintenance fees. A number of states have adopted time-share regulations to protect consumers and require proper disclosure (a prospectus is often required) before purchasing. Many states require people selling time-shares to hold a real estate license.

**COMPLETE THE SECTION 3 REVIEW EXERCISES AND COMPARE YOUR ANSWERS
WITH THE SOLUTIONS AT THE END OF THE CHAPTER.**

SECTION 3

REVIEW EXERCISES

1. Name the parties to a trust arrangement.

    a. _____

    b. _____

    c. _____

2. Name the type of trust arrangement that best matches each description.

    a. _____ Can retain control of the trust

    b. _____ Also called inter vivos trusts

    c. _____ Cannot be changed once created

    d. _____ Created by a will

3. Determine whether the description best fits a condominium or a cooperative.

    a. _____ Occupant holds shares

    b. _____ Occupants receive tax bills for their individual units

    c. _____ Occupant has a proprietary lease

    d. _____ Occupant receives a deed

Are the following statements true (T) or false (F)?

4. ____ The trustee is a fiduciary.

5. ____ An occupant in a cooperative actually owns personal property.

6. ____ One of the uses for a trust is to assist in estate planning purposes.

7. ____ When land is included in a trust, the benefit interest is real property.

8. ____ Investors in a real estate investment trust receive certificates of ownership.

Supply the term that best matches each of the following descriptions.

9. _____ A lease given by the corporation in a cooperative, allowing the shareholder to occupy a unit in the building

10. _____ The party who creates a trust

11. _____ Ownership in a multiunit building in which each unit is separately owned along with a percentage of the common elements

12. _____ A trust created by the owner during her lifetime

13. _____ A document that legally establishes a condominium

14. _____ Ownership of a time interval in a property

15. _____ An arrangement in which investors place title to real estate in a trust that is managed for the profit and benefit of the investors

16. _____ Rules used to run a condominium

17. _____ A three-party arrangement in which title to assets is held by a trustee

18. _____ Ownership of shares in a corporation that gives the owner the right to occupy a unit in a multiunit building

19. _____ A trust created by the owner after his death

20. _____ The party who holds title to assets held in a trust

21. _____ A trust in which the only asset is real estate

22. _____ A group of owners that controls the common elements in a condominium and enforces bylaws

SOLUTIONS
FOR SECTION REVIEW EXERCISES

SECTION 1

1. a. Entirety   b. Tenants in common   c. Community property
   d. Joint tenancy (also entirety)

2. a. Interest   b. Time   c. Title   d. Possession

3. FALSE Right of survivorship means that the property passes to the remaining tenants.

4. TRUE

5. TRUE

6. FALSE Joint tenants must be expressly stated, otherwise it is assumed to be a tenancy in common.

7. TRUE

8. TRUE

9. TRUE

10. Tenants in common

11. Tenancy by the entirety

12. Community property

13. Severalty

14. Right of partition

15. Joint tenancy

16. Right of survivorship

SECTION 2

1. a. Corporation or S corporation   b. General partnership
   c. Limited liability company (LLC)   d. Limited partnership   e. Syndication

2. TRUE

3. TRUE

4. FALSE One of the advantages of the corporate form of ownership is continuity of life.

5. TRUE

6. TRUE

7. Corporation

8. Limited partnership

9. Limited liability company

10. Joint venture

11. Partnership

12. S corporation

13. General partnership

SECTION 3

1. a. Trustor   b. Trustee   c. Beneficiary

2. a. Revocable trust   b. Living trusts   c. Irrevocable trusts
   d. Testamentary trust

3. a. Cooperative   b. Condominium   c. Cooperative   d. Condominium

4. TRUE

5. TRUE

6. TRUE

7. FALSE The beneficial interest created by a trust is personal property.

8. TRUE

9. Proprietary lease

10. Trustor

11. Condominium

12. living trust (inter vivos trust)

13. Declaration

14. Time-sharing

15. REIT

16. Condominium bylaws

17. Trust

18. Cooperative

19. Testamentary trust

20. Trustee

21. Land trust

22. Condominium owners' association

THIS IS THE LAST CHAPTER IN THE UNIT. TAKE THE UNIT III DIAGNOSTIC TEST

UNIT III
DIAGNOSTIC TEST

1. If Sarah owns a life estate, she could be prohibited from doing which of the following?

   a. Selling her ownership interest
   b. Leasing her ownership interest
   c. Leaving her interest in a will
   d. Living on the property

2. A tenant's lease requires the payment of all the property's operating expenses in addition to the rent. This type of lease is called a

   a. net lease.
   b. gross lease.
   c. variable lease.
   d. percentage lease.

3. Which of the following most likely would be considered community property if a couple lived in a community property state?

   a. Property owned by either spouse prior to the marriage
   b. Property purchased after they were married
   c. Property inherited by either spouse
   d. Property that was a gift to either spouse

4. If Amy grants a life estate to Bob and specifies that the property shall be transferred to Charley on the death of Bob, then

   a. Amy has a reversionary right.
   b. Bob is the remainderman.
   c. Charley is the remainderman.
   d. Charley has a reversionary right.

5. A tenant's lease requires that the amount of rent be based on the gross revenues of the business occupying the property. This type of lease is a

   a. net lease.
   b. gross lease.
   c. percentage lease.
   d. renegotiated lease.

6. In which of the following situations would ownership in severalty occur?

   a. A husband and wife sharing ownership in the same property
   b. Two or more people with the same ownership interest in the property
   c. Property owned by one person
   d. Two or more people holding the same form of ownership in a property

7. A portion of the homeowner's real estate is protected from creditors through which legal life estate?

   a. Dower
   b. Curtesy
   c. Special assessment
   d. Homestead

8. An apartment house has ten units that rent for $595 each per month and ten units that rent for $860 each per month. If the owner remodels the property at a cost of $15,000 and wishes to recover the cost within 6 months, how much will each unit's monthly rent need to be increased?

   a. $60
   b. $125
   c. $250
   d. $750

9. The right of survivorship is a characteristic of

   a. a cooperative.
   b. tenancy in common.
   c. joint tenancy.
   d. a condominium.

10. In states that recognize a homestead exemption the homeowner is protected against

   a. mechanics' liens.
   b. unsecured creditors.
   c. real estate tax liens.
   d. zoning changes.

11. Two days after a tenant's lease expired the owner discovered that the tenant was still in possession of the property. Which of the following describes the current occupancy?

    a. Encroachment
    b. Tenancy at sufferance
    c. Periodic tenancy
    d. A defeasible estate

12. Ellen, Jane and Tom were concurrent owners of a parcel of real estate. Jane died, and her interest passed according to her will to become part of her estate. Jane was a

    a. joint tenant.
    b. tenant by the entirety.
    c. limited partner.
    d. tenant in common.

13. Bob deeded a property to Katy and provided in the deed that if Katy ever used the property for the sale of alcoholic beverages, title would revert to Mary. The estate created by Bob is a

    a. life estate.
    b. fee simple absolute.
    c. defeasible estate.
    d. leasehold estate.

14. Kevin still has five months remaining on a one-year apartment lease. When Kevin moves to another city, he transfers possession of the apartment to Lois for the entire remaining term of the lease. Lois pays rent directly to Kevin. In this situation Kevin is a(n)

    a. sublessor.
    b. assignor.
    c. sublessee.
    d. lessor.

15. The ownership of shares of stock rather than real estate is a characteristic of

    a. condominiums.
    b. cooperatives.
    c. community property.
    d. land trusts.

16. John deeded a property to Bob for life and then to Mary when Bob dies. Mary has a

    a. life estate.
    b. remainder interest.
    c. fee simple estate.
    d. reversion interest.

17. Jack has a one-year leasehold interest in a shopping mall. The interest automatically renews itself at the end of each year. Jack's interest in the property is called a tenancy

    a. from period to period.
    b. at will.
    c. for years.
    d. at sufferance.

18. A resident of a unit in a multiunit building has a proprietary lease right. Title to the resident's building is held under which form of ownership?

    a. Joint tenancy
    b. Cooperative
    c. Condominium
    d. Land trust

19. Mary has a life estate in a property. As a life tenant Mary may

    a. convey her estate by will.
    b. commit waste.
    c. leave the estate to her heirs.
    d. lease the property.

20. Which of the following best describes a net lease?

    a. A lease-to-purchase agreement in which the landlord agrees to apply part of the monthly rent toward the ultimate purchase price of the property
    b. An agreement in which the tenant pays a fixed rent and the landlord pays all taxes, insurance and other charges on the property
    c. A lease in which the tenant pays rent plus maintenance and property charges
    d. A lease in which the tenant pays the landlord a percentage of the monthly income derived from the tenant's commercial use of the property

21. Which of the following forms of ownership includes the unities of time, title, interest and possession?

    a. Ownership in severalty
    b. Tenancy in common
    c. Joint tenancy
    d. Tenancy at sufferance

22. A life estate based on the life of a person other than the life tenant is called

    a. a remainder.
    b. a reversion.
    c. pur autre vie.
    d. curtesy.

23. A tenant who has a lease for a definite period of time that will terminate when the time has expired has a(n)

    a. periodic estate.
    b. estate at will.
    c. estate for years.
    d. estate at sufferance.

24. Which of the following is a characteristic of tenants in common?

    a. Each tenant is assumed by law to hold an equal interest in the land.
    b. Each tenant has an undivided interest in the property.
    c. Each tenant rents his or her portion of the property.
    d. Each tenant has the right of survivorship.

25. Sarah has a freehold estate in parcel of real estate that is not inheritable. The type of estate that Sarah has is a

    a. fee simple estate.
    b. defeasible estate.
    c. fee absolute estate.
    d. life estate.

26. A lease of fixed length that continually renews itself for like periods of time until notice is given to terminate is called a(n)

    a. periodic estate.
    b. estate at will.
    c. estate for years.
    d. estate at sufferance.

27. Bob has a fee simple ownership of a unit in a multiunit building, as well as ownership interest in a percentage of the common elements. Bob must have a

    a. cooperative.
    b. condominium.
    c. joint venture.
    d. syndication.

28. The system that recognizes private ownership of land is known as

    a. eminent domain.
    b. the allodial system.
    c. the government system.
    d. the feudal system.

29. A suit of partition is best described as a(n)

    a. court action to break up a co-ownership.
    b. action by local government to acquire private land.
    c. developer subdividing lots.
    d. challenge by property owners to a zoning change.

30. Mary, Bob and Fred are joint tenants in a tract of land Fred conveys his interest to Vern. Which of the following statements is true?

    a. Mary, Bob and Vern are tenants in common.
    b. Mary and Bob are still joint tenants.
    c. Mary, Bob and Vern are joint tenants.
    d. Vern has ownership in severalty.

31. John has a lease arrangement in which he pays a fixed rent and the landlord pays all the operating expenses of the property. John has a

    a. gross lease.
    b. net lease.
    c. percentage lease.
    d. ground lease.

32. A clause in a tenant's apartment lease that grants the tenant the right to renew the lease if notice is given before a specified date is called a(n)

    a. sublease clause.
    b. lease option clause.
    c. right of first refusal clause.
    d. assignment clause.

33. If a husband and wife own property as joint tenants and the wife conveys her interest to their son, the husband and the son will own the property as

    a. joint tenants.
    b. tenants in common.
    c. tenants by the entirety.
    d. tenants in severalty.

34. An "estate" in land refers to

   a. the amount of land owned.
   b. encumbrances on the property.
   c. the legal rights a person has in the property.
   d. how the property may be used.

35. The form of ownership that requires that the owners must be married is

   a. ownership in severalty.
   b. joint tenancy with right of survival.
   c. tenancy in common.
   d. tenancy by the entirety.

36. Jane held fee simple ownership to a vacant lot adjacent to a hospital and was persuaded to make a gift of the lot. She wanted to have some control over its use, so her attorney prepared her deed to convey ownership of the lot to the hospital "as long as it is used for hospital purposes." After completion of the gift, the hospital will own a

   a. fee simple estate.
   b. leasehold estate.
   c. life estate.
   d. defeasible estate.

37. A partition action is best defined as a

   a. subdivision of land.
   b. court proceeding to dissolve co-ownership of property.
   c. conversion of rental units to condominiums.
   d. conveyance of a life estate.

38. A father conveys ownership of his residence to his daughter but reserves for himself a life estate in the residence. The interest the daughter owns during her father's lifetime is

   a. pur autre vie.
   b. a remainder.
   c. a reversion.
   d. a leasehold.

39. A deed conveying title to a property to a town so long as the properly is used for "recreational purposes" conveys a:

   a. fee simple absolute.
   b. fee simple defeasible.
   c. leasehold interest.
   d. statutory life estate.

40. Mary purchases an apartment building and is told by her attorney that her ownership rights can continue forever and that no other person claims to be the owner or has any ownership control over the property. Mary holds a

   a. life estate.
   b. fee simple interest.
   c. determinable fee estate.
   d. statutory life estate.

41. Bob wishes to transfer two-thirds of his property to his wife and one-third to his son. This can be accomplished if they hold title as

   a. tenants in common.
   b. joint tenancy.
   c. tenants in severalty.
   d. tenants by the entirety.

42. All of the following are true regarding water rights of property owners *except*

   a. littoral rights refer to property bordering large bodies of water.
   b. under prior appropriation, owners must get permission to divert water.
   c. if water is nonnavigable, ownership extends to the water's edge.
   d. property bordering water may lose land through erosion.

43. A husband and wife plan to buy a house together, but each wants to leave his or her interest in the property in a will to their respective children from previous marriages. This can be accomplished by holding title as

   a. tenants in common.
   b. joint tenants.
   c. tenants in severalty.
   d. tenants by the entirety.

44. Bob, Ted and Alice are joint tenants. Alice sells her interest to Mary, and then Bob dies. Which of the following is now true?

   a. Ted and Mary are tenants in common.
   b. Bob's heirs, Mary and Ted are all joint tenants.
   c. Ted and Mary are joint tenants.
   d. Bob's heirs and Ted are joint tenants.

45. The husband's life estate in the wife's property is called

    a. curtesy.
    b. entirety.
    c. dower.
    d. homestead.

46. Of the four unities for joint tenancy, the one that also is required for tenants in common is:

    a. time.
    b. title.
    c. interest.
    d. possession.

47. A commercial lease calls for a minimum rent of $1,200 per month plus 4 percent of the annual gross business exceeding $150,000. If the total rent paid at the end of one year was $19,200, how much business did the tenant do during the year?

    a. $159,800
    b. $250,200
    c. $270,000
    d. $279,200

48. Dave and Sara are married. Under the laws of their state, any real property that either owns at the time of their marriage remains separate property. Further, any real property acquired by either party during the marriage (except by gift or inheritance) belongs to both of them equally. This form of ownership is called

    a. tenancy by the entirety.
    b. tenancy in common.
    c. community property.
    d. tenancy in severalty.

49. An advantage of using an S corporation rather than a regular corporation is

    a. less liability for the shareholders.
    b. officers have more control over the corporation.
    c. avoidance of double income taxation.
    d. property is exempt from real estate taxes.

50. Mary purchases an interest in a house located in the Easy Life Resort community. Mary is entitled to the right of possession only between August 1 and August 15 of each year. The type of ownership most likely purchased by Mary is

    a. cooperative.
    b. condominium.
    c. time-share.
    d. land trust.

U N I T

I I I

UNIT III
DIAGNOSTIC TEST
ANSWER SHEET

This sheet is perforated for easy pullout. Write your answers on this sheet as you complete the exercises. Refer to the diagnostic worksheet after completing the test to evaluate your strong and weak content areas. Review material in the appropriate chapter and sections.

1. _____

2. _____

3. _____

4. _____

5. _____

6. _____

7. _____

8. _____

9. _____

10. _____

11. _____

12. _____

13. _____

14. _____

15. _____

16. _____

17. _____

18. _____

19. _____

20. _____

21. _____

22. _____

23. _____

24. _____

25. _____

26. _____

27. _____

28. _____

29. _____

30. _____

31. _____

32. _____

33. _____

34. _____

35. _____

36. _____

37. _____

38. _____

39. _____

40. _____

41. _____

42. _____

43. _____

44. _____

45. _____

46. _____

47. _____

48. _____

49. _____

50. _____

UNIT
IV

TRANSFERRING
REAL ESTATE

CHAPTER 10

TRANSFERRING TITLE

At some point an owner of real estate may want to transfer the property to others. This chapter discusses how title to real estate is transferred. *Section 1* covers various methods by which title is transferred. *Section 2* covers several types of deeds that are used to transfer title. *Section 3* covers the parts of a deed. Remember to use the Study Tool Kit to reference key information and to update your progress checklist.

Learning Objectives

Track your progress as you work through the chapter by checking each learning objective when you complete it.

_____ List and describe the methods by which title to real estate can be transferred.

_____ List and describe the general requirements for a will.

_____ Describe a spouse's rights concerning wills.

_____ List and describe several types of involuntary transfer.

_____ List and describe the covenants included in a general warranty deed.

_____ Describe the function and purpose of the various types of deeds included in the chapter.

_____ List and describe the parts of a deed.

_____ List the general requirements for a deed.

Key Terms and Phrases

Track your progress as you work through the chapter by checking each term when you understand its meaning.

_____ Accession	_____ Devisee
_____ Acknowledgment	_____ Executor(trix)
_____ Adverse possession	_____ Further assurance
_____ Bargain and sale deed	_____ General warranty deed
_____ Beneficiary	_____ Grant deed
_____ Bequest	_____ Grantee
_____ Codicil	_____ Granting clause
_____ Covenant against encumbrances	_____ Grantor
_____ Deed	_____ Habendum clause
_____ Delivery and acceptance	_____ Holographic will
_____ Descent	_____ Intestate
_____ Devise	_____ Involuntary alienation

____ Nuncupative will

____ Probate

____ Quiet enjoyment

____ Quitclaim deed

____ Renouncing the will

____ Seisin

____ Special purpose deeds

____ Special warranty deed

____ Testate

____ Testator(trix)

____ Transfer tax

____ Voluntary alienation

____ Warranty forever

METHODS OF TRANSFERRING TITLE TO REAL ESTATE

Alienation is the legal term for transferring title to real estate. Title to real estate can be transferred either by **voluntary alienation,** with the owner's control and consent, or by **involuntary alienation,** without the control or consent of the owner. Figure 10.1 illustrates different methods of transferring title.

TRANSFER BY VOLUNTARY ALIENATION

Transfer by Will

If a person dies leaving a will we refer to this as having died **testate.** The deceased person who made the will is called a **testator** (if a male) or a **testatrix** (if a female). Disposition of property under a will is called a **devise** for real property (the "giver" is called *devisor*) and a **bequest** (or legacy) for personal property, including money. The party receiving property under a will is called a **devisee** for real property and a **beneficiary** (or legatee) for personal property.

EXAMPLE: A person making a will *devises* the house to a son and *bequeaths* an automobile to a daughter.

The will is filed with the *probate court* where the decedent resided. The legal process of **probate** is performed to (1) determine the validity of the will, (2) pay the debts of the estate and (3) distribute the estate's remaining assets. The person named in the will to oversee the administration of the will's provisions is called an **executor** (if a male) or an **executrix** (if a female).

An administrator (male) or administratrix (female) is appointed by the court when no will exists or no one was named in the will to oversee settlement of the estate.

Note: Some states have adopted the term personal representative to replace the terms executor, executrix and administrator. A personal representative refers to anyone responsible for administering an estate.

A **holographic will** is created by the *testator's writing* and is not witnessed. Several states recognize holographic wills as binding.

A **codicil** is an *amendment* or *addition* to a will. It must be dated, signed and witnessed, just as a will.

FIGURE 10.1
Methods of
Transferring Title

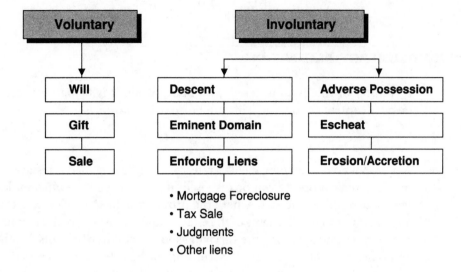

A **nuncupative** will is created *verbally* by a person who is near death. These wills usually can be used only to dispose of personal property.

Requirements for Making a Will

The requirements for making a legally valid will vary by state but generally include the following:

- *Legal age*—The testator must be of *legal age*. This is usually either 18 or 21 years of age.
- *Sound mind*—The testator must be of *sound mind* when the will is made. This means that the person must understand that a will is being drafted, the property he or she owns, and to whom it is being left.
- *In writing and signed*—The will must *usually* be in *writing, dated* and *signed by the testator*. Writing can include typed, printed or handwritten.
- *Free will*—The person making the will must not be under any *undue influence*.
- *Last will*—Proper language must be included in the will declaring it to be the *last will* of the testator.
- *Witnessed*—The will must be signed in the presence of two or more adult *witnesses* who are not beneficiaries under the will. Holographic wills are not witnessed.

Spouse's Rights

In most states, the surviving spouse is granted *additional rights* to the deceased spouse's property by statute.

- The surviving spouse has the option of **renouncing the will** and receiving benefits under state law. The surviving spouse receives a percentage of the estate as defined by state law.
- A will usually cannot supersede laws of *dower* and *curtesy* in states where these are recognized. (Dower and curtesy are covered in Chapter 7.)

Transfer by Gift or Sale

Two common ways title to real estate is *voluntarily* transferred are by *gift* and by *sale*. The owner either gives or sells the property to another party.

TRANSFER BY INVOLUNTARY ALIENATION

A transfer of title is considered *involuntary* when it is being transferred without the owner's control or consent. This can be done several ways.

Transfer by Descent

A person who dies *without a will* is referred to as having died **intestate.** In this situation the deceased's property will be disposed of according to the *intestacy laws* (also called *laws of descent*) in the state where the property is located. The court will appoint an *administrator* to pay the debts of the estate and then dispose of the remaining assets. The property is divided among the surviving spouse, children, parents, brothers and sisters, and other heirs of the deceased, according to the rules in the state's descent laws. The rules for the disposition of property through **descent** vary from state to state. Transferring title by descent is an example of *involuntary alienation* because the state, not the deceased, determines the disposition of the property.

Eminent Domain

Eminent domain is the government power to take private land for the public good through the process of *condemnation*. (Chapter 3, Government Powers, covers eminent domain.)

Lien Foreclosure Process

This includes foreclosure for various reasons, such as

- delinquent real estate taxes and special assessments,
- enforcement of mechanics' liens,
- enforcement of mortgage liens and
- enforcement of judgment liens. (Chapter 5 covers liens.)

Escheat

If a person dies *without a will* and has *no heirs*, the property will pass to the state through the government power of escheat. (Chapter 3, Government Powers, covers escheat.)

Adverse Possession

A person can obtain title to real estate by **adverse possession** (also called *title by prescription*). This is accomplished by using the property of another without the owner's consent and meeting other legal requirements. Requirements for acquiring title by adverse possession vary among states, but they generally contain the following provisions:

- *Use—Continuous use* of land for a number of years. If the use also includes a claim and color of title with payment of taxes, the time period may be reduced. Claim and color of title occurs when a legal instrument (such as a deed) appears to give someone title but is defective. Also, *tacking* (adding together) the time periods of subsequent adverse possessors may be permitted in some states.

- *Hostile*—The use is without the owner's consent or knowledge.
- *Open*—The use must be visible or well-known to others (also called *notorious*).

EXAMPLE: Erecting a fence or the construction of an improvement would be judged open use.

- *Exclusive*—Possession must be exclusive. Therefore, use cannot be shared with the owner.

EXAMPLE: A co-owner of a property cannot claim sole ownership through adverse possession.

 Note: Some land cannot be claimed under adverse possession. This includes land under Torrens and government-owned land. (Torrens is covered in Chapter 11.)

Transfer by Accession

Accession refers to additions to the land through natural or human causes. Human causes include *improvements* such as *fixtures* installed by a tenant that become part of the real estate. Natural causes include *accretion* (the gradual accumulation of land).

EXAMPLE: A property bordering a river receives increased land through the gradual deposit of sand carried by the river.

TRANSFER TAXES

Some states and local governments have passed **transfer tax** laws that require that tax stamps be purchased when title to real estate is transferred. The requirements of the laws and the amount of the tax vary but generally provide for the following:

- *Stamps* are purchased and attached to the deed.
- The amount of the tax is based on the selling price of the property.
- The tax is normally due when the *deed is recorded* and is normally paid by the *seller* of the property.
- The tax rate is assessed by states and local government entities where the property is located.
- Some types of transactions are *exempted* from the tax. These include transfers of government-owned properties, properties owned by tax-exempt organizations (e.g., churches, nonprofit groups), gifts of property and releases of security interests (release or reconveyance deeds).

BEFORE READING THE NEXT SECTION, COMPLETE THE SECTION 1 REVIEW EXERCISES AND COMPARE YOUR ANSWERS WITH THE SOLUTIONS AT THE END OF THE CHAPTER.

SECTION 1
REVIEW EXERCISES

1. Supply the term pertaining to wills that best matches each description.

   a. _____ Oversees the administration of the will's provisions

   b. _____ A woman who makes a will

c. _____ A house that is included in the will

d. _____ A person who receives an automobile under the will

e. _____ Verbal will made near death

f. _____ A person named to receive a house under a will

g. _____ A yacht that is included in the will

h. _____ Created in the testator's handwriting and not witnessed

i. _____ An amendment or change to the will

2. Name the requirement of a will that best matches each description.

a. _____ Should not be oral

b. _____ Cannot be beneficiaries of the will

c. _____ No undue influence to make the will

d. _____ Usually 18 or 21 years old

e. _____ Intended to be the final disposition of the property

f. _____ Cannot be legally insane

3. Supply the term pertaining to adverse possession that best matches each description.

a. _____ The use of the property by the adverse possessor is visible to others.

b. _____ The adverse possessor is the only party in possession of the property.

c. _____ The adverse possessor does not have the permission of the owner to use the property.

d. _____ The adverse possessor actually is using the property over time.

Are the following statements true (T) or false (F)?

4. ____ A person who complies with the state laws for adverse possession can acquire title to any parcel of land.

5. ____ Transfer taxes assessed when real estate is sold usually are paid by the seller of the property.

6. ____ One of probate's objectives is to pay the debts of the estate.

7. ____ If a person dies without a will, the property will be disposed of by following the federal laws of descent.

8. ____ All real estate transactions are subject to state transfer taxes.

Supply the term that best matches each of the following descriptions.

9. _____ An action taken by a surviving spouse to receive increased benefits from the deceased spouse's estate as defined by state law

10. _____ A tax imposed by state and local law when title to real estate passes from one party to another

11. _____ Rules that are followed to determine the disposition of property for someone who has died intestate

12. _____ Transferring title with the owner's consent

13. _____ The legal process of settling a person's will

14. _____ Having died and left a will

15. _____ Taking title to real estate through use of the property without the owner's consent

16. _____ Transferring title without the owner's consent

17. _____ Having died without leaving a will

TYPES OF DEEDS

A **deed** is a written instrument that conveys ownership interests in real estate from a grantor to a grantee. A *grantor* is the party *giving* an ownership interest. A *grantee* is the party *receiving* the ownership interest. There are many types of deeds, but this sections focuses on the ones that are used most frequently. (Ownership interests are covered in Chapter 7.)

EXAMPLE: In a real estate sales transaction the seller is the grantor (gives title) and the buyer is the grantee (receives title).

GENERAL WARRANTY DEED

The **general warranty deed** provides the greatest protection for the *grantee* because the grantor provides various *covenants* or *guarantees* that good and marketable title is being given to the grantee. (See Chapter 11, Recording Title, for a description of good and marketable title.) Because of the guarantees included in this type of deed, the general warranty deed gives the grantee the greatest assurance of title and is therefore the most desirable.

Covenants found in general warranty deeds include *seisin, encumbrances, quiet enjoyment, further assurance* and *warranty forever.*

Covenant of Seisin

Seisin (also spelled seizin) gives assurance that the grantor has the power and authority to convey title and has the type of ownership interest that is being conveyed by the deed.

EXAMPLE: Able gives Baker a general warranty deed that states that Able is conveying fee simple ownership. In fact, Able has only a determinable fee. The covenant of seisin is violated.

EXAMPLE: Able gives Baker a general warranty deed conveying title to a property, but in fact, the property is held in tenancy by the entirety and Able's spouse has not signed the deed. This is a violation of seisin because Able does not have sole power to convey the title.

Covenant Against Encumbrances

The **covenant against encumbrances** gives assurance that there are no encumbrances on the property except those stated in the deed.

EXAMPLE: Able gives Baker a general warranty deed that does not list any encumbrances when, in fact, there is a mortgage lien on the property. The covenant against encumbrances is violated, and Able may be liable to Baker for damages.

Covenant of Quiet Enjoyment

The covenant of **quiet enjoyment** provides assurance that the title being given by the grantor is good against other parties. In other words, the grantee may use the property without interference because no one else has a superior title claim to the property.

Covenant of Further Assurance

With the covenant of **further assurance,** the grantor promises to perform any reasonable acts necessary to correct defects in the title.

EXAMPLE: Able gives Baker a deed that contains a misspelling of Able's name. Through the covenant of further assurance, Able has agreed to provide any additional documents necessary to correct the mistake.

Covenant of Warranty Forever

The covenant of **warranty forever** gives assurance that the grantor will pay for expenses to defend the title if it is challenged by someone claiming superior title or compensation for losses if the title fails. This covenant is also called *warranty of title.*

 Note: To be legally entitled to a general warranty deed, the purchaser should be sure this provision is specified in the sales contract. If the contract does not specify the type of deed to be given, the seller could provide a quitclaim or other type of deed that would not be as desirable to the purchaser.

SPECIAL WARRANTY DEED

Because of the risk, sellers may not want to provide covenants or guarantees against title defects that occurred before they held title to a property. Sellers may limit their risk by giving a buyer a **special warranty deed** (also called a *limited warranty deed*). The special warranty deed does not contain all of the guarantees included in a general warranty deed. Rather, it warrants that the grantor has title and limits the grantor's liability to encumbrances against the property that occurred *after* he or she acquired the title. The grantor could include additional warranties by specifically stating them in the deed.

This type of deed is usually used by persons acting on behalf of the owner, such as executors, administrators or custodians.

EXAMPLE: A person files for bankruptcy and the property is sold to satisfy creditors. The trustee handling the property gives a special warranty deed to the buyer that guarantees title against claims only during the time the trustee held the title.

BARGAIN AND SALE DEEDS

Bargain and sale deeds usually have no expressed warranties. Some deeds add a covenant that the title is free from encumbrances while the grantor held title. Those without covenants are similar to quitclaim deeds. In either case there is an implication that the grantor holds title and has the right to convey it.

QUITCLAIM DEEDS

A **quitclaim deed** provides the *least protection* to the *grantee.* While a quitclaim deed conveys whatever title is held by the grantor (if any), the grantor does not provide any covenants with the deed. Quitclaim deeds are often used to cure technical defects in a title and to eliminate the potential claims against the property from persons with an uncertain or potential interest in the property.

EXAMPLE: Able's name is misspelled on the title. To correct the misspelled name, Able executes a quitclaim deed with the correct spelling.

GRANT DEEDS

Grant deeds are similar to special warranty deeds. The grantor is not providing a warranty against acts of previous owners. The grantor is ensuring only that no encumbrances were incurred while title was held by the grantor (except those that may be stated in the deed) and that the grantor has not conveyed title to anyone else.

SPECIAL PURPOSE DEEDS

Special purpose deeds are used in many states to handle frequently occurring transactions. These deeds are used in particular situations and usually take the form of either quitclaim or special warranty deeds. Listed below are a few of the special purpose deeds.

- *Administrator's deed*—When a person dies *intestate,* the court appoints an administrator to dispose of the deceased person's assets and pay the debts of the estate. An *administrator's deed* is used to convey title to purchasers of the real estate.
- *Executor's deed*—When a person dies *testate,* an executor is appointed to dispose of the assets. An *executor's deed* is given to the grantee to convey title to assets of the estate.
- *Sheriff's deed*—Used to transfer title to property sold by court order to satisfy a judgment.
- *Guardian's deed*—If a person is legally incompetent, the court appoints a guardian to administer the assets. A person acquiring title from the guardian is given a *guardian's deed* to convey title.
- *Referee's deed*—Used to convey title to property in a *foreclosure sale.*
- *Tax deed*—Used to convey title to property sold for delinquent taxes.
- *Deed in trust*—Used to establish a land trust. The *trustor* (the party creating the trust) is the *grantor* and gives the deed to the *trustee.* The deed in trust usually accompanies the trust agreement that outlines the trustee's actions. (Trusts are covered in Chapter 9.)
- *Trustee's deed* (also called *deed of reconveyance*)—Used by a trustee to convey title *out* of a trust.
- *Trust deed* (also called *deed of trust)*—Used when a lender requests security for repayment of a real estate loan. (Trust deed is covered in Chapter 20, Loan Instruments.)
- *Release deed* (also called a *deed of release*)—Used by a lender to release the claim against the property created by the trust deed.
- *Deed in lieu of foreclosure*—If a borrower is in default on a loan secured by the property, he or she may give the lender a *deed in lieu of foreclosure.* The grantor is giving the lender title to the property in exchange for terminating the loan. (Deed in lieu of foreclosure is covered in Chapter 21.)
- *Gift deed*—Used to convey real estate as a gift.

 Tip: Deed in trust, trust deed, trustee's deed and release deed sound similar but they perform different functions. See Figure 10.2 for a summary of the functions each performs.

FIGURE 10.2
Deeds

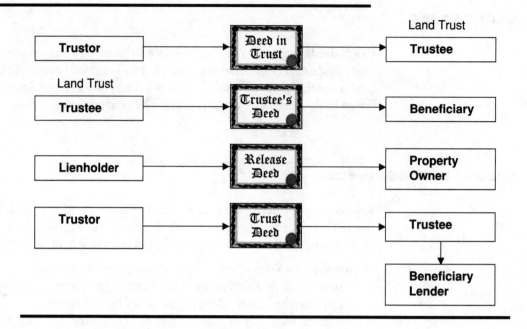

BEFORE READING THE NEXT SECTION, COMPLETE THE SECTION 2
REVIEW EXERCISES AND COMPARE YOUR ANSWERS WITH THE
SOLUTIONS AT THE END OF THE CHAPTER.

SECTION 2
REVIEW EXERCISES

1. Name the guarantee (covenant) being given by the grantor that best matches each description.

   a. _____ The grantee wants assurance that the title being given by the grantor is superior to anyone else's claim.

   b. _____ The grantee wants assurance that there are no liens or easements on the property.

   c. _____ The grantee wants assurance that the grantor will defend the title against claims from others.

   d. _____ The grantee wants assurance that the grantor will correct defects in the title.

   e. _____ The grantee wants assurance that the grantor has the authority to convey title.

2. Name the type of deed used with trusts that best matches each description.

   a. _____ Used in connection with a real estate loan

   b. _____ Used to transfer title out of the trust

   c. _____ Used to transfer title into the trust

Are the following statements true (T) or false (F)?

3. ____ A home equity loan lien on the property is not included in the general warranty deed given by the grantor. The covenant against seisin is violated.

4. ____ A quitclaim deed imposes the least liability on the grantee.

5. ____ Bargain and sale deeds can come with or without covenants.

Supply the term that best matches each of the following descriptions.

6. _____ A type of deed that contains no guarantees and is frequently used for clearing technical defects in the title

7. _____ The party receiving an ownership interest

8. _____ A deed similar to a special warranty deed in which grantors guarantee only that there are no encumbrances for the time they held title

9. _____ A written agreement that transfers title from one party to another

10. _____ A type of deed that includes several covenants or guarantees given by the grantor

PARTS OF A DEED

A deed can transfer title only if it is in proper legal form and conforms to the requirements of the state in which the property is located. Thus, a deed must include all of the parts *required by state law*. This section discusses the various parts that may be included in a deed and a list of basic deed requirements.

REQUIRED PARTS OF A DEED

Grantor

The **grantor** is the party giving title. The grantor's name should be the same name used when title was acquired, otherwise the discrepancy must be explained. Other guidelines for the grantor:

- There can be no misspellings in the grantor name(s).
- The *marital status* of the grantor should be identified.
- The grantor must have *legal capacity.* This generally means to be an adult (usually 18) and mentally competent. (See Chapter 14 for details on competent parties.)
- The deed must be *signed;* the signature may be that of an attorney-in-fact. In some states the grantor's spouse must also sign (even if the spouse's name is not on the title) to release marital and homestead rights. In most states a grantor who cannot write may sign by a mark, usually an "X," in the presence of witnesses.
- In some states the grantor's signature must be witnessed. This is called **acknowledgment.**
- Deeds conveyed by corporations must be signed by an authorized *corporate officer,* and some states may require that the *corporate seal* be attached to the deed.

Grantee

The **grantee** is the party receiving title to the property. The name of the grantee is required; however, the grantee's *signature is not necessary.* The grantee does not have to have legal capacity; however, the grantee must have been alive when *the deed was delivered.*

Consideration

Consideration is anything of value being given in exchange for title. In a deed this is usually stated as a dollar amount given to the grantor. (Chapter 14 covers consideration.)

Granting Clause

The **granting clause** (also called *words of conveyance*) states the grantor's intention to transfer title to the grantee and the type of ownership interest being conveyed. The granting clause also indicates the type of deed being used. Typical granting clauses for some deeds are

- "Grant, sell and convey with general warranty of title," in a warranty deed;
- "Grant, bargain and sell," in a bargain and sale deed;
- "Release, convey and quitclaim," in a quitclaim deed.

Habendum Clause

The **habendum clause** defines or limits the estate that is being granted to the grantee. Any limitations to the estate being conveyed should be included in this clause. This clause *must agree* with the granting clause. If there is a difference between the clauses, the estate described in the *granting clause takes precedence*. This clause starts with the words "To have and to hold."

EXAMPLE: "To have and to hold for the life of the grantee" creates a life estate.

Reservations or Exceptions

This section of the deed is used to describe limits to the estate being conveyed. The grantor would use this section to keep a right.

EXAMPLE: The grantor may keep an easement on the property.

Deed Restrictions (Subject to Clause)

Deed restrictions limit future use of the property. While these restrictions could cover almost anything, they cannot be used to discriminate. (Chapter 4 covers deed restrictions.)

Legal Description

A legal description of the property must be included in the deed to clearly identify the property being conveyed. A *street address is insufficient* because it may change over time and does not identify the exact boundaries of the property. (Chapter 6 covers legal descriptions.)

Appurtenances

Appurtenances are used to convey all property rights associated with the land.

EXAMPLE: Transfer of riparian rights or easements belonging to the land.

Acknowledgment

An **acknowledgment** is a voluntary declaration before a *notary public* or *officer of the court*. The acknowledgment verifies that the grantor's *signature is genuine* and the signing is a *voluntary act*. It is designed to prevent forged documents. In some states an acknowledgment is not needed to make the deed valid but is needed to record the deed in the public records.

Delivery and Acceptance

The moment title actually passes is at the time of **delivery and acceptance:** when the grantor *delivers* a valid deed that is *accepted* by the grantee. Silence by the grantee or recording of the deed is considered acceptance. The delivery may be to the grantee directly or a third party such as the *escrowee.* If the deed is delivered to the escrowee, title passes *when the deal is finished* but reverts back to the time when the deed was delivered to the escrowee. (Chapter 12 covers closing in escrow.)

Recording

Recording the deed in the public records is necessary for the title to be good against third parties. (Chapter 11 covers recording title.)

REQUIREMENTS FOR A VALID DEED

Deed requirements vary among states; however, the basic requirements usually include some or all of the following:

- The deed must be *in writing* (required by the statute of frauds).
- The *names* of grantor and grantee must appear.
- The grantor must have *legal capacity* (cannot be a minor or legally incompetent person).
- *Consideration* must be described.
- A *granting clause* or words of conveyance must be included.
- A *habendum clause* must define the quality and quantity of the ownership interest being conveyed.
- There must be a *legal description* of the property being transferred.
- The deed must be *signed* by the *grantor.*
- There must be *delivery and acceptance* of the deed.
- To be legally effective against third parties, the deed should be *recorded.*

COMPLETE THE SECTION 3 REVIEW EXERCISES AND COMPARE YOUR ANSWERS WITH THE SOLUTIONS AT THE END OF THE CHAPTER.

SECTION 3
REVIEW EXERCISES

1. Name the part of a deed that best fits each description.
   a. _____ Party who must sign the deed
   b. _____ Starts with the words "To have and to hold"
   c. _____ Describes the property being transferred
   d. _____ Something of value that is given
   e. _____ States the type of ownership being given

   Are the following statements true (T) or false (F)?

2. ____ If there is a difference between the habendum and granting clauses, the habendum clause takes precedence.

3. ____ Both the grantor and the grantee are usually required to sign the deed to make it valid.

4. ____ An acknowledgment is needed in all states to make a deed valid.

5. ____ The purpose of deed restrictions is to limit the future use of the property.

Supply the term that best matches each of the following descriptions.

6. _____ A declaration verifying that the signature on the deed is genuine

7. _____ Defines or limits the estate being conveyed

8. _____ The party receiving title

9. _____ The moment when title to property actually passes

SOLUTIONS
FOR SECTION REVIEW EXERCISES

SECTION 1

1. a. Executor(trix)   b. Testatrix   c. Devise   d. Beneficiary
   e. Nuncupative will   f. Devisee   g. Bequest   h. Holographic will   i. Codicil
2. a. In writing and signed   b. Two or more witnesses   c. Free will
   d. Legal age   e. Last will   f. Sound mind
3. a. Open   b. Exclusive   c. Hostile   d. Use
4. FALSE Some land cannot be claimed by adverse possession. This includes land under Torrens and land owned by the government.
5. TRUE
6. TRUE
7. FALSE Rules for disposing of property through descent are state laws.
8. FALSE Some types of transactions are exempted from transfer taxes. These typically include transactions between government bodies, partition transfers and transfers from nonprofit organizations.
9. Renouncing the will
10. Transfer taxes
11. Intestacy laws or laws of descent
12. Voluntary alienation
13. Probate
14. Testate
15. Adverse possession
16. Involuntary alienation
17. Intestate

SECTION 2

1. a. Quiet enjoyment   b. Encumbrances   c. Warranty forever
   d. Further assurance   e. Seisin
2. a. Trust deed (deed of trust)   b. Trustee's deed   c. Deeds in trust
3. FALSE The covenant against encumbrance would be violated.
4. FALSE The deed imposes the least liability on the grantor since there are no guarantees included in the deed.
5. TRUE
6. Quitclaim deed
7. Grantee
8. Grant deed
9. Deed
10. General warranty deed

SECTION 3

1. a. Grantor   b. Habendum clause   c. Legal description   d. Consideration
   e. Granting clause
2. FALSE The granting clause will take precedence.

3. FALSE Only the grantor (the party giving title) is required to sign the deed. The grantee's name must be given, but it is usually not necessary to have the signature.

4. FALSE In some states it is not needed to make the deed valid, although it may be needed to record the deed.

5. TRUE

6. Acknowledgment

7. Habendum clause

8. Grantee

9. Delivery and acceptance

CHAPTER 11
RECORDING TITLE

The last chapter discussed various ways in which title to real estate can be transferred. This chapter covers recording title and using what are called *evidences of title*. *Section 1* covers general information regarding public records and recording. *Section 2* covers three evidences of title. *Section 3* covers title insurance, which is a fourth evidence of title. Remember to use the Study Tool Kit to reference key information and to update your progress checklist.

Learning Objectives

Track your progress as you work through the chapter by checking each learning objective when you complete it.

____ Explain why title recording is important.

____ Explain the difference between constructive and actual notice.

____ List and describe four evidences of title.

____ Describe the process of recording under the Torrens system.

____ Explain the differences between lender's and owner's title policies.

____ List and describe the parts of a title insurance policy.

____ Describe the different coverages provided by title insurance and coverage exceptions.

Key Terms and Phrases

Track your progress as you work through the chapter by checking each term when you understand its meaning.

____ Abstract

____ Abstract of title with lawyer's opinion

____ Actual notice

____ Certificate of title

____ Chain of title

____ Color of title

____ Commitment to insure

____ Constructive notice

____ Gap

____ Marketable title

____ Perfecting title

____ Quiet title lawsuit

____ Subrogation

____ Title cloud

____ Title insurance

____ Title report

____ Torrens system

PUBLIC RECORDS AND RECORDING

NECESSITY FOR RECORDING

The reason for recording real estate documents in the public records is to give *legal, public* and *constructive notice* to the world of an ownership interest in real estate. This accomplishes two objectives. *First,* purchasers of real estate can rely on the public records to determine the condition of title, and *second,* recording provides protection for owners with existing interests in the property.

Recording acts are laws explaining the rules for recording real estate documents; they vary by state and county. Under recording acts all documents are recorded in the county where the land is located. The recording function is usually performed by either a recorder of deeds or the county clerk.

Note: Some liens, such as real estate tax liens, usually are not recorded.

Notice

There are two types of notice, constructive notice and actual notice.

1. **Constructive notice** refers to information that has been made public. The law presumes a person knows information that has been made available to the public. Therefore, buyers and other interested parties are presumed to have inspected the public records and to have knowledge of all information in the records. Possession of the property also gives constructive notice of possible rights.

   EXAMPLE: A lien is listed in the county's records for a property. If the buyers fail to inspect the records and later find out about the lien, they cannot hold the sellers responsible for not disclosing it because the law assumes the buyers inspected the public records and therefore knew of the lien.

2. **Actual notice** refers to information a person has actually gained by reading, seeing or hearing.

   EXAMPLE: In the example listed above if the buyers did inspect the public records before purchasing the property, they would have seen a record of the lien and therefore had actual knowledge.

ESTABLISHING TITLE

Cloud on Title

A **title cloud** (also called *title defect*) is any claim or encumbrance that may impair an owner's title on the property. The process of removing defects is called **perfecting title** (also called *clearing clouds on the title*).

Title Search

A *title search* (also called a *title examination*) is an examination of the public records to determine who has rights in the property and the condition of the title (what defects, if any, there are on the title).

The title records are referenced through property *indexes*. A county may maintain a number of indexes, including alphabetical indexes by grantor or grantee names and by property number, among others. A search also will include a check of *tax records* to determine whether there are any delinquent tax payments and of *court records* to determine whether there are any judgments against the property.

Abstract

An **abstract** is a history of all documents affecting title. It is prepared by an abstractor after searching the public records. Documents affecting title include deeds, easements, tax liens, mortgage liens and releases, and judgments.

Chain of Title

A **chain of title** is a listing of all the conveyances from owner to owner of the property up to the present. If an owner is missing, it is called a **gap**.

Quiet Title Lawsuit

If there is a defect in the title or uncertainty as to a party's legal rights in the property, a **quiet title lawsuit** can be initiated to remove clouds on the title.

Documents Not Recorded

Not all documents need to be recorded. Real estate taxes and special assessments need not be recorded. Other liens that by law are against all property of a person do not have to be recorded.

Marketable Title

A **marketable title** is one that is free from *major* defects that would deter potential buyers of the property. Major defects could include mortgagees' and mechanics' liens because a buyer probably would not want to take title with these encumbrances. The four types of evidences of title covered in Sections 2 and 3 are used as proof that title is marketable.

Tip: Remember that marketable title does not mean the title must be free from all defects because a buyer may accept the property with certain defects, such as a subdivision's deed restrictions or an existing mortgage.

Color of Title

Color of title refers to a claim of title that appears to be good but is not.

EXAMPLE: A gives to B a deed for land which A does not own. In this example A gives the appearance of title.

FOREIGN LANGUAGE DOCUMENTS

Documents written in a language other than English usually *do not* provide constructive notice. Recording statutes may require that an English translation be prepared and filed with the foreign language document.

BEFORE READING THE NEXT SECTION, COMPLETE THE SECTION 1
REVIEW EXERCISES AND COMPARE YOUR ANSWERS WITH THE
SOLUTIONS AT THE END OF THE CHAPTER.

SECTION 1
REVIEW EXERCISES

1. List the types of records that might be referenced in a title search.

   a. _____

   b. _____

   c. _____

2. What does the system of public recording for real estate accomplish?

   a. _____

   b. _____

Are the following statements true (T) or false(F)?

3. ____ The law assumes prospective buyers know information that is in the public records.

4. ____ A buyer is interested in a property located in county A, but both the buyer and seller live in county B. The prospective buyer should inspect the public records in county A.

5. ____ A prospective buyer inspects the public records and sees a document written in Polish, which the buyer does not speak. The buyer still is considered to have notice of the document's contents.

6. ____ All documents must be recorded to be valid.

7. ____ A gap may occur in an abstract.

8. ____ A property owner who needs to clear a problem with the title may file a quiet title lawsuit.

Supply the term that best matches each of the following descriptions.

9. _____ The process of removing a cloud on a property's title

10. _____ A brief history of all documents affecting title

11. _____ A listing of all of the property's conveyances up to the present

12. _____ Title free from defects that would deter potential buyers

13. _____ Information the law presumes the public knows

14. _____ Appears to be title but is not

15. _____ Information gained by seeing, hearing or reading

16. _____ A claim or encumbrance that may impair the owner's title

SECTION 2
EVIDENCES OF TITLE

EVIDENCES OF TITLE

In a real estate transaction the grantee (the party acquiring title) wants some assurance that the grantor is the actual owner of the property and is giving *marketable title*. We can't *guarantee* that a person is the property owner because there could have been mistakes or forgeries in the past, resulting in defects in that person's ownership. However, we can obtain *evidence* or *proof* of the ownership. There are four generally recognized evidences that can be used to establish ownership of the property: (1) abstract with attorney's opinion, (2) Torrens certificate, (3) certificate of title and (4) title insurance.

Abstract of Title with Lawyer's Opinion

As described in Section 1, an abstract is a brief history of the documents affecting title. An abstractor researches the public records and creates the abstract for the property. This search must be done with care, or the abstractor could be liable for negligence. The abstractor does not *guarantee the title* or give an *opinion* of the condition of the title.

The buyer's lawyer examines the abstract and writes a report called *Attorney's Opinion of Title.* Thus, there is an **abstract of title with lawyer's opinion.** The lawyer is providing an opinion of the title's status but does not provide any guarantees of title.

The Torrens System

The **Torrens system** of land registration is used for *assuring* and *recording* title. This system is used in only a small number of states. The procedure for registration is as follows:

1. A written application to register the title is made to the court in the county where the land is located. The court has the title examined by official title examiners, who report the results to the court.
2. A public notice is issued so that anyone who wishes to can contest the title.
3. If the examination results are satisfactory and there are no successful challenges to the title the court directs the Registrar of Titles to register the applicant's title. In Torrens the *registration rather than delivery of the deed passes title.*
4. Once registered, a *Torrens certificate* is prepared in duplicate with signature cards to guard against forgeries. The Torrens certificate lists the type of title and any encumbrances against the property.

Under Torrens a certificate holder who has suffered a loss due to a successful claim against the title may file a claim for reimbursement against the registrar. The registrar is not required to go to court to defend the certificate holder. In some states, a cash indemnity fund is usually maintained to cover claims.

Tip: Remember, land held in Torrens cannot be acquired by adverse possession.

Certificate of Title

A **certificate of title** is prepared by a title examiner. After examining the public records, the examiner issues a certificate expressing an opinion of the title status. The certificate states the name of the owner and lists liens and other encumbrances. The registrar keeps the original certificate of title and issues a duplicate to the owner. No abstract is prepared with the certificate.

Special Note

Abstracts and certificates do not guarantee title, because there could be undetected defects.

EXAMPLE: Deeds issued by legally incompetent persons, forged deeds, deeds without release of marital rights (dower, curtesy), failure of a co-owner to join in the conveyance.

Title Insurance

The last evidence of title is *title insurance.* This is discussed in Section 3.

Tip: Note that a deed by itself is not considered sufficient evidence of title. A deed will transfer whatever ownership the grantor actually has but is not evidence the grantor has any ownership rights.

BEFORE READING THE NEXT SECTION, COMPLETE THE SECTION 2 REVIEW EXERCISES AND COMPARE YOUR ANSWERS WITH THE SOLUTIONS AT THE END OF THE CHAPTER.

SECTION 2
REVIEW EXERCISES

1. Name the evidence of title that best fits each description.
   a. _____ Used for recording and assuring title
   b. _____ A document prepared after researching the public records
   c. _____ A report written by a lawyer after reviewing an abstract
   d. _____ Method of registration that includes a court proceeding
   e. _____ The combination of a lawyer's opinion and an abstract
   f. _____ A public hearing held before title is recorded
   g. _____ Issued by a title examiner after reviewing the public records and expressing an opinion of the title

Are the following statements true (T) or false (F)?

2. ____ A deed is usually considered an evidence of title.
3. ____ Evidences of title are used to guarantee that title is good.
4. ____ Torrens certificates are issued in duplicate.
5. ____ A Torrens certificate holder who has suffered a loss may be compensated by the Torrens system.

SECTION 3
TITLE INSURANCE

DESCRIPTION

A title company issues a **title insurance** policy that agrees to indemnify the owner against loss due to title defects. The policy is issued after an acceptable title search has been performed, and a one-time premium is charged when the policy is issued.

POLICY TYPES

Various forms of title insurance policies are issued, depending on which party is to be protected.

A *mortgagee's* or *lender's title insurance policy* protects the lender against known and hidden title defects.

An *owner's title insurance policy* protects the property owner.

There are several differences between an owner's and a lender's policy.

- An owner's policy insures for the amount paid for the property, whereas a lender's policy insures for the loan amount and decreases as the loan is repaid.
- A lender's policy has no exceptions for claims that could be determined from physical inspection of the property, whereas an owner's policy may include such exceptions.
- A lender's policy is *assignable* (to subsequent owners of the loan), whereas an owner's policy is not.

A *leasehold policy* insures that lessees (renters) have a valid lease from the owner.

A *certificate of sale policy* insures a purchaser of real estate at a court sale.

POLICY COVERAGE

Like other types of insurance, title policies may be written for different coverage levels. As a general rule coverage for all title policies includes the cost of defending the title against claims. Through **subrogation** the title company obtains the insured's legal rights to defend a claim against the title.

Standard coverage insures against defects found in public records, forged documents, incompetent grantors, incorrect marital statements, undisclosed spousal interests and improperly delivered deeds.

Extended coverage insures against standard risks plus defects found only by inspection of the property, or by a survey, unrecorded liens and easements, mining claims and water rights and rights of parties in possession of the property.

Policies do *not* cover title defects and liens listed in the policy, title defects known to the buyer or changes in land use as a result of zoning changes.

TITLE INSURANCE PROCESS

1. The title company receives a request for a title insurance policy and examines the public records (title search).
2. The results of the title search are reviewed and a **title report** is issued. The report lists anyone who has an ownership interest in the property.
3. A *preliminary binder,* which is the **commitment to insure,** is issued by the title company.
4. A title policy is issued by the title company.

PARTS OF A POLICY

Agreement to insure—The maximum amount the company will pay is listed. This is usually the face amount of the policy. In the event of a claim, the insurance company pays the legal costs to defend the title.

Description of the subject matter—this includes

- A description of the estate or interest being insured.
- A legal description of the property and improvements.

Schedule of exceptions—This section lists discovered defects and encumbrances not insured by the policy. Standard exceptions include unrecorded documents, such as special assessments and mechanics' liens; loss by government action, such as eminent domain and zoning changes; and losses due to the rights of parties in possession of the property.

Conditions and stipulations—This section describes how the company will handle claims under the policy. It includes the right of subrogation if the company elects to fight the claim.

Endorsements—This section includes any additional coverages purchased by the insured.

COMPLETE THE SECTION 3 REVIEW EXERCISES AND COMPARE YOUR ANSWERS WITH THE SOLUTIONS AT THE END OF THE CHAPTER.

SECTION 3
REVIEW EXERCISES

1. List the type of title insurance policy that best fits each description.

   a. _____ Based on the loan amount

   b. _____ Used by renters

   c. _____ Protects buyer's ownership interest in the property

   d. _____ Used by a purchaser at a court sale

   e. _____ Has a decreasing insured amount as the loan is repaid

2. List the part of a title insurance policy that best fits each description.

   a. _____ Lists defects not insured by the policy

   b. _____ Includes any additional coverages purchased by the insured

   c. _____ Includes the maximum amount that will be paid under the policy

   d. _____ Describes the property and improvements

   e. _____ Includes the right of subrogation

Are the following statements true (T) or false (F)?

3. ____ A lender's policy is assignable; an owner's policy is not.

4. ____ An annual insurance premium is charged for most title insurance policies.

5. ____ Unrecorded liens and easements are included in standard insurance coverages.

Supply the term that best matches each of the following descriptions.

6. _____ A binder issued by the title insurance company

7. _____ Gives the title insurance company the right to defend against a claim

SOLUTIONS
FOR SECTION REVIEW EXERCISES

SECTION 1

1. a. Title record indexes   b. Tax records   c. Court records
2. a. Purchasers can determine the condition of title.
   b. Provides protection for current owner's interests in the property.
3. TRUE
4. TRUE
5. FALSE Documents written in a language other than English usually do not provide notice.
6. FALSE Some liens, such as special assessments and real estate taxes, do not have to be recorded.
7. FALSE Gaps occur in a chain of title.
8. TRUE
9. Perfecting title
10. Abstract
11. Chain of title
12. Marketable title
13. Constructive notice
14. Color of title
15. Actual notice
16. Title cloud

SECTION 2

1. a. Torrens   b. Abstract of title   c. Attorney's opinion of title   d. Torrens
   e. Abstract of title with lawyer's opinion   f. Torrens   g. Certificate of title
2. FALSE A deed does not provide evidence of the grantor's ownership interest in the property.
3. FALSE Because of the possibility of past recording mistakes or fraud, title cannot be guaranteed.
4. TRUE
5. TRUE

SECTION 3

1. a. Lender's policy   b. Leasehold policy   c. Owner's policy
   d. Certificate of sale policy   e. Lender's policy
2. a. Schedule of exceptions   b. Endorsements   c. Agreement to insure
   d. Description of the subject matter   e. Conditions and stipulations
3. TRUE
4. FALSE Title insurance is usually a one-time premium, to be paid at closing.
5. FALSE Protection from these defects is included in extended title insurance coverage.
6. Commitment to insure
7. Subrogation

CHAPTER 12
REAL ESTATE CLOSINGS

The ultimate objective in a real estate transaction is to transfer title in the property. The real estate closing is the final step in that process. *Section 1* describes the closing process and the Real Estate Settlement Procedures Act (RESPA), which is the critical law to be followed during closings. *Section 2* describes the preparation of the closing statement and how to perform proration calculations. *Section 3* includes an example of completing a residential real estate closing statement. Remember to use the Study Tool Kit to reference key information and to update your progress checklist.

Learning Objectives

Track your progress as you work through the chapter by checking each learning objective when you complete it.

____ Identify and explain the difference between the two types of closing methods.

____ Identify where closings would likely be held and who would act as the closing agent.

____ Describe the process of closing in escrow.

____ List the escrow agent's duties.

____ Describe the purpose of RESPA.

____ List the types of transactions that are and are not covered by RESPA.

____ Describe the various RESPA requirements, including those related to disclosure, kickbacks and escrow monies.

____ Identify the types of expenses the buyer and seller incur at closing.

____ Describe the difference between prepaid and accrued expenses.

____ List the three approaches used to calculate prorations.

____ Calculate prepaid and accrued expenses, using the actual number of days in the year approach.

____ Calculate prepaid and accrued expenses, using the actual number of days in the month approach.

____ Calculate prepaid and accrued expenses, using the statutory month approach.

Key Terms and Phrases

Track your progress as you work through the chapter by checking each term when you understand its meaning.

____ Accrued expenses	____ Escrow closing
____ Actual number of days in month method	____ Final walkthrough
	____ Prepaid expenses
____ Actual number of days in the year method	____ Prorated expenses
____ Closing agent	____ Real Estate Settlement Procedures Act (RESPA)
____ Closing statement	____ Settlement statement
____ Doctrine of relation back	____ Statutory month method
____ Good faith estimate	____ Uniform Settlement Statement (HUD-1)
____ Escrow agent	

SECTION 1

THE CLOSING PROCESS AND RESPA

THE CLOSING PROCESS

The two common methods used to perform closings are (1) a face-to-face closing meeting held by all of the parties (or their representatives) or (2) an **escrow closing,** in which an *escrow agent* is appointed to handle all of the closing activities without the parties present.

The following activities are usually performed in the closing process:

- An *exchange of documents,* including evidence of marketable title by the seller and delivery of the deed to the buyer
- The preparation of a *closing statement* that shows all the financial entries of the transaction and the net amount owed by the buyer and due to the seller
- *Disbursement of funds,* including payment for the property to the seller

Where Closings Are Held

The closing can be held at any location that is mutually agreeable to the parties involved in the transaction. Closings are normally held at one of the following locations:

- The buyer's lending institution
- The office of either the buyer's or seller's lawyer
- The title company
- The escrow company
- The broker's office

Closing Agent

The **closing agent** prepares the closing statement, schedules the closing meeting and conducts the meeting. One of the following usually acts as the closing agent:
- A representative of the title company
- Lawyer for either the buyer or seller

- A representative of the lender

Closing in Escrow

Escrow Agent. The **escrow agent** is a disinterested (neutral) third party who coordinates the closing activities. The escrow agent is usually a lawyer, a title company, a lending institution's escrow department or an escrow company. A broker who acts as an escrow agent may *not take a commission* in the transaction because he or she would not be considered a neutral third party.

The Escrow Procedure. The buyer and seller select an escrow agent and enter into an *escrow agreement* that includes details of the transaction and instructions to the escrow agent. When the escrow agreement is signed, the broker delivers the earnest money to the escrow agent. Escrow agent duties usually include the following:

- Order the title to be examined to assure marketable title
- Collect all documents related to the transaction
- Deposit and disburse funds
- Record the deed and mortgage (if a loan is used to purchase property)
- Return parties to former status if sale cannot be completed

Doctrine of Relation Back. The **doctrine of relation back** pertains to the *effective date* that title passes if the closing is performed in escrow. The general rule is that *title passes when the deed is delivered.* However, in an escrow closing a period of time may pass while the escrow agent collects all of the documents and monies necessary to complete the transaction. The deed may be delivered to the escrow agent prior to completion of the transaction. In this situation title will not actually pass until the *transaction is completed* by the escrow agent; however, through the doctrine of relation back, title will have passed *as of the date the deed was delivered into escrow.* Thus, the death of either the buyer or the seller before the transaction is complete will not invalidate the transaction.

EXAMPLE: A seller deposits a deed with the escrow agent and dies. Later all escrow conditions are met. The deed passes title to the buyer *as of the date it was delivered to the escrow agent.*

Closing Documents

A closing usually requires that a large number of documents be delivered at the closing meeting or to the escrow agent. Some of the typical documents delivered by the buyer and seller are listed below.

- *The deed*—The seller delivers a deed of the type (e.g., general warranty deed) specified in the sales contract.
- *Current receipts*—The seller provides receipts showing that the real estate taxes, water bills and other property expenses have been paid.
- *Property inspection reports*—The seller provides inspection reports covering termite inspections, septic systems, etc.
- *Lien releases*—The seller provides documentation showing the release of liens and easements on the property.
- *Bill of sale*—A bill of sale is used to transfer any personal property included in the sale.
- *Loan documentation*—The buyer's lender provides various loan documents to be signed by the buyer.
- *Survey*—The buyer is usually required to obtain a current survey.
- *Homeowner's insurance policy*—The buyer must show evidence that the property is adequately insured as required by the lender.

- *Title insurance*—If required by the sales contract, the seller may provide title insurance or other evidence of title, such as an abstract. The buyer may provide the title policy if required by the lender. (Evidences of title are covered in Chapter 11.)
- *Certificate of occupancy*—The seller may be required to provide a certificate of occupancy, approved by the local government, if the building is new construction or has been improved.

IRS Reporting

To report the seller's sales proceeds to the IRS, Form 1099-S must be completed by the closing agent for all residential real estate transactions. The seller's social security number and sales price are included on the form. If the closing agent does not report the transaction, the responsibility shifts to the lender. If there is no lender, the broker is responsible and, ultimately, the parties to the transaction.

Property Inspection

On the day of closing, or shortly before, the buyer usually inspects the property being purchased. This is also called a **final walkthrough.** The purpose is to ensure that fixtures and personal property included in the transaction are still present, that no damage has been done to the property and that any required repairs have been made. The buyer also should verify that all appliances are operating.

REAL ESTATE SETTLEMENT PROCEDURES ACT (RESPA)

Purpose of RESPA

The purpose of the **Real Estate Settlement Procedures Act (RESPA)** is to ensure that buyers and sellers in a residential real estate transaction are informed of all settlement costs. RESPA, which is administered by the Department of Housing and Urban Development (HUD), *does not* set prices for settlement services.

Transactions Covered by RESPA

1. Loans made on one- to four-unit *residential* property (includes condos and cooperatives).
2. Real estate transactions financed using *new purchase mortgage loans.*
3. A *federally related* first mortgage. This includes
   - loans made by banks and thrifts insured by the Federal Deposit Insurance Corporation (FDIC);
   - loans insured by the Federal Housing Administration (FHA) or guaranteed by the Department of Veterans Affairs (VA);
   - loans administered by the Department of Housing and Urban Development (HUD); and
   - loans intended to be sold in the secondary mortgage market to GNMA, FNMA or FHLMC.
     (FDIC, FHA, VA, and the secondary mortgage market will all be discussed in the Unit VII chapters.)
4. Transactions involving loan refinance are covered if the *original loan* was covered by RESPA.

Transactions Not Covered by RESPA

While most *residential* real estate transactions are covered by RESPA, there are a few exceptions. These exceptions occur

- if the only financing in the transaction is by the seller, such as in an installment sales contract.
- if the buyer pays all cash for the property.
- if the buyer assumes the seller's mortgage (here there would be no *new* first mortgage).

RESPA Requirements

1. Special Information Booklet. A HUD booklet called "Settlement Costs, A HUD Guide" must be given to the borrower when *the loan application is filed* or *mailed within three business days.*

    Part 1 of the book describes settlement procedures, the nature of charges and the buyer's rights under RESPA. *Part 2* of the book explains the Uniform Settlement Statement and each item that appears on the statement.

2. Good faith estimate of settlement costs. The lender must provide a **good faith estimate** of the closing costs the borrower may incur at the time of the loan application or within three business days (Disclosure Statement Form 5121). If the lender requires that a particular title company or other service provider be used, the lender must disclose whether it has a business relationship with that provider and estimate the charges.

3. Uniform Settlement Statement (Form HUD-1). The **Uniform Settlement Statement** (Form **HUD-1**) must be used. This statement details all the financial particulars of the transaction. The lender must itemize all of the finance charges on the statement and must retain the closing statements for two years.

4. Prohibition against kickbacks. RESPA prohibits referral fees (kickbacks) between the lender and settlement service providers. Commission splitting between brokers is permitted under this law.

    The lender must provide the borrower with the name, address and telephone number of any service provider involved in the transaction.

    EXAMPLE: Lawyers and title insurance companies used by the lender.

    RESPA also prohibits the seller from requiring that the buyer purchase title insurance from a particular title company as a condition of the sale.

5. Controlled business arrangements. Congress amended RESPA and created an exception to the prohibition against kickbacks between service providers. If the party referring the buyer has a business relationship with the service provider, fees paid are *not considered kickbacks* if
    - the business arrangement is disclosed to the buyer.
    - a written estimate of charges is disclosed to the buyer.
    - the buyer is not required to use a particular service provider.

6. Rules for escrows monies. The lender often requires that a reserve for payment of real estate taxes and property insurance be established in an escrow account with the lender. RESPA provides limitations on the reserve amount the lender can collect from the buyer at closing.

    Lenders can collect an amount sufficient to pay the accrued expenses plus two months (or $\frac{1}{6}$ of the yearly amount). Once payments begin, the borrower cannot be required to pay more than $\frac{1}{12}$ the annual taxes in each month.

7. Other RESPA provisions
    - The lender is prohibited from charging a fee for the preparation of the settlement statement.
    - Borrowers or their agents are allowed to view the settlement statement one business day prior to closing.
    - Lawsuits for RESPA violations must be filed in a U.S. district court within one year of the violation.

TRUTH-IN-LENDING ACT

If the real estate transaction includes a mortgage loan, then the Truth-in-Lending Act may apply and its disclosure provisions must be followed. The purpose of this law is to inform the buyer of the cost of borrowing money. This law is discussed in detail in Chapter 23.

BEFORE READING THE NEXT SECTION, COMPLETE THE SECTION 1 REVIEW EXERCISES AND COMPARE YOUR ANSWERS WITH THE SOLUTIONS AT THE END OF THE CHAPTER.

SECTION 1
REVIEW EXERCISES

1. For each of the following transactions determine whether they would or would not be covered under RESPA.

   a. _____ Purchase of a three-unit dwelling, using a real estate loan, in which the owner will occupy one of the units.

   b. _____ Purchase of a single-family residence in which the buyer assumes the existing mortgage

   c. _____ Purchase of a condo using a real estate loan

   d. _____ Purchase of a store using a real estate loan

   e. _____ Purchase of a single-family residence using an installment sale contract loan

Are the following statements true (T) or false (F)?

2. ____ When closing in escrow, the seller's broker holds the earnest money until closing.

3. ____ Under RESPA, a HUD booklet describing settlement costs must be given to the seller.

4. ____ An IRS Form 1099-S must be completed by the closing agent for all residential closing transactions.

5. ____ The escrow agent usually disburses funds, collects documents and orders a title examination.

6. ____ Under RESPA, standard fees are set for real estate closings.

7. ____ When closing in escrow, the broker and seller enter into an escrow agreement.

8. ____ Under RESPA, the amount of reserve money held by the lender to pay taxes is limited to the accrued amount at the time of closing plus two months.

9. ____ The deed is delivered to the escrow agent on June 1 and the closing is completed on June 8. In this situation title will pass on June 8.

Supply the term that best matches each of the following descriptions.

10. _____ A form that details financial information of the transaction, required by RESPA to be used at closings

11. _____ The law requiring that certain disclosures be made as part of the closing process

12. _____ The final inspection of the property by the buyer shortly before the closing

13. _____ A closing procedure in which all of the closing details are handled by an appointed agent rather than by a face-to-face meeting between buyer and seller

14. _____ The party that conducts the closing meeting
15. _____ An estimate provided to the buyer of the expected closing costs the buyer will incur
16. _____ In escrow closings, it refers to the effective date that title passes rather than the actual date the deed was delivered

---

SECTION 2

THE CLOSING STATEMENT AND PRORATIONS

PREPARATION OF THE CLOSING STATEMENT

The **closing statement** (also called a **settlement statement**) is used for a detailed accounting of funds in a real estate transaction. Closing statements are usually prepared by the escrow agent, title company or the lawyers for the buyer and the seller. While brokers are usually not involved in the preparation of the closing statement, they should understand the information it includes and how it is completed.

DISPOSITION OF CHARGES

There are a number of charges involved in a real estate closing. These may be charged (debited on the closing statement) to the buyer or the seller. Listed below are the common charges included in a closing and what party usually incurs the charge.

Note: RESPA does not specify which party pays for the various fees. This is left to local custom and laws.

Charges Usually Paid by the Buyer

* *Recording fees*—The buyers pay fees to record their title.

EXAMPLE: Recording fees for the deed.

* *Loan fees*—The buyer (borrower) pays fees associated with obtaining or assuming a loan.

EXAMPLE: Points on loans, loan application fee and credit report.

* *Title fees*—The buyer (borrower) is responsible for title fees required to satisfy the lender.

EXAMPLE: Lender's title insurance policy.

* *Appraisal*—Whichever party ordered the appraisal pays; however, the buyer is usually required by the lender to order an appraisal and therefore usually is charged.
* *Insurance*—Homeowner's insurance is usually prepaid by the buyer at closing.
* *Survey*—A spot survey is a map showing the dimensions and location of improvements on the lot. The buyer's lender usually requires the survey and therefore, the buyer is charged.

The sales contract may require that the seller furnish a survey, in which case the seller would be charged.

- *Real estate taxes*—Any real estate taxes that were *prepaid* by the seller are reimbursed by the buyer.
- *Inspection fees*—An inspection by a professional inspection company for structural, electrical or plumbing defects may be paid by the buyer.
- *Lawyer's fees*—Fees for a lawyer hired by the buyer.
- *Buyer's broker commission*—If buyers hire a real estate broker to represent them, they may be required to pay a commission to the broker.

Charges Usually Paid by the Seller

- *Seller's broker commission*—It the broker was hired by the seller to sell this property, the seller will pay the commission.
- *Recording fees*—The seller is responsible for fees needed to clear title.

EXAMPLE: Satisfaction of a mechanic's lien or release of the existing mortgage lien.

- *State transfer tax*—Most states require a transfer tax, and this often is paid by the seller.
- *Title fees*—The seller is usually responsible for fees to prove good title.

EXAMPLE: Owner's title policy or an abstract of title.

- *Real estate tax*—Any real estate taxes that have *accrued* and not been paid are the responsibility of the seller.
- *Inspection fees*—Some municipalities require a building and or termite inspection. Also, soil and septic system tests may be required.
- *Lawyer's fees*—Fees for a lawyer hired by the seller.

PRORATIONS

Some expenses involved in a real estate transaction are not entered in total but must be prorated (shared) between the buyer and seller. **Prorated expenses** are either accrued or prepaid.

Prepaid expenses have been paid by the seller *in advance*. The seller should be reimbursed (credited) and the buyer debited.

EXAMPLE: Property insurance, heating fuel in the property's tank.

Accrued expenses are expenses that have been accumulated by the seller but not paid. The buyer should be reimbursed for the expense (credited) and the seller debited.

EXAMPLE: Interest on the seller's mortgage, if assumed by the buyer, is usually accrued.

Guidelines for Prorations

Techniques and practices for calculating prorations vary by the custom practiced in the property's location. These are general guidelines followed in handling prorations.

- Prorations *include the day of closing.* Often the day of closing is usually a day of expense and income for the seller.
- *Proration calculations* are usually computed using the 30 days in a month method (the statutory month method or actual number of days in the year method). Proration calculations will be explained in more detail later in the section.

- *Interest on the mortgage* is usually *paid in arrears,* meaning it is charged at the end of the month. This is an accrued expense, and if the mortgage is being assumed by the buyer, the buyer should be credited for the days the seller occupied the property since the last mortgage payment.
- *Special assessments* are due at the beginning of the year. Whoever is the owner on this date is responsible for the entire payment and it is not prorated.
- *Rent security deposits* are not prorated. They are credited in total to the buyer and debited to the seller.
- *Rent payments* are prorated using the actual number of days in the month method (see below). The rents are usually prepaid, so the buyer is credited and the seller debited.
- *Real estate taxes* could be paid in advance, paid in arrears, or a combination of both, depending on state and local government taxing rules where the property is located. If *prepaid,* the *seller* is *credited,* and if paid *in arrears* (accrued), the *buyer is credited.*

Methods of Prorations

While the rules and customs for performing proration calculations vary among states, three generally accepted methods are used.

1. Actual Number of Days in the Year Method

    The **actual number of days in the year method** calculates the proration using the actual number of days in the proration period. This is the most accurate method.

    Step 1. Divide the yearly expense by 365 days (366 days for a leap year) to determine the daily charge.

    Step 2. Calculate the actual number of days in the proration period.

    Step 3. Multiply the daily charge by the actual number of days in the proration period.

2. Statutory Month Method

    The **statutory month method** assumes that every month has 30 days. This method also can use a statutory year, which assumes there are 360 days in the year (i.e., 30 days × 12 months = 360 days).

    Step 1. Divide the yearly expense by 12 to find the *monthly* charge.

    Step 2. Divide the monthly charge by 30 to find the *daily* charge.

    Step 3. Multiply the monthly and daily charges by the number of months and days in the proration period.

3. Actual Number of Days in the Month Method

    The **actual number of days in the month method** is a variation of the statutory month method. A monthly charge is calculated like the statutory month method but uses the actual number of days in the month of closing to find the daily charge.

    Step 1. Divide the yearly expense by 12 to find the *monthly* charge.

    Step 2. Divide the monthly charge by the actual number of days in the month of closing to find the *daily* charge.

    Step 3. Multiply the monthly and daily charges by the number of months and days, respectively, in the proration period.

Prorating Accrued Expenses

Following is an example of prorating an *accrued expense* using the three proration methods discussed above.

Facts. Real estate taxes are paid in arrears at the end of the year. Closing is on July 22. The yearly tax bill is $3,400. What is the prorated amount to be debited to the seller and credited to the buyer? (If the current year's tax bill has not yet been issued, the parties usually agree to use last year's bill and adjust for any known changes, such as a change in assessment.)

Using the Actual Number of Days in the Year Method.

Step 1. Calculate the daily charge: $3,400 ÷ 365 = $9.315 per day.

Step 2. Calculate the actual number of days: Jan., 31 + Feb., 28 + Mar., 31 + Apr., 30 + May, 31 + June, 30 + July, 22 = 203 total days.

Step 3. Multiply the daily charge by the number of days: $9.315 × 203 = $1,890.945. Seller owes the buyer $1,890.95.

Using the Statutory Month Method.

Step 1. Calculate the monthly charge: $3,400 ÷ 12 = $283.333 per month.

Step 2. Calculate the daily charge: $283.333 ÷ 30 = $9.444 per day.

Step 3. Apply monthly and daily charges:

$$\begin{array}{cc} \$\ 283.333 & \$\ 9.444 \\ \times\quad\quad 6 & \times\quad\quad 22 \\ \hline \$1,699.998\ + & \$207.768 \end{array} = \$1,907.766.\ \text{Seller owes the buyer \$1,907.77.}$$

Using the Actual Number of Days in the Month Method.

Step 1. Calculate the monthly charge: $3,400 ÷ 12 = $283.333 per month.

Step 2. Calculate the daily charge: $283.333 ÷ 31 = $9.139 per day.

Step 3. Apply monthly and daily charges:

$$\begin{array}{cc} \$\ 283.333 & \$\ 9.139 \\ \times\quad\quad 6 & \times\quad\quad 22 \\ \hline \$1,699.998\ + & \$201.058 \end{array} = \$1,901.056.\ \text{Seller owes the buyer \$1,901.06.}$$

Hint: When computing prorations carry all answers to three decimals and round to the nearest cent (two decimals) after the last step. This will ensure a more accurate answer.

Prorating Prepaid Expenses

Following is an example of prorating a *prepaid* expense using the statutory and actual number of days methods discussed above.

Facts. The monthly homeowner's association fee has been prepaid on the first of the month. The fee is $150 per month. Closing is on July 23. What is the prorated amount to be credited to the seller and debited to the buyer?

Using the Actual Number of Days in the Month/Year Method.

Step 1. Calculate the daily charge: (use 31 days since closing is in July). $150.00 ÷ 31 = $4.839 per day.

Step 2. Calculate the actual number of days: July 23 through July 31 = nine days to prorate.

Step 3. Multiply daily charge by number of days: $4.839 × 9 = $43.551. The buyer owes the seller $43.55.

Using the Statutory Month Method.

Step 1. Calculate the daily charge: $150 ÷ 30 = $5 per day.

Step 2. Calculate the number of days to prorate: July 23 through July 31 = eight (total number of days).

Step 3. Apply the daily charge: $5 × 8 = $40 that buyer owes the seller.

**BEFORE READING THE NEXT SECTION, COMPLETE THE SECTION 2
REVIEW EXERCISES AND COMPARE YOUR ANSWERS WITH THE
SOLUTIONS AT THE END OF THE CHAPTER.**

SECTION 2
REVIEW EXERCISES

In each of the following situations determine the amount and appropriate closing statement entries. Use the statutory month or year method and include the day of closing in all prorations.

1. The rent for a two-unit apartment building was paid on the first of the month. The apartments rented for $900 and $600, and closing is on June 15.

   Buyer _____ $ _____
   Seller _____ $ _____

2. The buyer assumes the $50,000 mortgage on a property set for closing on April 20. The loan is at 10 percent and has been paid through March 31.

   Buyer _____ $ _____
   Seller _____ $ _____

3. Heating oil in the tank of an apartment building cost $.80 a gallon. There are 100 gallons in the tank, and the closing is to be held on March 18.

   Buyer _____ $ _____
   Seller _____ $ _____

4. The annual real estate taxes of $1,200 have been paid through the end of the year. The closing is scheduled for November 15.

   Buyer _____ $ _____
   Seller _____ $ _____

5. The annual real estate taxes of $3,600 have not been paid. The closing is scheduled for the last day in February.

   Buyer _____ $ _____
   Seller _____ $ _____

6. A three-year insurance policy was purchased by the seller for $36,000 on May 10, 1994. The remainder of the policy term will be transferred to the buyer at closing, which is scheduled for August 20, 1995.

   Buyer _____ $ _____
   Seller _____ $ _____

Are the following statements true (T) or false (F)?

7. ____ Closing statements usually are prepared by the seller's broker.

8. ____ Recording fees to transfer title usually are paid by the buyer.

9. ____ Homeowner's insurance usually is a prepaid item for the buyer at closing.

10. ____ Transfer taxes charged by the state usually are paid by the buyer at closing.

11. ____ Rent security deposits are an example of an expense that needs to be prorated at closing.

Supply the term that best matches each of the following descriptions.

12. _____ A method of proration using the actual number of days in the proration period

13. _____ An expense that has occurred but has not been paid

14. _____ A document used for detailing the financial information in a closing

15. _____ Expenses that are shared between the buyer and seller

16. _____ A method of proration that treats every month as if it had 30 days

17. _____ An expense that has been paid but not yet incurred

18. _____ A variation of the statutory month method that takes into account the actual number of days in the month of closing

SECTION 3

PREPARATION OF A CLOSING STATEMENT

STATEMENT FORMAT

Several formats may be used for the settlement statement. The format in the example in this section (see Figure 12.1) uses the HUD Uniform Settlement Statement (Form HUD-1). Also, because local customs determine which party is to be charged certain closing expenses, some of the charges on the settlement statement in the example may be treated differently in various areas of the country.

The Uniform Settlement Statement is divided into several sections. Sections A through I contain administrative information regarding the transaction. Sections J, K and L contain the transaction's financial information.

Borrower's (Buyer's) Transaction Entries (Section J)

- *Borrower's debits*—These are listed in lines 100 through 112 and are totaled on line 120.
- *Borrower's credits*—These are listed in lines 201 through 219 and are totaled on line 220.
- *Final entries*—The borrower's total credits (line 302) are subtracted from the borrower's total charges (line 301) to determine the cash due from (or to) the borrower at closing (line 303).

Seller's Transaction Entries (Section K)

- *Seller's credits*—These are listed in lines 400 through 412 and are totaled on line 420.
- *Seller's debits*—These are listed in lines 501 through 519 and are totaled on line 520.
- *Final entries*—The seller's total debits (line 602) are subtracted from the seller's total credits (line 601) to determine the cash due to (or from) the seller at closing (line 603).

Settlement Charges for Both the Borrower (Buyer) and Seller (Section L)

This section lists all of the settlement charges in the transaction. The buyer's settlement charges are in the left column and the seller's in the right column and are totaled on line 1400.

REAL ESTATE SETTLEMENT EXAMPLE

Following is information pertaining to a typical real estate closing and instructions on how to complete the closing statement. The closing settlement statement in Figure 12.1

FIGURE 12.1
Settlement Statement

A. **Settlement Statement**

U.S. Department of Housing
and Urban Development

OMB No. 2502-0265 (Exp. 12-31-86)

B. Type of Loan

1. ☐ FHA 2. ☐ FmHA 3. ☐ Conv. Unins.	6. File Number	7. Loan Number	8. Mortgage Insurance Case Number
4. ☐ VA 5. ☒ Conv. Ins.	951359PT	123456	

C. Note: This form is furnished to give you a statement of actual settlement costs. Amounts paid to and by the settlement agent are shown. Items marked "(p.o.c.)" were paid outside the closing; they are shown here for informational purposes and are not included in the totals.

D. Name and Address of Borrower	E. Name and Address of Seller	F. Name and Address of Lender
Andy & Anne Thrift 33 E. Main St. Anytown	Bob & Betty Smart 123 Easy St. Anytown	1st National Bank of Anytown 888 Commercial Ave. Anytown

G. Property Location	H. Settlement Agent
123 Easy Street Anytown	ABC Title Company

	Place of Settlement	I. Settlement Date
	ABC Title Company Anytown	8/15/

J. Summary of Borrower's Transaction		K. Summary of Seller's Transaction	
100. Gross Amount Due From Borrower		**400. Gross Amount Due To Seller**	
101. Contract sales price	150,000.00	401. Contract sales price	150,000.00
102. Personal property		402. Personal property	
103. Settlement charges to borrower (line 1400)	5,705.01	403.	
104.		404.	
105.		405.	
Adjustments for items paid by seller in advance		*Adjustments for items paid by seller in advance*	
106. City/town taxes to		406. City/town taxes to	
107. County taxes to		407. County taxes to	
108. Assessments to		408. Assessments to	
109.		409.	
110.		410.	
111.		411.	
112.		412.	
120. Gross Amount Due From Borrower	155,705.01	**420. Gross Amount Due To Seller**	150,000.00
200. Amounts Paid By Or In Behalf Of Borrower		**500. Reductions In Amount Due To Seller**	
201. Deposit or earnest money	50,000.00	501. Excess deposit (see instructions)	
202. Principal amount of new loan(s)	100,000.00	502. Settlement charges to seller (line 1400)	10,490.00
203. Existing loan(s) taken subject to		503. Existing loan(s) taken subject to	
204.		504. Payoff of first mortgage loan 1st. Nat.	48,199.95
205.		505. Payoff of second mortgage loan	
206.		506.	
207.		507.	
208.		508.	
209.		509.	
Adjustments for items unpaid by seller		*Adjustments for items unpaid by seller*	
210. City/town taxes to		510. City/town taxes to	
211. County taxes 1/1/ to 8/15/	1,500.01	511. County taxes 1/1/ to 8/15/	1,500.01
212. Assessments to		512. Assessments to	
213.		513.	
214.		514.	
215.		515.	
216.		516.	
217.		517.	
218.		518.	
219.		519.	
220. Total Paid By/For Borrower	151,500.01	**520. Total Reduction Amount Due Seller**	60,189.96
300. Cash At Settlement From/To Borrower		**600. Cash At Settlement To/From Seller**	
301. Gross Amount due from borrower (line 120)	155,705.01	601. Gross amount due to seller (line 420)	150,000.00
302. Less amounts paid by/for borrower (line 220)	(151,500.01)	602. Less reductions in amt. due seller (line 520)	(60,189.96)
303. Cash ☒ From ☐ To Borrower	4,205.00	**603. Cash** ☒ To ☐ From Seller	89,810.04

Previous Edition Is Obsolete

Great Lakes Business Forms, Inc.
Form No. 2384

HUD-1 (3-86)
RESPA, HB 4305.2

To Reorder Call: Great Lakes Business Forms, Inc.
Nationally 1-800-253-0209 Michigan 1-800-358-2643

FIGURE 12.1
(Continued)

L. Settlement Charges		Paid From Borrower's Funds at Settlement	Paid From Seller's Funds at Settlement
700. Total Sales/Broker's Commission based on price $ 150,000.00 @ % =			
Division of Commission (line 700) as follows:			
701. $ 8,000.00 to Sell Quick Realty			
702. $ to			
703. Commission paid at Settlement			8,000.00
704.			
800. Items Payable In Connection With Loan			
801. Loan Origination Fee %		250.00	
802. Loan Discount 2 %		2,000.00	
803. Appraisal Fee to Accurate POC $250 b		POC	
804. Credit Report to Information POC $ 50 b		POC	
805. Lender's Inspection Fee			
806. Mortgage Insurance Application Fee to			
807. Assumption Fee			
808.			
809.			
810.			
811.			
900. Items Required By Lender To Be Paid In Advance			
901. Interest from 8/16/ to 8/30/ @$ 25.00 /day (15 days)		375.00	
902. Mortgage Insurance Premium for months to			
903. Hazard Insurance Premium for 1 years to Failsafe Ins.		320.00	
904. years to			
905.			
1000. Reserves Deposited With Lender			
1001. Hazard insurance 3 months@$ 26.67 per month		80.01	
1002. Mortgage insurance months@$ per month			
1003. City property taxes 9 months@$ 200.00 per month		1,800.00	
1004. County property taxes months@$ per month			
1005. Annual assessments months@$ per month			
1006. months@$ per month			
1007. months@$ per month			
1008. months@$ per month			
1100. Title Charges			
1101. Settlement or closing fee to ABC Title Company		200.00	
1102. Abstract or title search to			
1103. Title examination to			
1104. Title insurance binder to			20.00
1105. Document preparation to			
1106. Notary fees to			
1107. Attorney's fees to		350.00	380.00
(includes above items numbers:)			
1108. Title insurance to ABC Title Company		150.00	460.00
(includes above items numbers:)			
1109. Lender's coverage $ 100,000			
1110. Owner's coverage $ 150,000			
1111.			
1112.			
1113.			
1200. Government Recording and Transfer Charges			
1201. Recording fees: Deed $ 50.00 ; Mortgage $ 10.00 ; Releases $ 70.00		60.00	70.00
1202. City/county tax/stamps: Deed $; Mortgage $			
1203. State tax/stamps: Deed $ 1,500.00 ; Mortgage $			1,500.00
1204.			
1205.			
1300. Additional Settlement Charges			
1301. Survey to Able Survey Company		120.00	
1302. Pest Inspection to Acme Pest Control			60.00
1303.			
1304.			
1305.			
1400. Total Settlement Charges (enter on lines 103, Section J and 502, Section K)		5,705.01	10,490.00

I have carefully reviewed the HUD-1 Settlement Statement and to the best of my knowledge and belief, it is a true and accurate statement of all receipts and disbursements made on my account or by me in this transaction. I further certify that I have recieved a copy of HUD-1 Settlement Statement.

_____   _____

Borrowers   Sellers

The HUD-1 Settlement Statement which I have prepared is a true and accurate account of this transaction. I have caused or will cause the funds to be disbursed in accordance with this statement.

_____   _____

Settlement Agent   Date

has been prepared using this information. Entries on the settlement statement are explained, including all proration calculations.

Closing Information

Bob and Betty Smart listed their house at 123 Easy Street with SellQuick Realty. The listing agreement included payment of a commission based on 6 percent for the first $50,000 and 5 percent on the remainder of the actual selling price. Andy and Anne Thrift signed a contract with the Smarts to buy the property for $150,000. The terms of the contract specified that the Thrifts would make an earnest money/down payment of $50,000, and the rest ($100,000) would be financed by a conventional loan from a lender. Because the loan-to-value ratio will not exceed 80 percent, the Thrifts will not have to purchase mortgage insurance. The closing date is set for August 15 at ABC Title Company, which charges a $200 closing fee.

The rate on the Thrifts' new mortgage is 9 percent, and the monthly payments are due on the last day of the month (in arrears). Because the Thrifts' loan is paid in arrears, interest for the remainder of August will be due at closing and the first full monthly payment (for the month of September) will be due on October 1. The Thrifts' also will pay the $10 fee to record the lender's mortgage lien. In obtaining the new loan the Thrifts will be charged an appraisal fee of $250 from Accurate Appraisal Corp. and $50 from Information Credit Corp. These two charges will be noted as POC (paid outside closing) on the Settlement Statement because they were paid to the lender at the time of the loan application. To obtain the loan the Thrifts also paid a loan origination fee of $250 and two discount points. The Smarts have an existing mortgage on the house from First National Bank with a balance of $48,000 as of August 1. Their loan rate is 10 percent, and the monthly payments for interest and principal are $550.

The real estate taxes are paid in arrears and have not been paid for this year. The taxes for the year are estimated to be $2,400. The Thrifts' lender requires them to deposit $9/12$ of the anticipated real estate taxes into a reserve account. The Thrifts must pay a one-year hazard insurance premium of $320 to the FailSafe Insurance Company and, in addition, their lender requires that a reserve to cover three months of the premium be deposited. The Smarts provided evidence of title using a title insurance binder that cost them $20. The Smarts paid the owner's title insurance policy of $460 and the Thrifts the lender's title insurance policy of $150. The Smarts will pay a $70 fee to record documents that clear their title and the transfer tax, which is based on 1 percent of the selling price. The Smarts also will pay $60 for a termite inspection and legal fees of $380. The Thrifts will pay the survey fee of $120, a $50 fee to record their new title and a $350 legal fee.

According to the contract, all prorations are to be made using 30 days in the month.

An explanation of the closing statement entries on Figure 12.1 follows.

- *Purchase price*—The purchase price of $150,000 is listed under the borrower's transactions on line 101 and the seller's transactions on line 401.
- *Earnest money/down payment*—The selling price less the amount of the purchase price not financed is listed under amounts paid by the borrower on line 201.

$$\$150,000 - \$100,000 \text{ loan} = \$50,000$$

- *Seller's mortgage entry*—The seller owes the lender the balance of the existing loan plus interest that has accrued from the first of the month to the day of closing.

    Yearly interest = $\$48,000 \times .10 = \$4,800$
    Daily interest = $\$4,800 \div 360 \text{ days} = \$13.33$
    Interest (August 1–15) = $\$13.33 \times 15 \text{ days} = \$199.95$
    Payoff balance = $\$48,000 + \$199.95 = \$48,199.95$

The loan payoff amount of $48,199.95 is put on line 504.

- *Buyer's mortgage entries*—The interest on the new loan is paid at the end of the month (in arrears). This is an accrued expense that must be prorated from the day of closing through the end of the month:

Yearly interest = $100,000 × .09 = $9,000
Daily interest = $9,000 ÷ 360 = $25
Interest (August 16–30) = $25.00 × 15 days = $375

The $375 in interest is paid by the borrower (buyer) to the lender at closing and is included on line 901. The borrower's loan of $100,000 (which will be paid by the lender on the borrower's behalf) is included on line 202.

- *Loan fees*—To obtain the new loan, the Thrifts were required to pay several expenses. These included an appraisal fee ($250) on line 803 and a credit report fee ($50) on line 804. Because these were paid outside closing, they are not included in the borrower's or seller's columns. The Thrifts also paid a loan origination fee ($250) on line 801 and two discount points ($100,000 × .02 = $2,000) on line 802 to the lender.

- *Real estate tax entries*—The taxes for this year have not been paid. This is an accrued expense that must be prorated from the beginning of the year through the closing date. Because the buyers will have to pay the tax bill, the prorated amount is included on lines 211 and 511 (items unpaid by the seller).

Monthly rate = $2,400 ÷ 12 = $200
Daily rate = $200 ÷ 30 = $6.667
Prorated tax = 7 months × $200 ($1,400) + 15 days × $6.667 ($100.01) = $1,500.01

The lender requires a reserve to cover the real estate tax expense that has been incurred from the start of the year through the first mortgage payment. Because the first payment is due on October 1, a reserve of nine months will be required at closing and is included on line 1004.

$2,400 (yearly tax) ÷ 12 = $200 (per month) × 9 = $1,800.

- *Property insurance*—The first year's premium must be paid at closing and is included on line 903. The lender requires a reserve of three months toward the next year's premium, which is included on line 1001.

$320 (1 year premium) ÷ 12 = $26.67 (per month) × 3 = $80.01

- *Broker's commission*—Information regarding the commission to be paid by the seller is included on lines 700 through 703.

(.06 × $50,000 = $3,000) + (.05 × $100,000 = $5,000) =
$3,000 + $5,000 = $8,000

- *Transfer tax*—The transfer tax usually is paid by the seller. The transfer tax rate is set by local government. In this problem it is 1 percent of the selling price and is included on line 1203.

$150,000 × .01 = $1,500

- *Title insurance*—In this problem the Smarts paid the owner's title insurance policy of $460 and the Thrifts the lender's title insurance policy of $150. These are included on line 1108 and the coverage amounts on lines 1109 and 1110. The Smarts also paid a title insurance binder ($20), included on line 1104.

- *Recording fee*—The seller pays recording fees to clear the title, and the buyer pays fees to record the new title. The recording fees included in the problem are $70 for releases to clear title (seller) and fees of $50 and $10 to record the deed and mortgage (buyer). These are included on line 1201.

- *Legal fees*—Legal fees are allocated to the party who hired the lawyer. In this problem both parties used the services of a lawyer and the fees are included on line 1107.

- *Survey*—Often the survey is ordered as a requirement of the buyer's lender. This expense ($120) is included on line 1301.
- *Termite inspection*—The seller is usually responsible for inspections (and expenses to correct defects). This expense ($60) is included on line 1302.
- *Final entries*—The difference between the gross amount due from the borrower (line 120) and the amount paid for the borrower (line 220) is the amount of cash due from the borrower at closing (line 303). The difference between the gross amount due to the seller (line 420) and the reduction for the seller (line 520) is the amount of cash due to the seller at closing (line 603).

**THERE ARE NO REVIEW QUESTIONS FOR THIS SECTION
AND THIS IS THE LAST CHAPTER IN THE UNIT.
TAKE THE UNIT IV DIAGNOSTIC TEST.**

SOLUTIONS
FOR SECTION REVIEW EXERCISES

SECTION 1

1. a. Covered—RESPA covers residential one- to four-unit property.
   b. Not covered—RESPA covers transactions in which there is a *new* first mortgage.
   c. Covered—RESPA covers residential property, including condos.
   d. Not covered—RESPA does not cover commercial property transactions.
   e. Not covered—RESPA covers transactions using a loan from a federally insured lender.

2. FALSE Once an escrow agreement has been signed, the broker gives the earnest money to the escrow agent.

3. FALSE The booklet, "Settlement Costs, A HUD Guide," must be given to the borrower at the time of the loan application or within three business days after.

4. TRUE

5. TRUE

6. FALSE RESPA does not set closing costs. Its purpose is to inform the parties of the closing costs.

7. FALSE An escrow agreement is between the buyer and seller.

8. TRUE

9. FALSE Through the doctrine of relation back, title will pass as of June 1.

10. Uniform Settlement Statement (HUD-1)

11. RESPA

12. Final walkthrough

13. Escrow closing

14. Closing agent

15. Good faith estimate

16. Doctrine of relation back

SECTION 2

1. $900 + $600 paid for the month of June. $1,500 ÷ 30 = $50 per day.
   $50 × 15 days = $750.
   Because the rent is prepaid, credit the buyer and debit the seller.

2. $50,000 × .10 = $5,000 annual interest.
   $5,000 ÷ 360 days × 20 days = $277.78
   Because interest is paid in arrears, this is an accrued expense; credit the buyer and debit the seller.

3. $100 × $.80 = $80
   Because this is a prepaid expense, debit the buyer and credit the seller.

4. $1,200 ÷ 12 = $100 × 1 month = $100
   $100 ÷ 30 × 15 days = $50 + $100 = $150
   Because this is a prepaid expense, debit the buyer and credit the seller.

5. $3,600 ÷ 12 = $300 × 2 months = $600
   Because this is an accrued expense, credit the buyer and debit the seller.

6. 1997 year 5 months 10 day
   <u>1995 year 8 months 20 day</u>
     1 year 8 months 20 days

   $36,000 ÷ 3 = $12,000 per yr. $12,000 ÷ 12 = $1,000 per mo. $1,000 ÷ 30 = $33.333 per day. (1 year = $12,000) + (8 months, $1,000 × 8 = $8,000) + (20 days, 20 ×

$33.333 = $666.67).

$12,000 + $8,000 + $666.67 = $20,666.67

Because this is a prepaid expense, debit the buyer and credit the seller.

7. FALSE Closing statements are usually prepared by the buyer's or the seller's lawyer, the escrow agent or the title company.

8. TRUE

9. TRUE

10. FALSE The seller is usually required to pay the tax.

11. FALSE Rent security deposits are credited in total to the buyer and debited to the seller. Rent payments may be prorated.

12. Actual number of days in the year method

13. Accrued expense

14. Closing statement

15. Prorated expenses

16. Statutory month method

17. Prepaid expense

18. Actual number of days in the month method

U N I T IV
DIAGNOSTIC TEST

1. A person who died leaving a valid will is called a(n)

   a. devisee.
   b. testator.
   c. legatee.
   d. intestate.

2. A lender's title policy is used by the lender to protect its interests. This type of policy

   a. covers the buyer's equity in the property.
   b. covers one-half of the buyer's equity in the property.
   c. does not cover any of the buyer's equity in the property.
   d. covers the amount of buyer's equity negotiated between the buyer and lender.

3. A property is sold on March 15. The annual insurance of $840 and annual water bill of $120 were prepaid in full on January 1. If these payments are prorated, what amount will be credited to the seller at closing?

   a. $200
   b. $385
   c. $760
   d. $960

4. The owner of a parcel of land died. The owner was not married, and the probate court determined the disposition of the land in accordance with state statutes. In this situation the owner died

   a. testate.
   b. with right of survivorship.
   c. with a will.
   d. intestate.

5. Fran bought two acres in a distant county, never went to see the land, and did not use the property. Harold moved his mobile home onto the land, had a water well drilled and lived there for 22 years. Harold may become the owner of the land if he has complied with the state law requirements for

   a. escheat.
   b. avulsion.
   c. adverse possession.
   d. voluntary alienation.

6. The seller paid the annual insurance premium of $720 for the coming year on April 1. If the closing for the sale of the house is on August 15, what prorated amount will be credited to the seller?

   a. $180
   b. $270
   c. $450
   d. $480

7. Which of the following best describes the covenant of quiet enjoyment?

   a. The grantor promises to obtain and deliver any instrument needed to make the title good.
   b. The grantor guarantees that if the title fails in the future, the grantor will compensate the grantee.
   c. The grantor guarantees that the title will be good against the title claims of third parties.
   d. The grantor warrants she is are the owner of the property and has the right to convey title.

8. An owner's title insurance policy usually lasts

   a. throughout the life of the mortgage.
   b. as long as the property is owned by the same owner.
   c. for one year, and renewable every year after.
   d. from 15 to 30 years, depending on the type of coverage.

9. Which of the following properties is exempt from RESPA requirements for a first mortgage?

   a. A single family house
   b. A condominium
   c. A shopping mall
   d. A three flat that is occupied by the owner

10. To acquire property by adverse possession, one must prove which of the following?

    a. A hidden use of the property
    b. Existence of the owner's deed
    c. A use that was done sporadically
    d. Hostile use

11. A borrower takes out a mortgagee's title insurance policy. The premium for the policy usually will be paid

    a. monthly, as part of the mortgage payment.
    b. semiannually, with the real estate tax.
    c. annually, with the homeowner's insurance policy.
    d. once, when the policy is issued.

12. A title search in the public records may be conducted by

    a. only attorneys and abstractors.
    b. anyone.
    c. only attorneys, abstractors and real estate brokers.
    d. anyone who obtains a court order under the Freedom of Information Act.

13. The purchase of a house is contingent on the inclusion of the refrigerator. Title to the refrigerator is conveyed by

    a. the sales contract.
    b. a rider in the sales contract.
    c. the deed.
    d. a bill of sale.

14. All of the following are characteristics of the Torrens system for registering property *except*

    a. Torrens is in widespread use throughout the country.
    b. a written application to register title is made in the county where the land is located.
    c. a Torrens certificate is prepared that lists the type of title and any encumbrances.
    d. a public notice is issued so that anyone who wishes can contest the title.

15. The sale of a residence is scheduled to close on September 8, and the yearly real estate taxes in the amount of $1,800 have not been paid. What entry for the real estate taxes should be made on the closing statement?

    a. Credit to the seller of $1,240
    b. Credit to the buyer of $1,240
    c. Debit to the seller of $560
    d. Debit to the buyer of $560

16. Title to real estate usually passes to the grantee at the time the deed is

    a. written.
    b. executed.
    c. delivered.
    d. acknowledged.

17. A prospective property buyer obtains a lawyer's statement indicating the title's quality as of a certain date. The buyer has obtained

    a. title insurance.
    b. a title opinion.
    c. a title abstract.
    d. a title search.

18. The Real Estate Settlement Procedures Act (RESPA) applies to real estate transactions that include

    a. federally related loans.
    b. loans made by private individuals.
    c. loans carried back by the seller.
    d. all cash transactions.

19. Condemnation and escheat are two examples of

    a. voluntary alienation.
    b. adverse possession.
    c. transfer of title by descent.
    d. involuntary alienation.

20. The Torrens System is best described as a method of

    a. describing property.
    b. measuring land.
    c. registering property.
    d. subdividing property.

21. The sale of a residence is scheduled to close on April 18, and the yearly real estate taxes in the amount of $2,400 have been prepaid. Prorations include the day of closing. What entries for the real estate taxes should be made on the closing statement?

 a. Credit the seller and debit the buyer $719.99
 b. Debit the seller and credit the buyer $719.99
 c. Credit the seller and debit the buyer $1,679.99
 d. Debit the seller and credit the buyer $1,679.99

22. The grantee receives greatest protection with what type of deed?

 a. Quitclaim
 b. General warranty
 c. Bargain and sale deed
 d. Special warranty

23. When an abstract of title is prepared, the abstractor

 a. insures the title.
 b. issues a certificate of title.
 c. prepares a history of the title after inspecting the public records.
 d. inspects the property.

24. Title to real estate may be transferred during a person's lifetime by

 a. devise.
 b. voluntary alienation.
 c. descent.
 d. escheat.

25. Which of the following forms of deeds imposes the greatest liability on the grantor?

 a. Special warranty
 b. Quitclaim
 c. General warranty
 d. Bargain and sale

26. The coverage in a standard title insurance policy protects the buyer from

 a. recorded liens that were not reported.
 b. the rights of the parties in possession of the property.
 c. encroachments.
 d. zoning violations.

27. A deed contains a promise that the title conveyed will be good against court actions brought by third parties who seek to establish a superior claim to the property. This is an example of which covenant?

 a. Seisin
 b. Further assurance
 c. Quiet enjoyment
 d. Warranty forever

28. If a grantor wishes to limit the warranties given in the deed to only those defects in a title that originated during the grantor's ownership, the grantor will use a

 a. special warranty deed.
 b. quitclaim deed.
 c. general warranty deed.
 d. bargain and sale deed.

29. Which of the following statements best explains why instruments affecting real estate are recorded?

 a. Failing to record will void the transfer.
 b. The instruments must be recorded to comply with the terms of the statute of frauds.
 c. Recording proves the execution of the instrument.
 d. Recording gives constructive notice to the world of the rights and interests of a party in the real estate.

30. A real estate closing is scheduled for September 14, and all prorations include the day of closing. The buyer has agreed to assume the seller's mortgage, which has an interest rate of 8 percent and a balance of $65,325 as of September 1. How should interest on the loan be prorated?

 a. Debit the buyer $203.23
 b. Debit the seller $203.23
 c. Debit the buyer $232.32
 d. Debit the seller $232.32

31. The process that occurs when the state acquires title to property because no heirs can be found is called

 a. eminent domain.
 b. escheat.
 c. adverse possession.
 d. statutory redemption.

32. A title insurance policy that includes standard coverages protects the insured against

    a. rights of parties in possession of the property.
    b. existing encroachments.
    c. forgery.
    d. hidden physical defects.

33. The buyer in a real estate sales transaction most likely would require which type of deed from the seller?

    a. Quitclaim deed
    b. Warranty deed
    c. Bargain and sale deed
    d. Trustee's deed

34. RESPA includes which of the following requirements?

    a. A good faith estimate of finance costs must be given to the buyer.
    b. It sets prices that may be charged for settlement services.
    c. An informational booklet regarding closing costs must be given to the buyer.
    d. The buyer is allowed to rescind the sales contract under certain conditions.

35. When the amount of land is increased gradually through natural causes, the process is called

    a. erosion.
    b. avulsion.
    c. accretion.
    d. appreciation.

36. Which of the following best describes a chain of title?

    a. A list of the successive owners of the property up to the present
    b. A summary of all of the documents affecting title to a property
    c. A document that protects the owner against defects in the title
    d. A method of measuring land

37. When land area decreases gradually through natural causes, the process is called

    a. erosion.
    b. avulsion.
    c. accretion.
    d. appreciation.

38. Settlement of a real estate transaction is being handled by an escrow agent. Which of the following duties will the agent perform?

    a. Preparing the purchase agreement
    b. Collecting and disbursing funds
    c. Preparing loan documents
    d. Obtaining insurance for the property.

39. Tom signed a deed transferring ownership of a property to Lois. To provide evidence that Tom's signature is genuine, Tom executed a declaration before a notary. This declaration is known as an

    a. affidavit.
    b. affirmation.
    c. acknowledgment.
    d. estoppel.

40. Prorations of expenses in a real estate closing are typically calculated as of the date

    a. the loan is approved.
    b. the sale contract is signed.
    c. title is transferred.
    d. of the buyer's walkthrough.

41. Which of the following statements is true regarding a quitclaim deed?

    a. It includes no expressed or implied warranties or guarantees.
    b. It warrants against encumbrances known by the grantor.
    c. It warrants that the grantor will indemnify the grantee if the title is successfully challenged by a third party.
    d. It warrants that the grantor's title is good against third parties.

42. The documents referred to as evidence of title to real estate include

    a. security agreements.
    b. title insurance.
    c. the mortgage.
    d. a general warranty deed.

43. The requirements for a valid deed usually include

    a. the grantor's signature.
    b. an acknowledgment.
    c. witnesses.
    d. the address of the grantee.

44. A statement that the person signing the deed is the person he or she claims to be and is doing so of his or her own free will is called a(n)

    a. notarization.
    b. acknowledgment.
    c. witnessing.
    d. recording.

45. Title to a parcel of real estate is transferred through descent. In this situation the transaction is

    a. intestate succession.
    b. property reverting to the government.
    c. creating a trust agreement.
    d. transfer through a will.

46. To carry out the wishes of the deceased, a will names a personal representative known as a(n)

    a. administrator(trix).
    b. executor(trix).
    c. attorney-at-fact.
    d. trustee.

47. The provisions of RESPA must be followed in which of the following real estate transactions?

    a. Every real estate transaction
    b. Those involving an installment sales contract
    c. All transactions involving commercial property
    d. Residential transactions financed by federally related mortgage loans

48. The buyer in a real estate transaction wishes to receive fee simple ownership in the property. The clause in the deed that will define the extent of the estate granted to the buyer is the

    a. habendum clause.
    b. subordination clause.
    c. defeasance clause.
    d. alienation clause.

49. A person performs hostile, visible, exclusive and continuous possession of another's property for a prescribed period of time. This person may acquire title to the property through

    a. voluntary alienation.
    b. adverse possession.
    c. escheat.
    d. descent.

50. Someone who wishes to remove a cloud on the title typically would use a

    a. bargain and sale deed.
    b. quitclaim deed.
    c. special warranty deed.
    d. general warranty deed.

U N I T IV
DIAGNOSTIC TEST
ANSWER SHEET

This sheet is perforated for easy pullout. Write your answers on this sheet as you complete the exercises. Refer to the diagnostic worksheet after completing the test to evaluate your strong and weak content areas. Review material in the appropriate chapter and sections.

1. _____

2. _____

3. _____

4. _____

5. _____

6. _____

7. _____

8. _____

9. _____

10. _____

11. _____

12. _____

13. _____

14. _____

15. _____

16. _____

17. _____

18. _____

19. _____

20. _____

21. _____

22. _____

23. _____

24. _____

25. _____

26. _____

27. _____

28. _____

29. _____

30. _____

31. _____

32. _____

33. _____

34. _____

35. _____

36. _____

37. _____

38. _____

39. _____

40. _____

41. _____

42. _____

43. _____

44. _____

45. _____

46. _____

47. _____

48. _____

49. _____

50. _____

REAL ESTATE
BROKERAGE

CHAPTER 13

AGENCY AND REAL ESTATE BROKERAGE

In most real estate activities a broker acts as an agent working for a principal. Agency is an important topic because it affects a broker's conduct and liability. *Section 1* covers an overview of agency, the types of agents and how agencies are created and terminated. *Section 2* covers specific duties agents owe their principals and the principals' duties to agents. *Section 3* covers the types of agency arrangements that a broker may have with a seller, a buyer, both a seller and a buyer, and with sales associates who are employed by the broker. Remember to use the Study Tool Kit to reference key information and to update your progress checklist.

Learning Objectives
Track your progress as you work through the chapter by checking each learning objective when you complete it.

____ Describe the concept of a fiduciary.

____ List three types of agents and describe how they differ.

____ List and describe four ways an agency can be created.

____ List and describe eleven ways an agency can be terminated.

____ List and describe five agent's duties to the principal.

____ List and describe four principal's duties to the agent.

____ Describe what a broker must disclose to potential buyers.

____ List and describe four agency situations involving a broker.

____ Describe the difference between an employee and an independent contractor.

____ Describe two antitrust practices and how they affect real estate brokers.

Key Terms and Phrases
Track your progress as you work through the chapter by checking each term when you understand its meaning.

____ Agent

____ Agency

____ Agency by estoppel

____ Agency by necessity

____ Agency coupled with an interest

____ Antitrust laws

____ As-is sale

____ Brokerage

____ Broker-sales associate agreement

____ Caveat emptor

____ Commingle

____ Designated agent

____	Dual agency	____	Misrepresentation
____	Employee	____	Price fixing
____	Errors and omissions insurance	____	Procuring cause
____	Expressed agency	____	Puffing
____	Fiduciary	____	Real estate assistant
____	Fraud	____	Seller disclosure statement
____	General agent	____	Special agent
____	Implied agency	____	Stigmatized property
____	Independent contractor	____	Subagent
____	Latent defects	____	Transactional brokerage
____	Market allocation	____	Universal agent

SECTION 1
DEFINING AGENCY RELATIONSHIPS

BROKERAGE

Most real estate professionals engage in the practice of **brokerage**. Real estate brokerage is bringing parties together for the purchase, rent or exchange of real estate in exchange for a fee. In performing this service agency relationships are usually created between the brokers and the parties they represent.

AGENCY

An **agent** is a person who represents, or acts on behalf of, another person, called a *principal*, in activities involving third parties. The relationship between agents and principals is called an **agency**. If the agent uses the assistance of other agents, they are called **subagents**. Certain agency relationships are considered **fiduciary**, meaning they are relationships involving great trust and confidence between the principal and the agent, and the agent must act with *high standards of care*.

EXAMPLE: A seller hires a broker to sell her house. This is a *fiduciary* agency, in which the seller is the principal, the broker is the agent.

Different agency relationships (e.g., broker and seller, broker and buyer) are covered in Section 3.

Levels of Agencies

Agents can be classified based on the level of authority they are given by the principal. There are three levels of agencies that can be established.

1. A **universal agent** represents the principal in *all matters* that can be legally delegated to others. An unlimited power of attorney can create this type of agency.

2. A **general agent** represents the principal in a *particular business* or *related range of activities*. The agent can sometimes bind the principal to any contracts agreed to while

operating within the scope of the agency. A general power of attorney can create this type of agency.

EXAMPLE: A property manager represents the principal on activities necessary to manage the property.

3. A **special agent** is limited to representing the principal in a *specific transaction*.

EXAMPLE: A broker is usually hired as a *special agent*. Brokers are hired to represent their principal in a single transaction, namely the sale or purchase of a property.

4. A **designated agent** is one of the broker's salespeople authorized to act as the agent for one of the parties in a real estate transaction. This allows other salespeople in the broker's office to act as agents for the other party.

EXAMPLE: Bob is a salesperson who negotiates a listing contract with a seller. Bob's broker, with the written consent of the seller, designates Bob to act as the agent of the seller. Other salespeople in the office can represent buyers of the property without creating a dual agency.

Creating an Agency

Requirements. Two requirements for creating an agency are (1) the *capacity of the parties*—the principal can empower an agent to do only what the principal is empowered to do, and (2) a *legal purpose* for the agency.

How Agencies Are Created. An **expressed agency** (by appointment) is created by an oral or a written agreement. A listing agreement is generally used to create an agency relationship between the broker and seller. While written listing agreements are typically preferred, state laws and regulations determine whether listings must be in writing to be enforceable.

EXAMPLE: A listing agreement between the seller and the broker creates an expressed agency.

An **implied agency** is created by the parties' action or conduct.

EXAMPLE: A couple advertises their house for sale offering "a 5 percent commission to licensed brokers bringing an acceptable purchase offer." A broker brings in an acceptable offer to the seller. The broker may be entitled to a commission as an agent of the seller by an implied agency.

An **agency by estoppel** (ostensible agency) is created when a principal, through his statement or actions, leads a third person to believe someone is his agent and the third person relies on it. In this situation the principal will be "estopped" from denying the agency.

EXAMPLE: A broker tells a buyer she is an agent of a homeowner and provides information on the house. The buyer calls the owner about the house, relaying the conversation with the broker. The homeowner confirms he is selling and neither confirms nor denies the broker is his agent. If the house is sold to the buyer the seller may be *estopped* from denying there was an agency with the broker and may owe the broker a commission.

An **agency by necessity** is created in an emergency, and it may be unnecessary to gain the consent of the principal to create an agency.

EXAMPLE: A broker lists a house that the seller has already vacated. The broker learns that a storm has damaged the roof. The broker may act as an agent of the owner and order the roof to be repaired to avoid further damage to the house.

TERMINATION OF AN AGENCY

There are a number of ways an agency can be terminated. These can be divided into two types: (1) termination by *acts of the parties* and (2) termination by *operation of law.*

Termination by Acts of the Parties

- *Performance*—Completion of the agency's purpose.

EXAMPLE: A broker with a listing sells the property. The agency created by the listing agreement is now over.

- *Mutual agreement*—Both parties can agree to end the agency.
- *Discharged by the principal*—If discharged, the broker may be able to sue for breach of contract. The broker can recover only damages actually sustained. However, if the sale is close to being completed, the broker may be able to recover the commission.

EXAMPLE: A broker has a 90-day listing with the seller. The seller discharges the broker after 30 days. The broker may recover advertising and other expenses.

- *Resignation*—An agent may resign at any time. However, the agent may be liable for breach of contract.
- *Abandonment*—An agent may abandon without explicitly stating it. Inactivity for an unreasonable period would suggest abandonment and terminate the agency. This may also result in breach of contract.

Termination by Operation of Law

- *Expiration of term*—If no term is specified, the agency may be terminated after a "reasonable" period.
- *Death or incapacity of the parties*—Death or incapacity (includes insanity) of either the principal or the agent.
- *Change in the law*—If the purpose of the agency becomes *illegal,* the agency is terminated.
- *Destruction* or *condemnation by eminent domain* of the property.

EXAMPLE: If a listed house burns down before sale, the agency created by the listing agreement is terminated.

- *Bankruptcy*—If either party files for bankruptcy, the agency may be terminated.

AGENCY COUPLED WITH AN INTEREST

If the agent has an interest in the subject of the agency, it is called an **agency coupled with an interest.** This agency *cannot be ended* by either revocation by the principal or death of the principal until the agent's interest has ended.

EXAMPLE: A developer and a real estate broker enter into a partnership to build condominiums. The developer will coordinate construction of the condos and the broker will list the units for sale. Because the broker has an ownership interest, the broker's listing cannot be revoked by the developer, nor will it be terminated if the developer dies.

**BEFORE READING THE NEXT SECTION, COMPLETE THE SECTION 1
REVIEW EXERCISES AND COMPARE YOUR ANSWERS WITH THE
SOLUTIONS AT THE END OF THE CHAPTER.**

SECTION 1

REVIEW EXERCISES

1. In each of the following situations list how the agency was terminated. The first answer is given as an example.
   a. The broker finds a buyer for the property that was listed.
   b. _____Performance_____ On January 1 the sellers list their property with a broker for 30 days. On February 1, the broker has not yet found a buyer for the property.
   c. _____ A listing broker is dissatisfied with the seller and informs the seller to find another broker to list the property.
   d. _____ Both the seller and the broker agree to end the listing.
   e. _____ The owner of a listed property is declared insane by the county.
   f. _____ A seller is unhappy with the way the listing broker is marketing the property and fires the broker.
   g. _____ A listing broker does absolutely nothing to market the seller's property.
   h. _____ A listed house is suddenly blown to pieces by a tornado.

Are the following statements true (T) or false (F)?

2. ____ An agency usually ends if the principal dies.
3. ____ An agency coupled with an interest can be terminated when the principal dies.
4. ____ The agency created between a buyer or seller and a real estate broker is considered a fiduciary relationship.
5. ____ Brokers are usually considered to be special agents.

Supply the term that best matches each of the following descriptions.

6. _____ The relationship between agents and principals
7. _____ An agency created because of an emergency situation
8. _____ Represents the principal in all activities
9. _____ An agency created by words (either oral or written)
10. _____ An agency in which the agent has an interest in the property
11. _____ Bringing parties together for the purchase, rent or exchange of real estate
12. _____ Parties who assist the agent
13. _____ Represents the principal in a particular business or related range of activities
14. _____ The party who acts on behalf of a principal
15. _____ An agency created by the action of the parties
16. _____ Relationship involving great trust and confidence
17. _____ Represents the principal in a specific transaction
18. _____ An agency created when a third person relies on the actions or statements of the principal in dealing with a purported agent

SECTION 2

PRINCIPAL AND AGENT DUTIES

 Hint: To help remember the agent's duties, think of the acronym COALD: Care, Obedience, Accounting, Loyalty and Disclosure.

AGENT'S DUTIES TO THE PRINCIPAL

Care

The broker must exercise *reasonable care and skill.* Brokers who are careless in their actions may be liable for *negligence.* They must perform with the *skill and knowledge customary* in the real estate business.

EXAMPLE: A broker accepts a listing at below market price because the broker was not familiar with the area and did not attempt to determine the fair market value of similar properties in the area. The broker could be considered negligent and liable to the seller for damages.

Obedience

Brokers must follow the principals' instructions and use their best efforts to carry out the agency. The duty of obedience does *not apply* to *unlawful* instructions by the principal.

EXAMPLE: The seller instructs the broker not to tell prospective buyers of certain hidden defects in the property, as required by local law. The broker must not obey the seller's illegal instructions.

Accounting

The broker must account for all funds received on behalf of the principal. State real estate licensing laws specify rules for handling funds received by the broker that belong to others. In general, brokers must deposit all funds into special escrow or trust accounts and cannot **commingle** (mix) their own monies with funds received. The broker also must maintain *detailed records* and *copies of documents* related to transactions.

Loyalty

The broker owes total loyalty to the principal. The duty of loyalty means that brokers may not act in their own self-interest. This means brokers

- may not take advantage of confidential information to the disadvantage of the principal.
- may not buy property they have listed *without the knowledge and consent* of the principal.
- must disclose to purchasers any interest they may have in the property sold.
- may not profit beyond the agreed commission. The broker may not accept kickbacks or finder's fees if related to the agency.

EXAMPLE: A broker is a joint tenant in a property that is for sale. The broker must disclose the ownership interest in the property to prospective buyers.

An agent must maintain *confidentiality* of information by not disclosing facts to others that may adversely affect the principal.

EXAMPLE: A broker representing the seller cannot disclose to the buyer that the seller is willing to accept a lesser price.

EXAMPLE: A broker representing the buyer cannot disclose to the seller that the buyer is willing to make a higher offer.

Dual Agency. **Dual agency** is representing both parties in the same transaction. It is very difficult to be 100 percent loyal to both parties, thus increasing the possibility of a breach of loyalty. *Prior written disclosure* and *consent* by all parties is now required in most states for a dual agency to be legal. *Undisclosed* dual agency may be *fraudulent,* even if it was unintentional or accidental.

Note: Disclosure must be made early in the negotiating process. The broker cannot wait to disclose until the contract is signed.

Disclosure or Notice

The broker must keep the principal informed of all material facts involving the transaction.

EXAMPLE: Because of improving market conditions, the asking price for a property the broker has listed is now too low. The broker must inform the principal (the seller) of this fact, so that the seller can decide if the price should be changed.

AGENT'S DUTIES TO OTHERS (THIRD PARTIES)

While a broker's primary duties are owed to the principal, brokers also must be careful in their relations with *third parties.* A third party is anyone other than the broker's principal. Brokers have responsibilities imposed by the law to act with *honesty* and *fair business dealings,* with skill and care and with *proper disclosure* of known facts. There is the potential for being liable for fraud or misrepresentation, and brokers must be knowledgeable of the type of conduct they may and may not use.

Misrepresentation and Fraud

Misrepresentation is the misstatement of a fact. The *intentional* misrepresentation of a fact is **fraud.** A contract to purchase property obtained through fraud or misrepresentation may be disaffirmed (ended), and the broker may be liable for any resulting damages.

EXAMPLE: A broker reviews the listing sheet on a house and tells prospective buyers that the real estate taxes on a house they are looking at are $2,000 a year. In fact, the broker does not know that there is a $1,000 tax exemption on the property that the buyers would not qualify for, and it is not known by the broker or referenced on the listing sheet. This probably would be regarded as *misrepresentation.*

EXAMPLE: In the same situation, however, suppose the broker *knows* that there is a $1,000 tax exemption on the property that the buyers would not qualify for that is not referenced on the listing sheet. This probably would be regarded as *fraud.*

Note: Fraud also is considered to be the intentional concealment or nondisclosure of defects.

Fraud versus Puffing

Some statements that appear to be fraudulent are actually puffing and may be allowed under the law. **Puffing** includes statements of *opinion* and exaggerating a property's benefits.

EXAMPLE: A broker tells prospective buyers that "This house is the most beautiful one in the neighborhood." Even though the house may be unattractive and not present itself very well, there is no misrepresentation or fraud because the broker's statement is an *opinion*.

Errors and Omissions Insurance

To protect themselves from financial loss due to liability for errors, mistakes and negligence, many brokers and salespersons purchase **errors and omissions insurance.** The broker pays an annual fee to an insurance company that, in turn, defends the broker and pays legal costs and judgments. The insurance will *not cover* intentional deception, misrepresentation or negligence, nor will it usually cover fair housing and antitrust violations.

DISCLOSURE

Caveat emptor means "Let the buyer beware." Under this doctrine buyers buy at their own risk and should examine the property being purchased. In real estate transactions buyers should inspect both the *property* and the *public records*. In recent years the law has changed to provide the buyer with more protection and *weaken* the concept of caveat emptor. Today, in many states, sellers and brokers must reveal any **latent defects** in the property. Latent defects are those that are *hidden* and would not be discovered by an ordinary inspection. Some brokers have sellers sign a **seller disclosure statement** listing any defects in the property when the property is listed. The statement can then be shown to prospective buyers. Some states prescribe a mandatory seller disclosure statement.

Stigmatized Property

Disclosure usually refers to *physical* defects in the property. **Stigmatized property,** that is, property that has been the scene of a crime, suicide or some other undesirable event, may not need to be disclosed, depending on state law.

As-Is Sales

Some real estate sales contracts include a clause stating that the property is being sold "*as is.*" In an **as-is sale** the seller will not fix any problems; however, the owner *still must disclose known hidden defects* in the property.

PRINCIPAL'S DUTIES TO AGENT

- *Care*—The principal must act to avoid negligently damaging the agent.

- *Cooperation*—The principal must not hinder an agent (the broker) from performing his or her duties. The principal may not undermine the broker to avoid paying the commission.
- *Reimbursement and indemnification*—The broker is entitled to be reimbursed for all authorized and necessary expenses incurred on the principal's behalf that may have been related to the sale.

EXAMPLE: The owners of a house listed by the broker have already moved out of state. The broker is entitled to reimbursement for minor repairs on the house that were arranged by the broker.

- *Compensation*—When the broker has fulfilled the terms of the agreement, the principal owes the broker a commission.

COMMISSIONS

To earn a commission, the broker must

- be *licensed* (usually in the state where the property is located).
- be *employed* by the seller or buyer (accomplished by the listing agreement). If not employed, the broker is called a *volunteer.*
- be the *procuring cause.* To be the **procuring cause,** the broker must have done something that resulted in completion of the transaction. This includes activities such as showing the house to the buyer, placing advertisements for the house in newspapers and conducting open houses.

When Is the Commission Earned?

It is customary to make the commission *payable* when the seller delivers the deed. However, a broker technically has *earned* the commission once the seller accepts an offer from a *ready, willing* and *able* buyer. If the transaction is not completed *because the seller defaults* and the broker has found a person ready to buy on the seller's terms, the broker is generally *entitled to a commission.*

EXAMPLE: A broker brings a ready, willing and able buyer; however, the sellers change their mind and refuse to sell the property or refuse to correct defects in the title or cannot deliver possession as stipulated in the contract. In these situations the broker may be entitled to a commission.

Salesperson's Compensation

Normally a broker divides the commission with the salesperson(s) involved with the sale. The salesperson may *receive compensation only from the employing broker.* The salesperson may not receive any type of compensation from the seller, buyer or other brokers.

Compensation to Unlicensed Individuals

It is illegal in most states for a broker to share the commission with someone who does not have a real estate license. This includes payment of finder's fees and other premiums.

EXAMPLE: A broker gives an unlicensed individual part of his commission for referring a buyer who purchased a house through the broker.

ANTITRUST VIOLATIONS

The purpose of the federal **antitrust laws** is to protect competition. Common antitrust violations that can occur in real estate practice are *price fixing* and *market allocation.*

The commission rate must be completely *negotiable between the principal and the agent.* **Price fixing** occurs when brokers conspire to establish a standard commission rate rather than letting the rate be set by the open market. While a broker's office can establish a commission rate, it must do so *independently of any other broker.*

EXAMPLE: Brokers in a certain area meet and agree to accept only listings that have a 6 percent commission rate. This is price fixing.

Market allocation occurs when brokers agree to divide the market among themselves and not compete in each other's areas. This prevents competition because a seller could list a home with only one broker.

EXAMPLE: Four brokers in a suburb meet and agree to divide the suburb into four areas. Each broker is "assigned" an area and will take listings only in his or her area. This is market allocation.

Tip: Market allocation can occur not only by geographic area but also by price range, type of property or some other criterion.

EXAMPLE: Brokers in an area meet and agree that certain brokers will handle residential property under $150,000; others, residential property over $150,000; others, commercial property; and others, condominiums. This is market allocation.

The broker can receive a maximum of three years in prison and $100,000 in fines for violations of antitrust laws. Corporations can be fined up to $1 million. If the broker is successfully sued for an antitrust violation in a civil suit, the court can award *triple* damages, plus lawyers' fees and court costs.

**BEFORE READING THE NEXT SECTION, COMPLETE THE SECTION 2
REVIEW EXERCISES AND COMPARE YOUR ANSWERS WITH THE
SOLUTIONS AT THE END OF THE CHAPTER.**

SECTION 2
REVIEW EXERCISES

1. Name the duty breached by the broker as an agent of the seller in each of the following situations.

   a. _____ The broker receives a check for earnest money from a buyer and deposits it into the real estate office's general operating account.

   b. _____ A broker representing the seller tells the buyer that the seller is going through a divorce and is very anxious to sell as quickly as possible.

   c. _____ The broker's actions result in negligence.

d. _____ The seller has refused to consider lowering the listing price but, thinking she will get more offers, the broker lowers it without the seller's knowledge.

e. _____ A broker represents both the buyer and seller in the same sales transaction and has not disclosed this to either party.

f. _____ A buyer has made an offer acceptable to the seller; however, the broker fails to qualify the buyer to determine if he can reasonably afford the house and does not provide copies of the listing and sales contracts as required.

g. _____ Two days before the closing the broker writes a check from the transaction's earnest money to pay a utility bill that is due.

h. _____ The broker continues to hold open houses while the seller is out of town, despite being told by the seller not to do so.

i. _____ The listing broker receives an offer from a salesperson in the broker's office and a second offer from another real estate office but tells the seller only of the first offer.

Are the following statements true (T) or false (F)?

2. ____ A broker tells prospective buyers that a house should have good appreciation in the future. If the value of the house does not actually rise in the future, the broker has committed fraud.

3. ____ A broker is legally entitled to a commission only when the deed is delivered by the seller.

4. ____ Because it is theoretically impossible to represent both parties in the same transaction, dual agencies are always illegal.

5. ____ The doctrine of *caveat emptor* is weaker under current laws than it was in past years.

6. ____ Both price fixing and market allocation are illegal because they prevent competition.

7. ____ The broker probably would have to disclose to a prospective buyer that a house had been the scene of a murder.

8. ____ A seller is so impressed with a salesperson working for the listing broker that the seller gives the salesperson an extra $1,000 as a bonus without the broker's knowledge. The salesperson can accept the bonus because the broker is the seller's agent.

9. ____ If a property is being sold "as is," the broker does not have to disclose all material defects.

10. ____ Errors and omissions insurance will pay for judgments against the broker for mistakes as long as they were not intentional acts to deceive the buyer.

11. ____ A broker is legally entitled to a commission if the seller signed a listing agreement with the broker, the broker showed the house to the buyer (i.e., is the procuring cause of the sale) and the broker holds a real estate license in the state where the house is located.

Supply the term that best matches each of the following descriptions.

12. _____ The intentional misstatement of a fact

13. _____ An illegal practice in which brokers conspire to establish a standard commission rate

14. _____ A contract clause indicating the seller will not fix any problems with the property

15. _____ Representing both parties in the same transaction

16. _____ An illegal practice in which brokers agree to divide the market among themselves and not compete in each other's areas

17. _____ The unintentional misstatement of facts

18. _____ A listing by the seller of any property defects

19. _____ Laws designed to protect free competition

20. _____ Statements of opinion and exaggeration by the broker

21. _____ The concept that buyers make purchases at their own risk

22. _____ A type of insurance coverage that protects brokers from loss due to errors, mistakes and negligence

23. _____ Hidden defects in the property

24. _____ Property that has been involved with some undesirable event, such as a crime or suicide

25. _____ Something done by the broker that resulted in completion of the sales transaction

---

SECTION 3

THE BROKER-PRINCIPAL RELATIONSHIP

The broker-principal relationship can take several forms. The broker can be (1) an agent of the seller, (2) an agent of the buyer or (3) an agent of both the seller and the buyer (dual agency). Figure 13.1 shows the relationships of the parties in various broker-principal agency situations. An agency relationship also exists between brokers and their sales associates.

THE BROKER AS AGENT OF THE SELLER (SELLER AGENCY)

A real estate broker can act as an agent of the seller, who is the principal. This agency is established by a *listing agreement* (discussed in Chapter 15). The broker as agent assists in the negotiations but *cannot bind* the principal.

Cooperating Brokers/Subagency/Designated Agency

A broker may hire sales associates and belong to a multiple listing service (MLS) to help market properties. In these situations only the broker is the agent of the seller. The sales associates who work for the broker and cooperating brokers in the MLS may or may not be considered *subagents of the seller*. In states that recognize designated agency, the listing broker may identify one or more salespeople as designated agents of the seller.

Disclosure

As stated in Section 1, under the duty of loyalty, brokers and sales associates cannot buy, sell or have any interest in the real estate unless they notify all parties in writing.

If the broker is an agent of the seller, disclosure must be made to potential buyers *prior to the start of negotiations*, informing them of the agency relationship between the broker and seller.

FIGURE 13.1
Agency Relationships

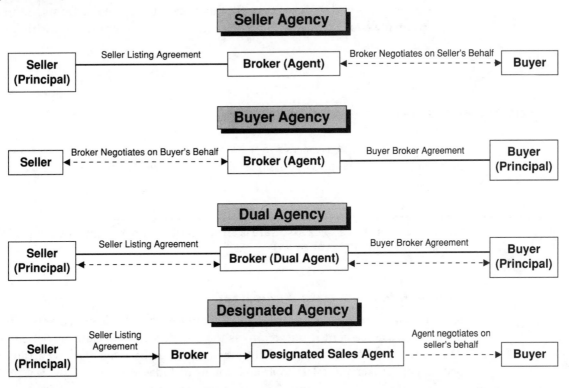

THE BROKER AS AGENT OF THE BUYER (BUYER AGENCY)

Traditionally, brokers have been agents of the sellers of residential property. However, a recent trend in brokerage is for brokers to be agents of the buyers. The parties enter into a *buyer agency agreement,* and the broker is hired to find the buyer a property.

Typical services provided by brokers to buyers include

- locating properties that fit the buyer's requirements;
- assisting in negotiations with the seller and offering advice on offers;
- providing consultation on securing financing; and
- providing information on market conditions.

If the broker is an agent of the buyer, disclosure must be made *prior to the start of negotiations* to informing sellers of the agency relationship between the broker and buyer.

THE BROKER AS AGENT OF SELLER AND BUYER (DUAL AGENCY)

Dual agency occurs when a broker represents both the buyer and seller in the same transaction. As was explained in Section 2, dual agency is legal when *proper disclosure* is given and written consent is obtained from the parties. With the increased use of buyer agency, brokers may find themselves representing a buyer who is interested in one of the broker's own listings. In this situation the broker represents both buyer and seller, and a dual agency has been created. Proper disclosure must be made to the parties.

A broker may designate an individual(s) in the broker's real estate company to be the *designated agent(s)* of a principal. The other salespeople are then free to act as agents for the other party in the transaction. In this situation salespeople from the same real estate company could represent both sides in a real estate transaction without there being a dual agency.

THE BROKER-SALES ASSOCIATE RELATIONSHIP

Brokers may hire sales associates to work for them. Because salespersons cannot work independently, all of the sales associates' activities are performed *in the name of the broker.*

Tip: Remember that a sales associate is an agent of the broker and not of the broker's principal (i.e., the buyer or seller).

Broker-Sales Associate Agreement

Sales associates are agents of brokers and should have written agreements with their brokers. This agreement is referred to as the **broker-sales associate agreement** and is dated and signed by the parties. The agreement formalizes the working arrangement between the broker and salespeople and usually includes

- how compensation will be determined;
- responsibilities and duties of the sales associate;
- who is to pay fees, dues and expenses; and
- verification of independent contractor status (if applicable).

The handling of compensation and expenses can be set up in various ways.

- Some brokers pay for all office expenses and some promotional expenses.
- Some brokers make the sales associates pay advertising and other promotion expenses of listed properties.
- Some brokers allow sales associates to draw money from an account against future commissions.
- Some brokerages are 100 percent commission offices. In these offices a sales associate receives 100 percent of the commission and pays a monthly fee to the broker plus marketing and other expenses, rather than dividing the commission with the broker.

Responsibility of the Broker

Brokers are responsible for the real estate activities of all salespeople licensed under them. Sales associates are agents of the broker, and all real estate activities are *performed in the broker's name.*

EXAMPLE: A salesperson completes a listing contract with a seller. Even though the seller is dealing with the salesperson, the agreement is between the seller and the salesperson's employing broker. (This would also be true for a broker/buyer agreement.)

Employee versus Independent Contractor

Sales associates who work for brokers are either **independent contractors** or **employees.** The distinction between the two statuses (1) has tax ramifications, (2) determines if benefits (other than commission) can be offered by the broker and (3) affects the sales associate's work responsibilities.

Independent Contractor. Under independent contractor status the broker *controls* what the sales associate will do but cannot control *how it will be done.* Because the sales associate is not an employee, the broker does not withhold Social Security (FICA), unemployment and income taxes. In addition, the broker cannot offer sales associates health or life insurance, pension plans, profit sharing and so forth.

IRS Test for Independent Contractor. The IRS uses three tests to determine whether the salesperson is to be treated as an independent contractor.

1. Does the person have a current *real estate license?*
2. Is there a *written contract* with the person stating that he or she will not be treated as an employee?
3. Is at least 90 percent of the person's income *based on sales* and not the number of hours worked?

Salespersons who do *not meet* these tests may lose their independent contractor status.

Employee. For sales associates with employee status the broker withholds income, FICA and unemployment taxes; may offer benefits; and can require that sales associates work certain hours, attend meetings and comply with all other office rules.

Note: While sales personnel in a broker's office may be independent contractors, secretaries and clerical help are usually employees.

Transaction Brokerage

A **transactional broker** (also referred to as a *facilitator* or *coordinator*) is *not an agent of either party.* A transactional broker's function is simply to introduce buyers and sellers to one another and let them negotiate directly. The broker helps both parties with the necessary paperwork and other formalities involved with the closing of the transaction and is expected to treat all parties honestly and competently. Because they do not negotiate on behalf of either the buyer or the seller, they must not disclose confidential information to either party and must disclose known defects in the property.

Real Estate Assistants

Real estate assistants are hired by either the broker or salesperson to help perform administrative tasks associated with real estate transactions. An assistant may or may not have a real estate license. The extent to which the assistant can help the broker or salesperson with transactions is often determined by state license laws. Depending on state law, an assistant may perform duties ranging from clerical and secretarial functions to office management, telemarketing, market strategy development, placing advertisements, arranging appointments to show houses and direct contact with customers and clients.

**COMPLETE THE SECTION 3 REVIEW EXERCISES AND COMPARE YOUR ANSWERS
WITH THE SOLUTIONS AT THE END OF THE CHAPTER.**

REVIEW EXERCISES

1. List whether salespersons are being treated as employees or independent contractors in each of the following situations.

   a. _____ The broker does not withhold income tax from the salesperson's commission.

   b. _____ The broker includes the salesperson in the company's health insurance plan.

   c. _____ The broker requires salespersons to attend weekly sales meetings.

   d. _____ The broker requires salespersons to pay their own licensing fees and operating expenses and provide their own cars.

   e. _____ The broker withholds Social Security tax from the salesperson's commission.

   f. _____ The broker includes the salesperson in the company's profit-sharing plan.

Are the following statements true (T) or false (F)?

2. ____ When a listing is entered into an MLS, the brokers in the MLS always will be subagents of the seller.

3. ____ The broker establishes an agency with the seller with a listing agreement that gives the broker the right to bind the seller.

4. ____ Disclosure identifying the party the broker represents must be made *before* the start of negotiations.

5. ____ A broker-sales associate agreement usually includes who will pay fees and expenses and how compensation will be determined.

6. ____ Tests used by the IRS to determine whether a sales associate is to be treated as an independent contractor include an agreement stating the sales associate will not be treated as an employee and the existence of a current real estate license.

Supply the term that best matches each of the following descriptions.

7. _____ A working relationship between the broker and the broker's sales agents in which the broker controls what the agent will do but not how it will be done

8. _____ A written agreement between the broker and the broker's sales agents

9. _____ A working relationship between broker and sales agents in which the broker has control over how the agents will perform their duties

SOLUTIONS
FOR SECTION REVIEW EXERCISES

SECTION 1

1. a. Performance   b. Expiration   c. Resignation   d. Mutual agreement
   e. Incapacity   f. Discharge by the principle   g. Abandonment
   h. Destruction of the property
2. TRUE
3. FALSE This will not end the agency unless the agent's interest has also ended.
4. TRUE
5. TRUE
6. Agency
7. Agency by necessity
8. Universal agent
9. Expressed agency
10. Agency coupled with an interest
11. Brokerage
12. Subagents
13. General agent
14. Agent
15. Implied agency
16. Fiduciary
17. Special agent
18. Agency by estoppel

SECTION 2

1. a. Accounting   b. Loyalty   c. Care   d. Obedience   e. Loyalty
   f. Care   g. Accounting   h. Obedience   i. Disclosure
2. FALSE This is a statement of opinion and not of fact; therefore, it is not fraud.
3. FALSE While it is customary to pay the commission at that time, the commission is technically earned when the seller accepts an offer from a ready, willing and able buyer.
4. FALSE Prior written disclosure and consent by both buyer and seller generally will make a dual agency legal.
5. TRUE
6. TRUE
7. FALSE Generally, disclosure relates to physical defects in the property, not to stigmatized property.
8. FALSE A salesperson can accept compensation only from the employing broker.
9. FALSE An as-is sale means only that the seller will not correct problems with the property. Defects still must be disclosed.
10. TRUE
11. TRUE
12. Fraud
13. Price fixing
14. "As is"
15. Dual agency

16. Market allocation

17. Misrepresentation

18. Seller disclosure statement

19. Antitrust laws

20. Puffing

21. Caveat emptor

22. Errors and omissions

23. Latent defects

24. Stigmatized property

25. Procuring cause

SECTION 3

1. a. Independent contractor   b. Employee   c. Employee
   d. Independent contractor   e. Employee   f. Employee

2. FALSE Under an *optional subagency* MLS policy the seller can choose whether to have the brokers in the MLS be subagents.

3. FALSE The agreement creates the agency with the seller; however, the broker can only assist in negotiations and cannot bind the seller.

4. TRUE

5. TRUE

6. TRUE

7. Independent contractor

8. Broker-sales associate agreement

9. Employee

CHAPTER 14
REAL ESTATE CONTRACTS

Contracts play an important part in real estate transactions. This chapter covers some of the basic principles of contracts and the real estate sales contact, which is the most common contract used by brokers. *Section 1* covers general contract concepts and real estate sales contracts. *Section 2* covers the required elements that contracts must have to be valid. *Section 3* covers how contracts can be ended and legal remedies available if one of the parties breaches. Remember to use the Study Tool Kit to reference key information and to update your progress checklist.

Learning Objectives

Track your progress as you work through the chapter by checking each learning objective when you complete it.

____ Explain the difference between express and implied contracts.

____ Explain the difference between unilateral and bilateral contracts.

____ Explain the difference between executory and executed contracts.

____ Explain the difference between valid, void and voidable contracts.

____ List and explain the rules for handling earnest money deposits.

____ List and explain the five required elements of a contract.

____ Explain the effect of contracts made under duress, through fraud or through trickery.

____ List the types of contracts that must be in writing.

____ Explain what is considered legally sufficient consideration.

____ List the various ways a contract can be discharged.

____ List the buyer's remedies if the seller defaults.

____ List the seller's remedies if the buyer defaults.

Key Terms and Phrases

Track your progress as you work through the chapter by checking each term when you understand its meaning.

____	Assignment	____	Duress
____	Bilateral contracts	____	Earnest money
____	Binder	____	Equitable title
____	Breach of contract	____	Escrow account
____	Consideration	____	Executed contracts
____	Contingencies	____	Executory contracts
____	Contract	____	Express contracts

____	Implied contracts	____	Statute of frauds
____	Installment sales contracts	____	Statute of limitations
____	Liquidated damages	____	Time is of the essence
____	Meeting of the minds	____	Trust account
____	Mirror image offer	____	Unenforceable contract
____	Mutual assent	____	Unilateral contracts
____	Novation	____	Valid contract
____	Offer and acceptance	____	Vendor and Purchaser Risk Act
____	Option	____	Void Contract
____	Parol evidence	____	Voidable contract
____	Riders	____	Waste
____	Specific performance		

SECTION 1

GENERAL CONTRACT CONCEPTS

A **contract** is a legally enforceable agreement between two or more parties to do or not to do something. Many different types of contracts are used in real estate. These include sales contracts, listings, leases and property management agreements. The two most common types used by real estate brokers are listing contracts (discussed in Chapter 15) and sales contracts, which are discussed later in this section.

GENERAL RULES REGARDING CONTRACTS

A property owner may prepare any document involved in a transaction, such as a bill of sale or sales contract. However, real estate brokers generally *may not* prepare any of these documents, otherwise they will be engaging in the unauthorized practice of law. If the broker is found to have been practicing law, the contract may be held unenforceable and the commission lost, and the broker may face possible loss of license, fines and jail.

While rules and practices vary among states, the following are some general rules for brokers regarding completion of contracts:

- They may only fill in the blanks and make deletions in a preprinted contract form. If the pre-printed contract requires extensive deletions and changes, it should be redrafted by a lawyer.
- They may give only factual information so that a contract can be formed.
- They may not give legal advice or interpret the contract.
- They may attach preprinted **riders,** which are additional clauses or agreements that become part of the contract.

 Note: Before signing a real estate sales contract or other legal documents, the parties to the transaction should be advised to have the documents examined by their lawyers.

Contracts can be changed by the parties; however, any changes to a contract must be *signed* or *initialed* by all signers.

The words **time is of the essence** in a contract mean that time limits in the contract must be met. Parties not meeting the time limits may be liable for breach of contract.

A **binder** is a short version of an agreement between the parties and includes all the essential terms. It is signed by the parties and is effective until the longer, more complex contract is completed.

EXAMPLE: A buyer and seller may sign a binder for the purchase of a house. This will legally bind the parties to the transaction until a detailed sales contract is drafted.

A deed or contract executed on a Sunday or legal holiday is valid and enforceable.

CLASSIFICATION OF CONTRACTS

Contracts can be classified in several ways.

Express or Implied Contracts

Express contracts are those in which the parties show their intentions by *words* (either oral or written words).

EXAMPLE: Real estate listings and sales contracts are express contracts.

In **implied contracts** the parties' intentions are shown by their *acts and conduct*.

EXAMPLE: If you get into a cab there is an implied agreement that the driver will take you where you want to go and you will pay the fare.

Unilateral or Bilateral Contracts

In **unilateral contracts** one party makes a *promise* to persuade a second party to *act*. The party making the promise is obligated to keep the promise only if the second party acts. The second party is not legally obligated to act.

EXAMPLE: A homeowner offers to pay a commission to any broker who finds a buyer for her home. No broker is obliged to find a buyer, and the owner will be obligated to pay a commission only if one of the brokers finds a buyer.

In **bilateral contracts** *both* parties *promise* to do something.

EXAMPLE: A real estate sales contract is a bilateral contract. Usually the buyer promises to pay money for the property and the seller promises to transfer title at closing.

Hint: To simplify: Unilateral contracts are a promise for an act and bilateral contracts are a promise for a promise.

Executed or Executory Contracts

Executed contracts have been completed. All parties have performed the contract provisions.

EXAMPLE: At closing a real estate sales contract is executed.

Executory contracts have not been completed. Some of the terms remain to be carried out.

EXAMPLE: A listing contract is executory until the broker finds a ready, willing and able buyer.

Valid, Void, Voidable and Unenforceable Contracts

A **valid contract** contains all of the required contract elements and is binding on both parties. (The required elements of a contract are discussed in Section 2.)

A **void contract** does not meet all of the required contract elements. Because it is missing one or more contract elements, it actually is not a contract and has no legal effect.

EXAMPLE: In a listing contract the seller requires the house to be sold to a buyer of a specific ethnic group. This is illegal, and the listing contract is void.

A **voidable contract** is one in which at least one of the parties has the power to either *rescind* (cancel) or *enforce* the contract at will.

EXAMPLE: Contracts with minors are generally voidable at the option of the minor. (Section 2 discusses contracts with minors.)

An **unenforceable contract** appears to be valid but is not legally enforceable by either party in a court of law.

Options

An **option** is a separate contract. In a typical option contract the buyer is given a right for a fixed period of time to purchase property at a specified price. An option is an example of a unilateral contract.

EXAMPLE: A family gives the seller $1,000 for an *option to buy* a house for $150,000 within the next five days. The family does not have to buy the house but has the right to do so if it chooses. In either case the seller keeps the $1,000.

In the example above something of value (called *consideration*) is given by both parties. The family has given $1,000, and the seller has *given up the right to sell* the property to someone else for five days.

Note: Remember that while the buyer in an option contract has the right to purchase the property, he or she is not required to do so.

REAL ESTATE SALES CONTRACTS

A real estate sales contract is an agreement between the buyer and seller that specifies the terms and conditions for the sale of real estate. The sales contract is probably the most important document in a real estate transaction because it sets out the terms of the transaction and establishes the legal rights and obligation of the parties. There is no specific form for a real estate sales contract; however, Figure 14.1 lists the type of information usually included.

FIGURE 14.1
Information Usually Included in a Real Estate Sales Contract

- Price of the property and how the purchaser will pay
- Legal description or street address of the property
- Amount of earnest money and when it is to be paid
- Personal property to be left with the real estate
- Type of deed the seller will deliver
- Closing date and any prorations to be made
- When possession of the property will occur
- Names of the buyer and seller
- Title evidence required

Earnest Money

The buyer usually is required to deliver a cash deposit to show his or her intention to complete the transaction. This is called **earnest money** and is held by the seller's broker or lawyer. The amount of the earnest money is determined by *agreement of the parties,* and most contracts specify that the money should be given to the seller if the buyer defaults.

The parties to a contract can agree in advance on **liquidated damages,** which is an amount of money to be paid as compensation if one of the parties breaches contract. A typical example of liquidated damages is the forfeiture of the earnest money by the buyer to the seller if the buyer defaults.

Rules for handling earnest money deposits by the broker are set by state law and generally provide the following:

- The money is to be held in an **escrow** or a **trust account.** This is a special account used when someone (the broker) holds money for another party (the buyer).
- Brokers cannot *commingle* (commingle means *to mix*) their own money with the earnest money.
- Brokers do not need to open a separate escrow account for each transaction and can include the money from several transactions in one escrow account.
- The earnest money cannot be used by the broker because it belongs to the buyer.
- The broker must maintain complete records of all escrow account transactions.
- Written permission from both the buyer and seller may be needed to release the funds.

Mirror Image Offer

An offer for the full purchase price that meets all of the seller's terms is called a **mirror image offer** because it mirrors the terms of the listing contract. If the seller rejects this offer, the broker is usually entitled to a commission because a buyer was found who fulfilled the terms of the listing agreement with the broker.

Equitable versus Legal Title

When a buyer and seller have signed a real estate sales contract, the buyer does not receive the *legal title* because that will be delivered later by a deed. However, the buyer does receive **equitable title,** which means that the law recognizes some ownership interest by the buyer even though he or she is not yet the owner of record.

The Vendor and Purchaser Risk Act

Many states have adopted the **Vendor and Purchaser Risk Act,** which provides that the seller will bear any loss that occurs to the property from the signing of the sales contract until title passes or the buyer takes possession.

Note: If the damages were minor and repaired by the seller, the sales contract would still be in force.

Contingencies

Real estate sales contracts typically include conditions called **contingencies** that must be satisfied before the contract is enforceable. The most common contingencies include the following:

- *Mortgage contingency*—Makes the contract conditioned on the buyer's obtaining a mortgage with the terms specified in the contingency.
- *Property sale contingency*—Makes the contract conditioned on the sale of the purchaser's current home. This protects the buyer from owning two homes at the same time.
- *Inspection contingency*—Makes the contract conditioned on obtaining the results of specified inspections. Inspections could include those for termites, lead-based paint, radon gas, septic systems and the condition of the structure and mechanical systems.

The seller may lose valuable time if the property is not on the market while the buyer's contingencies are being satisfied. To minimize this, the seller may insist on an escape clause permitting the continued marketing of the property to other buyers. The original buyer may retain the right to drop the contingencies (referred to as a kick out clause) within a specified period of time if the seller receives a better offer from another buyer.

Installment Sales Contracts

Installment sales contracts are also known as selling *"under contract," land contracts, contracts for deed* or *articles of agreement.* With this type of sales contract the seller receives a down payment and finances the balance owed by the buyer. An important characteristic of installment sales contracts is that *title remains with the seller* (vendor). The buyer (vendee) takes possession and is obligated to pay taxes, maintenance and insurance and also gets equitable title. The buyer takes *actual* title when the loan balance is paid and the seller delivers the deed. The buyer may not commit **waste;** that is, the buyer may not do anything that would *reduce the value* of the property.

BEFORE READING THE NEXT SECTION, COMPLETE THE SECTION 1 REVIEW EXERCISES AND COMPARE YOUR ANSWERS WITH THE SOLUTIONS AT THE END OF THE CHAPTER.

SECTION 1
REVIEW EXERCISES

1. Name the contract classification that best fits each description.

   a. _____ A contract created by the action or conduct of the parties

   b. _____ A contract in which one party promises to act if the other party acts

   c. _____ A contract created by the words of the parties

   d. _____ A contract in which both parties promise something

Are the following statements true (T) or false (F)?

2. ____ When a buyer and seller sign a real estate sales contract, the buyer receives actual title.

3. ____ Because the buyer takes immediate possession of the property under an installment sales contract, the buyer receives title when the contract is signed.

4. ____ A broker cannot combine the earnest money deposits from several real estate transactions involving unrelated parties into the same account.

5. ____ In an installment sales contract the buyer is obligated to pay the real estate taxes and insurance on a property even though title does not pass until the loan is paid.

Supply the term that best matches each of the following descriptions.

6. _____ Time limits stated in the contract that must be met

7. _____ A short version of the contract that includes all of the essential contract terms

8. _____ A contract in which the parties have performed all of the provisions

9. _____ An agreement that does not meet all of the required contract elements

10. _____ A contract that appears to be valid but is not legally enforceable

11. _____ A law that defines which party suffers a loss if the property is destroyed before the closing

12. _____ A sales contract in which the buyer takes possession of the property but the seller retains title until the loan is paid

13. _____ A cash deposit showing good faith on the part of the buyer

SECTION 2
THE REQUIRED ELEMENTS OF A CONTRACT

For contracts to be valid and enforceable, they must contain certain elements. This section will discuss five required elements of a contract: (1) legally competent parties, (2) offer and acceptance (also referred to as *meeting of the minds*), (3) reality of consent, (4) consideration and (5) legality of object.

LEGALLY COMPETENT PARTIES

The parties to the contract must be *legally competent* (have the legal capacity to enter into the contract). This generally means that they have sufficient mental capacity, are of legal age and have the authority to act.

The legal age (also called the age of majority by the minor) varies among states but usually is the age of 18. Contracts with a minor are voidable (by the minor). An exception is a contract with a minor for necessities like food and shelter. These contracts are enforceable. In some states contracts with a minor are void by statute.

Note: A sales contract for the purchase of real estate probably would not be considered a necessity, but leases or rent agreements would be.

Legal competency of the parties also means that neither of the parties is suffering a mental handicap. A person under the influence of alcohol or drugs may be considered temporarily insane and any contract entered into by that person is therefore *voidable*. If a mentally disabled person has a legal guardian, his or her contracts are *void*. If such a person has no legal guardian, the contracts are *voidable*.

OFFER AND ACCEPTANCE

An offer must be made by one party and accepted by another party. **Offer and acceptance** is also called a **meeting of the minds**, meaning the parties agree on the terms. Agreement by the parties is also called **mutual assent**. The parties must have full and accurate knowledge of the terms and conditions of the contract, otherwise the contract will be void.

Requirements for Offers

To be a legal offer, the following requirements must be met:

- *Contractual intent*—The person making the offer must appear to intend that the offer be legally binding.

EXAMPLE: Two friends at a party are talking about their houses. In jest, one offers to buy the other's house for "one hundred million dollars." There is no contractual intent.

- *Communicated*—An offer must be communicated to the offeree.
- *Definite terms*—The terms must be definite enough to allow the courts to determine the intention of the parties.

Terms of a real estate sales contract should include

- identity of the parties,
- description of the subject matter,
- time for performance and
- the price to be paid.

An offer will be terminated under any of the following circumstances:

- *Expiration of the time period* stated in the offer or, if not stated, a reasonable period of time (In this case the offer has *expired* or *lapsed*.)
- *Withdrawal* of the offer at any time *before it is accepted*
- *Death* or *insanity* of either party
- *Destruction* of the property
- *Changing* the offer *terms* (creates a *counteroffer* and terminates the original offer)
- *Rejection* of the offer

Tip: The offeree must agree to every item of the offer. If any changes are made, it is a counteroffer and the original offer has ended.

REALITY OF CONSENT

Assent by the parties to a contract must be freely given (called *reality of consent*).

Contracts under Duress

Duress is the use of *force* or the *threat of force* to obtain an agreement. The consenting party must not be coerced or pressured into the contract. Duress includes both physical force and mental stress. Contracts made under duress are *voidable* at the option of the innocent party.

Contracts under Undue Influence

The parties must not be prevented from acting under their own free will. This can occur when one party places special trust or confidence in another party. This includes relationships such as lawyer/client or doctor/patient. Contracts under *undue influence are voidable* at the option of the innocent party.

EXAMPLE: A son has taken care of his elderly father's financial affairs for a number of years, and the father has become totally reliant on the advice of his son. The son then convinces his father to sell him a large tract of land at a price far below market value. The sale may be voided by the courts for undue influence.

Contracts under Misrepresentation or Fraud

Contracts made under *fraud, tricks, misrepresentation* or *mutual mistake* are *voidable* at the option of the injured party. The fraud must be relied and acted on by the party to his or her detriment.

EXAMPLE: A broker shows a house to a buyer who wants to be in a particular school district. The broker states that the house is in the district desired by the buyer when, in fact, the broker knows that the school boundaries have recently changed and the house is now in another school district. Because of fraud there is no mutual agreement and the buyer can rescind the contract.

LEGALLY SUFFICIENT CONSIDERATION

Consideration is what the parties agree to give each other. Consideration can be anything of *value*, including money, property, personal services, a promise to act, giving up a right to act or love and affection.

EXAMPLE: In a real estate sales contract the buyer is giving a promise to pay *money* and the seller is giving a promise to convey *title* to the property.

 Note: The values of the considerations given by the parties do not have to be equal. One party could sell a house for an amount that is below market value and it still would be considered sufficient consideration.

LEGALITY OF OBJECT

The purpose of the contract must not be illegal or against public policy. It would be contradictory for the courts to enforce contracts that will break the law.

EXAMPLE: Bob, who is not a licensed broker, sells the house of his neighbor. Bob cannot sue for a commission because all states require that an agent be licensed to be entitled to a commission.

Note: Ignorance of the law is not an excuse. If the parties entered into the contract not knowing that the contract's purpose was illegal, it will still be void.

PROPER LEGAL FORM

Proper legal form is *not* a required element for *all* contracts. However, it does apply to some contracts that must be in writing to be enforceable.

Statute of Frauds

Every state has adopted the **statute of frauds,** which requires that certain types of contracts be in writing to be enforceable. A contract that is not in writing, as required by the statute of frauds, cannot be enforced in court. Contracts that must be in writing to be enforceable include

- contracts for the sale of real estate;
- land contracts, options to purchase, deeds and mortgages; and
- contracts not to be performed within one year of the date created.

EXAMPLE: A lease for more than one year has to be in writing to be enforceable.

Parol Evidence Rule

Verbal evidence is called **parol evidence.** The concept of parol evidence means that oral evidence will not be allowed to alter or replace a written contract. Oral evidence may be allowed, however, if the written contract is incomplete or ambiguous or to show fraud or undue influence.

Statute of Limitations

State laws sets time limits under **statute of limitations** for starting legal proceedings. The length of time varies among states and according to the type of legal action sought. Time limits to start legal action for breach of contract generally vary from three to seven years.

BEFORE READING THE NEXT SECTION, COMPLETE THE SECTION 2 REVIEW EXERCISES AND COMPARE YOUR ANSWERS WITH THE SOLUTIONS AT THE END OF THE CHAPTER.

SECTION 2
REVIEW EXERCISES

1. Name the contract requirement that corresponds to each description.

a. _____ An agreement under duress

b. _____ An agreement with a minor

c. _____ A counteroffer

d. _____ An agreement made by using trickery

e. _____ Agreeing to something illegal

f. _____ Rejection of an offer

g. _____ An agreement with someone who is intoxicated

h. _____ Exerting undue influence on a party to an agreement

Are the following statements true (T) or false (F)?

2. ____ The legal age to be considered an adult in most states is 21.

3. ____ A person under the influence of drugs or alcohol is considered to be suffering a mental handicap.

4. ____ An offer can be terminated by a rejection, a counteroffer or expiration.

5. ____ An oral contract for a six-month real estate lease is valid.

Supply the term that best matches each of the following descriptions.

6. _____ A meeting of the minds

7. _____ A party who has legal capacity

8. _____ Anything of value given by parties to a contract

9. _____ Requires that certain contracts must be in writing to be enforceable

10. _____ Oral evidence not allowed to contradict a written contract

SECTION 3
ENDING THE CONTRACT

This section discusses how contracts are terminated (discharged), what happens if a party breaches (defaults on) the contract and how parties may withdraw from a contract.

DISCHARGE OF A CONTRACT

- *Complete performance*—If all of the contract terms are completed, the contract is discharged.
- *Partial performance*—Partial performance may be enough to end the contract if the party for whom the acts have not been done agrees in writing.
- *Substantial performance*—If some of the contract details are not completed, there still may be sufficient performance to fulfill the contract. Substantial performance may be sufficient to force payment (minus any damages caused by the uncompleted details) even if the other party does not agree.
- *Impossibility of performance*—If an act required by the contract cannot be legally accomplished, the contract is ended.

EXAMPLE: Destruction of the property before the closing will end the sales contract.

- *Mutual agreement of the parties*—The parties to the contract may mutually agree to cancel and end the contract.
- *Operation of law*—The law may terminate the contract.

EXAMPLE: A contract that was created as a result of fraud may be terminated by the court.

DEFAULT—BREACH OF A CONTRACT

In general a **breach of contract** occurs when a party fails to comply, without legal excuse, with the key terms of the contract. A breach of contract is also referred to as *default*. In a real estate sales contract, when a buyer or seller defaults, the other party has the following alternatives:

Buyer's Remedies if the Seller Defaults

- *Rescind* or *terminate* the contract and recover the earnest money.
- Sue for **specific performance.** This action forces the seller to go through with the terms of the contract.
- Sue the seller for the actual money lost (*compensatory damages*).

Seller's Remedies if the Buyer Defaults

- *Rescind* or *terminate* the contract. Any earnest money must be returned (liquidated damages).
- Declare the contract *forfeited* and possibly retain any earnest money.
- Sue for specific performance to force the buyer to go through with the terms of the contract.
- Sue the buyer for the actual money lost (*compensatory damages*).

Note: Rescission cancels the contract and restores the parties to their original positions; forfeiture is recognizing default by one of the parties.

WITHDRAWING FROM CONTRACTS

A party may end involvement with the contract without actually terminating the contract through an *assignment* or *novation*.

In an **assignment** a party's rights and obligations under the contract are transferred (assigned) to someone else. An assignment cannot occur if it is prohibited by the contract. If obligations are assigned, the new obligor is *primarily* liable and the old obligor is *secondarily* liable.

EXAMPLE: If a loan is assumed by the buyer of a property, it is an assignment of the duties in the loan contract.

Tip: Contracts requiring performance related to some personal quality or unique ability cannot be transferred. These are called personal services contracts.

Novation is the substitution of a new contract for an old one between the same or new parties (called novation of the parties). The parties must intend to discharge the old contract.

EXAMPLE: A lender allows the buyer to assume the seller's loan and releases the seller from further liability. The new agreement replaces the old loan agreement.

**COMPLETE THE SECTION 3 REVIEW EXERCISES AND COMPARE YOUR ANSWERS
WITH THE SOLUTIONS AT THE END OF THE CHAPTER.**

SECTION 3
REVIEW EXERCISES

1. Name the method used to terminate a contract that corresponds to each description.
   - a. _____ All but minor details in the contract are completed.
   - b. _____ A provision in the contract cannot be legally completed.
   - c. _____ All terms of the contract are complete.
   - d. _____ Parties agree to end the contract.
   - e. _____ Enough of the terms are fulfilled to end the contract.
   - f. _____ The contract is terminated by law.

Are the following statements true (T) or false (F)?

2. ____ A contract may not be terminated until all of the terms have been completed.

3. ____ If either the buyer or the seller breaches a real estate sales contract, the other party may sue for damages or specific performance.

4. ____ An assignment of obligations in a contract effectively relieves the party of those obligations.

Supply the term that best matches each of the following descriptions.

5. _____ A suit to force another party to complete the contract terms

6. _____ Transferring contract rights or obligations

7. _____ Substituting a new contract for an old one

SOLUTIONS

FOR SECTION REVIEW EXERCISES

SECTION 1

1. a. Implied contract   b. Unilateral contract   c. Express contract
   d. Bilateral contract

2. FALSE The buyer receives *equitable title* when the sales *contract is signed*. The buyer receives *legal title* when the *deed is delivered*.

3. FALSE The buyer does not receive title until the loan is repaid to the seller.

4. FALSE The broker cannot commingle personal money with earnest money deposits but deposits from any number of transactions can be put into the same escrow account.

5. TRUE

6. Time is of the essence

7. Binder

8. Executed contract

9. Void contract

10. Unenforceable contract

11. Vendor and Purchaser Risk Act

12. Installment sales contract

13. Earnest money deposit

SECTION 2

1. a. Reality of consent   b. Competent parties   c. Offer and acceptance
   d. Reality of consent   e. Legal object   f. Offer and acceptance
   g. Competent parties   h. Reality of consent

2. FALSE The legal age for adults in most states is 18.

3. TRUE

4. TRUE

5. TRUE

6. Mutual assent

7. Competent parties

8. Consideration

9. Statute of frauds

10. Parol evidence rule

SECTION 3

1. a. Substantial performance   b. Impossibility of performance
   c. Complete performance   d. Mutual agreement   e. Partial performance
   f. Operation of law

2. FALSE Contracts can be terminated for partial or substantial performance.

3. TRUE

4. FALSE The new obligor is primarily liable and the old obligor is secondarily liable.

5. Specific performance

6. Assignment

7. Novation

CHAPTER 15
LISTING AGREEMENTS

The last chapter introduced general contract principles and some characteristics of real estate sales contracts. In this chapter you learn about the listing contract used by brokers when they are hired. *Section 1* covers the various types of listing agreements. *Section 2* covers requirements for creating listing agreements and how they are terminated. Remember to use the Study Tool Kit to reference key information and to update your progress checklist.

Learning Objectives

Track your progress as you work through the chapter by checking each learning objective when you complete it.

____ List and explain five types of listing agreements used by brokers.

____ Explain the difference between exclusive-agency and exclusive-right-to-sell listing contracts.

____ List and describe the information found in most listing contracts.

____ Calculate the broker's commission.

____ Calculate the selling price in a net listing.

____ List and explain the different ways a listing agreement can be terminated.

Key Terms and Phrases

Track your progress as you work through the chapter by checking each term when you understand its meaning.

____ Broker protection clause

____ Competitive market analysis (CMA)

____ Exclusive-agency listing

____ Exclusive-right-to-sell listing

____ Listing contract

____ Multiple listing

____ Multiple-listing service (MLS)

____ Net listing

____ Open listing

SECTION 1
TYPES OF LISTING AGREEMENTS

A **listing contract** is an agreement between a broker and a seller in which the broker is hired as an agent of the seller to find a ready, willing and able buyer for the seller's real estate.

OPEN LISTING

An **open listing** is also called a *simple listing* or *general listing*. With this type of listing the seller may employ any number of brokers at the same time, but the seller owes a commission only to the broker who sells the property. If the seller sells the property, the broker is not entitled to a commission.

EXAMPLE: Able gives several brokers in the area an open listing to sell the house. Broker Baker brings in a buyer for the house. Baker is entitled to a commission.

EXAMPLE: Able gives several brokers in the area an open listing to sell the house. Before any of the brokers brings a buyer for the house, Able finds a buyer. No commission is owed to any of the brokers.

EXCLUSIVE-AGENCY LISTING

With an **exclusive-agency listing** the seller employs *only one broker*. Just as in an open listing, the broker is not entitled to a commission if the owner sells the property.

EXAMPLE: Able gives Baker an exclusive-agency listing. Before Baker can find a buyer, Able sells the property. No commission is owed to the broker.

EXAMPLE: Able gives Baker an exclusive-agency listing. Broker Cain approaches Able with a buyer. Able cannot agree to let Cain work for him under the terms of the exclusive agency agreement with Baker. Cain will have to work with Baker.

EXCLUSIVE-RIGHT-TO-SELL LISTING

Under an **exclusive-right-to-sell listing** the seller *employs one broker*. But unlike the exclusive-agency listing, if a broker other than the listing broker sells the property, the listing broker still will be paid a commission. Even if the property is sold by the owner, the broker will be entitled to a commission. This is the most common form of listing agreement used by brokers.

A **broker protection clause** (also called a *carryover provision* or a *holdover provision*) provides that even after the listing has expired, the listing broker is entitled to a commission if the property is sold to anyone introduced to the property during the listing period. A period of time is specified in the provision and usually parallels the time period of the listing. To prevent a dual listing, the clause will not be enforced if the seller relists with a new broker. Characteristics of open and exclusive listing agreements are included in Figure 15.1.

Tip: The exclusive-agency and exclusive-right-to-sell listing agreements sound the same, but a significant difference is the circumstance in which a broker is entitled to receive a commission.

Type of Listing	Agent	Commission
Open	Many brokers	Only to broker who sells property
Exclusive agency	One broker	To listing broker if not sold by owner
Exclusive right to sell	One broker	To listing broker no matter who sells

FIGURE 15.1
Comparison of Listings

MULTIPLE LISTING

A **multiple listing** actually refers to a service provided by brokers rather than to a specific type of listing. It is created by a clause included in an exclusive listing agreement that allows the broker to turn over listing information to a multiple-listing service within a specified period of time.

A **multiple-listing service** is usually referred to as an **MLS**. The MLS is an organization of brokers who agree to share listing information. This provides greater exposure for a broker's listing and also makes information on other listed properties available to all brokers.

NET LISTING

Unlike other listing agreements, which typically calculate the commissions as a percentage of the selling price, a **net listing** states the amount that the seller is to receive (the net amount) from the sale of the property. The broker's commission is any amount *above the net amount* due to the seller. The broker sets the asking price for the property. This type of listing is *illegal* in many states and discouraged in others because of the potential for fraud by brokers.

EXAMPLE: A seller wants to net $90,000 from the sale of the property. The broker sells the property for $110,000. The seller gets $90,000, and the broker's commission is $20,000.

BUYER BROKER AGREEMENTS

Traditionally, sellers sign listing contracts with real estate brokers to sell their properties. Chapter 13, however, discussed the growing concept of buyer brokerage. The buyer and broker may enter into an agreement in which the broker represents the buyer in the purchase of a property. These agreements can be similar to the exclusive-right-to-sell contracts with sellers. Under an exclusive agreement, the broker may earn a commission from the buyer even if the buyer purchases a house without the assistance of the broker. Also, the signing of more than one broker's contract could result in the buyer's owing more than one commission. A buyer broker agreement typically would include the following:

- The term of the agreement, listing the beginning and ending dates.
- General characteristics of the property being sought by the buyer. This includes the type of property (e.g., residential, commercial), price range and location.
- A list of the broker's obligations during the term of the agreement. These could include assisting the buyer in locating and inspecting available properties, assisting the buyer in obtaining information on available properties, assisting the buyer in preparing offers and

negotiating terms, assisting the buyer in obtaining financing, monitoring closing procedures and deadlines.

- A list of the buyer's obligations during the term of the agreement. These could include providing information to assist the broker, such as financial information to assess the buyer's ability to secure financing, and conducting all negotiations in good faith.

BEFORE READING THE NEXT SECTION, COMPLETE THE SECTION 1 REVIEW EXERCISES AND COMPARE YOUR ANSWERS WITH THE SOLUTIONS AT THE END OF THE CHAPTER.

SECTION 1
REVIEW EXERCISES

1. Name the type of listing agreement that best corresponds to each description.

   a. _____ The broker will receive a commission no matter who sells the property.

   b. _____ Information will be shared with other brokers.

   c. _____ The seller can hire numerous brokers.

   d. _____ One broker is hired but will not receive a commission if the property is sold by the seller.

   e. _____ The seller will receive a predetermined amount from the sales price.

Are the following statements true (T) or false (F)?

2. ____ The exclusive-agency listing is the most desirable listing for a broker.

3. ____ Several brokers can be hired under an exclusive-agency listing.

4. ____ Because of the potential for fraud, net listings are illegal in many states.

Supply the term that best matches each of the following descriptions.

5. _____ An organization of brokers who share listing information.

6. _____ An agreement between a broker and a seller to market the seller's property in exchange for a commission.

SECTION 2
CREATING AND TERMINATING LISTINGS

INFORMATION INCLUDED IN LISTINGS

There is no standard listing contract that is used throughout the country. A wide variety of forms are used, depending on local state rules, customs and broker or MLS preferences. While there is no standard format, certain information is required in most listing contracts.

- *The type of listing*—Defines whether the listing is an exclusive-agency, exclusive-right-to-sell or an open listing. It also gives the broker authority to act on the seller's behalf.

- *Names and signatures of broker and seller*—The broker (or in some areas the broker's associates) and all parties with an ownership interest in the property should be included on the contract.
- *Date*—The date the contract is signed by the parties.
- *Length*—The time period the listing is to be in effect.
- *Listing price of the property*—The *seller* ultimately decides the listing price for the property. However, the broker may help the seller determine the price by performing a **competitive market analysis (CMA).** The CMA is performed by reviewing recent sales of similar properties in the area and other competing properties currently on the market, to arrive at a price range for the listed property. Chapter 19 discusses the appraisal methods used to determine the market value of property.
- *Commission*—This includes the amount of the broker's commission, when it is to be paid and how the commission will be determined (i.e., a percentage of the sales price or a flat fee). Commission calculations will be discussed later in this section.
- *Property description*—The address or legal description of the property.
- *Discrimination*—Marketing of the property must comply with all federal, state and local fair housing laws.
- *Antitrust practices*—The commission amount is set by agreement between the seller and the broker and not set by any government or trade organization.
- *Earnest money deposits*—The handling and depositing of earnest money deposits. Should include a provision regarding the disposition of the earnest money if the buyer or seller defaults.
- *Personal property*—Personal property that is to be left with the real estate and any fixtures that are to be removed by the seller should be clearly identified.
- *Marketing the property*—Permission by the seller for the broker to place sale signs, advertise and market the property.
- *MLS*—Permission by the seller for the broker to submit the listing information to the MLS.
- *Possession*—Proposed date for possession of the property by the buyer. The seller should take into consideration time needed to make moving arrangements.
- *Homeowner warranty program*—If the seller is willing to pay for a homeowner warranty program for the property, this should be included.
- *Termination*—Under what circumstances the contract can be terminated.
- *Broker protection clause* or *holdover provision*—The terms for any *carryover provision* that provides the payment of a commission to the broker after the listing has expired.

COMMISSION CALCULATIONS

Calculating the Amount of Commission

The commission *amount* is usually calculated as a *percentage of the selling price.* The formula for the calculation is Commission Amount = Selling Price × Commission Rate, or

$$C = SP \times R,$$

where C = *commission amount,* SP = *selling price* and R = *commission rate.*

EXAMPLE: A house sells for $150,000, and the broker is to receive a 6 percent commission. The amount of the commission is $9,000 ($150,000 × .06 [6%] = $9,000).

Calculating the Commission Rate

We can also find the broker's commission *rate,* using the same information as above.

Formula: $R = C \div SP$

.06 = $9,000 \div $150,000

Calculating the Selling Price

If we know the amount of the commission (income) and the commission rate, we can turn the formula around and find the *selling price*. Using the amounts in the example above, we can find the selling price.

Formula: $SP = C \div R$

$150,000 = $9,000 \div .06

Calculating the Selling Price—Net Listing

If the broker wishes to make a 6 percent commission under a net listing and the seller wants $90,000, the amount to the seller is known but the selling price is not. To find the selling price for the property to satisfy both the seller and the broker, do the following;

Net to seller $\div$ (100% $-$ R)

100% $-$ 6% = 94%, and $90,000 $\div$ .94 = $95,745

TERMINATION OF LISTING AGREEMENTS

Listing contracts may be terminated for all of the following reasons:

- *Performance by the broker*—When the broker has successfully sold the property, the listing agreement is complete.
- *Expiration of time stated in the agreement*—The listing agreement should include a definite period of time. When this time period is over, the listing agreement is terminated. *Automatic extensions* of the listing time periods are discouraged and are illegal in some states. As noted in Section 1, brokers may include a protection clause.
- *Abandonment by the broker*—If the broker has done nothing to market the property, the seller may be able to terminate the listing.
- *Revocation by the owner*—The seller can revoke the listing but may be liable to the broker for damages.
- *Renunciation by the broker*—The broker can renounce the listing but may be liable to the owner for damages.
- *Death, insanity or bankruptcy of either party*—These will usually cancel the listing.
- *Destruction of the property*—Destruction of the property makes it impossible to perform the agreement.
- *Mutual consent*—The parties may mutually agree to end the listing.
- *A change in the property use*—If the use of the property changes significantly, the listing may be terminated.
- Transfer of title by operation of law.

EXAMPLE: The owner files bankruptcy and the property is sold to satisfy the creditors, or the property is condemned through eminent domain.

COMPLETE THE SECTION 2 REVIEW EXERCISES AND COMPARE YOUR ANSWERS WITH THE SOLUTIONS AT THE END OF THE CHAPTER.

SECTION 2

REVIEW EXERCISES

1. Name the type of provision found in a listing contract that best fits each description.

   a. _____ The amount the broker will earn

   b. _____ Permission to place a sign on the property

   c. _____ The listing price

   d. _____ Specifies that the agreement is an exclusive-right-to-sell listing

   e. _____ The legal address of the property

   f. _____ Provides for the broker to get a commission after the listing has expired

   g. _____ Must comply with all fair housing laws

   h. _____ What property is to be left with the real estate

2. Supply the correct formula and use it to calculate the amount of commission, using the following information: A house sells for $180,000 and the broker is to receive a 5 percent commission.

   _____

3. Supply the correct formula and use it to calculate the commission rate, using the following information: A house sells for $160,000 and the broker earns a commission of $9,600.

   _____

4. Supply the correct formula and use it to calculate the selling price, using the following information: The broker earns a commission of $10,000, which is a 5 percent commission.

   _____

Are the following statements true (T) or false (F)?

5. ____ It is the broker's responsibility to decide the listing price of the property.

6. ____ The commission amount is set by the broker's local MLS rules.

7. ____ If the property is destroyed before being sold, the listing agreement is terminated.

Supply the term that best matches each of the following descriptions.

8. _____ A review of the sales of similar properties in the area to arrive at a price range for the property

9. _____ Entitles the broker to a commission after the listing contract has expired

SOLUTIONS
FOR SECTION REVIEW EXERCISES

SECTION 1

1. a. Exclusive-right-to-sell listing   b. Multiple listing   c. Open listing
   d. Exclusive-agency listing   e. Net listing
2. FALSE The exclusive-right-to-sell listing is the most desirable listing for a broker because it increases the opportunity to collect a commission.
3. FALSE Only one broker is hired under an exclusive-agency listing.
4. TRUE
5. Multiple listing service (MLS)
6. Listing contract

SECTION 2

1. a. Commission   b. Marketing the property   c. Price of the property
   d. Type of listing   e. Property description   f. Carryover provision
   g. Discrimination prohibition   h. Personal property
2. Commission Amount = Selling Price × Commission Rate ($C = SP \times R$)
   $9,000 = $180,000 × .05
3. Commission Rate = Commission Amount ÷ Selling Price ($R = C \div SP$)
   6% = $9,600 ÷ $160,000
4. Selling Price = Commission Amount ÷ Commission Rate ($SP = C \div R$)
   $200,000 = $10,000 ÷ .05
5. FALSE It is the seller's responsibility to decide the listing price of the property.
6. FALSE The commission amount is set by agreement between the broker and the seller.
7. TRUE
8. Competitive market analysis (CMA)
9. Carryover provision

CHAPTER 16

REAL ESTATE LICENSING LAWS

All of the states and the District of Columbia require that real estate people be licensed. This chapter presents *general* licensing rules, but because licensing laws differ, readers should find out what the specific rules are in their own areas. *Section 1* covers the purpose and administration of licensing laws, who must be licensed, who is exempt from licensing and the different license categories. *Section 2* covers licensing requirements, rules for operating a real estate business, suspending and revoking licenses and recovery funds. Remember to use the Study Tool Kit to reference key information and to update your progress checklist.

Learning Objectives

Track your progress as you work through the chapter by checking each learning objective when you complete it.

____ Describe the reasons for licensing real estate professionals.

____ List activities that generally require a real estate license.

____ List activities that usually do not require a real estate license.

____ Describe the differences between a broker, a salesperson and an associate broker.

____ Describe the purpose of reciprocal agreements and nonresident licenses.

____ List and describe the licensing requirements.

____ List and describe the requirements for running a real estate business.

____ Describe some of the ways a license can be suspended or revoked.

____ Describe the purpose and operation of a recovery fund.

Key Terms and Phrases

Track your progress as you work through the chapter by checking each term when you understand its meaning.

____ ARELLO   ____ Nonresident license

____ Associate broker   ____ Reciprocal agreements

____ Blind ads   ____ Recovery fund

____ Broker's license   ____ Salesperson's license

____ Commingling funds

ADMINISTRATION OF LICENSING LAWS

Licensing law requirements vary among states, but all are intended to accomplish the following:

- *Evaluate the competency* of persons seeking licenses
- *Protect the public* from dishonest and unprofessional licensees
- *Maintain high standards* in the real estate profession

LICENSING AGENCIES

Each licensing law is administered by a licensing authority, usually called a *real estate commission, department* or *board*. Administration of the licensing law includes activities such as

- issuing and renewing licenses,
- preparing licensing forms,
- establishing content and structure of licensing tests,
- collecting fees,
- conducting disciplinary hearings,
- setting standards for real estate schools and
- imposing penalties.

The licensing authority adopts *rules* and *regulations* to assist in the administration of the licensing laws.

ARELLO

The Association of Real Estate License Law Officials (**ARELLO**) is a federation of real estate law officials to assist each other in the administration and enforcement of license laws in the United States. This organization promotes uniform policies and standards for license law administration. While state licensing laws vary, many of their major provisions are similar because they are based on the model recommended by ARELLO.

WHO IS REQUIRED TO BE LICENSED

Persons are usually required to be licensed if they (1) perform or offer to perform the following *services* (2) *for another* and (3) *for compensation* or the promise of compensation:

- *Sell* real estate
- *List* real estate for sale
- *Purchase* real estate
- Negotiate the *exchange* of real estate
- *Lease* or rent real estate (e.g., rental referral services)
- *Manage* real estate

Other activities that *may* require a real estate license (depending on the state) include

- auctioning real estate;
- selling cemetery lots;
- sale of campground lots;
- sale of mineral, oil and gas rights;
- sale of time-shares;
- negotiating mortgage loans (mortgage brokers);
- managing property; and
- subdividing and developing real estate.

WHO IS EXEMPT FROM THE LAWS

Licensing laws generally *do not* require licensing of the following persons:

- Owners selling or leasing their own property
- Salaried employees managing or leasing properties owned by their employer (if the employer's principal occupation is *not* dealing in real estate)
- Someone acting under a power of attorney (also called an attorney-in-fact)
- An attorney-at-law (if performing the normal duties as a lawyer)
- A person selling real estate under court order (e.g., a receiver, a trustee, an administrator or an executor handling a deceased's estate or a guardian)
- Public officials and employees while performing their regular duties

LICENSE CATEGORIES

Types of licenses vary among states but generally fall into two categories.

1. *Broker license:* A person holding a **broker's license** may own or manage a real estate business. All states allow brokers to hire other licensed brokers or salespersons to sell real estate.
2. *Salesperson license:* A person holding a **salesperson's license** must be employed by a broker. A salesperson performs real estate activities under the direction, guidance and responsibility of the employing broker. Persons holding salesperson's licenses may not operate their own real estate businesses.

Associate broker: Some states issue a special license called an **associate broker** or broker-salesperson license. Persons holding this designation have passed the broker's exam and are qualified to hold the broker's license but are working for other brokers rather than running their own businesses.

Note: In everyday language a real estate agent refers to any licensee (broker or salesperson) who participates in real estate transactions.

Tip: The basic license distinction is that a broker can hire salespeople and other brokers, but a salesperson must work for a broker.

CORPORATIONS AND PARTNERSHIP LICENSES

A real estate business may take the form of a corporation or partnership. Rules regarding the licensing of corporation officers and partners vary among states. Generally, the people running a business (officers or partners) must have *brokers' licenses.*

NONRESIDENT (RECIPROCAL) LICENSES

A person must be licensed in the state where he or she conducts real estate transactions. To facilitate situations in which a licensee wishes to be involved in real estate transactions in another state, **reciprocal agreements** have been developed between most states. These agreements provide for the granting of out-of-state, **nonresident licenses** to brokers or salespeople who wish to sell real estate in more than one state. The reciprocal agreement includes requirements that must be met before a nonresident license is granted. When operating out-of-state, the licensee may be required to file a *notice of consent* with the state of which he or she is not a resident. This permits that state to receive legal summonses on behalf of the nonresident licensee and makes it easier for a resident of the state to serve a summons against the out-of-state licensee.

LICENSE RENEWAL OR TRANSFER

Licenses remain in effect for the period of time specified in the licensing laws. Some states require payment of only a renewal fee, others require completion of *continuing education* or additional requirements.

A broker or salesperson may wish to *transfer* his or her license to another broker. This is allowed under licensing laws if certain conditions and procedures are followed.

BEFORE READING THE NEXT SECTION, COMPLETE THE SECTION 1 REVIEW EXERCISES AND COMPARE YOUR ANSWERS WITH THE SOLUTIONS AT THE END OF THE CHAPTER.

SECTION 1

REVIEW EXERCISES

1. Name the type of license associated with each of the following descriptions.
   a. _____ A broker hired by another broker
   b. _____ An entry-level real estate license
   c. _____ Able to hire other brokers and salespersons
   d. _____ Employed by a broker to conduct real estate transactions

2. For each of the following activities determine whether it probably would require a license.
   a. _____ An owner hires someone to list his or her property for sale
   b. _____ A house is advertised as "For sale by owner"

    c. _____ A person negotiates an exchange of buildings between
          two property owners

    d. _____ An employee of the city leases park land to various
          businesses

Are the following statements true (T) or false (F)?

3. ____ One of the reasons for licensing real estate professionals is to provide a source of
income for the state.

4. ____ Licensing authorities adopt rules and regulations to help administer licensing laws.

5. ____ Associate brokers hire salespeople to work for them.

Supply the term that best matches each of the following descriptions.

6. _____ A license granted to brokers operating in another state

7. _____ Licensee in charge of a real estate office

8. _____ A federation of real estate law officials to assist each other
in the administration and enforcement of license laws

9. _____ A broker employed by another broker

10. _____ Agreements between states that make it easier for brokers
to obtain an out-of-state license

SECTION 2
LICENSING REQUIREMENTS

REQUIREMENTS FOR LICENSING

Requirements for licensing vary among states, but most require the following:

- *Age*—Applicants must be a minimum age, usually 18 years.
- *Education*—Applicants must complete a minimum number of hours in real estate education
courses. While the number of hours required varies by state, brokers are usually required to
complete more hours of instruction than salespersons.
- *Examination*—A written examination is required to obtain either a broker's or a salesperson's
license. State license laws specify length of examinations, scores needed for passing and
rules for retaking exams. Most states use professional testing services to develop and administer licensing exams.
- *Experience*—Broker applicants may be required to have a stated minimum amount of experience as salespersons. Because the salesperson license is considered an entry-level license,
there is no experience requirement.
- Applicants must not have had a real estate license or other professional license revoked
within a specified period of time.
- Applicants must not have been convicted of certain types of crime.
- Background checks, including personal character references, credit reports, or fingerprints,
may be made.
- Submission of an application and payment of the appropriate licensing fees to the state.

A growing number of states require the completion of additional hours of real
estate education *for license renewal*. The purpose is to keep licensees current in various
real estate topics.

OPERATING A REAL ESTATE BUSINESS

Licensing laws include rules mandating how a real estate business must be run. While the rules vary among states, they commonly include the following areas:

- A *definite place of business* must be maintained in the state.
- Real estate businesses are allowed to operate one or more *branch offices.*
- Brokers must maintain detailed *records* of all transactions and monies received. Copies of documents used in transactions must be maintained and all records may be inspected by the state.
- Brokers are required to maintain *escrow* or *trust accounts* and all monies received from clients must be placed in the account. Brokers are not allowed to commingle their own money with the client's. **Commingling funds** is mixing the broker's business or personal money with the client's money, usually by placing both in the same account.

Tip: Remember that brokers can't commingle their own money with the clients', but they usually can consolidate funds from different clients.

- *Fraudulent advertising* may not be used by brokers. Advertising that does not include the broker or real estate company name gives the impression that the property is not being handled by a broker. These are called **blind ads** and cannot be used.

SUSPENDING OR REVOKING A LICENSE

One of the ways the state exercises control over brokers and salespersons is the power to suspend or revoke their licenses. State laws list numerous reasons for suspending or revoking real estate licenses. These generally include violation of the state's licensing act, committing misrepresentation or fraud, commingling personal money with clients' funds, obtaining a license through the use of fraud, negligence or conviction of certain types of crimes.

Disciplinary Hearings

When a complaint against a licensee is received, an investigation is conducted by the state. Based on the results of the investigation, a formal hearing may be held by a disciplinary board. A decision to impose a fine or to suspend or revoke a license may result from the hearing.

Additional Penalties

In addition to having their licenses suspended or revoked, licensees may face court ordered *fines* or *imprisonment* for criminal violations of state laws.

REAL ESTATE RECOVERY FUND

Most states have established real estate **recovery funds** to provide *compensation to the public* for financial losses caused by actions of real estate licensees. Losses typically could result from violations of the licensing act, fraud, discrimination, forgery or misrepresentation. The recovery fund balance is usually maintained by fees paid by brokers and salespersons.

Anyone seeking reimbursement from the fund must follow the procedures and requirements included in the licensing rules. Usually a judgment against the licensee must first be obtained, and the injured party must have been unsuccessful in trying to collect on the judgment before money will be paid out of the fund.

> **Tip: Don't confuse the purpose of the recovery fund. It is to reimburse the public, not licensees.**

SURETY BONDS

Another method of protecting the public in some states is the requirement that a *bond* be *posted with the state* before a license is issued. The bond money then is used for payment of an uncollectible judgment against a licensee.

COMPLETE THE SECTION 2 REVIEW EXERCISES AND COMPARE YOUR ANSWERS WITH THE SOLUTIONS AT THE END OF THE CHAPTER.

SECTION 2
REVIEW EXERCISES

Are the following statements true (T) or false (F)?

1. ____ A salesperson's license does not require real estate experience.

2. ____ Because salespeople are new to the field of real estate, education requirements are generally greater than those for brokers.

3. ____ Applicants who recently had their insurance licenses revoked probably would be denied real estate licenses.

4. ____ The primary purpose of requiring that continuing education courses be completed when licenses are renewed is to prevent anyone not active in real estate from renewing a license.

5. ____ Salespersons who lie on their license applications probably will lose their licenses when it is discovered.

6. ____ Someone who suffers financial damages due to the actions of a licensee usually can obtain compensation from the recovery fund immediately after obtaining a judgment against the licensee.

7. ____ Bonding a licensee is used by some states to protect the licensee from loss.

Supply the term that best matches each of the following descriptions.

8. _____ An account operated by the state that can be used to pay uncollectible judgments against licensees

9. _____ Advertising used by the broker that does not include the broker's name or the name of the real estate company

10. _____ Mixing the broker's personal money with the client's

SOLUTIONS
FOR SECTION REVIEW EXERCISES

SECTION 1

1. a. Associate brokers are hired by another broker.   b. Salesperson license is an entry-level real estate license. A salesperson must work under the direction of a broker.   c. Brokers are able to hire other brokers and salespersons.   d. A salesperson is employed by a broker to conduct real estate transactions.

2. a. Listing property for sale requires a real estate license.   b. An owner selling his or her house without the assistance of a broker would not require a license.   c. Negotiating an exchange of property requires a real estate license.   d. Government employees selling or leasing property as part of their jobs do not have to be licensed.

3. FALSE Raising funds is not one of the reasons for licensing real estate professionals.

4. TRUE

5. FALSE Associate brokers work for brokers and cannot hire salespeople to work for them.

6. Nonresident license

7. Broker

8. ARELLO

9. Associate broker

10. Reciprocal agreement

SECTION 2

1. TRUE

2. FALSE The education requirements for brokers are generally greater than those for salespeople.

3. TRUE

4. FALSE The primary purpose of requiring that continuing education courses be completed when licenses are renewed is to keep licensees current in various real estate topics.

5. TRUE

6. FALSE Someone who suffers financial damages due to the actions of a licensee can obtain compensation from the recovery fund only after unsuccessfully attempting to obtain compensation under the judgment.

7. FALSE Bonding a licensee is used by some states to protect the public from loss caused by actions of the licensee.

8. Recovery fund

9. Blind ad

10. Commingling funds

CHAPTER 17
FAIR HOUSING LAWS

Real estate licensees must comply with fair housing laws that exist at the federal, state and local levels or face severe and expensive penalties. In this chapter you learn about several federal fair housing laws, as well as unethical practices. *Section 1* covers unethical practices and federal fair housing laws. *Section 2* covers a detailed discussion of the Fair Housing Act of 1968. *Section 3* covers enforcement of fair housing laws. Remember to use the Study Tool Kit to reference key information and to update your progress checklist.

Learning Objectives

Track your progress as you work through the chapter by checking each learning objective when you complete it.

____ List and describe the three unethical practices covered in the chapter.

____ List the real estate included under the different fair housing acts.

____ Describe the objectives and major provisions of the Americans with Disabilities Act.

____ List the groups protected under the 1968 Fair Housing Act and its subsequent amendments.

____ List the property exempt from the 1968 Fair Housing Act.

____ List and describe the type of discriminatory acts that are prohibited under the 1968 Fair Housing Act.

____ Describe the significance of the *Jones v. Mayer* court case.

____ Describe the HUD process for handling a complaint under the 1968 Fair Housing Act.

____ Describe the options for filing a complaint in a federal district court.

Key Terms and Phrases

Track your progress as you work through the chapter by checking each term when you understand its meaning.

____ Administrative law judge

____ Americans with Disabilities Act

____ Blockbusting

____ Civil Rights Act of 1866

____ Civil Rights Act of 1964

____ Conciliation agreement

____ Department of Housing and Urban Development (HUD)

____ Fair Housing Act of 1968

____ Fair Housing Amendments Act

____ Housing and Community Development Act

____ *Jones v. Alfred H. Mayer Company*

____ Mortgage Disclosure Act of 1975

____ Redlining

____ Steering

____ Substantially equivalent laws

UNETHICAL PRACTICES AND FAIR HOUSING ACTS

UNETHICAL PRACTICES

Three unethical (and illegal) practices are discussed here. Two of them, blockbusting and steering, are specifically prohibited by federal fair housing laws, discussed later in the chapter.

Blockbusting

Blockbusting is inducing homeowners to sell, often at below market prices by making representations that members of a certain minority group are entering the area. Blockbusters purchase the homes from frightened owners at low prices, then sell them to other home buyers at much higher prices, thus making a significant profit.

Steering

Steering is directing home seekers or renters to particular areas to maintain the homogeneity of the area, thus "steering" them away from other areas. This limits the client's housing choices and promotes segregation. Clients should be the ones who decide where they want to look.

EXAMPLES: A broker shows a Hispanic home buyer only houses in Hispanic neighborhoods.

A broker shows a white home buyer only houses in white neighborhoods.

A broker shows a Catholic home buyer only houses in Catholic neighborhoods.

Redlining

Redlining is the practice of refusing to make loans to purchase, construct or repair a dwelling in a specific area without regard to the qualifications of the applicant. Applicants can be refused loans only on the basis of economic reasons, not because they live in a specific area. Redlining also can be a refusal to sell insurance policies on property for the same reason. The **Mortgage Disclosure Act of 1975** was passed to counteract redlining. Lenders with assets in excess of $10 million must make annual reports by census tracts of all mortgage loans made or purchased.

FEDERAL FAIR HOUSING LAWS

A number of federal laws have been passed regarding fair housing practices. These are discussed in the remainder of this section and are summarized in Figure 17.1.

Civil Rights Act of 1866

The **Civil Rights Act of 1866** was the earliest federal fair housing act. This law prohibits any type of discrimination based on *race* in *any* real estate transaction (sale or rental), *without exception*. Little was done to enforce this law for many years.

Civil Rights Act of 1964

The **Civil Rights Act of 1964** prohibits discrimination in all housing that receives federal funding. This law affected only a limited percentage of houses.

Fair Housing Act of 1968

The federal **Fair Housing Act of 1968** (as amended in 1988) is contained in Title VIII of the Civil Rights Act of 1968. This law greatly expanded fair housing coverage, to affect the majority of housing in the country. This law has been amended twice, so that today it prohibits discrimination based on *color, race, national origin, religion, sex, familial status (families with children under 18)* and *people with mental or physical handicaps* when *selling* or *renting* residential property. This law is discussed in more detail in Section 2.

 Note: State and local laws may protect not only the classes covered by federal laws but also additional classes.

Jones v. Alfred H. Mayer Company (1968). In *Jones v. Alfred H. Mayer Company* the Supreme Court upheld the Civil Rights Act of 1866, which prohibits racial discrimination in the sale or rent of *any property*. This denies any exceptions in the Civil Rights Act of 1968 related to discrimination based on race.

Americans with Disabilities Act of 1990

The **Americans with Disabilities Act** protects employment and accessibility rights of individuals with mental and physical disabilities, including AIDS and alcoholism. Provisions under this act include the following:

- Individuals with disabilities cannot be denied access to public transportation, any public accommodation or any commercial facility. ADA does not apply to residential property unless the property has some commercial use.

EXAMPLE: A model sales office in an apartment complex would need to comply with ADA.

- Public accommodations include hotels, restaurants and offices. Commercial facilities include factories.
- Public accommodations and commercial facilities must be *newly constructed* or *altered* to meet accessibility standards if *readily achievable*.
- Readily achievable means easily accomplished without much difficulty or expense. Criteria for determining if the public accommodation and commercial facility can be made accessible are included in the act.
- If readily achievable, structural, architectural and communication barriers must be removed.

EXAMPLE: Changes to make facilities accessible include widening doors, making cuts in the curb, lowering telephones, installing ramps and installing toilets and grab bars in restrooms.

The act is enforced by the U.S. Attorney General. Penalties include fines of up to $50,000 for the first offense, $100,000 for subsequent offenses and injunctions against operation of an offending business.

FIGURE 17.1
Fair Housing Laws

Civil Rights Act of 1866	Civil Rights Act of 1964	Fair Housing Act of 1968
Prohibits discrimination based on race Applies to all real estate	Only housing receiving Federal funds	Prohibits discrimination for many groups Covers selling and leasing Covers most residential property

Jones v. Mayer	Americans with Disabilities Act
Enforced Civil Rights Act of 1866 Includes sale or rent of any property	Includes persons with physical and mental disabilities Protects employment and accessibility rights Affects public accommodations and commercial facilities

**BEFORE READING THE NEXT SECTION, COMPLETE THE SECTION 1
REVIEW EXERCISES AND COMPARE YOUR ANSWERS WITH THE
SOLUTIONS AT THE END OF THE CHAPTER.**

SECTION 1
REVIEW EXERCISES

1. Name the law that best fits each description.

   a. _____ Prohibits discrimination based on race only

   b. _____ Broadens the number of classes protected against discrimination

   c. _____ Buildings to be made accessible to everyone

   d. _____ Prohibits racial discrimination in *all* housing

   e. _____ Prohibits discrimination in a limited amount of housing

   f. _____ Enforces the 1866 Civil Rights Act

   g. _____ Defines a number of activities that are prohibited as discriminatory

   h. _____ Requires lenders to provide information to detect redlining

Are the following statements true (T) or false (F)?

2. ____ It is redlining if a lender refuses to make construction loans to residents in certain areas because "they don't pay their loans."

3. ____ Public accommodations must be altered to meet accessibility requirements under the Americans with Disabilities Act no matter what the cost.

4. ____ There are four exceptions to housing covered by the Civil Rights Act of 1866.
5. ____ A person with mental illness would be included under the Americans with Disabilities Act.
6. ____ To avoid steering, the broker should let prospective house buyers determine what areas they want to see.

Supply the term that best matches each of the following descriptions.

7. _____ Refusing to make loans or issue insurance policies in areas populated by a protected class

8. _____ For profit, inducing owners to sell based on representations that minorities are moving into the area

9. _____ Channeling home seekers to certain areas because of their race, color or religion

SECTION 2
THE FAIR HOUSING ACT OF 1968

GROUPS PROTECTED UNDER THE ACT

The 1968 Fair Housing Act and its subsequent amendments prohibit discrimination based on sex, color, race, religion, national origin, handicap or familial status. (Some cities, states and counties have added additional protected classes.)

Exceptions:
1. Illegal drug abusers are not protected under the handicap class.
2. Anyone who poses a threat to the health and safety of the public is not protected under the handicap class.
3. Housing for elderly people is exempt from the familial status protection if
   - all units are occupied by persons age 62 or older or
   - at least 80 percent of the units are occupied by at least one person age 55 or older.

GROUPS NOT COVERED

While the act covers many groups, some still are *not* covered. These include groups based on

- marital status,
- age and
- occupation.

ACTIVITIES PROHIBITED UNDER THE ACT

Under this law you cannot perform the following discriminatory acts:

- Refuse to sell, rent, negotiate or otherwise make unavailable any dwelling.

EXAMPLE: An apartment owner refuses to rent any units to persons of a specific national origin because of fear that many of the building's tenants will move out.

- Change the terms or conditions of the sale.

EXAMPLE: A developer offers to pay the first three months' loan payments on houses purchased in a recently completed development. However, the developer will not offer the purchase incentive to members of a particular religion, to discourage them from buying houses in the development.

- Restrict the sale or rental of property to certain groups through statements or advertisements.

EXAMPLE: Advertising that states that certain groups are "preferred" renters in an apartment complex.

EXAMPLE: An apartment manager tells all of the tenants that members of a particular race will never be allowed to rent in the building.

- Represent that a building is not for sale, rent or inspection when, in fact, it is.

EXAMPLE: A couple telephones a broker and makes an appointment to see a house that is for sale. The broker meets them at the house, and on discovering they are of a particular national origin, he tells them that the owner has taken the house off the market. In fact, the house is still on the market and the broker is lying.

- For profit influence owners to sell or rent because of the possible entry into the area of people of a certain race, color, religion or other protected class. This is *blockbusting* or *panic peddling*.

EXAMPLE: A broker tells owners that they had better sell as soon as possible because an ethnic minority is moving into the area and the value of the house will drop.

Note: Even general statements to homeowners, such as "The neighborhood is changing," could be considered by the courts to be blockbusting.

- *Alter the terms* or *conditions* of a home loan or *deny a loan* to any person *purchasing* or *repairing* a house on the basis of other than economic reasons.

EXAMPLE: Because of their minority status, a lender tells a couple applying for a home improvement loan that they will be charged a higher rate because there is a greater risk they will default on the loan.

- Refuse membership or put conditions on participation in a multiple-listing service or other real estate organization.

EXAMPLE: A multiple-listing service will not accept listings from a certain ethnic group because it feels they are "too difficult to work with."

- Harass persons exercising their fair housing rights.

Discriminatory Advertising

Under the act discriminatory advertising cannot be used. This means any advertising that shows preference based on any of the classes protected under the act.

EXAMPLE: An apartment ad that states "Seeking Adult Renters Only."

EXAMPLE: Ads for the sale of houses or rentals in apartment buildings that show pictures with people of only one race.

Note: Advertising includes print ads, billboards, direct mail and promotional materials such as flyers and handouts.

REAL ESTATE TRANSACTIONS EXEMPTED UNDER THE ACT

While most property is covered by the act there are *four exemptions*. Note that these exemptions apply only if *two* conditions are met: (1) A real estate broker was not used and (2) discriminatory advertising was not used.

1. Sale or rent of a *single-family* home if *owned* by the seller, under the following conditions:
   - The seller does not own more than three single-family dwellings at one time.
   - If the seller was not living in the house or was not the most recent resident at the time of the sale, only one sale is exempt within a 24-month period.
2. *Rentals* in buildings with *four or fewer family units* if the *owner occupies* one of the units.
3. *Religious organizations* may restrict dwelling units they own or operate for other than commercial purposes to members of their religion if the organization does not otherwise discriminate in accepting its membership.
4. *Private clubs* may restrict rental or occupancy of its units to its members if the lodging is not run commercially.

Tip: While most residential and vacant property intended for residential use is covered under the 1968 Fair Housing Act, commercial property is not included.

AMENDMENTS TO THE FAIR HOUSING ACT OF 1968

In 1974 the **Housing and Community Development Act** added *sex* as a protected class. In 1988 protected classes under the Fair Housing Act were extended by the **Fair Housing Amendments Act** to include *families with children under 18* (familial status) and *people with mental or physical handicaps*.

Familial Status

Familial status is defined as covering an adult(s) with children under 18, a person who is pregnant and a person who has legal custody of a child or is in the process of securing legal custody.

Easy Accessibility by People with Physical Disabilities under the 1988 Amendment

- Affects new multifamily buildings (those with four or more units) built or designed for occupancy after March 31, 1991.
- Doors must be wide enough to allow passage by people in wheelchairs.
- Kitchens and bathrooms must be designed to allow wheelchairs to maneuver.

FIGURE 17.2
*Equal Housing
Opportunity
Poster*

U.S. Department of Housing and Urban Development

EQUAL HOUSING
OPPORTUNITY

We Do Business in Accordance With the Federal Fair Housing Law
(The Fair Housing Amendments Act of 1988)

It is Illegal to Discriminate Against Any Person Because of Race, Color, Religion, Sex, Handicap, Familial Status, or National Origin

- ◼ In the sale or rental of housing or residential lots
- ◼ In advertising the sale or rental of housing
- ◼ In the financing of housing

- ◼ In the provision of real estate brokerage services
- ◼ In the appraisal of housing
- ◼ Blockbusting is also illegal

Anyone who feels he or she has been discriminated against may file a complaint of housing discrimination:
    1-800-424-8590 (Toll Free)
    1-800-424-8529 (TDD)

**U.S. Department of Housing and
Urban Development
Assistant Secretary for Fair Housing and
Equal Opportunity
Washington, D.C. 20410**

Previous editions are obsolete

form **HUD-928.1** (3-89)

- Environmental controls and light switches must be within easy reach.
- Bathroom walls must be strong enough to support grab bars.

Note: Although similar in intent, the law is distinct from the Americans with Disabilities Act (ADA), which generally applies to public structures such as office buildings.

- Also, in all residential property tenants with disabilities must be allowed to make reasonable alterations, at their expense, to provide them with accessibility to their apartments.

A regulation issue subsequent to the 1972 amendment instituted the *equal housing opportunity poster*. See Figure 17.2 for a sample of the poster. This poster is provided by the U.S. Department of Housing and Urban Development (HUD) and includes

- the equal housing logo,
- the equal housing opportunity slogan and
- an equal housing statement.

Failure to display this sign in the broker's office may be *considered evidence* of *discrimination* in the event a discrimination complaint is made against the broker.

BEFORE READING THE NEXT SECTION COMPLETE THE SECTION 2 REVIEW EXERCISES AND COMPARE YOUR ANSWERS WITH THE SOLUTIONS AT THE END OF THE CHAPTER.

SECTION 2
REVIEW EXERCISES

In each of the following situations determine whether the transaction would be covered under the 1968 Fair Housing Law and why or why not.

1. An apartment building owner passes out flyers in the neighborhood stating units are available for rent to non-Hispanic, single males.

2. A developer offers low-rate loans to purchasers of new homes in a subdivision if the buyers are Caucasian single females.

3. An apartment owner refuses to rent to convicted drug abusers.

4. A property owner refuses to sell a vacant lot intended for residential use to people of a certain ethnic group.

5. A homeowner refuses to sell to buyers who are lawyers.

6. A property manager of an office building refuses to rent space to companies owned by a certain ethnic group.

7. The owner of a three-unit building who lives in one of the units and rents the other two without the help of a broker rents only to couples without children.

Are the following statements true (T) or false (F)?

8. ____ The discriminatory advertising rules under the act include handouts and billboards.

9. ____ Familial status under the act includes pregnant women.

10. ____ Tenants with disabilities must be allowed to make reasonable changes in residential property to provide accessibility to their apartments.

11. ____ Discriminatory advertising is permitted as long as a real estate broker is not involved in the transactions

12. ____ A broker does not display the HUD equal housing opportunity poster in the office. In suing for discrimination, the plaintiff may use the fact that the poster was not displayed as evidence of discrimination.

Supply the term that best matches each of the following descriptions.

13. _____ A protected class that refers to an adult with children under 18, a person who is pregnant or a person in legal custody of a child

14. _____ Added sex as a protected class

15. _____ Added families with children and people with handicaps as protected classes

---

SECTION 3

ENFORCEMENT OF THE FAIR HOUSING LAWS

COMPLAINTS FILED WITH HUD
(UNDER THE 1968 FAIR HOUSING ACT)

Enforcement of the 1968 act falls primarily to the U.S. **Department of Housing and Urban Development (HUD)**; however, complaints can be made to *both* HUD and to the federal *district courts*. The act includes procedures to be followed and these are described here.

- A person must file a complaint with HUD within *one year* after the discriminatory act occurs.
- After the complaint is filed, HUD investigates and gives a decision within *100 days*.
- HUD bears the costs of discovery and investigation of the complaint.
- During the 100 days HUD may be able to mediate the complaint and have the parties sign a **conciliation agreement.**
- If the state or local government has fair housing laws that have been ruled **substantially equivalent** to the federal law, HUD must refer the complaint to a state or local agency.
- Any of the parties (or HUD) can elect to go to a federal district court and have the charge of discrimination heard there.
- If parties do not elect to have charges heard in federal court, they are heard by a HUD **administrative law judge.**
- The HUD administrative law judge can award actual damages; grant an injunction or equitable relief; or grant civil penalties up to $50,000. Either party can appeal the administrative law judge's decision to a U.S. district court within 30 days.

EXAMPLE: A landlord discriminates by refusing to rent to a member of a minority group. The HUD judge could order the property owner to rent to the plaintiff.

The *Office of Equal Opportunity,* under HUD, administers the act.

CIVIL SUIT FILED IN FEDERAL DISTRICT COURT

A suit can be filed in a *federal court*, either under the 1866 Civil Rights Act or the 1968 Fair Housing Act.

Under the 1968 Fair Housing Act,

- a suit must be filed within *two years* after the discriminatory act.
- if a HUD administrative law judge has started a hearing or HUD has achieved a conciliation agreement with the parties, they may not file a civil suit in a federal district court.

Under the 1866 Civil Rights Act, the time limits are set by state statutes of limitations. The court may award an injunction, actual damages and punitive damages with no limit.

ACTION TAKEN BY THE DEPARTMENT OF JUSTICE

The U.S. *Attorney General* and the U.S. Department of Justice may initiate a suit in federal court if

- one of the parties elects this option,
- there is a breach of conciliation agreement or
- there is a pattern or practice of discrimination or a number of persons have been injured and the case raises an issue of general public importance.

For cases involving a breach of conciliation agreement or pattern of discrimination, the federal court may provide injunctive relief, award monetary damages and assess a civil penalty up to $50,000 (and up to $100,000) for repeat violations.

RESPONSIBILITY OF THE LICENSEE

Intent

A person bringing a discrimination complaint under the fair housing laws may *not* have to prove that the defendant had *knowledge or intent* to discriminate. All that has to be proved is that the *discriminatory act occurred*. Brokers who are charged with discrimination cannot use as a defense that they didn't *know* they were discriminating or that they did not *intend* to discriminate.

 Note: Citing any past service the broker may have performed on behalf of the protected class initiating the suit is of little value to a broker's defense.

Testing

The courts have held that it is permissible for real estate offices to be *tested for discriminatory practices*. Undercover volunteers posing as prospective buyers or renters may visit sales or rental offices to determine whether customers are being treated equally.

Education

The best way to prevent discrimination violations is to be *knowledgeable about fair housing laws* and stay current with changes in the law. The National Association of REALTORS® (NAR) has had a Code of Ethics for its members since 1913. Licensees should understand the code and use it as a suggested set of conduct standards. Information can be obtained from professional organizations such as the NAR and by attending continuing education seminars given by various groups and schools.

COMPLETE THE SECTION 3 REVIEW EXERCISES AND COMPARE YOUR ANSWERS WITH THE SOLUTIONS AT THE END OF THE CHAPTER.

SECTION 3
REVIEW EXERCISES

Are the following statements true (T) or false (F)?

1. ____ Persons who feel they have been discriminated against have up to two years to contact HUD.

2. ____ HUD may try to end the complaint and encourage voluntary compliance through a conciliation agreement.

3. ____ HUD administers the 1968 Fair Housing Act.

4. ____ The party bringing the complaint pays the costs associated with the investigation of the complaint.

5. ____ A home buyer brings a discrimination complaint against a broker. The buyer must prove that the broker intended to discriminate against the buyer.

Supply the term that best matches each of the following descriptions.

6. _____ State or local government fair housing laws that are similar to the federal fair housing laws

7. _____ The successful result of mediation between the parties in a discrimination complaint

8. _____ A judge that operates under HUD in resolving discrimination complaints

9. _____ Primarily responsible for enforcement of the 1968 Fair Housing Act

---

THIS IS THE LAST CHAPTER IN THE UNIT. TAKE THE UNIT V DIAGNOSTIC TEST

SOLUTIONS
FOR SECTION REVIEW EXERCISES

SECTION 1

1. a. Civil Rights Act of 1866   b. Fair Housing Act of 1968
   c. Americans with Disabilities Act   d. Civil Rights Act of 1866
   e. Civil Rights Act of 1964   f. *Jones v. Mayer*   g. Fair Housing Act of 1968
   h. Mortgage Disclosure Act

2. TRUE The lender is denying the loans based on a geographical generalization rather than on the actual financial qualifications of the loan applicants.

3. FALSE Buildings must be altered if readily achievable (accomplished without undue difficulty or expense).

4. FALSE The Civil Rights Act of 1866 covers all racial discrimination in housing with no exceptions. There are four exceptions in the Civil Rights Act of 1968.

5. TRUE

6. TRUE

7. Redlining

8. Blockbusting

9. Steering

SECTION 2

1. Covered: Discrimination by restricting the rental of property to certain groups is prohibited.

2. Covered: Changing the terms or conditions of sale to the detriment of any of the protected classes is prohibited.

3. Not covered: Drug abusers are not covered under the handicap status.

4. Covered: Vacant land is intended for residential use.

5. Not covered: Occupation is not one of the protected classes.

6. Not covered: Commercial property is exempted.

7. Not covered: This is one of the transactions exempted under the act.

8. TRUE

9. TRUE

10. TRUE

11. FALSE Discriminatory advertising can never be used.

12. TRUE

13. Familial status

14. Housing and Community Development Act 1974

15. Fair Housing Amendments Act

SECTION 3

1. FALSE The time period is one year.

2. TRUE

3. TRUE

4. FALSE These costs are paid by HUD.

5. FALSE The buyer has to prove only that a discriminatory act occurred and not that the broker had knowledge of the act or intended to discriminate.

6. Substantially equivalent laws

7. Conciliation agreement

8. Administrative law judge

9. Department of Housing and Urban Development (HUD)

U N I T V
DIAGNOSTIC
TEST

1. Which of the following is true if a broker is acting as an agent of the seller?

   a. The broker can disclose personal information to a buyer if it increases the likelihood of a sale.
   b. The broker can agree to a change in the selling price without the seller's approval.
   c. The broker can accept a commission from the buyer without the seller's approval.
   d. The broker is obligated to tell the seller that the buyer is considering making a higher offer to purchase the property.

2. During negotiations for the sale of an empty lot, a property seller misrepresents to the buyer that the land is suitable for constructing an office building. The sales contract they sign is

   a. valid.
   b. void.
   c. voidable by the buyer.
   d. voidable by either party.

3. An owner expects to net $130,000 from the sale of her property after paying the broker a 6 percent commission. To meet both the seller's net amount and the broker's commission, the property must sell for

   a. $7,800.
   b. $137,800.
   c. $138,298.
   d. $180,000.

4. The primary purpose for real estate licensing laws is to

   a. raise revenue for the state licensing agencies.
   b. protect the real estate industry from being oversaturated with licensees.
   c. protect the public.
   d. ensure that licensees are adequately trained to market real estate.

5. A real estate broker shows homes in certain neighborhoods only to persons of a particular ethnic group. This practice is called

   a. blockbusting.
   b. redlining.
   c. steering.
   d. panic peddling.

6. Which of the following is a similarity between an exclusive- right-to-sell and an exclusive-agency listing?

   a. Under both, the seller retains the right to sell the real estate without the broker's help and without paying the broker a commission.
   b. Both types of listings give the responsibility for representing the seller to only one broker.
   c. Under both, the seller authorizes only one particular salesperson to show the property.
   d. Both types of listings are open listings.

7. The party who holds legal title to real property when the property seller and buyer enter into an installment sales contract is the

   a. vendor.
   b. vendee.
   c. closing agent.
   d. buyer.

8. A real estate broker and his client create a fiduciary relationship when

   a. they enter into a listing agreement.
   b. a sales contract is signed by the seller and buyer.
   c. the real estate transaction is closed.
   d. the buyer secures a loan commitment.

9. The statute of frauds requires that a contract for the sale of real estate be

   a. recorded.
   b. acknowledged.
   c. accompanied by earnest money.
   d. in writing.

10. Which of the following statements about real estate licensing laws is true?

    a. License laws are the same for each state.
    b. Licensing guidelines are established by the federal government.
    c. The primary purpose of license laws is to ensure that buyers pay a fair price for property.
    d. Licenses may be suspended or revoked under state license laws.

11. A contract in which one of the parties has used duress to obtain consent usually can be rescinded

    a. by the party who used duress to obtain consent.
    b. by either of the parties.
    c. only if both parties mutually agree to rescind the contract.
    d. by the innocent party.

12. An owner residing in a single-family home wishes to sell the house without the help of a broker. The owner has not sold any other homes in the past few years and does not use discriminatory advertising. Under these circumstances may the owner discriminate on the basis of race when selling the property?

    a. No, because this is prohibited under the 1968 Civil Rights Act.
    b. Yes, because this falls under exceptions in the 1968 Civil Rights Act.
    c. Yes, because discrimination under the fair housing laws applies only to real estate brokers.
    d. No, because this is prohibited under the 1866 Civil Rights Act.

13. Which of the following statements is true regarding an option-to-purchase contract?

    a. It keeps an offer to purchase open for a specified period of time.
    b. The seller will owe the broker a commission if the buyer does not exercise the option.
    c. It requires that the buyer purchase the property.
    d. It gives the buyer a lien on the property.

14. A couple purchasing property for the first time do not know how they want to take title to the property and ask the selling broker for advice. The broker should advise them to

    a. discuss it with the lender.
    b. take title as tenants in common.
    c. take title in joint tenancy.
    d. consult an attorney.

15. A contract for the sale of real estate that does not state the consideration to be paid for the property is considered to be

    a. valid.
    b. void.
    c. voidable.
    d. unenforceable.

16. The owners of a house enter into a listing agreement with a broker. Under the terms of the listing if the owners sell the house themselves, they are still required to pay the broker a commission. The type of listing agreement with the broker must be a(n)

    a. exclusive-agency listing.
    b. exclusive-right-to-sell listing
    c. net listing.
    d. open listing.

17. Which of the following statements is true regarding land contracts?

    a. The buyer takes possession of the property.
    b. The seller receives a lien on the property.
    c. The buyer has legal title to the property.
    d. The seller provides no financing for the transaction.

18. Under state licensing laws a licensed salesperson in a real estate transaction may receive commissions from a(n)

    a. seller.
    b. buyer.
    c. employing broker.
    d. cooperating broker.

19. Under a listing agreement, the broker is entitled to sell the property for any price, as long as the seller receives $90,000. The broker may keep any amount over $90,000 as a commission. This type of listing is called a(n):

   a. net listing.
   b. exclusive-right-to-sell listing.
   c. exclusive-agency listing.
   d. open listing.

20. The 1968 federal Fair Housing Act does not cover discrimination based on

   a. national origin.
   b. race.
   c. gender.
   d. marital status.

21. Which of the following statements best describes the prospective buyer's situation if the seller makes a counteroffer?

   a. The buyer is relieved of any obligation under his original offer.
   b. The buyer is obligated to accept the counteroffer.
   c. The buyer remains obligated to the terms of the original offer.
   d. The buyer is obligated to make a new offer if the counteroffer is not accepted.

22. The selling broker tells a buyer that there are no special assessments on the property. Relying on this information, the buyer agrees to a sales contract on the property. The buyer later learns that there is a large special assessment on the property for recently installed curbs and sidewalks. The buyer refuses to close. Which of the following is true in this situation?

   a. The broker may collect a commission from the seller.
   b. The buyer may rescind the contract for sale.
   c. The buyer must complete the closing.
   d. The seller may sue the buyer for specific performance.

23. Which of the following is an essential requirement for a valid contract?

   a. Acknowledgment by a notary public
   b. Time is of the essence
   c. Competent parties
   d. Legal description

24. A broker was given a 90-day exclusive-agency listing by the seller. The broker advertised the property and ran several open houses. Forty days later the seller sold the property to a neighbor. The broker was entitled to

   a. the full commission.
   b. no commission.
   c. a partial commission.
   d. reimbursement from the seller for all marketing expenses.

25. A prospective buyer pays a seller $2,000 for a four-week option to purchase the seller's property for $200,000. After two weeks the buyer contacts the seller and offers to buy the property for $180,000. In this situation which of the following is true?

   a. The buyer's new offer voids the contract.
   b. The seller may sue the buyer for breach of contract.
   c. The seller may accept the lower offer.
   d. The buyer has violated contract law.

26. A broker sold a residence for $85,000 and received $5,950 as her commission in accordance with the terms of the listing. What was the broker's commission rate?

   a. 6 percent
   b. 7 percent
   c. 7.25 percent
   d. 7.5 percent

27. A prospective buyer makes an offer to purchase that is received by the seller. The seller then changes some of the terms and sends it back to the buyer. In this situation the buyer is:

   a. bound by the offer sent to the seller for a reasonable period of time.
   b. bound by the seller's terms.
   c. not bound by the offer sent to the seller.
   d. considered the offeror.

28. The Civil Rights Act of 1866 prohibits discrimination based on

   a. physical or mental handicap.
   b. owners with children.
   c. race only.
   d. race, creed and national origin.

29. A broker receives four offers to purchase a property during an open house and is finally able to contact the seller later that evening. The broker should present

    a. only the highest offer to the seller.
    b. all four offers at the same time in no specific order.
    c. offers from the broker's office first and then the other offers.
    d. only the best offer to the seller.

30. All of the following types of real estate fall under the 1968 federal Fair Housing Act *except*

    a. houses.
    b. apartment buildings.
    c. office buildings.
    d. condominiums.

31. The broker tells a prospective buyer that a property is connected to the city's water supply. After signing a contract, the buyer discovers that the property depends on wells and not the city's water source and refuses to close. Which of the following is true?

    a. The buyer must comply with the terms of the sales contract.
    b. The broker may collect a commission from the seller.
    c. The buyer may rescind the sales contract.
    d. The seller may sue the buyer for specific performance.

32. The law requiring that certain contracts be in writing to be enforceable is called the

    a. statute of limitations.
    b. statute of frauds.
    c. parol evidence rule.
    d. blue-sky law.

33. Susan wants to net $120,000 on the sale of her house after paying the broker a 6 percent commission. What price must Susan's house sell for?

    a. $7,200
    b. $124,200
    c. $127,200
    d. $127,660

34. To maintain their license, real estate brokers and salespersons must

    a. submit a new license application.
    b. retake and pass a license examination.
    c. meet any continuing education requirements.
    d. sell a minimum number of houses.

35. Which of the following protected classes was added under the 1988 Fair Housing Amendments Act?

    a. Gender
    b. Familial status
    c. Race
    d. Marital status

36. A broker who has a listing contract to sell a parcel of land for an owner is what type of agent?

    a. General
    b. Special
    c. Universal
    d. Common

37. The buyer in a real estate transaction refuses to perform the provisions of the contract. Which of the following actions would allow the seller to force the contract provisions to be carried out?

    a. Novation
    b. Suit to quiet title
    c. Suit for specific performance
    d. Rescission

38. A broker is entering into a real estate listing with a seller and wants to be paid a commission regardless of who finds the buyer. What type of listing agreement should the broker use?

    a. Net listing
    b. Open listing
    c. Exclusive-agency listing
    d. Exclusive-right-to-sell listing

39. On Monday the Smiths make an offer in writing to purchase a house for $120,000, including all draperies in the house. The offer was to expire on Saturday at noon. The sellers responded in writing on Thursday, accepting the $120,000 offer but excluding the draperies. On Friday, while the Smiths were considering the sellers' reply, the sellers decided to accept the original purchase offer that included the draperies and stated their decision in writing. Which of the following is true at this point in the negotiations?

   a. The Smiths are legally bound to purchase the house but have the right to insist that the draperies be included.
   b. The Smiths are not legally bound to purchase the house.
   c. The Smiths must buy the house and are not entitled to the draperies.
   d. The Smiths must buy the house but may deduct the value of the draperies from the $120,000.

40. A broker has a listing on a house that contains a provision that the house is to be sold in "as-is" condition. The broker learns of a major hidden defect in the property. When showing the property to a prospective purchaser, the broker should

   a. advise the buyer of the defect.
   b. point out that the house will be sold in "as-is" condition.
   c. mention the defect to the buyer only if asked.
   d. inform the buyer that the seller has told him of no defects.

41. The real estate sales contract states that John will purchase the property only if John's wife approves the sale by the following Saturday. The wife's approval is a

   a. reservation.
   b. binder.
   c. contingency.
   d. consideration.

42. A broker receives a commission of $6,500 on the sale of a property. If the commission is based on 6 percent of the first $100,000 of the sales price and 5 percent of the remainder, what is the sale price of the property?

   a. $260,000
   b. $180,000
   c. $110,000
   d. $80,000

43. The amount of commission to be earned in a real estate transaction is determined by

   a. a local board of REALTORS®.
   b. the multiple-listing service.
   c. the state real estate commission.
   d. negotiation between the seller and the broker.

44. When purchasing a parcel of real estate, the amount of the buyer's earnest money deposit is determined by

   a. agreement between the buyer and seller.
   b. local law according to the price of the property.
   c. an amount equal to the listing broker's commission.
   d. agreement between buyer and broker.

45. A homeowner has an exclusive-agency listing with a broker but finds a buyer for the property without the assistance of the broker. The listing broker is entitled to

   a. no commission.
   b. the full commission.
   c. reimbursement for expenses.
   d. one-half of the commission.

46. A buyer is told by the seller's broker that "this is the most attractive house in the subdivision" when there are other houses that actually look better. This statement is an example of

   a. fraud.
   b. misrepresentation.
   c. dual agency.
   d. puffing.

47. The broker/owner of a real estate company does not require that salespeople be in the office at certain hours or attend meetings and does require that they pay their own business expenses. The sales staff

   a. are employees.
   b. are independent contractors.
   c. can participate in the company's profit sharing.
   d. can be covered under the company's health insurance.

48. A salesperson wishes to purchase a property listed by the real estate company that employs the broker. The salesperson may do so under which of the following conditions?

    a. The salesperson's real estate company has an exclusive-agency listing on the property.
    b. The sellers are informed that the buyer is a licensed salesperson.
    c. The salesperson purchases the property at the full asking price with no contingencies.
    d. The listing has first been published in the MLS.

49. During the period of time after a real estate sales contract is signed but before title actually passes the status of the contract is

    a. voidable.
    b. executory.
    c. unilateral.
    d. implied.

50. A prospective buyer asks the listing broker if the sellers will accept $10,000 less than the asking price of the property. The listing broker knows the seller probably will accept such an offer. The broker should answer the buyer's question by telling the buyer

    a. that the seller will not accept an offer that low.
    b. that the seller is anxious to sell and probably will accept less than the listing price.
    c. to submit the offer and the seller will decide.
    d. that the seller is looking for an offer in the amount proposed by the buyer.

UNIT **V**
DIAGNOSTIC TEST
ANSWER SHEET

This sheet is perforated for easy pullout. Write your answers on this sheet as you complete the exercises. Refer to the diagnostic worksheet after completing the test to evaluate your strong and weak content areas. Review material in the appropriate chapter and sections.

1. _____

2. _____

3. _____

4. _____

5. _____

6. _____

7. _____

8. _____

9. _____

10. _____

11. _____

12. _____

13. _____

14. _____

15. _____

16. _____

17. _____

18. _____

19. _____

20. _____

21. _____

22. _____

23. _____

24. _____

25. _____

26. _____

27. _____

28. _____

29. _____

30. _____

31. _____

32. _____

33. _____

34. _____

35. _____

36. _____

37. _____

38. _____

39. _____

40. _____

41. _____

42. _____

43. _____

44. _____

45. _____

46. _____

47. _____

48. _____

49. _____

50. _____

UNIT VI

REAL ESTATE VALUATION

CHAPTER 18

THE APPRAISAL PROCESS

One of the services provided by the real estate industry is property appraisal. Appraisals are needed in a variety of real estate activities, such as determining value for obtaining a loan, insurance purposes, property tax assessments, estate valuations, a potential investor or condemnation procedures to determine proper compensation. Even though real estate brokers and salespeople are not required to be certified professional appraisers, it is important that they have an understanding of appraisal concepts and process. An appraisal is an estimate of value, and *Section 1* introduces the term *value* and identifies its elements. *Section 2* explains several principles that affect value. *Section 3* discusses the appraisal process and the appraisal profession, along with new appraisal regulations and certification requirements. Remember to use the Study Tool Kit to reference key information and to update your progress checklist.

Learning Objectives

Track your progress as you work through the chapter by checking each learning objective when you complete it.

____ Define the concept of value as used in real estate appraisal.

____ List and describe four elements of value.

____ List and describe each of the principles of value used in appraisal.

____ List and describe the steps that make up the appraisal process.

____ Describe the appraisal certification requirements.

Key Terms and Phrases

Track your progress as you work through the chapter by checking each term when you understand its meaning.

____ Anticipation	____ Conformity
____ Appraisal	____ Contribution
____ Appraisal Foundation	____ Cost
____ Appraisal Institute	____ FIRREA
____ Appraisal Qualifications Board	____ Highest and best use
____ Appraisal Standards Board	____ Increasing and diminishing returns
____ Assemblage	____ Member of the Appraisal Institute (MAI)
____ Change	____ Market value
____ Competition	____ Plottage

____	Price	____	Substitution
____	Progression	____	Supply and demand
____	Regression	____	Uniform Residential Appraisal Report (URAR)
____	Senior Residential Appraiser (SRA)		

THE CONCEPT OF VALUE

Appraisal is the process of estimating and supporting an *opinion of value*. The economic concept of value is a critical component of most real estate activity. It is important to realize that the appraisal value is the appraiser's *opinion* of the property's worth and the appraisal process requires some *subjective judgments* by the appraiser. As a result, appraisal is not an exact science, and it is not unusual for three appraisers to produce three different values for the same property.

MULTIPLE MEANINGS OF VALUE

The word *value* has many meanings, and a parcel of real estate may have *many values at one time*. The reason for this is that the value of a property is affected by the purpose for which the value is being determined.

EXAMPLE: A county tax assessor assigning an assessed value to the property for real estate tax purposes will place heavy emphasis on the selling price of similar properties. An insurance company, however, may value the property differently because it is more concerned with the cost of replacing damaged structures.

Market Value

A real estate appraiser estimates the **market value** (sometimes called the *fair market value*) of the property. The market value has the following characteristics:

- The *most probable* price that a property will bring (not the highest or average price).
- Payment must be in cash or its equivalent.
- Buyer and seller must be *unrelated* and acting *without undue pressure*.
- The property must be exposed to the *open market* for a *reasonable period* of time.
- Buyer and seller must be *well informed* of the market conditions and the property's use and defects.

Note: The Appraisal Institute defines market value as the most probable price in terms of money that a property will bring in a competitive and open market under all conditions requisite to a fair sale, the buyer and seller each acting prudently and knowledgeably, and assuming the price is not affected by undue stimulus.

Market Value/Price/Cost

While *market value* refers to the amount knowledgeable parties will agreed to in an open market, **price** refers to the amount for which the property *actually sold*. These two amounts may be different because a variety of extenuating circumstances might have surrounded the transaction and affected the price paid for the property. The **cost** of a property is the amount of money used to construct improvements plus the value of the land. Theoretically, market value, price and cost should be the same, but this is seldom the case.

EXAMPLE: A property owner purchases a lot and builds a house for a *cost* of $70,000. Ten years later the owner is thinking of selling and has the house appraised at a *market value* of $150,000. Shortly before selling, the owner's son gets married, and the owner decides to help the young couple by selling the house to them for a *price* of $100,000.

BASIC ELEMENTS OF VALUE

We know that an appraiser estimates value; however, for property (or any product or service) to have value, it must have the four characteristics of demand, utility, scarcity and transferability.

1. *Demand*—The property must be needed or wanted by someone who has the purchasing power to obtain it.

EXAMPLE: If because of high interest rates potential buyers who want to purchase property cannot get a mortgage, the value of property diminishes.

2. *Utility*—The property must have a useful purpose or satisfy a need. The more useful a property is, the more likely someone will pay for it.
3. *Scarcity*—The type of property must have some degree of rareness. This refers to the supply of similar property in relation to the demand for it.

EXAMPLE: Air has great utility and is needed by everyone; however, it is usually not scarce and thus may not have value.

EXAMPLE: In places where water is scarce it has great value.

EXAMPLE: Due to zoning restrictions, commercial property may be very scarce in a particular city. This creates higher values for the few available commercial buildings.

4. *Transferability*—The ability to transfer title to the property to someone else.

 Hint: A method of remembering the four characteristics of value is that the first letters of the characteristics spell the word DUST (i.e., Demand, Utility, Scarcity and Transferability).

BEFORE READING THE NEXT SECTION, COMPLETE THE SECTION 1 REVIEW EXERCISES AND COMPARE YOUR ANSWERS WITH THE SOLUTIONS AT THE END OF THE CHAPTER.

SECTION 1
REVIEW EXERCISES

1. Name the element of value that best fits each description.

a. _____ Wanted by someone with the purchasing power to obtain it

b. _____ Refers to the supply of something in relation to the demand for it

c. _____ Satisfies a need

d. _____ Ability to pass title to someone else

Are the following statements true (T) or false (F)?

2. ____ The appraiser's objective is to estimate the market price of the property.

3. ____ A parcel of real estate may have many values at one time.

4. ____ The market value is the highest price the property will bring on the open market.

Supply the term that best matches each of the following descriptions.

5. _____ The total in dollars for replacing the land and constructing the improvements on the property

6. _____ The most probable price for a property if payment is made in cash and the parties are knowledgeable, well informed, and acting without pressure

7. _____ What a property actually sells for

8. _____ The process of estimating and supporting an opinion of value

PRINCIPLES OF VALUE

Various underlying economic principles affect the value of real estate. Several of the more important principles are listed here along with a description of each.

Anticipation—The value of a property may increase or decrease based on a potential purchaser's belief that some *future* event will benefit or detract from the value of the property.

EXAMPLE: The value of a commercial property may increase if a potential buyer believes a major highway interchange will be built close to it.

Change—Real estate conditions, both physical and economic, do not remain constant, and this, in turn, changes value. Property may physically change though normal wear and tear or sudden changes such as fire or storms. Economically, real estate may change because of zoning changes, tax law changes and changes in the marketplace. Changes in real estate usually are not noticeable on a day-to-day basis, but they can be seen over time.

 Note: Most real estate passes through a cycle of (1) growth, (2) stability, (3) decline, (4) renewal.

Competition—When substantial profits are being made, competition will be attracted. Increased competition may result in less profit in the long term.

EXAMPLE: If office rents are high and property owners are making substantial profits, builders and investors will be motivated to build more office buildings. The increased supply of office space will then reduce the rental rates and, therefore, profits to the property owners.

Conformity—The maximum value for a property is reached when it conforms to the surrounding land use. In some areas conformity is accomplished through zoning laws.

EXAMPLE: A single-family residence may not reach its full value if it is located in an industrial area.

Contribution—The value of an improvement is equal to its contribution to the added value of the property. If there is an existing improvement, its contribution to the property would equal the reduction in the property's value if the improvement were absent. This principle is used to make adjustments in the sales comparison approach (an approach covered in Chapter 19).

EXAMPLE: A house with a garage is worth more than a house without one. The difference in value between the two houses represents the contribution of the improvement (the garage).

Tip: An improvement's contribution to the value of the property may not be equal to its cost. Building a swimming pool may cost $15,000 but may only increase the value of the property by $10,000. Thus, the swimming pool's contribution is $10,000.

Highest and Best Use—Each property has one legal use that gives that property its greatest value.

EXAMPLE: A parcel of land with a house is that property's highest and best use if the land is zoned for single family residence.

This principle recognizes that a parcel of land can be used for several purposes and that the *existing use* of a property *may not* be its highest and best use. This is important to an appraiser because estimating the value of the property according to its current use may not indicate its true value.

EXAMPLE: Consider a house located on property that is zoned for commercial use and is located next to a busy shopping center. That property's highest and best use would be for a commercial structure rather than its current residential use.

Note: Remember, the highest and best use of a property may change if conditions change. For example, if the above property is rezoned, its highest and best use may change.

Increasing and Diminishing Returns—Returns refers to the relationship between the cost of an improvement and the value it adds (its contribution) to the property. A certain number of improvements may add substantial value to the property (*increasing return*) but adding more than that number will add less value or no value (*diminishing return*).

EXAMPLE: Adding a second bedroom to a one-bedroom house may substantially increase its value, but as additional bedrooms are added, the increase in value will be smaller, and eventually value will not increase at all.

> **Note: When excessive improvements are made to a property so that they no longer add value, the property is referred to as overimproved property.**

Plottage—By combining or consolidating adjacent lots into one larger lot, the resulting land value will be higher than the sum of the values of the separate lots. **Assemblage** is the process of merging the lots.

EXAMPLE: Zoning laws may allow the building of a two-story office building on a 50,000-square-foot lot. However, if two of these lots are combined, the zoning law allows a ten-story office building to be built. Thus, by combining the two lots the total value is increased.

Progression—The value of a *poorer* property will *increase* if it is near *better* property.

EXAMPLE: The worth of an older, smaller home will be *enhanced* if larger homes are constructed near it.

Regression—The value of a *better* property will be *lessened* by the presence of *poorer* properties.

EXAMPLE: The worth of a large, lavish house will *decrease* if it is located in a neighborhood of smaller, more modest houses.

Substitution—The maximum value of a property is equal to the cost of purchasing or constructing equally desirable properties.

EXAMPLE: If two similar houses are for sale, the lower-priced house generally will be purchased first.

Supply and Demand—Property values will be affected both by the supply of property and by buyer demand for it.

Value *increases* if supply decreases or if demand increases.
Value *decreases* if supply increases or if demand decreases.

EXAMPLE: The first houses sold in a new development will most likely be lower in price, and the price for the houses will rise as the supply decreases.

BEFORE READING THE NEXT SECTION, COMPLETE THE SECTION 2 REVIEW EXERCISES AND COMPARE YOUR ANSWERS WITH THE SOLUTIONS AT THE END OF THE CHAPTER.

SECTION 2

REVIEW EXERCISES

1. Name the economic principle that best fits each description.

   a. _____ A property's value is diminished by $10,000 because it lacks a garage.

   b. _____ An owner adds a fourth bedroom to her home and realizes a significant gain in property value. The addition of a fifth bedroom a year later results in only a modest increase in value.

    c. _____ A prospective buyer believes a suburb will be passing a rent control ordinance.

    d. _____ After reviewing a property, a buyer decides that its greatest value could be realized if a strip mall were built on it.

    e. _____ A developer decides to assemble four adjacent lots so that an office building can be built.

    f. _____ A property's value passes through a renewal phase.

    g. _____ A property owner's house is worth approximately the same as other similar houses on the block.

    h. _____ A homeowner's property value suffers because it is next to a house that has become rundown.

    i. _____ A homeowner's property value benefits because it is next to a house that recently has been renovated.

Are the following statements true (T) or false (F)?

2. ____ A property's highest and best use is always the existing use of the property.

3. ____ The principle of contribution provides that the value of the property will increase by the cost of any improvements.

4. ____ The highest and best use of a property may change.

Supply the term that best matches each of the following descriptions.

5. _____ The value of property is maximized if it is used in the same way as neighboring properties.

6. _____ The value of real estate does not remain constant.

7. _____ Effect on the value of property based on some future event.

8. _____ Effect of an improvement on a property's value.

9. _____ Property values change as these two forces adjust themselves in the real estate market.

10. _____ Process of merging lots.

11. _____ The value of a better property will decrease if it is near a poorer quality property.

12. _____ Combining lots to increase the value of the new larger lot over the sum of the smaller ones.

13. _____ The value of a poorer property will increase if it is near a better quality property.

14. _____ The one legal use that provides a property its greatest value.

15. _____ The maximum value of a property is equal to the cost of purchasing an equally desirable property.

_____ **SECTION 3**

APPRAISAL PROCEDURES

DESCRIPTION OF THE APPRAISAL PROCESS

In estimating property value an organized and systematic set of procedures is used to collect and organize data and arrive at the appraised value. While the process used by

FIGURE 18.1
Summary of the
Appraisal Process

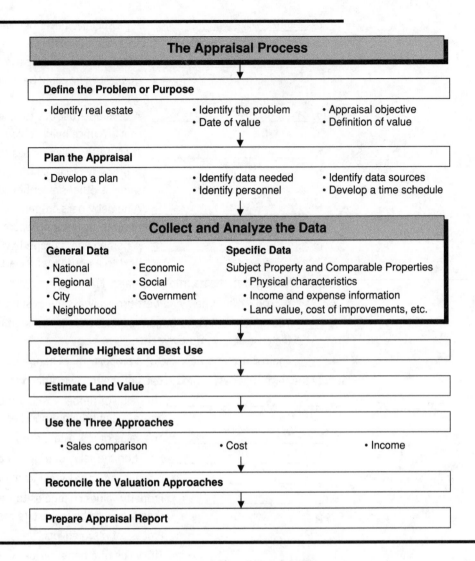

appraisers may vary, most follow a process similar to the one presented in this section (see Figure 18.1). The appraisal process generally consists of eight steps:

1. Define the problem or purpose
2. Plan the appraisal
3. Collect and analyze the data
4. Determine highest and best use
5. Estimate land value
6. Use the three approaches
7. Reconcile the valuation approaches
8. Prepare the appraisal report

1. Define the Problem or Purpose

The first step in any appraisal process is to identify the *purpose* of the appraisal, the *type of value* to be estimated, the *real estate* to be appraised and the *date* of valuation. The purpose of the appraisal will influence the type of data to be collected and the approach used. (The approaches to estimating value are discussed in Chapter 19.)

EXAMPLE: If the appraisal is for a loan on a residence, the market data approach should be used.

2. Plan the Appraisal

After defining the problem the appraiser must *develop a plan and time schedule*, identify personnel needed, identify the *types of data* needed and identify *data sources*. Data can be collected from numerous sources, and those pertinent to a particular appraisal need to be identified. Following is a partial list of information sources:

Assessor's office	Chamber of Commerce
Attorneys/Lawyers	Cost manuals
Brokers	Newspapers
Builders	Recorder of Deeds

3. Collect and Analyze the Data

After identifying the data sources in step 2, the appraiser can collect and analyze the appropriate data. Collecting and analyzing data is critical to an accurate appraisal. Data can be divided into categories.

- *General data*—Information about the nation, region, city and neighborhood. This could include detailed information about economic, social and government-related conditions.

EXAMPLE: If the appraiser notes that the local economic base indicates an expansion of employment and population, a lower vacancy rate might be used in the appraisal.

- *Specific data*—Information about the subject property, as well as comparable properties. Depending on the appraisal approach(es) used, data may include construction costs, income and expense information, land value and property improvements. Data should be verified whenever possible by checking the information from two different sources.

4. Determine Highest and Best Use

The highest and best use of the land is determined both as if it were vacant and by its best use as improved property. Current and potential uses of the property are considered in the analysis.

5. Estimate Land Value

The value of the land alone is estimated by comparing the selling prices of similar properties that recently have been sold.

6. Use the Three Approaches

Using the data collected in step 3, apply the appropriate appraisal approaches and arrive at an estimate of value. The three approaches used are sales comparison, cost and income. These are discussed in Chapter 19. While not all the approaches may be relevant for a particular property, the general practice is to use all three unless reasons can be given for their exclusion. Using all three approaches acts as a control. While the values obtained from each method may be different, they should be reasonably close. If one result is significantly different, it may indicate that the data used were incorrect, a calculation error was made or the method is inappropriate to use on that property.

7. Reconcile the Valuation Approaches

Each of the approaches used in step 6 to estimate value probably will produce different values for the property. A *reconciliation* or *correlation* step is performed to arrive at an opinion of the market value. In this step the appraiser analyzes the facts and results for each of the approaches and uses professional judgment to assign different weights to each method in forming an opinion of the value. In some cases one approach may be better than the others for a particular property and may be relied on more heavily.

EXAMPLE: If the property being appraised is an office building, the method that would be assigned the greatest weight probably would be the income approach.

8. Prepare the Appraisal Report

The last step is to prepare a formal written report for the client. There are various formats for the appraisal report: a letter report, a short form report, a narrative report or the Uniform Residential Appraisal Report (URAR). The format will depend on the information need and the purpose of the appraisal.

EXAMPLE: A lender may want the appraisal on a URAR form acceptable to the secondary mortgage market. An out-of-state investor considering purchase of a 300-unit apartment building may want a narrative report.

The most common appraisal report form used today and the form most government agencies use is the **Uniform Residential Appraisal Report (URAR)** form. The following government agencies require the use of this form: Fannie Mae, Federal Home Loan Mortgage Corporation (FHLMC), Housing and Urban Development (HUD), Department of Veterans Affairs (VA) and Farmers Home Administration (FmHA). The URAR includes a brief summary of the property and site, a neighborhood analysis, and analysis of the calculations used in the three approaches. The report must include the license or certificate number of the individual performing the appraisal.

The past few years have seen a growing awareness of environmental risks and their effect on the use and value of real estate. In response to this the Uniform Standards of Professional Appraisal Practice (USPAP) and Fannie Mae appraisal regulations require that licensed and certified appraisers recognize and report environmental conditions as part of the appraisal report.

APPRAISAL ORGANIZATIONS

There are several professional appraisal organizations in the United States. The American Institute of Real Estate Appraisers (AIREA) and Society of Real Estate Appraisers (SREA) were two well-known appraisal associations that were organized during the 1930s. Both organizations offered designations that could be obtained by meeting education, experience and competence requirements. In 1991 they were united into one organization called the **Appraisal Institute.** The Appraisal Institute offers the following appraiser designations:

- **Member of the Appraisal Institute (MAI).** This is the highest designation and requires at least 4,500 hours of appraisal experience.
- The **Senior Residential Appraiser (SRA).** For residential appraisers, this designation requires at least 3,000 hours of appraisal experience.

While a person performing services as an appraiser need not be associated with these organizations, there are advantages to being a member. The designations offered indicate that the appraiser has demonstrated professional competence by meeting education and experience requirements and passing examinations.

The Appraisal Foundation

The **Appraisal Foundation** is a private, nonprofit organization composed of representatives from all the major appraisal organizations and other related professional groups. The *objectives* of the foundation are to establish uniform appraisal standards, develop minimum criteria for the certification and recertification of qualified appraisers and maintain systems for the certification and recertification of qualified appraisers.

The *goal* of the foundation is to disseminate qualification criteria to the states and other government entities to help them in their appraiser certification and recertification programs. The foundation maintains two independent boards to accomplish these objectives.

1. The **Appraisal Qualifications Board** establishes minimum criteria for state-certified appraisers and endorses uniform examinations for certification.
2. The **Appraisal Standards Board** sets minimum standards for appraisals performed in federally related transactions.

APPRAISAL REGULATION

FIRREA

The Financial Institutions Reform, Recovery, and Enforcement Act of 1989 (**FIRREA**) was passed as a result of the troubles experienced by the savings and loan industry. Title XI of FIRREA is called the *Real Estate Appraisal Reform Amendments* and was intended to upgrade the professionalism and competency of appraisers. FIRREA requires that appraisals of property involved in federally related transactions be made by licensed or certified appraisers.

USPAP Standards

The Appraisal Standards Board created *mandatory* real estate appraisal *requirements* known as the Uniform Standards of Professional Appraisal Practice or USPAP. USPAP consists of ten standards that are revised and updated periodically by the Appraisal Foundation through its Appraisal Standards Board. In preparing an appraisal an appraiser must employ recognized methods and techniques and follow specific requirements for the analysis. All states require that certified or licensed appraisers comply with these standards.

The Appraisal Report

FIRREA established required regulations for the appraisal report. These included regulations governing content, characteristics and certification of reports.

APPRAISER QUALIFICATIONS

- Each state must establish and administer a system for licensing and certifying appraisers that is consistent with criteria established by the Appraisal Foundation and Title XI of FIRREA. State plans for regulating appraisers are approved by the Appraisal Subcommittee of the Federal Financial Institutions Examination Council (FFIEC).
- Appraisal course providers are approved by state licensing authorities.
- Certification requirements:

In most states *three classes of license/certification* exist for appraisers. The requirements and types of real estate transactions vary for each class of license/certification. All three have educational and experience requirements and require passing an appraisal exam.

1. Licensed Real Estate Appraiser—Qualified to appraise single-family homes and two- to four-unit residential buildings if transaction amount is less than $1 million, nonresidential property if transaction amount is less than $250,000.
2. Certified Residential Real Estate Appraiser—Qualified to appraise single-family homes and two- to four-unit residential buildings regardless of transaction amount, nonresidential property if transaction amount is less than $250,000.
3. Certified General Real Estate Appraiser—Qualified to appraise all types of real estate.

Qualifications for both licensed and certified appraisers include ten hours per year of continuing education.

SECTION 3
REVIEW EXERCISES

1. Name the step of the appraisal process that best fits each description.

a. _____ The market data, cost and income analysis is performed.

b. _____ This step includes the type of value to be estimated.

c. _____ The appraiser correlates the results to arrive at a value.

d. _____ This step includes information about the area where the property is located, as well as about the property itself.

e. _____ The last step in the process can take many formats.

f. _____ The appraiser identifies the types of data needed and data sources.

Are the following statements true (T) or false (F)?

2. ____ If the three approaches to estimating value are used properly, the appraiser should expect to see the same amounts from all three.

3. ____ Appraisal reports may take different formats, depending on the information needed and the purpose of the report.

4. ____ Under FIRREA regulations each state must establish and administer a system for licensing and certifying appraisers.

5. ____ The Appraisal Institute offers the MAI and SRA designations.

6. ____ A licensed real estate appraiser is qualified to appraise single-family homes and residential buildings of four units or more.

7. ____ General data collected during the appraisal process include information on land value, construction costs and property improvements.

8. ____ If a URAR report is being used, the appraisal must be done by a licensed or certified appraiser.

Supply the term that best matches each of the following descriptions.

9. _____ The highest designation awarded by the Appraisal Institute, it requires 4,500 hours of appraisal experience

10. _____ Sets minimum criteria for state-certified appraisers

11. _____ Act that includes amendments intended to improve the competency of appraisers

12. _____ The appraisal form most government agencies use

13. _____ Awarded by the Appraisal Institute, requires 3,000 hours of appraisal experience

14. _____ Sets minimum standards for appraisals used in federally related transactions

15. _____ A private, nonprofit group that establishes uniform appraisal standards

SOLUTIONS
FOR SECTION REVIEW EXERCISES

SECTION 1

1. a. Demand   b. Scarcity   c. Utility   d. Transferability
2. FALSE The appraiser estimates the market value of the property.
3. TRUE
4. FALSE The market value is the most probable price that a property should bring.
5. Cost
6. Market value
7. Price
8. Appraisal

SECTION 2

1. a. Contribution   b. Increasing and diminishing returns   c. Anticipation
   d. Highest and best use   e. Plottage   f. Change   g. Substitution
   h. Regression   i. Progression
2. FALSE The existing use of a property may not be its highest and best use.
3. FALSE An improvement's cost may be greater than the change in property value.
4. TRUE
5. Conformity
6. Change
7. Anticipation
8. Contribution
9. Supply and demand
10. Assemblage
11. Regression
12. Plottage
13. Progression
14. Highest and best use
15. Substitution

SECTION 3

1. a. Use of the three approaches   b. Define the problem
   c. Reconciliation of valuation approaches   d. Collect and analyze the data
   e. Prepare appraisal report   f. Appraisal planning
2. FALSE Using the three approaches acts as a control. The values from each probably will be different but should be reasonably close.
3. TRUE
4. TRUE
5. TRUE
6. FALSE Licensed real estate appraisers are qualified to appraise residential buildings of two to four units.
7. FALSE This is specific data about the subject property.
8. TRUE
9. Member of the Appraisal Institute (MAI)

10. Appraisal Qualifications Board
11. FIRREA
12. Uniform Residential Appraisal Report (URAR)
13. Senior Residential Appraiser (SRA)
14. Appraisal Standards Board
15. Appraisal Foundation

CHAPTER 19

METHODS OF ESTIMATING VALUE

The last chapter presented general appraisal concepts and how the overall appraisal process is performed. This chapter covers the various approaches used by appraisers to estimate the market value of real estate. *Section 1* covers the sales comparison approach, *Section 2* covers the cost approach, *Section 3* covers the income approach. Each approach is generally considered suitable for specific types of properties. In addition, *Section 4* covers two shorter methods for estimating value; the gross rent multiplier and the gross income multiplier. A summary of the steps used in the approaches is included in Figure 19.1. Remember to use the Study Tool Kit to reference key information and to update your progress checklist.

Learning Objectives

Track your progress as you work through the chapter by checking each learning objective when you complete it.

____ List the three approaches used to estimate value and the steps used in each of these approaches.

____ Identify which type of real estate is most suitable for each appraisal approach.

____ Calculate the market value, using each of the three approaches.

____ Distinguish between reproduction cost and replacement cost.

____ List the three types of depreciation.

____ Calculate the capitalization rate for a property.

____ Calculate the market value using the gross rent multiplier and gross income multiplier.

Key Terms and Phrases

Track your progress as you work through the chapter by checking each term when you understand its meaning.

____ Capitalization rate

____ Comparable property

____ Cost approach

____ Curable depreciation

____ Economic obsolescence

____ Functional obsolescence

____ Gross income multiplier (GIM)

____ Gross rent multiplier (GRM)

____ Income approach

____ Incurable depreciation

____ Physical deterioration

____ Replacement cost

____ Reproduction cost

____ Sales comparison approach

____ Subject property

THE SALES COMPARISON APPROACH

The first approach for estimating value is the **sales comparison approach** (sometimes called the *market data approach*). This approach uses information from the sale of similar properties that have recently sold and compares it to the subject property. This is a two step process. *First,* data on sales of similar properties (called *comparables*) must be collected and *second,* adjustments must be made to the comparable sales data to make them reflect the subject property.

- The **subject property** is the property being appraised.
- **Comparable properties** are similar to the subject property and have recently been sold.

MAKING ADJUSTMENTS

One of the physical characteristics of real estate (covered in Chapter 1) is *nonhomogeneity,* that is, no two parcels of real estate are exactly alike. Because of the differences between the comparable properties and the subject property, adjustments must be made to the sales price of the comparables.

Tip: The goal of adjustments is to make the sales price of comparable properties equal to the subject property. Therefore all adjustments are made to the comparable properties, not to the subject property.

Adjustment Rules

Add to the sale price if features *are present (or are superior)* in the subject property and *are not present (or are inferior)* in the comparable property.

    Subtract from the sale price if features *are not present (or are inferior)* in the subject property and *are present (or are superior)* in the comparable property.

EXAMPLE 1: The *comparable* house has one bedroom and sold for $150,000. The *subject* property has two bedrooms. It is estimated that this feature adds $20,000 to the value of the property. What adjustment should be made?

SOLUTION: *Add* $20,000 to the sales price of the *comparable,* making it $170,000. We add to the sales price because the feature (i.e., two bedrooms) is not present in the comparable property.

EXAMPLE 2: The *comparable* house has a two-car garage and sold for $150,000. The subject property does not have a garage, and it is estimated that this feature adds $15,000 to the value of the property. What adjustment should be made?

SOLUTION: *Subtract* $15,000 from the sales price of the *comparable* property, making it $135,000.

FIGURE 19.1
*Summary of Steps Used
in the Approaches to
Estimating Value*

APPROACHES TO ESTIMATING VALUE

SALES COMPARISON

1. Collect data on comparable properties
2. Make adjustments to comparables

COST APPROACH

1. Estimate current cost of construction improvements
2. Estimate accrued depreciation (Physical, Functional, Economic)
3. Deduct depreciation from construction costs
4. Add the land value

INCOME APPROACH

1. Estimate potential gross income
2. Estimate effective gross income
3. Estimate net operating income (NOI)
4. Estimate capitalization rate
5. Apply capitalization rate to net income

GROSS RENT MULTIPLIER

1. Divide sales price of comparables by gross monthly rent
2. Apply multiplier to fair market rent of the subject property

GROSS INCOME MULTIPLIER

1. Divide sales price of comparables by gross annual income
2. Apply multiplier to gross annual income of subject property

Tip: Remember, when deciding whether to add or subtract for a feature, it is the sales price of the comparable property that is being adjusted, not the value of the subject property. Therefore, if a feature makes the comparable property better than the subject property, we reduce the comparable's sales price; if the feature is lacking in the comparable property, we add to its sales price.

Reasons for Making Adjustments

Adjustments to the sales price of the comparable property should be made for a variety of reasons. These can be categorized into four areas.

1. *Terms or conditions of sale*—The sale may not have a standard loan arrangement. Favorable loan terms may be offered by the seller, or the existing loan on the property may have an assumable mortgage at a favorable rate. Presumably these would make the property more attractive to the buyer and increase its value.
2. *Date of sale*—Economic conditions may have changed since the comparable property was sold. As a general rule it is best to use properties that have sold within *the past six months,* although this time period can be extended if property prices have remained relatively stable.
3. *Location*—The subject property may be located in a different part of the neighborhood or in a different neighborhood altogether.
4. *Physical condition and features*—This category covers a wide range of property characteristics, including age of the building, lot size, landscaping, construction, number of rooms, square footage of living space, construction of the property, inclusion or absence of a garage and air conditioning.

Hint: Another way of remembering how to adjust for a property's feature is to use "SBA" or "CBS."

SBA = if Subject Better, Then Add or **CBS = If Comparable Better, Then Subtract**

FIGURE 19.2
Sales Comparison Approach

Property Feature	Subject Property	Comparable #1		Comparable #2		Comparable #3		Comparable #4	
Sales price		$148,000		$142,000		$151,000		$148,500	
Date sold		Current	$0	Current	$0	Current	$0	Current	$0
Age	10 years	15 yrs.	$2,000	20 yrs.	$4,000	5 yrs.	($500)	10 yrs.	$0
Location	Good	Poorer	$3,000	Better	($2,000)	Same	$0	Same	$0
Lot Size	80′ × 125′	40′ × 125′	$3,000	60′ × 125′	$2,000	80′ × 200′	($2,000)	80′ × 125′	$0
Landscaping	Good	Better	($500)	Same	$0	Poorer	$500	Same	$0
Style	Ranch	Ranch	$0	Ranch	$0	Ranch	$0	Ranch	$0
Construction	Brick	Brick	$0	Brick	$0	Brick	$0	Brick	$0
Number of rooms	6	6	$0	6	$0	6	$0	6	$0
Number of bedrooms	3	2	$4000	3	$0	4	($4000)	3	$0
Number of baths	2	1½	$1000	2½	($1,000)	1	$2,000	2	$0
Sq. ft. of living space	1,800	1,500	$2,000	2,000	($1,200)	3,000	($4,000)	1,800	$0
Basement	Full	Slab	$3,000	Full	$0	Full	$0	Full	$0
Garage	2-car	1-car	$2,000	2-car	$0	3-car	($2,000)	2-car	$0
Condition—exterior	Good	Poorer	$1,000	Good	$0	Better	($1,000)	Good	$0
Condition—interior	Average	Average	$0	Average	$0	Average	$0	Average	$0
Other improvements	None	None	$0	None	$0	None	$0	None	$0
Net adjustments		$20,500		$1,800		$11,000		$0	
Adjusted sales price		$168,500		$143,800		$140,000		$148,500	

Note: Comparables with the highest degree of similarity (i.e., the fewest adjustments) are given more weight in reconciling the adjusted sales prices of the comparables to determine the most probable value. Because comparable #4 has no adjustments, the value of the subject property would probably be $148,500.

Setting a Dollar Amount for Adjustments

An adjustment for the difference in *market value* must be estimated by the appraiser for each of the differences between the subject property and comparable properties. (Note that the adjustment is not based on the cost of correcting the differences.) In determining the amount of adjustments the general rule is that the more *alike* the comparable property features are to those or the subject property, the *fewer* and *smaller* the adjustments. In determining the amount of the adjustments the appraiser determines from the marketplace what the average buyer will pay for the differences being compared.

Finding the Adjusted Sales Price

Three to five comparables usually provide a sufficient basis for estimating the value. To use more than this number of comparables probably would add little to the accuracy of the estimate, making the extra effort of little value. The sales price for each of the comparable properties is changed by the *net adjustments* calculated in the analysis. This results in an *adjusted sales price* for the comparables. The adjusted sales prices of the comparable properties create a probable value range for the subject property. A single value then can be selected from this range.

Note: If the supply of comparable properties is more than adequate, choose the comparables that require the least number of adjustments.

TYPE OF PROPERTY BEST SUITED FOR THIS APPROACH

Because the sales comparison approach depends on the availability of similar properties that recently have sold, it is ideally suited for *residential property.* There usually is an ample supply of recently sold houses to enable the performance of an appraisal. However, this approach can be used for any type of property for which other similar properties are available for comparison purposes.

Figure 19.2 illustrates the sales comparison approach for a residential property by comparing the subject property with four comparable properties.

Note: Brokers and salespeople often use a simplified version of this approach for residential real estate when helping sellers set a likely selling price for their property. This is usually referred to as a Competitive Market Analysis or Comps or CMA.

BEFORE READING THE NEXT SECTION, COMPLETE THE SECTION 1 REVIEW EXERCISES AND COMPARE YOUR ANSWERS WITH THE SOLUTIONS AT THE END OF THE CHAPTER.

SECTION 1
REVIEW EXERCISES

1. Name the three approaches for estimating real estate value.
   a. _____
   b. _____
   c. _____

Are the following statements true (T) or false (F)?

2. ____ When making adjustments under the sales comparison approach we always adjust the subject property.

3. ____ When making adjustments under the sales comparison approach, if the comparable property has a superior feature we reduce the sales price.

4. ____ If there are a number of comparable properties to use, choose the comparables that require the most adjustments.

5. _____ How many comparable properties are usually required to form a sufficient basis for estimating value using the sales comparison approach?

6. List the four areas for making adjustments under the sales comparison approach.
   a. _____
   b. _____
   c. _____
   d. _____

7. What type of property is best suited for the sales comparison approach?
   _____

Supply the term that best matches each of the following descriptions.

8. _____ Property similar to the subject property that has recently sold

9. _____ The property being appraised

10. _____ The sales price of the *comparable* properties after adjustments are made

FIGURE 19.3
Cost Approach to Estimating Value

Estimate Value of Improvements
  (replacement or reproduction cost)
  1,800 sq. ft. @ $85 per sq. ft. = $153,000

Less Depreciation $ 3,000
  Physical deterioration = $84,000
  Functional obsolescence =
  Economic obsolescence = $ 0
  Total depreciation   ($7,000
Depreciated Value of the Improvements $146,000

Estimate Land Value
  Size 80′ × 120′ @$400 per front ft. = $32,000
  Site improvements
    (walks, landscaping, driveways) = $34,000
      Total Land Value $136,000
Estimated Value of the Property $182,000

SECTION 2
THE COST APPROACH

The second approach to estimating the value of property is the **cost approach.** The objective of this approach is to estimate the value of the subject property based on the cost of purchasing a similar parcel of land and constructing similar improvements. Figure 19.3 provides an illustration using this approach.

STEPS IN USING THE COST APPROACH

1. Estimate *current cost of constructing buildings* and other *improvements* on the subject property. There are several methods for determining the current cost of construction, and these are discussed later in the section.
2. Estimate amount of *accrued depreciation* (depreciation that has already occurred). Depreciation refers only to improvements on the property because land does not depreciate.

    Three types of depreciation are included in this step: (1) physical deterioration, (2) functional obsolescence, (3) economic obsolescence (also called external obsolescence). These are discussed in more detail later in the section.

3. Deduct the accrued depreciation from the construction costs determined in step 1.
4. Add the value of the land. (The land value is determined assuming the land was *vacant* and put to its *highest and best use.*

The sales comparison approach described above could be used to determine the land value. The location of the subject property and any improvements are compared with similar properties and the appropriate adjustments are made.)

Hint: Formula for Cost Approach
Value = Cost to Replace − Depreciation + Land Value

TYPE OF PROPERTY BEST SUITED FOR THIS APPROACH

The cost approach to estimating value can be used for any improved property, but it is ideally suited to the appraisal of *special-purpose* buildings, such as churches, schools and government-owned property, because few other properties of this type are sold and thus available to use as comparables. This approach can also be used for estimating the value of *newly constructed houses.*

APPROACHES FOR ESTIMATING CURRENT COST OF CONSTRUCTION

Step 1 in the cost approach estimates the current cost of construction. There are *two approaches* used to estimate the cost of construction. These are the **reproduction cost** approach and the **replacement cost** approach.

Reproduction Cost Approach

The *reproduction cost approach* calculates the current construction costs to *duplicate* improvements on the subject property *exactly* as it originally was constructed. This means constructing the property with the same favorable and unfavorable features and materials.

Replacement Cost Approach

The *replacement cost approach* calculates the current construction costs to produce improvements *similar* or *equivalent* to those of the subject property. This means constructing improvements with similar functionality to the original but not necessarily a replica. Replacement cost is the *more practical choice* and is frequently used in appraising because it eliminates obsolete features and takes advantage of current construction materials and techniques.

Hint: Reproduction = Exactly like the improvements
Replacement = Similar to the improvements

Methods for Determining Reproduction or Replacement Costs

The following methods are used by appraisers to determine the reproduction or replacement cost of improvements on the subject property.

- *The Square-Foot Method:* This is the *most common method used* to estimate costs. The cost per square foot of recently built buildings similar to the subject building is multiplied by the number of square feet in the subject building. This method is *simple to prepare* and is reasonably accurate.
- *The Cubic-Foot Method:* This method follows the same procedure as the square foot method but uses cubic feet of space instead of square feet of area. The formula for calculating cubic feet is Cubic feet = Length × Width × Height.
- *The Unit-in-Place Method:* This method is based on measuring the construction cost of *individual building components.*

EXAMPLE: An appraiser evaluates the foundation, heating unit, plumbing fixtures, etc., calculating the material, labor and overhead costs of each. Then the costs for all components are added together to determine the total cost.

- *The Quantity Survey Method:* Using this method, a list of all materials to replace the current improvements is made (brick, lumber, etc.). Next, the current costs of the materials and installation are estimated. Added to these costs are indirect building costs (the builder's profit, building permits, survey). The total represents the replacement cost of the improvements.

   This method is *very accurate;* however, it is also very detailed and time consuming. For this reason it usually is used only for appraising historical property.

- *The Index Method:* This method uses an index that *reflects the increase in construction costs* for the geographic area. The original cost of the subject property is multiplied by the index to estimate the value. This method is the *least accurate* because it generalizes the increase in construction costs over time rather than taking into account the specific characteristics of the subject property. This method is useful to check the estimates reached by the other methods.

ESTIMATING THE AMOUNT OF ACCRUED DEPRECIATION

Step 2 in the cost approach to estimating value is to calculate the amount of *accrued depreciation.* There are three classes of depreciation used in the cost approach: *physical deterioration, functional obsolescence* and *economic obsolescence.* Depreciation can also be classified as either *curable* or *incurable.*

Tip: Depreciation used in appraisal is not the same as depreciation calculated for accounting purposes. The later will be discussed in Chapter 26, Real Estate Investments.

Curable versus Incurable Depreciation

With **curable depreciation,** the cost of correcting or "*curing*" the defect does not exceed the *increase in property value.* **Incurable depreciation** is not *cost effective* to correct because the cost would exceed any increase in property value. Examples of each are included in the following discussion of depreciation classes.

Hint: The test of curability is whether the cost to cure is less than the value that would be added.

- **Physical deterioration**—This type of depreciation refers to the loss of value due to physical wear and tear on buildings and other improvements caused by use, age or negligence.
   Curable—Repairs are economically feasible, considering the life of the building.

EXAMPLE: Preventive maintenance such as painting and minor repairs.

   Incurable—Features are not easily corrected.

EXAMPLE: The foundation on a house is severely cracked and crumbling, requiring extensive work to replace.

- **Functional obsolescence**—This type of depreciation refers to the loss of value owing to poor design and features that make the building outdated.
   Curable—Features are not fashionable, but they can be corrected at low cost.

EXAMPLE: Plumbing fixtures or outdated equipment that can easily be replaced.

Incurable—Building design features are not easily corrected.

EXAMPLE: Because of the house's poor floor plan, one bedroom cannot be reached without going through a second bedroom. Extensive remodeling would be required to redesign the floor plan.

Note: Functional obsolescence also includes features in the property not fully valued in the marketplace. EXAMPLE: a marble sink with solid gold faucet handles.

- **Economic obsolescence**—This type of depreciation is also called *external obsolescence* because it refers to the loss of value due to forces that are external to the subject property.
  Incurable—Economic obsolescence is *always incurable* because the owner of the subject property has no control over it.

EXAMPLE: A house is located near a factory that emits pollutants.

Breakdown Method

When estimating the amount of depreciation, the breakdown method is usually used. This method breaks down depreciation into the three categories discussed above with separate estimates for curable and incurable depreciation in each class.

BEFORE READING THE NEXT SECTION, COMPLETE THE SECTION 2 REVIEW EXERCISES AND COMPARE YOUR ANSWERS WITH THE SOLUTIONS AT THE END OF THE CHAPTER.

SECTION 2
REVIEW EXERCISES

1. What three types of depreciation are used in the cost approach?
   a. _____
   b. _____
   c. _____

Are the following statements true (T) or false (F)?

2. ____ The reproduction cost approach calculates current construction costs to produce improvements that are equivalent to the subject property.

3. ____ Using the replacement cost approach takes advantage of current construction materials and techniques.

4. ____ Economic obsolescence can be both curable and incurable.

5. List the methods used to determine the cost of improvements on the subject property.
   a. _____
   b. _____
   c. _____
   d. _____
   e. _____

6. Name the type of depreciation for each of the following examples.

a. _____ Bedrooms with no closets

b. _____ An apartment building located near a noisy factory

c. _____ A building with defective air-conditioning equipment

d. _____ A condo building located in an area with traffic congestion

7. List the four steps to estimating value using the cost approach.

a. _____

b. _____

c. _____

d. _____

8. What type of property is best suited for the cost approach?

_____

Supply the term that best matches the each of the following descriptions.

9. _____ Cost of duplicating property *exactly* as it is constructed

10. _____ Cost of producing improvements similar or equivalent to the subject property

11. _____ Cost of curing the defect does not exceed the increase in property value

12. _____ Cost of curing the defect exceeds the increase in property value

13. _____ Refers to the physical wear and tear on the property

14. _____ Refers to obsolete features in the building

15. _____ Refers to features external to the building

SECTION 3

THE INCOME APPROACH

The third approach for estimating the value of property is the **income approach.** Use of this approach is based on the assumption that anticipated net income produced by the property can be used to determine its value. There are *five steps* to estimate value using this approach.

STEPS IN USING THE INCOME APPROACH

1. Estimate the annual *potential gross income.* This step includes an estimate of anticipated income from rent as well as income from other sources such as vending machines and laundry facilities. *Market rents* should be used to compute this figure, not rents currently used in the building.

2. Estimate the annual *effective gross income.* Because it is unlikely that all of the units will be rented at all times, an *allowance* for *anticipated vacancies* and *uncollectible rent* must be made. This amount is deducted from the potential gross income.

FIGURE 19.4
Income Approach to
Estimating Value

Potential Gross Annual Income		)
Market Rent (10 units × $500 × 12 mos.)		$ 60,000)
Other income (Vending machines, fees)		2,000
Subtotal		$ 62,000
Less vacancy and collection losses (@5%)		($ 3,100)
Effective Gross Income		$ 58,900
Expenses:		
Fixed Expenses:		
Real Estate Taxes	$7,000	
Insurance	1,500	
Total	$8,500	
Variable Expenses:		
Maintenance	$1,000	
Utilities	4,200	
Repairs	1,200	
Decorating	700	
Legal and Accounting	500	
Total	$7,600	
Total Expenses		($16,100)
Annual Net Operating Income		$ 42,800
Capitalization Rate = 10%		
Estimated Value of Property	($42,800 ÷ .10)	$428,000

3. Estimate the annual *net operating income (NOI)*. Determine the anticipated annual operating expenses for running the property and *deduct* this amount from effective gross income. Typical operating expenses are included in Figure 19.4.

Tip: Mortgage expense, depreciation and capital improvements are not considered operating expenses and should not be considered in this step.

4. Estimate the **capitalization rate** (rate of return). The capitalization rate is the rate of return or *yield* that an investor expects from investing money in the property. The capitalization rate to be used in the appraisal is found by comparing *NOI* with the *sales prices* of similar properties that recently have sold.

   To find the capitalization rate, divide net income by the sales price of similar buildings recently sold (Net Income ÷ Value = Rate).

EXAMPLE: A property has net income of $15,000 and sells for $100,000. The capitalization rate for this property is 15 percent ($15,000 ÷ $100,000 = 15%).

   An appraiser determines the capitalization rate for recently sold properties similar to the subject property. This rate then is used to estimate the value of the subject property.

5. Estimate the property value. The last step is to apply the *capitalization rate* (step 4) to the subject property's annual *NOI* (step 3).

   To find the value, divide net income by the capitalization rate (Net Income ÷ Rate = Value).

Note: There is a relationship between the capitalization rate (rate of return) and risk. If the property had a greater risk, the investor would seek a higher return on the property. On a property with lower risk, the investor would probably accept a lower rate of return.

Current interest rates also affect the capitalization rate. If interest rates are high an investor will seek a higher capitalization rate to match the greater returns offered by other investments.

EXAMPLE: If the net income found in step 3 was $30,000, and the rate was 15 percent, the value of the property would be $200,000 ($30,000 ÷ 15% = $200,000).

Under the income approach, changes in the capitalization rate and operating expenses for a building produce the following changes in the building's value:

Value *decreases* if   *Rate* increases *or*
                         Expenses increase

Value *increases* if   *Rate* decreases *or*
                         Expenses decrease

TYPE OF PROPERTY BEST SUITED FOR THIS APPROACH

This approach is used for properties that produce income. With apartment buildings and commercial properties, such as shopping centers and office buildings, this approach can be used.

An example of the income approach to estimating value is included in Figure 19.4.

BEFORE READING THE NEXT SECTION, COMPLETE THE SECTION 3 REVIEW EXERCISES AND COMPARE YOUR ANSWERS WITH THE SOLUTIONS AT THE END OF THE CHAPTER.

SECTION 3
REVIEW EXERCISES

1. List the five steps to estimate value using the income approach.

    a. _____

    b. _____

    c. _____

    d. _____

    e. _____

Are the following statements true (T) or false (F)?

2. ____ Annual operating costs are deducted from the potential gross income to determine effective gross income.

3. ____ Operating expenses used in the income approach include insurance and depreciation costs.

4. What is the formula for finding the capitalization rate?

_____

5. What is the formula for applying the capitalization rate to find the value of the subject property?

_____

6. List the effect on value in the following situations:
   a. _____ Rate increases
   b. _____ Rate decreases
   c. _____ Expenses increase
   d. _____ Expenses decrease

7. What type of property is best suited for the income approach?

_____

Supply the term that best matches each of the following descriptions.

8. _____ Anticipated income from rent and all other sources
9. _____ Potential gross income less uncollected rent and vacancies
10. _____ Effective gross income less operating expenses
11. _____ The yield an investor will expect for investing money in the property

GROSS RENT AND GROSS INCOME MULTIPLIERS

The **gross rent multiplier (GRM)** and **gross income multiplier (GIM)** are shorter variations of the more detailed income approach. Each of these variations compares the *sales price* of a property with its *expected income*. Because the GRM and GIM use *gross income* and a property may have unusually high or low expenses, they may provide only a rough estimate of value.

TYPE OF PROPERTY BEST SUITED FOR THESE APPROACHES

- GRM—Because single-family residences and smaller (one- to four-unit) residential apartment buildings usually produce only a rental income, the *gross rent multiplier* is used. This relates the *sales price* to *monthly rental income.*
- GIM—Commercial and industrial properties, as well as larger residential apartment buildings, usually generate income from rent as well as other sources (e.g., concessions). They are valued using their *annual* income from all sources.

FORMULAS FOR FINDING THE GRM AND GIM

GRM = Sales Price ÷ Gross Monthly Rent (Income)

EXAMPLE: A property recently sold for $96,000 and the gross monthly rent is $725. The GRM would be 132.4 ($96,000 ÷ $725 = 132.4).

GIM = Sales Price ÷ Gross Annual Income

EXAMPLE: A commercial property recently sold for $360,000 and the gross annual income is $40,000. The GIM would be 9 ($360,000 ÷ $40,000 = 9).

APPLYING THE GRM AND GIM

To find the value of a subject property, an appraiser establishes a GRM by using the sales price and rental income from at least *four properties similar* to the subject property. The GRM can then be applied to the subject property's *fair market rental* to determine its value. The GIM can be found the same way.

Formulas for Applying the GRM and GIM

Estimated Market Value = Gross Monthly Rent × GRM

EXAMPLE: A property has gross monthly rental income of $860 and the GRM is 132.4. The value of the property is $113,864 ($860 × 132.4 = $113,864).

Estimated Market Value = Gross Annual Income × GIM

EXAMPLE: A property has gross annual income of $50,000 and the GIM is 9. The value of the property is $450,000 ($50,000 × 9 = $450,000).

Note: The GIM and GRM are popular because they are simple to use. However, simplicity is also their weakness because they do not take into account variations for vacancy, uncollected rents and various expenses on the property.

COMPLETE THE SECTION 4 REVIEW EXERCISES AND COMPARE YOUR ANSWERS WITH THE SOLUTIONS AT THE END OF THE CHAPTER.

SECTION 4
REVIEW EXERCISES

1. What is the formula for finding the GRM?

2. What is the formula for finding the GIM?

3. What is the formula for applying the GRM to a subject property?

4. What is the formula for applying the GIM to a subject property?

5. Calculate the GRM if a property sells for $125,000 and the gross monthly rent is $900.

6. Calculate the GIM if a property sells for $125,000 and the gross annual income is $10,800.

7. Calculate the property value if the GRM is 126.5 and the gross monthly rent is $1,200.

8. Calculate the property value if the GIM is 10.5 and the gross annual income is $12,000.

_____

9. What type of property is best suited for the GRM?

_____

10. What type of property is best suited for the GIM?

_____

Supply the term that best matches each of the following descriptions.

11. _____ A number by which a property's gross monthly rent is multiplied to estimate its value

12. _____ A number by which a property's gross annual income is multiplied to estimate its value

---

THIS IS THE LAST CHAPTER IN THE UNIT. TAKE THE UNIT VI DIAGNOSTIC TEST.

SOLUTIONS
FOR SECTION REVIEW EXERCISES

SECTION 1

1. a. The sales comparison approach (also called the market data approach)
   b. The cost approach   c. The income approach
2. FALSE When making adjustments under the sales comparison approach we always adjust the comparable properties and not the subject property.
3. TRUE
4. FALSE If there are a number of comparable properties to use, choose the comparables that require the *least* adjustments.
5. Three to five
6. a. Terms or conditions of sale   b. Date of sale   c. Location
   d. Physical condition or features
7. Residential property
8. Comparable property
9. Subject property
10. Adjusted sales price

SECTION 2

1. a. Physical deterioration   b. Functional obsolescence
   c. Economic obsolescence
2. FALSE The reproduction cost approach calculates current construction costs to produce improvements that are *exactly* like the subject property.
3. TRUE
4. FALSE Because external (economic) obsolescence refers to forces external to the property, it is always considered incurable.
5. a. Square-foot method   b. Cubic-foot method   c. Unit-in-place method
   d. Quantity survey method   e. Index method
6. a. Functional obsolescence   b. Economic obsolescence
   c. Physical deterioration   d. Economic obsolescence
7. a. Estimate the current cost of constructing improvements   b. Estimate the amount of accrued depreciation   c. Deduct depreciation from construction costs   d. Add the value of the land
8. Special purpose buildings
9. Reproduction cost
10. Replacement cost
11. Curable depreciation
12. Incurable depreciation
13. Physical deterioration
14. Functional obsolescence
15. Economic obsolescence

SECTION 3

1. a. Estimate annual potential gross income   b. Estimate annual effective gross income   c. Estimate annual net operating income   d. Estimate the capitalization rate   e. Apply the capitalization rate to the property's net income

2. FALSE An allowance for vacancies and uncollected rents is deducted from the potential gross income to determine effective gross income.

3. FALSE Operating expenses used in the income approach do not include depreciation costs because these are not an actual cash outlay.

4. Capitalization Rate = Net Income ÷ Value

5. Value = Net Income ÷ Capitalization Rate

6. a. Value decreases   b. Value increases.   c. Value decreases.
   d. Value increases.

7. Properties that produce income (e.g., apartment buildings and commercial properties)

8. Potential gross income

9. Effective gross income

10. Net operating income

11. Capitalization rate

SECTION 4

1. GRM = Sales Price ÷ Gross Monthly Rent (Income)

2. GIM = Sales Price ÷ Gross Annual Income

3. Value = GRM × Gross Monthly Rent

4. Value = GIM × Gross Annual Income

5. GRM = $125,000 ÷ $900 = 138.9

6. GIM = $125,000 ÷ $10,800 = 11.6

7. Value = 126.5 × $1,200 = $151,800

8. Value = 10.5 × $12,000 = $126,000

9. The type of property best suited for the GRM is residential property because it usually generates only rental income.

10. The type of property best suited for the GIM is commercial and industrial property because income may be generated from sources other than rent.

11. Gross rent multiplier

12. Gross income multiplier

UNIT VI
DIAGNOSTIC TEST

1. The income approach would be best used in appraising a(n)

   a. single-family residence.
   b. church.
   c. apartment building.
   d. school.

2. The sales comparison (market data) approach can be used effectively in an appraisal if

   a. current construction costs are available.
   b. the property generates income.
   c. depreciation for the property can be calculated.
   d. there are recent sales of similar properties.

3. One of the concepts used in appraisal is "highest and best use," which refers to

   a. the property's current use.
   b. the legal use that will yield the greatest return.
   c. acquiring title to the property through long-standing use.
   d. acquiring a zoning variance for a more valuable use.

4. Which of the following methods is used to calculate the gross rent multiplier?

   a. Divide the sales price by the gross monthly rent
   b. Multiply the capitalization rate by net income
   c. Divide net income by the capitalization rate
   d. Multiply gross rent by the capitalization rate

5. An appraiser is using the cost approach to estimating the value of a property. Which of the following steps would the appraiser use?

   a. Estimate the market value of the land
   b. Determine the capitalization rate
   c. Determine the vacancy rate
   d. Identify several similar buildings that have recently sold

6. When performing an appraisal of real estate, the appraiser is estimating the property's

   a. selling price.
   b. depreciable basis.
   c. market value.
   d. utility value.

7. In the cost approach to estimating value, the type of depreciation that is always considered incurable is

   a. physical deterioration.
   b. functional obsolescence.
   c. economic obsolescence.
   d. market obsolescence.

8. What is the gross income multiplier for a property if the annual gross income from a building is $66,000, net operating income is $29,500 and the building sells for $561,000?

   a. 6.5   c. 8.1
   b. 7.2   d. 8.5

9. Reconciliation refers to which of the following?

   a. Loss of value due to any cause
   b. Separating the value of the land from the total value of the property to compute depreciation
   c. The process by which an appraiser determines the highest and best use for a parcel of land
   d. Analyzing the results obtained by the different approaches to value to determine a final estimate of value

10. To determine the listing price of a residential property, a broker most likely would use a(n)

    a. income analysis.
    b. cost analysis.
    c. competitive market analysis.
    d. assessment analysis.

11. To determine the listing price of a church, an appraiser most likely would use a(n)

    a. income analysis.
    b. cost analysis.
    c. market analysis.
    d. data comparison analysis.

12. If an expensive home is built in an area consisting of less expensive homes, its value will be affected by the concept of

    a. functional obsolescence.
    b. regression.
    c. contribution.
    d. progression.

13. In performing an appraisal of a single-family residence, the appraiser reduced its value because of functional obsolescence. The appraiser was referring to

    a. proximity to a waste incinerator.
    b. special assessments on the property.
    c. a cracked foundation.
    d. a one-car garage.

14. To determine the listing price of an office building, an appraiser most likely would use a(n)

    a. income analysis.
    b. cost analysis.
    c. market analysis.
    d. data comparison analysis.

15. According to the principle of conformity, the highest value for a house is obtained if its location is

    a. next to an office building.
    b. in a residential development.
    c. near a shopping center.
    d. across the street from a church.

16. Which of the following would an appraiser most likely consider functional obsolescence?

    a. Deterioration of the property
    b. Location next to a noisy factory
    c. A leaky roof
    d. A house in an exclusive area with a one car garage

17. A competitive market analysis (CMA) is frequently prepared by a real estate agent to estimate the most probable sales price of a property. This method is based on the

    a. gross rent multiplier.
    b. cost approach.
    c. market data approach.
    d. income approach.

18. The last house in a new development sold for twice the price paid for the first houses sold in the same development. The higher price is a result of

    a. supply and demand.
    b. conformity.
    c. progression.
    d. contribution.

19. Which of the following appraisal methods requires that the appraiser calculate the amount of accrued depreciation?

    a. Cost approach
    b. Income approach
    c. Sales comparison approach
    d. Gross income multiplier

20. Which of the following is considered economic obsolescence?

    a. A leaky roof
    b. Abandoned buildings in the area
    c. Outmoded plumbing fixtures
    d. A cracked foundation

21. A group of investors making very high profits from a shopping mall most likely would be concerned with the principle of

    a. conformity.
    b. progression.
    c. competition.
    d. contribution.

22. An appraiser calculates the replacement cost of a building when using the

    a. cost approach.
    b. sales comparison approach.
    c. income approach.
    d. gross rent multiplier.

23. An appraiser estimating the value of a property with a net income of $40,000 decides to use an 8 percent capitalization rate instead of a 10 percent rate. Use of the lower rate results in

   a. a 2 percent decrease in the appraised value.
   b. a $100,000 increase in the appraised value.
   c. a $100,000 decrease in the appraised value.
   d. no change in the appraised value.

24. The economic effect of an improvement on a property's value is indicated by the appraisal principle of

   a. reproduction.
   b. contribution.
   c. progression.
   d. diminishing returns.

25. Capitalization is the process by which annual net operating income is used to

   a. estimate value.
   b. determine cost.
   c. establish depreciation.
   d. determine tax savings.

26. An appraiser who calculates the cost of reproducing a building is finding the

   a. present value of the building.
   b. current cost to duplicate the building.
   c. depreciated value of the building.
   d. current cost to build a similar building using cheaper materials.

27. A property has a monthly net income of $1,800, and an appraiser believes a 9 percent rate of return is appropriate for the property. Its value would be estimated at

   a. $20,000.   c. $240,000.
   b. $21,600.   d. $2,400,00.

28. An investor who follows the concept that "the whole is worth more than the parts" is using the concept of

   a. depreciation.
   b. progression.
   c. plottage.
   d. contribution.

29. An appraiser who calculates the cost of constructing an older building using modern techniques and materials is finding the building's

   a. unit cost.
   b. replacement cost.
   c. reproduction cost.
   d. operating cost.

30. Physical deterioration is a result of which of the following?

   a. Cracked sidewalks
   b. Poor floor plan
   c. Location next to a noisy airport
   d. Out-of-date fixtures

31. For anything to have value which of the following characteristics must be present?

   a. Scarcity
   b. Competition
   c. Anticipation
   d. Balance

32. Harold constructs an eight-bedroom brick house with a tennis court, a greenhouse and an indoor pool in a neighborhood of modest two-bedroom and three-bedroom frame houses on narrow lots. The value of Harold's house is likely to be affected by what principal?

   a. Progression
   b. Assemblage
   c. Change
   d. Regression

33. The appraised value of a residence with four bedrooms and one bathroom would probably be reduced because of

   a. external obsolescence.
   b. curable physical deterioration.
   c. functional obsolescence.
   d. incurable physical deterioration.

34. An investor is willing to pay a premium for a commercial property because he believes there will be an increase in the area's population. The investor's decision is based on the concept of

   a. anticipation.
   b. competition.
   c. conformity.
   d. contribution.

35. An appraiser estimating the value of vacant land is using the

   a. sales comparison approach.
   b. income approach.
   c. cost approach.
   d. gross income multiplier approach.

36. When using the sales comparison approach, all of the following are important characteristics in selecting comparables *except*

   a. sale dates of the properties.
   b. location of the properties.
   c. cost to the sellers.
   d. number of rooms.

37. An investor investigates the zoning code for a property to determine how much should be offered for the property. The investor's decision will be based on the concept of

   a. anticipation.
   b. competition.
   c. highest and best use.
   d. contribution.

38. An appraiser is asked to determine the value of an existing shopping center. The appraiser will probably give the most weight to which of the approaches to estimating value?

   a. Income approach
   b. Cost approach
   c. Market data approach
   d. Index method

39. Which of the following is deducted from potential gross income to calculate gross effective income when using the income approach?

   a. Legal expenses
   b. Repairs
   c. Loan payments
   d. Vacancy loss

40. Estimating the value of property requires a systematic set of procedures. The first step in the appraisal process is typically to

   a. develop an appraisal plan.
   b. collect general data on the area.
   c. define the purpose of the appraisal.
   d. estimate the value of the land.

41. What is the value of a property that produces gross income of $94,000 if the GIM is 8.5?

   a. $66,583   c. $132,706
   b. $110,588   d. $799,000

42. An appraiser would use the cost approach as the primary appraisal method for a

   a. parking garage.
   b. condominium.
   c. shopping mall.
   d. public school.

43. An investor purchased a property for $450,000. If the property has annual net income of $36,000, the capitalization rate on the investment is

   a. 6.6 percent.
   b. 8 percent.
   c. 9 percent.
   d. 12.5 percent.

44. If appraising a newly built single-family house, an appraiser would be most interested in the

   a. cost of constructing the house.
   b. capitalization rate of the house.
   c. location of the house.
   d. gross rent multiplier.

45. To calculate the monthly gross rent multiplier of a property

   a. multiply the monthly gross income by 12.
   b. divide the purchase price by the gross monthly income.
   c. divide the capitalization rate by the monthly gross income.
   d. divide the annual gross income by the purchase price.

46. Using the cost approach, an appraiser determines that the value of a property is $230,000. If the appraiser estimated the cost of replacing the structures on the property at $160,000 and the land value as $90,000, what was the amount of accrued depreciation estimated by the appraiser for the property?

   a. $10,000   c. $60,000
   b. $20,000   d. $90,000

47. An apartment building has six units that rent for $750 each per month. If the purchase price of the property is $486,000, the property's annual gross income multiplier is

    a. 7.   c. 54.
    b. 9.   d. 108.

48. An appraiser calculates a separate value for the land when using the

    a. sales comparison approach.
    b. income approach.
    c. cost approach.
    d. gross rent multiplier approach.

49. If an appraiser uses more than one appraisal method and assigns different weights to the results of each, she is using

    a. substitution.
    b. contribution.
    c. replacement.
    d. reconciliation.

50. An apartment building has a capitalization rate of 6 percent. If the expenses on the property increase by $6,000 while the rents remain the same, the property value will

    a. remain unchanged.
    b. increase by $6,000.
    c. decrease by $36,000.
    d. decrease by $100,000.

VI
UNIT VI

UNIT VI
DIAGNOSTIC TEST
ANSWER SHEET

This sheet is perforated for easy pullout. Write your answers on this sheet as you complete the exercises. Refer to the diagnostic worksheet after completing the test to evaluate your strong and weak content areas. Review material in the appropriate chapter and sections.

1. _____
2. _____
3. _____
4. _____
5. _____
6. _____
7. _____
8. _____
9. _____
10. _____
11. _____
12. _____
13. _____
14. _____
15. _____
16. _____
17. _____

18. _____
19. _____
20. _____
21. _____
22. _____
23. _____
24. _____
25. _____
26. _____
27. _____
28. _____
29. _____
30. _____
31. _____
32. _____
33. _____
34. _____

35. _____
36. _____
37. _____
38. _____
39. _____
40. _____
41. _____
42. _____
43. _____
44. _____
45. _____
46. _____
47. _____
48. _____
49. _____
50. _____

UNIT
VII

REAL ESTATE
FINANCE

CHAPTER 20

LOAN INSTRUMENTS

Because few real estate transactions are cash sales, an understanding of real estate financing is important. This chapter discusses some basic lending concepts and documents used in real estate loans. *Section 1* covers the three primary financing instruments, which are the note, mortgage and deed of trust. *Section 2* covers the mortgage document in more detail. Remember to use the Study Tool Kit to reference key information and to update your progress checklist.

Learning Objectives

Track your progress as you work through the chapter by checking each learning objective when you complete it.

____ List and describe the three theories of mortgage law.

____ List and describe the three primary loan documents involved with a real estate loan.

____ List the differences and similarities between a mortgage and a trust deed.

____ List and describe the three parties involved in a deed of trust.

____ List and describe the mortgagor's duties.

____ List and describe the mortgage clauses.

Key Terms and Phrases

Track your progress as you work through the chapter by checking each term when you understand its meaning.

____ Acceleration clause	____ Mortgagee
____ Alienation clause	____ Mortgagor
____ Deed of trust	____ Prepayment clause
____ Defeasance clause	____ Promissory note
____ Equity	____ Release deed
____ Hypothecation	____ Satisfaction of mortgage
____ Intermediary theory	____ Senior mortgage
____ Junior mortgage	____ Subordination agreement
____ Lien theory	____ Title theory
____ Mortgage	

TYPES OF LOAN INSTRUMENTS

LENDING CONCEPTS

Mortgagor—The **mortgagor** is the *borrower*, also called the *obligor*, who gives the lender a pledge to pay the loan (the mortgage).

Mortgagee—The **mortgagee** is the *lender*, also called the *obligee*, who receives the pledge to pay the loan (the mortgage).

Hypothecation—The borrower may *pledge property* as collateral to secure a loan without giving up possession. By doing this the borrower **hypothecates** the property.

Senior and Junior Mortgages

A property may have several mortgages (loans) attached to it. The first loan taken out on the property is called the *first mortgage,* the next mortgage taken is called the *second mortgage* and so on. The first mortgage holder has priority over subsequent mortgages; therefore, the first mortgage is called the **senior mortgage** and the rest are **junior mortgages.** The holder of the senior mortgage can voluntarily take a lower priority than a junior loan holder through a **subordination agreement.**

EXAMPLE: A lender with a first lien on a vacant property may subordinate that mortgage to a second lender who is providing a loan for construction of buildings on the property.

Equity

Equity is the difference between the *value* of the property and the value of *loans* against the property. Changes in an owner's equity depend on changes in the loan amount and property value.

____ Equity = Property Value – Property Debt

____ Equity increases if value increases and/or debt decreases

____ Equity decreases if value decreases and/or debt increases

EXAMPLE: A property is worth $180,000 with a mortgage of $100,000. The owner's equity is $80,000. If the owner takes a second loan for $20,000 the equity will be $60,000.

MORTGAGE LAW

The states interpret mortgage law using the following three *legal theories:*

1. *Title theory states*—Some states follow **title theory,** in which the mortgage conveys *ownership* to the mortgagee. On default by the mortgagor the mortgagee may take possession of the property. A *defeasance clause* in the mortgage provides that title reverts to the mortgagor when the loan is paid.
2. *Lien theory states*—The majority of states are **lien theory** states. The mortgage creates only a *lien* on the property and title remains with the mortgagor. If the mortgagor defaults, the lender must foreclose on the lien.
3. *Intermediary theory states*—Some states have modified these theories and are called **intermediary theory** or *modified lien theory* states. In these states title remains with the mortgagor, but the mortgagee may take title to the property if the mortgagor defaults.

LOAN INSTRUMENTS

Promissory Note

The **promissory note** is a contract between the borrower and the lender. The borrower promises to pay the lender the loan amount following specified terms. It is a personal obligation of the borrower. The borrower is also called the *obligor* and the lender is the *obligee.* One of the characteristics of a note is that it is a *negotiable instrument.* This means that the holder of the note (the lender) may transfer its rights to another party. (This is similar to endorsing a check, which is a negotiable instrument, over to someone else.) Thus, the lender may sell the note to investors.

Essential elements of a note:

- It must be in *writing.*
- The obligor and obligee must have *contractual capacity.*
- There must be a *promise* to pay a *definite amount* by the obligor.
- There must be *definite terms* of payment.
- It must be *signed* by the borrower.
- It must be voluntarily *delivered* by the borrower and *accepted* by the lender.

Mortgage

A **mortgage** is a contract between the mortgagor and the mortgagee, providing security for the debt by *creating a lien* on the property. The mortgage is covered in more detail in Section 2.

Note: In some areas it is common practice to incorporate both the note and the mortgage in one document.

Deed of Trust

A **deed of trust,** also called a *trust deed,* involves *three parties* (a mortgage involves two: the mortgagor and the mortgagee). Its purpose is the same as a mortgage, to secure a loan.

Parties to a deed of trust:

- *Trustor*—the mortgagor (the borrower)
- *Trustee*—a third party (usually a bank or title company)
- *Beneficiary*—the mortgagee (the lender)

When a loan is made, the borrower conveys title to the trustee for the lender's benefit. The title remains in trust until the loan is paid. The trustee is given *naked title* or *bare legal title* rather than *actual title,* meaning that the trustee does not have the rights usually associated with ownership, such as possession of the property. The lender usually holds the deed of trust for safekeeping. Figure 20.1 compares a mortgage with a deed of trust.

Default. State rules on a trust deed foreclosure vary, but in general the process is faster, less expensive and less complex than judicial foreclosure with a mortgage. If the borrower defaults, the lender delivers the deed of trust to the trustee with instructions to sell the property. The property is sold at a trustee's sale and the loan is repaid.

Ending a Deed of Trust. When the loan is repaid, the trustee issues a **release deed** or a *trustee's reconveyance deed.* This deed can be recorded to provide notice in the public records that the lender's beneficial interest in the property is over.

FIGURE 20.1
Mortgage and
Deed of Trust

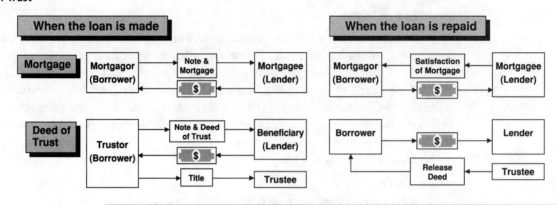

BEFORE READING THE NEXT SECTION, COMPLETE THE SECTION 1
REVIEW EXERCISES AND COMPARE YOUR ANSWERS WITH THE
SOLUTIONS AT THE END OF THE CHAPTER.

SECTION 1
REVIEW EXERCISES

1. Name the mortgage theory that best fits each description.

   a. _____ Title remains with the borrower.

   b. _____ Title remains with the borrower but the lender may take
   title if the borrower defaults.

   c. _____ Mortgage gives title to the lender.

2. What is the effect on a property's equity in each of the following situations?

   a. _____ An owner makes an extra loan payment.

   b. _____ An owner remodels the kitchen in her home.

   c. _____ Because of overbuilding, a subdivision's market value
   drops.

   d. _____ An owner takes out a home equity loan.

Are the following statements true (T) or false (F)?

3. ____ A mortgage and deed of trust are similar because both involve three parties.

4. ____ A mortgage and deed of trust are similar because both provide security for a loan.

5. ____ A mortgage and deed of trust are different because it is more difficult for the lender
   to recover its money under a deed of trust if the borrower defaults.

6. ____ A promissory note is a negotiable instrument giving the lender the right to sell the
   loan.

Supply the term that best matches each of the following descriptions.

7. _____ An agreement between a borrower and a lender in which
   the borrower commits to pay the lender the loan amount
   following specific terms

8. _____ The party who gives the lender a pledge to pay a loan

9. _____ An agreement between three parties for the purpose of
   securing a real estate loan

10. _____ An agreement between a borrower and a lender that provides security for the loan by creating a lien on the property

11. _____ The party who receives a pledge to pay a loan

12. _____ A deed given by a trustee when a loan is repaid

13. _____ The difference between the value of a property and the value of any loans against it

14. _____ Pledging property as security for a loan without giving up possession

---

SECTION 2
THE MORTGAGE

MORTGAGE REQUIREMENTS

The following are needed for a valid mortgage: a written agreement, both parties with the capacity to contract, a valid debt (the note provides evidence of this), a legal description of the property being pledged, the mortgaging clause (pledges or grants the property as security), any other terms or covenants, signature of the mortgagor and acceptance by the mortgagee.

MORTGAGOR'S DUTIES

Clauses in the mortgage documents usually include several *covenants,* which are promises made by the borrower to the lender. There is no single standardized mortgage, but the following are common promises included in a mortgage:

- *Promise to pay*—The mortgagor promises to repay the debt according to the terms in the note.
- *Real estate taxes*—The borrower promises to pay all real estate taxes on the property.
- *Insurance*—The borrower promises to maintain adequate insurance on the property.
- *Good repair*—The borrower promises to keep the property in good condition (also called *preservation and maintenance* or *covenant against waste*).
- *Removal*—The borrower promises not to remove or demolish any buildings or fixtures because it may cause loss of value.

Mortgage Clauses
- A **prepayment clause** describes the borrower's rights and obligations if the loan is prepaid.
- The **acceleration clause** allows the lender to demand immediate payment of the loan balance if the borrower breaks the terms of the note or mortgage.

Hint: Think of the accelerating clause as "speeding up" the remaining loan payments so that they are all due immediately.

- The **defeasance clause** provides that when the loan is paid in full, the mortgage is void. A document called a **satisfaction of mortgage** (if a mortgage was used) or *release deed* (if a trust deed was used) is issued by the lender. The satisfaction or release should be promptly recorded in the county where the mortgage was recorded to indicate that the mortgage lien has been extinguished.

Hint: To remember the purpose of the defeasance clause think of the mortgage as being defeated, or ended.

- The **alienation clause** allows the lender to make the entire loan balance due if title to the property is transferred (alienated). This is also called a *due-on-sale clause.* This prevents the loan from being assumed without the lender's consent.
- An *escalator clause* allows the lender to change the interest rate under certain conditions.
- A *late payment clause* is used to assess a penalty for late loan payments.

COMPLETE THE SECTION 2 REVIEW EXERCISES AND COMPARE YOUR ANSWERS WITH THE SOLUTIONS AT THE END OF THE CHAPTER.

SECTION 2
REVIEW EXERCISES

1. Name the mortgage clause that best fits each description.
   a. _____ Ends the mortgage when the loan is paid
   b. _____ The lenders can demand all the payments immediately if the borrower does not follow the terms of the note
   c. _____ Lists any costs associated with paying the loan off early
   d. _____ Prevents the loan from being assumed by someone else

Are the following statements true (T) or false (F)?

2. ____ A release deed is issued by the lender under the alienation clause.

3. ____ Common duties of the mortgagor in a mortgage are to keep the property repaired and maintain adequate insurance on the property.

4. ____ An escalator clause allows the lender to change the interest rate on the loan.

Supply the term that best matches each of the following descriptions.

5. _____ A document issued by the lender that releases the lien on the property

6. _____ Allows the lender to demand the entire loan balance immediately if title to the property is transferred

7. _____ Allows the lender to demand immediate payment of the entire loan balance if the borrower breaks the terms of the note

8. _____ Determines the borrower's rights and duties if the loan is prepaid

9. _____ Provides that the mortgage lien is released when the loan is repaid

SOLUTIONS
FOR SECTION REVIEW EXERCISES

SECTION 1

1. a. Lien theory   b. Intermediary theory   c. Title theory
2. a. Equity increases because debt on the property decreases.
   b. Equity increases because the value of the property will increase.
   c. Equity decreases because the value of the property decreases.
   d. Equity decreases because the loan amounts against the property increase.
3. FALSE A mortgage involves two parties (mortgagor and mortgagee) and a deed of trust involves three parties (trustor, trustee and beneficiary).
4. TRUE
5. FALSE It is easier for the lender to recover the loan amount under a deed of trust than it is using the foreclosure process under a mortgage.
6. TRUE
7. Promissory note
8. Mortgagor
9. Deed of trust
10. Mortgage
11. Mortgagee
12. Release deed
13. Equity
14. Hypothecation

SECTION 2

1. a. Defeasance clause   b. Acceleration clause   c. Prepayment clause
   d. Alienation clause
2. FALSE It is issued as a result of the defeasance clause.
3. TRUE
4. TRUE
5. Satisfaction of mortgage
6. Alienation clause
7. Acceleration clause
8. Prepayment clause
9. Defeasance clause

CHAPTER 21

LENDING PRACTICES

This chapter discusses how loans are made and who provides the funds. *Section 1* covers the process for originating loans. *Section 2* covers the providers of mortgage money and the secondary mortgage market where real estate loans are bought and sold. *Section 3* covers foreclosure of real estate loans and the mortgagor's redemption rights. Remember to use the Study Tool Kit to reference key information and to update your progress checklist.

Learning Objectives

Track your progress as you work through the chapter by checking each learning objective when you complete it.

_____ List and describe the steps involved in the loan process.

_____ Qualify a borrower by using the two qualifying ratios.

_____ Explain the different uses of points.

_____ Explain the difference between *assumption* and *subject to*.

_____ List and describe the various sources of mortgage money.

_____ Describe the difference between mortgage brokers and mortgage bankers.

_____ Explain the effects of the secondary mortgage market.

_____ Describe the difference between conforming loans and portfolio loans.

_____ List and describe the entities that participate in the secondary mortgage market.

_____ List and describe the different types of foreclosure proceedings.

_____ Explain the difference between statutory and equitable redemption.

Key Terms and Phrases

Track your progress as you work through the chapter by checking each term when you understand its meaning.

_____ Assumption of mortgage

_____ Certificate of sale

_____ Commercial banks

_____ Conforming loans

_____ Credit unions

_____ Deed in lieu of foreclosure

_____ Deficiency judgment

_____ Discount points

_____ Disintermediation

_____ Equitable right of redemption

_____ Escrow account

_____ Fannie Mae

_____ Federal Home Loan Mortgage Corporation (FHLMC)

_____ Foreclosure

_____ Government National Mortgage Association (GNMA)

_____ Judicial foreclosure

____	Lis pendens	____	Power of sale clause
____	Loan-to-value ratio	____	Private mortgage insurance (PMI)
____	Mortgage banking company	____	Private mortgage packagers
____	Mortgage bond financing	____	REIT
____	Mortgage broker	____	Savings banks
____	Mutual savings banks	____	Secondary mortgage market
____	Nonjudicial foreclosure	____	Statutory right of redemption
____	PITI	____	Strict foreclosure
____	Points	____	Subject-to mortgage
____	Portfolio lenders		

SECTION 1
THE LOAN PROCESS

QUALIFYING FOR A LOAN

Qualifying the Buyer

The lender must assess the borrower's financial ability to pay the loan. To make this evaluation, the following analysis is performed.

Loan application—The borrower provides information on employment, credit history, assets (including investment account balances and property owned), liabilities (current loan amounts owed) and other personal information. Most lenders use the *Uniform Residential Loan Application* form for all loans (including FHA and VA) secured by one-family to four-family properties.

Credit evaluation—Information in the application, such as employment history and assets, is *verified*. The lender orders a *credit report* to determine financial information such as the number of other loans and balances, payment histories and personal bankruptcies. Two *qualifying ratios* are usually applied to ensure that the borrower's monthly income is sufficient to meet the housing expense (**PITI** = principal, interest, taxes and insurance).

1. *Payment-to-Income Ratio*—Using this ratio (also called the *Front-end ratio*), the PITI should not be more than 25 percent to 30 percent of the borrower's gross monthly income (FHA is 29 percent, and VA does not use this ratio).

EXAMPLE: A loan applicant has gross monthly income of $2,000 and the PITI is $700. The applicant would not qualify because the PITI exceeds 30 percent of monthly income ($700 ÷ $2,000 = 35%). In this situation the loan applicant would qualify for a PITI up to $600 ($2,000 × .3 = $600).

2. *Debt-to-Income Ratio*—Using this ratio (also called the *Back-end ratio*), the PITI and long-term debt (loans of six months or longer) should not be more than 33 percent to 38 percent of the borrower's monthly gross income (FHA and VA is 41 percent).

EXAMPLE: A loan applicant has gross monthly income of $2,000, the PITI is $700 and the applicant has a car loan with a $200 monthly payment. The applicant would not qualify because the PITI plus other debt exceeds 33 percent ($700 + $200 ÷ $2,000 = 45%). In this situation the loan applicant would qualify for a PITI up to $460 ($2,000 × .33 − $200 = $460).

Prequalifying

Buyers seeking a loan often have a lender prequalify them for a loan. The lender collects the buyers' financial information, performs a credit check and determines the maximum loan amount for which the buyers will qualify. Knowing the maximum loan amount provides the buyers an estimate of the housing price range they may be able to afford.

Using Automation in the Loan Origination Process

Two approaches to loan origination recently have been developed: computerized loan origination (CLO) and automated underwriting systems (AUS). Using a CLO, a real estate agent helps a prospective buyer answer questions on a computer screen, which allows a lender's underwriter to make an approval decision. Using an AUS system, a mortgage broker enters the buyer's financial information into the computer, and in a couple of minutes the system determines if the buyer qualifies for the loan. If the system cannot make the loan decision automatically, it may refer it to the lender's underwriters for analysis and a manual decision. With an AUS system a broker could plug a laptop computer into a phone jack (possibly in the buyer's home) and obtain a loan decision for the buyer. Freddie Mac and Fannie Mae now have their own AUS systems available.

Qualifying the Property

The real estate is the lender's security for the loan, and the lender will have an *appraisal* performed to determine the property's value. (Chapters 18 and 19 cover property appraisal.)

The lender also applies a qualifying ratio to the property. The loan amount may not exceed a certain percentage of the property's market value. This is called a **loan-to-value ratio** (*LTV*). Lenders generally require that loans be less than 80 percent of the property's value. A borrower seeking a loan with less than a 20 percent down payment may be required to seek private mortgage insurance (covered later in this section) or a VA or an FHA loan (covered in Chapter 22).

EXAMPLE: A buyer wants to purchase a house at $160,000, and the lender agrees to make an 80 percent LTV loan. The appraisal confirms the property value at $160,000. The maximum loan amount the lender will give is $128,000 ($160,000 × .80). The buyer needs a down payment of $32,000.

Qualifying the Title

To ensure that the lender's mortgage is a *first lien*, a *title search* is performed on the property. (Chapter 11 covers title searches.)

CLOSING THE LOAN TRANSACTION

If the lender decides that the loan can be made, a *loan commitment* is sent to the borrower, indicating the amount and rate the lender is committing to the loan. The borrower is notified of the closing date. At the closing the loan is given and title to the property is conveyed. (Chapter 12 covers closing.)

Servicing the Loan

Once the loan is closed, it must be serviced. *Servicing* includes a variety of activities including processing the loan payments, paying real estate taxes and insurance, providing tax information to the IRS and providing the customer with loan

FIGURE 21.1
*Borrower's Rights
Regarding Loan
Servicing*

**Disclosure Requirements
(disclosed within 3 days of loan application)**

– Estimate of whether servicing will be retained or transferred
– % of loans for which servicing was transferred in last 3 years
– % of loans lender expects to sell in the next 12 months
– A summary of borrower's rights with loan servicers

Borrower's Rights with Loan Servicers

– Written acknowledgment sent to borrower within 20 days of a request for assistance
– Servicer must correct problems within 60 days
– Servicer may not report anything to credit bureau during dispute period

Rights if Loan Servicing Is Transferred

– Before 15 days of transfer, the name, address and toll free number of the new servicer must be sent
– Before 15 days of transfer, borrower must be notified of new and old servicer department telephone numbers for handling questions
– Within 15 days after transfer, new servicer must send information on handling questions
– Within 60 days after transfer, misdirected payments may not result in late penalty

information. If the loan is sold to investors, the lender may continue to service the loan and earn a fee.

Because of consumer complaints when loan servicing was transferred by lenders, Congress has enacted rules to protect borrowers from mistakes and abuses by loan servicing companies. Rules issued by HUD in 1994 prescribe a nationally standardized disclosure notice to alert the loan applicant to the lender's servicing practices. There are also new rules when a loan is transferred to another servicer. These rules are summarized in Figure 21.1.

Escrow Accounts

Most loan agreements require that the borrower make monthly payments into an **escrow account** (also called an *impound account* or a *reserve account*) so the lender can pay the real estate taxes and property insurance premiums. The lender normally collects one twelfth of the estimated annual expenses each month. Several states require that interest be paid on the escrow money.

EXAMPLE: The annual real estate taxes on a property are $2,400 and the insurance is $600. The lender collects an additional $250 ($200 for taxes and $50 for insurance) each month.

Private Mortgage Insurance (PMI)

In 1957 the Mortgage Guaranty Insurance Corp. (MGIC), also called "Magic," established a private mortgage insurance program to *insure conventional loans* with *low down payments*. Today several companies offer private mortgage insurance that allows lenders to make loans with only 5 percent to 10 percent down.

Private mortgage insurance (PMI) insures the top 20 percent of the loan. When the LTV drops below a certain percentage, the insurance is no longer needed and can be ended. This is not true of FHA-insured loans (covered in Chapter 22), which insure the entire loan. Borrowers are normally charged a fee (approximately 1 percent) at closing and an annual fee of less than 1 percent each year the insurance is in force.

EXAMPLE: A lender is willing to make a loan for $80,000, but the borrower needs $100,000. The lender agrees to make the loan if the borrower purchases mortgage insurance for the loan amount from $80,000 to $100,000.

Points

A **point** is *1 percent of the loan amount.* There are two uses of points in real estate lending.

1. *Loan origination fees*—Lenders charge a variety of fees to originate a loan. Some lenders itemize each of these, while others combine them by charging points as an origination fee.

EXAMPLE: A lender charges a one point loan origination fee. If the amount of the loan is $80,000 the fee is $800.

2. *To increase yield*—If the lender wants to raise the yield on the loan (the profit the lender actually will make), it can charge **discount points.** In this case the points are actually *prepaid interest.* Calculating the increased yield on the loan using points becomes a little difficult, but a general guideline is that *eight points equals a 1 percent increase in the yield* (or one point increases the yield by ⅛ percent).

EXAMPLE: A lender charges a borrower an interest rate of 8 percent. To raise the yield to 8.5 percent, the lender charges 4 points. If the loan is for $100,000, the lender will charge $4,000 ($100,000 × 4%) at closing.

ASSUMPTIONS VERSUS SUBJECT-TO MORTGAGES

- **Subject-to mortgage**—When a buyer purchases a property *subject to an existing loan,* the buyer acknowledges the existence of the debt but takes no personal liability for the loan. Even though the buyer continues making loan payments, the seller remains personally liable for the loan. If the buyer stops making payments, the lender may hold the seller liable for the remaining balance.
- **Assumption of mortgage**—When a buyer purchases a property and *assumes* the loan, the buyer becomes primarily liable for the debt. If the buyer defaults on the loan, the lender will look to the buyer first. However, the seller is still on the original note, so the lender can look to the seller if the buyer does not pay the loan. If the buyer released the seller when the loan was assumed, then only the buyer is liable.

BEFORE READING THE NEXT SECTION, COMPLETE THE SECTION 1 REVIEW EXERCISES AND COMPARE YOUR ANSWERS WITH THE SOLUTIONS AT THE END OF THE CHAPTER.

SECTION 1
REVIEW EXERCISES

1. Name the step in the loan qualifying process that best fits each description.

a. _____ A ratio that compares the applicant's gross income to the proposed PITI

b. _____ Verification of a loan applicant's employment history and assets

c. _____ Lender's comparison of the property's value and the proposed loan amount

d. _____ Information provided by borrowers consisting primarily of what they own and what they owe

e. _____ Search of the public records to discover any liens on the property

f. _____ Ratio that compares the applicant's gross income to the proposed PITI and long-term debt

Are the following statements true (T) or false (F)?

2. ____ The front-end qualifying ratio is used by the lender to determine if the applicant will need private mortgage insurance.

3. ____ To raise the yield on a loan from 7 percent to 8 percent, a lender should charge approximately two discount points at closing.

4. ____ A point is a percent of the property's selling amount.

5. ____ Mortgage insurance is used to insure the entire loan.

Supply the term that best matches each of the following descriptions.

6. _____ Provides insurance for the lender when the loan-to-value ratio exceeds 80 percent

7. _____ Used to raise the yield on the loan

8. _____ Buyer makes payments but is not personally liable for the loan

9. _____ Describes the borrower's monthly housing expense

10. _____ Buyer becomes primarily liable for the loan

11. _____ An account with the lender that holds money to pay real estate taxes and insurance

12. _____ Used by the lender as a qualifying ratio for the property

13. _____ A percent of the loan amount

SECTION 2

PROVIDERS OF MORTGAGE MONEY

Providers of mortgage money can generally be divided into two categories: (1) *primary sources of funds,* where loans are made either directly by the lender or through intermediaries, and (2) the *secondary market,* where loans made in the primary market are bought and sold to investors.

PRIMARY SOURCES OF LOANS

Savings Banks

Savings banks (formerly savings and loan associations) are also called *thrifts* and *savings associations.* These institutions traditionally have been an important source of funds for loans to purchase or construct owner-occupied residential housing. Savings banks invest a major portion of their assets in real estate loans. Thrifts can be either federally or state chartered and are regulated by state and federal agencies.

Commercial Banks

In recent years **commercial banks** have surpassed savings banks in the number of mortgage loans originated and the amount of money invested in mortgage loans. Banks also make real estate construction and home improvement loans. Banks are either federally (nationally) chartered or state chartered. National banks are supervised by the *Comptroller of the Currency*, are members of the *Federal Reserve System (FRS)* and have the term *National* in their title. State-chartered banks are regulated by state agencies, and membership in the FRS is optional.

Mutual Saving Banks

Mutual saving banks are similar to savings banks, are mutually owned (no stockholders) and are located primarily in the northeastern states. They are very active in mortgage lending. Because they seek low-risk loans, they make many FHA and VA loans. They are state chartered.

Credit Unions

Credit unions are cooperative organizations that maintain savings accounts for their members. They provide some financing for residential and nonresidential loans. They also make home improvement loans to depositors.

Life Insurance Companies

Life insurance companies deal with correspondents (*intermediaries*) such as mortgage bankers rather than individual borrowers. They invest in loans to large-scale commercial and industrial properties and also in packages of FHA and VA residential mortgage loans purchased in the secondary market. (The secondary market is covered later in the section.)

Mortgage Banking Company

Mortgage banking companies (also called *mortgage companies*) originate loans with either their own funds or money borrowed from other institutions. They package these loans and sell them to investors. The mortgage banker usually continues to service the loans, even after they are sold, receiving a fee for its services. They are regulated by state law. Since the 1980s the volume of loan originations has shifted from thrifts to mortgage companies. Mortgage companies now account for more than half of the originations of single-family loans.

Mortgage Broker

Mortgage brokers do not make loans; rather they act as intermediaries between borrowers and lenders. They take the loan information and "shop" for the lender offering the best rates and terms. They earn a finder's fee, usually 1 percent or more of the loan amount, when they successfully match a borrower with a lender. Once the loan is made, the mortgage broker is not involved with servicing the loan.

Tip: Do not confuse mortgage banker and mortgage broker. They sound similar but perform different functions. The mortgage banker loans money and services loans, whereas the mortgage broker brings borrowers and lenders together.

Pension Funds

Pension funds invest in real estate loans primarily through mortgage bankers and mortgage brokers.

Real Estate Investment Trusts (REITs)

REITs are owned by investors that make loans to large commercial real estate projects. These are covered in more detail in Chapter 9.

Individuals

Sellers of houses sometimes provide loans to buyers. Other *individuals* or *groups of investors* lend money for real estate.

Government Programs

State and local governments have enacted various programs to provide home financing, often at preferred interest rates, to home buyers in their areas. With **mortgage bond financing,** municipalities raise funds by selling tax-exempt bonds and use the money to provide low-rate mortgages. The objective is usually to assist low-to-middle-income, first-time buyers to purchase a home.

U.S. Department of Agriculture

The Rural Economic and Community Development (RECD) services and Farm Service Agency (FSA) are agencies of the U.S. Department of Agriculture (USDA). The RECD administers loan programs to help purchase or improve properties in rural areas. Loans are made to residential property and rural improvement projects such as water lines. Agricultural loans made to farms, chicken houses, etc., are administered by the FSA. These loan programs were formerly administered by the Farmers Home Administration (called Farmer Mac.)

SECONDARY MORTGAGE MARKET

Because the mortgage and the note it secures can be assigned to someone else, the lender can sell the loan to an investor in the **secondary mortgage market.** The borrower may be unaware of the sale because it does not affect his or her rights or obligations and the original lender may continue to service the loan (for a fee from the investor). Loans can be sold *directly between lenders* or they can be sold to *organizations* that actively participate in the secondary market.

Effects of the Secondary Market

The secondary mortgage market accomplishes two objectives: (1) It circulates the mortgage money supply and (2) it standardizes loan requirements.

1. *Circulates the mortgage money supply*—Because the secondary market is *national,* lenders in one area who have made loans can sell them and receive cash with which to make new loans. Investors in other areas that have cash but are not making loans can buy loans. This gives mortgages *liquidity* (ability to be converted to cash). This is especially important because it counteracts **disintermediation,** an outflow of funds from savings institutions. If disintermediation occurs, the lender can sell more of its loans and use the cash to cover the outflow of funds.

EXAMPLE: A lender has made several loans totaling $1 million. The lender packages the loans and sells them to investors. The lender receives cash and now can make more loans.

2. *Standardizes loan requirements*—Because loans are packaged together for investors, they must follow standard guidelines (e.g., limits on LTVs and loan amounts) and use standard

loan forms (e.g., appraisal forms, closing statements, notes). If the loans were all different, investors could not be sure what they were buying, thus increasing their risk and making them less willing to invest.

Loans that follow guidelines established by federal regulations in the secondary market are called **conforming loans.** Some lenders do not sell their loans and are called **portfolio lenders** because they keep the mortgages in their loan portfolios.

Fannie Mae

The largest participant in the secondary market is **Fannie Mae,** formerly known as the Federal National Mortgage Association. It was started in 1938 as a government agency to purchase FHA-insured loans. It was reorganized in 1968 as a private corporation with shares traded on the New York Stock Exchange.

Today Fannie Mae provides a secondary market for *VA, FHA and conventional loans.* It purchases "pools" or "packages" of large blocks of loans from lenders and then issues *mortgage-backed securities* to investors. The income investors receive from the securities is derived from the loans that "back them up." Fannie Mae is the largest single private mortgage purchaser. Mortgage banking firms are actively involved in originating and servicing loans for Fannie Mae.

Government National Mortgage Association

The **Government National Mortgage Association (GNMA),** also known as "Ginnie Mae," was created in 1968 when Fannie Mae was reorganized. GNMA is a wholly owned government corporation under the Department of Housing and Urban Development (HUD) and provides a secondary market for *VA and FHA loans* (not conventional loans).

GNMA has a *mortgage-backed securities program* selling guarantee certificates called *Ginnie Mae Pass-Through Certificates* to investors. These certificates are backed by FHA and VA loans, and as the loans are paid, the proceeds are "passed though" to the certificate holders.

GNMA sometimes works with Fannie Mae under special assistance programs called *tandem programs,* used when mortgage money is tight. Fannie Mae buys higher-risk, lower-yield (usually FHA) loans at market rates, and GNMA guarantees payment and absorbs the difference in the yield, making FHA loans attractive.

Federal Home Loan Mortgage Corp.

The **Federal Home Loan Mortgage Corporation (FHLMC),** also known as "Freddie Mac," was created by Congress in 1970. Shares in FHLMC are sold publicly.

FHLMC works with savings banks to provide a secondary market for their loans. Unlike Fannie Mae and GNMA, most of the loans FHLMC handles are conventional loans. FHLMC sells *mortgage participation certificates (PCs)* and *guaranteed mortgage certificates (GMCs)* backed by pools of mortgage loans.

Private Conduits

Private mortgage packagers also are active in the secondary market. These organizations purchase and pool mortgages from loan originators for sale in the secondary market. Some specialize in areas not serviced by Fannie Mae, GNMA or FHLMC, such as *jumbo loans* (loans with balances exceeding limits set by Fannie Mae, GNMA and FHLMC). Private mortgage packagers include Sears, Roebuck and General Electric.

**BEFORE READING THE NEXT SECTION, COMPLETE THE SECTION 2
REVIEW EXERCISES AND COMPARE YOUR ANSWERS WITH THE
SOLUTIONS AT THE END OF THE CHAPTER.**

SECTION 3
REVIEW EXERCISES

1. Name the primary source of loans that best fits each description.

   a. _____ Very active in mortgage lending, especially making VA and FHA loans; similar to savings and loans

   b. _____ Act as intermediaries between borrowers and lenders

   c. _____ Maintain savings accounts for their members while providing primarily home improvement and home equity real estate loans

   d. _____ Seeks investors to pool their money and to make loans to large commercial real estate projects

   e. _____ Originates loans and packages them to investors; may use its own money or money borrowed from other lenders; also services loans

   f. _____ Invest in packages of real estate loans primarily from mortgage bankers and brokers

   g. _____ Provides loans to people in rural areas

   h. _____ Traditionally an important source of loans for residential property but role has greatly diminished in recent years

   i. _____ Deal with intermediaries rather than individual borrowers; provide money for large industrial and commercial real estate projects

   j. _____ Are either federally or state chartered and make real estate mortgage, construction and home improvement loans

2. Name the organization in the secondary mortgage market that best fits each description.

   a. _____ Works closely with thrifts to provide a secondary market for their loans

   b. _____ Handles FHA, VA and conventional loans; the largest mortgage purchaser

   c. _____ Often purchase and pool nonstandardized loans for selling in the secondary market

   d. _____ Wholly owned government corporation that provides a secondary market for VA and FHA loans

Are the following statements true (T) or false (F)?

3. ____ Mortgage brokers originate and service real estate loans.

4. ____ The secondary mortgage market helps circulate the mortgage money supply and subsidize loan programs.

5. ____ Fannie Mae, GNMA and FHLMC all issue some type of investment securities backed by the loans they hold.

Supply the term that best matches each of the following descriptions.

6. _____ The outflow of funds from savings institutions

7. _____ Loans that follow the established guidelines of the secondary mortgage market

8. _____ A government agency that guarantees loans to help purchase or improve properties in rural areas

9. _____ The process of selling tax-exempt bonds by municipalities to raise money for low-rate loans to first-time home buyers

10. _____ Lenders that do not sell to investors loans that they originate

SECTION 3

FORECLOSURE AND REDEMPTION

FORECLOSURE METHODS

If the buyer defaults and does not fulfill the mortgage terms, the lender can enforce its right of foreclosure. **Foreclosure** is the liquidation of the asset to satisfy the debt. Two approaches to foreclosure are (1) **judicial foreclosure**, in which the matter is brought to the court in a lawsuit, and (2) **nonjudicial foreclosure**, which is handled in a process that does not involve the courts. These are summarized in Figure 21.2.

Judicial Foreclosure

Judicial foreclosure is also called *foreclosure by sale*, and there are two types:

1. *By judicial sale.* The lender uses the acceleration clause in a mortgage and then files suit of foreclosure. Proper notice is given according to local laws, and if the borrower does not pay the loan, the court will order the property sold. The property is sold to the highest bidder at sale. Proceeds are used to pay the lienholders in order of priority. Any amount remaining is paid to the borrower.

2. *By strict foreclosure.* **Strict foreclosure** is also judicial foreclosure, but there is no sale of the property by the court. Instead the court issues a decree that gives title to the lender and ends the debt. The mortgagor loses all rights and equity in the property and usually has no redemption rights. The mortgagee has no rights to a deficiency judgment. This is not a common method of foreclosure because the mortgagor loses all equity in the property.

Nonjudicial Foreclosure

There are two types of *nonjudicial foreclosure.*

1. *Power of sale clause.* A **power of sale clause** is included in the mortgage, giving the lender the right to sell the property if the mortgagor defaults without going through a fore-closure suit. If there is a trust deed, the trustee is usually given the power of sale.

    A *notice of default* is sent to the borrower and filed with the county recorder. Notice of the public sale is given in the newspaper. The property is sold at a public auction to the highest bidder. If the sale price were not enough to satisfy the debt, the lender would have to go to court to obtain a *deficiency judgment.*

2. *Deed in lieu of foreclosure.* A **deed in lieu of foreclosure** may be used rather than going through the process of foreclosure. Sometimes called a "friendly foreclosure," the mortgagee accepts a deed in satisfaction of the debt. If the property is worth more than the loan balance, the lender may pay the difference in cash to the borrower. The mortgagor

FIGURE 21.2
Foreclosure Processes

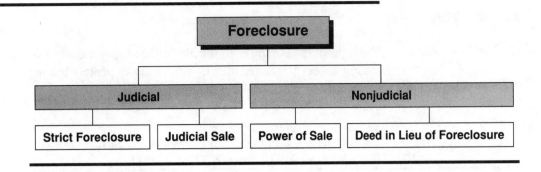

has no redemption rights. A disadvantage to the mortgagee is that title is taken subject to any other existing liens.

Lis Pendens

When a foreclosure lawsuit (or other lawsuit that may affect a property) is filed in court, a **lis pendens** notice is also filed with the county recorder's office where the property is located. A lis pendens gives *public notice* that a legal action is pending against the property. This makes it difficult for the owner to dispose of the property prior to the outcome of the suit. Any purchaser's ownership would be subject to the results of the lawsuit.

Deficiency Judgments

If the net sale proceeds (the selling amount less costs of the sale) are insufficient to pay the debts, the note holder may seek a **deficiency judgment,** which is a *personal judgment* against the debtor. This means that the lender may be able to attach the borrower's personal assets. Most states allow deficiency judgments, although the rules vary among states.

EXAMPLE: A property sells for $100,000 at a foreclosure sale, but the mortgage loan is for $110,000. The lender can try to get a deficiency judgment for $10,000 against the borrower's personal assets.

REDEMPTION

Two types of *redemption rights* may be available to the borrower.

1. *Equitable redemption.* **Equitable right of redemption** is the owner's right to redeem the property *before the foreclosure sale.* Usually the lender must be paid the amount currently due (in some states it may be the entire loan balance) plus any costs, and the loan will be reinstated.
2. *Statutory redemption.* Many states have passed laws establishing a statutory period of time *after the sale* during which the property can be redeemed by the owner. The **statutory right of redemption** usually requires the payment of the debt, interest and any associated costs. The winner at a foreclosure sale receives a **certificate of sale** entitling him or her to a deed *after the redemption period* is over.

POSSESSION

The right of the borrower to remain in the property during and after foreclosure varies among states. A receiver may be appointed to protect the property from *waste* by the borrower.

**COMPLETE THE SECTION 3 REVIEW EXERCISES AND COMPARE YOUR ANSWERS
WITH THE SOLUTIONS AT THE END OF THE CHAPTER.**

SECTION 3
REVIEW EXERCISES

1. Name the type of judicial or nonjudicial foreclosure method that best fits each description.

   a. _____ The lender has the right to have the property sold if the borrower defaults, without going through the court.

   b. _____ The lender files a suit in court seeking a decree that will give title to the property to the lender.

   c. _____ The lender accepts title to the property from the borrower in exchange for ending the debt.

   d. _____ The lender uses the acceleration clause in the mortgage and then files a suit to have the property sold and the loan paid.

Are the following statements true (T) or false (F)?

2. ____ Strict foreclosure is not commonly used because the mortgagor loses all equity in the property.

3. ____ If a lender starts a foreclosure suit, it would be useful also to file a lis pendens.

4. ____ In a judicial sale foreclosure the lender starts the process by using the acceleration clause.

Supply the term that best matches each of the following descriptions.

5. _____ A foreclosure process that does not involve the courts

6. _____ The owner's right to redeem the property after the foreclosure sale

7. _____ A judgment against the debtor's personal assets if the sale of the real estate is not sufficient to satisfy the loan

8. _____ The owner's right to redeem the property before the foreclosure sale

9. _____ The process of liquidating assets to satisfy a debt

10. _____ A notice in the public records of a lawsuit involving a particular property that may result in a claim against the property

11. _____ A foreclosure process that is brought to court in a lawsuit

12. _____ Given to the winner at a foreclosure sale entitling him or her to a deed after the redemption period is over

SOLUTIONS
FOR SECTION REVIEW EXERCISES

SECTION 1

1. a. Buyer qualification: front-end qualifying ratio   b. Buyer qualification: credit evaluation   c. Qualifying the property: loan-to-value ratio   d. Buyer qualification: loan application   e. Qualifying the title   f. Buyer qualification: back-end qualifying ratio

2. FALSE The loan-to-value ratio is used by the lender to determine if the applicant will need private mortgage insurance.

3. FALSE It takes approximately eight points to raise the yield of a loan by 1 percent.

4. FALSE It is a percent of the loan amount.

5. FALSE Mortgage insurance covers the top portion of the loan.

6. Private mortgage insurance (PMI)

7. Discount points

8. Subject-to mortgage

9. PITI

10. Assumption of mortgage

11. Escrow account

12. Loan-to-value ratio

13. Point

SECTION 2

1. a. Mutual saving banks   b. Mortgage brokers   c. Credit unions   d. REIT   e. Mortgage banking company   f. Pension funds   g. RECD or FSA   h. Savings banks/thrifts   i. Life insurance companies   j. Commercial banks

2. a. FHLMC   b. Fannie Mae   c. Private conduits   d. GNMA

3. FALSE Mortgage brokers do not make or service loans. They serve as intermediaries between borrowers and sellers.

4. FALSE The secondary mortgage market helps circulate the mortgage money supply and standardizes loan requirements.

5. TRUE

6. Disintermediation

7. Conforming loans

8. RECD or FSA

9. Mortgage bond financing

10. Portfolio lenders

SECTION 3

1. a. Nonjudicial foreclosure: by power of sale clause   b. Judicial foreclosure: by strict foreclosure   c. Nonjudicial foreclosure: deed in lieu of foreclosure   d. Judicial foreclosure: by judicial sale

2. TRUE

3. TRUE

4. TRUE

5. Nonjudicial foreclosure

6. Statutory right of redemption
7. Deficiency judgment
8. Equitable right of redemption
9. Foreclosure
10. Lis pendens
11. Judicial foreclosure
12. Certificate of sale

CHAPTER 22

TYPES OF REAL ESTATE LOANS

This chapter covers the different loan plans that can be used to finance real estate. *Section 1* covers several of the common loan plans. *Section 2* covers loans that are insured or guaranteed by an agency of the federal government. Remember to use the Study Tool Kit to reference key information and to update your progress checklist.

Learning Objectives

Track your progress as you work through the chapter by checking each learning objective when you complete it.

____ List and describe the key components of an ARM.

____ Explain the concept of amortization.

____ Describe key features of the various financing techniques included in Section 1.

____ Explain the difference between conventional and nonconventional loans.

____ List the characteristics of FHA loans.

____ List the characteristics of VA loans.

Key Terms and Phrases

Track your progress as you work through the chapter by checking each term when you understand its meaning.

____ Adjustable rate mortgage (ARM)

____ Amortized loan

____ Balloon loan

____ Biweekly loan

____ Blanket loan

____ Budget loan

____ Buydown

____ Construction loan

____ FHA loan

____ Fifteen-year loan

____ Graduated payment mortgage (GPM)

____ Home equity loan

____ Impound account

____ Land contract

____ Mortgage insurance premium (MIP)

____ Negative amortization

____ Open-end loan

____ Package loan

____ Purchase-money mortgage (PMM)

____ Reverse annuity mortgage (RAM)

____ Teaser rates

____ Term loan

____ Upfront mortgage insurance premium (UFMIP)

____ VA loan

____ Wraparound loan

MORTGAGE PLANS

ADJUSTABLE RATE MORTGAGE

The interest rate on an **adjustable rate mortgage (ARM)** changes at fixed intervals based on a preselected *economic index*. Because the lender has some protection from interest rate fluctuations, the loan is less risky; therefore, the initial rate on an ARM is *usually lower than that on a fixed rate* loan.

Components of this type of loan include the following:

- *Index*—Interest rate changes are tied to an index. Popular indexes are the one-year Treasury Bill Index (prepared by the Federal Reserve Board) and the Cost of Funds Index (prepared by the 11th District Federal Home Loans Bank). Other common indexes are three- and five-year U.S. Treasury securities and six-month Treasury bills.
- *Margin*—The margin is *added* to the *index rate* and does not change over the life of the loan. The margin represents the lender's operating costs and profit.

EXAMPLE: A borrower has an ARM tied to the one-year T-bill rate with a margin of 2.25. If the T-bill rate is 6 percent, the loan rate will be 8.25 percent.

- *Adjustment interval*—How often the rate can change. A common adjustment period is one year, but it could be monthly, quarterly or any period.
- *Rate caps*—Caps place limits on rate changes. Three common types of caps are (1) increase at *each rate change*, (2) increase in *any year* and (3) total increase over *life of the loan*.
- *Payment cap*—Limits the amount the monthly payments can increase during any one year. If rates rise sharply but the payments do not owing to the payment cap, *negative amortization* could result.
- *Teaser rates*—ARMs may be offered with very low rates (e.g., 2 percent) called **teaser rates.** The attractive rate is usually for only the first year, with sharp annual rate jumps required starting in the second year.
- *Convertible feature*—Allows the borrower to convert to a fixed-rate loan during specified periods in the life of the loan. Fees and other conditions usually accompany this feature.

AMORTIZED LOAN

An **amortized loan** requires periodic payment of both interest and principal. The most commonly used plan has monthly payments of a *constant amount*. Because each payment is calculated on the remaining loan balance, the *initial payments* consist *mostly of interest* with little applied toward principal. With each payment the loan balance decreases so that *more* of the payment is *applied to the principal* and less to the interest. Figure 22.1 illustrates changes in the interest and principal components as an amortized loan is paid.

In a *fully amortized loan* the payments are sufficient in size and number so that the loan balance is reduced to zero with the last payment.

Negative amortization occurs when the payments are not large enough to cover the interest expense. The unpaid interest is added to the balance. Because the loan balance increases with each payment rather than decreasing, it is called *negative amortization*.

FIGURE 22.1
Allocation of Payments
to Interest and Principal

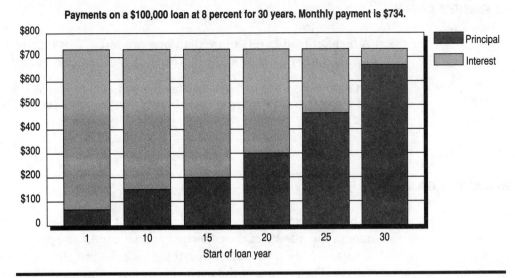

Payments on a $100,000 loan at 8 percent for 30 years. Monthly payment is $734.

If the payments reduce but do not fully extinguish the debt, it is a *partially amortized* loan. A balloon payment is required at the end of the loan term.

BALLOON LOAN

In a **balloon loan** the payments do not fully amortize the loan. The remaining loan balance is included with the last payment (called a *balloon payment*). As discussed earlier, balloon loans can be *partially amortized* loans.

EXAMPLE: To help sell their home a couple agrees to finance the sale because high interest rates have reduced buyer activity. They give the buyer a 30-year amortized loan with a three-year balloon. The buyer now can purchase the property, pay the sellers monthly payments and have three years (when the balloon is due) to find a lower rate loan.

BIWEEKLY MORTGAGES

A **biweekly loan** is amortized the same way as other loans with monthly payments, but the borrower makes a payment *every two weeks* equal to one-half the normal monthly payment. The borrower makes the equivalent of an *extra month's payment each year* (i.e., 26 half-size payments equal 13 full-month payments instead of 12). This saves the borrower interest and the loan is paid off quicker.

EXAMPLE: A borrower with a 30-year loan might make payments of $1,000 a month, or $12,000 a year. A biweekly loan would be $500 every two weeks, or $13,000 a year ($500 × 26).

EXAMPLE: A borrower who takes out a 30-year fixed rate loan for $100,000 at 7.25 percent and makes monthly payments will pay approximately $145,580 in interest. The borrower who had a biweekly loan at the same rate would pay $108,602 in interest ($36,987 less), and the loan would be paid off in approximately 23 years.

BLANKET LOAN

A **blanket loan** covers more than one property. This type of loan contains a *partial release clause* that releases the lien on individual properties as the loan is paid.

EXAMPLE: A developer plans to build 50 houses. Rather than obtaining 50 individual loans, the developer uses a blanket loan to cover all of them. As the developer builds and sells the lots, the partial release clause releases the liens on the lots sold.

BUDGET LOAN

A **budget loan** is an *amortized loan* that not only collects principal and interest each month *but also* 1/12 of the estimated annual cost of the property's real estate taxes and insurance. The total monthly payment includes principal, interest, taxes and insurance (PITI). The portion of the payment for taxes and insurance is placed in an **impound account** (also called an *escrow* or *reserve account*).

BUYDOWNS

A loan **buydown** occurs when a party, usually someone other than the borrower, pays an interest subsidy to the lender. In exchange for the upfront fee paid to the lender, the loan *rate is reduced,* usually for the *first couple of years,* and then rises.

EXAMPLE: To help sales, a developer offers buyers a buydown of 3 percent the first year, 2 percent the second year and 1 percent the third year to those who purchase a new home.

CONSTRUCTION LOAN

Construction loans provide funds for building real estate projects. The lender commits to the full loan amount but usually disburses the money as the work is completed (called *draws*). Interest is charged only on the amount disbursed.

Because construction loans are for a short term, permanent financing for longer terms (to repay the construction loan) also must be arranged. The permanent financing on the construction loan is known as a *takeout* or *standby loan.*

FIFTEEN-YEAR LOAN

The **fifteen-year loan** is actually a fully amortized loan with a 15-year term. Reducing the term of the loan saves the borrower a significant amount of interest with only a moderate increase in the monthly payment.

EXAMPLE: A $100,000 loan at a 9 percent rate for both 30- and 15-year terms:

Step 1: 30 years = $805 per month × 360 = $289,800
15 years = $1,015 per month × 180 = $182,700

Step 2: Subtract the $100,000 principal from each
$289,800 – $100,000 = $189,800 interest
$182,700 – $100,000 = $82,700 interest

Step 3: Interest saved: $189,800 – $82,700 = $107,100

GRADUATED PAYMENT MORTGAGE

A **graduated payment mortgage (GPM),** also called a *flexible payment plan,* provides for smaller payments in the early years of the loan and larger payments in later years. Generally payments stabilize after five to ten years. This loan was designed to help first-time buyers whose income was not large enough to qualify for a larger loan but who had good future earnings potential. Because the smaller payments in the initial years will not cover the interest expense, the loan has *negative amortization,* which is reversed as payments rise in later years.

HOME EQUITY LOAN

Homeowners wishing to utilize the equity they have in their property may use a **home equity loan.** This is usually a *second (junior)* mortgage on the property, based on the amount of equity, and can be for either a *fixed amount* or a *line of credit.* The interest rate usually is adjustable and based on the lender's prime rate. The total loan-to-value ratio is usually limited to 80 percent or less.

EXAMPLE: A lender agrees to give a home equity loan on a property at a rate of 3 percent over prime. The property is appraised at $160,000 and has a $60,000 first mortgage. The line of credit may be determined as follows: $160,000 × .80 = $128,000 – $60,000 = $68,000 line of credit.

 Note: Home equity loans have increased in popularity in recent years because tax laws have eliminated deduction of interest on loans not secured by real estate.

LAND CONTRACT

A **land contract** is also called an *installment contract* or a *contract for deed.* The seller accepts a down payment from the buyer and finances the rest of the purchase price. Unlike other types of financing, *title remains with the seller* (called the *vendor*) until the loan is repaid. The buyer (called the vendee) takes possession and is responsible for real estate taxes, insurance and upkeep. If the buyer defaults, the seller usually can regain possession of the property and keep any money paid by the buyer.

OPEN-END LOAN

With an **open-end loan** the mortgagor may borrow up to the *original amount of the loan* using the same property as security. Any additional funds are provided at *prevailing rates.*

PACKAGE LOAN

A real estate transaction may include both real and personal property. Rather than get a second loan for the personal property, a **package loan** can be used to finance *both* the *real* and the *personal property.*

EXAMPLE: A buyer uses a package loan to finance the purchase of a new house when the builder included the stove, refrigerator and other personal property in the sales price.

EXAMPLE: A buyer uses a package loan to finance the purchase of a commercial property that includes office furniture and equipment in the sales price.

PURCHASE-MONEY MORTGAGE

A **purchase-money mortgage (PMM)** is also called a *take-back* mortgage. The owner finances, or "takes back," part of the selling price. Title passes to the buyer and the seller retains a lien right. The seller usually takes a second lienholder position because the buyer's lender will want to be the senior lienholder. PMMs are usually short-term loans with a balloon payment.

Tip: Note that land contracts and purchase money loans are similar in that both involve seller financing but are different in determining when title passes.

REVERSE ANNUITY MORTGAGE

Reverse annuity mortgages (RAMs) are designed for elderly people who have *little or no debt* on their property and wish to convert the property's *equity into income.* The lender pays the borrower a fixed amount each month, based on the owner's life expectancy and value of the property. As payments are made to the borrower they are added to the loan amount. Because the borrower does not make payments, interest charges are also added to the loan balance. Usually, borrowers do not have to repay the loan until they sell, die or move out of the property. Rather than payment of a fixed amount, some variations of the RAM allow for a line of credit so that the owners can decide how much they want to borrow (up to the assigned credit limit) by writing a check.

TERM LOAN

In a **term loan** (also called a *straight loan*) the payments *include only interest,* and the full amount of the principal is due at the end of the loan period. These are *nonamortizing* loans, usually with a *short term* (three to five years). At the end of the loan the borrower either sells the property to pay the balance or refinances the loan.

 Note: Until the 1930s, the term loan was the usual method of financing real estate.

WRAPAROUND LOAN

A **wraparound loan** also is called an *all-inclusive loan.* It is a new, junior loan that is larger (*provides additional funds*) than the existing first loan. The *new lender assumes the payments* on the original loan and the borrower makes *one payment to the new lender.*

EXAMPLE: To facilitate the sale of their house, the sellers agree to make a wraparound loan to the buyers. The house is selling for $150,000 and has an assumable $80,000 loan at 6 percent. The buyers have a $25,000 down payment and the sellers make a $125,000 wraparound loan at 7 percent. The buyers make their monthly payment to the sellers, who continue to make payments on the original loan. The sellers earn the 1 percent difference on the $80,000 loan and 7 percent on the additional $45,000.

 Note: A wraparound loan should not be used if it involves a property sale with an enforceable due-on-sale clause. The existing loan must be assumable.

BEFORE READING THE NEXT SECTION, COMPLETE THE SECTION 1 REVIEW EXERCISES AND COMPARE YOUR ANSWERS WITH THE SOLUTIONS AT THE END OF THE CHAPTER.

SECTION 1
REVIEW EXERCISES

1. Name the type of loan that applies to each situation.

a. _____ To help their son buy a house, the parents agree to pay the lender a fee at closing in exchange for a lower interest rate loan for their son.

b. _____ So that they can qualify for a larger loan to purchase their home, a young couple recently entering the work force wants a loan with lower initial monthly payments that will increase at predetermined intervals over the first few years.

c. _____ A borrower is paid every other week and wants a loan that requires that payments be made with the same frequency as her pay.

d. _____ A home buyer believes interest rates will go down in the future and seeks a loan that will take advantage of this situation.

e. _____ A buyer would like to find a loan that will cover the purchase of the house as well as the appliances in it.

f. _____ A developer wants a loan that will cover all five of his parcels of real estate.

g. _____ The lender provides a short-term loan with the money disbursed to a general contractor as work is completed.

h. _____ An elderly couple with no existing mortgage on their home would like to find a loan arrangement that would allow them to take advantage of the equity in their property without forcing them to move.

i. _____ A homeowner wishes to sell her property but wants to receive the sale proceeds over several years by financing the sale and retaining the title until the loan is paid.

j. _____ A homeowner wishes to sell his property and decides to provide part of the financing to prospective buyers to make the property more attractive.

k. _____ A buyer wants a loan that will take advantage of the current low-rate, assumable loan on the property while providing her with the additional funds she needs to purchase the house.

2. Name the component of an adjustable rate mortgage that best fits each of the following descriptions.

a. _____ Describes how often the rate can change

b. _____ Limits the amount the payments can change

c. _____ A very low initial interest rate that may rise significantly in the second year

d. _____ Represents the lender's profit on the loan

e. _____ Allows the borrower to change from an adjustable rate to a fixed rate loan during certain time periods

f. _____ Places limits on the rate changes

g. _____ Rate changes tied to this

Are the following statements true (T) or false (F)?

3. ____ In an installment sales contract the buyer is responsible for paying the real estate taxes and insurance but does not have title to the property.

4. ____ The payment made on a biweekly loan is equal to one-fourth the payment amount of a standard 30-year amortized loan with the same loan amount.

5. ____ In a construction loan the lender agrees to the total loan but does not give the funds out at one time.

6. ____ Adjustable-rate loans are usually offered at rates higher than fixed-rate loans.

7. ____ In an amortized loan the initial payments consist mostly of interest.

8. ____ If a blanket loan covers four properties and one of the properties is sold, the entire loan must be paid off to release the lien.

Supply the term that best matches each of the following descriptions.

9. _____ In this loan arrangement a portion of the property's real estate taxes and insurance is collected by the lender as part of the loan payment.

10. _____ This loan is based on the homeowners' equity in their property and usually is an adjustable-rate loan and a second (junior) mortgage. The interest usually is deductible for income tax purposes.

11. _____ This fully amortized loan with a 15-year term reduces the term from 30 to 15 years and saves the borrower interest with only a moderate increase in the payment amount.

12. _____ Under this loan arrangement the loan balance increases with each payment rather than decreasing because the payment amount is not sufficient to cover the interest.

13. _____ In this loan the interest rate changes at fixed intervals based on a preselected economic index.

14. _____ An account that is maintained by the lender holds money collected from the borrower for the payment of real estate taxes and insurance and also is called an *escrow* or *reserve account.*

15. _____ This loan requires periodic payments of both interest and principal.

16. _____ The payments on this loan do not fully amortize the loan balance. The remaining loan balance is included in the last payment, called a *balloon payment.*

17. _____ Under this loan arrangement the mortgagor may borrow additional money up to the original amount of the loan using the same property as collateral.

18. _____ Payments on this kind of loan include only interest; the loan balance is due at the end of the loan period. Also called a *straight loan,* these are nonamortizing loans for short terms.

<hr>

SECTION 2

GOVERNMENT INSURED AND GUARANTEED LOANS

CONVENTIONAL AND NONCONVENTIONAL LOANS

One way of grouping loans is as conventional or nonconventional loans. A *conventional loan* is one that is *not* insured or guaranteed *by a government agency.* The lender assumes the full risk of default in a conventional loan. *Nonconventional loans* include FHA-insured and VA-guaranteed loans. Because the government agencies provide some protection to the lender, the loans can be made with smaller down payments.

FHA LOANS

The National Housing Act of 1934 established the *Federal Housing Administration (FHA).* The purpose of the FHA is to stimulate housing by establishing better ways of financing mortgage loans. Today, there are a number of **FHA loan** programs that are

administered by the *Department of Housing and Urban Development (HUD)*. FHA loans
have the following characteristics:

- *Loan insurance*—Loan is insured by the FHA up to certain limits.
- *Lending source*—Loans are made by an FHA-*approved lender,* not by the FHA.
- *Discount points*—These can be charged by the lender and paid by either the seller or the buyer.
- *Amount of down payment*—Low down payment, generally a minimum 3 percent to 5 percent down, in contrast to conventional loans requiring down payments of 20 percent.
- *Loan limit*—The maximum loan amounts insured by the FHA vary by area of the country to reflect regional differences in housing costs. These amounts change periodically.
- *Insured commitment*—To determine the maximum insured loan amount for a residence, two calculations must be performed. One calculation is made with *closing costs added* and *one without,* with the *lesser amount* used for the commitment. There also are variations of the calculations, depending on whether the property value/price exceeds $50,000 or is $50,000 or less.
    1. Properties Exceeding $50,000
        a. *With closing costs*—Lesser of (1) the sales price or (2) the appraised value + 100 percent of the closing costs. The commitment equals 97 percent of the first $25,000, 95 percent of the next $100,000 and 90 percent of the remaining amount.

EXAMPLE: A house sells for $110,000, and the appraisal is $100,000 with closing costs of $1,000. What is the maximum insured commitment?

Step 1. $100,000 = Lesser of sales price or appraisal
Step 2.   +   1,000 = 100% of $1,000 closing costs
Step 3. $101,000 = Value for calculating commitment
Step 4.   24,250 = 97% of first $25,000
Step 5.   + 72,200 = 95% of $76,000
Step 6. $ 96,450 = Maximum insured commitment

        b. *Without closing costs*—Multiply the lesser of (1) the sales price or (2) the appraised value by 97.75 percent.

EXAMPLE: Same facts as the preceding example.

Step 1. $100,000 = Lesser of the sales price or appraisal
Step 2. $ 97,750 = $100,000 × .9775

        Because the result of the first calculation (a) is *smaller,* the *maximum insured commitment* is $96,450.

    2. Properties $50,000 or Less
        The only differences between calculations for these properties versus those over $50,000 are (1) the first calculation (a, Step 4) uses 97 percent on the entire amount and (2) the second calculation (b, Step 2) uses 98.75 percent.
        a. With closing costs

EXAMPLE: A house sells for $48,000 and the appraisal is $45,000 with closing costs of $1,000. What is the maximum insured commitment?

Step 1. $45,000 = lesser of the sales price or appraisal
Step 2.   + 1,000 = 100% of $1,000 closing costs
Step 3. $46,000 = Value for calculating commitment
Step 4. $44,620 = $46,000 × .97

        b. Without closing costs

EXAMPLE: Same facts as the preceding example.

> Step 1. $45,000 = Lesser of the sales price or appraisal
> Step 2. $44,438 = $45,000 × .9875
>
> Because the result of the second calculation (b) is *smaller*, the *maximum insured commitment* is $44,438.

 Note: Whatever the results of the calculation, the loan amount cannot exceed the maximum mortgage limit set by HUD for the region.

- *Insurance premium*—A one-time mortgage insurance fee of 1.75 percent to cover the FHA insurance is paid at closing. This is called the **upfront mortgage insurance premium (UFMIP).** In addition, a **mortgage insurance premium (MIP)** with an annual rate of .5 percent is paid on the outstanding loan balance as part of the borrower's monthly payment. The term of the MIP (how many years it will be charged) is based on (1) the year the loan was originated and (2) the loan-to-value ratio.

EXAMPLE: On a $100,000 loan the UFMIP is $2,250 ($100,000 × .0225) and the MIP is $41.67 per month ($100,000 × .005 ÷ 12).

- *Qualifying ratios*—Two qualifying ratios are set by HUD for FHA loans:
  a. *Housing-expense ratio* (also called the *front-end ratio*)—Principal, interest, taxes and insurance (PITI) + MIP + homeowner's dues and assessments (if any) usually may not exceed 29 percent of monthly effective gross income.
  b. *Total fixed obligation ratio* (also called the *back-end ratio*)—PITI + MIP + recurring expenses (debt of ten more months or payments of more than $100 a month) usually may not exceed 41 percent of monthly effective gross income.
- *Interest rate*—Not set by FHA or HUD. Allowed to fluctuate with the market.
- *Appraisal*—Property must be appraised by an *FHA-approved appraiser.*
- *Closing costs*—Borrowers can finance 100 percent of the closing costs.
- *Assumption*—All FHA loans are assumable, but the rules vary depending on the *date the loan was made.*
  a. *Loans made prior to December 1, 1986,* are freely assumable with no qualification of the buyer (can be owner-occupied or an investor).
  b. *Loans made between December 1, 1986, and December 14, 1989,* require credit approval of the buyer assuming the loan (can be owner-occupied or an investor).
  c. *Loans made after December 14, 1989,* require complete qualification of the buyer assuming the loan. Also, loans will be made or assumed only to owner-occupied properties (*no investor loans*).
- *Prepayment penalty*—There is no prepayment penalty if proper notice (30 days before the prepayment) is given to lender.
- *Environmental notice*—For loans on properties built before 1978, the FHA requires that the borrowers sign a lead-based paint notice statement on or before the date of the sales contract.

Common FHA Loan Programs

- *Section 203(b)* is the most popular home mortgage program. A highly leveraged loan for the *purchase* or *construction* of *one- to four-unit* family residences insures
  a. 97 percent of first $25,000 of appraised value (i.e., 3 percent down).
  b. 95 percent of the next $100,000.
  c. 90 percent of the remaining value up the maximum loan limit set by HUD.

Adjustable rate mortgages (ARM) are also offered under this program.

- *Section 203(k),* called the Rehabilitation Mortgage Insurance Program, insures financing for both the *acquisition* and *rehabilitation* (repairs and improvements) of *residential* property of *one to four units* that are at least one year old. It is available to both owners of and investors in a residence. A buyer does not have to get a higher note construction loan for the remodeling. ARMs are also offered under this program.
- *Section 213* insures loans on cooperative housing.
- *Section 221(d)(2)* is designed for low- or moderate-income families.
- *Section 234(c)* insures loans on condominiums. Rules are similar to the 203(b) loans. (There is no UFMIP required by these loans.)
- *Section 245* insures graduated payment mortgages (GPM). There are five repayment plans available under this program.
- *Section 251* insures ARMs. Caps on the interest rate are 1 percent per year and 5 percent over the loan life.

VA LOANS

The Servicemen's Readjustment Act of 1944 established protection to lenders for loans made to approved veterans. The government *guarantees* loans made by approved lenders. These loans are administered by the *Department of Veterans Affairs* (still called the *VA*). **VA loans** have the following characteristics:

- *Qualifications*—Only a veteran or the nonremarried spouse of a veteran who died from a service-related disability or in the line of duty qualifies for a loan.
- *Eligibility*—Borrower must meet *minimum service times,* which vary depending on calendar dates of service. In general there are three groups of qualifying periods:
  1. 90 days' active duty during any one of four wartime periods (WWII, Korea, Vietnam and Persian Gulf).
  2. 181 days' active duty during the time periods between the four war periods.
  3. 24 months' active duty during the period from September 8, 1980, to August 2, 1990.
  4. 181 days' active duty (persons currently on active duty).

     In addition, certain members of the National Guard and Reserves with more than six years of service now are eligible.
- *Lending source*—Loans are made by a VA-approved lender. In locations where a lending institution is not available, the VA may make direct loans to veterans.
- *Eligible property*—Loans are for *purchase* or *construction* of one- to four-unit residences. Borrower must occupy the property.
- *Discount points*—Points can be charged by the lender and paid by *either* the seller or the buyer.
- *Qualifying ratios*—There are two qualifying ratios set by the VA for loans. The *applicant must qualify under both.*
  1. *Residual income ratio*—Gross income is reduced by certain expenses (federal, state and social security taxes; property maintenance; utilities) to determine net income. Net income is then reduced by the estimated house payments (PITI) + long-term debt (debt of six more months or payments of more than $100 a month) to determine *residual balance available for family support.* The residual balance must meet standard amounts established by the VA for various regions of the country.
  2. *Total fixed obligation ratio*—The PITI + homeowners' association dues + long-term debt can not exceed 41 percent of monthly gross income.
- *Loan limits*—There is no limit on the amount of the loan (however, there are limits on the amount the VA will guarantee).

FIGURE 22.2
VA Loan Guarantee

VA LOAN GUARANTEE

Loan Amount	Guarantee
0–$45,000	50% of the loan
$45,000–$144,000	40% of the loan
over $144,000	Lesser of 25% or $50,750

- *Loan guarantee*—Guarantees are based on the size of the loan and are summarized in Figure 22.2. The guarantee limits are changed periodically by the VA and apply to loans for the purchase, construction, repair or alteration of the residence.
- *Amount of down payment*—Lenders determine the maximum loan amount they will make with no money down, but it is usually set at four times the veteran's loan guarantee. Because the maximum loan guarantee is $50,750, the maximum loan amount with no down payment is $203,000 ($50,750 × 4).
- *Entitlement*—The veteran must apply for a *certificate of eligibility* from the VA, which includes the *maximum loan amount guarantee* for the veteran. This is set by the VA, based on income and current VA eligibility limits.
- *Reusing the entitlement*—To obtain a full new guarantee entitlement, the veteran must pay off the previous loan or obtain a release of liability and substitution of eligibility by a veteran purchaser if the loan is assumed. If the first loan was assumed and there is no release and substitution, the loan amount is deducted from the current entitlement amount.
- *Appraisal*—Property must be appraised by a VA appraiser. The VA reviews the appraisal and issues a *certificate of reasonable value (CRV)*, setting the maximum VA loan amount for the property.
- *VA funding fee*—A funding fee is paid by the borrower in cash at closing or is included in the loan amount. The amount of the fee is based on the size of the down payment and is calculated as a percentage of the loan, as summarized in Figure 22.3. Disabled veterans are not required to pay a funding fee.
- *Loan origination fee*—Charged to the borrower by the lender, and may not exceed 1 percent of the loan amount.
- *Prepayment penalty*—None is allowed.
- *Assumption*—There is no due-on-sale clause. All VA loans are assumable, *even to nonveterans.* For loans made after March 1, 1988, the buyer must be qualified; prior to this date qualification was not required. If the loan is assumed by a buyer, the veteran is secondarily liable if the buyer defaults. To avoid liability, the veteran must arrange with the VA for a *release of liability.* Lenders may charge an assumption fee, and the VA requires payment of a .5 percent fee.
- *Interest rate*—The loan rate is not set by the VA. It is allowed to fluctuate with the market.

Note: Because the rules for FHA and VA loans are frequently changed, a person thinking of using one of these loans should inquire with the local FHA or VA field offices and local lenders who make these loans.

FIGURE 22.3
VA Funding Fee

VA FUNDING FEE

Down Payment	Amount of Fee
Less than 5%	2.25% (Reservists 2.75%)
5%–10%	1.50% (Reservists 2.25%)
over 10%	1.25% (Reservists 2.00%)

**COMPLETE THE SECTION 2 REVIEW EXERCISES AND COMPARE YOUR ANSWERS
WITH THE SOLUTIONS AT THE END OF THE CHAPTER.**

SECTION 2
REVIEW EXERCISES

1. For each of the following descriptions determine whether it applies to FHA loans, VA loans or both.

   a. _____ Loans assumable under certain conditions

   b. _____ Loan program administered by HUD

   c. _____ Available for veterans and nonveterans alike

   d. _____ Loans insured up to certain limits

   e. _____ Down payments as little as no money down

   f. _____ Charges a monthly insurance fee

   g. _____ Loans cannot have a prepayment penalty

   h. _____ Loan limits set by the government

   i. _____ Loans guaranteed up to certain limits

   j. _____ Discount points may be charged by the lender and can be paid by either the buyer or seller

   k. _____ Interest rates not set by the government

   l. _____ Requires that borrower have a certificate of eligibility before a loan can be given

   m. _____ Requires that borrower pay a funding fee at closing

Are the following statements true (T) or false (F)?

2. ____ Veterans may reuse their entitlements to get a new VA loan.

3. ____ The mortgage insurance premium (MIP) charged on FHA loans is paid at closing.

4. ____ FHA loans can be obtained from HUD.

5. ____ In determining the maximum insured loan amount, the FHA takes into consideration the sales price or appraised value and the closing costs.

6. ____ The qualifying ratios for VA and FHA loans are generally higher than for conventional loans.

Supply the term that best matches each of the following descriptions.

7. _____ The federal agency that administers FHA loans

8. _____ A loan program administered by the Department of Veterans Affairs and guaranteed by the government

9. _____ A loan that is not insured or guaranteed by the federal government

10. _____ A one-time mortgage insurance fee to cover FHA insurance

11. _____ Loan programs administered by HUD and insured by the federal government

SOLUTIONS

FOR SECTION REVIEW EXERCISES

SECTION 1

1. a. Buydown loan   b. Graduated payment mortgage   c. Biweekly loan
   d. Adjustable rate mortgage   e. Package loan   f. Blanket loan
   g. Construction loan   h. Reverse annuity mortgage   i. Land contract
   j. Purchase-money mortgage   k. Wraparound loan

2. a. Adjustment interval   b. Payment cap   c. Teaser rate   d. Margin
   e. Convertible feature   f. Rate cap   g. Index

3. TRUE

4. FALSE The biweekly loan payment is equal to one-half the loan amount of a standard 30-year amortized loan.

5. TRUE

6. FALSE Initial rates on ARMs are usually less than on fixed-rate loans because the lender has some protection from interest rate fluctuations.

7. TRUE

8. FALSE Blanket loans provide the release of liens on individual properties.

9. Budget loan

10. Home equity loan

11. Fifteen-year loan

12. Negative amortization

13. Adjustable rate mortgage

14. Impound account

15. Amortized loan

16. Balloon loan

17. Open-end mortgage

18. Term loan

SECTION 12

1. a. FHA and VA   b. FHA   c. FHA   d. FHA   e. VA   f. FHA
   g. FHA and VA   h. FHA   i. VA   j. FHA and VA   k. FHA and VA
   l. VA   m. VA

2. TRUE

3. FALSE The upfront mortgage insurance premium charged on FHA loans is paid at closing. The MIP is charged as part of the monthly payments.

4. FALSE FHA loans are provided by FHA-approved lenders, not directly from a government agency.

5. TRUE

6. TRUE

7. Department of Housing and Urban Development (HUD)

8. VA loans

9. Conventional loan

10. Upfront mortgage insurance premium (UFMIP)

11. FHA loan

_____
_____
_____
_____

CHAPTER 23

LENDING LAWS AND GOVERNMENT ACTIVITIES

This chapter discusses the government's involvement in real estate lending and several important laws that affect the lending process. *Section 1* covers government activities, most importantly, the government agencies that regulate and monitor the lending industry. *Section 2* covers two laws that involve loan origination, the Truth-in-Lending Law and the Equal Credit Opportunity Act. *Section 3* covers three bank reporting laws intended to monitor lending practices to ensure there is no discrimination. Remember to use the Study Tool Kit to reference key information and to update your progress checklist.

Learning Objectives

Track your progress as you work through the chapter by checking each learning objective when you complete it.

_____ List and describe three ways that the government regulates the country's money supply.

_____ Describe the role of the FDIC in the lending industry.

_____ Describe the role of the OTS in the lending industry.

_____ Identify the types of transactions that are covered by the Truth-in-Lending Act.

_____ Describe the disclosures to the borrower required by the Truth-in-Lending Act.

_____ Describe the advertising disclosures required by the Truth-in-Lending Act.

_____ Describe the penalties for violations of the Truth-in-Lending Act.

_____ Identify which groups are protected by and requirements of the Equal Credit Opportunity Act.

_____ Describe the purpose of the Fair Credit Reporting Act.

_____ Identify provisions of the Fair Credit Reporting Act if credit is denied.

_____ Describe the purpose of the Community Bank Reinvestment Act.

_____ Describe the purpose of the Home Mortgage Disclosure Act.

Key Terms and Phrases

Track your progress as you work through the chapter by checking each term when you understand its meaning.

____	Annual percentage rate (APR)	____	Home Mortgage Disclosure Act
____	Community Bank Reinvestment Act	____	Office of the Comptroller of the Currency (OCC)
____	Consumer Credit Protection Act	____	Office of Thrift Supervision (OTS)
____	Discount rate	____	Open market activities
____	Equal Credit Opportunity Act	____	Regulation Z
____	Fair Credit Reporting Act	____	Reserve requirement
____	Federal Deposit Insurance Corporation (FDIC)	____	Truth-in-Lending Act
____	Federal Reserve System	____	Usury laws
____	FIRREA		

SECTION 1
GOVERNMENT ACTIVITIES

THE FEDERAL RESERVE SYSTEM

The **Federal Reserve System** (called "the Fed") was established by Congress in 1913 to help maintain a sound credit and economic environment and to counteract inflation and deflation trends. The country is divided into 12 reserve districts, each with a district reserve bank. All *nationally chartered banks* must join the Fed and purchase stock in the district reserve banks.

The Fed regulates the flow of money and interest rates by controlling the *discount rate* and *reserve requirements* of its member banks and through its *market activities*.

The **reserve requirement** refers to the portion of a member bank's deposits that *may not be loaned*. By adjusting the reserve requirement, the Fed affects the amount of money available, which influences interest rates and the economy.

- If the reserve requirement is *increased,* the money supply drops, interest rates increase and the economy slows.
- If the reserve requirement is *reduced,* the money supply increases, interest rates decrease and the economy expands.

EXAMPLE: The Fed raises the reserve requirements for banks from 5 percent to 6 percent. A bank that takes in $1,000,000 in deposits now must keep on reserve $60,000 instead of $50,000. Thus, it has $10,000 less to lend out.

The second way the Fed regulates the money supply is through the **discount rate.** The discount rate is the interest rate charged other banks by the Fed for loans.

- If the rate is *increased,* less money is loaned, the money supply drops and the economy slows.
- If the rate is *reduced,* borrowing is encouraged, the money supply increases and the economy expands.

EXAMPLE: The Fed raises the discount rate for banks from 6 percent to 7 percent. A bank normally charges 2 percent above the discount rate when making loans. The bank now will have to charge 9 percent instead of 8 percent. Fewer borrowers will want or can afford to take the loans with the higher rates, and the bank will make fewer loans.

The third way the Fed regulates the money supply is through its **open market activities.** The Fed can buy or sell U.S. Treasury Securities. By doing so it changes the money supply.

- If it *sells* securities, the money supply decreases (draws money from investors) and the economy slows.
- If it *purchases* securities, the money supply increases (pays for securities with dollars) and the economy expands.

See Figure 23.1 for a summary of the effects on the money supply for the methods used by the Fed.

FIGURE 23.1
FED Action and Effects on the Money Supply

Action Taken by the FED	Money Supply	Interest Rates
Reserve Requirement—Increase	Decrease	Increase
Reserve Requirement—Decrease	Increase	Decrease
Discount Rate—Increase	Decrease	Increase
Discount Rate—Decrease	Increase	Decrease
FED sells securities	Decrease	Increase
FED buys securities	Increase	Decrease

THE FINANCIAL INSTITUTIONS REFORM, RECOVERY AND ENFORCEMENT ACT (FIRREA)

FIRREA was passed in 1989 to address the savings and loan crisis of the 1980s. FIRREA restructured the regulatory and deposit insurance systems and closed or reorganized insolvent savings and loans.

Federal Deposit Insurance Corporation

The **Federal Deposit Insurance Corporation (FDIC)** was established in 1934 to insure bank deposits. It was given increased responsibilities under FIRREA. FDIC insures customer deposits in savings and commercial banks.

Regulatory Agencies

Created by FIRREA, the **Office of Thrift Supervision (OTS)** is part of the Treasury Department and is responsible for monitoring and regulating the savings and loan industry. The **Office of the Comptroller of the Currency (OCC)** is responsible for monitoring and regulating the nationally chartered banking industry.

**BEFORE READING THE NEXT SECTION, COMPLETE THE SECTION 1
REVIEW EXERCISES AND COMPARE YOUR ANSWERS WITH THE
SOLUTIONS AT THE END OF THE CHAPTER.**

REVIEW EXERCISES

1. What will be the probable effect on mortgage loan interest rates as a result of each of the following actions taken by the Fed?

   a. _____ The discount rate is reduced.

   b. _____ The reserve requirement is reduced.

   c. _____ The Fed purchases securities.

   d. _____ The discount rate is increased.

   e. _____ The reserve requirement is increased.

   f. _____ The Fed sells securities.

Are the following statements true (T) or false (F)?

2. ____ The Federal Deposit Insurance Corporation (FDIC) provides protection for deposits in banks only.

3. ____ All banks and thrifts must join the Federal Reserve System.

4. ____ The Fed controls the money supply and affects interest rates through its market operations.

Supply the term that best matches each of the following descriptions.

5. _____ A law passed to address the savings and loan crisis of the 1980s

6. _____ The portion of a bank's deposits that may not be loaned

7. _____ A government agency that manages two insurance funds used to insure deposits in both commercial banks and thrifts

8. _____ Established by Congress in 1913 to help maintain a sound credit and economic environment and counteract inflation and deflation trends

9. _____ Responsible for monitoring and regulating the nationally chartered banking industry

10. _____ The interest rate charged by the Fed to other banks for loans

11. _____ An agency that is part of the Treasury Department and is responsible for monitoring and regulating thrifts

LAWS AFFECTING LOAN ORIGINATIONS

USURY LAWS

Usury laws limit the interest rate lenders can charge borrowers. Usury laws are passed by states and vary, depending on the type of loan. (Usury laws usually do not apply to most mortgage loan situations.)

THE TRUTH-IN-LENDING ACT

Purpose of the Law

The **Truth-in-Lending Act** (referred to as **Regulation Z**) is part of the **Consumer Credit Protection Act**. It is implemented by the Federal Reserve System's Regulation Z, became effective in 1969 and has subsequently been amended. The purpose of the act is to force lenders to inform borrowers of the true cost of obtaining a loan. The primary disclosures that must be made are (1) the finance charge, (2) the annual percentage rate, (3) the amount financed and (4) the total payments.

Generally the law applies to a person or business that "regularly extends consumer credit." Regular is defined as more than *five real estate loans* or *more than 25 consumer loans* in a calendar year. The law applies to

- real estate loans secured by the borrower's *residence* (regardless of amount);
- *non–real estate* consumer loans up to $25,000; and
- new loans, refinancing or consolidation loans.

It does *not* apply to the following:

- business, commercial or agricultural loans of more than $25,000;

EXAMPLE: A loan to renovate a commercial property is not covered because it is an income/business loan.

- loans to corporations or government agencies; or
- assumption of a real estate loan by a new borrower.

Required Disclosures

Finance Charges

- The total finance charge and the interest rate must be disclosed before the loan is completed. The *finance charge* is the total dollar amount the loan will cost over its entire life.
- Other charges that must be disclosed include interest charges, discount points or buydown fees, loan finder's fees, servicing fees and required life insurance.
- Not included in finance charges are title and legal fees such as title examinations, title insurance, legal fees, appraisal fees, survey fees, notary fees, credit reports and preparing deeds.

Annual Percentage Rate (APR). The finance charge must be stated as an **annual percentage rate (APR)**. The APR includes the interest rate and other loan costs and represents the true yearly cost of credit. The APR is rounded to the nearest ⅛ percent.

Finance charges included in the APR are application fees, prepaid mortgage interest, discount points or buydown fees, loan finder's fees, servicing fees, mortgage insurance premium, disclosure fees, lender inspection fees, closing fees and tax service fees.

Amounts. The act requires disclosure of

- the total amount of the payments (the total amount the borrower will have paid after making all of the scheduled payments) and
- the amount financed (the amount of credit provided by the lender).

Other Disclosures. Other required disclosures include the lender's identity; the number, amount and time installments are due; description of prepayment penalties; late payment charges; required insurance; filing fees; description of the security used as collateral (house, car); any required deposits; description of the assumption policy; adjustable rate features (if an ARM); and itemization of the amount financed.

Note: The Truth-in-Lending Act requires disclosure of loan information but does not establish or require specific interest rates or other finance charges.

Disclosure Timing

All required disclosures must be made *in writing* and either given to the borrower at the *time of the loan application* or sent *within three business days.*

Right of Rescission

The law requires a "cooling-off" period in which the borrower has the *right to rescind* (cancel) the contract up to midnight of the *third business day* following the signing of the loan documents.

- This right *can be waived* by the borrower for financial reasons.
- The right of rescission applies to most consumer loans but does *not apply* to loans to *purchase or construct a home.*
- If *refinancing* with a new lender, the right of rescission applies. If refinancing with the same lender, *only additional money* added to the original loan (if any) may be rescinded.

Restrictions on Credit Advertising

The Truth-in-Lending Act does not *require* creditors to advertise credit terms, but if they advertise *some credit terms,* called *trigger terms,* they must include additional disclosures.

- *Trigger terms* include the (1) amount of down payment, (2) number of payments, (3) amount of any payment, (4) period of payments and (5) amount of any finance charges.
- *Required disclosures* include the (1) cash price or amount of loan; (2) amount of required down payment; (3) number, amount and frequency of payments; (4) APR; and (5) total of all payments (unless it refers to a first mortgage on property being purchased).

Note: General phrases may be used, such as "favorable financing terms available," without triggering disclosure requirements.

Violations of the Law

Violations of the Truth-in-Lending Act can result in civil penalties and fines paid to the borrower including twice the amount of the finance charge up to $1,000, actual damages, and attorney fees and current costs. Violations of the act can also result in criminal penalties including fines for each violation and a prison sentence. In addition, if the required disclosures were not made, the buyer has up to three years to cancel the loan.

FEDERAL EQUAL CREDIT OPPORTUNITY ACT

Purpose of the Act

The Federal **Equal Credit Opportunity Act** was passed to protect borrowers from discrimination when seeking a loan. A lender should deny a borrower credit based only on *reasonable business reasons*.

Groups Protected

The act prohibits discrimination against credit applicants based on race, color, sex, marital status, age, religion, national origin, income from public assistance or alimony or child support or an applicant's exercise of any right under the Consumer Credit Protection Act.

Exceptions to the Act

Individuals without contractual authority are not protected under the act.

EXAMPLE: Minors can be denied credit, and this would not be discrimination based on age.

Requirements under the Act

- Lenders must inform credit applicants in writing of the reason for rejection within 30 days.
- Creditors must retain records of applications for 25 months.
- If the loan applicant has paid for an appraisal used by the lender to evaluate the application, the applicant is entitled to a copy of the appraisal. This is true whether or not the loan is approved, and the copy must be requested in writing.

Penalties under the Act

Violations of the Federal Equal Credit Opportunity Act can result in actual or punitive damages assessed against the lender and awarded to the borrower. Lawsuits must be filed against the lender within two years of the violation.

REAL ESTATE SETTLEMENT PROCEDURES ACT (RESPA)

RESPA requires disclosure of loan costs for federally related loans (on one to four residential units) involving a first mortgage. Federally related loans are those made by a federally insured or regulated lender. This law is covered in more detail in Chapter 12.

**BEFORE READING THE NEXT SECTION, COMPLETE THE SECTION 2
REVIEW EXERCISES AND COMPARE YOUR ANSWERS WITH THE
SOLUTIONS AT THE END OF THE CHAPTER.**

SECTION 2
REVIEW EXERCISES

1. Name the law that best matches each of the following descriptions.
   a. _____ Must disclose the amount financed

b. _____ Requires disclosure for certain costs at closing

c. _____ Must disclose the annual percentage rate

d. _____ Sets limits on interest rates

e. _____ Provides protection from discrimination when applying for a loan

f. _____ Applies to non–real estate loans up to $25,000

g. _____ Credit applicants given the reason for rejection

h. _____ Must disclose any prepayment penalties

i. _____ Provides for a cooling off period in certain situations

j. _____ The applicant entitled to a copy of the appraisal

k. _____ Prescribes rules for advertising credit

Are the following statements true (T) or false (F)?

2. ____ The Truth-in-Lending Act applies to most business loans.

3. ____ Disclosures under the Truth-in-Lending Act must be given to the borrower at closing or sent within five business days of the loan application.

4. ____ Under the Federal Equal Credit Opportunity Act the lender cannot deny an applicant a loan because the primary source of income is from alimony.

5. ____ Under the Truth-in-Lending Act all finance charges plus the interest rate must be disclosed before the loan is completed.

Supply the term that best matches each of the following descriptions.

6. _____ Represents the true yearly cost of credit

7. _____ The right to end the loan agreement within certain time periods

8. _____ Intended to force lenders to inform borrowers of the true costs of obtaining a loan

9. _____ Intended to protect borrowers from discrimination when applying for loans

10. _____ Limit interest rates lenders can charge borrowers

BANK REPORTING ACTS

FAIR CREDIT REPORTING ACT

Purpose of the Act

The **Fair Credit Reporting Act** of 1977 regulates the action of credit bureaus and the use of consumer credit information.

Provisions of the Act

- *Access to lenders' files*—If consumers are denied credit, lenders must make information in customers' credit files available to them.
- *Correcting credit files*—If consumers' credit files include credit reports that have errors, consumers have the right to have these corrected.
- *Credit information suppliers*—If denied a loan by a creditor, the consumer must be given the name and address of the credit bureau that supplied the credit information.

- *Credit bureau information*—If requested by the consumer, the credit bureau must supply the consumer with information included in the credit file.
- *Restricting access to credit files*—Access to information in the credit files is limited to inquiries (1) for credit, insurance or employment; (2) by court order; (3) with the consumer's permission.

COMMUNITY BANK REINVESTMENT ACT

Purpose of the act—The **Community Bank Reinvestment Act** was passed to prevent *redlining* and *discrimination* by lenders. The act is designed to ensure banks "meet the credit needs of the community."

   Provisions of the act—Lenders must prepare community reinvestment statements that include

- a definition of the community in which they conduct their lending business;
- a list of the credit products they offer in each community;
- lending activity information by territory (must be made available for public inspection); and
- affirmative programs that meet the community's credit needs.

   To comply with the act, lenders must make a reasonable percentage of loans in their business areas.

HOME MORTGAGE DISCLOSURE ACT (REGULATION C)

Purpose of the act—The purpose of the **Home Mortgage Disclosure Act** is to prevent *redlining* and *discrimination*.

   Provisions of the act—The lender must make annual disclosures of the number of mortgage and home improvement loans made by geographic area.

COMPLETE THE SECTION 3 REVIEW EXERCISES AND COMPARE YOUR ANSWERS WITH THE SOLUTIONS AT THE END OF THE CHAPTER.

SECTION 3
REVIEW EXERCISES

Are the following statements true (T) or false (F)?

1. ____ Under the Home Mortgage Disclosure Act the lender must disclose where it is making loans.
2. ____ Under the Fair Credit Reporting Act access to information in a credit bureau's files is limited to court orders and certain inquiries.
3. ____ Under the Community Bank Reinvestment Act the lender must make a reasonable percentage of loans in its business area.
4. ____ Under the Fair Credit Reporting Act anyone seeking a loan must be given the name and address of the credit bureau used by the lender.

Supply the term that best matches each of the following descriptions.

5. _____ Law passed to ensure that banks meet the lending needs in the communities where they are located

6. _____ Law passed to regulate consumer credit information

7. _____ Law passed to prevent real estate lenders from redlining

SOLUTIONS
FOR SECTION REVIEW EXERCISES

SECTION 1

1. a. Rates will decrease   b. Rates will decrease   c. Rates will decrease
   d. Rates will increase   e. Rates will increase   f. Rates will increase

2. FALSE The FDIC administers two insurance funds, one for banks and the other for savings and loans (thrifts).

3. FALSE Only nationally chartered banks must join the FED.

4. TRUE

5. Financial Institutions Reform, Recovery and Enforcement Act (FIRREA)

6. Reserve requirement

7. Federal Deposit Insurance Corporation (FDIC)

8. Federal Reserve System (the Fed)

9. Office of the Comptroller of the Currency (OCC)

10. Discount rate

11. Office of Thrift Supervision (OTS)

SECTION 2

1. a. Truth-in-Lending Act   b. Real Estate Settlement Procedures Act (RESPA)
   c. Truth-in-Lending Act   d. Usury laws   e. Equal Credit Opportunity Law
   f. Truth-in-Lending Act   g. Equal Credit Opportunity Law   h. Truth-in-Lending Act   i. Truth-in-Lending Act   j. Equal Credit Opportunity Law   k. Truth-in-Lending Law

2. FALSE The act does not apply to business loans.

3. FALSE The disclosures must be in writing and sent within three business days of the loan application.

4. TRUE

5. TRUE

6. Annual Percentage Rate (APR)

7. Right to rescind

8. Truth-in-Lending Act

9. Equal Credit Opportunity Act

10. Usury laws

SECTION 3

1. TRUE

2. FALSE If the consumer's permission is obtained, information can be given out for other reasons.

3. TRUE

4. FALSE This requirement applies to consumers who have been denied credit by the lender.

5. Community Bank Reinvestment Act

6. The Fair Credit Reporting Act

7. Home Mortgage Disclosure Act

THIS IS THE LAST CHAPTER IN THE UNIT. TAKE THE UNIT VII DIAGNOSTIC TEST.

UNIT VII
DIAGNOSTIC TEST

1. When using a deed of trust in a real estate loan, title to the property is held by the

   a. seller.
   b. lender.
   c. trustor.
   d. trustee.

2. Discount points charged by the lender on a loan are computed as a percentage of the

   a. loan amount.
   b. closing costs.
   c. sales price.
   d. down payment.

3. The Federal Housing Administration (FHA) has developed several loan programs designed to

   a. insure housing loans.
   b. provide funding for housing loans.
   c. guarantee housing loans.
   d. buy and sell housing loans.

4. Lenders are required to disclose the total cost of borrowing under

   a. the Equal Credit Opportunity Act.
   b. Regulation Z.
   c. the federal Fair Housing Act.
   d. the Real Estate Settlement Procedures Act (RESPA).

5. If the borrower defaults, a mortgage clause that allows the lender to require that all of the loan payments be due immediately is called a(n)

   a. acceleration clause.
   b. due-on-sale clause.
   c. alienation clause.
   d. defeasance clause.

6. A buyer purchased a house for $160,000 and obtained an 80 percent loan at 9 percent with 1½ points. How much will the buyer have to pay for the points charged by the lender?

   a. $1,600
   b. $1,920
   c. $2,400
   d. $14,400

7. Wraparound mortgages are second (junior) mortgages on the property and include

   a. real and personal property as security for the loan.
   b. the original loan plus an additional loan amount.
   c. interest only payments.
   d. several parcels of land.

8. Tom purchased a new house for $175,000. He made a down payment of $15,000 and obtained a $160,000 mortgage loan. The builder of Tom's house paid the lender a fee to reduce Tom's loan rate by 3 percent for the first year and 2 percent for the second year. This type of loan arrangement is a

   a. buydown mortgage.
   b. wraparound mortgage.
   c. package mortgage.
   d. blanket mortgage.

9. The purpose of the alienation clause in a mortgage is to

   a. prevent the loan from being assumed.
   b. prevent the loan from being sold.
   c. allow for interest rate changes to be made.
   d. allow negative amortization to accrue.

10. The defeasance clause in a mortgage

   a. prevents the loan from being assumed.
   b. prevents the loan from being sold.
   c. allows for interest rate changes to be made.
   d. cancels the mortgage when the loan is repaid.

11. A purchaser obtains a fixed-rate loan to finance a home. Which of the following characteristics is true of this loan?

    a. The loan cannot be sold in the secondary market.
    b. The amount of interest to be paid is predetermined.
    c. The monthly payment amount will fluctuate each month.
    d. The loan's interest rate will change according to an index.

12. The Federal National Mortgage Association (Fannie Mae) performs which of the following?

    a. Originates loans to home buyers
    b. Buys and sells mortgages
    c. Guarantees VA loans
    d. Insures FHA loans

13. The Federal Housing Administration (FHA) is part of the

    a. Federal National Mortgage Association (FNMA).
    b. Federal Home Loan Mortgage Association (FHLMC).
    c. Department of Housing and Urban Development (HUD).
    d. Federal Reserve System (Fed).

14. A buyer purchased a property for $100,000. The buyer makes a down payment of $10,000, finances $80,000 with a new loan and asks the seller to take back a second mortgage for the balance. The second mortgage is called a(n)

    a. purchase-money mortgage.
    b. installment mortgage.
    c. blanket mortgage.
    d. bridge loan.

15. Fran purchased her house for cash 30 years ago. Today, Fran receives a monthly check from the bank that supplements her pension income. Fran most likely has obtained a(n)

    a. graduated payment mortgage.
    b. reverse annuity mortgage.
    c. adjustable rate mortgage.
    d. blanket mortgage.

16. In a loan that requires periodic payments that do not fully amortize the loan balance by the final payment, what term best describes the final payment?

    a. Variable
    b. Acceleration
    c. Balloon
    d. Graduated

17. The party that gives a deed of reconveyance when a real estate loan is repaid is the

    a. mortgagor.
    b. trustor.
    c. trustee.
    d. mortgagee.

18. A developer received a loan that covers five parcels of real estate and provides for the release of the mortgage lien on each parcel when certain payments are made on the loan. This type of loan arrangement is called a

    a. package loan.
    b. purchase-money loan.
    c. blanket loan.
    d. wraparound loan.

19. The type of activity a mortgage broker usually performs is

    a. making loans from its own funds.
    b. servicing mortgage loans.
    c. matching borrowers and lenders.
    d. selling mortgage-backed securities.

20. The mortgagor's right to regain property following a mortgage foreclosure is known as the right of

    a. redemption.
    b. alienation.
    c. satisfaction of mortgage.
    d. mortgage acceleration.

21. Borrowers seeking Federal Housing Administration (FHA) loans should go to

    a. the Federal Reserve Bank.
    b. the Department of Housing and Urban Development (HUD).
    c. the Federal Housing Administration (FHA).
    d. a qualified lending institution.

22. Liquidation of a loan through periodic payments that include principal and interest is called

   a. alienation.
   b. redemption.
   c. amortization.
   d. acceleration.

23. To comply with advertising requirements under the Truth-in-Lending Act, an ad should state

   a. "9% annual interest."
   b. "9% interest."
   c. "9% annual percentage rate."
   d. "9% compounded interest."

24. An individual's right to inspect her file at a credit bureau is included in

   a. the Truth-in-Lending Act.
   b. the Equal Credit Opportunity Act.
   c. Regulation Z.
   d. the Fair Credit Reporting Act.

25. If a borrower fails to make the loan payments when due, the lender can demand immediate payment of the entire balance under the

   a. acceleration clause.
   b. alienation clause.
   c. prepayment clause.
   d. defeasance clause.

26. A borrower's house can be used as collateral for a loan while the borrower continues to occupy the property through the process of

   a. acceleration.
   b. alienation.
   c. hypothecation.
   d. subordination.

27. After a borrower's house is foreclosed by the lender, the borrower may regain the property by exercising the right of

   a. redemption.
   b. quiet enjoyment.
   c. defeasance.
   d. alienation.

28. Funds for Federal Housing Administration loans are usually provided by

   a. the Federal Housing Administration.
   b. the Federal Reserve System.
   c. qualified lenders.
   d. the Department of Housing and Urban Development.

29. A loan that allows the borrower to obtain additional money at a later time is called a(n)

   a. open-end loan.
   b. blanket loan.
   c. installment loan.
   d. blanket loan.

30. A new mortgage that is subordinate to an existing mortgage and includes the existing mortgage amount plus additional money is a

   a. blanket mortgage.
   b. purchase-money mortgage.
   c. package mortgage.
   d. wraparound mortgage.

31. The borrower's right to rescind a new consumer loan within three business days is provided by

   a. the Equal Credit Opportunity Act.
   b. RESPA.
   c. the Community Bank Reinvestment Act.
   d. the Truth-in-Lending Act.

32. The Equal Credit Opportunity Act makes it illegal for lenders to refuse credit or discriminate because an applicant

   a. has bad credit history.
   b. is an unmarried woman.
   c. is a single parent who cannot afford the loan payments.
   d. is unemployed with no assets.

33. A house is purchased using a fixed-rate, fully amortized mortgage loan. Which of the following statements is true regarding this mortgage?

   a. Each payment amount is the same.
   b. A balloon payment will be made at the end of the loan.
   c. The principal amount in each payment is greater than the interest amount.
   d. Each payment reduces the principal by the same amount.

34. The clause that makes the mortgage void when the loan is repaid is called the

    a. defeasance clause.
    b. alienation clause.
    c. acceleration clause.
    d. prepayment clause.

35. An owner who no longer wants to be primarily responsible for a mortgage should find a buyer willing to

    a. subordinate the loan.
    b. give a wraparound loan.
    c. take the property subject to the loan.
    d. assume the loan.

36. Which of the following best describes the secondary market?

    a. Lenders who deal exclusively in second mortgage loans
    b. The major originator of mortgage loans for single-family residences
    c. Where loans are bought and sold after they have been originated
    d. The major originator of FHA and VA loans

37. The purchasers of a new home take out a loan that requires them to pay a mortgage insurance premium (MIP). The type of loan the purchasers have is a(n)

    a. conventional loan.
    b. VA loan.
    c. FHA loan.
    d. FNMA loan.

38. Which of the following statements is true of VA loans?

    a. They are available only to veterans who served in combat.
    b. They are guaranteed by the government.
    c. They are made by the VA.
    d. They cannot be assumed.

39. A borrower obtains a $100,000 mortgage loan for 30 years at 7½ percent interest. If the monthly payments of $902.77 are credited first to interest and then to principal, what will be the balance of the principal after the borrower makes the first loan payment?

    a. $99,772
    b. $99,722
    c. $99,097
    d. $100,000

40. The clause that gives the lender the right to end the loan if title to the property is transferred is called a(n)

    a. acceleration clause.
    b. alienation clause.
    c. defeasance clause.
    d. graduated clause.

41. A lender making a loan with an interest rate of 9¼ percent wishes to raise the yield on the loan to 9¾ percent If it takes approximately 8 points to raise the yield 1 percent, how many points must the lender charge?

    a. 2
    b. 3
    c. 4
    d. 8

42. All of the following buy and sell loans in the secondary market *except*

    a. FHA.
    b. GNMA.
    c. FNMA.
    d. FHLMC.

43. Which of the following describes the monthly loan payments on an amortized loan?

    a. The principal portion of the payment decreases.
    b. Equal amounts are applied to interest and principal.
    c. There is no change in the portion applied to the principal.
    d. The interest portion of the payment decreases.

44. Under the Truth-in-Lending Act (Regulation Z), which of the following is *not* a component of the annual percentage rate for a loan?

    a. The loan interest rate
    b. The loan origination fee
    c. Discount points
    d. The broker's commission

45. Which of the following statements regarding VA loans is correct?

    a. A VA loan can be used to purchase rental property.
    b. VA loans may be up to 100 percent of the property's appraised value.
    c. A veteran who has obtained one VA loan can never obtain another.
    d. The lender is protected because the loan is guaranteed.

46. The primary purpose of the Truth-in-Lending Act (Regulation Z) is to

    a. protect the lender against defaulting loans.
    b. establish minimum interest rates.
    c. provide the borrower with information on the loan costs.
    d. prevent discrimination against loan applicants.

47. If a lender agrees to make a loan based on an 80 percent loan-to-value ratio, what is the amount of the loan if the property appraises for $114,500 and the sales price is $117,000?

    a. $83,200
    b. $91,300
    c. $91,600
    d. $92,900

48. The type of loan that provides for interest only payments to be made is called a(n)

    a. term loan.
    b. amortized loan.
    c. wraparound loan.
    d. graduated payment loan.

49. A homeowner borrowed $120,000, to be repaid in monthly installments of $820 at 8 percent annual interest. How much of the borrower's first monthly payment was applied to reducing the principal amount of the loan?

    a. $10
    b. $20
    c. $800
    d. $820

50. A borrower has an 8 percent, fixed rate, amortizing loan. If the current loan balance is $56,000, how much interest will the borrower pay in the next loan payment?

    a. $373.33
    b. $480
    c. $4,480
    d. $5,600

U N I T VII
DIAGNOSTIC TEST
ANSWER SHEET

This sheet is perforated for easy pullout. Write your answers on this sheet as you complete the exercises. Refer to the diagnostic worksheet after completing the test to evaluate your strong and weak content areas. Review material in the appropriate chapter and sections.

1. _____
2. _____
3. _____
4. _____
5. _____
6. _____
7. _____
8. _____
9. _____
10. _____
11. _____
12. _____
13. _____
14. _____
15. _____
16. _____
17. _____

18. _____
19. _____
20. _____
21. _____
22. _____
23. _____
24. _____
25. _____
26. _____
27. _____
28. _____
29. _____
30. _____
31. _____
32. _____
33. _____
34. _____

35. _____
36. _____
37. _____
38. _____
39. _____
40. _____
41. _____
42. _____
43. _____
44. _____
45. _____
46. _____
47. _____
48. _____
49. _____
50. _____

UNIT VIII

SPECIALITY TOPICS

CHAPTER 24

PROPERTY MANAGEMENT

One of the specialized services performed by real estate professionals is property management. Owners of investment property such as apartment and office buildings often hire professionals to manage the property. In this chapter you learn some basic information on property management. *Section 1* covers objectives and activities of property managers. *Section 2* covers the property management agreement between the owner and the property manager. *Section 3* covers basic concepts of homeowner's property insurance. Remember to use the Study Tool Kit to reference key information and to update your progress checklist.

Learning Objectives

Track your progress as you work through the chapter by checking each learning objective when you complete it.

____ Describe the primary objectives of a property manager.

____ List and describe the major activities performed by a property manager.

____ List and describe techniques a manager may use to attract quality tenants.

____ List and describe four types of maintenance.

____ List and describe four strategies a property manager can use to manage risk.

____ Describe the purpose and requirements of the ADA.

____ List the information that should be included in a property management agreement.

____ List and describe professional organizations associated with the property management profession.

____ Describe the protection provided by liability coverage.

____ Describe the difference between claims settled under the standard settlement and full replacement methods.

____ Calculate the amount reimbursed in a claim processed under the coinsurance rule.

____ Describe the purpose and characteristics of the National Flood Insurance Program.

____ List the types of transactions that would require federal flood insurance.

Key Terms and Phrases

Track your progress as you work through the chapter by checking each term when you understand its meaning.

____ Actual cash value	____	Coinsurance clause
____ All-risks policy	____	Endorsement
____ Americans with Disabilities Act (ADA)	____	Full replacement coverage
____ Building Owners and Managers Association (BOMA)	____	Homeowner's policy

____	Institute of Real Estate Management (IREM)	____	Perils
____	Liability coverage	____	Property management agreement
____	Management plan	____	Standard settlement
____	National Flood Insurance Program (NFIP)	____	Subrogation

_____ **SECTION 1**

PROPERTY MANAGEMENT OBJECTIVES AND ACTIVITIES

GROWTH OF PROPERTY MANAGEMENT

As the size and complexity of both residential and commercial buildings have grown, so has the use of property managers. Property managers are used in various types of real estate, including residential (apartment buildings, condominiums, townhomes), commercial (office buildings, hotels, shopping malls) and industrial (industrial parks, warehouses).

Many real estate companies have created separate property management staffs, and larger corporations have established property management departments to handle the property they own. In most states property managers offering their services to the public *must be licensed* either as property managers or as real estate brokers.

PROPERTY MANAGEMENT OBJECTIVES

The overall objectives of the property manager are to (1) preserve, and enhance if possible, the value of the property and (2) generate income (3) while achieving the owner's objectives. These three objectives are interrelated.

EXAMPLE: A manager could increase income on the property by stopping all maintenance expenses. While increasing income, this would ultimately reduce the property's value.

PROPERTY MANAGEMENT ACTIVITIES

The property manager usually acts as an *agent of the owner* and therefore owes all of the duties under the laws of agency to the principal (the owner). These are the same duties discussed in real estate brokerage in Chapter 13. Activities performed by property managers can be distributed among three areas: (1) *administration* activities, including preparing budgets and reporting to the owner; (2) *marketing* activities, including finding and selecting tenants; and (3) *physical management* activities, including maintenance, rehabilitation, insuring the property and addressing environmental requirements. The rest of this section covers typical property management activities.

Developing a Management Plan

The property manager should develop a long-range **management plan** that incorporates the owner's objectives. The plan should detail what the manager hopes to accomplish and how it will be done. Before the plan can be developed, the manager should perform an analysis of the property, market conditions in the area and the owner's objectives.

Budgeting and Controlling Expenses

The manager prepares an annual operating budget. The budget contains an estimate of income and expenses and should take into consideration the owner's long-range plans for the property. The budget can be used to gauge how successfully the management plan is working. A reserve fund should be created to address unanticipated expenses.

Leasing the Property

Perhaps the most important function a manager performs is the selection of quality tenants. Tenants who are destructive, cause problems with other tenants and are delinquent with their rent can create significant expenses and lost revenue. A variety of methods to attract suitable tenants to the building are used, including developing a marketing strategy to stress favorable qualities of the property that would appeal to tenants, offering attractive rent rates and offering rent incentives such as a free month(s) rent, paying for moving costs, or extensive decorating or remodeling.

Note: When selecting tenants, a manager may not discriminate on the basis of race, color, religion, sex, national origin, family status or physical disabilities. In addition, state and local laws may extend protection to other groups.

Hint: A high vacancy rate does not mean that the rental rates are too high, because there can be other problems with the property, such as poor maintenance. A very low vacancy rate also does not guarantee the property is properly managed, because the rent being charged may be too low.

Collecting Rents

A manager's collection policy should be consistent, firm and handled in a businesslike manner. Tenants are usually informed in the lease agreement when the rent is due and the penalties if the rent is not paid on time. If a tenant breaks the terms of the lease, the manager must follow the legal procedure for evicting that tenant from the property. State and local laws vary, and the manager should be familiar with them and act in conjunction with legal counsel. (Eviction is covered in Chapter 8.)

MAINTAINING THE PREMISES

A critical function for the manager is maintenance of the property. The manager must develop a cost-effective maintenance plan that satisfies the tenants but meets the property's budget. There are several types of maintenance.

- *Preventive maintenance*—Regularly scheduled work that prolongs the life of the building and its operating components and avoids the cost of corrective maintenance later.

EXAMPLE: Regularly scheduled maintenance on heating and air-conditioning equipment, cleaning of common areas such as pools and health equipment.

- *Corrective maintenance*—Repairs to keep the building functioning.

EXAMPLE: Fixing air conditioners, furnaces, leaking faucets.

- *Routine maintenance*—Most frequently occurring maintenance; includes the regular cleaning, painting and minor repairs.

EXAMPLE: Vacuuming the hallways, washing walls.

- *Construction*—Includes renovating and improving existing facilities or building new facilities.

EXAMPLE: Building an addition or redesigning the interior to meet a tenant's needs.

Risk Management

Risk management is minimizing or eliminating the potentially enormous losses that can result from fire, water, accidents or other causes. There are four strategies a property manager can pursue after analyzing the risk that something will happen and the potential loss that may occur.

1. *Avoid the risk*—This can often be done by removing the source of the risk or not engaging in certain activities.

EXAMPLE: If allowing alcohol at parties held in an apartment development's "community room" has caused liability risks in the past, the manager could change the rules and not allow alcohol to be served in the room.

2. *Share the risk*—The amount of the risk to be shared will depend on the amount of the *insurance deductible.*
3. *Control the risk*—The manager can take preventive measures to minimize the risk.

EXAMPLE: To minimize the liability risk associated with the property's swimming pool, the manager could hire lifeguards, restrict the hours of operations and so forth.

4. *Transfer the risk*—This is usually done by taking out insurance against the risk.

The property manager usually works with an insurance agent who is familiar with the type of property involved to decide on the appropriate insurance coverage. But although the manager and insurance agent may make recommendations, the final decision is made by the property owner. Property insurance, including types of coverage and methods for settling claims, is covered in more detail in Section 3.

Hiring and Supervising Employees

The manager may be responsible for hiring and supervising employees to perform maintenance and other services. For some properties contracts with outside vendors are used instead of employees.

Record Keeping and Reporting

The manager must keep accurate and complete records that present a clear picture to the owner. The frequency and level of detail for reporting should be determined by the owner.

Complying with Environmental Regulations

Numerous *environmental regulations* have been passed in recent years, at the federal, state and local levels. These are increasing the amount of time and effort required by the property manager to respond to environmental problems.

EXAMPLE: Hazardous wastes produced by the property's tenants must be properly disposed of; the property may be the subject of an environmental audit; or it may contain asbestos, lead or other dangerous materials.

Complying with the Americans with Disabilities Act

The **Americans with Disabilities Act** (ADA) was passed in 1990 and affects the property manager's responsibilities. While property managers are not expected to be ADA experts, they should be familiar with the major provisions of the law. The manager is usually responsible for obtaining an audit to determine if the building meets ADA requirements and implementing a plan to correct any part of the property not in compliance. Title III of ADA pertains to commercial property open to the public (called *Places of Public Accommodation*). These properties must conform to ADA rules regarding access to the facilities if it can be done in a readily achievable manner (i.e., done easily and at a reasonable cost).

EXAMPLE: To meet the ADA requirements, a property manager may need to install a ramp for wheelchair access, an automotive dropoff zone near the entrance, braille markings on elevator buttons and lower, well-maintained public telephones.

BEFORE READING THE NEXT SECTION, COMPLETE THE SECTION 1 REVIEW EXERCISES AND COMPARE YOUR ANSWERS WITH THE SOLUTIONS AT THE END OF THE CHAPTER.

SECTION 1
REVIEW EXERCISES

1. Name the three overall objectives of a property manager.

   a. _____

   b. _____

   c. _____

2. This section classified the property manager's activities in three areas. Name the area associated with each of the following activities.

   a. _____ Running an advertising campaign to attract new tenants

   b. _____ Preparing reports to the manager

   c. _____ Insuring the property

   d. _____ Preparing an operating budget

   e. _____ Performing an environmental audit on the building

   f. _____ Qualifying tenants

3. What type of maintenance best describes each of the following activities?

   a. _____ Washing the walls in the building's hallways

   b. _____ Cleaning and lubricating the heating equipment

   c. _____ Building enclosed parking spaces for tenants

   d. _____ Draining the pool and resealing the bottom

e. _____ Changing burned-out lightbulbs

f. _____ Painting the lobby

4. Name the risk strategy that best describes each of the following.

a. _____ Hiring a security guard to patrol the grounds

b. _____ Extending the insurance coverage to include a risky activity

c. _____ Closing the pool to prevent accidents

d. _____ Decreasing the amount of the deductible on an insurance policy

Are the following statements true (T) or false (F)?

5. ____ In preparing the operating budget the property manager would take into consideration the owner's long-range plan for the property.

6. ____ A low vacancy rate means that the property is being well managed.

7. ____ It is probable that the manager of a large office building is licensed either as a property manager or a broker.

8. ____ Probably the most important function performed by a property manager is selecting tenants.

9. ____ Property managers are usually agents of the owners.

10. ____ The property manager usually is responsible for making sure the property conforms to the ADA rules.

Supply the term that best matches each of the following descriptions.

11. _____ A law that requires property that is open to the public to include features that facilitate access to the building

12. _____ A document developed by the property manager that outlines the owner's objectives and how the manager intends to meet them

SECTION 2

THE PROPERTY MANAGEMENT AGREEMENT AND PROFESSIONAL ORGANIZATIONS

PURPOSE OF THE AGREEMENT

To establish their working relationship, the manager and property owner enter into a **property management agreement.** The agreement creates an agency relationship in which the manager acts as a general agent of the owner. The agreement is a contract between the parties and should be in writing.

PROVISIONS OF THE AGREEMENT

Management agreements could cover many different areas but should include the following:

- *Identify the parties*—The owner's and manager's names and the date the agreement is created.

- *Description of the property*—This could cover one building or several. If any recreational facilities on the property are also to be managed, they should be specified.
- *Time period*—The time period covered by the agreement.
- *Statement of owner's purpose*—The owner's overall goals for the property should be made clear to the manager. These will be critical in developing the management plan, budgeting and making management decisions.

EXAMPLE: An owner wants to substantially increase the property's value. The manager might develop a plan to increase maintenance on the property to improve its appearance, add amenities, remodel older parts of the property and perhaps construct additions.

EXAMPLE: An owner wants to substantially increase the property's net income. The manager might develop a plan to cut the property's operating expenses, defer maintenance and increase rental rates.

- *Description of the manager's responsibilities*—All of the manager's duties should be described in the agreement.
- *Extent of manager's authority*—This part of the agreement should detail what authority the manager will have, as well as any exceptions or limitations.

EXAMPLE: The manager may have authority to contract for repairs up to a certain dollar amount, with larger amounts requiring the owner's consent.

EXAMPLE: The manager may be given the authority to hire and supervise employees and set rental rates.

- *Manager's fee*—The manager's fee could be determined in several ways: a flat fee, a percentage of the gross income (typically 5 percent to 8 percent) based on occupancy rates, the number of units in the property or a combination of methods. Fees also could be affected by the size of the building and competitiveness in the local market.

EXAMPLE: The manager's fee is based on 6 percent of the annual gross income on the property. If there are 10 units renting at $700 per month, the annual commission will be $5,040 (12 × $700 × 10 × .06 = $5,040).

Note: The management fee is negotiated between the manager and the owner. Any type of standard fee schedule agreed on among property management companies for property management services would be price fixing, which is illegal under the antitrust laws.

- *Reporting*—The frequency and level of reporting should be specified in the agreement. Reports usually include financial and operating information. Reports are used by the owner and manager to assess the current operation and formulate future plans.

PROPERTY MANAGEMENT ORGANIZATIONS

Established in 1933, the **Institute of Real Estate Management (IREM)** is the largest property management organization and is affiliated with the National Association of REALTORS®. IREM awards the following designations to individuals who have met the institute's educational requirements:

- Certified Property Manager (CPM)
- Accredited Resident Manager (ARM) (for on-site managers)

The **Building Owners and Managers Association (BOMA)** comprises local associations that include primarily owners and managers of office buildings. The Building Owners and Managers Institute (BOMI) provides educational programs for property managers and awards the following designations:

- Real Property Administrator (RPA)
- Systems Maintenance Administrator (SMA)
- Facilities Management Administrator (FMA)

Other organizations include The National Apartment Association, The National Association of Residential Property Managers and The International Council of Shopping Centers.

BEFORE READING THE NEXT SECTION, COMPLETE THE SECTION 2 REVIEW EXERCISES AND COMPARE YOUR ANSWERS WITH THE SOLUTIONS AT THE END OF THE CHAPTER.

SECTION 2
REVIEW EXERCISES

1. Name the section in the property management agreement that covers each of the following areas.

   a. _____ The owner's overall goals for the property
   b. _____ Compensation to be paid to the property manager
   c. _____ The names of the owner and property manager
   d. _____ Information provided to the owner by the property manager
   e. _____ Identifying the building and facilities to be managed
   f. _____ The length of time the agreement is for
   g. _____ A listing of the manager's duties

Are the following statements true (T) or false (F)?

2. ____ If the property manager is to manage more than one of the owner's buildings, there should be a separate management agreement for each.

3. ____ The owner's overall goals for the property are critical in developing the management plan, budgeting and making management decisions.

4. ____ The fee arrangement for the property manager usually follows a formula prescribed by the Institute of Real Estate Management.

Supply the term that best matches each of the following descriptions.

5. _____ An association primarily of owners and managers of office buildings

6. _____ The largest property management organization; affiliated with the NAR

7. _____ A document that establishes the working relationship between the building owner and the property manager

SECTION 3
HOMEOWNERS' INSURANCE POLICIES

POLICY CLASSIFICATIONS

Property owners run the risk of substantial losses due to physical catastrophes such as fires, tornadoes or floods or a lawsuit filed by someone who is injured on the property. Hazards or risks such as these are called **perils,** and insurance can be obtained to minimize the owner's losses. Several types of standardized insurance policies, providing different levels of coverage, are available. Policy standards have been developed by the Insurance Services Office (an industry group that provides services to underwriters). A brief description of these follows.

- HO-1   Basic coverage (covers 11 perils)
- HO-2   Broad coverage (covers 18 perils)
- HO-3   Special broad coverage (provides HO-5 coverage for the dwelling and HO-2 coverage for personal property)
- HO-4   Designed for renters and covers their personal property on the premises (covers perils the same as HO-2)
- HO-5   Comprehensive coverage (also called an **all-risks policy**) covers all perils except those stated in the policy
- HO-6   Designed for condominium and cooperative owners (similar to tenants [HO-4] coverage of personal property)
- HO-8   Designed for older homes and insures for *actual cost* (not replacement cost) because the cost of duplicating an older home usually would exceed its market value (perils in the HO-1 policy form covered)

POLICY ENDORSEMENTS

An **endorsement** can be added to a basic policy to change its terms. A common reason for endorsements is to add a special coverage. An endorsement may also be called a *rider.*

EXAMPLE: A homeowner's computer equipment is not covered by the insurance company's basic policy, so an endorsement is added to extend the coverage to include the equipment.

LIABILITY COVERAGE

Liability coverage provides protection against claims from others for injury or property damage caused by the owner's negligence. Insurance policies protect the owner from liability claims, including the legal costs of defending the suit and any damages up to the limit of the policy.

EXAMPLE: A neighbor's child is hurt when a swing set breaks while the child is playing with the owners' daughter in the backyard. A liability claim may be filed against the property owner for not properly maintaining the equipment.

HOMEOWNER'S POLICY

A **homeowner's policy** can be bought for residential property and has several advantages. It *packages* several types of coverage, both property and liability, into one policy and costs less than if the policies were bought separately. In addition there is only *one premium* to be paid.

INSURANCE FOR BUSINESS PROPERTY

Buildings being rented or used for commercial purposes are not covered by homeowners' policies. A *business package policy* is available and includes coverage and characteristics similar to the homeowners' policies. The general types of coverages include

- loss to buildings and other structures,
- business interruption for earnings lost as a result of damage to the property,
- loss of contents and other personal property and
- losses from liability. (This is an important coverage because the property will frequently be visited by others.)

LENDER'S INSURANCE REQUIREMENTS

A lender usually will require that a borrower carry extended insurance on the property securing a loan. The reason is to safeguard the lender's collateral for the loan. The loan agreement usually requires the first year's policy premium to be prepaid by the closing date, and the policy must be kept in force during the term of the loan. The lender's name is on the policy with the owner's, and any checks issued by the insurance company for property damages will be payable to *both the owner and the lender.*

PRIVATE HOME WARRANTY PROGRAMS

In many areas the buyer or seller of a used house can purchase a home warranty policy through an insurance company. The broker also can purchase the policy as an incentive to market a listing. These policies usually cover from one to three years and include the plumbing, electrical and heating systems; air-conditioning; hot water tank; and major appliances. The policies usually include a deductible, exclusions, limitations and specific requirements.

INSURANCE CLAIMS

- **Standard settlement**—Under a standard settlement the insurance company settles for the **actual cash value** of the property. Actual cash value means that depreciation will be subtracted from the original cost of the property (this includes either personal or real property that is damaged).

FIGURE 24.1
*Methods of
Settling Claims*

Full Replacement	=	Cost of the property
Standard Replacement	=	Cost of the property – depreciation
Coinsurance Clause	=	(Amount of coverage ÷ amount of coverage required) × amount of loss

EXAMPLE: A stereo system cost $2,000 when purchased two years ago. The insurance company calculates its useful life at five years, so it will deduct two years of depreciation ($2,000 ÷ 5 × 2 = $800) and pay the claim for $1,200 ($2,000 – $800).

- **Full replacement coverage**—With full replacement coverage, the insurance company pays for replacing the property, whatever the current cost, with no reduction for depreciation.
- **Coinsurance clause**—Most policies have a coinsurance clause, which means the owner assumes some of the risk. If damage occurs, the policy will pay the full replacement cost up to the policy limit *if the coverage has been kept at a certain percentage (usually 80 percent) of replacement cost.* If coverage is at less than 80 percent, the insurance company will pay either (1) the actual cash value of the loss (replacement costs less depreciation) or (2) a percentage of the replacement cost calculated as follows:

> Claim payment = (the *coverage carried* divided by the amount of *coverage required* in the policy) multiplied by the *amount of the loss.*

See Figure 24.1 for a summary of the methods used in calculating claims.

 Note: It is critical that a homeowner's policy be reviewed periodically to ensure that the amount of coverage has kept pace with the rising costs of construction. Some policies include an inflation guard clause that automatically adjusts the coverage based on current construction costs.

SUBROGATION

A **subrogation** clause in a policy prevents the insured from collecting for a loss from both the insurance company and the party that caused the damage. Under this clause the insurance company assumes all the rights of the insured to sue the party at fault when it pays the claim. The insurance company can then sue that party, if it chooses, to recover its money.

NATIONAL FLOOD INSURANCE ACT OF 1968

Purpose of the Act

Congress created the **National Flood Insurance Program (NFIP)** to help provide property owners with coverage against losses due to flooding. The program is administered by the Federal Insurance Administration, which is part of the *Federal Emergency Management Agency (FEMA).*

Obtaining Insurance

Homeowners can buy coverage if their community participates in NFIP. This means that the community has agreed to take steps to manage and control local flooding. More than 18,000 communities belong to the program nationwide. Flood insurance can be obtained from licensed insurance agents working for private insurance companies. The insurance is guaranteed by the government.

Transactions Covered under the Act

Flood insurance is *required* equal to the amount of the loan balance (or value of the property) for all types of buildings if

- the property is located in a designated floodplain area (these have been designated by FEMA) and
- the owner is seeking a loan from a federally regulated, supervised or insured lender (i.e., FDIC) or an FHA, a VA, an FNMA, a Fannie Mae or a GNMA loan.

If a property is located in an area newly designated as a floodplain, the lender must require flood insurance for all loans made in the area (referred to as *forced placement*). If the owner/borrower does not comply within 45 days, the lender is required to provide insurance and may charge borrowers reasonable fees for costs incurred by the lender to obtain the insurance.

COMPLETE THE SECTION 3 REVIEW EXERCISES AND COMPARE YOUR ANSWERS WITH THE SOLUTIONS AT THE END OF THE CHAPTER.

SECTION 3
REVIEW EXERCISES

1. Name the method used to settle the claim in each of the following situations.

   a. _____ In determining the settlement the insurance adjuster considers the amount of insurance coverage on the property in relation to its replacement value.

   b. _____ Appliances in the house were destroyed and the insurance adjuster takes into consideration their age in determining the settlement.

   c. _____ The insurance company settles with the homeowner for the cost of purchasing new appliances destroyed in a fire.

Are the following statements true (T) or false (F)?

2. ____ Liability coverage in a policy pays for the amount of the legal claim but not the cost of defending the claim.

3. ____ A lender will require a borrower to carry insurance on the property to protect the borrower from loss.

4. ____ To add special coverage in a policy, an endorsement is added.

5. ____ A large house built at the end of the nineteenth century probably should be insured for replacement cost.

6. ____ In a homeowner's policy there are several types of coverages but only one policy premium to be paid.

7. ____ Homeowners seeking flood insurance in a designated floodplain area can obtain it through the Federal Insurance Administration.

8. ____ Flood insurance coverage under the National Flood Insurance Program (NFIP) can be obtained in all communities.

Supply the term that best matches each of the following descriptions.

9. _____ Protection against claims from others for injuries caused by the owner's negligence

10. _____ A rider added to an insurance policy

11. _____ Hazards or risks that may be covered by insurance policies

12. _____ A package of several types of coverage available to homeowners

13. _____ A clause in the insurance policy whereby the owner may take on some of the risk if the house is insured for less than a certain percentage of the replacement cost, stated in the policy

14. _____ A program administered by a division of the Federal Emergency Management Agency (FEMA) that helps provide coverage to homeowners for losses due to flooding

15. _____ A method of settling an insurance claim in which depreciation is subtracted from the original cost of the property

16. _____ A clause in the policy that prevents the insured from collecting from both the insurance company and the party causing the loss

17. _____ A method of settling an insurance claim in which no depreciation is subtracted from the cost of replacing the property

SOLUTIONS
FOR SECTION REVIEW EXERCISES

SECTION 1

1. a. Preserve property value   b. Generate income   c. Meet the owner's objectives
2. a. Marketing   b. Administration   c. Physical management   d. Administration
   e. Physical management   f. Marketing
3. a. Routine maintenance   b. Preventive maintenance   c. Construction
   d. Preventive maintenance   e. Corrective maintenance   f. Routine maintenance
4. a. Control the risk   b. Transfer the risk   c. Avoid the risk   d. Share the risk
5. TRUE
6. FALSE While the property may be well managed, it is not guaranteed because the rents being charged may be too low or there may be other circumstances that result from poor management decisions.
7. TRUE
8. TRUE
9. TRUE
10. TRUE
11. Americans with Disabilities Act
12. Management plan

SECTION 2

1. a. Statement of owner's purpose   b. Management fee   c. Identity of the parties   d. Reporting   e. Description of the property   f. Time period   g. Description of the manager's responsibilities
2. FALSE The agreement can cover one or more buildings. The buildings to be managed should be described in the property description part of the agreement.
3. TRUE
4. FALSE There are many ways the fee can be determined. The management fee is negotiated between the owner and the manager, and any standard fee schedule agreed on among management firms may be considered price fixing, which is illegal under the antitrust laws.
5. Building Owners and Managers Association (BOMA)
6. Institute of Real Estate Management (IREM)
7. Property management agreement

SECTION 3

1. a. Coinsurance clause   b. Actual cash value   c. Full replacement
2. FALSE Liability coverage typically includes the legal costs of defending the suit.
3. FALSE The purpose of requiring the borrower to insure the property is to protect the lender's loan collateral (the property).
4. TRUE
5. FALSE Older homes should be insured for actual cost because the cost of duplicating the damaged party would be more expensive than replacing the home with current construction features.
6. TRUE
7. FALSE Flood insurance is obtained from licensed insurance agents.

8. FALSE Homeowners can buy coverage under the plan only if their community participates in NFIP.
9. Liability coverage
10. Endorsement
11. Perils
12. Homeowner's policy
13. Coinsurance clause
14. National Flood Insurance Program (NFIP)
15. Actual cash value
16. Subrogation
17. Full replacement coverage

CHAPTER 25

TAX ADVANTAGES OF HOME OWNERSHIP

This chapter discusses several tax advantages of owning a home. The purpose of the chapter is to provide enough information to *familiarize* the reader with some of the tax rules but *not* enough to become a tax expert. *Section 1* covers income deductions that can be taken by the homeowner. *Section 2* covers how gain on the home can be excluded from tax liability. Keep in mind that the tax rules are complicated and there are always exceptions. The reader is advised to consult expert tax help whenever making a decision with tax ramifications. Remember to use the Study Tool Kit to reference key information and to update your progress checklist.

Learning Objectives

Track your progress as you work through the chapter by checking each learning objective when you complete it.

_____ List the type of expenses that can be taken as deductions.

_____ List the limitations on interest deductions.

_____ Calculate the tax savings of a deduction to the taxpayer/homeowner.

_____ Calculate the gain on the sale of a principal residence.

_____ List the requirements for qualifying for an exclusion of the gain on the sale of a home.

_____ Describe the characteristics of an installment sale.

Key Terms and Phrases

Track your progress as you work through the chapter by checking each term when you understand its meaning.

_____ Acquisition debt

_____ Adjusted cost basis

_____ Capital gain

_____ Deductions

_____ Installment sale method

_____ Principal residence

INCOME TAX DEDUCTIONS

DEDUCTIONS

Taxpayers are allowed to deduct from (reduce) their income for certain expenses. These are called **deductions** to income. Some of the expenses related to owning a home can be deducted, and these are discussed in this section.

MORTGAGE INTEREST

Generally, interest paid on loans secured by a taxpayer's first and second homes is deductible. There are some limitations to this, however.

- The loan amount used to acquire, construct or improve the residence cannot exceed $1 million. This is called the **acquisition debt.**
- Interest on a home equity loan is deductible if the loan does not exceed $100,000. The money for these loans can be used for any purpose.
- All home loans *combined* cannot exceed the *market value* of the home.

EXAMPLE: A home has a market value of $200,000 and the homeowner bought the home with a $120,000 mortgage. The homeowner now takes a home equity loan for $60,000. The combined debt does not exceed the market value of the home; therefore, any interest paid may be deductible.

Mortgage Origination Fees (Points)

A point is 1 percent of the loan amount and it is one of the charges for obtaining a loan. If the points are for the use of the money and not for services, they are deductible. Points are deductible in the year they are paid by the taxpayer. (A note of caution: The rules pertaining to the IRS treatment of points have changed frequently.)

If points are paid when *refinancing* a loan, they cannot be deducted in the year paid. They must be *deducted over the life of the loan.* If the property is sold before the refinanced loan has been paid, the owner can deduct the remaining portion of the points not yet deducted.

EXAMPLE: A homeowner pays $3,600 in points when refinancing a 15-year loan. The owner can deduct $20 for each monthly payment ($20 = $3,600 ÷ 180 payments).

Mortgage Prepayment Penalties

Penalties for paying a loan off early are deductible as interest in the year they are paid.

REAL ESTATE TAXES

The annual ad valorem property taxes on a residence are deductible in the year they are paid. Special assessments usually are not deductible as a real estate tax. However, they usually are used to pay for improvements to the property and can be used to reduce the taxable gain when the property is sold. If the special assessment is used to finance maintenance or repairs, such as fixing the street, they may be deductible as property taxes.

Note: Depreciation, maintenance and other property expenses are not deductible for a residence but may be deductible on investment property (see Chapter 26).

TAX SAVINGS OF DEDUCTIONS

The taxpayer/owner of a residence can reduce his or her income taxes based on the amount of the deductions and the owner's tax rate (also called the *tax bracket*). Personal tax rates are 15 percent, 28 percent, 31 percent, 36 percent and 39.6 percent. The amount an owner's taxes may be reduced can be determined by multiplying the owner's tax rate by the amount of the deductions.

EXAMPLE: An owner in the 28 percent tax bracket paid $5,400 in deductible interest and $2,300 in real estate taxes. The taxes were reduced by $2,156 ($5,400 + $2,300 × .28).

BEFORE READING THE NEXT SECTION, COMPLETE THE SECTION 1 REVIEW EXERCISES AND COMPARE YOUR ANSWERS WITH THE SOLUTIONS AT THE END OF THE CHAPTER.

SECTION 1
REVIEW EXERCISES

Are the following statements true (T) or false(F)?

1. ____ When obtaining a loan for the purchase of a home, points paid to the lender for the use of the money must be deducted over the life of the loan.

2. ____ All real estate taxes such as ad valorem and special assessments are deductible in the year they are paid.

3. ____ Generally, taxpayers can deduct interest only on loans secured by their primary residence.

4. ____ A taxpayer purchasing a house pays points for obtaining a loan and then is charged a prepayment penalty a year later when the property is sold and the loan is repaid. The points and prepayment penalty are allowed as interest deductions on the owner's tax return.

5. ____ One limitation on deducting interest on a residence is that the total amount of all the loans on the home cannot be more than its market value.

Supply the term that best matches each of the following descriptions.

6. _____ Expenses that taxpayers are allowed to reduce their income

7. _____ An income tax term used to describe money borrowed to purchase, construct or improve a residence

EXCLUDING CAPITAL GAIN

When a taxpayer sells a house, it is usually a taxable event. The gain or loss must be computed on the sale of the property to determine if any income tax is due. The profit from the sale or exchange of an *asset* (such as real estate) is called a **capital gain**.

Note: A loss from the sale of a principal residence cannot be taken by the owner on his or her tax return.

CALCULATION OF GAIN OR LOSS

The amount of gain from the sale of a principal residence is the difference between the *net sales price* and the *adjusted cost basis*.

The *net sales price* (also called the amount realized) is the selling price *less* selling expenses.

EXAMPLE: A homeowner sells her home for $150,000 and pays the broker $7,500, her lawyer $300 and transfer taxes of $150. The *net sales price* is $142,050 ($142,050 = $150,000 – $7,500 – $300 – $150).

The **adjusted cost basis** is the owner's original cost *plus* buying expenses, *plus* capital improvements, *less* certain deductions. Deductions include the nontaxable gain deferred from the sale of a prior residence and any depreciation or casualty losses taken.

EXAMPLE: The homeowner in the example above bought the house several years ago for $80,000. There were purchase costs of $800, improvements have been made totaling $5,200 over the years and a casualty loss of $3,000 was taken. In addition, there was a deferred gain from a prior sale of $10,000. The *adjusted cost basis* of the owner's property is $73,000 ($73,000 = $80,000 + $800 + $5,200 – $3,000 – $10,000).

To compute the gain or loss, subtract the adjusted cost basis from the net sales price.

EXAMPLE: The *capital gain* for the homeowner in the example above is $69,500 ($69,500 = $142,500 net sales price – $73,000 adjusted cost basis)

Figure 25.1 summarizes the formulas used to calculate the gain on the sale of a residence.

FIGURE 25.1
Formulas Used in Calculating the Gain on a Principal Residence

Capital Gain or Loss = Net Sales Price – Adjusted Cost Basis

Net Sales Price = Selling Price – Selling Expenses

Asset's Basis = Cost of the Asset + Buying Expenses

Adjusted Basis = Original Basis + Capital Improvements
  – Deferred Gains from Previous Residences

IMPROVEMENTS VERSUS REPAIRS

Improvements are additions that add value to the property. Repairs are expenditures to maintain the current condition of the property.

EXAMPLE: A homeowner paints the house, fixes some windows, replaces a broken gutter and adds aluminum siding to the house. All except the aluminum siding are repairs.

DETERMINE THE CAPITAL GAIN EXCLUSION

The tax laws allow a taxpayer who sells his or her **principal residence** to exclude the gain on the sale if certain conditions are met. A principal residence is considered for tax purposes to be the primary place where the taxpayer resides. The taxpayer may reside in more than one place (i.e., may have a summer home), but only can have one principal residence. Therefore, second homes and summer homes do not qualify.

In general, some or all of the gain from the sale is excluded from income taxes if

- the taxpayer owned and used the property as his or her principal residence for at least two of the five years before the sale. A prorated exemption can be claimed if sold before two years because of a job-related move or for health reasons.
- the exclusion cannot be used more than once every two years.
- the exclusion is limited to $250,000 for taxpayers filing singly and $500,000 for married couples filing joint returns.

Installment Sales

The seller pays tax on the gain from the sale of real estate in the year the gain is collected. In most cases the entire gain is received in the same year as the sale. Under the **installment sale method** the gain is received from the buyer over a number of years, and the seller recognizes the gain for taxes over the same period. The seller finances the portion of the purchase price that is received in future installments. The IRS will *impute* (i.e., assign) an interest rate on the purchase balance if the sales contract does not provide for one or if the rate in the contract is below market rates. Another requirement is that the sales price must be more than $3,000, and at least one payment must be due six months after the date of sale.

**COMPLETE THE SECTION 2 REVIEW EXERCISES AND COMPARE YOUR ANSWERS
WITH THE SOLUTIONS AT THE END OF THE CHAPTER.**

SECTION 2
REVIEW EXERCISES

1. Name the result of each of the following calculations.

a. _____ Cost of the property plus capital expenditures less certain deductions

b. _____ Subtract the adjusted cost basis from the net sales price

c. _____ Subtract selling expenses from the selling price

2. What are the requirements for *excluding* the gain on the sale of a personal residence?

a. _____

b. _____

c. _____

Are the following statements true (T) or false(F)?

3. ____ Using an installment sale is a method of spreading the taxable gain from the sale of the property over more than one year.

4. ____ If a married couple wishes to use the capital gain exclusion on the sale of their residence, they must have lived in the residence for two of the last five years.

5. ____ If an owner spends money on items that maintain the current condition of the property, they are considered repairs and not improvements.

Supply the term that best matches each of the following descriptions.

6. _____ The primary location where the taxpayer resides

7. _____ The original cost of an asset plus capital improvements less certain deductions

8. _____ A method to sell real estate in which the gain on the sale is received from the buyer over several years and recognized as a taxable gain over the same period

9. _____ Expenses that can be used to reduce an owner's income taxes

10. _____ The profit from the sale of an asset

SOLUTIONS
FOR SECTION REVIEW EXERCISES

SECTION 1

1. FALSE Points can be deducted in the year they are paid. Points paid when refinancing a loan must be deducted over the length of the loan.

2. FALSE Special assessments are usually not deductible but are used to adjust the property's basis when computing the gain on the sale of the property.

3. FALSE Generally, interest can be deducted on a taxpayer's first and second homes.

4. TRUE

5. TRUE

6. Deductions

7. Acquisition debt

SECTION 2

1. a. Adjusted cost basis   b. Taxable gain   c. Net sales price

2. a. Limited to $250,000 ($500,000 for married couples filing jointly).

   b. The owner must have lived in the house at least two of the previous five years.

   c. The exclusion may be used once every two years.

3. TRUE

4. TRUE

5. TRUE

6. Principal residence

7. Adjusted cost basis

8. Installment sale method

9. Selling expenses

10. Capital gain

CHAPTER 26
REAL ESTATE INVESTMENTS

Despite unfavorable changes in the tax laws and uncertainty in the real estate market the past few years, millions of Americans still own investment real estate. This chapter discusses some of the basic concepts of real estate investments. This topic is complicated, and anyone interested in pursuing real estate as an investment should seek professional advice from a tax accountant, lawyer or investment specialist. *Section 1* covers some of the basic investment terms, advantages and disadvantages of investing in real estate. *Section 2* covers some of the tax rules regarding real estate investments. *Section 3* covers some of the types of real estate investments. Remember to use the Study Tool Kit to reference key information and update your progress checklist.

Learning Objectives

Track your progress as you work through the chapter by checking each learning objective when you complete it.

____ Explain the key investment terms included in Section 1.

____ List the advantages and disadvantages of real estate investments.

____ Describe the differences between the three types of income as defined by the tax code.

____ Describe the limits on deducting passive losses.

____ Describe the two exceptions to the limits on passive income losses.

____ Describe the kind of property that can be included in a tax-deferred exchange.

____ Describe the three types of exchanges.

____ Describe the components used in calculating depreciation.

____ Calculate depreciation using the straight-line method.

____ List and describe four different real estate investment types.

Key Terms and Phrases

Track your progress as you work through the chapter by checking each term when you understand its meaning.

____ Accelerated cost recovery system (ACRS)

____ Active income

____ Appreciation

____ Basis

____ Blue-sky laws

____ Boot

____ Capital gain/loss

____ Cash flow

____ Depreciable basis

____ Depreciation

____ Direct exchange

____ Equity

____ Leverage

____ Like-kind property

____ Liquidity

____	Multiple exchange	____	Section 1031
____	Passive income	____	Starker exchange
____	Portfolio income	____	Straight-line method
____	Pyramiding	____	Syndication
____	Real estate mortgage investment conduit (REMIC)	____	Tax credits
		____	Tax shelter
____	Risk	____	Useful life

SECTION 1

TERMINOLOGY, ADVANTAGES AND DISADVANTAGES OF REAL ESTATE INVESTMENTS

INVESTMENT TERMS

Cash flow refers to the dollars remaining after all expenses of ownership have been paid. Cash flow may be *positive* or *negative*.

EXAMPLE: A property has yearly income of $100,000 and operating expenses (i.e., maintenance, mortgage payments, taxes) of $90,000. The property has a *positive cash flow* of $10,000 for the investor ($100,000 income – $90,000 expenses).

EXAMPLE: A property has yearly income of $100,000 and operating expenses (i.e., maintenance, mortgage payments, taxes) of $110,000. The property has a *negative cash flow* of $10,000, requiring the owner to invest additional money ($100,000 income – $110,000 expenses).

Leverage is the use of borrowed funds (often referred to as *other people's money*) to finance the purchase of an investment.

EXAMPLE: Bob purchases investment property for $1 million with 10 percent down. Bob is leveraging his investment by using the lender's money to purchase a property costing ten times what he could afford to purchase by himself.

The difference between the *adjusted basis* in a property and the *net selling price* results in a **capital gain** (i.e., a profit) or **loss**.

EXAMPLE: An investor's basis in a property is $400,000. The property is sold for $500,000. The investor has a capital gain of $100,000 ($500,000 selling price – $400,000 adjusted basis).

An owner's **basis** is the investor's initial cost for the property. The basis is adjusted (to find the *adjusted basis*) by *adding* any improvements made and *deducting* depreciation expenses taken.

EXAMPLE: An investor purchases a property for $200,000. Improvements—a swimming pool and new driveway—are added for $100,000, and depreciation of $50,000 is taken. The investor's adjusted basis is now $250,000 ($200,000 + $100,000 – $50,000).

Appreciation is the increase in property value over a period of time. It can be caused by inflation or by the intrinsic value of the property (characteristics of the property that others view as valuable).

EXAMPLE: A parcel of property that is in the center of an affluent and rapidly growing neighborhood increases in value (appreciates) because of its location.

Equity is the property's value minus any debt.

EXAMPLE: A property is worth $400,000 and has loans of $300,000 against it. The owner's equity is $100,000 ($400,000 value – $300,000 debt).

Liquidity is the speed at which an investment can be converted to cash.

EXAMPLE: An investor owns 100 shares of IBM. The stock is a *liquid investment* because it can be sold quickly and converted to cash.

Risk is the possibility of loss from an investment. In general, the *higher the investment risk,* the *higher the return* the investor will demand.

Any tax-deductible expense is a **tax shelter** because it "shelters" (reduces) taxable income.

ADVANTAGES OF REAL ESTATE INVESTMENTS

Recent tax law changes and economic conditions in some areas have made real estate investment less attractive than in the past, but there still are several significant advantages. These include the following:

- *High rate of return*—In the past few years local economic conditions and overabundance of investment real estate in some areas have produced poor returns for investors. In general, however, real estate investments have historically produced a favorable rate of return for their owners in relation to other types of investment.
- *Tax advantages*—Tax advantages for real estate have been limited by the Tax Reform Act of 1986; however, there are still some tax benefits.
- *Inflation hedge*—In some areas real estate values have fluctuated and not kept pace with inflation. Overall, however, real estate usually increases in value over time to provide a hedge against inflation.
- *Leverage*—Real estate can be highly leveraged (i.e., the investor may be able to borrow up to 80 percent or more of the purchase price), resulting in greater buying power and possibly a higher return on equity.

EXAMPLE: An investor obtains financing for 90 percent of the cost of an investment property. By investing $20,000, an investor can purchase a property worth $200,000.

EXAMPLE: For the investment in the example above, after the first year the property is worth $210,000 (a 5 percent increase). The owner's return on investment is 50 percent ($20,000 investment + $10,000 increase = .5). This is a very simplistic example but shows the potential affect of leverage.

- *Equity buildup*—As the property's value rises and the loan is paid down, its equity increases. By using the property's equity, an investor can refinance and obtain additional money, which can then be used to buy additional investment property. This is called **pyramiding.**

DISADVANTAGES OF REAL ESTATE INVESTMENTS

There are several disadvantages to investing in real estate. These include the following:

- *Illiquidity*—Real estate is not a liquid investment. Real estate investments usually involve a long-term commitment of funds. Investors needing access to their invested funds may suffer a loss trying to sell quickly.

    Reasons why real estate investments are not liquid include the following: (1) Real estate is nonhomogeneous (no two parcels are alike). Because of this it takes longer to match buyers and sellers. (2) There is no national real estate market (real estate markets are local and can vary substantially). (3) There is no formal marketplace (such as the stock exchanges for stocks) to speed the process of buying, selling or exchanging properties.

- *Need for expert help*—Real estate investments often require the expertise of several professionals. These may include property managers, tax accountants and lawyers.
- *Management effort*—Physical and mental effort, either by the investor or by a professional property manager, is needed to manage the investment.
- *Risk*—As in any investment there is always the possibility of risk. In real estate investments the risks include a decrease or lower-than-expected rise in property value or cash flow.

**BEFORE READING THE NEXT SECTION, COMPLETE THE SECTION 1
REVIEW EXERCISES AND COMPARE YOUR ANSWERS WITH THE
SOLUTIONS AT THE END OF THE CHAPTER.**

SECTION 1

REVIEW EXERCISES

1. Name the advantage of investing in real estate that best fits each if the following statements.

   a. _____ The investment value probably will increase at least as fast as inflation.

   b. _____ The value-to-debt ratio of the property increases, allowing the investor to borrow additional money for new investments.

   c. _____ Investors can make as much as or more than they could in other investments.

   d. _____ Investors usually can deduct their investment expenses.

   e. _____ Investors do not have to pay for the property in cash.

2. Name the disadvantage of investing in real estate that best fits each of the following statements.

   a. _____ Time and effort are required to protect the investment.

   b. _____ The property's value or income may decrease.

   c. _____ The investor's funds cannot be taken out of the investment quickly.

   d. _____ Expertise is required to protect and run the investment.

Are the following statements true (T) or false (F)?

3. ____ It may take longer for investors to get access to funds invested in real estate than in other types of investments because no parcels of real estate are exactly alike.

4. ____ Cash flow from the property can be either positive or negative.

5. ____ The difference between the net selling price of a property and the purchase price of a replacement property is the capital gain.

6. ____ On a lower-risk investment an investor should expect a higher return.

Supply the term that best matches each of the following descriptions.

7. _____ Use of borrowed money to purchase investments

8. _____ An asset's initial cost to an investor

9. _____ The dollars remaining from income after all expenses have been paid

10. _____ Obtaining additional investment property by borrowing on the equity of existing investments

11. _____ A property's value less any loans against it

12. _____ The difference between an asset's adjusted basis and the net selling price

13. _____ To lower (or protect) taxable income through tax-deductible expenses

SECTION 2
TAX RULES AND REAL ESTATE INVESTMENTS

Tax rules affecting real estate frequently change; therefore, it is always advisable to seek professional tax help when making real estate investment decisions.

TAX RATES

Taxes are applied to a taxpayer's taxable income. This is the amount that remains after deductions and adjustments to income are applied. There are several individual tax rates: 15 percent, 28 percent, 31 percent, 36 percent and 39.6 percent. Individual refers to *personal income taxes* versus *corporate tax rates*. However, the maximum tax rates for capital gains depend on how long the property is held and the taxpayer's tax rate (bracket).

TYPES OF INCOME

For tax purposes income is classified as either ordinary income or capital gain income.
   Ordinary income includes three types:

1. **Active income** includes wages, tips, commissions, jury duty fees, bonuses and similar income.
2. **Passive income** includes income from activities in which the taxpayer does not *materially participate*. This includes income from limited partnerships and certain rental activities.
3. **Portfolio income** includes income from interest, stock dividends, capital gains, royalties and annuity income.

   Capital gain income results from the sale of capital assets. Capital gains (and losses) are either *short term*, if the asset is held for less than 12 months, or *long term*, if held for more than 12 months. Capital gains (whether long or short term) are added to taxable income. Capital *losses* can be deducted, *up to $3,000 in a year*. Losses that exceed the limit can be carried over to subsequent years.

TYPES OF INVESTORS

An *active investor* is an investor who materially participates in managing the property on a regular and substantial basis. A *passive investor* is an investor who does not materially participate in managing the activity.

LIMITS ON DEDUCTING LOSSES

Passive Income Losses

- Real estate losses are considered *passive losses* and can be used only to *offset other passive income*. Losses from passive income *cannot offset* either *active* or *portfolio* income.
- *Unused* passive losses (also called *suspended losses*) can be carried over to later years indefinitely. This may happen either because they exceed passive income or because there are only passive losses and no passive income to offset.

EXAMPLE: An investor has two properties. One makes a profit of $10,000 and the other has a loss of $15,000. The investor can offset the $10,000 income with the loss but must carry forward the remaining $5,000 loss (the suspended loss), and it cannot be used to offset active income.

- If an investment in a passive activity is sold and there are unused passive losses, the losses may be used to offset any gain from the sale of the investment.

Exceptions to Passive Loss Limitation

Lower Income. Investors with lower income have a limited ability to deduct losses for real estate against nonpassive income (i.e., wages).

- An investor with adjusted gross income of less than $100,000 can use passive losses in *rental real estate* up to $25,000 to offset any other income.
- If over $100,000, the loss that can be deducted is reduced by $1 for every $2 dollars of income over $100,000, up to $150,000. No losses are allowed for income over $150,000.

To be eligible to take the loss, investors must (1) *actively participate* (at least making major managerial decisions) in their rental property and (2) hold at least a 10 percent interest in the investment. Passive investors (i.e., investors in real estate syndications) cannot use the losses against nonpassive income.

Real Estate Activity. Starting in 1994, investors who spend at least 750 hours per year or 50 percent of their working time in real estate brokerage, leasing, development, management, construction, acquisitions or conversions can deduct losses from rental property against ordinary income. Investors qualifying under this exception are not limited to the $25,000 maximum annual tax loss described above.

EXCHANGES

Real estate exchanges are used to trade properties and defer (not eliminate) tax on any gain. These also are called **Section 1031** exchanges, referring to the section in the IRS code that authorizes them. To be eligible as a tax-deferred exchange, the properties must be of *like kind* and held for use in a *trade or business* or for *investment*.

Like-kind property refers to personal property that is exchanged for other personal property and real property that is exchanged for other real property. It does not matter what kind of real property is being exchanged. An office building can be exchanged for a vacant lot or a store exchanged for an apartment building. Personal residences and foreign property do not qualify for exchanges.

If any cash or other nonqualifying property is received in *addition* to the like-kind property, this is called **boot.** The value of boot is taxable to the party receiving it.

EXAMPLE: Investor *A* exchanges a building worth $200,000 for investor *B*'s building worth $150,000, a car worth $20,000 and $30,000 in cash. Investor *A* has a taxable boot of $50,000 ($20,000 car + $30,000 cash).

Direct exchanges occur if two parties are willing to trade like-kind properties with each other in the same transaction. This type of exchange seldom occurs.

Because it is often difficult to find two parties willing to swap properties, exchanges usually involve more than two properties in the same transaction. These are called **multiple exchanges** and still are considered tax-deferred exchanges.

EXAMPLE: *A, B* and *C* have apartment buildings of different sizes and want to exchange properties. *A* acquires *C*'s property, *B* acquires *A*'s property and *C* acquires *B*'s property.

If a seller cannot find like-kind property immediately, a *delayed exchange* might be used to defer the gain. This is called a **Starker exchange** (named after a 1979 court case that recognized this type of arrangement). Under a Starker exchange the proceeds from the sale of property are held beyond the control of the seller until the seller can locate like-kind property in which to invest the proceeds. Some strict time limits apply.

- The property to be acquired in the exchange must be identified in writing within 45 days of the closing date of the sale of the old property.
- Closing on the like-kind property found for the exchange must take place within 180 days after the closing of the sale of the old property.
- Property acquired in an exchange between related parties must be held for at least two years.

The intermediary holding the money from the sale must be someone the seller can't control. The IRS will not accept a spouse, a close family member or someone who has been an agent of the seller (i.e., the seller's lawyer, accountant or real estate broker). A lawyer or trust company hired just to handle the transaction is acceptable.

Note: Because exchanges are subject to a number of IRS rules that must be strictly adhered to, guidance from professionals familiar with real estate exchanges is advisable.

DEPRECIATION

Depreciation is a deductible expense that allows the cost of an asset to be recovered over the asset's useful life. Depreciation deductions can be taken only on property used in a trade or business or in the production of income. An owner's residence *cannot* be depreciated because it is not used in a business, nor can land because it does not wear out.

Depreciation Components

The **depreciable basis** of the property is the amount that may be depreciated. For real estate property it is generally the price of the property plus acquisition costs minus the value of the land.

The **useful life** of an asset is the number of years the asset will be useful to the investor, as determined by IRS tax laws.

Straight-Line Method

Using the **straight-line method,** equal amounts of depreciation are taken annually over the asset's useful life. To calculate depreciation using this method, divide the basis by the number of years of useful life. For real property the useful life is

- *27.5 years* for residential property and
- *39 years* for nonresidential property.

The useful life for property placed in service prior to January 1, 1987, varies, based on the date of service.

EXAMPLE: A residential real estate investment property placed in service after January 1, 1987, had been bought for $250,000, with a land value of $50,000. The depreciable basis is $200,000 ($250,000 price – $50,000 land). The yearly depreciation deduction would be $7,273 ($200,000 basis ÷ 27.5 years).

Accelerated Cost Recovery System

The **Accelerated Cost Recovery System (ACRS)** is an alternative method of calculating depreciation. Under ACRS more depreciation is taken in earlier years (called *accelerated depreciation*) and less in later years. ACRS can be used only for *personal property* and real estate put in service *prior to January 1, 1987.*

TAX CREDITS

Tax credits are direct reductions of tax rather than deductions against income. Credits are allowed for rehabilitation of older buildings, low-income housing projects and historic property.

**BEFORE READING THE NEXT SECTION, COMPLETE THE SECTION 2
REVIEW EXERCISES AND COMPARE YOUR ANSWERS WITH THE
SOLUTIONS AT THE END OF THE CHAPTER.**

SECTION 2
REVIEW EXERCISES

1. What type of income (for tax purposes) best describes each of the following?

   a. _____ Income from rent

   b. _____ A salary received by an employee

   c. _____ Gain from the sale of a capital asset

   d. _____ Interest from a certificate of deposit

   e. _____ Commissions received by a real estate broker

Are the following statements true (T) or false (F)?

2. ____ Residential real estate exchanged for commercial real estate does not qualify under the tax rules for tax-deferred like-kind exchanges.

3. ____ Long-term capital gains are for property held less than 12 months.

4. ____ In a Starker delayed exchange the proceeds from the sale of the first property can be held by the investor's real estate broker until reinvested in the new property.

5. ____ Investors who are active in managing their investments or engage in certain real estate activities may be able to use losses from real estate investments to reduce active or portfolio income.

6. ____ A taxpayer with a large capital loss cannot deduct the loss if it's over $3,000.

7. ____ Losses from real estate investments are considered passive losses.

8. ____ Depreciation expense on an investor's residence is not allowed under the tax laws.

Supply the term that best matches each of the following descriptions.

9. _____ Personal property exchanged for other personal property or real estate exchanged for other real estate

10. _____ A tax-deductible expense that allows the cost of an asset to be recovered over its useful life

11. _____ Like-kind exchanges involving more than two properties

12. _____ The amount of an asset that may be depreciated

13. _____ Tax-deferred exchange of property held for use in a trade or business or an investment

14. _____ A method of depreciating an asset in which equal amounts of depreciation are taken annually over the asset's useful life

15. _____ A delayed exchange of properties that qualifies as a tax-deferred exchange

16. _____ The length of time an asset will be useful to the owner, as defined by the IRS

17. _____ An alternative method of calculating depreciation in which more depreciation is taken in earlier years and less in later years

18. _____ Additional cash or nonqualifying property received as part of a like-kind exchange that is taxable to the recipient

19. _____ A direct reduction of tax

20. _____ A like-kind exchange involving two parties trading properties

SECTION 3
INVESTMENT TYPES

DIRECT OWNERSHIP

A common form of investment is direct ownership of the property. Title to the property can be held by individuals, corporations or partnerships that control and manage the property directly. There is a wide selection of properties for real estate investment. These include vacant land, houses, condominiums, shopping centers and apartment and office buildings of many sizes. Selecting the type of property for investment by direct ownership requires matching, among other things, the investors' capital, tolerance for risk, and capability to manage the property.

REAL ESTATE INVESTMENT SYNDICATIONS

In general, a **syndication** is a business venture in which two or more people invest their money in a real estate project. The form of ownership used by a syndication could be tenancy in common, joint tenancy, general or limited partnership, or corporation. When used for real estate investments, however, they are usually limited partnerships. (Chapter 9 covers forms of ownership in more detail.) Syndications generate profit for investors when they buy, sell or develop real estate. They can be small groups of associated investors (called *private syndications*) or much larger groups (called *public syndications*) with hundreds or thousands of investors.

Because syndications solicit and pool investors' funds much like stock, they often come under securities registration laws. These are administered by the federal Securities and Exchange Commission and state real estate regulator departments. Federal and state disclosure laws also have been enacted to protect investors from fraud. In general these laws outline fraudulent practices, require the registration of securities prior to sale and require full disclosure by providing a *prospectus* to all potential investors. State laws, commonly referred to as **blue-sky laws,** were passed to protect the public from fraudulent investing schemes (which only gave the investor a piece of the blue sky). These typically apply to limited partnerships and securities being offered within the state.

 Note: Real estate salespeople selling shares in syndications may be required to obtain securities licenses and special state registration.

REAL ESTATE INVESTMENT TRUSTS

Real estate investment trusts (REITs) allow small investors to participate in real estate investments similar to mutual funds for stocks. A trust is formed and allows investors (called *beneficiaries*) to purchase real estate investment trust certificates issued by the REIT. The REIT then uses the funds to purchase real estate and mortgages. The investment certificates can be traded on major stock exchanges.

REITs are not subject to federal income taxes as long as certain conditions are met, including that at least 75 percent of the REIT's income must be from real estate investments, 95 percent of its profits must be distributed to the investors and it must have at least 100 beneficiaries.

REAL ESTATE MORTGAGE INVESTMENT CONDUIT

The **real estate mortgage investment conduit** (REMIC) was created by the Tax Reform Act of 1986. REMICs may issue multiple classes of investor securities backed by a pool of mortgages. Securities classes can be for *residual interests* or *regular interests*. Holders of residual securities (only one class can be issued) receive distributions when loans in the pool are paid. Holders of regular securities (one or more classes can be issued) receive payments based on a fixed or variable rate.

COMPLETE THE SECTION 3 REVIEW EXERCISES AND COMPARE YOUR ANSWERS WITH THE SOLUTIONS AT THE END OF THE CHAPTER.

SECTION 3
REVIEW EXERCISES

1. Name the type of real estate investment that best fits each description.

   a. _____ Title to the investment property is usually held in the form of a limited partnership that generates profits for the limited partners.

   b. _____ Securities issued to investors are backed by pools of mortgages.

   c. _____ Title to the property is held by the people who manage the property.

   d. _____ Investors are called beneficiaries and purchase investment certificates.

Are the following statements true (T) or false (F)?

2. ____ Holders of securities issued by REMICs will receive their money either when the loans in the pool are paid or on a fixed payment schedule.

3. ____ If REITs follow rules prescribed by the IRS, the income investors receive from the trusts is not subject to federal income tax.

4. ____ The investors capability to manage should be considered in selecting the type of property for investment by direct ownership.

5. ____ Securities registration laws often apply to syndications.

Supply the term that best matches each of the following descriptions.

6. _____ Laws passed to protect the public from fraudulent investing schemes

7. _____ Investor securities, backed by mortgage loan pools, issued to investors

8. _____ A business venture that usually takes the form of a limited partnership

9. _____ Funds from the issuance of investment trust certificates to investors used to purchase real estate investments for the benefit of the investors

SOLUTIONS
FOR SECTION REVIEW EXERCISES

SECTION 1

1. a. Inflation hedge   b. Equity buildup   c. High rate of return
   d. Tax advantages   e. Leverage
2. a. Management effort   b. Risk   c. Not liquid   d. Need expert help
3. TRUE
4. TRUE
5. FALSE The capital gain is the difference between the adjusted basis in a property and its net selling price.
6. FALSE The higher the investment risk, the higher the return that can be expected by the investor.
7. Leverage
8. Basis
9. Cash flow
10. Pyramiding
11. Equity
12. Capital gain
13. Tax shelter

SECTION 2

1. a. Passive income   b. Active income   c. Portfolio income   d. Portfolio income
   e. Active income
2. FALSE Like-kind property exchange is defined as real estate for real estate. It does not matter what type of real estate is being exchanged.
3. FALSE Assets must be held longer than 12 months.
4. FALSE The proceeds must be held by someone outside the control of the investor.
5. TRUE
6. FALSE The taxpayer can deduct up to a maximum of $3,000 in any one year but any additional loss can be carried over to subsequent years.
7. TRUE
8. TRUE
9. Like-kind property
10. Depreciation
11. Multiple exchanges
12. Depreciable basis
13. Section 1031 (like-kind exchange)
14. Straight-line method
15. Starker exchange
16. Useful life
17. Accelerated Cost Recovery System (ACRS)
18. Boot
19. Tax credits
20. Direct exchange

SECTION 3

1. a. Syndication   b. Real estate mortgage investment conduit (REMIC)
   c. Direct ownership   d. Real estate investment trust (REIT)

2. TRUE

3. FALSE The trust does not have to pay taxes on the income, but the money distributed to investors is taxable to them.

4. TRUE

5. TRUE

6. Blue-sky laws

7. Real estate mortgage investment conduit (REMIC)

8. Syndication

9. Real estate investment trusts (REIT)

THIS IS THE LAST CHAPTER IN THE UNIT. TAKE THE UNIT VIII DIAGNOSTIC TEST.

UNIT VIII
DIAGNOSTIC TEST

1. Which of the following is *not* covered in a homeowner's insurance policy?

   a. A claim by someone who was injured on the property
   b. The garage
   c. The house
   d. The land

2. During the year, a homeowner paid an average of $375 a month for interest on a mortgage. If the owner was in the 28 percent income tax bracket and all the interest for that year was deductible from taxable income, approximately how much less was the income tax bill as a result of this deduction?

   a. $28
   b. $105
   c. $375
   d. $1,260

3. The extent of a property manager's authority is found in the

   a. licensing laws.
   b. local zoning laws.
   c. association by-laws.
   d. management agreement.

4. Which of the following is true of the lender's insurance requirements regarding the borrower's homeowner's insurance policy?

   a. The lender's name is on the policy with the owner.
   b. The loan agreement will usually require that the first year's policy premium be paid in monthly installments with the loan payments.
   c. After the first five years of the loan, continuation of homeowner's insurance is at the option of the borrower.
   d. Any checks issued by the insurance company for damages will be payable to the lender.

5. Which of the following expenses may homeowners take as a deduction on their income tax returns?

   a. Costs to improve the property
   b. Property insurance costs
   c. Interest paid on the mortgage
   d. Depreciation calculated on a straight-line basis

6. An investor uses borrowed funds to finance the purchase of an investment. The investor is using the principle of

   a. liquidity.
   b. cash flow.
   c. leverage.
   d. equity.

7. Typical functions of a property manager include all of the following *except*

   a. maintaining quality service with the lowest possible expenses.
   b. generating the highest return for the owner.
   c. selling the property at the highest price for the owner.
   d. keeping the property in good repair.

8. A homeowner's insurance policy provides that any claims will be settled using a standard settlement. Which of the following is *not* true for a claim being settled under this policy?

   a. The company will settle for the actual cash value of the property.
   b. Depreciation will be deducted from the original cost of any personal property damaged or destroyed.
   c. The insurance will pay for the current cost of replacing the property.
   d. Depreciation will be deducted from the original cost of any real property damaged or destroyed.

9. A couple buy a home and pay $22,000 in mortgage interest in the first year. If they are in the 28 percent income tax bracket and can deduct all of the interest, how much will they save in income taxes the first year?

   a. $616
   b. $2,200
   c. $6,160
   d. $22,000

10. A prospective investor in a limited partnership is given a disclosure statement that explains the partnership's objectives and plans. The investor was probably given a(n)

    a. operating statement.
    b. prospectus.
    c. equity statement.
    d. commitment.

11. Jane has a basis of $60,000 in her primary residence. She sells the house for $150,000. The broker's commission was 6 percent and other selling expenses totaled $500. What is the gain on Jane's transaction?

    a. $9,000
    b. $80,500
    c. $90,000
    d. $140,000

12. A homeowner's insurance policy provides that any claims will be settled using a coinsurance clause. Which of the following is true for this policy?

    a. The owner assumes none of the risk under this policy.
    b. The amount of coverage should be periodically reviewed to ensure it meets the coinsurance clause requirements.
    c. The insurance will pay for full replacement cost if coverage is kept at a certain percentage of the *original cost*.
    d. If the coinsurance clause ratio is not met, the claim will be paid at full replacement cost.

13. Mary is preparing her income tax return and lists the following expenses she paid during the year on her house: $9,500 in interest on a mortgage loan, a $1,000 loan origination fee paid in obtaining the loan,. $800 in real estate taxes and a $450 homeowner's insurance premium. How much may Mary deduct on her income tax return?

    a. $9,800
    b. $10,500
    c. $11,300
    d. $11,750

14. A property generates a positive cash flow for its owner when the property's income exceeds

    a. depreciation and operating expenses.
    b. depreciation and mortgage expenses.
    c. mortgage payments only.
    d. mortgage payments and operating expenses.

15. If a property manager chooses an insurance policy with a high deductible, the risk management technique being used is

    a. avoiding risk.
    b. sharing risk.
    c. controlling risk.
    d. transferring risk.

16. Most homeowner's insurance policies include a deductible clause. Which of the following is true regarding deductible clauses?

    a. Usually a larger deductible amount will increase the premium.
    b. One purpose of deductibles is to discourage the filing of high dollar claims.
    c. The deductible amount for a homeowner's policy is usually less than $50.
    d. They require that the owner pay the initial amount of the claim up to the deductible amount.

17. Which of the following *cannot* be deducted from a homeowner's income tax return as an interest expense in the year they are paid?

    a. Points paid to refinance a loan
    b. Interest on a second residence
    c. Interest to improve a residence
    d. Mortgage prepayment penalties

18. The investment principle of liquidity can best be described as

    a. the speed at which the investment can be converted to cash.
    b. using other people's money to finance the purchase of an investment.
    c. the property's value less any debt against the property.
    d. increasing a property's value over a period of time.

19. Repairing a faulty air-conditioning unit is considered

    a. preventive maintenance.
    b. corrective maintenance.
    c. routine maintenance.
    d. construction maintenance.

20. Which of the following transactions involving properties located in a floodplain does *not* require federal flood insurance?

    a. The buyer is seeking a VA loan.
    b. The buyer is seeking an FHA loan.
    c. The buyer is seeking an FNMA loan.
    d. The buyer is seeking seller financing.

21. To compute the gain on the sale of a residence for tax purposes, the taxpayer subtracts the

    a. selling expenses from the selling price.
    b. selling price from the original purchase price.
    c. selling expenses from the purchase price.
    d. adjusted cost basis from the net sales price.

22. An investment property was purchased six years ago for $120,000. At the time of the purchase the property was worth $132,000 and the land was valued at $10,000. If the investor used straight-line depreciation with a 31½ year life, what is the present book value of the property?

    a. $88,550
    b. $96,600
    c. $99,045
    d. $110,000

23. Periodically draining the Jacuzzi in the property's health room to clean and inspect its condition is considered

    a. preventive maintenance
    b. corrective maintenance.
    c. routine maintenance.
    d. construction maintenance.

24. A typical homeowner's insurance policy does not cover

    a. theft of personal property.
    b. flood damage.
    c. liability for someone injured on the property.
    d. damage to the house's contents.

25. What is the maximum capital gains tax exclusion available to homeowners who file as single taxpayers?

    a. $125,000
    b. $225,000
    c. $250,000
    d. $500,000

26. A partnership considering an investment in real estate would be correct in considering which of the following potential advantages?

    a. Liquidity of the investment
    b. Use of leverage
    c. Level of expert help needed
    d. Effort required to manage the investment

27. A homeowner's insurance policy provides that any claims will be settled using an 80 percent coinsurance clause. If the home carries $60,000 in insurance coverage and costs $100,000 to replace, how much will the insurance company pay if a house fire caused $25,000 in damages?

    a. $5,000
    b. $18,750
    c. $20,000
    d. $25,000

28. A husband and wife filing a joint tax return realize a capital gain of over $625,000 on the sale of their residence. In this situation

    a. if either is over 55 they will not have to pay tax on the amount over $500,000.
    b. they can defer paying tax on any of the gain if they purchase another house for at least $625,000.
    c. they will have to pay tax on the entire $625,000.
    d. $125,000 will be considered taxable income on their tax return.

29. A homeowner who wished to recognize the taxable gain on the sale of his or her residence over a number of years would use

    a. an installment sale.
    b. a tax exchange.
    c. an all-cash sale.
    d. a sale using a purchase-money mortgage.

30. Which of the following would be a potential disadvantage if investing in real estate?

    a. Liquidity of the investment
    b. Use of leverage
    c. Hedge against inflation
    d. Allowable depreciation expenses to offset income

U N I T VIII
DIAGNOSTIC TEST
ANSWER SHEET

This sheet is perforated for easy pullout. Write your answers on this sheet as you complete the exercises. Refer to the diagnostic worksheet after completing the test to evaluate your strong and weak content areas. Review material in the appropriate chapter and sections.

1. _____	11. _____	21. _____
2. _____	12. _____	22. _____
3. _____	13. _____	23. _____
4. _____	14. _____	24. _____
5. _____	15. _____	25. _____
6. _____	16. _____	26. _____
7. _____	17. _____	27. _____
8. _____	18. _____	28. _____
9. _____	19. _____	29. _____
10. _____	20. _____	30. _____

STUDY TOOL
KIT

PROGRESS CHART

UNIT I / UNIT II / UNIT III

CHAPTERS AND SECTIONS	1.1	1.2	1.3	2.1	2.2	3.1	3.2	3.3	4.1	4.2	5.1	5.2	5.3	6.1	6.2	6.3	7.1	7.2	7.3	8.1	8.2	8.3	9.1	9.2	9.3
Read each section																									
Complete review exercise																									
Review solutions to review exercise																									
Check off Learning Objectives and Key Terms																									
Complete Unit Diagnostic Test																									
Review solutions to Unit Diagnostic Test																									

UNIT IV / UNIT V

CHAPTERS AND SECTIONS	10.1	10.2	10.3	11.1	11.2	11.3	12.1	12.2	12.3	13.1	13.2	13.3	14.1	14.2	14.3	15.1	15.2	16.1	16.2	17.1	17.2	17.3
Read each section																						
Complete review exercise																						
Review solutions to review exercise																						
Check off Learning Objectives and Key Terms																						
Complete Unit Diagnostic Test																						
Review solutions to Unit Diagnostic Test																						

UNIT VI / UNIT VII / UNIT VIII

CHAPTERS AND SECTIONS	18.1	18.2	18.3	19.1	19.2	19.3	19.4	20.1	20.2	21.1	21.2	21.3	22.1	22.2	23.1	23.2	23.3	24.1	24.2	24.3	25.1	25.2	26.1	26.2	26.3
Read each section																									
Complete review exercise																									
Review solutions to review exercise																									
Check off Learning Objectives and Key Terms																									
Complete Unit Diagnostic Test																									
Review solutions to Unit Diagnostic Test																									

This chart should be used to track your progress in the book. Additional blank lines are provided in the event you would like to track other study activities by chapter (i.e., rereading the chapter, retaking the section exercises, etc.).

UNIT I: INTRODUCTION TO REAL ESTATE
CHAPTER 1   Introduction to Real Estate
        2   Real Estate Concepts

UNIT II: REAL ESTATE LAW
CHAPTER 3   Government Powers
        4   Encumbrances
        5   Encumbrances: Liens
        6   Legal Descriptions

UNIT III: REAL ESTATE OWNERSHIP
CHAPTER 7   Freehold Interests in Real Estate
        8   Leasehold Estates in Real Estate
        9   Forms of Ownership

UNIT IV: TRANSFERRING REAL ESTATE
CHAPTER 10   Transferring Title
        11   Recording Title
        12   Real Estate Closings

UNIT V: REAL ESTATE BROKERAGE
CHAPTER 13   Agency and Real Estate Brokerage
        14   Real Estate Contracts
        15   Listing Contracts
        16   Real Estate Licensing Laws
        17   Fair Housing Laws

UNIT VI: REAL ESTATE VALUATION
CHAPTER 18   The Appraisal Process
        19   Methods of Estimating Value

UNIT VII: REAL ESTATE FINANCE
CHAPTER 20   Loan Instruments
        21   Lending Practices
        22   Types of Real Estate Loans
        23   Lending Laws and Government Activities

UNIT VIII: SPECIALTY TOPICS
CHAPTER 24   Property Management
        25   Tax Advantages of Home Ownership
        26   Real Estate Investments

LIST OF REAL ESTATE ABBREVIATIONS

Laws

ADA	Americans with Disabilities Act
CERCLA	Comprehensive Environmental Resource, Compensation, and Liability Act
FIRREA	Financial Institutions Reform, Recovery, and Enforcement Act
NEPA	National Environmental Policy Act
NFIP	National Flood Insurance Program
RESPA	Real Estate Settlement Procedures Act
UCC	Uniform Commercial Code

Organizations and Government Agencies

ARELLO	Association of Real Estate License Law Officials
BOMA	Building Owners and Managers Association
BOMI	Building Owners and Managers Institute
DVA	Department of Veterans Affairs
EPA	Environmental Protection Agency
FDIC	Federal Deposit Insurance Corporation
FEMA	Federal Emergency Management Agency
FHA	Federal Housing Authority
FHLMC	Federal Home Loan Mortgage Corporation
FmHA	Farmers Home Administration
FNMA	Federal National Mortgage Association
FRS	Federal Reserve System
GNMA	Government National Mortgage Association
HUD	Department of Housing and Urban Development
IREM	Institute of Real Estate Management
IRS	Internal Revenue Service
MGIC	Mortgage Guarantee Insurance Corp.
NAR	National Association of REALTORS®
OCC	Office of the Controller of Currency
OTS	Office of Thrift Supervision
VA	(See DVA) Veterans Administration

Common Terms

ACRS	Accelerated cost recovery system
APR	Annual percentage rate
ARM	Adjustable rate mortgage
CC&R	Covenants, Conditions & Restrictions
CMA	Competitive market analysis
CPM	Certified property manager
CRV	Certificate of reasonable value
GIM	Gross income multiplier
GPM	Graduated payment mortgage

GRM	Gross rent multiplier
LLC	Limited liability company
LTV	Loan-to-value ratio
MAI	Member of the Appraisal Institute
MIP	Mortgage insurance premium
MLS	Multiple-listing service
NOI	Net operating income
PITI	Principal, interest, taxes and insurance
PMI	Private mortgage insurance
PMM	Purchase-money mortgage
POB	Point of beginning
PUD	Planned unit development
RAM	Reverse annuity mortgage
REIT	Real estate investment trust
S&Ls	Saving and loan associations
UFMIP	Upfront mortgage insurance premium
URAR	Uniform Residential Appraisal Report
USPAP	Uniform Standards of Professional Appraisal Practice

Acronyms To Help Remember Key Concepts

PETE	Government powers: Police powers, Eminent domain, Taxes, and Escheat
TTIP	Unities for joint tenancy: Time. Title, Interest, Possession
DUST	Elements of value: Demand, Utility, Scarcity, Transferability
CPUD	Bundle of rights: Control, Possession, Use, Disposition
MCI	Approaches to appraising: Market data, Cost, Income
COALD	Agent's duties to principal: Care, Obedience, Accounting, Loyalty, Disclosure
CBS	Adjustments in the market data approach: Comparable Better Subtract
SBA	Adjustments in the market data approach: Subject Better Add

SUMMARY OF LAWS AFFECTING REAL ESTATE

This section of the Study Tool Kit includes a brief description of some important laws and regulations that affect real estate. Many of the laws listed in this section have had amendments passed in later years. The description given includes the provisions of both the original act and subsequent amendments.

Air Quality Act (1967)

Requires that the EPA establish and enforce air quality standards. Also gives citizens and special interest groups the right to sue alleged polluters. Recent amendments to the law have added new standards to protect areas with clean air from deteriorating.

Americans with Disabilities Act (1990)

Protects employment and accessibility rights of individuals with physical and mental impairments. "Places of public accommodations" (hotels, restaurants, etc.) must be newly constructed or modified to remove architectural barriers to the disabled. Examples of changes include widening doors, making curb cuts in sidewalks, installing ramps and installing raised toilet seats and grab bars in restrooms.

Civil Rights Act of 1866

The earliest federal fair housing act. Prohibits discrimination in the sale or rent of real estate based on race. This law affects all housing.

Civil Rights Act of 1964

Prohibits discrimination based on race. Only affects housing that receives federal funds, thus limiting the percentage of housing affected.

Civil Rights Act of 1968

The federal Fair Housing Act was included in the Civil Rights Act of 1968. Prohibits discrimination based on race, gender, religion, national origin, color, mental or physical handicap and familial status (families with children) when selling or renting residential real estate. Affects most residential housing of one to four units.

Coastal Zone Management Act (1972)

Its purpose is to preserve, protect, develop and restore or enhance coastal resources for future generations. Develops management programs for use of coastal land and water resources. An amendment in 1976 created a fund to help states provide public facilities and manage growth in coastal areas.

Community Bank Reinvestment Act (1977)

Encourages banks to meet the credit needs of their communities to prevent redlining and discrimination. Lenders must prepare community reinvestment statements defining their business areas and must make a reasonable percentage of loans in those areas. A lender's credit activities are subject to audit by government agencies. Implementation of the act is defined through Regulation BB issued by the Federal Reserve System.

Comprehensive Environmental Response, Compensation, and Liability Act (1980)

This act was passed to correct the environmental problems caused by abandoned hazardous waste sites. Sites containing hazardous substances are identified, action is taken to ensure the sites are cleaned up and reimbursement for cleanup expenses is sought from the parties responsible for creating the problem.

Consumer Credit Protection Act (1960)

Provides consumer rights in the areas of credit reporting, disclosure of credit terms, inaccurate and unfair credit billing and credit card practices. Provisions of this act that affect real estate lending are found in the Truth-in-Lending and Fair Credit Reporting acts (see Truth-in-Lending Act and the Fair Credit Reporting Act).

Equal Credit Opportunity Act (1974)

Protects borrowers from discrimination when seeking a loan. Prohibits lenders from denying a loan on the basis of race, color, age, religion, national origin, gender, marital status or applicant's receipt of funds from public assistance, alimony or child support. Lenders also cannot discriminate against applicants who exercised any right under the Consumer Credit Protection Act. An applicant must be notified of the lender's credit decision within 30 days of the loan application. A reasonable reason for denial of a loan must be given if requested by the applicant. An applicant's income from a steady part-time job must be included in the lender's loan decision.

Fair Credit Reporting Act

Intended to protect consumers from inaccurate credit bureau information. Allows consumers to correct inaccurate information on credit reports and requires that credit bureau reports be kept confidential.

Fair Housing Act of 1968 (See Civil Rights Act of 1968)

Fair Housing Amendment Act (1988)

An amendment to the 1968 Fair Housing Act that added families with children (familial status) and people with mental and physical handicaps as protected classes.

Federal Flood Insurance Program (1968)

Created by the National Flood Insurance Act (see the National Flood Insurance Act).

Financial Institutions Reform, Recovery and Enforcement Act (FIRREA) (1989)

Also called the Savings and Loan (S&L) bailout bill, it was intended to address the problem of failing financial institutions and implement reforms to prevent the problem from happening again. FIRREA also was intended to upgrade the professionalism and competency of the appraisal profession. It created mandatory real estate appraisal requirements known as the Uniform Standards of Professional Appraisal Practice (USPAP). It also required that each state establish and administer a system for licensing and certifying appraisers.

Home Mortgage Disclosure Act (1975)

Also referred to as Regulation C. The purpose of this act is to prevent redlining and discrimination by lenders. Lenders are required to provide information on lending activities by geographic area to government agencies.

Housing and Community Development Act (1974)

An amendment to the 1968 Fair Housing Act. Added gender (sex) as a protected class.

Interstate Land Sales Full Disclosure Act (1968)

Requires developers of subdivisions with 25 or more lots to file a property report for prospective buyers for subdivisions with 100 or more lots, and a statement of record with the Office of Interstate Land Sales and also with the Department of Housing and Urban Development (HUD). These must be filed before the developer promotes or offers the land lots for sale or lease. Applies to land sold or leased in interstate commerce.

Jones v. Alfred E. Mayer

A 1968 U.S. Supreme Court civil rights case. The court ruled that the 1866 Civil Rights Act, prohibiting discrimination based on race in all housing, would be enforced.

National Environmental Policy Act (NEPA) (1969)

Promotes efforts to reduce damage to the environment. Requires the filing of an Environmental Impact Statement with the Environmental Protection Agency (EPA) to ensure that proposed land projects do not adversely affect the environment.

National Flood Insurance Act (1968)

This act created the Federal Flood Insurance Program (NFIP) to help provide property owners with coverage for losses due to flooding. The program makes flood insurance available at reasonable rates to property owners in flood-prone areas. Communities that agree to take steps to manage and control local flooding can participate in the NFIP. Owners seeking loans on property in a designated floodplain are required to obtain flood insurance.

Real Estate Settlement Procedures Act (RESPA) (1974)

Regulates closing and settlement procedures in federally related mortgage transactions. Provides for disclosure to the buyer and seller of real estate settlement costs, requires that an information booklet explaining the nature of real estate settlement services be provided to the buyer, requires the use of a common closing statement format and prohibits unearned kickbacks.

Regulation Z

Regulations issued by the Federal Reserve System implementing the Truth-in-Lending Act (See Truth-in-Lending Act).

Resources Conservation and Recovery Act (1976)

Defines hazardous material and sets safety standards for its transportation, storage, use, treatment, disposal and cleanup. Gives the Environmental Protection Agency the authority to make state grants for hazardous waste treatment programs.

Sherman Antitrust Act (1890)

Prohibits restraints and monopolies in business that inhibit free competition. Activities of real estate agents fall under this act. Examples of antitrust activities for which real estate agents could be sued include price fixing and market allocation.

Statutes of Frauds

Intended to prevent fraudulent contracts by requiring that certain contracts must be in writing. All states have adopted statutes of frauds.

Contracts that must be in writing to be enforceable include

- contracts for the sale of real estate;
- land contracts, options to purchase, deeds and mortgages;
- contracts not to be performed with in one year of the date created; and
- contracts for the sale of personal property over $500.

Statutes of Limitations

Set time limits within which certain actions must be brought to court. The time limits vary by state and types of legal action (generally between three and seven years). After the time expires, the action may not be enforced in court.

Superfund Amendments and Reauthorization Act (1986)

This act defines stringent cleanup standards for sites containing hazardous substances and expands liability for the cleanup costs. Current owners may be held responsible even though the problem was created by previous owners.

Truth-in-Lending Act (1968)

Part of the Consumer Protection Credit Act and implemented by the Federal Reserve's Regulation Z. The purpose of the act is to inform borrowers of costs associated with loans. The law requires various disclosures by the lender, including the finance charge and the annual percentage rate (APR).

Uniform Partnership Act

A model act adopted by most states establishes the legality of the partnership form of ownership. Also provides that title to real estate can be held in the partnership name.

Uniform Vendor and Purchaser Risk Act

This law has been adopted in many states. It is used to determine which party will suffer the loss if property in a real estate sales transaction is damaged or destroyed before legal title has passed to the buyer. The risk of loss does not pass from the seller (vendor) to the buyer (vendee) until either (1) title has passed to the buyer or (2) the buyer has taken possession of the property. This is true unless provisions in the purchase agreement state otherwise.

Water Pollution Control Act (1972)

Establishes regulatory programs to restore and maintain the quality of the country's waters. Provides standards for water pollution controls. Includes effluent limitations, water quality standards, municipal pollution controls and waste treatments. Establishes pollution discharge programs and state grants for construction of sewage treatment plants.

REAL ESTATE INTERNET SITES

INTRODUCTION

This section of the Study Tool Kit provides a brief description of Internet sites that include useful information for anyone interested in real estate. Internet sites are constantly changing and the information in this section was accurate at the time of printing.

REAL ESTATE ORGANIZATIONS

American Institute of Architects (AIA) - http://www.aiaonline.com

Includes information on the organization as well as materials and resources for architects.

American Society of Home Inspectors (ASHI) - http://www.ashi.com

Association for home inspectors. Members must pass the ASHI examination and meet continuing education requirements.

Building Owners and Managers Association International (BOMA) - http://www.bomi.edu.org

This association is made up of owners, managers, investors, and developers of commercial buildings. It includes the Building Owners and Managers Institute (BOMI), which provides educational programs for property owners and managers.

Federal Home Loan Mortgage Corp (FHLMC) - http://www.freddiemac.com

Also known as "Freddie Mac." This site provides information on FHLMC financial mortgage backed securities, services and housing initiatives.

Federal National Mortgage Association (FNMA) http://www.fanniemae.com

Also known as "Fannie Mae." This site includes information on FNMA financial mortgage backed securities, services and housing initiatives, lists of FNMA-owned properties in all 50 states.

Government National Mortgage Association (GNMA) - http://www.ginniemae.com

Also known as "Ginnie Mae." This site includes information on GNMA financial mortgage backed securities, services and housing initiatives.

National Association of Home Builders - http://www.nahb.com

Includes a large database of building industry and home improvement information.

National Association of Real Estate Brokers (NAREB) - nareb@aol.org

Conducts research, educational and certification programs. Its objectives are to promote high standards of conduct in the real estate profession and protect the public from unethical or fraudulent practices.

National Association of REALTORS® (NAR) - http://www.realtor.com

Information about the various REALTOR® associations, funding a home, moving tips, mortgages and products from the REALTOR® bookstore.

National Association of Remodeling Industry - http://www.nari.com

Includes basic information a homeowner needs before starting a home remodeling project. Also provides links to remodelers and suppliers in local areas.

Real Estate Educators Association (REEA) - http://www.realed.holhowww.com

Members of this organization are involved in all aspects of real estate education.

GOVERNMENT AGENCIES

Department of Housing and Urban Development (HUD) - http://www.hud.gov

Information on community development loans and initiatives, affordable housing opportunities, HUD homeless assistance programs and environmental regulations.

Department of Veterans Affairs (DVA) - http://www.va.gov

A federal government agency created to assist veterans. Their site includes history of the VA and information on programs for veterans.

Environmental Protection Agency - http://www.epa.gov

The EPA's mission is to protect human health and safeguard the natural environment. The site includes EPA projects and programs and definitions for commonly used terminology.

Federal Deposit Insurance Corporation (FDIC) - http://www.fdic.gov

An agency of the Federal Reserve System, it insures bank and thrift deposits. The site includes statistical information on the banking industry, banking laws and regulations.

Federal Emergency Management Agency (FEMA) - http://www.fema.gov

Among its activities it administers the National Flood Insurance Program (NFIP).

Internal Revenue Service (IRS) - http://www. irs.ustreas.gov

The IRS site includes federal tax forms, publications and information on new tax laws.

Federal Housing Authority (FHA) - http://www.hud.gov

A division of the Department of Housing and Urban Development (HUD), the FHA's principal role is to insure residential mortgages.

Federal Reserve System (the "FED") - http://www.frb.gov

Established by Congress to help maintain a sound credit and economic environment and counteract inflation and deflation trends. This site includes the purpose and function of the FED, information from the Federal Open Market Committee, financial statistics and regulations regarding enforcement action.

National Safety Council - http://www.nsc

This site includes the National Lead Information Center, which provides information on environmental lead poisoning.

Office of the Controller of Currency (OCC) - http://www. occ.treas.gov

The OCC is responsible for monitoring and regulating the thrift industry.

US Census Bureau - http://www.census.gov

This site includes statistical social, demographic and economic information.

OTHER SITES PROVIDING REAL ESTATE INFORMATION

IRED - http://www.ired.com

A real estate directory with links to thousands of real estate bulletin boards

FedStats - http://www.fedstats.gov

The Federal Interagency Council on Statistical Policy maintains this site to provide easy access to statistics produced by more than 70 federal government agencies. Also includes links to many federal government agency Internet sites.

US Geological Survey (USGS) - http://www.USGS

The USGS provides information to describe and understand the Earth. The site includes laws and regulations governing USGS activities, its history and mapping products and services.

National Fair Housing Advocate - http://www.fairhousing.com

Includes news and information regarding the issues of housing discrimination.

REAL ESTATE MATH REVIEW

Math plays an important role in the real estate business and is used in every real estate transaction. Realizing this, state licensing officials include math questions in the state licensing examinations. To be a real estate professional and pass the licensing examinations, applicants must be familiar with simple mathematical concepts and formulas. The thought of having to solve math problems on a licensing test creates apprehension for many people studying real estate, but this should not be the case because the math involved usually consists of simple arithmetic. To solve real estate math problems, all that is required is the ability to read and analyze the facts carefully, identify the correct formula or process and solve using addition, subtraction, multiplication and division.

This section of the Study Tool Kit explains some of the basic mathematical concepts used most frequently in real estate transactions and licensing examinations. These include measurement, area and volume, fractions, and percentages and decimals. There are also practical examples of applying mathematics to real estate situations.

HINTS FOR SOLVING MATH PROBLEMS

Read the question carefully to determine what information is being asked for.

Take note of the measurements or units given in the problems and the measurements asked for in the answers (e.g., annual, semiannual or monthly amounts).

If using a calculator, be careful to place the decimal in the proper position when entering numbers.

Try working math problems backward, using the various answers to determine which one matches the information given in the problem.

Key Terms

____ *Annual* – Yearly.

____ *Area* – The number of square units (square feet, square yards, etc.) in a two-dimensional (length, width) space.

____ *Capitalization (Cap) Rate* – Used to calculate the rate of return on an investment.

____ *Front Foot* – A measurement of the width (in feet) of a property's side that faces the frontage (the main street).

____ *Mill* – Equal to 1/10 of a cent or $.001. Used to express a tax rate.

____ *Percent* – Means "per hundred" and represents a portion of a whole expressed as 100. Percentages can be less than or greater than 100.

____ *Perimeter* – Total length of the boundary of a two-dimensional figure (square, rectangle, etc.).

____ *Principal* – The amount of money borrowed.

____ *Quarterly* – Four times per year.

____ *Volume* – The number of cubic units (cubic feet, cubic yards, etc.) contained in a three-dimensional (height, length and width) space.

FIGURE H-1
Measurements and Formulas Used in Real Estate

Linear Measurements

1 Foot = 12 Inches
1 Yard = 3 Feet
1 Rod = 16½ Feet
1 Chain = 66 Feet
1 Mile = 5,280 Feet

Square Measurements

1 Sq. Foot = 144 Sq. Inches
1 Sq. Yard = 9 Sq. Feet
1 Acre = 160 Sq. Rods
1 Acre = 43,560 Sq. Feet
1 Sq. Mile = 640 Acres
1 Section = 1 Sq. Mile
1 Township = 36 Sections

Cubic Measurements

1 Cu. Foot = 1,728 Cu. Inches
1 Cu. Yard = 27 Cu. Feet

Circular Measurements

Circle = 360 Degrees
1 Degree = 60 Minutes
1 Minute = 60 Seconds

Formulas

Area of Square = 1 Side × 1 Side
Area of Rectangle = Width × Length
Area of Triangle = ½ Base × Height
Volume of Cube or Rectangle = Length × Width × Height

MEASUREMENTS

Measurements are used in calculations to find perimeter, area and volume. *Linear measurement* measures the distance from one point to another. Some measurements commonly used in real estate are included in Figure H.1.

Converting Units of Measurement

a. Convert square feet to square inches = No. of square feet × 144.

EXAMPLE: *How many square inches does three square feet equal? (3 × 144 = 432 sq. in.)*

b. Convert square inches to square feet = No. of square inches ÷ 144.

EXAMPLE: *How many square feet does 432 square inches equal? (423 ÷ 144 = 3 sq. ft.)*

c. Convert square yards to square feet = No. of square yards × 9.

EXAMPLE: *How many square feet does three square yards equal? (3 × 9 = 27 sq. ft.)*

d. Convert square feet to square yards = No. of square feet ÷ 9.

EXAMPLE: *How many square yards does 27 square feet equal? (27 ÷ 9 = 3 sq. yds.)*

e. Convert square yards to square inches = No. of square yards × 1,296.

EXAMPLE: *How many square inches does three square yards equal? (3 × 1,296 = 3,888 sq. in.).*

f. Convert square inches to square yards = No. of square inches ÷ 1,296.

EXAMPLE: *How many square yards does 3,888 square inches equal? (3,888 ÷ 1,296 = 3 sq. yds.)*

g. Convert cubic feet to cubic yards = No. of cubic feet ÷ 27.

EXAMPLE: *How many cubic yards does 381 cubic feet equal? (381 ÷ 27 = 3 cu. yds.)*

h. Convert square feet to acres = No. of square feet ÷ 43,560.

EXAMPLE: How many acres does 130,680 square feet equal? (130,680 ÷ 43,560 = 3 acres)

FRACTIONS

A fraction has a numerator (the top number) and a denominator (the bottom number) divided by a bar.

Types of Fractions

a. Proper fractions (also called simple fractions): The numerator is smaller than the denominator (i.e., expresses a value less than 1).

EXAMPLE: ¼, ½, ¾, ¹⁵⁄₁₆

b. Improper fractions: The numerator is larger than the denominator (i.e., expresses a value greater than 1).

EXAMPLE: ³⁄₂, ⁴⁄₃, ⁶⁄₅, ¹²⁄₁₁

c. Mixed number: A whole plus a fraction.

EXAMPLE: 1½, 2¾, 5⅜

Simplifying Fractions

Fractions should always be simplified (reduced to their lowest terms). This is done by finding the highest number by which both the numerator and the denominator can be divided evenly.

EXAMPLE: ⁴⁄₆ = ²⁄₃, ³⁄₆ = ½, ⁸⁄₁₆ = ½

Multiplying Fractions

1. Multiply the numerators.
2. Multiply the denominators.
3. Reduce to lowest terms.

EXAMPLE: ²⁄₄ × ⁸⁄₁₂ = ¹⁶⁄₄₈ = ⅓

Dividing Fractions

Invert the divisor (the fraction you are dividing by), then solve the same as multiplication.

EXAMPLE: ¾ ÷ ⅔ = ¾ × ³⁄₂ = ⁹⁄₈ = 1⅛

PERCENTAGES AND DECIMALS

Percentages

Percent (%) means "per hundred" or per hundred parts.

EXAMPLE: 50% = 50 parts of 100 (or ½)

FIGURE H.2
Common Symbols Used

a = area
b = base
d = depth
h = height
l = length
v = volume
w = width
d and h are interchangeable

cu. = cubic
ft. = feet
in. = inches
sq. = square
′ = feet
″ = inches

× = multiply
÷ or / = divide

Converting a Percent to a Decimal

To use a percent in a mathematical calculation, it must be converted to a decimal. Drop the percent sign (%) and move the decimal two places *to the left* (i.e., divide the percentage by 100).

EXAMPLE: 1% = .01, 10% = .10, 20% = .20, 150% = 1.50 or 1.5

Converting Decimals and Fractions to a Percent

To convert a decimal, move the decimal point two places *to the right* and add the percent sign (i.e., multiply by 100). To convert a fraction to a percent, divide the numerator by the denominator and convert the resulting decimal number to a percent.

EXAMPLE: .01 = 1%, .10 = 10%, .75 = 75%, 1.2 = 120%
$\frac{1}{2}$ = 1 ÷ 2 = .5 = 50%, $\frac{3}{4}$ = 3 ÷ 4 = .75 = 75%

Converting a Percent to a Simple Fraction

Drop the percent sign (%), place the percentage over 100, then reduce to a simple fraction.

EXAMPLE: 1% = $\frac{1}{100}$, 10% = $\frac{10}{100}$ = $\frac{1}{10}$, 20% = $\frac{20}{100}$ = $\frac{1}{5}$, 150% = $\frac{150}{100}$ = 1$\frac{1}{2}$

Adding and Subtracting Decimals

To add or subtract decimals, place the decimal points directly over one another and then add or subtract.

EXAMPLE:

$$
\begin{array}{r}
234.56 \\
+562.23 \\
\hline
796.79
\end{array}
\qquad
\begin{array}{r}
653.78 \\
-432.65 \\
\hline
221.13
\end{array}
$$

Multiplying and Dividing Decimals

When multiplying, count the number of decimal places in the numbers being multiplied, then move the decimal in the answer to the left the same number of places. When dividing, move the decimal in the dividing number (the divisor) to the right to make it a whole number. Then move the decimal the same number of spaces to the right in the number being divided (the dividend).

EXAMPLE:

$$
\begin{array}{r}
6.11 \\
\times 4.23 \\
\hline
25.8453
\end{array}
$$

$$80.5 \div .25 = 8050 \div 25 = 322$$

or

$$.25\overline{)80.5} \quad = 25\overline{)8050}^{\,322}$$

PERIMETER, AREA AND VOLUME

Performing calculations to find the perimeter, area and volume of land, buildings and other objects is done frequently in the real estate business. When computing the area and volume, the symbols and abbreviations in Figure H.2 are often used.

Perimeter

To find the perimeter, add all of the exterior dimensions.

a. The perimeter of the tract of land shown below is 100' + 55' + 75' + 60'+ 50' + 45 = 385'.

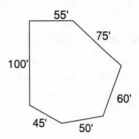

b. The perimeter of the building shown below is 80' + 30' + 50' + 10' + 30' + 40' = 240'.

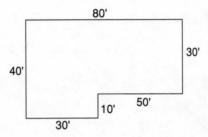

Area of a Square

A square has four sides of the same length. To calculate the area of a square, multiply one side by another. This is the same as finding the square of one of the sides.

Area = 1 side × 1 side

EXAMPLE: The area of the square below is 10' × 10' = 100 sq. ft.

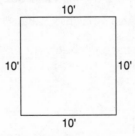

Area of a Rectangle

Any surface with four straight sides is called a quadrilateral. A rectangle is a quadrilateral in which the sides are joined at right angles and the opposite sides are the same length and are parallel to each other. To find the area, multiply the length by the width.

Area = Width × Length or a = w × l

EXAMPLE:

The area of the rectangle below is 10′ × 20′ = 200 sq. ft.

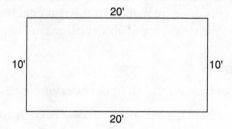

Area of a Parallelogram

A parallelogram is a quadrilateral with two sets of parallel sides. To find the area, the height is multiplied by the base. The height is the perpendicular distance between the parallel sides.

Area = Height × Base or a = h × b

EXAMPLE:

The area of the parallelogram below is 200′ × 75′ = 15,000 sq. ft.

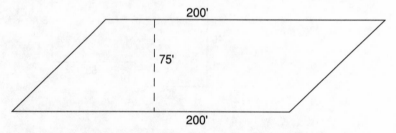

Area of a Trapezoid

A trapezoid is a quadrilateral with only one pair of parallel sides. The parallel sides are called *bases* and the nonparallel sides are called *legs*. To find the area, the height is multiplied by one half of the sum of the parallel sides (the bases). The height is the perpendicular distance between the parallel sides.

Area = Height × ½(Base 1 + Base 2) or a = ½(b₁+b₂)

EXAMPLE: The area of the trapezoid below is
25′ × .5(20′ + 30′)
25′ × 25′ = 625 sq. ft.

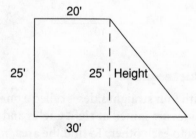

Area of a Triangle

A triangle is a three-sided figure. To find the area, multiply the base times the height and divide by 2.

$$\text{Area} = (\text{Base} \times \text{Height}) \div 2 \text{ or } a = (b \times h)$$

EXAMPLE: The area of the triangle below is
$(60' \times 40') \div 2 = 2,400' \div 2 = 1,200$ sq. ft.

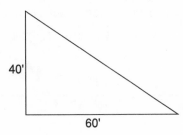

Computing the Volume of a Cube

To calculate the volume of a cube, multiply Length × Width × Height ($l \times w \times h$).

EXAMPLE: The volume of the cube below is
$25' \times 25' \times 25' = 15,625$ cu. ft.

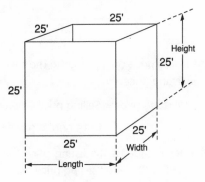

COMMISSION CALCULATIONS

a. Calculate the total commission owed on the sale of a property. The commission rate is 6 percent and the sales price is $150,000.

Commission amount = Sales price × Rate of commission

$150,000 × .06 = $9,000

b. Calculate the total commission owed on the sale of a property. The commission rate is 6 percent on the first $50,000 of the sales price and 5 percent on the remainder of the sales price. The property sold for $150,000.

Commission amount = Sales price × Rate of commission

(.06 × $50,000 = $3,000) + (.05 × $100,000 = $5,000)
$3,000 + $5,000 = $8,000

c. Calculate a commission split. The commission rate charged by a real estate company is 6 percent of the selling price and the company's salesperson receives 60 percent of the commission. The property sold for $110,000. How much commission was received by the company and how much by the salesperson?

$$\text{Commission amount} = \text{Sales price} \times \text{Rate of commission}$$
$$\text{Commission Split} = \text{Commission amount} \times \% \text{ received}$$

$$\$110,000 \times .06 = \$6,600$$
$$\$6,600 \times .6 = \$3,960 \text{ (salesperson) and } \$6,600 \times .4 = \$2,640 \text{ (company)}$$

d. Calculate the rate of commission. The commission amount was $6,000 and the sales price was $120,000.

$$\text{Commission rate} = \text{Amount of commission} \div \text{Sales price}$$

$$\$6,000 \div \$120,000 = .05, \text{ or } 5\%$$

CALCULATING THE SALES PRICE

Calculate the sales price of a property. The commission rate was 6 percent and the amount of commission was $6,000.

$$\text{Sales price} = \text{Amount of commission} \div \text{Commission rate}$$
$$\$6,000 \div .06 = \$100,000$$

LISTING CALCULATIONS

a. Calculate the listing price on a property. The selling price was $135,000, which was 90 percent of the listing price.

$$\text{Listing price} = \text{Selling price} \div \text{Percentage of listing price}$$

$$\$135,000 \div .9 = \$150,000$$

b. Calculate the percentage of the listing price the seller accepted. The listing price on the property was $160,000 and its selling price was $140,000.

$$\text{Percentage of listing price} = \text{Selling price} \div \text{Listing price}$$

$$\$140,000 \div \$160,000 = 87.5\%$$

c. Calculate the selling price on a net listing. The seller expects to net $90,000, and the broker expects to make 6 percent commission on the sale.

$$\text{Selling price} = \text{Net to seller} \div (100\% - \text{Commission rate})$$

$$\$90,000 \div (100\% - 6\%) = \$90,000 \div .94 = \$95,745$$

INSURANCE CALCULATIONS—PROPERTY INSURANCE

a. Calculate the annual homeowner's premium if the policy has a face value of $220,000 and the premium rate is $4.75 per $1,000.

$$\text{Annual premium} = (\text{Policy value} \div \$1,000) \times \text{Rate}$$

$$(\$220,000 \div \$1,000) \times \$4.75 = \$1,045$$

b. Calculate the face value of a homeowner's insurance policy. The annual premium rate is $4.25 per $1,000 of face value and the annual premium is $892.50.

Policy value = (Annual premium ÷ Premium rate) × $1,000

($892.5 ÷ $4.25) × $1,000 = $210,000

INSURANCE CALCULATIONS—TITLE INSURANCE

Calculate the total premium of a title insurance policy that covers both the owner (mortgagor) and the lender (mortgagee). The property sold for $180,000 and the owner financed the purchase with a $140,000 mortgage. The premium for the owner's coverage is $4.25 per $1,000 of face value and the premium for the lender's coverage is $3.50 per $1,000 of face value.

Owner's policy premium = (Value of property ÷ $1,000) × Premium rate
($180,000 ÷ $1,000) × $4.25 = $765

Lender's policy premium = (Amount of the loan ÷ $1,000) × Premium rate
($140,000 ÷ $1,000) × $3.50 = $490

Total premium = Owner's policy premium + Lender's policy premium
$765 + $490 = $1,255

INSURANCE CALCULATIONS—MORTGAGE INSURANCE

Private mortgage insurance is required by lenders when making a mortgage with a very high loan-to-value ratio. Calculate the borrower's monthly mortgage insurance premium (P) if the mortgage (m) is for $110,000 and the annual premium is ¾ percent (r) of the original loan amount paid in monthly installments.

Monthly insurance premium = (Loan amount × Annual premium rate) ÷ 12 months

($110,000 × .0075) ÷ 12 = $68.75

LOAN CALCULATIONS

a. Calculate the annual interest and monthly interest on a nonamortizing loan (simple interest loan). The loan balance is $90,000 and the annual interest rate is 8 percent.

Annual interest = Loan balance × Interest rate

Monthly interest = Yearly interest ÷ 12

$90,000 × .08 = $7,200

$7,200 ÷ 12 = $600

b. Calculate the amount of a loan payment that is applied to the loan balance (principal). The beginning loan balance is $75,000, the interest rate is 9 percent and the loan payment is $600.

Payment to principal = Loan payment − (Loan balance × Interest rate ÷ 12)

Principal = (Loan balance × Interest Rate ÷ 12) − Loan payment

$75,000 × .09 ÷ 12 = $562.5
$600 − $562.50 = $37.50

c. Calculate the total amount of interest paid on a loan. The beginning loan balance is $60,000, the interest rate is 9 percent, the loan term is 15 years and the monthly loan payment is $609.

Total interest = Total amount paid − Amount borrowed

15 years × 12 months = 180 months
180 × $609 = $109,620 total amount paid
$109,620 − $60,000 = $49,620 interest paid

d. Calculate the amount paid in points. One point equals 1 percent of the loan amount. The loan amount is $80,000, and the lender requires payment of 3½ points.

Dollars in points = Loan amount × Number of points

$80,000 × .035 = $2,800

e. Calculate the number of points paid. One point equals 1 percent of the loan amount. The loan amount is $75,000, and the borrower paid $2,250.

Number of points = Amount paid in points ÷ Loan amount × 100

$2,250 ÷ $75,000 × 100 = 3 points

f. Calculate the loan-to-value ratio. The loan amount is $70,000 and the property is worth $87,500.

Loan-to-value ratio = Loan amount ÷ Property value

$70,000 ÷ $87,500 = .80 = 80% loan-to-value ratio

REAL ESTATE TAX CALCULATIONS

a. Calculate the tax rate. The assessed property in a taxing district is $275,000,000 and income from taxes need to meet its budget is $15,000,000.

Tax rate = Tax income ÷ Assessed value

$15,000,000 ÷ $275,000,000 = .0545

This rate also can be expressed as 5.45%, 54.5 mills or $5.45 per $100 of assessed value.

b. Calculate the assessed value of a property. The market value of the property is $178,000, and property is assessed at a rate of 20 percent of market value.

Assessed value = Property's market value × Assessed rate

$178,000 × .2 = $35,600

c. Calculate the real estate tax on a property. The assessed value of the property is $40,000, and the tax rate is $3.75 per $100 of assessed value.

$$\text{Real estate tax} = (\text{Assessed value} \div 100) \times \text{Tax rate}$$

$$(\$40,000 \div \$100) \times \$3.75 = \$1,500$$

d. Calculate the market value of a property. The property was assessed at 80 percent of market value, the tax rate is 5 percent and the amount of the tax is $1,875.

$$\text{Market value} = (\text{Real estate tax} \div \text{Tax rate}) \div \text{Assessment rate}$$

$$\$1,875 \div .05 = \$37,500$$

$$\$37,500 \div .8 = \$46,875$$

TRANSFER TAX CALCULATIONS

Calculate the amount of the transfer tax (T). A property sold for $168,000 (P). The state transfer tax was based on the sales price at a rate of $1 per thousand ($R_1$), and the county transfer tax was $.50 per thousand ($R_2$).

$$T = (P \times R_1) + (P \times R_2)$$

$$(\$168,000 \times .001 = \$168) + (\$168,000 \times .0005 = \$84)$$

$$\$168 + \$84 = \$252$$

CAPITALIZATION CALCULATIONS

Capitalization calculations are used frequently by investors and in appraising properties that generate operating income. The capitalization rate is based on the amount invested and the annual net income from the property. Investors use it to calculate the rate of return they will receive on the money they invest and to determine the appropriate purchase price for a property based on its net income.

a. Calculate the capitalization rate. A property is worth $635,000 and generates net income of $50,800.

$$\text{Capitalization rate} = \text{Net operating income} \div \text{value of the property}$$

$$\$50,800 \div \$635,000 = .08 \text{ or } 8\%$$

b. Calculate the value of a property using the capitalization rate. A property generates net income of $63,000, and the capitalization rate is 9 percent.

$$\text{Property value} = \text{Net operating income} \div \text{Capitalization rate}$$

$$\$63,000 \div .09 = \$700,000$$

c. Calculate the net income of a property using the amount invested and the capitalization rate. An investor paid $350,000 for a property that returns a capitalization rate of 9 percent to the investor.

$$\text{Net operating income} = \text{Property value} \times \text{Capitalization rate}$$

$$\$350,000 \times .09 = \$31,500$$

DEPRECIATION CALCULATIONS

a. Calculate the amount of yearly and accumulated depreciation. A property was purchased four years ago for $450,000. The value of the land was $80,000 and the property was depreciated at 3 percent per year.

Yearly depreciation = (Original value − Land Value) × Rate of depreciation

Accumulated depreciation = (Yearly depreciation × Number of years depreciated)

$$(\$450,000 − \$80,000) × .03 = \$11,100$$

$$\$11,100 × 4 = \$44,400$$

b. Calculate the original value of a property. A property was purchased six years ago and has been depreciated at a rate of 3 percent per year. The remaining depreciable balance is $360,800. The value of the land at the time purchase was $40,000.

Property's original value = Remaining balance ÷ (Years depreciated
× Rate of depreciation − 100%) + Land value

$$\$360,800 ÷ (6 × .03 − 1) = \$440,000 + \$40,000 = \$480,000$$

LEASE CALCULATIONS

Calculate the annual rent on a percentage lease. The rent charged is $500 a month plus 4 percent of gross sales, and the tenant had gross sales of $230,000 in the year.

Annual rent = (Monthly rent × 12 months) + (.04 × Gross sales)

$$\$500 × 12 = \$6,000$$
$$.04 × \$230,000 = \$9,200$$
$$\$6,000 + \$9,200 = \$15,200$$

Legal Description Calculations

A circle = 360 degrees; One degree = 60 minutes; One minute = 60 seconds

Number of acres = 640 (acres in a section) ÷ denominators in description:
Calculate the number of acres in the S½, NW¼, SE¼ = 640 ÷ 4 ÷ 4 ÷ 2 = 20 acres

Proration Calculations

a. Actual number of days in the year proration method = Yearly expense ÷ 365 (366 for leap yrs.) × No. of days in proration period
b. Actual number of days in the month proration method = Yearly expense ÷ 12 ÷ No. of days in closing mos. × No. of days in proration period
c. Statutory month proration method = Yearly expense ÷ 12 ÷ 30 days × No. of days in proration period

Commission Calculations

a. Commission amount = Selling price × Commission rate
b. Commission rate = Amount of commission ÷ Selling price
c. Selling price = Amount of commission ÷ Commission rate

MATH REVIEW PRACTICE EXERCISES

1. If a real estate broker earned a commission of $7,500 at a rate of 6 percent, the selling price of a property was
   a. $75,000.
   b. $79,787.
   c. $120,000.
   d. $125,000.

2. If a property sold for the amount of its assessed value, the annual tax on the property is $1,200 and the tax rate is $1.50 per $100 of assessed value, the selling price of the property was
   a. $1,200.
   b. $1,800.
   c. $8,000.
   d. $80,000.

3. The annual rent in a lease agreement is to be 3.5 percent of the tenant's gross sales with a minimum annual rent of $6,800. What will be the amount of the rent if the sales are $236,000?
   a. $6,800
   b. $8,260
   c. $15,060
   d. $82,600

4. How many acres does a rectangular parcel of land contain if it is 120 feet deep and 20 yards wide?
   a. .06 acre
   b. .17 acre
   c. 6 acres
   d. 17 acres

5. A salesperson earned $60,000 in commissions, which was 30 percent of the commissions earned by the office last year. The total amount of commissions earned by the office last year was
   a. $78,000.
   b. $180,000.
   c. $200,000.
   d. $20,000,000.

6. What is the market value of a commercial building if its gross income is $82,000, its operating expenses are $10,000 and an investor expects a capitalization rate of 9 percent?
   a. $80,000
   b. $800,000
   c. $920,000
   d. $911,111

7. A building with an economic life of 25 years is four years old and its current value is $218,400. The original value of the building was
   a. $225,000.
   b. $252,944.
   c. $260,000.
   d. $273,000.

8. An investor bought a condominium for $48,000. A year later the investor sold it for $52,000. What rate of return did the investor receive on the property?
   a. .083%
   b. 7.7%
   c. 8.3%
   d. 83%

9. The dimensions of a rectangular house are 68 feet by 87 feet. The square footage of the house is
   a. 155 sq. ft.
   b. 174 sq. ft.
   c. 5,916 sq. ft.
   d. 24,025 sq. ft.

10. A property sold for $262,500 and the broker earned a 6 percent commission on the sale. The broker earned
    a. $1,575.
    b. $4,375.
    c. $5,750.
    d. $15,750.

11. The real estate tax rate in mills for a taxing body that includes properties totaling $42,000,000 in assessed value and a budget of $1,890,000 is
    a. 4.5 mills.
    b. .22 mills.
    c. 45 mills.
    d. 22 mills.

12. A homebuyer makes a small down payment and receives a mortgage for $148,000 but must pay a monthly ½-point premium for private mortgage insurance (PMI). The monthly PMI premium is
    a. $61.67.
    b. $74.00.
    c. $616.67.
    d. $740.

13. The current value of an eight-year-old building is $210,000, and it has an economic life of 50 years. Its original value was
    a. $250,000.
    b. $252,000.
    c. $260,000.
    d. $410,000.

14. An investor bought a tract of land for $320,000. A year later the investor divided the tract into four parcels and sold each for $92,000. What rate of return did the investor make on the properties?
    a. .5%
    b. 34%
    c. 1.5%
    d. 15%

15. A property has a mortgage of $86,000 with an interest rate of 8.5% paid annually. The amount of interest paid for the year is
    a. $609.16.
    b. $731.
    c. $7,310.
    d. $73,100.

16. A building sold for $152,000, which was 85 percent of the listing price. The listing price was
    a. $101,333.
    b. $129,200.
    c. $178,824.
    d. $281,200.

17. A buyer obtained a loan for $94,500 and, as part of the loan agreement, paid the lender 3 points at closing. How much did the buyer pay the lender at closing?
    a. $283
    b. $2,820
    c. $2,835
    d. $28,350

18. What is the perimeter of the house shown here?

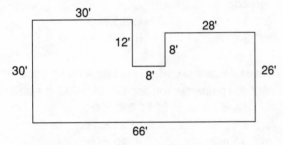

    a. 170 ft.
    b. 192 ft.
    c. 208 ft.
    d. 230 ft.

19. A landowner wishes to install a fence around the perimeter of the property illustrated. How many feet of fencing will the owner need to complete the job?

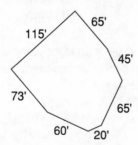

    a. 333 ft.
    b. 378 ft.
    c. 343 ft.
    d. 443 ft.

20. A property has a loan of $77,000 with an annual interest rate of 9.25%. The amount of the monthly interest payment is
    a. $594.
    b. $712.
    c. $5,935.
    d. $7,123.

21. An owner wishes to have a landscaping company spray her lot with weed killer. The landscaping company charges $.50 per 100 square feet. How much will it cost for the lot to be sprayed?

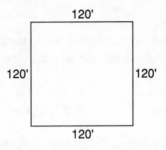

    a. $7.20
    b. $72
    c. $720
    d. $7,200

22. What is the area of the parcel of land shown here?

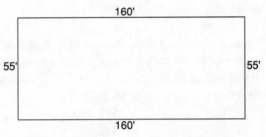

    a. 430 sq. ft.
    b. 8,800 sq. ft.
    c. 3,025 sq. ft.
    d. 25,600 sq. ft.

23. What is the volume of the cube illustrated?

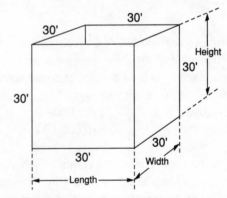

    a. 90 cu. ft.
    b. 900 cu. ft.
    c. 2,700 cu. ft.
    d. 27,000 cu. ft.

24. What is the area of the triangle?

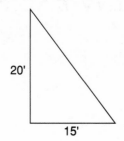

20'

15'

a. 75 sq. ft.   c. 300 sq. ft.
b. 150 sq. ft.   d. 3,000 sq. ft.

25. What is the area of the parcel of land shown?

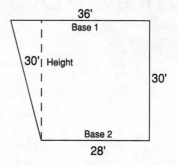

36'
Base 1

30' | Height

30'

Base 2
28'

a. 124 sq. ft.   c. 1,920 sq. ft.
b. 960 sq. ft.   d. 30,240 sq. ft.

SOLUTIONS TO THE MATH REVIEW EXERCISES

1. **d** Sales price = Commission ÷ Rate
$7,500 ÷ .06 = $125,000

2. **d** Annual tax ÷ Tax rate = Selling price
$1,200 ÷ .015 = $80,000

3. **b** Sales × Lease rate = Rent
(Or the minimum rent, whichever is higher)
$236,000 × .035 = $8,260

4. **b** 20 yards × 3 = 60 feet
120 feet × 60 feet = 7,200 sq. ft.
7,200 sq. ft. ÷ 43,560 sq. ft. = .17 acre

5. **c** $60,000 ÷ .3 = $200,000

6. **b** Gross income – Operating expenses ÷ Capitalization rate = Value
$82,000 – $10,000 ÷ .09 = $800,000

7. **c** 100% ÷ 25 = 4% depreciation each year
4 yr. × 4% = 16% depreciated (100% – 16% = 84% left)
$218,400 ÷ .84 = $260,000

8. **c** $52,000 – $48,000 = $4,000 profit
$4,000 ÷ $48,000 = 8.3%

9. **c** 68 ft. × 87 ft. = 5,916 sq. ft.

10. **d** $262,500 × .06 = $15,750

11. **c** $1,890,000 ÷ $42,000,000 = .045 = 45 mills

12. **a** $148,000 × .005 = $740
$740 ÷ 12 = $61.67

13. **a** 100% ÷ 50 = 2% depreciation each year
8 yrs. × 2% = 16% depreciated (100% – 16% = 84% left)
$218,400 ÷ .84 = $250,000

14. **d** $92,000 × 4 = $368,000
$368,000 – $320,000 = $48,000 profit
$48,000 ÷ $320,000 = 15%

15. **c** $86,000 × .085 = $7,310

16. **c** $152,000 ÷ .85 = $178,824

17. **c** $94,500 × .03 = $2,835

18. **c** 66 + 30 + 30 + 12 + 8 + 8 + 28 + 26 = 208 ft.

19. **d** 60 + 73 + 115 + 65 + 45 + 65 + 20 = 443 ft.

20. **a** $77,000 × .0925 ÷ 12 = $593.54 = $594

21. **b** 120 × 120 = 14,400 sq. ft. ÷ 100 = 144 × $.50 = $72

22. **b** 160 × 55 = 8,800 sq. ft.

23. **d** Volume = height × width × length
30 × 30 × 30 = 27,000 cu. ft.

24. **b** Area = ½ (base × height)
20 × 15 ÷ 2 = 150 sq. ft.

25. **b** Area = ½ height × (base 1 + base 2)
.5 × 30 × (36 + 28)
15 × 64 = 960 sq. ft.

COMPREHENSIVE PRACTICE EXAMINATIONS

Most state licensing agencies use examinations as one of the methods for determining the candidate's qualifications for licensing. The purpose of an exam is to measure the candidate's knowledge of various real estate topics as part of their evaluation for licensing. Most states use professional testing services to help develop and administer the licensing examinations, but some have developed their own tests. The format of most state licensing examinations consists of questions in a four-option, multiple-choice format with one correct answer for each question. The test is usually divided into two parts. One part (generally 80 to 100 questions) covers general real estate topics, and the second (30 to 50 questions) covers laws and practices specific to the state. The rest of this section includes information and tips to help you successfully complete the licensing examination.

Preparation for the Test

- Learn all you can about the test administered in your state. Examination information can usually be obtained from either the testing service used by the state or the state agency that administers licensing.
- Register for the test date and site location as early as possible because your preferred test date and site may fill up quickly.
- Visit the test site before the test date to locate parking and determine how long the commute will be to the test site.
- The night before, assemble all items needed for the test. These could include identification for access to the site, a watch, any fees required to be paid at the test site, a calculator (test to be sure it is working), extra batteries for the calculator, pens, pencils and erasers.
- The evening before the test quickly review topics you feel are critical or have given you the most trouble and then get to bed early. Do not stay up all night trying to study. You will probably answer more questions wrong if you are sleepy and not mentally alert.

Studying

- There is no substitute for commitment and hard work. Plan ahead to invest an adequate amount of time in reading, studying and practicing your testing skills.
- Spend adequate time studying the definition of key real estate terms. Each chapter in this book starts with a list of key terms covered in the chapter and highlights them in bold in the text. The Glossary is a good place to study the vocabulary of real estate.
- Practice test taking by using the Unit Diagnostic Tests in this book, as well as the practice tests in this section. Remember that practice tests are not a substitute for studying. Do not try to memorize the answers because subtle changes in the question you may encounter on the licensing test may change the correct answer.
- Practice taking tests under conditions similar to those you will be operating under at the licensing exam.
- When practicing with tests, note the areas you continue to have trouble with and focus your time on restudying those topics.

Taking the Test

- Arrive at the test site early to avoid rushing and putting extra pressure on yourself. Use the extra time to relax, use the bathroom and mentally prepare yourself.

- Listen to the test proctor's instructions carefully, review the test material given to you and note if anything is missing.
- Budget your time and pace yourself in working through the questions. Although you should work as quickly as you can, do not rush through the questions because this increases the risk of careless errors such as hitting a wrong key on your calculator.
- Do not spend too much time on a question the first time through the test. You will not know the answer to every question, and some questions may be long or confusing to you. Skip these and return to them after answering the other questions.
- Take mental breaks to avoid fatigue. Mental fatigue may cause careless mistakes, so if necessary, stop and close your eyes for a minute or two and then resume the test.
- Carefully mark your answers. Whether you use a paper answer sheet or a computer, make sure the answers you are entering match the number of the question.
- Do not change an answer unless you are very sure it is incorrect, because your first answer is usually the best.
- **Read carefully.** You must read each question carefully and completely. Do not skim through the question. Read **all** the possible choices before making a selection.
- Watch for key words. Words such as *not, must, always, except* and so forth are usually critical to selecting the best answer. When you encounter these terms, circle or highlight them in case you need to return to the question so you won't miss them.
- Find the *best* answer. Some answers may be at least partially correct, but only one can be the best answer.
- Eliminate obviously incorrect answers. When reading all of the answers, cross out those that you are sure are wrong. If you return to the question, you will not waste time considering these answers again.
- Mark up the test. Usually only the answer sheet is used for grading. Next to the questions write notes, calculations or question marks for unsure answers; circle or highlight key words or phrases or anything else that will help you analyze the question.
- Use *all* the necessary information given but *only* the information given. Remember to use all of the relevant facts in selecting the answer, but do not start reading facts that are not there into the question. (Some tests may have questions with extraneous facts that are not necessary in selecting the correct answer.)
- Review. If you finish answering the questions early, review the questions, if for no other reason than to be sure you did not make careless mistakes in recording your answers, in your computations, and so forth. Very often applicants fail the test by only a few points, and there is no extra credit for finishing early.

COMPREHENSIVE PRACTICE EXAMINATION I

1. An investor purchasing an apartment building obtains a loan from a local bank. In this transaction the investor is the
   a. lessee.
   c. vendor.
   b. grantor.
   d. mortgagor.

2. *F* and *K* enter into an agreement, *K* will mow *F*'s lawn every week during the summer. Later, *K* decides to go into a different business. *V* would like to assume *K*'s obligation to mow *F*'s lawn. *F* agrees and enters into a new contract with *V. F* and *K* tear up their original agreement. This is known as
   a. assignment.
   c. substitution.
   b. novation.
   d. rescission.

3. One of the requirements of the Real Estate Settlement Procedures Act (RESPA) is that the lender must provide the purchaser with a
   a. title report.
   b. good-faith estimate of closing costs.
   c. written explanation if the purchaser's loan application is denied.
   d. mortgage insurance policy.

4. *L* placed title to her building in a trust, with *L* as the beneficiary. When *L* died, *L*'s will directed the trustee to sell the building and distribute the proceeds of the sale to *L*'s heirs. The trustee sold the building in accordance with the will. What type of deed was delivered at closing?
   a. Trustee's deed
   b. Trustor's deed
   c. Deed in trust
   d. Reconveyance deed

5. Which of the following activities usually requires a real estate license?
   a. City employee selling city property
   b. Attorney at law selling a property he had listed
   c. Trustee selling property under court order
   d. Attorney-in-fact following the instructions of the principal

6. A homeowner is preparing her income tax return. Which of the following expenses may she deduct from income on her tax return?
   a. Homeowner's insurance premium
   b. Depreciation expense
   c. Maintenance expenses
   d. Real estate taxes

7. An apartment manager decides to minimize the threat of criminal activity on the property by adding security cameras and new electronic locks with pass keys on all of the entrance doors to the building. This form of risk management is known as
   a. avoiding the risk.
   b. controlling the risk.
   c. retaining the risk.
   d. transferring the risk.

8. Land in the SW¼ of the SE¼ of the NW¼ of the S½ of a section is valued at $3,000 per acre. The total value of the property is
   a. $15,000.
   c. $120,000.
   b. $30,000.
   d. $480,000.

9. A broker receives a check for earnest money from a buyer on Friday and deposits the money in his personal checking account over the weekend. This action may expose the broker to a charge of
   a. commingling.
   c. subrogation.
   b. novation.
   d. accretion.

10. An investor wishes to measure the return from a real estate investment. To accomplish this, the investor would most likely use the property's
    a. cash flow .
    b. capitalization rate.
    c. depreciation schedule.
    d. debt expense.

11. A veteran wishes to refinance her home with a VA-guaranteed loan. The lender is willing, but insists on charging 3½ discount points. In this situation, the veteran
   a. can refinance with a VA loan, provided the lender does not charge the discount points .
   b. can refinance with a VA loan, provided the lender charges no more than two discount points.
   c. cannot refinance because VA-guaranteed loans cannot be used for refinancing an existing loan.
   d. can proceed with the loan and pay the discount points.

12. A home buyer obtains a loan that only partially amortizes the principal. This type of loan must include a
   a. subordination clause.
   b. balloon payment.
   c. prepayment penalty.
   d. usury rate clause.

13. A lender probably would allow a higher loan-to-value ratio when making a loan on
   a. commercial property.
   b. unimproved land.
   c. a single-family residence.
   d. agricultural land.

14. Who bears the liability for the rent payments under a lease agreement if the lease is assigned by the lessee?
   a. The assignor remains primarily liable.
   b. The assignee is primarily liable and the assignor has secondary liability.
   c. The assignor is liable to the assignee.
   d. The assignee becomes liable and the assignor is released.

15. A lender requires that the buyer purchase mortgage insurance before agreeing to make the loan. The title insurance policy premium will be paid
   a. annually.
   b. each month with the mortgage payment.
   c. semiannually until the mortgage is paid.
   d. when the title policy is issued.

16. The buyer in a real estate transaction is given a deed that includes the phrase "to have and to hold." The part of the deed this would be in is the
   a. defeasance clause.
   b. habendum clause.
   c. legal description clause.
   d. alienation clause.

17. Licensed salespeople can legally receive commissions from
   a. their employing brokers.
   b. brokers from cooperating real estate offices.
   c. other salespeople in their offices.
   d. sellers.

18. A characteristic of real estate salespeople who are independent contractors is that they usually receive
   a. more than 50 percent of their income in the form of a monthly salary or hourly wage.
   b. company-provided health insurance and other benefits.
   c. reimbursement for documented business expenses.
   d. more than 90 percent of their income based on sales production.

19. A borrower seeking a real estate loan is required to get a certificate of reasonable value. What type of loan is the buyer seeking?
   a. VA loan
   b. Loan with private mortgage insurance
   c. FHA loan
   d. Loan requiring flood insurance

20. In performing an appraisal of an office building using the cost approach, the appraiser makes an adjustment for functional obsolescence. The appraiser is referring to
   a. a large number of interior pillars on each floor.
   b. several cracked windows.
   c. an unfavorable zoning change.
   d. poor landscaping.

21. To be legally enforceable, a contract for the sale of real estate must be
   a. accompanied by an earnest money deposit.
   b. in writing.
   c. recorded in the county records.
   d. acknowledged by a notary.

22. An owner is calculating the taxable gain on the sale of investment property. Which of the following would be included in the calculation?
   a. Improvements to the property
   b. Maintenance expenses
   c. Amount of real estate taxes paid
   d. The cost of repairs

23. A buyer wishes to continue making the payments on the seller's existing low-interest mortgage. The buyer will not be permitted to do this if the mortgage includes a(n)
    a. defeasance clause.
    b. subordination clause.
    c. alienation clause.
    d. acceleration clause.

24. A young couple looking to purchase a house prefer to find one near a school. Their preference for certain areas is referred to as
    a. situs.
    b. nonhomogeneity.
    c. scarcity.
    d. modifications.

25. A mechanic's lien can be filed against a recently built house by the
    a. store that provided furniture for the house.
    b. roofer who installed the new roof.
    c. newspaper that ran advertising used in selling the house.
    d. company that moved the furniture into the house.

26. B's home is the smallest in a neighborhood of large, expensive houses. The effect of the other houses on the value of B's home is known as
    a. regression.
    b. progression.
    c. substitution.
    d. contribution.

27. A homeowner and a broker enter into a listing agreement for the sale of the owner's house. In the agency relationship created by the listing contract
    a. the homeowner is the agent.
    b. the broker is the principal.
    c. the homeowner is the principal.
    d. neither the homeowner or broker is the principal.

28. A father dies and leaves a gift of real property to his son. The real estate is considered a(n)
    a. bequest.
    b. devise.
    c. escheat.
    d. chattel.

29. If the economy is expanding too rapidly and the Federal Reserve wishes to slow the economy down and reduce inflation, it could
    a. increase the reserve requirement for banks.
    b. decrease the discount rate.
    c. reduce the income tax rates.
    d. buy government securities.

30. The grantor wishes to give the grantee a deed that provides the grantee with the least assurance of good and clear title. The grantor should give a
    a. general warranty deed.
    b. special warranty deed.
    c. quitclaim deed.
    d. bargain and sale deed.

31. A buyer and seller enter into a real estate sales contract. A clause in the contract states that "time is of the essence." This means
    a. time periods for contract terms will be strictly enforced.
    b. all terms of the contract must be performed.
    c. there can be no extensions to the contract.
    d. the contract cannot be assigned.

32. The mortgagee's right to declare the entire loan balance due immediately if the mortgagor is in default is called a(n)
    a. acceleration clause.
    b. defeasance clause.
    c. alienation clause.
    d. forbearance clause.

33. A real estate broker wishes to use a listing that assures the broker a commission no matter who sells the property. The broker should use a(n)
    a. exclusive-agency listing.
    b. exclusive-right-to-sell listing.
    c. net listing.
    d. open listing.

34. T is a real estate broker employed by M. When T finds a property that M might be interested in buying, T is careful to find out as much as possible about the property's owners and why their property is on the market. T's efforts to keep M informed of all facts that could affect a transaction is the duty of
    a. care.
    b. loyalty.
    c. obedience.
    d. disclosure.

35. A landlord most likely would be guilty of discrimination if the lease agreement included a clause stating that renters
    a. must pay a security deposit.
    b. must provide character references.
    c. may not have children living in the apartment.
    d. may not keep pets in the apartment.

36. Tenant D's landlord has sold the building where D lives to the state so that an expressway can be built. D's lease has expired, but the landlord permits D to stay in the apartment until the building is torn down. D continues to pay the rent as prescribed in the lease. What kind of tenancy does D have?
    a. Holdover tenancy
    b. Month-to month tenancy
    c. Tenancy at sufferance
    d. Tenancy at will

37. A general warranty deed assures the buyer that the
    a. property conforms with zoning laws.
    b. property meets construction codes.
    c. title is good against third parties.
    d. property is free from latent defects.

38. An owner's house was recently appraised at $120,000. Based on the appraisal, it has appreciated 20 percent in the four years since it was purchased. The purchase price of the property was
    a. $80,000   c. $100,000
    b. $96,000   d. $126,000

39. To calculate the amount of real estate taxes on a property
    a. multiply the assessed value by the tax rate.
    b. multiply the selling price by the tax rate.
    c. divide the assessed value by the tax rate.
    d. divide the selling price by the tax rate.

40. M conveys the ownership of an office building to a nursing home. The nursing home agrees that the rental income will pay for the expenses of caring for M's parents. When M's parents die, ownership of the office building will revert to M. The estate held by the nursing home is a
    a. life estate with remainder.
    b. legal life estate.
    c. pur autre vie life estate.
    d. leasehold estate.

41. Z wishes to obtain an easement by prescription over X's land. One of the requirements Z will have to prove is a(n)
    a. hostile use.
    b. periodic use.
    c. agreement with the owner.
    d. hidden use.

42. An investor intends to purchase a commercial property and then lease it at an annual rent of $70,000. Annual expenses are estimated at $12,000. If an 8 percent return is expected on the investment, what should the investor pay for the property?
    a. $63,043   c. $725,000
    b. $580,000   d. $875,000

43. Which of the following statements regarding escrow accounts is true
    a. Brokers can commingle their own money in the account.
    b. Escrow accounts must pay interest.
    c. A broker cannot maintain more than one escrow account.
    d. Earnest money must be deposited into an escrow account.

44. A borrower was delinquent on his mortgage, and the lender started a foreclosure action. The borrower has the right to regain ownership of the real estate through the right of
    a. estoppel.   c. condemnation.
    b. subrogation.   d. redemption.

45. A buyer withdraws a full-price offer to purchase a home prior to acceptance by the seller. In this situation the earnest money
    a. must be returned to the buyer less broker expenses.
    b. must be returned to the seller.
    c. must be returned to the buyer.
    d. is split between the buyer and seller.

46. A tenant receives a proprietary lease through the purchase of stock in the corporation that owns the building. The tenant must be living in a
    a. condominium.
    b. planned unit development.
    c. syndication.
    d. cooperative.

47. A real estate sale is closing on November 10. The real estate taxes of $1,800, which were due on January 1 for the current year, have been paid in full by the seller. If prorations are made using a 360-day year, what is the seller's entry on the closing statement?
    a. $250 credit   c. $250 debit
    b. $1,550 credit   d. $1,550 debit

48. *F* signed a 90-day listing agreement with a broker. Two weeks later, *F* was killed in an accident. What is the present status of the listing?
    a. The listing agreement is binding on *F*'s estate for the remainder of the 90 days.
    b. Because *F*'s intention to sell was clearly defined, the listing agreement is still in effect, and the broker may proceed to market the property on behalf of *F*'s estate.
    c. The listing agreement is binding on *F*'s estate only if the broker can produce an offer to purchase the property within the remainder of the listing period.
    d. The listing agreement was terminated automatically when F died.

49. The owner of commercial property believes the stores occupying the property will have significantly increased sales in the next few years. In negotiating a new lease with the stores the property owner should ask for a
    a. ground lease.   c. gross lease.
    b. percentage lease.   d. net lease.

50. A homeowner gave open listings to three local real estate brokers. The brokers in this situation
    a. will each receive an equal share of the commission if one of them sells the property.
    b. will earn a share of the commission if the owner sells the property.
    c. will each have the chance to earn the whole commission.
    d. are entitled to reimbursement for expenses if one of them sells the property.

51. An appraiser calculates depreciation when using the
    a. cost approach.
    b. market data approach.
    c. income approach.
    d. gross income multiplier.

52. A lender making a VA loan wishes to increase the loan yield from 6.5 percent to 7 percent by charging discount points. The number of discount points to be charged is
    a. 2.   c. 6.
    b. 4.   d. 8.

53. *X, Y,* and *Z* organize a partnership that purchases a tract of land that contains one-half of a section. The number of acres owned by the partnership is
    a. 40 acres.   c. 320 acres.
    b. 160 acres.   d. 640 acres.

54. *Z* bought a house for $120,500. It appraised for $125,500 and previously sold for $118,250. Based on these facts, if *Z* applies for an 80 percent mortgage, what will be the amount of the loan *Z* will receive?
    a. $94,600   c. $100,000
    b. $96,400   d. $106,750

55. If the annual gross income for a property is $168,000 and the gross income multiplier is 8.5, what is the estimated value of the property?
    a. $197,640   c. $1,680,000
    b. $1,428,000   d. $1,976,471

56. A licensed real estate salesperson working for the listing broker completed a difficult transaction. The seller wished to reward the salesperson with a bonus. The salesperson can receive the compensation from
    a. the broker only.
    b. the seller only.
    c. either the broker or seller.
    d. no one; the salesperson cannot receive the bonus.

57. The type of interest held by the owner of a property with a condition subsequent is a
    a. defeasible estate.
    b. leasehold estate.
    c. legal life estate.
    d. remainder interest.

58. Valley Place is a condominium community with a swimming pool, tennis courts and bike trail. These amenities are most likely owned by the
    a. Valley Place condominium board.
    b. corporation in which the unit owners hold stock.
    c. local government where the property is located.
    d. condominium unit owners.

59. Which of the following loan programs provides the borrower the greatest leverage by requiring the smallest down payment?
    a. A conventional loan
    b. An FHA loan
    c. A VA loan
    d. A conventional loan with private mortgage insurance

60. Which of the following laws is known as Regulation Z?
    a. Real Estate Settlement Procedures Act
    b. Fair Housing Act
    c. Truth-in-Lending Law Act
    d. Fair Credit Reporting Act

61. A contract in which one party makes a promise and the other party performs some action is called
    a. unilateral contract.
    b. bilateral contract.
    c. multilateral contract.
    d. multipurpose contract.

62. Which of the following easements would an owner seek from the court to gain access to property that is landlocked?
    a. Easement by prescription
    b. Easement in gross
    c. Commercial easement
    d. Easement by necessity

63. A buyer and seller soon will be closing on a transaction involving the purchase of an apartment building. The expense that most likely would be prorated on the closing statement is
    a. real estate taxes.
    b. recording fees.
    c. title insurance.
    d. rent security deposit.

64. A tenant holds a leasehold estate that renews itself automatically unless notice is given by the owner. The tenant's estate is called a(n)
    a. periodic estate.
    b. estate for years.
    c. estate at sufferance.
    d. estate at will.

65. If an apartment building is appraised using a capitalization rate of 10 percent, what is the effect on its value for each dollar that expenses are reduced?
    a. $10 increase   c. $10 decrease
    b. $1 increase   d. $1 decrease

66. Two brothers own a building in joint tenancy. One of the brothers dies, leaving his entire estate to a friend and nothing to his wife. Title to the deceased brother's property will be
    a. held by the surviving brother.
    b. held by the deceased brother's wife.
    c. held by the deceased brother's friend.
    d. split between the deceased brother's friend and his wife.

67. In calculating the gain on a house the owner's cost basis in the property is affected by
    a. a swimming pool that was added.
    b. the amount of repairs made.
    c. the remaining loan balance.
    d. the amount of real estate taxes paid.

68. The purchaser of a property records the deed given to her by the seller in the public records in the county where the property is located. The type of notice created by this action is referred to as
    a. public notice.
    b. actual notice.
    c. official.
    d. constructive notice.

69. X, Y, and Z decide to take title to a recently purchased property as tenants in common. In this situation each of them
    a. has right of survivorship.
    b. has exclusive right of possession.
    c. must have an equal ownership interest.
    d. can sell their ownership interest without the consent of the others.

70. A homeowner entering into a real estate transaction decides to use a contract for deed. Which of the following statements best describes this transaction?
    a. It is an option to purchase real estate.
    b. It involves the sale of real estate and owner financing.
    c. It is the same as a sale and leaseback.
    d. It requires that the vendee construct a building.

71. A homeowner applies for a home equity loan with a local bank. The homeowner may be entitled to a three-day right of rescission under the provisions of
    a. Regulation Z.
    b. RESPA.
    c. the statute of frauds.
    d. the statue of limitations.

72. G is a real estate salesperson employed by broker T. What is G's share of the commission if the sales price of a property is $195,000 and G is entitled to 65 percent of the 7½ percent commission?
    a. $950.63   c. $9,506.25
    b. $8,872.50   d. $95,062.50

73. An owner selling or leasing her property is exempt from the provisions of the federal Fair Housing Act of 1968 if
    a. the property has more than four units.
    b. the owner occupies one of three units in the building.
    c. discriminatory advertising is used.
    d. the owner lists the property with a real estate broker.

74. An appraiser uses the unit-in-place method while performing an appraisal. Which approach to estimating value must the appraiser be using?
    a. Market data
    b. Cost
    c. Income
    d. Sales comparison

75. A store owner renting space in a shopping mall is responsible for paying the property's taxes, insurance and maintenance expenses. The store owner must have a(n)
    a. gross lease.
    b. net lease.
    c. percentage lease.
    d. indexed lease.

76. A deed being used to convey title to two people who are not married to each other does not specify how they are taking title. It will be presumed that ownership in the property is held as
    a. joint tenants.
    b. tenancy by the entirety.
    c. tenancy in common.
    d. community property.

77. To a real estate appraiser, economic obsolescence in a property could be the result of
    a. outmoded fixtures.
    b. location next to an undesirable property.
    c. lack of adequate ventilation and air-conditioning.
    d. poor design.

78. A tenant who continues to occupy an apartment after breaking the terms of the lease is a
    a. tenant at will.
    b. periodic tenant.
    c. tenant at sufferance.
    d. tenant from period to period.

79. Redlining would most likely be practiced by
    a. real estate broker.
    b. landlords.
    c. property developers.
    d. lenders.

80. Transactions covered by the Real Estate Settlement Procedures Act include those with
    a. business loans.
    b. loans to shopping malls.
    c. first mortgages.
    d. second mortgages.

ANSWER GRID FOR COMPREHENSIVE PRACTICE EXAMINATION

1. _____

2. _____

3. _____

4. _____

5. _____

6. _____

7. _____

8. _____

9. _____

10. _____

11. _____

12. _____

13. _____

14. _____

15. _____

16. _____

17. _____

18. _____

19. _____

20. _____

21. _____

22. _____

23. _____

24. _____

25. _____

26. _____

27. _____

28. _____

29. _____

30. _____

31. _____

32. _____

33. _____

34. _____

35. _____

36. _____

37. _____

38. _____

39. _____

40. _____

41. _____

42. _____

43. _____

44. _____

45. _____

46. _____

47. _____

48. _____

49. _____

50. _____

51. _____

52. _____

53. _____

54. _____

55. _____

56. _____

57. _____

58. _____

59. _____

60. _____

61. _____

62. _____

63. _____

64. _____

65. _____

66. _____

67. _____

68. _____

69. _____

70. _____

71. _____

72. _____

73. _____

74. _____

75. _____

76. _____

77. _____

78. _____

79. _____

80. _____

COMPREHENSIVE PRACTICE EXAMINATION II

1. Which of the following types of property are usually exempt from real estate taxes?
   a. Small shopping centers
   b. Small office complexes
   c. Privately owned day care facilities
   d. City parks

2. A buyer and seller both sign a purchase contract for a house. The buyer at this point in the transaction has acquired a property interest known as
   a. statutory title
   b. actual title
   c. equitable title
   d. determinable title

3. Before closing a real estate transaction, the lender provides the buyer and seller with statements of fees and charges they may incur. By doing this the lender is complying with the
   a. Truth In Lending Act.
   b. Equal Credit Opportunity Act.
   c. Real Estate Settlement Procedures Act.
   d. Community Bank Reinvestment Act.

4. What was the selling price of a house if the real estate broker earned a commission of $8,400, which was 7 percent of the selling price?
   a. $84,000   c. $120,000
   b. $90,322   d. $1,200,000

5. A borrower repays the debt on property foreclosed by the lender. By doing this the borrower may now regain the property under the right of
   a. adverse possession.
   b. condemnation.
   c. reversion.
   d. redemption.

6. A house sells for $120,000 with a commission rate of 6 percent. The selling broker received 40 percent and the listing broker the rest. If the listing broker splits his share of the commission evenly with the listing salesperson, the salesperson will receive
   a. $4,320.   c. $2,160.
   b. $2,880.   d. $1,440.

7. An investor's commercial building has annual gross income of $33,000 and expenses of $12,000 for maintenance and repairs, $38,000 for depreciation, $8,500 for real estate taxes and $120,000 for loan payments, which include $110,000 in interest. The annual cash flow on the property is
   a. $78,500.   c. $189,500.
   b. $151,500.   d. $199,500.

8. Section number 1 is located in which corner of a township?
   a. Northeast corner.
   b. Northwest corner.
   c. Southeast corner.
   d. Southwest corner.

9. The bylaws of a condominium building association require that owners who are considering selling their units offer them for sale to the other condo owners first. If other owners do not want to purchase the unit, it can be offered for sale to the general public. This requirement is known as
   a. prior acceptance.
   b. right of first refusal.
   c. covenant of seisin.
   d. defeasance requirement.

10. A lender charges the borrower a rate of 8 percent plus six discount points on a 30-year loan. The lender's yield on the loan is
    a. 8 percent   c. 8.5 percent
    b. 8.25 percent   d. 8.75 percent

11. *X* conveys a life estate to *Y* with instructions that the property will pass to *Z* when *Y* dies. *Z*'s interest in the property while *Y* is alive is best described as
    a. pur autre vie.   c. redemption.
    b. remainder.   d. reversion.

12. A seller signed a real estate sales contract under duress. This contract would probably be considered
    a. breached.   c. voidable.
    b. void.   d. valid.

13. What was the selling price of a property that sold for the amount of its assessed value if its annual real estate tax was $768 and the tax rate was $8 per $100 of assessed value?
    a. $9,600
    b. $61,400
    c. $96,000
    d. $960,000

14. X, Y, and Z own an undivided interest in a parcel of real estate, with X owning a one-half interest while Y and Z each own a one-quarter interest. The form of ownership under which they hold title to the property is
    a. tenancy in common.
    b. joint tenancy.
    c. tenancy by the entirety.
    d. severalty.

15. X is the manager of the LiveWell apartment complex. Which of the following activities would X be least likely to perform?
    a. Coordinating repairs and improvements
    b. Negotiating new leases
    c. Preparing an income tax strategy for the owner
    d. Preparing an operating budget

16. In the cost approach to estimating value, the appraiser makes use of the
    a. owner's original cost of the building.
    b. estimated current replacement cost of the building.
    c. sales prices of similar buildings in the area.
    d. assessed value of the building.

17. Which of the following actions by a broker probably would be considered blockbusting?
    a. Directing home seekers to certain areas based on their race
    b. Soliciting listings from homeowners by creating a fear of racial changes in the area
    c. Refusing to show listings to potential buyers based on their national origin
    d. Refusing to grant loans to persons in a certain area

18. A borrower's monthly loan payment includes $583.33 in interest. If the loan balance is $80,000, what is the borrower's interest rate on the loan?
    a. 8.25 percent
    b. 8.5 percent
    c. 8.75 percent
    d. 9 percent

19. The approach to estimating value that includes determining the value of the land and adding the value of improvements is the
    a. cost approach.
    b. income approach.
    c. market data approach.
    d. gross rent multiplier approach.

20. Which of the following facts may a broker, as an agent of the seller, disclose to a prospective buyer without the permission of the seller?
    a. Hidden defects on the property
    b. The original amount paid by the owner for the property
    c. The lowest price the seller is willing to accept
    d. Circumstances requiring the owner to sell quickly

21. A borrower pays $1,800 in interest over a three-month period on an $80,000 nonamortizing loan. What is the interest rate on the borrower's loan?
    a. 6 percent
    b. 8 percent
    c. 9 percent
    d. 10 percent

22. A family is going to keep their furniture in a storage facility for six months until their new home is ready for occupancy. If the storage space is 32 by 160 by 10 feet high and the facility charges $1 per cubic yard each month, what will the monthly storage cost be to the family?
    a. $1,896.30
    b. $5,120.00
    c. $5,688.89
    d. $17,066.67

23. If a developer wants to build a commercial building closer to the street than is permitted by the local zoning ordinance because the shape of the lot makes a standard setback impossible, the developer should seek a
    a. variance.
    b. nonconforming use permit.
    c. conditional use permit.
    d. density zoning permit.

24. A buyer and seller enter into an agreement that gives the buyer the option to purchase the property within a specified period of time. Which of the following is true regarding the agreement?
    a. The buyer is not obligated to purchase the property.
    b. Any consideration given by the buyer must be returned if the property is not purchased.
    c. The buyer cannot assign the option to someone else.
    d. Consideration is not required from the buyer to have a valid option.

25. A tenancy (estate) for years is best described as a tenancy
    a. without the consent of the property owner.
    b. created by the death of the owner.
    c. created through long-standing use.
    d. that ends on a specific date.

26. Several homes valued at $300,000 to $400,000 are built in an area where an existing home valued at $150,000 is located. As a result, the value of the existing home increases. The real estate principle of value that applies to this situation is called the principle of
    a. substitution.
    b. improvement.
    c. progression.
    d. principle of increasing and diminishing returns.

27. Whose signature is necessary for an offer to purchase real estate to become a valid contract?
    a. Buyer's only
    b. Buyer's and seller's
    c. Seller's only
    d. Seller's and seller's broker's

28. A real estate salesperson who has a written contract with his broker that specifies that he will not be treated as an employee and whose entire income is from sales commissions rather than an hourly wage is probably a(n)
    a. real estate assistant.
    b. employee.
    c. subagent.
    d. independent contractor.

29. A broker took a listing and later discovered that the client had been declared incompetent by a court. What is the current status of the listing?
    a. The listing is unaffected because the broker acted in good faith as the owner's agent.
    b. The listing is of no value to the broker because the contract is void.
    c. The listing is the basis for recovery of a commission from the client's guardian or trustee if the broker produces a buyer.
    d. The listing may be renegotiated between the broker and the client, based on the new information.

30. The listing and selling brokers in a real estate transaction split the commission equally. If the commission rate was 6 percent and the selling broker received $3,600, what was the selling price of the property?
    a. $36,000   c. $80,000
    b. $60,000   d. $120,000

31. A brother and sister own an apartment building as joint tenants. The brother dies and has personal debts of several thousand dollars but no assets other than his ownership in the building. Which of the following statements is true?
    a. The sister is liable for the debts.
    b. The sister is liable for the debts if she continues ownership of the building.
    c. The brother's creditors can seize the building.
    d. The sister owns the building and has no obligation for the debts.

32. If a person believes she has been the victim of a discriminatory practice by a real estate broker, how long does she have to file a complaint under the Fair Housing Laws?
    a. 30 days after the alleged discriminatory act occurred
    b. 6 months after the alleged discriminatory act occurred
    c. 1 year after the alleged discriminatory act occurred
    d. There is no time limit

33. Several investors decide to enter into a partnership as limited partners. Which of the following statements is true regarding the investors in the partnership?
   a. Each of them may be responsible for all of the partnership debts.
   b. They are limited as to the amount of profits they may receive.
   c. Their liability is limited regarding the amount of losses they may incur.
   d. They may take an active role in managing the partnership.

34. A deed conveys ownership to the grantee "as long as the existing building is not torn down." What type of estate does this deed create?
   a. Determinable fee estate
   b. Fee simple absolute estate
   c. Nondestructible estate
   d. Life estate pur autre vie

35. A lender makes a 30-year loan at a rate of 8.75 percent. If the lender wishes to earn a yield of 9 percent on the loan, how many discount points must the lender charge?
   a. One   c. Three
   b. Two   d. Four

36. If a broker is estimating the market value of a house being listed for sale, which appraisal method should the broker use?
   a. Gross rent multiplier method
   b. Income method
   c. Cost method
   d. Market data method

37. The states in which the lender holds title to the mortgaged real estate are known as
   a. title-theory states.
   b. lien-theory states.
   c. statutory states.
   d. strict title forfeiture states.

38. Which of the following phrases, when placed in a print advertisement, would comply with the requirements of the Truth-in-Lending Act (Regulation Z)?
   a. "12 percent interest"
   b. "Rate of 12 percent"
   c. "12 percent annual interest"
   d. "12 percent annual percentage rate"

39. A person has inherited a building and after reviewing the public records determines that there is a problem with the title. Wishing to clear title to the property, the person initiates a
   a. quiet title suit.
   b. lis pendens.
   c. specific performance suit.
   d. condemnation suit.

40. A lender is willing to make a loan up to an LTV of 80 percent. If a property is valued at $160,000, the maximum amount the lender will loan on the property is
   a. $128,000.   c. $180,000.
   b. $160,000.   d. $220,000.

41. The market value for a parcel of land can be best described as
   a. the most probable price the property will sell for.
   b. the same as market price.
   c. the amount the seller wants the property to sell for.
   d. how much the property cost the seller.

42. Which of the following is a characteristic of mortgage loan brokers?
   a. They match borrowers and lenders.
   b. They service loans.
   c. They provide the loan funds.
   d. They buy and sell loans.

43. Title to personal property in a real estate transaction is transferred by a
   a. package mortgage.
   b. warranty deed.
   c. listing agreement.
   d. bill of sale.

44. W enters into a sale-leaseback agreement with X, under which X will become the owner of W's ranch. Which of the following statements is true of this arrangement?
   a. W retains title to the ranch.
   b. X receives possession of the property.
   c. X is the lessor.
   d. W is the lessor.

45. Involuntary alienation of title to real estate includes all of the following except
   a. adverse possession.
   b. a bequest.
   c. a tax sale.
   d. eminent domain.

46. The state wants to acquire a strip of land from several homeowners to build a highway. Does the state have the right to acquire the privately owned land?
    a. Yes. The state can acquire the land through its police powers.
    b. Yes. The state can acquire the land through its power of eminent domain.
    c. Yes. The state can acquire the land through its power of escheat.
    d. No. The US Constitution prevents the state from acquiring private land.

47. A travel agency is purchasing a large old mansion that has been converted to commercial property. The appraiser hired by the lender should give the greatest weight to the
    a. sales comparison approach.
    b. income approach.
    c. gross rent multiplier.
    d. cost approach.

48. A property manager leased three stores for a year. The monthly rent for the first store was $800 a month. The rent for the other two stores was 10 percent higher than the first store. If the property manager earned an 8 percent fee on the rent, what was the property manager's yearly fee?
    a. $205   c. $2,560
    b. $2,458   d. $3,072

49. If a house sold for $40,000 and the buyer obtained an FHA- insured mortgage loan for $38,500, how much money would the buyer pay in discount points if the lender charged four points?
    a. $385   c. $1,540
    b. $1,500   d. $1,600

50. The term *point of beginning* (POB) is used in which of the following methods of describing real estate?
    a. Plat method
    b. Rectangular survey system
    c. Metes-and-bounds method
    d. Lot and block method

51. The parties in a real estate transaction want to verify the authenticity of the signatures on the deed. To accomplish this, they should have the deed
    a. acknowledged.   c. notified.
    b. recorded.   d. verified.

52. A broker has listed a house for sale and under the terms of the listing agreement will receive a commission even if the sellers sell the property themselves. The type of listing being used is a(n)
    a. net listing.
    b. exclusive agency listing.
    c. exclusive-right-to-sell listing.
    d. open listing.

53. An investor's equity in a building is best described as the
    a. property's value less its debt.
    b. investor's cash investment less the property's value.
    c. investor's cash investment less depreciation.
    d. investor's total cash investment.

54. A building's current value is 133 percent more than its original cost. If the building was purchased five years ago for $96,000, its current value is
    a. $72,180.   c. $127,680.
    b. $98,880.   d. $721,805.

55. An appraiser has been hired by the lender to perform an appraisal on a house. In this situation the appraiser's objective is to
    a. estimate the market value.
    b. determine the cost.
    c. determine the market value.
    d. set a selling price.

56. *A, B,* and *C* own a parcel of real estate as joint tenants. *C* sells her interest to *X,* and then *B* dies. What is the result of these two events?
    a. *A* and *X* are tenants in common.
    b. *B*'s heirs, *A* and *X* are joint tenants.
    c. *B*'s heirs and *A* are joint tenants with *X* as a tenant in common.
    d. *B*'s heirs, *A* and *X* are tenants in common.

57. Under the Real Estate Settlement Procedures Act (RESPA) several disclosures are required to be made to the buyer. Which party is required under the act to make the disclosures?
    a. Broker   c. Title company
    b. Seller   d. Lender

58. If purchase of a lender's title insurance policy is required for obtaining a new loan, the cost of the policy would typically be shown on the settlement statement as a
    a. credit to the buyer.
    b. credit to the seller.
    c. debit to the buyer.
    d. debit to the seller.

59. A person is interested in purchasing a parcel of real estate and inspects the public records to obtain information about the title to the property. Which of the following documents would the person be most likely to discover?
    a. mortgage liens
    b. encroachments
    c. leases
    d. property surveys

60. The Torrens system is best described as a(n)
    a. appraisal system.
    b. title registration system.
    c. zoning system.
    d. mortgage insurance system.

61. A married couple filing a joint tax return sells the house they have been living in for the past five years. What is the maximum amount of capital gains they are allowed to exclude from their taxable income?
    a. $100,000
    b. $125,000
    c. $250,000
    d. $500,000

62. A first-time homebuyer finds that he is unlikely to qualify for a mortgage under current interest rates. His parents agree to pay a lump sum in cash to the lender at closing to offset the high rate. What type of loan is this?
    a. Balloon mortgage
    b. Term mortgage
    c. Reverse annuity mortgage
    d. Buydown mortgage

63. An investor's decision to purchase an apartment building was primarily based on a fraudulent income statement provided by the broker. The sale contract is
    a. valid.
    b. void.
    c. voidable.
    d. executed.

64. The Equal Credit Opportunity Act makes it illegal for lenders to refuse credit to or otherwise discriminate against which of the following applicants?
    a. Parent of two children who receives public assistance and who cannot afford the monthly mortgage payments
    b. New homebuyer who does not have a credit history
    c. A single person who receives public assistance
    d. An unemployed person with no identifiable source of income

65. How much was the total amount of commissions earned by a broker's office last year if a salesperson earned $80,000 in commissions, which was 10 percent of the commissions earned by the office?
    a. $88,000
    b. $800,000
    c. $880,000
    d. $8,000,000

66. The capitalization rate as used in the income approach to estimating the value of real estate is the
    a. minimum expense rate to make the property profitable.
    b. expected rate the property's value will increase.
    c. maximum rate the property owner can charge other investors.
    d. rate of return the property will earn for the investor.

67. As part of a loan agreement the lender requires that the borrower include an additional amount in the monthly loan payment, which will be held by the lender in a special account. This money will be used for
    a. service charges.
    b. delinquency charges.
    c. real estate taxes.
    d. property maintenance fees.

68. According to a broker's competitive market analysis (CMA), a property is worth $125,000. The homeowner bought the property for $90,000 and added $50,000 in improvements, for a total of $140,000. The property sold for $122,500. Which amount represents the property's market price?
    a. $90,000
    b. $122,500
    c. $125,000
    d. $140,000

69. In a settlement statement, how will a proration of prepaid water, gas and electric charges be reflected?
    a. Debit to the seller, credit to the buyer
    b. Debit to the buyer, credit to the seller
    c. Debit to the buyer only
    d. Credit to the seller only

70. To net the owner $84,000 after paying the broker a 6 percent commission, the selling price would have to be
    a. $89,040.
    b. $89,362.
    c. $90,000.
    d. $91,304.

71. One reason a lender might make a VA or an FHA loan rather than a conventional loan is
    a. income tax advantages.
    b. a higher interest rate.
    c. a longer loan term.
    d. lower risk.

72. After a seller accepted a buyer's offer, the buyer learned that the broker the buyer had hired to represent her was also an undisclosed agent of the seller. The buyer can
    a. withdraw the offer and not be subject to damages.
    b. withdraw the offer but be liable for damages to the broker.
    c. be forced to complete the purchase of the property.
    d. withdraw the offer but only with the consent of the seller.

73. A couple renting a house from its owner install new kitchen cabinets. What is the status of the cabinets when the lease ends and the tenants leave the property?
    a. The couple may not remove the cabinets.
    b. The cabinets stay, but the owner must reimburse the couple for the cost of the cabinets.
    c. The cabinets stay, but the couple is entitled to the increased property value as a result of the cabinets.
    d. The couple may remove the cabinets when they leave.

74. What is the area in square feet of a rectangular parcel of land that is 175 feet deep and 30 yards wide?
    a. 1,575 sq. ft.
    b. 5,250 sq. ft.
    c. 7,500 sq. ft.
    d. 15,750 sq. ft.

75. A broker listed a house owned by an elderly couple and earned a 9 percent commission when it sold. After the closing the couple learned that the same broker had listed several other houses in their area at a 6 percent commission rate. Under these circumstances the couple
    a. can rescind the contract with the broker.
    b. can receive damages for the difference between the commission rates.
    c. can have the broker's license revoked.
    d. have no recourse because the broker has done nothing wrong.

76. A home buyer obtained a conventional $68,000 amortized loan with an interest rate of 9 percent payable over 30 years. If the monthly payment is $525 the loan balance after the first payment is
    a. $67,475
    b. $67,490
    c. $67,985
    d. $68,000

77. A warehouse is in an area that has recently been zoned for residential use only. The building's continued use as a warehouse is best described as a(n)
    a. zoning variance
    b. nonconforming use
    c. illegal use
    d. amendment

78. A property purchased for investment six years ago for $132,000 is now worth $190,000. At the time of the purchase the value of the land was $18,000. If the investors are using straight-line depreciation over a 31½ year useful life, the current book value of the property is
    a. $21.714
    b. $92,286
    c. $110,381
    d. $114,000

79. A broker obtained an offer on one of his listings. Before he could contact the seller to present the offer, he received a second offer from another real estate company. What action should the broker take with the offers?
    a. Both offers should be presented to the seller at the same time.
    b. The offers should be presented in the order they were received by the broker.
    c. The broker should recommend the acceptance of the first offer.
    d. The broker should present the first offer and notify the seller that a second offer has also been received.

80. Which of the following is classified as a general lien?
    a. judgment lien
    b. mortgage lien
    c. second mortgage lien
    d. mechanic's lien

ANSWER GRID FOR COMPREHENSIVE PRACTICE EXAMINATION

1. _____

2. _____

3. _____

4. _____

5. _____

6. _____

7. _____

8. _____

9. _____

10. _____

11. _____

12. _____

13. _____

14. _____

15. _____

16. _____

17. _____

18. _____

19. _____

20. _____

21. _____

22. _____

23. _____

24. _____

25. _____

26. _____

27. _____

28. _____

29. _____

30. _____

31. _____

32. _____

33. _____

34. _____

35. _____

36. _____

37. _____

38. _____

39. _____

40. _____

41. _____

42. _____

43. _____

44. _____

45. _____

46. _____

47. _____

48. _____

49. _____

50. _____

51. _____

52. _____

53. _____

54. _____

55. _____

56. _____

57. _____

58. _____

59. _____

60. _____

61. _____

62. _____

63. _____

64. _____

65. _____

66. _____

67. _____

68. _____

69. _____

70. _____

71. _____

72. _____

73. _____

74. _____

75. _____

76. _____

77. _____

78. _____

79. _____

80. _____

U N I T I
DIAGNOSTIC WORKSHEET

CHAPTER 1
Introduction to Real Estate

No.	Answer	Correct
1	b	
4	b	
6	b	
8	c	
9	c	
15	c	
16	d	
18	d	
20	a	
22	b	
24	d	
26	b	
28	c	
30	b	
TOTAL NUMBER CORRECT		

CHAPTER 2
Real Estate Concepts

No.	Answer	Correct
2	c	
3	b	
5	b	
7	d	
10	a	
11	a	
12	b	
13	a	
14	d	
17	b	
19	c	
21	b	
23	b	
25	d	
27	b	
29	d	
TOTAL NUMBER CORRECT		

TEST SUMMARY

Enter Number Correct for Each Chapter	Correct
Chapter 1—Introduction to Real Estate	
Chapter 2—Real Estate Concepts	
TOTAL NUMBER CORRECT	

SCORE BREAKDOWN

Excellent = 30–27
Very Good = 26–24

Okay = 23–21
Poor = 20–0

SOLUTIONS TO UNIT I DIAGNOSTIC TEST

1. B Nonhomogeneity means that no two parcels of land are exactly alike because at least the location of the parcels must be different.

2. C Trade fixtures are personal property.

3. B An item's value or the price paid for an item is not one of the tests used to determine if it is a fixture.

4. B Commercial property includes retail stores and shopping malls.

5. B Common law is based on custom and usage.

6. B Scarcity means that the amount of land is finite and there may not be enough in certain areas to satisfy demand.

7. D Real property includes the earth's surface, above and below, things permanently attached and the rights to use them.

8. C Situs is an economic characteristic of real estate that refers to people's preference for certain areas.

9. C Industrial property includes factories, warehouses and research development buildings.

10. A The allodial system recognizes private ownership of land.

11. A Display counters, if installed and owned by the tenant, are considered trade fixtures and therefore personal property.

12. B With more real estate available prices will decrease.

13. A If real property is "severed" it becomes personal property.

14. D The time period during which an item has been attached is not one of the tests used to determine if it is a fixture.

15. C Wage levels affect the demand for real estate. People will be more willing to make major purchase commitments if they have better employment opportunities.

16. D The term REALTOR® is a registered trademark of the National Association of REALTORS®.

17. B Trade fixtures are the tenant's personal property and may be removed at any time.

18. D Commercial property includes office buildings, retail stores and shopping malls.

19. C If the mobile home is placed on a permanent foundation, it would most likely be considered real property.

20. A Fixity means that because real estate is immobile and a nonstandard product, investments in real estate are long term.

21. B The lumber is movable and not attached to the real estate at this point and is therefore personal property.

22. B The real estate industry provides several services besides brokerage.

23. B Trade fixtures are personal property and belong to the tenant.

24. D Modifications mean that changes in a parcel of land affect its value.

25. D The cabinets are fixtures and belong to the owner of the real estate.

26. B Special purpose property includes parks, cemeteries, schools and other property that does not fit the descriptions for other classes of real estate.

27. B Fixtures used in a trade or business are trade fixtures and are personal property.

28. C Because real estate is immobile, changes in the surrounding areas will greatly affect it, and it is easier to locate for assessing and collecting taxes by local governments.

29. D The definition of land does not include things artificially attached, such as fixtures.

30. B Scarcity means that there is a finite amount of land, and this will affect the value of property in areas with high demand.

U N I T II
DIAGNOSTIC WORKSHEET

CHAPTER 3
Government Powers

No.	Answer	Correct
1	c	
5	a	
10	d	
15	c	
19	c	
22	a	
25	b	
29	d	
33	b	
36	b	
38	d	
44	b	
47	b	
TOTAL NUMBER CORRECT		

CHAPTER 4
Encumbrances:
Easements and Deed Restrictions

No.	Answer	Correct
2	c	
6	b	
12	a	
16	b	
20	c	
23	d	
24	c	
28	c	
30	b	
37	d	
TOTAL NUMBER CORRECT		

SCORE BREAKDOWN

Excellent = 50–45
Very Good = 44–40

Okay = 39–35
Poor = 34–0

UNIT II
DIAGNOSTIC WORKSHEET

CHAPTER 5
Encumbrances: Liens

No.	Answer	Correct
3	b	
8	a	
9	c	
13	b	
17	d	
21	c	
26	a	
32	b	
34	c	
40	a	
41	a	
43	d	
45	c	
48	d	
50	c	
TOTAL NUMBER CORRECT		

CHAPTER 6
Legal Descriptions

No.	Answer	Correct
4	a	
7	c	
11	a	
14	b	
18	b	
27	a	
31	a	
35	d	
39	a	
42	b	
46	b	
49	b	
TOTAL NUMBER CORRECT		

TEST SUMMARY

Enter Number Correct for Each Chapter	Correct
Chapter 3—Government Powers	
Chapter 4—Encumbrances: Easements and Deed Restrictions	
Chapter 5—Encumbrances: Liens	
Chapter 6—Legal Descriptions	
TOTAL NUMBER CORRECT	

SCORE BREAKDOWN

Excellent = 50–45   Okay = 39–35
Very Good = 44–40   Poor = 34–0

SOLUTIONS TO UNIT II DIAGNOSTIC TEST

1. C The type of materials used in a building are usually controlled by building codes.

2. C Easements appurtenant "run with the land" and transfer to the new property owner.

3. B $\$90,000 \times .2 = 18,000 \div \$100 = 180 \times \$5 = \$900$.

4. A The metes-and-bounds method starts and ends at a point of beginning and describes the property using directions and reference points such as natural objects.

5. A A preexisting use that does not conform to current zoning laws is referred to as a *nonconforming use.*

6. B An easement by necessity is given to a property owner to enter (right of ingress) and exit (right of egress) the property.

7. C A township is six miles on each side, forming an area of 36 square miles.

8. A Real estate tax liens attach only to the real estate (specific) and are not voluntary.

9. C A mechanic's lien protects anyone furnishing labor or materials to real estate.

10. D Under the government power of escheat, property will revert to the government if the owner dies without a will and there are no heirs.

11. A Land is measured north and south of base lines.

12. A An encroachment is a physical intrusion on someone's land. Encroachments of long standing use may become easements by prescription.

13. B $\$800 \div \$22,000 = 3.6\%$.

14. B The 36 sections in a township are numbered starting with the northeast section (*section 1*) and proceeding west to section 6, then east again to section 12 and so on. The section in the northwest corner therefore is 6.

15. C Eminent domain is a government power that is exercised through the process of condemnation.

16. B An easement by prescription is created when these conditions are met.

17. D Ad valorem taxes are based on the assessed value of the property.

18. B Section 16 is set aside in each township to help support schools.

19. C Zoning powers are obtained by local governments through enabling legislation or home rule.

20. C Most utility easements are easements in gross.

21. C $\$20,000 \times .0525 = \$1,050 \times 1.45 = \$1,523$.

22. A The government power of eminent domain gives the government the right to take private land for the public good.

23. D Tacking on time periods among related parties pertains to gaining an easement by prescription.

24. C An easement is the right to enter someone else's land.

25. B Police powers are the government powers to regulate real estate for the public good. This is usually performed through zoning codes and building ordinances.

26. A $\$150,000 \times .2 = \$30,000 \times .05 = \$1,500$.

27. A Starting with the 640 acres in a section = $640 \div 2 = 320$; $320 \div 4 = 80$; $80 \div 4 = 20$ acres.

28. C An encroachment is a physical intrusion on someone's land.

29. D A nonconforming use is created through a change in the zoning law and not by a variance.

30. B An easement by necessity is given to a property owner to enter (right of ingress) and exit (right of egress) the property.

31. A Legal descriptions using the rectangular survey system require a principal meridian.

32. B Real estate tax liens generally take priority over other liens.

33. B The owner no longer would have to comply with the zoning ordinance if granted a variance.

34. C Mortgage liens attach only to the real estate (specific) and are voluntary.

35. D There are 640 acres (1 square mile) in a section.

36. B Planned unit developments (PUDs) are areas zoned for mixed uses.

37. D Because the easement is on Sam's land, he has the servient tenement and Bob has the easement right. While both parties may mutually agree to end the easement, Sam cannot unilaterally end it.

38. D Zoning codes regulate how property can be used.

39. A Townships are horizontal strips of land that are measured from base lines.

40. A Mechanic liens attach only to the real estate (specific) and are involuntary because they are created by law.

41. A Equitable redemption rights are effective before the tax sale.

42. B Ranges are vertical strips of land that are measured from the principal meridians.

43. D Judgment liens attach to all of a person's property (general) and are involuntary.

44. B An occupancy permit (also called *certificate of occupancy*) must be issued for new construction before it may legally be inhabited.

45. C Unpaid real estate taxes are generally given priority over other liens.

46. B 520' × 520' = 270,400 sq. ft.; 1,040 × 1,040 = 1,081,600 sq. ft.; 270,400 ÷ 1,081,600 = 25%.

47. B The government may condemn the property with or without the owner's consent.

48. D A judgment is a general lien resulting from a lawsuit against the owner.

49. B Metes and bounds describes the circumference of the property using direction, distances and reference points.

50. C Property owned by local, state and federal governments is exempt, but not privately owned property.

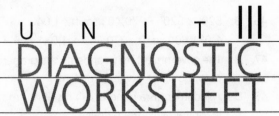

U N I T III
DIAGNOSTIC WORKSHEET

CHAPTER 7		
Freehold Interests in Real Estate		

No.	Answer	Correct
1	c	
4	c	
10	b	
13	c	
16	b	
19	d	
22	c	
25	d	
28	b	
34	c	
36	d	
38	b	
39	b	
40	b	
42	c	
45	a	
TOTAL NUMBER CORRECT		

CHAPTER 8		
Leasehold Interests in Real Estate		

No.	Answer	Correct
2	a	
5	c	
8	b	
11	b	
14	a	
17	c	
20	c	
23	c	
26	a	
31	a	
32	b	
47	c	
TOTAL NUMBER CORRECT		

SCORE BREAKDOWN

Excellent = 50–45
Very Good = 44–40

Okay = 39–35
Poor = 34–0

U N I T **III**
DIAGNOSTIC WORKSHEET

CHAPTER 9
Forms of Ownership

No.	Answer	Correct
3	b	
6	c	
7	d	
9	c	
12	d	
15	b	
18	b	
21	c	
24	b	
27	b	
29	a	
30	b	
33	b	
35	d	
37	b	
41	a	
43	a	
44	a	
46	d	
48	c	
49	c	
50	c	
TOTAL NUMBER CORRECT		

TEST SUMMARY

Enter Number Correct for Each Chapter	Correct
Chapter 7—Freehold Interests in Real Estate	
Chapter 8—Leasehold Interests in Real Estate	
Chapter 9—Forms of Ownership	
TOTAL NUMBER CORRECT	

SCORE BREAKDOWN

Excellent = 50–45

Very Good = 44–40

Okay = 39–35

Poor = 34–0

SOLUTIONS TO UNIT III DIAGNOSTIC TEST

1. C   A life estate is a noninheritable interest. Holders of life estates may not leave them to their heirs.

2. A   A net lease requires that the tenant pay some or all of the property's expenses in addition to a base monthly rent.

3. B   Property acquired after spouses are married (except for property acquired by gift or inheritance) is considered community property.

4. C   Because the property will transfer to Charlie after the death of the life tenant (Bob), Charlie has a remainder interest in the property.

5. C   A percentage lease is used when renting commercial property and the rent is based, all or partly, on the tenant's gross income.

6. C   Ownership in severalty is sole ownership.

7. D   The legal life estate of homestead protects against certain creditors.

8. B   Step 1: $15,000 ÷ 20 units (10 + 10) = $750. Step 2: $750 ÷ 6 = $125.

9. C   Joint tenancy provides that the surviving tenants will receive property held by the deceased joint tenant.

10. B   The homestead exemption usually protects only against creditors with general liens.

11. B   Continued occupancy of the property without the owner's consent is a considered a tenancy at sufferance.

12. D   Joint tenancy provides that the surviving tenants will receive property held by the deceased joint tenant.

13. C   A defeasible estate is a freehold estate that includes a condition. The estate will continue as long as the condition is met.

14. A   Kevin is subleasing the apartment to Lois and remains primarily liable for the rent.

15. B   In a cooperative, the corporation owns the building and issues shares to the owners.

16. B   Mary has a remainder interest because title will pass after Bob's life estate ends.

17. C   A lease for a definite period of time is an estate for years (also called an *estate for stated period*).

18. B   In a cooperative, the corporation owns the building and issues shares to the owners.

19. D   A life estate is not inheritable, and the life tenant may not do anything to destroy the property's value (called *waste*).

20. C   A net lease requires that the tenant pay some on all of the property's expenses in addition to a base monthly rent.

21. C   Joint tenancy requires the four unities.

22. C   Pur autre vie life estate means that it is based on "the life of another".

23. C   A lease for a definite period of time is an estate for years (also called an *estate for stated period*).

24. B   Each tenant in common holds an undivided interest in the land and cannot sell or rent only his or or her portion. Joint tenancy has right of survivorship.

25. D   Life estates are not inheritable.

26. A   A periodic estate continues to renew itself until notice to terminate is given.

27. B   Condominium owners own their own unit and own a portion of the common parts of the building and land.

28. B   The allodial system recognizes private ownership of land.

29. A   Owners in joint tenancy and tenancy in common can dissolve the co-ownership through partition.

30. B   When Fred conveyed his interest, Vern became a tenant in common with Mary and Bob as joint tenants.

31. A   In a gross lease the landlord pays all the operating expenses of the property. This is the most common type of lease.

32. B   A lease option clause gives the tenant the right to renew the lease within a specified date.

33. B   Conveying the ownership ends the joint tenancy so that the new tenancy is in common. The husband and son could agree to create a new joint tenancy.

34. C   Estate refers to the degree of ownership rights a person has in the property.

35. D   Tenancy by the entirety is a special form of tenancy between husband and wife.

36. D   Defeasible estates include a condition on the ownership.

37. B   Any of the co-owners of a property may ask the court to dissolve the co-ownership.

38. B   The daughter has a future ownership interest (a remainder interest) in the property and will become fee simple owner when her father dies.

39. B   A defeasible estate is a freehold estate that includes a condition. The estate will continue as long as the condition is met.

40. B   Fee simple estates provide the owner with the greatest ownership interest recognized by law.

41. A   Tenancy in common allows unequal ownership interest in the property.

42. C   If water is nonnavigable, ownership extends to the center of the water.

43. A   Tenancy in common allows the property to pass to their respective heirs. Joint tenancy and tenancy by the entirety has right of survivorship, and severalty is sole ownership.

44. A   When Alice sold her interest, Mary became a tenant in common with Bob and Ted as joint tenants. When Bob died Ted received Bob's share so that Ted is left as a tenant in common with Mary.

45. A   Curtesy is the husband's life estate in the wife's property.

46. D   All tenants in common have an equal right of possession.

47. C $1,200 × 12 = $14,400; $19,200 − $14,400 = $4,800 ÷ .04 = $120,000; $150,000 + $120,000 = $270,000.

48. C   Community property rules recognize property owned individually by the spouse or by both (community property).

49. C   An S corporation is taxed once like a partnership. Both S and regular corporations offer limited liability to the shareholders.

50. C   The holder of a time-share has the right to occupy the property for a specified period of time.

U N I T IV
DIAGNOSTIC
WORKSHEET

CHAPTER 10
Transferring Title

No.	Answer	Correct
1	b	
4	d	
5	c	
7	c	
10	d	
13	d	
16	c	
19	d	
22	b	
24	b	
25	c	
27	c	
28	a	
31	b	
33	b	
35	c	
37	a	
39	c	
41	a	
43	a	
44	b	

No.	Answer	Correct
45	a	
46	b	
48	a	
49	b	
50	b	
TOTAL NUMBER CORRECT		

CHAPTER 11
Recording Title

No.	Answer	Correct
2	c	
8	b	
11	d	
12	b	
14	a	
17	b	
20	c	
23	c	
26	a	
29	d	
32	c	
36	a	
42	b	
TOTAL NUMBER CORRECT		

SCORE BREAKDOWN

Excellent = 50–45
Very Good = 44–40

Okay = 39–35
Poor = 34–0

UNIT IV
DIAGNOSTIC WORKSHEET

CHAPTER 12
Closings

No.	Answer	Correct
3	c	
6	c	
9	c	
15	b	
18	a	
21	c	
30	b	
34	c	
38	b	
40	c	
47	d	
TOTAL NUMBER CORRECT		

TEST SUMMARY

Enter Number Correct for Each Chapter	Correct
Chapter 10—Transferring Title	
Chapter 11—Recording Title	
Chapter 12—Closings	
TOTAL NUMBER CORRECT	

SCORE BREAKDOWN

Excellent = 50–45
Very Good = 44–40

Okay = 39–35
Poor = 34–0

SOLUTIONS TO UNIT IV DIAGNOSTIC TEST

1. B The testator is the party who makes a will.

2. C A lender's policy covers the lender's interest (the loan amount) in the property.

3. C Step 1: $840 + $120 = $960. Step 2: $960 ÷ 12 = $80. Step 3: $80 ÷ 30 = $2.67. Step 4: $80 × 9 + $2.67 × 15 = $760. Because the expense is prepaid, the time period to prorate is from the closing date to the end of the year.

4. D If a property owner dies intestate (without a will) and the property is not held in joint tenancy, the court will dispose of the property according to the state's law of descent.

5. C State law defines the requirements for acquiring title to real estate through adverse possession.

6. C Step 1: $720 ÷ 12 = $60. Step 2: $60 ÷ 30 = $2 Step 3: $60 × 7 + $2 × 15 = $450. Because the expense is prepaid, the time period to prorate is from the closing date to April 1.

7. C Quiet enjoyment means that the grantee need not worry about other parties with superior claims against the property.

8. B Title insurance policies usually last as long as the property is owned by the same owner.

9. C Residential one- to four-unit property is covered under RESPA.

10. D Acquiring property through adverse possession requires hostile use for the time period prescribed by law, not by deed from the prior owner.

11. D Title insurance premium is usually paid once, when the policy is issued.

12. B The public records are open to anyone wishing to inspect them.

13. D Title to personal property is conveyed by a bill of sale.

14. A Torrens is used in only a few counties in the country.

15. B Step 1: $1,800 ÷ 12 = $150. Step 2: $150 ÷ 30 = $5. Step 3: $150 × 8 + $5 × 8 = $1,240.

16. C Title passes to the grantee with delivery and acceptance of the deed by the grantee.

17. B A title opinion is a statement of the condition of title at a certain point in time.

18. A RESPA applies to real estate transactions in which a federally related loan is made. These include loans made by lenders who are federally insured, FHA, and VA loans.

19. D Involuntary alienation is any method of transferring title without the owner's consent.

20. C The Torrens System is a method of registering property.

21. C Step 1: $2,400 ÷ 12 = $200. Step 2: $200 ÷ 30 = $6.666. Step 3: $200 × 8 + $6.666 × 12 = $1,679.99. Because the taxes are prepaid, the seller should receive credit for the unused portion of the taxes paid.

22. B A general warranty deed includes several guarantees given by the grantor to the grantee.

23. C An abstractor inspects the public records and prepares a brief history of all the documents affecting the title.

24. B Voluntary alienation is transferring property through gift or sale.

25. C A general warranty deed includes several guarantees by the grantor.

26. A The standard policy protects against mistakes in reporting liens that are in the public records, and extended coverage will protect against the rights of the parties in possession of the property.

27. C Quiet enjoyment means that the grantee need not worry about other parties with claims against the property.

28. A A special warranty deed guarantees only those defects to the title that occurred while the grantor was the owner.

29. D The public is given constructive notice of anything found in the public records.

30. B $65,325 × .08 = $5,226 (annual interest); $5,226 ÷ 12 ÷ 30 = $14.52 (daily interest); $14.52 × 14 days = $203.23. Because the buyer will have to make the loan payment at the end of the month, the seller is debited and the buyer is credited.

31. B When a property owner dies intestate leaving no heirs, property will eventually revert to the state through the government's power of escheat.

32. C Protection against forgery is included, while A and B are included in extended coverages. Physical defects are not covered under title insurance.

33. B   A buyer would most likely want the guarantees that accompany a warranty deed.

34. C   RESPA requires that a booklet describing the closing process and costs be given to the buyer by the lender.

35. C   Accretion is the gradual addition of land through a natural process.

36. A   A chain of title is a listing of all the owners of the property up to the present.

37. A   Erosion is the gradual reduction of land through a natural process.

38. B   The escrow agent collects and distributes all funds involved in the transaction.

39. C   Acknowledgments are made by notaries or officers of the court to indicate that the signatures on the deed are genuine.

40. C   Prorations are usually made as of the date title is transferred (typically the date of closing).

41. A   Quitclaim deeds include no warranties or guarantees.

42. B   Evidence of title includes title insurance, Torrens, certificate of title and abstract with lawyer's opinion.

43. A   A deed requires the grantor's signature. The remaining answers may be required in certain states for recording.

44. B   An acknowledgment is sometimes performed by a notary and is needed in some areas for recording.

45. A   States have laws of descent (also called intestacy laws) for situations in which the property owner died without a will.

46. B   The executor(trix) is also called the *personal representative* in some states.

47. D   RESPA was intended for residential transactions involving loans from federally insured lenders or VA or FHA loans.

48. A   The habendum clause includes the estate being transferred by the grantor.

49. B   By following the requirements for adverse possession as prescribed by state law, a person can acquire title to property.

50. B   A quitclaim deed includes no guarantees by the grantor and is often used to clear problems in the title.

UNIT V
DIAGNOSTIC WORKSHEET

CHAPTER 13
Agency and Real Estate Brokerage

No.	Answer	Correct
1	d	
14	d	
22	b	
31	c	
36	b	
40	a	
43	d	
46	d	
47	b	
48	b	
50	c	
TOTAL NUMBER CORRECT		

CHAPTER 14
Real Estate Contracts

No.	Answer	Correct
2	c	
7	a	
9	d	
11	d	
13	a	
15	b	
17	a	
21	a	
23	c	
25	c	
26	b	
27	c	
29	b	
32	b	
37	c	
39	b	
41	c	
44	a	
49	b	
TOTAL NUMBER CORRECT		

SCORE BREAKDOWN

Excellent = 50–45   Okay = 39–35
Very Good = 44–40   Poor = 34–0

UNIT V
DIAGNOSTIC WORKSHEET

CHAPTER 15
Listing Agreements

No.	Answer	Correct
3	c	
6	b	
8	a	
16	b	
19	a	
24	b	
33	d	
38	d	
42	c	
45	a	
TOTAL NUMBER CORRECT		

CHAPTER 16
Real Estate Licensing Laws

No.	Answer	Correct
4	c	
10	d	
18	c	
34	c	
TOTAL NUMBER CORRECT		

CHAPTER 17
Fair Housing Laws

No.	Answer	Correct
5	c	
12	d	
20	d	
28	c	
30	c	
35	b	
TOTAL NUMBER CORRECT		

TEST SUMMARY

Enter Number Correct for Each Chapter	Correct
Chapter 13—Agency and Real Estate Brokerage	
Chapter 14—Real Estate Contracts	
Chapter 15—Listing Agreements	
Chapter 16—Real Estate Licensing Laws	
Chapter 17—Fair Housing Laws	
TOTAL NUMBER CORRECT	

SCORE BREAKDOWN

Excellent = 50–45
Very Good = 44–40

Okay = 39–35
Poor = 34–0

SOLUTIONS TO UNIT V DIAGNOSTIC TEST

1. D In a listing agreement a seller hires a broker and establishes a fiduciary relationship of special trust and confidence. The broker's actions must be for the benefit of the principal/seller.

2. C A contract entered into by misrepresentation or fraud is voidable by the innocent party.

3. C $130,000 ÷ (100% − 6%) = $130,000 ÷ .94 = $138,298.

4. C The purpose of the licensing laws is to protect the public from unqualified and unethical people in real estate.

5. C Steering is channeling home buyers to particular areas based on the buyers' ethnic or racial characteristics rather than on their purchasing preferences.

6. B In both listings the seller hires only one broker to market the property. Under an exclusive-agency listing, however, the seller can sell the property without owing a commission.

7. A The seller (vendor) holds title to the property under an installment sales contract.

8. A A listing agreement creates a fiduciary relationship between a real estate broker and his or her client.

9. D The statute of frauds requires that certain contracts be in writing, including real estate sale contracts.

10. D Real estate licensing laws outline rules under which licenses may be suspended or revoked by the state licensing authority.

11. D Contracts made under duress are voidable by the innocent party.

12. D The 1866 Civil Rights Act prohibits discrimination based on race without exceptions.

13. A The option gives the buyer the right to purchase the property for the time period stated in the contract.

14. D Brokers may not give legal advice.

15. B Consideration is one of the essential requirements of a contract. Without it there is no contract.

16. B An exclusive-right-to-sell listing requires that the principal pay the broker a commission no matter who sells the property.

17. A The buyer takes possession of the property but title remains with the seller until the loan, provided to the buyer by the seller, is paid.

18. C Sellers and buyers have an agency relationship with the broker, not with the broker's salespeople. Licensed salespersons may accept commissions from only their employing brokers.

19. A In a net listing the broker sets the selling price and the seller receives a predetermined amount.

20. D Marital status is not a protected class under the 1968 federal Fair Housing Act.

21. A A counteroffer ends the original offer.

22. B Misrepresentation by the selling broker may allow the buyer to rescind the contract.

23. C To have a valid contract, competent parties are required.

24. B Under an exclusive-agency listing the owner agrees to work with one broker; however, the owner does not have to pay the broker a commission if the owner sells the property.

25. C The option gives the buyer the right to purchase the property at the price stated in the option. However, the buyer does not have to purchase the property and may offer any amount that the seller is willing to accept.

26. B $5,950 ÷ $85,000 = 7%.

27. C When the seller changed the terms, a counteroffer was created that ended the buyer's offer.

28. C The 1866 Civil Rights Act covered only discrimination based on race.

29. B The agent's duty of notice requires that all offers should be presented to the seller at the same time.

30. C Business property is not included under the Fair Housing Act of 1968.

31. C Misrepresentation by the selling broker may allow the buyer to rescind the contract.

32. B The statute of frauds requires that certain contracts be in writing to be enforceable.

33. D $120,000 ÷ .94 = $127,660.

34. C In most states licensees are required to take continuing education courses before renewing their licenses.

35. B Familial status and handicapped status were added by the act.

36. B A special agent represents the principal in a specific transaction. The broker is hired only to sell the house.

37. C A suit for specific performance is used to force the terms of the contract to be carried out.

38. D Under an exclusive-right-to-sell listing the broker is entitled to a commission no matter who sells the property.

39. B The sellers' counteroffer that excluded the draperies ended the Smith's original offer.

40. A A broker should inform the buyer of any hidden defects in the property.

41. C A contingency is a condition on which the contract is based.

42. C Step 1: $100,000 × .06 = $6,000. Step 2: $6,500 − $6,000 = $500. Step 3: $500 ÷ .05 = $10,000. Step 4: $10,000 + $10,000 = $110,000.

43. D The amount of commission is completely negotiable between the principal and agent. Brokers cannot conspire to set standard commission rates.

44. A The amount of earnest money deposit is always negotiated between the buyer and seller. There are no laws specifying the amount of the deposit.

45. A Under an exclusive-agency listing the owner does not have to pay the broker a commission if the owner sells the property.

46. D Brokers can make statements of opinion called puffing and not be liable for fraud or misrepresentation.

47. B Independent contractors cannot be required to attend meetings or maintain specific work hours and must pay their own income taxes and business expenses. They are not eligible for benefits from the broker because they are not employees.

48. B The salesperson must give proper disclosure to the sellers that he or she is licensed.

49. B Contracts in which some or all of the terms have yet to be completed are called executory.

50. C The duty of loyalty requires that the broker act in the best interests of the seller. The broker should not divulge information that might hurt the seller and should try to obtain the best offer from the buyer.

UNIT IV
DIAGNOSTIC WORKSHEET

CHAPTER 18
The Appraisal Process

No.	Answer	Correct
3	b	
6	c	
9	d	
12	b	
15	b	
18	a	
21	c	
24	b	
28	c	
31	a	
32	d	
34	a	
37	c	
40	c	
TOTAL NUMBER CORRECT		

TEST SUMMARY

Enter Number Correct for Each Chapter	Correct
Chapter 18—The Appraisal Process	
Chapter 19—Methods of Estimating Value	
TOTAL NUMBER CORRECT	

CHAPTER 19
Methods of Estimating Value

No.	Answer	Correct
1	c	
2	d	
4	a	
5	a	
7	c	
8	d	
10	c	
11	b	
13	d	
14	a	
16	d	
17	c	
19	a	
20	b	
22	a	
23	c	
25	a	
26	b	
27	c	
29	b	
30	a	
33	c	
35	c	
36	c	
38	a	
39	d	
41	d	
42	d	
43	b	
44	c	
45	b	
46	b	
47	b	
48	c	
49	d	
50	d	
TOTAL NUMBER CORRECT		

SCORE BREAKDOWN

Excellent = 50–45   Okay = 39–35

Very Good = 44–40   Poor = 34–0

SOLUTIONS TO UNIT VI DIAGNOSTIC TEST

1. C The income approach would be best used to appraise property that generates income, such as an apartment building.

2. D The sales comparison approach uses information from the sale of similar properties to calculate the value.

3. B A property's highest and best use is the legal use that gives the owner the greatest return. The property's current use may not be its highest and best use.

4. A The gross rent multiplier is the relationship between the value of the property and the income produced by the property.

5. A The value of the land is included in estimating value using the cost approach.

6. C An appraisal is an estimate of the property's market value.

7. C Of the three types of depreciation, economic obsolescence is always considered to be incurable.

8. D GRM = value ÷ annual gross income ($561,000 ÷ $66,000 = 8.5).

9. D Different approaches to estimating value may be used for a single property. The last step in the appraisal process is to reconcile the results of using these approaches.

10. C Brokers normally use a competitive market analysis by comparing the selling price of similar properties to help determine the value of residential property.

11. B Appraisers normally use a cost analysis to determine the value of property that does not generate income and does not have similar properties to determine the value.

12. B Regression is the concept that the value of a better property may be adversely affected by the presence of poorer properties.

13. D Functional obsolescence refers to outmoded (obsolete) features on the property.

14. A Appraisers normally use an income analysis to determine the value of property that generates income, such as an office building.

15. B To attain its maximum value, a property should be located in an area of similar properties.

16. D Functional obsolescence refers to outmoded or poorly designed features in a property.

17. C The market data (also called *sales comparison*) approach uses information from similar properties that have sold to determine the subject property's value.

18. A As the supply of houses decreases, the demand and the price increase.

19. A Accrued depreciation is subtracted from the cost of replacing the property's structures in the cost approach.

20. B Economic obsolescence refers to conditions external to the subject property.

21. C The high profits may attract other investors who will build competing shopping malls, potentially reducing profits.

22. A The cost of replacing buildings on the property is a step used in the cost approach.

23. C Income ÷ Rate = Value. $40,000 ÷ .08 = $500,000 versus $40,000 ÷ .10 = $400,000.

24. B Contribution is the effect of improvements on the property's value.

25. A The annual net operating income of a property is divided by the capitalization rate to determine the property's value under the income approach.

26. B Reproducing the building is duplicating its features.

27. C $1,800 × 12 = $21,600; $21,600 ÷ .09 = $240,000.

28. C Assembling properties is done because the plottage value of the new, larger property is greater than the sum of the values of the individual properties.

29. B The cost of replacing the building is used in the cost approach. Reproducing the building is replicating its features and would probably not take advantage of modern materials and building techniques.

30. A Physical deterioration is the result of wear and tear on the property.

31. A To have value there must be demand, utility, scarcity and transferability (DUST).

32. D Regression means that the value of a better property will suffer if it is located near poorer properties.

33. C Functional obsolescence refers to outmoded or poorly designed features in a property.

34. A Anticipation affects the value of the property based on some future benefit or detriment potential purchasers believe will occur.

35. C Estimating the value of land is found in the cost approach.

36. C The amounts paid by sellers of comparable properties have no effect on the comparable values.

37. C Each property has a highest and best use that provides the property its greatest value.

38. A The income approach is most suitable for commercial property.

39. D An amount for anticipated vacancies is subtracted from potential gross income. The other expenses are subtracted from effective gross income to find net income.

40. C The purpose of the appraisal must be first defined prior to appraisal planning.

41. D $94,000 × 8.5 = $799,000.

42. D Estimating the value of special purpose property such as a public school is best performed by the cost approach.

43. B $36,000 ÷ $450,000 = 8%.

44. C In appraising residential property the location of the property is important.

45. B The gross rent multiplier (GRM) is found by dividing the sales price by the gross monthly rent. The GRM is a shorter variation of the more detailed income approach.

46. B Using the cost approach, the value of the property = replacement cost plus the land value less depreciation. $230,000 = $160,000 + $90,000 − $20,000.

47. B $750 × 6 × 12 = $54,000; $486,000 ÷ $54,000 = 9.

48. C The cost approach adds the value of the land to the cost of constructing structures on the property.

49. D The reconciliation (also called correlation) process analyzes the various results to arrive at a value.

50. D $6,000 ÷ .06 = $100,000 decrease

U N I T VII
DIAGNOSTIC
WORKSHEET

CHAPTER 20
Loan Instruments

No.	Answer	Correct
1	d	
5	a	
9	a	
10	d	
17	c	
25	a	
26	c	
33	a	
34	a	
39	b	
40	b	
TOTAL NUMBER CORRECT		

CHAPTER 21
Lending Practices

No.	Answer	Correct
2	a	
6	b	
11	b	
12	b	
19	c	
20	a	
27	a	
28	c	
35	d	
36	c	
41	c	
42	a	
TOTAL NUMBER CORRECT		

UNIT VII
DIAGNOSTIC
WORKSHEET

CHAPTER 22
Types of Real Estate Loans

No.	Answer	Correct
3	a	
7	b	
8	a	
13	c	
14	a	
15	b	
16	c	
18	c	
21	d	
22	c	
29	a	
30	d	
37	c	
38	b	
43	d	
45	b	
47	c	
48	a	
50	a	
TOTAL NUMBER CORRECT		

CHAPTER 23
Lending Laws and Government Activities

No.	Answer	Correct
4	b	
23	c	
24	d	
31	d	
32	b	
44	d	
46	c	
49	b	
TOTAL NUMBER CORRECT		

TEST SUMMARY

Enter Number Correct for Each Chapter	Correct
Chapter 20—Loan Instruments	
Chapter 21—Lending Practices	
Chapter 22—Types of Real Estate Loans	
Chapter 23—Lending Laws and Government Activities	
TOTAL NUMBER CORRECT	

SCORE BREAKDOWN

Excellent = 50–45
Very Good = 44–40

Okay = 39–35
Poor = 34–0

SOLUTIONS TO UNIT VII DIAGNOSTIC TEST

1. D   The trustee is a neutral party to the transaction who acts if the borrower defaults or the loan is paid.

2. A   Points are always computed as a percentage of the loan balance. For example, 3 points charged on a $100,000 loan equals $3,000 ($100,000 × .03).

3. A   The FHA insures loans made under its various loan programs.

4. B   The purpose of the Truth-in-Lending Act (also referred to as *Regulation Z*) is to inform the borrower of all the loan costs.

5. A   An acceleration clause "accelerates" all of the loan payments so that they are due immediately.

6. B   Step 1: $160,000 × .8 = $128,000 (the amount of the loan). Step 2: $128,000 × .015 = $1,920.

7. B   A wraparound loan is used to advance the borrower enough funds to pay the original loan plus additional funds. The lender giving the loan takes over the payments of the original loan.

8. A   In a buydown mortgage, the lender is given a fee to reduce the interest rate on the loan.

9. A   An alienation clause (also called a *due-on-sale clause*) allows the lender to end the loan if title passes.

10. D   A defeasance clause protects the mortgagor by ending the mortgage when the loan is paid.

11. B   Because the rate will not change, the amount of interest the borrower will pay on the loan amount can be predetermined.

12. B   The purpose of FNMA is to provide a secondary market for loans. It buys and sells loans to investors.

13. C   The Federal Housing Administration (FHA) is an agency of HUD.

14. A   In a purchase-money mortgage the seller finances a portion of the purchase price. In an installment loan the seller usually provides all of the financing for the purchase.

15. B   With a reverse annuity mortgage the lender makes payments to the borrower and adds the amount to the loan balance. The loan does not have to be repaid until the house is sold or the owner dies.

16. C   A balloon is a larger payment due at the end of the loan to pay off the remaining balance.

17. C   In a trust deed situation, the trustee releases the beneficiary's (the lender's) claim on the property by issuing a release deed.

18. C   A blanket loan covers more than one parcel of real estate and allows the mortgage lien to be released on individual parcels when a predetermined amount of the loan is paid.

19. C   The function of mortgage brokers is bringing the borrower and lender together. Mortgage brokers do not service loans.

20. A   Mortgagors may redeem their foreclosed property through redemption rights (either equitable or statutory).

21. D   FHA loans are originated by qualified FHA lenders and not by a government agency.

22. C   As each payment of the loan is made, a portion is used to pay down (amortize) the loan balance.

23. C   The Truth-in-Lending Act requires that the annual percentage rate (i.e., APR) be included in advertisements.

24. D   The Fair Credit Reporting Act provides certain rights to consumers, including the right to inspect their files maintained at the credit bureaus.

25. A   The acceleration clause allows the lender to accelerate all of the remaining loan payments.

26. C   Hypothecation is pledging property as security for a loan without giving up possession of the property.

27. A   Redemption rights allow the borrower to stop foreclosure processing or regain the property after the sale. The rights of redemption vary by state.

28. C   Under the FHA loan programs, HUD insures the loans but does not provide loan money. FHA-approved lenders make the loans.

29. A   An open-end loan allows the borrower to obtain additional money up to the original loan amount.

30. D   A wraparound mortgage is a new, junior mortgage that is larger than the existing first loan.

31. D   The Truth-in-Lending Act (Regulation Z) allows the borrower three business days to rescind the loan for certain consumer loans.

32. B Under the Equal Credit Opportunity Act, lenders must make credit decisions based on economic reasons, not on the applicant's marital status or gender.

33. A Because the rate is fixed, the payment amounts are the same. The amount of each payment applied to the principal and interest varies as the loan is repaid.

34. A A defeasance clause protects the mortgagor by ending the mortgage when the loan is paid.

35. D A full assumption relieves the owner of primary responsibility for the loan.

36. C The secondary market does not originate loans; it buys and sells loans made by primary lenders.

37. C FHA loans charge the borrowers a mortgage insurance premium.

38. B VA loans are guaranteed by the government, but the VA does not make the loans.

39. B Step 1: $100,000 × .075 = $7,500 ÷ 12 = $625. Step 2: $902.77 − $625 = $277.77. Step 3: $100,000 − $277.77 = $99,722.23.

40. B An alienation clause (also called a *due-on-sale clause*) allows the lender to end the loan if title passes.

41. C If 8 points equal 1 percent, then ¾ − ¼ = 2/4 or ½ = 4 points.

42. A The FHA insures loans through its various loan programs but does not buy and sell loans.

43. D As loan payments are made, the balance is reduced, so that the amount of interest is less.

44. D The annual percentage rate must include most costs for obtaining the loan. Brokers' commissions are not considered part of these costs.

45. B One of the attractive features of VA loans is a low or, in some cases, no downpayment.

46. C The Truth-in-Lending Act requires that the lender provide the borrower with information on the loan costs so that the borrower can make a better-informed decision on the loan.

47. C $114,500 × .8 = $91,600.

48. A Payments on a term loan (also called a *straight loan*) include only interest, with the balance due at the end of the loan term.

49. B $120,000 × .08 = $9,600 ÷ 12 = $800; $820 − $800 = $20.

50. A Each payment is calculated on the outstanding loan balance. $56,000 × .08 = $4,480; $4,480 ÷ 12 = $373.33.

UNIT VII
DIAGNOSTIC WORKSHEET

CHAPTER 24
Property Management

No.	Answer	Correct
1	d	
3	d	
4	a	
7	c	
8	c	
12	b	
15	b	
16	d	
19	b	
20	d	
23	a	
24	b	
27	b	
TOTAL NUMBER CORRECT		

CHAPTER 25
Tax Advantages of Home Ownership

No.	Answer	Correct
2	d	
5	c	
9	c	
11	b	
13	c	
17	a	
21	d	
25	c	
28	d	
29	a	
TOTAL NUMBER CORRECT		

CHAPTER 26
Real Estate Investments

No.	Answer	Correct
6	c	
10	b	
14	d	
18	a	
22	c	
26	b	
30	a	
TOTAL NUMBER CORRECT		

TEST SUMMARY

Enter Number Correct for Each Chapter	Correct
Chapter 24—Property Management	
Chapter 25—Tax Advantages of Home Ownership	
Chapter 26—Real Estate Investments	
TOTAL NUMBER CORRECT	

SCORE BREAKDOWN

Excellent = 30–27
Very Good = 26–24

Okay = 23–21
Poor = 20–0

SOLUTIONS TO UNIT VIII DIAGNOSTIC TEST

1. D   Land would not be covered in the policy because it is assumed that land cannot be destroyed.

2. D $375 × 12 = $4,500 × .28 = $1,260.

3. D   The property management agreement defines the manager's rights and duties.

4. A   The lender's name is added to the insurance policy, and any checks issued by the insurance company for damages will be payable to both the lender and the owner.

5. C   Interest paid on a loan secured by a person's home can usually be taken as a deduction.

6. C   Leverage is using other people's money to finance the purchase of an investment.

7. C   Property managers are usually not hired to sell the property.

8. C   Under full replacement coverage, insurance will pay for the current cost of replacing the property. Under a standard settlement, depreciation is deducted.

9. C $22,000 × .28 = $6,160.

10. B   Federal and state laws generally require full disclosure by providing a prospectus to all potential investors.

11. B $150,000 – $500 – $9,000 ($150,000 × .06) = $140,500; $140,500 – $60,000 = $80,500.

12. B   The insurance will pay for full replacement cost if coverage is kept at a certain percentage of the replacement cost of the property. Thus, it is important for the owner to periodically review the amount of coverage.

13. C   The $450 property insurance premium cannot be taken as an income tax deduction.

14. D   Cash flow on a property is the income generated less operating expenses and mortgage payments. Depreciation is not a cash expense.

15. B   By using a high insurance deductible, the property manager shares the risk of loss with the insurance company.

16. D   Policyholders must pay for damages up to the amount of the deductible. A larger deductible amount will usually decrease the premium.

17. A   Points to refinance a loan must be deducted over the life of the loan.

18. A   Liquidity is converting an asset to cash. Real estate is a nonliquid investment because it takes a relatively long time to sell.

19. B   Corrective maintenance includes repairs to keep the building functioning.

20. D   Only transactions in which the owner is seeking a loan from a federally insured lender or VA-, FHA-, FNMA-, GNMA- or FHLMC-related loans require flood insurance.

21. D   The taxable gain is the net sales price less the owner's adjusted cost basis in the property. The adjusted cost basis is the original cost of the residence plus any improvements made.

22. C $120,000 – $10,000 = $110,000; 100% ÷ 31.5 × 6 (years) = 19.05%; 19.5% × $110,000 = $20,955 depreciation; $110,000 – $20,955 = $89,045 + $10,000 = $99,045.

23. A   Preventive maintenance includes regularly scheduled work that prolongs the life of the building and equipment.

24. B   Flood insurance is covered by a separate policy.

25. C   The maximum capital gains exclusion amount is $250,000 for taxpayers filing singly and $500,000 for taxpayers filing joint returns.

26. B   Liquidity is converting an asset to cash and is a disadvantage to a real estate investment because real estate it takes a relatively long time to sell.

27. B $100,000 × .8 = $80,000; $60,000 ÷ $80,000 = .75; $25,000 × .75 = $18,750.

28. D   The amount that exceeds the capital gain exclusion limits ($500,000 if filing a joint return) is taxable income.

29. A   Under an installment sale the buyer agrees to pay the seller over a period of time rather than in one year. The seller/taxpayer recognizes the portion of the gain paid by the buyer in each year.

30. A   Real estate is not a liquid asset because it cannot be converted to cash quickly.

SOLUTIONS TO COMPREHENSIVE TEST 1

1. D The mortgagor is the borrower.

2. B A novation substitutes a new agreement for an old one.

3. B The purpose of RESPA is to inform the buyer of all closing costs.

4. A The trustee would provide the deed at closing.

5. B Attorneys at law must be licensed if acting as brokers and not as legal counsels.

6. D The primary expenses homeowners may deduct on their income tax returns are mortgage interest and real estate taxes.

7. B The apartment manager's actions are to control the liability risk for the property owner.

8. A 640 acres ÷ 4 = 160 ÷ 4 = 40 ÷ 4 = 10 ÷ 2 = 5 acres; 5 × $3,000 = $15,000.

9. A Brokers may not mix (commingle) their own money with money belonging to the parties in a real estate transaction.

10. B The capitalization rate is the rate of return from an investment.

11. D Lenders may charge and borrowers may pay discount points on VA-guaranteed loans.

12. B A balloon payment is a large payment at the end of a loan that is not completely amortized.

13. C Single-family residences provide safer collateral; therefore, lenders would be willing to make a higher leveraged loan.

14. B While the assignee is primarily liable, the assignor still has secondary liability.

15. D The title insurance premium is paid one time, when the policy is issued.

16. B The habendum clause defines the extent of the estate being conveyed.

17. A Because salespersons work for brokers, they can receive compensation only from the employing brokers.

18. D Independent contractors receive their income from commissions and not monthly or hourly wages.

19. A A certificate of reasonable value is required by the VA to obtain a loan.

20. A Functional obsolescence refers to outmoded or obsolete features of the property.

21. B The statue of frauds requires that contracts for the sale of real estate be in writing to be enforceable.

22. A Improvements are used to adjust the property's basis in determining the taxable gain or loss.

23. C An alienation clause (also called a *due-on-sale clause*) prevents the mortgage from being assumed by the buyer.

24. A Because of situs and immobility, the location of real estate has the greatest effect on its value.

25. B A mechanic's lien is a claim for materials or services provided to the real estate.

26. B Increasing the value of a house because the surrounding properties are better is referred to as *progression.*

27. C In a listing contract the seller (the principal) hires the broker (the agent) to sell the property.

28. B A devise is the gift of real property in a will, whereas a bequest involves personal property.

29. A Increasing the reserve requirements means banks will have less money to lend, thus slowing the economy.

30. C A quitclaim deed provides no guarantees by the grantor to the grantee.

31. A "Time is of the essence" means that the terms must be completed on time.

32. A An acceleration clause allows the lender to declare the remaining loan payments due immediately if the borrower defaults on the loan.

33. B An exclusive-right-to-sell listing requires that the seller pay a commission regardless of who sells the property.

34. D The duty of disclosure requires that the broker keep his or her principal informed of all relevant facts in the transaction.

35. C The Fair Housing Law prohibits owners from discriminating against families with children.

36. D In a tenancy at will the tenant possesses the property with the consent of the landlord, who can cancel it at any time.

37. C The grantor warrants good and clear title to the property.

38. C $120,000 \div 1.2 = $100,000.

39. A The amount of tax is calculated by multiplying the assessed value by the tax rate.

40. C The nursing home has a life estate based on the life of another (*M's* parents).

41. A The use must be without the owner's consent.

42. C $70,000 – $12,000 = $58,000 \div .08 = $725,000.

43. D The broker must put earnest money into an escrow account and not in the broker's personal or business account.

44. D The right of redemption allows the property owner to stop the foreclosure sale or regain the property after the sale. Rules for redemption vary by state.

45. C When an offer is withdrawn before acceptance there is no contract, and the earnest money must be returned to the buyer in full.

46. D In a cooperative the corporation purchases a building and gives the shareholders a proprietary lease right to occupy a unit in the building.

47. A $1,800 \div 360 days = $5 per day. $5 \times 50 days = $250. The seller is credited because the taxes are prepaid.

48. D A listing agreement will automatically terminate with the death of the seller.

49. B A percentage lease bases the amount of rent on the gross sales of the tenant.

50. C A commission is owed only to the broker who sells the property. If the owner sells the property, no commission is owed.

51. A The cost approach subtracts the amount of depreciation from the cost of the improvements in determining the value of the property.

52. B It takes approximately 8 points to raise the yield on the loan 1%; thus, an increase of ½% requires 4 points.

53. C Each section equals 640 acres. One-half is 320 acres.

54. B $120,500 \times .80 = $96,400.

55. B $168,000 \times 8.5 = $1,428,000.

56. A Salespersons can receive compensation only from their employing brokers.

57. A A condition subsequent is a type of defeasible (conditional) estate.

58. D The common areas of a condominium facility are owned by all the unit owners.

59. C VA loans can be obtained with little or no down payment.

60. C The Truth-in-Lending Act is also called Regulation Z, which is the federal regulation that defines the act.

61. A In a unilateral contract there is a promise for an action.

62. D An easement by necessity gives the owner the right of ingress and egress from the property.

63. A Real estate taxes need to be prorated based on the date of closing and the payment period.

64. A Periodic estates (also called *estates from period to period*) require notice to terminate.

65. A $1 \div .10 = $10. Because expenses decrease, the value increases.

66. A Joint tenancy has right of survivorship, which takes precedent over a will.

67. A Improvements adjust the owner's basis in the property.

68. D Placing documents in the public records provides constructive notice.

69. D Joint tenancy has right of survivorship and the unity of interest (equal owners). Tenants in common cannot exclude the other owners but can sell their interest without the other owners' consent.

70. B In an installment sales contract the seller provides financing and title passes to the buyer when the loan is repaid.

71. A The Truth-in-Lending Act (Regulation Z) provides for a three-day cooling-off period (right of rescission) in certain loan situations.

72. C $195,000 \times .075 = $14,625; $14,625 \times .65 = $9,506.25.

73. B Owner-occupied residential property of one to four units is exempted under the 1968 federal Fair Housing Act.

74. B The cost approach uses the unit-in-place method to estimate the current cost of constructing improvements on the property.

75. B Net leases require that the tenant pay some or all of the property's expenses in addition to a base rent amount.

76. C Tenants in common would be presumed. Joint tenancy must be specifically stated, and both tenancy by the entirety and community property are between married couples.

77. B   Undesirable effects owing to the location of the appraised property are caused by economic obsolescence, not functional obsolescence.

78. C   A tenant occupying the premises without the consent of the landlord is a tenant at sufferance.

79. D   Redlining is refusing to make loans or issue insurance policies in certain areas without regard to the applicant's qualifications.

80. C   RESPA covers transactions involving noncommercial property with first mortgages.

SOLUTIONS TO COMPREHENSIVE TEST 2

1. D   Government-owned land is usually exempt from property taxes.

2. C   Actual title is not conveyed until a deed is delivered, but the buyer acquires equitable title when the contract is signed.

3. C   The Real Estate Settlement Procedures Act (RESPA) requires disclosure of closing charges and fees.

4. C   Sales price = Commission ÷ Rate; $8,400 ÷ .07 = $120,000.

5. D   Borrowers may regain their property through the right of redemption.

6. C $120,000 × .06 = $7,200; $7,200 × .6 (60%) = $4,320; $4,320 × .5 = $2,160.

7. C $330,000 − $12,000 − $8,500 − $120,000 = $189,500.

8. A   Sections are numbered 1 through 36 beginning with number 1 in the northeast corner of a township.

9. B   The right of first refusal allows someone to purchase the property first before it is offered to the general public.

10. D   Each point raises the loan yield approximately ⅛ of a percent.

11. B   A remainder interest is given to a third party in a life estate.

12. C   The contract is voidable by the party who acted under duress.

13. C   Annual tax ÷ Tax rate = Selling price; $768 ÷ .008 = $96,000.

14. A   Different percentages of ownership can be held by tenants in common. Joint tenants hold equal ownership.

15. C   Property managers usually are not expected to supply income tax advice.

16. B   The current cost of replacing the improvements on the property is one of the steps in the cost approach to estimating value.

17. B   Blockbusting is inducing owners to sell by instilling fear of adverse changes in an area based on racial or ethnic changes.

18. C $583.33 × 12 = $6,999.96; $6,999.96 ÷ $80,000 = .0875.

19. A   The cost approach estimates the value of the land and improvements less depreciation.

20. A   Brokers must generally disclose all hidden defects in the property whether or not they are instructed to do so by the seller.

21. C $1,800 × 4 = $7,200; $7,200 ÷ $80,000 = 9%.

22. A   32′ × 160′ × 10′ = 51,200 cu. ft.; 51,200 ÷ 27 = $1,896.30.

23. A   A variance allows the owner an "exception" to the zoning laws.

24. A   While the option gives the buyer the right to purchase the property, it does not require the buyer to purchase.

25. D   A tenancy (estate) for years continues for a definite period of time.

26. C   The principle of progression refers to the value of a poorer property being enhanced by its proximity to better properties.

27. B   A real estate sales contract is an agreement between the buyer and seller.

28. D   Independent contractors are not paid a fixed salary and cannot be treated as employees.

29. B   One of the essential elements of a valid contract is competent parties.

30. D $3,600 × 2 = $7,200; $7,200 ÷ .06 = $120,000.

31. D   Joint tenancy has right of survivorship. As the surviving tenant the sister now owns the property and is not responsible for the brother's personal debts.

32. C   The Federal Fair Housing Act sets a time limit of one year after the discriminatory act occurred.

33. C   Limited partners are liable only to the extent of their investment.

34. A   A determinable fee estate is created as long as a condition is met by the grantee.

35. B   It takes approximately 8 discount points to raise the yield on a 30-year loan 1 percent (9 − 8.75 = .25% or ¼ or 2 points).

36. D   The market data (also called sales comparison) method of estimating value is best suited to houses because there should be an ample number of comparison properties to use.

37. A   A title-theory state allows the lender to hold title to the property being mortgaged.

38. D The annual percentage rate (APR) must be included when advertising financial terms.

39. A A quiet title suit is used to clear uncertainties in the title.

40. A $160,000 × .8 = $128,000.

41. A Market value is the most probable price the property will sell for if the buyers are negotiating freely with knowledge of the marketplace.

42. A Mortgage brokers bring real estate buyers (borrowers) and lenders together.

43. D Title to personal property is transferred by a bill of sale. A deed transfers title to real property.

44. C The buyer (X) leases the property back to the seller (W), who becomes the lessee.

45. B A bequest transfers property through the voluntary action of the owner.

46. B Through its government power of eminent domain, the state may acquire ownership of private land for the public good.

47. B Because the building is now commercial property, the income approach should be given the most weight in determining its market value.

48. B $800 × .10 + $800 = $880 (rent for the second and third stores); $800 + $880 + $880 = $2,560 (rent per month); $2,560 × 12 = $30,720 (annual rent); $30,720 × .08 = $2,457.60.

49. C $38,500 × .04 = $1,540.

50. C The metes-and-bounds method of describing real estate starts at a point of beginning, or POB.

51. A Deeds are acknowledged before a notary or officer of the court to provide assurance of the authenticity of the parties to the deed.

52. C An exclusive-right-to-sell listing provides that the listing broker is entitled to a commission no matter who sells the property.

53. A Equity in a property is equal to the difference between the property's value and its debt.

54. C $96,000 × 1.33 = $127,680.

55. A A real estate appraiser estimates market value. Buyers and sellers determine the value and actual selling price.

56. A When B died, her interest went to A (the surviving joint tenant). When C sold his interest, X became a tenant in common.

57. D RESPA requires that the lender make the required disclosures under the act.

58. C A lender's title policy is usually charged to the buyer because it is a cost of obtaining the loan.

59. A Mortgage liens are usually recorded. Leases and surveys are usually *not* recorded, and encroachments are physical intrusions on the property.

60. B The Torrens system is used to register title to real estate.

61. D The maximum gain from the sale of a residence that may be excluded from income is $250,000 for single taxpayers and $500,000 for married taxpayers filing a joint return.

62. D In a buydown mortgage someone other than the borrower pays the lender a fee at the start of the loan and the lender makes the loan at a lower interest rate for the first few years.

63. C The contract is voidable by the defrauded party.

64. C The lender can deny a loan based on the applicant's financial condition.

65. B $80,000 ÷ .1 = $800,000.

66. D The capitalization rate is the rate of return the property will earn for the owner.

67. C Money held in a special account (typically called a *reserve* or *escrow account*) by the lender is used to pay the real estate taxes and homeowner's insurance on the property.

68. B The property's market price is the actual sale amount.

69. B Prepaid expenses are charged to the buyer and the seller is reimbursed with a credit.

70. B $84,000 ÷ .94 = $89,362.

71. D Because the loans are insured or guaranteed by the government, there is lower risk to the lender.

72. A Because of the undisclosed dual agency, the buyer can withdraw from the transaction without damages.

73. A The cabinets are improvements and become part of the real estate. They are owned by the property owner.

74. D 30 yards × 3 = 90 feet; 175 feet × 90 feet = 15,750 sq. ft.

75. D The commission rate is negotiated between the broker and the principal.

76. C $68,000 × .09 = $6,120 (annual interest); $6,120 ÷ 12 = $510; $525 − $510 = $15 (toward principal); $68,000 − $15 = $67,985.

77. B A property that conforms to a previous zoning code but is no longer in compliance because of a zoning change may continue as a nonconforming use.

78. B $132,000 − $18,000 = $114,000 (depreciable basis); $114,000 ÷ 31.5 × 6 = $21,714.30 (depreciation); $114,000 − $21,714.30 = $92,285.70 (current book value).

79. A   All offers should be presented as soon as possible, and the seller must decide which offer to accept.

80. A   A judgment attaches to all of a person's property and is a general lien.

GLOSSARY

abstract of title A summary of all legal instruments affecting title to a property from the original source of the title to the present. If the buyer's lawyer examines the abstract and writes a report of the title's condition, it is called an *abstract and lawyer's opinion*.

accelerated cost recovery system (ACRS) An alternative method of calculating depreciation in which more depreciation is taken in earlier years and less in later years.

acceleration clause A clause in the mortgage that allows the lender to demand immediate payment of the loan balance if the borrower breaks the terms of the note or mortgage.

accession Acquiring additions to real estate as a result of adding a fixture or of accretion.

accretion The addition of land through natural forces.

accrued expense An expense that has occurred but not been paid.

acknowledgment A voluntary statement before a notary or officer of the court by a person who signed a document that indicates that the signature is genuine and made by the signer's free will.

acquisition debt An income tax term used to describe money borrowed to purchase, construct or improve a residence.

acre A measure of land equal to 43,560 square feet.

actual cash value A method of settling an insurance claim in which depreciation is subtracted from the original cost of the property.

actual eviction The removal of a tenant by the landlord because the tenant breached a condition of the lease.

actual notice Information a person has gained by actually reading, hearing or seeing.

actual number of days in the month method A variation of the statutory month method for prorating expenses at closing. It takes into account the actual number of days in the month of closing.

actual number of days in the year method A method of proration using the actual number of days in the proration period.

adjustable rate mortgage (ARM) A mortgage in which the interest rate changes at predetermined intervals according to a predetermined financial market index. There are usually ceilings (caps) that limit the amount the rate can change every year and over the life of the loan.

adjusted cost basis The original cost of an asset plus capital improvements less certain deductions. Used to determine the amount of gain or loss realized when the asset is sold.

administrative law judge Judges who operate under HUD in resolving discrimination complaints.

ad valorem tax A Latin term meaning *according to value*. It is a real estate tax based on the value of the property.

adverse possession A method of acquiring title to real property by using the property without the owner's consent and following statutory requirements.

agency The relationship between an agent and a principal.

agency by estoppel An agency created when a third person relies on the statements of the principal regarding a purported agent.

agency by necessity An agency created because of an emergency situation.

agency coupled with an interest A agency in which the agent is given an estate or interest in the property by the principal.

agent The party who acts on behalf of a principal.

air rights Rights a property owner has in the space above the surface of the property.

alienation clause The clause in a mortgage that allows the lender to make the entire loan balance due if title to the property is transferred. Also referred to as a *due-on-sale clause*.

allodial system A legal system that recognizes private ownership of land.

alluvion New deposits of land as the result of accretion.

Americans with Disabilities Act (ADA) A law that requires that property that is open to the public include features that facilitate access to the building. The ADA is designed to eliminate discrimination against individuals with disabilities by providing equal access to jobs, public accommodations, government services, public transportation and telecommunications.

amortization Systematic repayment of a debt through periodic installments. Loans can be fully amortized (the entire balance is extinguished), partially amortized (only part of the balance is paid) or negatively amortized (the balance increases).

annual percentage rate (APR) A term used in the Truth-in-Lending Act to represent the true yearly cost of a loan. The APR is a yearly rate and includes the loan's interest rate plus other loan fees.

anticipation A principle of value used in appraisal. The value of property may increase or decrease based on some future event that is expected to occur.

antitrust laws Laws designed to protect free competition.

appraisal The process of estimating and supporting an opinion of value.

Appraisal Foundation A private nonprofit group that establishes uniform appraisal standards.

Appraisal Qualifications Board A board of The Appraisal Foundation. Sets minimum criteria for state-certified appraisers and endorses uniform examinations for certification.

appreciation The increase in a property's value over a period of time, which can be caused by inflation or by the characteristics of the property.

appurtenant easements Easement rights belonging to properties that are adjacent to one another and pass with the property to new owners. Include water rights and rights-of-way.

ARELLO The Association of Real Estate License Law Officials. A federation of real estate law officials to assist each other in the administration and enforcement of license laws.

as is A contract clause indicating the seller will not fix any problems with the property.

assemblage The process of merging adjoining lots together. It is used to take advantage of the principle of value called *plottage*.

assessed value A value put on real and personal property by a taxing authority as a basis to calculate the amount of real estate tax.

assignment Transferring contract rights or obligations. In a lease situation, transferring all of the remaining terms of the lease to someone else.

associate broker A license category. A person holding this type of license has passed the requirements for a broker license but is employed by another broker.

assumption *See* loan assumption.

attachment The process of changing personal property to real property.

attorney-at-law A person licensed by the state to practice law.

attorney-in-fact A person appointed to act for another under a power of attorney.

avulsion The sudden removal of land by natural forces.

back-end qualifying ratio A ratio used by a lender to qualify a loan applicant. It compares the applicant's gross income with the proposed PITI and long-term debt.

balloon loan A loan in which the payments do not fully amortize the loan balance. The remaining loan balance is included in the last payment, called a *balloon payment*.

bargain and sale deed A deed that may come with or without guarantees. The only guarantee usually associated with this deed is a guarantee against encumbrances for the period the grantor held title.

base lines East-west lines that intersect with principal meridians. Used in the rectangular survey system.

basis The original cost of the property plus capital improvements less accrued depreciation. Used for accounting and income tax purposes.

bench mark Reference point used in metes-and-bounds descriptions.

beneficiary The party in a trust who benefits from the assets of the trust. Also, the party receiving personal property under a will.

bequest The disposition of personal property under a will.

bilateral contract A type of contract in which both parties promise to act.

bill of sale Transfers title to personal property in a transaction.

binder A short version of a contract that includes all of the essential contract terms.

biweekly loan A loan in which a payment is made every two weeks. Under this arrangement a borrower pays less interest and pays the loan off sooner than under a standard loan arrangement with monthly payments.

blanket loan A loan that covers more than one property and contains a partial release clause that releases the lien on individual properties as the loan is paid.

blind ad Advertising that does not include the broker's name or the name of the real estate company. State licensing laws usually prohibit blind ads.

blockbusting Inducing owners to sell or rent based on representations that persons of a particular race, religion, national origin, etc., are moving into the area.

blue-sky laws Laws passed to protect the public from fraudulent investment schemes.

boot Additional cash or nonqualifying property received as part of a like-kind exchange. Boot is taxable to the recipient.

borrower A person who receives a loan (also known as the *mortgagor*).

boundary lines Used in metes-and-bounds descriptions. They define the boundaries of a property.

broker One who acts as an intermediary on behalf of others for a fee.

brokerage Bringing parties together for the purchase, rent or exchange of real estate.

broker license A type of real estate license category that allows the licensee to operate a real estate office.

broker/sales associate agreement A written agreement between a broker and his or her sales agents.

budget loan A loan arrangement in which a portion of the property's real estate taxes and insurance is collected by the lender as part of the loan payment.

building codes Enacted by local governments under their police powers to protect the public from inferior construction practices.

Building Owners and Managers Association (BOMA) An association of owners and managers of primarily office buildings.

building permit Issued by local governments' building inspectors to allow construction of new buildings or alteration of existing structures.

bundle of legal rights A concept of land ownership under which an owner holds all legal rights (i.e., possession, enjoyment, disposition, etc.) to the land.

buydown A loan arrangement in which the lender is paid an interest subsidy in exchange for a reduced loan rate in the first years of the loan.

capital gain (loss) The profit (or loss) from the sale or exchange of an asset. It is computed as the difference between an asset's adjusted basis and the net selling price.

capitalization rate The rate of return or yield from a property that is expected by an investor. The rate is used in the income approach to estimating value and is determined by dividing a property's net income by its sales price.

carryover provision A clause in a listing agreement that provides that the broker may be entitled to a commission after the listing contract has expired.

cash flow The dollars remaining from income after all expenses have been paid. Cash flow can be either positive or negative.

caveat emptor A Latin phrase meaning *let the buyer beware*. Under this concept buyers make purchases at their own risk.

certificate of eligibility Issued by the VA to qualified veterans and includes the maximum loan amount guarantee for the veteran, which is set by the VA based on eligibility period and prior use.

certificate of occupancy A certificate of occupancy must be issued before a building can be legally occupied. It is issued only after the building is inspected to make sure it complies with building codes.

certificate of reasonable value (CRV) Sets the maximum VA loan amount for a property after it is appraised by a VA appraiser and the appraisal is reviewed by the VA.

certificate of sale Given to the winner at a foreclosure sale. It entitles the winner to a deed after the redemption period is over.

certificate of title A document signed by a lawyer or title examiner that states that the seller has marketable title

on a property. Unlike a title insurance policy, it does not provide protection against title defects not found in the public records.

chain of title A chronological history of all the conveyances of a property. Includes who purchased and sold the property and the dates. This information is obtained from the public records.

change A principle of value used in appraisal. States that real estate conditions, both physical and economic, do not remain constant, thus affecting the value of real estate.

chattel Another name for personal property.

closing The consummation of a real estate transaction. Includes delivery of the deed, signing of forms and disbursement of funds to complete the transaction.

closing agent The party that schedules and coordinates the closing process. Usually a representative of a title company or lender or the lawyer for the buyer or seller.

closing statement A document used for detailing the financial information (funds received and paid) in a closing.

cloud on title Anything that impairs the marketability of a title. Clouds include liens, easements and deed restrictions on the title.

codicil An amendment or addition to a will.

coinsurance clause A clause in the insurance policy whereby the owner may take on some of the risk if the house is insured for less than a certain percentage (usually 80 percent) of the replacement cost stated in the policy.

collateral Property pledged as security for a debt.

color of title A claim to title that is defective.

commercial banks Banks that are either federally or state chartered and that make mortgage, construction and home improvement loans.

commercial easement The right given to utility companies to go onto the land to maintain their equipment. A type of easement in gross.

commercial property Property used for businesses, such as stores and office buildings.

commingling Mixing the broker's personal or operating money with the client's, usually by placing both in the same account. This is illegal under real estate licensing laws.

commitment fee A fee paid by a potential borrower to the lender for the lender's promise to lend money at a specified rate within a certain time period.

commitment to insure A binder issued by an insurance company stating its intention to grant a policy to an applicant.

commitment to lend *See* loan commitment.

common elements In condominiums, the parts of the property used by all residents of the condominium building.

common law A body of laws based on custom and usage.

Community Bank Reinvestment Act A law passed to ensure that banks meet the lending needs in the communities where they are located and to prevent redlining.

community property Property acquired by a husband and wife after marriage. Property acquired prior to the marriage or obtained by gift or inheritance while they are married is owned separately.

comparable property Comparable properties are recently sold properties that are similar to the subject property. Used in the sales comparison approach to estimating value.

competent parties Parties who have legal capacity.

competition A principle of value used in appraisal. States that if substantial profits are being made competition will be attracted. The increased competition may reduce profit and property value.

competitive market analysis (CMA) A simplified version of the sales comparison approach used by brokers to help sellers set a likely selling price for property.

conciliation agreement The successful result of mediation between the parties in a discrimination complaint.

condemnation The legal process for taking of title to property under the government power of eminent domain.

condominium A form of property ownership in which each occupant of a multiunit building owns his or her dwelling unit separately and an undivided interest with other owners in the property's common elements (lobbies, hallways, etc.).

condominium bylaws Rules passed by the condominium owners' association that are used to administer the property.

condominium owners' association An association of all the owners in a condominium. They may elect a Board of Directors to oversee the administration and management of the condominium.

conforming loans Loans that follow the established guidelines of the secondary mortgage market.

conformity A principle of value used in appraisal. States that the value of property is maximized if it conforms to the surrounding land use.

consideration Anything of value given by parties to a contract.

construction loan A loan that provides funds for real estate projects. The lender usually disburses the money as work is completed (called *draws*).

constructive eviction Occurs when a tenant is forced to leave because the property becomes uninhabitable.

constructive notice Information that has been made public. The law presumes a person knows all information made available to the public.

contingency A provision in a contract requiring certain acts to be done before the contract is binding.

contract An agreement among competent parties to do or not to do some legal act(s) and supported by legal considerations.

contract for deed *See* installment sales contract.

contribution A principle of value used in appraisal. States that an improvement's value is equal to the value added to the property.

conventional life estate A life estate created by the acts of the parties rather than by statute.

conventional loan A loan that is not insured or guaranteed by a government agency. The lender assumes the full risk of default in a conventional loan.

cooperatives A form of property ownership in which a corporation owns the building and the tenants purchase shares in the corporation that give them a right to occupy a unit in the building.

corporation An artificial entity created by a corporate charter and run by a board of directors. A corporation can hold title to real estate.

correction lines Used in the rectangular survey method to compensate for the convergence of range lines due to the curvature of the earth.

cost In appraisal, the total in dollars of the value of the land and constructing the improvements on the property.

cost approach An approach to estimating the value of property through the concept of substitution. The value of the subject property is found by (1) estimating the cost of construction, (2) subtracting depreciation and (3) adding the land value.

covenants Guarantees given in deeds by the grantor. Covenants include seisin, encumbrances, further assurance, quiet enjoyment and warranty forever.

credit report A report issued by a service bureau detailing an individual's credit history.

credit unions Associations that maintain savings accounts for their members while providing primarily home improvement and home equity real estate loans.

curable depreciation Depreciation that is worth fixing. That is, the cost of fixing does not exceed the value of the property.

curtesy The husband's legal life estate in his wife's property.

datum Used to measure elevations. While cities may have several datums, the most commonly used is the USGS datum, which is based on sea level in New York Harbor.

debt-to-income ratio A ratio used by lenders to qualify borrowers. It is used to calculate the percentage of gross income allowed for the monthly PITI payment.

declaration A document that legally establishes a condominium. Also known as a *master deed* or *enabling declaration*.

deductible The amount an insured has to pay before the insurance company is liable.

deductions Expenses that taxpayers are allowed to include on their income tax returns to reduce their taxable income.

deed A written instrument that transfers title to real property from one owner (the grantor) to another (the grantee).

deed in lieu of foreclosure A type of nonjudicial foreclosure in which the lender accepts title to the property from the borrower in exchange for ending the debt.

deed of trust An agreement among three parties for the purpose of securing a real estate loan. Parties to the trust are the trustor (the borrower), the trustee (usually a title company or bank) and a beneficiary (the mortgagee). Used in many states in place of a mortgage.

deed restriction A clause in a deed that limits the owner's use of the property.

defeasance clause Stipulates that the mortgage lien is void when the loan is repaid.

defeasible fee estate An estate in which the holder has a fee simple title to the property that will end on the occurrence or nonoccurrence of some event.

deficiency judgment A judgment against a debtor's personal assets if the sale of real estate is not sufficient to satisfy the loan.

delivery and acceptance The time at which title to real estate passes, when a deed is delivered to and accepted by the grantee.

demographics Refers to characteristics of a population, such as age and economic status.

Department of Housing and Urban Development (HUD) One of the duties of this federal agency is to administer the FHA loan programs. Primarily responsible for enforcing the Fair Housing Law of 1968.

Department of Veterans Affairs A federal agency also known as the VA. One of its functions is to administer the guaranteed loan program for loans made to qualified veterans by approved lenders.

depreciable basis The total monetary value of an asset that is used to calculate depreciation.

depreciation (1) In appraisal, a loss of property value due to any cause. Depreciation is used in the cost approach to estimating value. *See also* cost approach, curable depreciation, economic obsolescence, functional obsolescence, incurable depreciation, physical deterioration. (2) For tax purposes, a deduction that allows the cost of assets used in business or as investment property to be recovered over a period of time. Noninvestment property (such as principal residences) cannot be depreciated. The rules for calculating tax-deductible depreciation are established by the IRS.

descent Rules used by state law to determine how title to property will pass if the owner died leaving no will.

designated agent A licensed person authorized by a broker to act as the agent for a specific principal in a real estate transaction.

devise The disposition of real property under a will.

devisee The party receiving real property under a will.

discount point Interest points charged by a lender to raise the yield on a loan. One point is equal to 1 percent of the loan amount.

discount rate The interest rate charged other banks by the Fed for loans. By adjusting the discount rate the Fed can control interest rates and the flow of money in the economy.

disintermediation The outflow of funds from savings institutions.

dominant tenement A tract of land that benefits from an easement appurtenant right.

dower The wife's legal life estate in her husband's property.

downzoning A change in zoning from higher-density to lower-density use. Often used to prevent overloading of public services in an area.

dual agency Representing both parties in the same transaction.

due-on-sale clause *See* alienation clause.

earnest money A deposit given by the potential buyer of real estate after a purchase contract is signed to demonstrate the buyer's good-faith intention to purchase the property. The money is held by a third party (usually the seller's broker) until closing.

easement The right to use another's land.

easement by necessity An easement right granted by law when there is no access to a person's land.

easement by prescription Acquiring an easement right by using the property without the owner's consent for the period of time stated by law.

easement in gross An easement right given to a person or corporation to enter someone's land for a specific purpose.

economic obsolescence Loss of value caused by variables external to the property. May result from economic, social or environmental forces such as zoning changes, etc. One of the three types of depreciation calculated in the cost approach to estimating value. The property owner has little or no control over these forces; therefore, this type of depreciation is always considered incurable.

effective gross income Used in the income approach to estimating value. Effective gross income is found by subtracting an allowance for vacancies and uncollected rent from potential gross income.

emblements Annual crops on a property that are raised by the owner.

eminent domain The government power to take private land for the public good. Compensation must be given to the owner of the property.

employee A working relationship between a broker and his or her sales agents in which the broker has control over how agents perform their duties. The broker can withhold for taxes and Social Security and offer benefits such as pensions, health insurance and profit sharing.

enabling legislation Laws passed by some states giving local governments the authority to establish local laws.

encroachment Illegal physical intrusion on another's land.

encumbrance A charge, claim or liability on the property.

endorsement A rider added to an insurance policy that changes the coverage.

Equal Credit Opportunity Act Protects borrowers from discrimination when applying for loans. A lender can deny a borrower credit based only on valid business reasons.

equalizer Adjusts property assessments so that they are equitable throughout a state.

equitable redemption A borrower's right to redeem property *before* a foreclosure sale.

equity A property's value minus any loans against it.

erosion The gradual loss of land through natural causes.

errors and omissions insurance A type of coverage that protects brokers from loss due to errors, mistakes and negligence.

escheat The government power to acquire land from owners who die without a will and leave no heirs.

escrow Placing something (e.g., money, documents or property) with a third party to be delivered to a designated person when certain conditions, such as the closing of a transaction, are fulfilled.

escrow account An account maintained with a lender to hold money to pay real estate taxes and insurance. Also used by brokers to hold buyers' earnest money that comes into brokers' possession during real estate transactions.

escrow closing A closing procedure in which an appointed agent handles all of the closing details rather than having them handled in a face-to-face meeting of buyer and seller.

estate for years A leasehold estate that continues for a definite period of time. This is the most common type of leasehold estate and usually requires no notice to terminate.

estate in land The degree, extent, quantity and nature of interest a person has in real property.

eviction The process of removing a tenant from the premises if a lease agreement is breached. Implemented by filing a suit for possession after giving sufficient notice to the tenant.

evidence of title Proof of ownership of property. Usually a certificate of title, an abstract of title with lawyer's opinion, title insurance or a Torrens registration certificate.

exclusive-agency listing A type of listing in which the seller hires a single broker. If the seller sells the property himself or herself, however, a commission is not owed the broker.

exclusive-right-to-sell listing A type of listing in which the seller hires a single broker. In this type of listing a commission is owed the broker no matter who sells the property.

executed contract A contract in which the parties have performed all of the provisions.

executor A male named in a will as the person to oversee the administration of a will's provisions.

executrix A female named in a will as the person to oversee the administration of a will's provisions.

expressed agency An agency created by words (either oral or written).

Fair Credit Reporting Act A law passed to regulate the action of credit bureaus and consumer credit information. It protects consumers from the reporting and use of inaccurate or obsolete credit information. A lender who rejects a loan request because of adverse credit bureau information must inform the borrower of the source of the information.

Fair Housing Act A federal law that prohibits discrimination in the sale and rental of housing based on race, color, religion, gender, handicap, familial status and national origin.

Fannie Mae Formally known as the Federal National Mortgage Association (FNMA). Operates in the secondary mortgage market. It handles FHA, VA and conventional loans and is the largest mortgage purchaser.

Federal Agricultural Mortgage Corporation A federal agency that establishes a secondary mortgage market for farm real estate loans.

Federal Deposit Insurance Corporation (FDIC) A government agency that manages two insurance funds used to insure deposits in both commercial banks and savings banks or thrifts.

Federal Home Loan Mortgage Corporation (FHLMC) A government agency that works closely with thrifts to provide a secondary market for their loans. Also known as "Freddie Mac."

Federal Housing Administration (FHA) The FHA is a division of the Department of Housing and Urban Development (HUD). The FHA's principal role is to insure residential mortgage loans made by private lenders.

Federal Reserve System Called *the Fed*, it was established by Congress in 1913 to help maintain a sound credit and economic environment and counteract inflation and deflation trends. The Fed regulates money supply and interest rates.

fee simple absolute The highest form of ownership recognized by the law. Another name for *fee simple estate*.

fee simple defeasible An estate that is subject to some condition to determine when it will begin or end. Also referred to as *determinable, conditional,* or *qualified fee.*

fee subject to condition precedent An estate that takes effect when a specified condition is performed. The estate ends when the condition is no longer met.

fee subject to condition subsequent An estate that includes a prohibited use of the property.

feudal system A system of ownership in which the land was controlled by the king, usually associated with England.

FHA loan A loan made by an approved lender and insured by the Federal Housing Administration.

fiduciary relationship A relationship that involves great trust and confidence.

fifteen-year loan A fully amortized loan with a 15-year term. Reducing the loan term from 30 to 15 years saves the borrower interest with only a moderate increase in the payment amount.

final walkthrough The final inspection of property by a buyer shortly before closing.

Financial Institutions Reform, Recovery and Enforcement Act (FIRREA) A federal law passed as a result of the troubles experienced by the savings and loan industry. The act included amendments intended to improve the competency of appraisers.

first mortgage A real estate loan that has priority over any subsequent mortgages.

fixed interest rate An interest rate that does not change during the loan term.

fixed rate mortgage A loan in which the interest rate does not change.

fixity An economic characteristic of real estate that refers to the fact that investments in real estate are for the long term.

fixture An item that was once personal property but has been attached to the real estate and become real property.

foreclosure The process of liquidating a borrower's assets to satisfy a debt.

fractional section Sections that are undersized (less than 260 acres). Used in the rectangular survey method for describing real estate.

fraud The intentional misstatement of a fact to induce someone to take a particular action.

Freddie Mac *See* Federal Home Loan Mortgage Corporation.

freehold estate An ownership interest in real estate for an indeterminable length of time.

friendly foreclosure The mortgagor in default conveys title to the lender to avoid a record of foreclosure. Also called *deed in lieu of foreclosure.*

front-end qualifying ratio A ratio used by a lender to qualify a loan applicant. It compares a loan applicant's gross income with the proposed PITI.

front foot A unit of linear measurement (in feet) of the side of a property that faces the street.

fruits of industry Items such as crops that are on but *not part of* the real estate.

fruits of nature Items such as bushes and trees that are on and *part of* the real estate.

full replacement coverage A method of settling an insurance claim in which no depreciation is subtracted from the cost of replacing the property.

functional obsolescence Loss of value caused by outdated features in the property, such as outdated bathroom fixtures. Functional obsolescence may be either curable or incurable. One of the three types of depreciation calculated in the cost approach to estimating value.

further assurance A guarantee in a deed by which the grantor promises to perform any reasonable acts necessary to correct defects in the title being given.

gap A defect in the chain of title that raises doubt as to the ownership of a parcel of real estate.

general agent Represents the principal in a related range of activities.

general lien A lien that applies to all of a person's property.

general partnership A partnership in which all of the partners are general partners and have unlimited liability and the right to manage the partnership.

general warranty deed A type of deed that provides the greatest protection to the grantee because the grantor provides various covenants (guarantees) that the title being given is good.

Ginnie Mae *See* Government National Mortgage Association.

good-faith estimate An estimate required by RESPA and provided to the buyer by the lender stating the expected closing costs the buyer will incur.

government lots Lots that are smaller than full quarter sections. Used in the rectangular survey system of describing real estate.

Government National Mortgage Association (GNMA) A wholly owned government corporation that provides a secondary market for VA and FHA loans. Also known as "Ginnie Mae."

government survey system *See* rectangular survey system.

graduated lease Allows for rent changes at set future dates. Also called a *variable lease.*

graduated payment mortgage (GPM) A loan program that has smaller loan payments in the early years of the loan and larger payments in later years. Designed for buyers who do not have sufficient income to qualify for larger loans but have good income potential.

grant deed Grantors provide assurance only that there were no encumbrances on the property while they held title. Similar to a special warranty deed.

grantee The party who receives an ownership interest in property.

granting clause States the grantor's intention to transfer title and the type of ownership interest conveyed. Also called *words of conveyance.*

grantor The party who gives an ownership interest in property.

gross income multiplier (GIM) A shortened method of estimating the value of income-producing property. The multiplier is found by dividing the selling price by gross annual income of comparable properties. The GIM is used to find the value of the subject property by multiplying the gross annual income of the subject property by the multiplier.

gross lease A lease agreement in which the tenant pays a fixed amount of rent and the owner pays all of the expenses of the building. This is the most common type of lease arrangement.

gross rent multiplier (GRM) A shortened method of estimating the value of income-producing rental property. The multiplier is found by dividing the selling price by the residential gross monthly rent of comparable properties. The GRM is used to find the value of the subject property by multiplying the gross monthly rent of the subject property by the multiplier. Usually used for single-family rental property.

ground lease A long-term lease of land (50 years or more) that usually requires that the tenant construct a building.

guide meridians In the rectangular survey method of describing real estate, every fourth range line is a guide meridian and is used in conjunction with correction lines to compensate for the curvature of the earth.

habendum clause A clause in a deed that defines or limits the estate being granted.

heirs Persons legally eligible to receive property of a decedent.

highest and best use The one legal use that provides a property with its greatest value. A principle of value used in appraisal.

holdover tenancy Occurs when a tenant remains on the property after the right to possess it has expired.

holographic will A will created in the testator's own handwriting and not witnessed.

home equity loan A loan based on a homeowner's equity in his or her property, usually an adjustable rate, second (junior) mortgage. The interest is usually deductible for income tax purposes.

Home Mortgage Disclosure Act A law passed to prevent real estate lenders from redlining. Lenders must make annual disclosures showing areas where loans are being made.

homeowner policy A package of several types of insurance coverage available to homeowners.

homeowners' association dues Fees imposed by a condominium or homeowners' association for maintenance of the common areas.

home rule powers Provisions in the constitutions of some states that give local governments the power to regulate real estate to protect the public health and safety.

homestead exemption A legal life estate that protects a portion of the value of an owner's principal residence from unsecured creditors. Rules are set by state law.

Housing and Community Development Act A 1974 amendment to the 1968 Fair Housing Act that added gender as a protected class.

HUD A standard settlement form required by RESPA. *See* Uniform Settlement Statement.

hypothecation Pledging property as security for a loan without giving up possession.

immobility A physical characteristic of real estate, meaning that land cannot be moved.

implied contract An agreement created by the actions of the parties.

impound account An account maintained by the lender that holds money collected from the borrower for the payment of real estate taxes and insurance. Also called an *escrow* or a *reserve account.*

improvements Additions to a property that are created artificially rather than by nature.

income approach An approach to estimating the value of property by finding the net income and applying it with the capitalization rate. The value of the subject property is estimated by (1) finding the annual potential gross income, (2) subtracting a vacancy rate to find the effective gross income, (3) subtracting operating expenses to find the net income, (4) finding the capitalization rate and (5) applying the capitalization rate to the subject property. *See also* capitalization rate.

increasing and diminishing returns The relationship between the cost of improvements and the value they add to the property. Improvements may initially add substantial value (increasing return) but will reach a point where they add less value (diminishing return). A principle of value used in appraisal.

incurable depreciation When present, the cost of fixing the property will be more than the increase in value or the corrections are not physically possible. Used in appraisal.

independent contractor A working relationship between a broker and his or her sales agents in which the broker can control what the agent will do but not how it will be done. The broker cannot withhold for taxes or Social Security or provide benefits. *See also* employee.

indestructibility A physical characteristic of real estate meaning that land cannot be destroyed.

index lease A lease agreement in which the rent changes are based on some common economic index.

industrial property Property used in industry, such as factories.

in gross *See* easement in gross.

installment sale method A method of selling real estate in which the gain on the sale is received from the buyer over several years and recognized as a taxable gain over the same period.

installment sales contract A sales contract in which the buyer takes possession of the property but the seller retains title until the loan is paid.

Institute of Real Estate Management (IREM) The largest property management organization. It is affiliated with the National Association of REALTORS®.

instrument A legal document such as a contract, deed or note.

insured loans A loan insured by FHA or a private mortgage insurance company that protects the lender against default.

intangible property Personal property represented by a document but that cannot be detected by the senses. Stock certificates are a representation of intangible property.

interim financing A short-term loan often used to finance real estate construction.

Interstate Land Sales Full Disclosure Act A federal law that regulates the sale of real estate across state lines (in interstate commerce) under certain conditions.

inter vivos trust A living trust created by an owner during his or her lifetime.

intestate Having died without making a will.

inverse condemnation Forcing the state to buy an owner's property if government action has forced loss of value or inability to use the property.

involuntary alienation Transferring title to real estate without the will and consent of the owner.

involuntary lien A lien that is created by law, either by statute or by a court.

joint tenancy Ownership by two or more people who own an undivided interest with right of survivorship. Four unities are required to create a joint tenancy: time, title, interest and possession.

joint venture A business entity created for a single project, usually intended to last a limited period of time.

judgment A decree issued by the court at the conclusion of a lawsuit. After recording in the county records, it usually becomes a general lien on the defendant's property.

judicial foreclosure Foreclosure procedures that use the courts. These procedures include judicial sale and strict foreclosure.

judicial sale A type of judicial foreclosure in which the lender uses the acceleration clause in the mortgage and then files a suit to have the property sold and the loan paid.

junior mortgage A loan that is subordinate to a prior mortgage.

laches Loss of legal rights because of failure to assert them on a timely basis.

land Includes the earth's surface, below to the center, above to infinity and all natural things attached.

land contract The seller accepts a down payment and finances the rest of the purchase price. Title to the property remains with the seller until the loan is repaid. Also called an *installment sales contract* and *contract for deed.*

landlocked Property that does not have access to a public road to enter or leave the land. This situation may create an easement by necessity.

land trust A trust in which real estate is the only asset.

latent defects Hidden defects in property.

lease option Gives the tenant the right to renew the lease if proper notice is given.

lease purchase An arrangement in which the tenant leases property for a period of time with the intention of purchasing it.

lease with option to buy Allows the tenant to purchase property within a specified time period, usually with pre-agreed terms.

legal description A precise method of describing a parcel of real estate. A description on documents used in the transfer of title to real estate that is acceptable to the courts.

legal life estates Life estate created by statute rather than by the actions of the parties. There are three common types, curtesy, dower and homestead.

lessee The tenant in a lease arrangement.

lessor The landlord/property owner in a lease arrangement.

leverage The use of borrowed money to purchase investments.

liability coverage Protection against claims by others for injuries caused by an owner's negligence.

license A personal privilege to enter another's land for a specific purpose.

lien A charge or claim against the property for a debt or obligation of the property owner.

lienee The party whose property is subject to a lien.

lienor The party holding the lien right.

life estate A noninheritable freehold estate based on the life (or lives) of named individuals.

life insurance companies A source of money for large industrial and commercial real estate projects. Deal with intermediaries rather than individual borrowers.

life tenant The party who owns a life estate in the property.

like-kind property As defined by the tax code (Section 1031), personal property that can be exchanged for other personal property or real estate that can be exchanged for other real estate.

limited liability company Incorporates the tax and liability advantages of corporations and limited partnerships.

limited partnership A type of partnership that includes at least one general partner and one or more limited partners. The limited partners cannot manage the business, and their liability is limited to the amount of their investment.

liquidity The speed at which an investment can be converted into cash.

lis pendens A notice in the public records of a lawsuit involving a particular property that may result in a claim against the property.

listing contract An agreement between an owner and a licensed broker in which the broker is employed to sell the real estate within a given time in return for a commission, to be paid by the owner.

littoral rights The rights of an owner with property bordering large bodies of water, such as the ocean.

loan assumption Occurs when someone other than the original borrower becomes primarily liable for the loan.

loan commitment A commitment by a lender to make a loan on a property for a stated amount within a certain period of time. Given to loan applicants when their credit has been approved by the lender.

loan-to-value ratio The relationship between the amount of a loan and the appraised value of a property. The ratio is expressed as a percentage of the appraised value.

lot-and-block system A method of describing real estate that references a parcel of land by lot and block numbers within a subdivision. Also called *recorded plat*.

management agreement A contract by which a property owner employs a property manager.

management plan A document developed by a property manager that outlines the owner's objectives and how the manager intends to meet them.

marketable title Title that is free from major defects that would deter potential buyers of the property.

market data approach *See* sales comparison approach.

market price The actual sales price of a property, usually different from the market value.

market segmentation Dividing real estate markets into submarkets.

market value The most probable price a property should bring if payment is made in cash and the buyer and seller are unrelated, well informed and acting without pressure.

mechanic's lien A claim against real property by suppliers of goods and services to the real estate.

Member of the Appraisal Institute (MAI) The highest designation awarded by the Appraisal Institute.

metes and bounds One of the common methods of describing real estate. The description starts at a point of beginning (POB) and describes the circumference of the property, ending at the POB.

mill An amount equal to one tenth of a cent ($.001). Sometimes used to express a real estate tax rate.

misrepresentation A false statement or concealment of a material fact.

modification The economic characteristic of real estate meaning that a change in one property affects the value of neighboring properties, either favorably or unfavorably.

monuments Monuments are fixed objects used in the metes-and-bounds method of describing real estate.

mortgage A contract between a borrower and a lender that provides security for the loan by creating a lien on the property.

mortgage banking company Originates loans and packages them to investors, who may use their own money or money borrowed from other lenders. They also service loans.

mortgage bond financing The process of selling tax-exempt bonds by municipalities to raise money for low-rate loans to first-time home buyers.

mortgage broker One who arranges a loan between a lender (mortgagee) and borrower (mortgagor) for a fee.

mortgagee The lender or obligee, who receives a pledge from a borrower to repay a loan.

mortgage insurance premium An insurance fee paid by the borrower either to the FHA or to a private mortgage insurer to protect the lender against default.

mortgagor The borrower or obligor, who gives the lender a pledge to repay a loan.

multiple listing A method of sharing listing information among brokers.

multiple-listing service (MLS) An organization composed of member brokers who agree to share their listing information with the intention of more quickly finding buyers for a property.

mutual savings banks Similar to savings banks, they use most of their funds for residential real estate loans.

National Association of REALTORS® A professional organization for the real estate industry.

National Flood Insurance Program (NFIP) A program administered by a division of the Federal Emergency Management Agency (FEMA) that helps provide coverage to homeowners for losses due to flooding.

necessity *See* easement by necessity.

negative amortization A loan arrangement in which the loan balance increases with each payment rather than decreasing because the payment amount is not sufficient to cover the interest.

negotiable instrument A written promise or order to pay a specific amount of money. The instrument may be transferred to someone else by endorsing the document. A mortgage note and checks are examples of negotiable instruments.

net income Gross income less operating expenses. Also called *net operating income*.

net lease A lease arrangement in which the tenant pays a fixed amount of rent plus some or all of the building's expenses.

net listing A listing in which a specified amount is due the seller and the broker's commission is any amount above that. This type of listing is illegal in some states because of the potential for fraud by the broker.

nonconforming loan A mortgage not eligible for sale and delivery to either FNMA or FHLMC for various reasons, including the loan amount, loan characteristics or underwriting guidelines.

nonconforming use A property's use that existed prior to the current zoning laws and is not in compliance with those laws.

nonhomogeneity An economic characteristic of real estate meaning that no two parcels of land are exactly alike.

nonjudicial foreclosure Foreclosure procedures used by lenders that do not involve the courts. Common types are power of sale clauses and deeds in lieu of foreclosure.

note A written promise to pay a sum of money at a stated rate during a specific term.

novation Substituting a new contract for an old one.

nuncupative will A will created orally by a person near death.

obsolescence Loss of value owing to being outmoded or less useful.

occupancy permit Issued by a local government body to establish that a property is suitable for habitation because it meets local safety and health standards.

Office of the Comptroller of the Currency (OCC) A government office responsible for monitoring and regulating the nationally chartered banking industry.

Office of Thrift Supervision (OTS) An agency that is part of the Department of the Treasury and responsible for monitoring and regulating thrifts.

oil and gas lease A lease under which a property owner receives rent from a company for allowing it to drill for oil and gas on the property.

open-end loan A loan arrangement whereby the mortgagor may borrow additional money up to the original amount of the loan using the same property as collateral.

open listing Listing in which the seller employs any number of brokers at the same time but owes a commission only to the broker who sells the property.

ordinary life estate An estate based on the tenant's life.

package mortgage A loan arrangement used to finance both real and personal property in a real estate transaction.

parol evidence rule Oral evidence will not be allowed to contradict a written contract.

partition The right of parties in a tenancy in common or joint tenancy to have the courts force the dissolution of the tenancies.

partnership An agreement between two or more persons to conduct a business. A partnership can be either limited or general. *See also* general partnership, limited partnership.

party wall A wall built on the line separating two properties. Because the wall is built partly on each property, each owner has an easement on the adjoining owner's land that is covered by the wall.

pension funds These funds invest in packages of real estate loans, primarily from mortgage bankers and brokers.

percentage lease A lease arrangement in which the rent is determined by a percentage of the tenant's gross income.

perfecting title The process of removing defects on the title.

perils Hazards or risks that may be protected against with insurance policies.

periodic estate A leasehold estate that continues for an indefinite period of time. Also called an *estate from period to period*.

personal property All property that is not classified as real property. The primary characteristic of personal property is mobility.

physical deterioration Loss of value caused by wear and tear on the building, such as a leaking roof or peeling paint. Physical deterioration may be either curable or incurable. One of the three types of depreciation calculated in the cost approach to estimating value.

PITI An acronym describing principal (P), interest (I), taxes (T) and insurance (I), the most common components of a mortgage payment.

planned unit development (PUD) Mixed-use developments of several acres that set aside areas for residences; commercial property; and public areas such as schools, parks, etc.

plat A property map recorded in plat books in the public records.

plat-of-survey method Also called recorded plat and lot-block-tract, this is one of the methods used to describe real estate. Divides land into blocks, lots and tracts.

plottage Combining lots to increase the value of the new larger lot over the sum of values of the smaller ones. A principle of value used in appraisal.

point of beginning In the metes-and-bounds method of describing real estate, the description begins and ends at the point of beginning.

points Points are interest, usually payable at closing. A point is 1 percent of the loan amount.

police powers Government powers that give the state and local governments the authority to pass laws to protect the public health and safety.

portfolio lenders Lenders who hold loans they originate rather than selling them to investors.

power of attorney A written instrument authorizing one person (called the *attorney-in-fact*) to act as an agent for another person.

property management agreement A document that establishes the working relationship between a building owner and a property manager. A contract between the parties that establishes an agency in which the manager is the agent and the owner is the principal.

prepaid expense An expense that has been paid but not yet incurred.

prepayment clause A mortgage clause that determines the borrower's rights and duties if the loan is prepaid.

prescriptive easement *See* easement by prescription.

price In appraisal, what a property actually sells for.

price fixing An illegal practice (violation of the antitrust laws) in which brokers conspire to establish a standard commission rate.

principal meridians Lines running north and south and intersected by base lines. Used in the rectangular survey system of describing real estate.

prior appropriation Ownership and use of water are controlled by the state, and property owners must apply to the state to appropriate (divert) water.

private conduits Organizations that often purchase and pool nonstandardized loans for selling in the secondary market.

private mortgage insurance (PMI) Insurance written by a private company that protects a mortgage lender against loss if a borrower defaults. The insurance is usually used when the loan-to-value ratio exceeds 80 percent. PMI insures the top 20 percent to 25 percent of the loan, and borrowers are charged a fee at closing as well as an annual fee.

probate The legal process of determining a will's validity, paying the debts of the estate and distributing the estate's remaining assets.

procuring cause The broker whose actions resulted in completion of the sales transaction.

progression The idea that the value of a poorer property will increase if it is near a better quality property. A principle of value used in appraisal.

promissory note A contract agreement between a borrower and a lender whereby the borrower commits to pay the lender the loan amount following specific terms. The note is a negotiable instrument, allowing the lender to sell the note to investors.

proprietary lease A lease given by the corporation that owns a cooperative apartment building to the shareholder, giving the shareholder the right as a tenant to one of the units in the building.

prorated expenses Expenses shared between the buyer and seller.

puffing Statements of opinion and exaggeration by the broker.

pur autre vie A type of life estate based on the life of someone other than the life tenant. Means *for the life of another.*

purchase-money mortgage A loan given by the seller to finance part of the purchase price. Also called a *take-back mortgage.*

pyramiding Obtaining additional investment property by borrowing on the equity of existing investments.

quiet enjoyment A guarantee in a deed that the title being given is good against third parties.

quiet title lawsuit Used to clear up defects or uncertainty in a title.

quitclaim deed A deed that conveys whatever interest, if any, is held by the grantor and does not provide the grantee with any guarantees.

range lines Lines that run north and south and are measured from the principal meridian. Used in the rectangular survey system of describing real estate.

ranges Strips of land running north and south and measured from the principal meridian. Used in the rectangular survey system of describing real estate.

raw land Land that has no improvements. Also called *unimproved land*.

real estate Land plus any artificial things permanently attached.

real estate assistant An individual who assists a broker or salesperson in the real estate business. Assistants may be licensed or unlicensed

Real Estate Investment Trust (REIT) Allows small investors to participate in real estate investments. Investors transfer title to real estate to a trustee, who manages the property for the benefit and profit of the investors. Funds from the issuance of investment trust certificates to investors are used to purchase real estate investments for the benefit of the investors.

Real Estate Mortgage Investment Conduit (REMIC) Issues investor securities backed by mortgage loan pools.

Real Estate Settlement Procedures Act (RESPA) The primary purpose of this federal law is to ensure that the parties in a residential real estate transaction are informed of settlement costs. The law's requirements include good-faith estimate of closing costs, use of HUD's settlement statement, providing a HUD information booklet and prohibiting kickbacks.

real property All components of real estate plus the legal rights and interests associated with its ownership.

REALTOR® A registered trademark of the NAR that can be used only by its members.

recapture clause Allows a lessor to take back the premises if a minimum sales amount is not met. Used in percentage leases.

reciprocal agreements (reciprocity) Agreements between states that make it easier for brokers to obtain licenses in other states.

recovery fund An account operated by the state used to pay uncollectible judgments against licensees.

rectangular survey system Established by Congress as a method of describing real estate. Established a grid of intersecting lines to describe the location of a property. Also known as the *government survey system*.

redemption The rights of an owner whose property is sold (or is being sold) to satisfy a lien against the real estate to recover the property. Redemption rights are commonly given when property is being sold to satisfy mortgage loans and real estate taxes. *See also* statutory redemption, equitable redemption.

redlining Refusing to make loans or issue insurance policies in certain areas, based on the presence of a protected class.

regression The idea that the value of a better property will decrease if it is near a poorer quality property. A principle of value used in appraisal.

Regulation Z Federal regulation issued by the Fed to implement the Truth-in-Lending Act. *See also* Truth-in-Lending Act.

release deed A deed given by a trustee when a loan is repaid. Also called a *trustee's deed of reconveyance*.

reliction The gradual subsiding of water leaving additional land.

remainder interest A third party who has a future ownership interest in property.

renouncing the will A spouse's election to receive the benefits of the estate that are allowed under state law rather than those given by the will.

replacement cost Estimates the current cost of constructing similar or equivalent improvements. Used in the cost approach to estimating value.

reproduction cost Estimates the current cost of constructing duplicates of the property improvements. Reproduction creates an exact replica, while replacement cost creates similar improvements. Used in the cost approach to estimating value.

reserve requirement The portion of a bank's deposits that may not be loaned. By adjusting the reserve requirement, the Fed can control interest rates and the flow of money in the economy.

residential property Property used for housing. Includes single-family housing, condos, cooperatives and apartment buildings.

reverse annuity mortgage A loan designed for elderly people with little or no debt on their houses. The lender pays the borrower a fixed amount of money each month based on the equity in the property and the owner's life expectancy. The loan is repaid when the owner dies, sells the house or moves out of the house.

reversion interest Under this arrangement property "reverts," returns, to the original owner.

right of first refusal In a lease arrangement, allows the tenant the opportunity to buy the property if the owner receives a purchase offer. In a cooperative or condominium, the corporation or condominium board can require the shareholders to offer their shares, or unit, to the corporation or board before selling them to others.

right of survivorship When tenants in a joint tenancy die, their ownership share goes to the surviving joint tenants.

riparian rights Rights pertaining to land bordering flowing water, such as streams or rivers.

run with the land Easement rights that are passed on to successive owners of the property.

sale and leaseback An arrangement whereby an owner sells property and then leases it back from the purchaser. Often used with commercial and industrial property.

sales comparison approach An approach to estimating the value of property by comparing the subject property with various similar (comparable) properties. The value of the subject property is found by (1) locating at least three comparable properties, (2) making adjustments for differences between the comparables and the subject property and (3) reconciling the adjusted sales price of the comparables.

salesperson license An entry level real estate license category. A person holding a salesperson license must be employed by a broker to perform selling activities.

satisfaction of mortgage A document issued by a lender verifying that a loan has been repaid.

savings banks Also called *thrifts*. Lenders that have traditionally been an important source of loans for residential property. Their role has greatly diminished in recent years.

scarcity An economic characteristic of real estate that refers to the finite amount of land.

S corporation A special form of corporation that is taxed like a partnership but has limited liability.

secondary mortgage market A market where existing mortgages are bought and sold. Mortgages are originated in the primary mortgage market.

Section 1031 The section of the IRS code that authorizes the deferment of tax on a gain through an exchange of like-kind property.

sections A land measure of one square mile or 640 acres used in the rectangular survey method of describing real estate. *See also* townships.

seisin A guarantee in a deed that the grantor has the power and authority to convey title.

seller disclosure statement A listing by a seller of any property defects.

Senior Residential Appraiser (SRA) A designation awarded by the Appraisal Institute to residential appraisers.

servient tenement A tract of land over which an appurtenant easement right runs.

severalty The same as sole owner.

severance The process of changing real property to personal property.

situs The economic characteristic of real estate that refers to people's preference for some areas over others.

special agent A representative of the principal in a specific transaction.

special assessment A special real estate tax for improvements that benefit the property.

special warranty deed A deed that limits the guarantee given by the grantor to encumbrances acquired while title

was held by the grantor. Used by someone acting on behalf of the owner, such as an executor or administrator.

specific lien A lien that applies to a specific property.

specific performance A suit to force another party to complete the contract terms.

spot survey Shows the location and size of buildings on a property.

Starker exchange A delayed exchange of properties that qualifies as a tax-deferred exchange.

statute of limitations The law pertaining to the period of time within which certain actions must be brought to court.

statutes of frauds State laws that require that certain contracts must be in writing to be enforceable.

statutory month method A method of proration that treats every month as if it had 30 days.

statutory redemption The borrower's right to redeem property *after* the foreclosure sale.

steering Channeling home seekers to areas on the basis of their race, color, religion, etc.

stigmatized property Property that has been involved with some undesirable event, such as a crime or suicide.

straight-line method A method of depreciating an asset in which equal amounts of depreciation are taken annually over the asset's useful life.

subagents Parties who assist the agent.

subject property The property that is being appraised. Used in appraisal.

subject-to mortgage An arrangement in which the buyer assumes the seller's mortgage and makes payments but is not personally liable for the debt.

sublease In a sublease the original tenant becomes the lessor and takes on a new tenant (a sublessee). The sublessee makes payments to the original tenant.

subordination agreement A written agreement between lienholders to change priority of their respective liens.

subrogation Obtaining the legal rights of another party. Used by title insurance companies to defend the insured title against lawsuits from other parties. This clause in the policy prevents the insured from collecting both from the insurance company and from the party causing the loss.

substantially equivalent laws State or local government fair housing laws that are similar to the federal fair housing laws.

subsurface rights Rights a property owner has in any material below the surface of the land.

suit for possession A lawsuit that initiates an action for eviction against the tenant.

suit to quiet title A court action to settle a cloud on the property's title.

supply and demand In the real estate market property values change as these two forces adjust themselves. As supply increases or demand decreases, values decrease. As supply decreases or demand increases, values increase.

survey A measurement and description of land. Surveys usually are required when property is sold or improvements are being made.

syndication Usually a limited partnership formed by two or more parties to operate a real estate investment.

tacking Combining successive periods of property use.

tangible property Property that can be seen and touched, such as a car.

taxation A government power by which local governments can raise revenue by taxing real estate.

tax shelter An investment intended to lower (or protect) taxable income through tax-deductible expenses.

tenancy at sufferance This tenancy occurs when a tenant wrongfully remains on the property after the right to possess has ended.

tenancy at will A form of tenancy whereby the tenant possesses the property with the consent of the landlord. The term is for an indefinite period of time and can be canceled without notice.

tenancy by the entirety A form of joint tenancy that exists between husband and wife.

tenancy in common A form of holding title in which two or more parties have an undivided interest in the property. They can hold unequal shares in the property, and there is no right of survivorship.

term loan A loan arrangement in which payments include only interest and the loan balance is due at the end of the loan period. They are usually nonamortizing loans for short terms. Also called a *straight loan*.

testamentary trust A trust created through a will after a property owner's death.

testate Having died and left a will.

testator A male person who has made a will.

testatrix A female person who has made a will.

thrifts *See* savings banks.

time is of the essence A clause in a contract that stipulates that time limits stated in the contract must be met.

time-share Ownership of a specified time interval in a property, usually recreational or resort property.

title The legal evidence of ownership rights to real property.

title insurance Insures the existence of rights in real estate and pays for losses to the insured because of successful claims to the title by other parties. A policy is issued after a search of the public records. There are lenders' and owners' policies.

title report The results of a search of the public records by a title insurance company. The report lists anyone who has an ownership interest in the property being examined.

title search A search of the public records to determine past and present facts regarding ownership of the property. Also called *title examination*.

Torrens system A system used for both assuring and recording title to real estate. This system is used in only a small number of states. When a property is registered in Torrens, a Torrens certificate establishing title to the owner on the certificate is issued by the registrator of title.

township lines Township lines are six miles apart, run east and west and are measured from the base lines. Used in the rectangular survey method of describing real estate.

townships Townships are square sections of land that are six miles on a side and contain 36 square miles, or sections. Used in the rectangular survey method of describing real estate. *See also* sections.

trade fixture A fixture that remains personal property and can be removed by the tenant.

transactional broker A licensee who does not act as the agent for either party in a real estate transaction. The broker's function is to assist the parties with the required paperwork and other activities in the transaction but not negotiate on behalf of either party.

transfer tax A tax on the transfer of real property that is assessed by state and local law. The seller in the real estate transaction is usually required to pay the tax.

trust A three-party arrangement (trustor, trustee, beneficiary) in which title to real estate or other assets is placed with the trustee.

trust deed A deed that creates security for a loan by conveying title to a trustee, who holds it as security for the benefit of the lender (the beneficiary). Also called a *deed of trust*.

trustee The party in a trust that holds title to the assets for the benefit of the beneficiary.

trustor The party that creates a trust by transferring title to assets to a trustee.

Truth-in-Lending Act A federal law implemented by Regulation Z that requires that lenders inform borrowers of the true costs of obtaining a loan. Primary disclosures include the finance charge, annual percentage rate, the amount financed and the total payments. The law also provides certain restrictions when advertising financing terms.

Uniform Residential Appraisal Report (URAR) The most common appraisal report form used today. Most government agencies use the form.

Uniform Settlement Statement (HUD-1) A form required by RESPA to be used at closings that details financial information of the transaction.

universal agent An agent who represents a principal in all activities.

useful life The length of time an asset will be useful to the owner and can be depreciated. For tax purposes this is defined by the IRS.

usury laws Laws passed by states that limit the interest rates lenders can charge borrowers.

vacancy levels The percentage of building units that are not occupied.

variable lease A lease agreement that allows for changes in the rent. May be an *index* or *graduated lease*.

variance An exception to the zoning law. Often granted if strict enforcement of the zoning law would force an undue hardship on the property owner.

vendee lien A lien that protects a buyer.

vendor lien A lien that protects a seller.

Vendor Purchaser Risk Act A law that defines which party suffers a loss if property is destroyed before closing a transaction.

voidable contract An agreement that can be rejected or disaffirmed by one or both of the parties.

void contract An agreement that does not satisfy the required contract elements and has no legal force or effect.

voluntary alienation Transferring title to real estate by the will and consent of the owner.

warranty forever A guarantee given in a deed that gives assurance that the grantor will pay for expenses to defend the title against claims by third parties.

waste Acts that injure a property and reduce its value.

wraparound loan A loan arrangement in which an existing loan on a property is assumed by a lender, who then gives the borrower a new, larger loan.

zoning ordinance Zoning laws regulate and control the use of land. An example of the government's police powers.

INDEX